Conflict

From Theory to Action

SECOND EDITION

Roxane S. Lulofs

Azusa Pacific University

Dudley D. Cahn

State University of New York, New Paltz

Allyn and Bacon

Boston • London • Toronto • Sydney • Tokyo • Singapore

Series Editor: Karon Bowers
Editorial Assisstant: Scout Reilly
Marketing Manager: Jackie Aaron
Production Editor: Christopher H. Rawlings
Editorial-Production Service: Omegatype Typography, Inc.
Composition and Prepress Buyer: Linda Cox
Manufacturing Buyer: Megan Cochran
Cover Administrator: Jennifer Hart
Electronic Composition: Omegatype Typography, Inc.

Copyright © 2000 by Allyn & Bacon
A Pearson Education Company
160 Gould Street
Needham Heights, MA 02494

Internet: www.abacon.com

Library of Congress Cataloging-in-Publication Data

Lulofs, Roxane Salyer.
    Conflict : from theory to action / Roxane S. Lulofs, Dudley D.
Cahn.—2nd ed.
      p. cm.
    Includes bibliographical references and index.
    ISBN 0-205-29030-2 (alk. paper)
     1. Conflict (Psychology). 2. Interpersonal conflict. 3. Conflict
management. I. Cahn, Dudley D. II. Title.
BF637.I48 L85   2000
303.6—dc21   98-47878
                                                                CIP

Printed in the United States of America
10 9 8 7 6 5 4 3   04 03 02

Contents

Preface   xi

PART I   *Understanding the Nature of Conflict*   *1*

1   *Introduction to the Study of Conflict*   *2*

     Objectives   *2*

     Key Terms   *2*

     A Perspective on Conflict   *3*
       Defining Conflict   3   •   Conflict Is Generally Viewed Negatively   6

     The Inevitability of Conflict   *9*
       Conflict Is a Fact of Life   9   •   Interpersonal Violence Is Not a Fact of Life   11

     The Consequences of Conflict   *12*
       Functions of Conflict   12   •   Conflict Communication as Productive or Destructive   13

     From Theory to Action   *17*

2   *People in Conflict: Values, Attitudes, and Beliefs*   *21*

     Objectives   *21*

     Key Terms   *21*

     Socialization and Conflict   *22*

     Attitudes toward Communication and Conflict   *23*
       Rhetorical Sensitivity and Communicator Style   23   •   Influences on Interpersonal Perception   24

     Functional Beliefs for Managing and Resolving Conflict   *28*
       Functional Belief One   28   •   Functional Belief Two   29   •   Functional Belief Three   30   •   Functional Belief Four   31   •   Functional Belief Five   32   •   Functional Belief Six   32   •   Functional Belief Seven   33   •   Functional Belief Eight   34   •   Functional Belief Nine   34

Attitudes Fostering Conflict Resolution   35

From Theory to Action   37

3   *Culture and Gender in Conflict*   39

Objectives   39

Key Terms   39

A Hierarchical Model of Cultural Understanding   42

The Hierarchical Model and Cultural Variability   44

The Challenge of Diversity   47

Sex, Gender, and Conflict   48

From Theory to Action   52

PART II   *Understanding How Conflict Works*   55

4   *Types of Conflict*   56

Objectives   56

Key Terms   56

Types of Conflict   57

Real versus Unreal Conflicts   58   •   Substantive versus Nonsubstantive
Conflicts   62   •   Real and Substantive Conflicts   64   •   Mere Disagreements
versus Interpersonal Conflicts   65

Issues as Indicators of Real and Substantive Conflicts   66

Behavioral Conflicts   66   •   Normative Conflicts—Issues of
Relationships   67   •   Personality Conflicts—Dispositions and Values   68

Moral Conflict   69

From Theory to Action   73

5   *The Process of Conflict: Phases and Cycles*   74

Objectives   74

Key Terms   74

Phase Theories of Conflict   75

Patterns and Cycles in Conflict   76
The Conflict Avoidance Cycle   77   •   The Chilling Effect: A Diminished
Communication Cycle   79   •   The Competitive Conflict Escalation Cycle   81

Conflict as a Process   87
The Prelude to Conflict   88   •   The Triggering Event   91   •   The Initiation of
Conflict   92   •   The Differentiation of Conflict   93   •   The Resolution of
Conflict   96

From Theory to Action   97

6   *Conflict Styles, Strategies, and Tactics   99*

Objectives   99

Key Terms   99

Conflict Styles, Strategies, and Tactics   100

Conflict Strategies and Tactics   104
Collaboration, Competition, and Avoidance   104   •   Other Strategies
and Tactics   107

Collaboration: The Preferred Style   109
Low Personal and Relationship Stress   109   •   High Personal and Relationship
Growth and Satisfaction   110   •   Phases of Collaboration   112

Case Studies of Cultural Differences in Conflict Resolution Styles   114
Criticisms of the Japanese, American, and Yugoslav Approaches
to Conflict Resolution   118

From Theory to Action   118

**PART III   *Analyzing Conflict: Theory and Reseach
in Interpersonal Conflict   121***

7   *Social-Psychological Perspectives of Conflict   123*

Objectives   123

Key Terms   123

Psychodynamic and Attribution Theories   124
Psychodynamic Theory   124   •   Attribution Theory   126

Relationship Theories   129
Social Exchange Theory   129   •   Game Theory   132   •   Systems Theory   133

Structural Theory   136
Trust   137   •   Uncertainty   139   •   Power   140

From Theory to Action   144

8   *A Communication Perspective on Conflict Behavior   148*

Objectives   148

Key Terms   148

Linear versus Transactional Views of Communication and Conflict   149
The Linear Model: Message Senders and Receivers   149   •   The Transactional
Model: People Communicating Together   150

Rules and Conflict Communication   151

Communication Competence and Conflict Behavior   153

Examining Goals and Effects in Conflict Situations   157
Instrumental Goals and Effects of Communication in Conflict   158   •   Relational
Goals and Effects of Communication in a Conflict   159   •   Identity Goals and
Effects of Communication in Conflict   161   •   Interrelationship of the Three
Types of Goals and Effects   163

From Theory to Action   164

9   *Research on Intimacy and Conflict   168*

Objectives   168

Key Terms   168

Intimate and Marital Conflict Issues   170

Relationship Life Cycle, Aging, and Conflict Style   178
Couple Type and Conflict Styles   178   •   Distressed and Nondistressed Couples
and Conflict Styles   180   •   Couple Complaints and Conflict Style   182   •
Family Strengths and Conflict Style   183

From Theory to Action   183

PART IV   *Effective Communication Behavior*   *187*

10   *Using the S-TLC System*   *189*

    Objectives   *189*

    Key Terms   *189*

    The S-TLC System   *190*
        Stop   190   •   Think   190   •   Listen   191   •   Communicate   191

    Thinking about Conflict: Analyzing Conflict Situations   *192*
        The Goal of Analysis   193   •   Dimensions of the Conflict Situation   194   •
        Conflict Pollutants   196   •   Cooperation versus Competition   198   •
        Trained Incapacities   199   •   Models for Analysis   201

    Listening in Conflict Situations   *203*

    From Theory to Action   *204*

11   *Choosing among the Communication Options in Conflict Situations*   *206*

    Objectives   *206*

    Key Terms   *206*

    Conflict Communication Options   *207*
        Nonassertive Communication (Avoidance or Accommodation) as an Option   207   •
        Aggressive Communication as an Option   208   •   Nonverbal Aggression (Physical
        Violence) as an Option   210   •   Verbal Aggression as an Option   211   •
        Passive-Aggressive Communication as an Option   214   •   Assertive
        Communication as an Option   216

    Communication Considerations: Which Conflict Communication Option Is Best?   *220*
        The Occasion (Including Time and Location)   221   •   The Other Person   221   •
        Your Needs   221

    From Theory to Action   *222*

12   *Effectively Confronting Others*   *225*

    Objectives   *225*

    Key Terms   *225*

The Interpersonal Conflict Ritual: Six Steps to Successful Confrontation   **226**

Preparation: Identify Your Problem, Needs, and Issues   227   •   Make a "Date" to
Sit Down and Talk   228   •   Interpersonal Confrontation: Talk to the Other about
Your Problem   228   •   Consider Your Partner's Point of View   232   •   Resolve
the Problem: Make an Agreement   233   •   Follow Up on the Solution: Set a Time
Limit for Reevaluation   233

Doing Conflict Messages: Using I-Statements   **233**

Components of I-Statements   236   •   General Tips on Being Assertive   238   •
Advantages of Using I-Statements   238   •   Challenges Associated with
I-Statements   239

Dealing with People Who Play Games   **239**

Confronting Difficult People   **240**

From Theory to Action   **243**

13   *Cooperative Negotiation in Win-Lose Conflicts*   **246**

Objectives   **246**

Key Terms   **246**

Conflicts over Two Types of Resources   **247**

Bargaining and Negotiation   **250**

The Nature of Bargaining in Formal Situations   250   •   Research on Formal
Bargaining   252   •   Informal Negotiation   254   •   Research on Tactics and
Strategies in the Negotiation Situation   254

Strategies for Tangible-Issue Conflicts   **256**

Principles of Reconciliation   261   •   Separate People from the Problem   265   •
Focus on Interests Rather Than Positions   265   •   Generate More
Options   266   •   Base Decisions on Objective Criteria   268   •   Converting
Competition into Cooperation   268

From Theory to Action   **270**

PART V   *Escalating and De-Escalating Conflict*   **273**

14   *The Escalation of Conflict: Anger and Stress*   **274**

Objectives   **274**

Key Terms   **274**

The Emotion of Anger   **275**

General Irritability   275   •   Anger as a Secondary Emotion   276   •   The
Process of Anger   277   •   Controlling Anger   278   •   Understanding Sources
of Anger   279   •   Responding to Another's Anger   281

Containing Escalation   *281*

Stress and the Escalation of Conflict   *282*
Sources of Stress   284   •   Facing the Expected Event   288   •   Facing
Unexpected Events   288   •   Facing Decision-Making Events   289
•   Facing a Situation of Competing or Difficult Roles   290   •   Ways to
Alleviate Stress   291

From Theory to Action   *292*

15   *Impression Management in Conflict Situations*   *293*

Objectives   *293*

Key Terms   *293*

Understanding the Demands of Face   *294*
Defining Face   294   •   Positive and Negative Face   295   •   Preventing
Face Threats   296   •   Reasons to Avoid Face Issues in Conflict   299

Embarrassment as a Face-Threatening Situation   *299*

Methods for Correcting One's Impression   *303*
Accounts   304   •   Apologies   307   •   Relationship Outcomes When Accounts
and Apologies Are Used   309

From Theory to Action   *312*

16   *After the Conflict: Forgiveness and Reconciliation*   *315*

Objectives   *315*

Key Terms   *315*

Conflicts and Relational Transgressions   *317*

Relational Transgressions   *317*
Transgressions and Their Effects   318   •   Regrettable Messages   320   •
Deception and Lies   320   •   When Conflict Turns to Violence   324

Conflict, Forgiveness, and Reconciliation   *325*
Part of the Social Fabric   326   •   Why People Don't Forgive or Restore
Relationships   327   •   What Is Forgiveness?   329   •   What Forgiveness
Is Not   331   •   Strategizing for Forgiveness   332   •   The Importance of
Creating Reconciliation   333   •   Receiving Forgiveness   336   •   Moving
beyond Victimization   336

From Theory to Action   *338*

Appendix A   Mediation as Third-Party Intervention   341

Settling Disputes through the Intervention of a Third Party   341

Mediation Compared to Adjudication   343

Who Are the Mediators?   345

When Should a Third Party Intervene?   347

Mediator Skills   348

Basic Communication Skills   348   •   Structuring the Process of Mediation   348   •
Reframing the Disputants' Statements and Positions   349   •   Expanding the
Information Resource   349

Mediators as Communication Rules Enforcers   349

The Mediation Process: Step by Step   350

The Mediator's Opening Statement: Setting the Rules   351   •   The Disputants'
Opening Statements: Identifying the Issues   352   •   Exchange: Clarifying the
Issues   352   •   Building an Agreement: Identifying Goals   353   •   The Written
Agreement   354   •   The Closing   355

Code of Ethics   355

Mediation in Educational Settings   356

School-Based Mediation Models   356   •   College-Based Mediation Models   357

In Summary   358

Appendix B   Example of a Conflict Assessment   360

References   364

Index   381

Preface

When we first started discussing conflict at the beginning of the semester, I really thought I had never experienced a major conflict in my life. When people talked about their conflicts in class, I used to think that something was wrong with them. First of all, I believed I had never experienced a really dramatic conflict and second of all, I couldn't believe that they were telling them to the whole class. What I didn't realize was that there were conflicts in my life and that I was just not dealing with them.

Although we may not always admit it or even know it, most of us encounter conflict quite frequently. Sometimes conflict is easily resolved, particularly when we find, simply through talking to the other person, that what you have is a false conflict. If you share a car with another person, for instance, you may assume that arranging to use the car that evening will be difficult. When you actually talk to that person, however, you may find that the other person has no plans for the car when you want it. You thought there was a conflict, but after talking to the other person, you found that there was none.

In other cases, though, communication with the other individual only reinforces what you anticipated—the two of you want different things, the other person does not see things your way, and you cannot get what you want from the situation. Business partners who disagree about the way in which a product should be marketed, for example, may understand each other's position quite clearly and still not agree with one another. If they want to be successful, however, they need to resolve their differences over the marketing of the product. At the very least, they must compromise or manage their conflict.

Conflict management is not always easy. Dealing effectively with conflict requires more than following simple communication rules—it requires that we make choices to act toward the other based on an understanding of the situation (including the conflict issue and the other person's likely responses) and a knowledge of what choices are most likely to help us achieve what we want, without making us feel that we have acted inappropriately. Thus, a *fundamental assumption* of this book is that *effective behavior in conflict situations requires an ability to analyze the situation and choose behavior appropriate to it, without sacrificing one's own values and beliefs.* It may not seem that people can reach agreement without making such a sacrifice, but we will show you how it can be done.

As we analyze situations, we are affected by our desire to appear competent to others. A *second assumption* that underlies the approach of this text is that *people are motivated to create and maintain favorable impressions of themselves with others, and this motivation may generate or exacerbate conflict situations.* This desire to maintain *face,* as Goffman termed it,[1] is important in conflict situations.

There are some writers who believe that face issues tend to distract people in conflict from focusing on more substantive issues such as the control of resources (e.g., money) or competing solutions to a problem.[2] We argue, however, that the impression people feel others have of them may be the central issue in the conflict, as the following narrative illustrates. Our desire to be seen by others as we see ourselves is a powerful motivator in all communication situations and must be seen as an integral motivator of action in conflict situations.

Effectiveness in conflict situations requires analysis, which is tempered by our desire to maintain a favorable impression by appearing competent to others. The third element is choice, which may be the most critical in conflict management. Although we cannot dictate others' responses, we *can* choose our own actions and thereby feel satisfied that we have done all we can to deal with a conflict directly. Conflict itself is neither good nor bad, but behaviors within a conflict can be evaluated that way. This idea of choice constitutes a *third assumption* in the approach of this textbook, which is that *people feel that they have acted most competently in conflict situations when they perceive that they chose their actions rather than simply reacted to the other person.* Consider how these three basic assumptions about conflict behavior are illustrated by this encounter between two friends who work together:

> My friend Jose, whom I have known for almost three years, asked me out to dinner. I accepted with the idea that we were just going out as friends. During dinner, however, Jose added a new twist to our relationship when he confessed that what he felt for me was more than friendship. Imagine my surprise and shock as I searched for the "right thing" to say. (Is there really ever a right thing to say in this situation?) I didn't want to hurt his feelings because I know how sensitive he is (he takes everything personally), but I also knew that I had to be honest with him and tell him I didn't feel the same way. I explained as best I could how I thought of him as a friend, and he seemed to take it rather well. The next day when a close friend of mine asked me how it went, I told her. Unfortunately, I did not count on her unusually big mouth, and soon quite a few people (including Jose) knew that I had refused Jose's affections (a nice way of saying he crashed and burned).
>
> To make a long story short, Jose no longer talks to me, and he only looks at me when I ask him a direct question, and even that is like pulling teeth. I really miss him as a friend. Not only do I feel bad because I hurt his feelings when I turned him down, but he also thinks that I made fun of him and is embarrassed that other people besides me know about his feelings. I have tried several times since our "date" to talk to him, but he denies that he is mad and leaves the room. I can see that it would be very hard for him to talk to me after what has happened, especially if he believes that I went out of my way to be cruel and make fun of him. Whatever the case, the fact that we are still not talking really bothers me. All I want is the opportunity to tell him my side of the story and to explain to him that I never intended for the story to get around work.

You can see from the beginning that the first assumption of effective conflict management was violated. The woman had no time to analyze the situation; she had to ad lib a response to a very surprising statement. Then, rather unthinkingly, she told someone about what had happened, and the word spread throughout their part of the organization.

In addition, it is obvious that impression management played a large part in the creation and maintenance of this conflict. Jose had no way of backing down from his attempt to make the relationship more serious, particularly because his unsuccessful attempt had become public knowledge. The woman, who had no intention of hurting his feelings or causing him embarrassment, nonetheless did so. This drive to manage impressions can lead us to pull back from others when our image has been damaged, to fight to restore the impression another has of us when that impression has been questioned, or to agree to plans we do not really like. Throughout this text, we will focus on the effect that thinking about one's impression has on the conflict choices a person makes.

A final note on the preceding example concerns the problems resulting from the conflict. It is not that conflict exists that created the problems for the narrator and Jose. It was the sense that neither felt as though the common knowledge about their encounter was really due to choices they made. Although both had tried to handle the incompatible expectations for the relationship in a caring manner, the gossip surrounding their encounter made the conflict larger and created a sense of being involved in something over which they had no control.

The title of this book reflects a progression through the process of conflict—from understanding theory to implementing appropriate action. We must understand why certain skills work before we can use them properly; thus, the book begins with our understanding of the nature of interpersonal conflict and the theories of conflict before discussing skills. In addition, throughout the book, we have tended to "privilege" relationship conflict over other types—that is, we have given a great deal of attention to conflicts over the very nature of the way people relate to one another. Our reason for doing so is that they have different dynamics than conflicts that occur, for example, over things like money or space. Resource-based conflicts may seem difficult, but they are fairly easy to diagnose and to manage. Conflicts over who we should be with respect to one another are more "slippery"— we may not even realize that our relationship is the source of problems and yet we feel a sense of dissatisfaction that generally may only be alleviated through conflict engagement.

Part I of the text is meant to help you understand what conflict is and what people bring to the conflict situation in the way of attitudes, beliefs, and values, as well as explaining the impact of cultural identity and gender on conflict processes. Part II explains the various forms in which conflict occurs, and how the process of conflict unfolds into both productive and destructive patterns, in addition to explaining the various ways and means people use to engage in conflict. Part III provides a theoretical perspective for understanding conflict behavior, examining both traditional and social-psychological theories and exploring an emerging communication perspective on conflict. Part IV is concerned with competent behavior in conflict situations: creating effective messages, avoiding aggressive behavior, listening to the other, and confronting the other in a productive manner. Part V provides tools for controlling destructive impulses in conflict encounters and in creating outcomes that are good for the long as well as the short term. We have also included two appendices—one examining mediation processes and another showing how the conflict assessment guide might be used by someone experiencing a conflict.

Throughout the book, you will encounter brief narratives and longer case studies. These are personal descriptions of conflict situations. Whenever possible, we have allowed these individuals to speak for themselves and have used their actual words. Although in conflict situations, our goal should be to try to understand how the other person feels and what he or she wants as a result of the conflict, we generally know only our own side of the story. Thus, many of the narratives and case studies included here present only one view of the conflict. Having read the feelings and perceptions of those involved in the conflicts, you should try to put yourself in the place of the speaker, attempt to understand the situation, and think about how *you* would deal with the issue.

Each chapter offers several applications, or exercises, designed for use inside and outside the classroom. Examples are drawn from a variety of situations familiar to students, including roommate difficulties, family problems, and work conflicts. As the book moves from theoretical concepts to the practice of conflict skills, more time is devoted to helping you identify effective conflict behaviors and learn how to acquire them.

This text moves from the general to the specific. It starts with the nature of conflict, examines various theories that explain conflict dynamics, and then moves to an understanding of different conflict situations. Once the theoretical foundation has been laid, the text turns to skills of analysis, productive attitudes, values, beliefs, and specific communication behaviors that are effective in conflict situations. As you read through this book, you will progress from an understanding of conflict processes, to understanding particular conflict situations, to adopting constructive attitudes and building skills that help achieve mutually satisfactory goals in conflict situations.

The one thing a textbook on conflict management cannot offer you is "communication magic." Despite the existence of books and magazine articles with titles such as *The Eight Essential Steps to Conflict Resolution*,[3] there are no easy ways to make conflicts disappear or to make you feel any better about the conflicts in your life. It is possible, however, to raise your level of understanding and to increase your ability to respond effectively and appropriately to the conflicts you experience. We hope that this will be a productive learning period for you as you embark on the study of conflict.

When studying conflict management, you will find it helpful to set two or three goals to meet during the semester or quarter. You will gain effective behaviors at a different pace than other readers, but most people are encouraged when they can see personal progress toward better conflict skills. Keeping a "conflict journal" also promotes personal growth because reflection on behaviors becomes more informed throughout the semester.

Consider your enrollment in a conflict course an adventure, and remember that periods of change can be stressful. Whenever you have had to move from one place to another, for example, it has probably taken longer than you expected and was more stressful than you anticipated. Just as moving can be difficult, rearranging or remodeling behaviors probably will take longer than you expect. Other people will not always behave in ways you will learn are best. Your life may seem messy as you move toward change. The result, however, will be greater satisfaction with your behavior in conflict situations.

Just a note on our writing style—whenever we use a story that one of us has generated, we'll refer to ourselves by name. It seemed to us to be a more personal note than referring to ourselves in the third person by writing "One of the authors . . . ."

Acknowledgments

A textbook isn't published without a great deal of collaboration among coauthors, their families, editors at the press, manuscript reviewers, colleagues, and stimulating students. Working together, they endeavor to publish the best book possible. This work is somewhat unique in that we, coauthors, had not met face-to-face nor talked on the telephone until over halfway through the project. Even then we met just once for a working dinner and talked once or twice on the telephone after that. Everything needed to write this textbook was accomplished via e-mail until toward the end when entire manuscripts were shipped back and forth via "snail mail." We have the electronic age to thank for bringing us together intellectually in cyberspace, where we found plenty of opportunities to collaborate.

Perhaps another unique aspect of this project is that Lee teaches his interpersonal conflict course entirely on-line and asynchronously under the auspices of the SUNY Learning Network. Roxane teaches a course in conflict management for undergraduates twice a year, and teaches a similar class in the master's of management program at Azusa Pacific University.

Back in the "real" world, we would like to thank Karon Bowers of Allyn and Bacon for her continuous support and encouragement and the staff at Omegatype for their expert help in preparing the manuscript for publication. We also thank our reviewers: Lori J. Carrell, University of Wisconsin, Oshkosh; Robert G. Chamberlain, Seattle Pacific University; Alice L. Crume, State University of New York, Brockport; G. Jon Hall, University of Northern Iowa; Suzanne McCorkle, Boise State University; Trudy Mills, Warner Pacific College.

Our colleagues have been wonderful sounding boards and sources of stimulating discussion about all aspects of the conflict process. Lee would especially like to thank Jess Alberts, Robert Bell, Charles Brown, William Benoit, Nancy Burrell, Daniel Canary, William Cupach, Clare Danielsson, Steve Duck, Frank Fincham, MaryAnne Fitzpatrick, John Gottman, James Halpern, Sally Lloyd, Gayla Margolin, Paul Mongeau, Robert Nye, Rory Remer, L. Edna Rogers, Michael Roloff, Teresa Chandler Sabourin, Pepper Schwartz, Brian Spitzberg, Stella Ting-Toomey, Robert Weiss, Dolf Zillmann. Roxane's appreciation goes to those who continue to be a support and encouragement to her as she writes: her family—Ed, Kathy, and David; APU colleagues David Bicker, Wanda Calnon, David Esselstrom, Monica Ganas, Diana Glyer and the St. Rita Society, Kevin Jones, Ray McCormick, Phil Nash, and David Weeks, EQG; and colleagues on other campus, especially Helen Sterk and Barbara Baker.

We appreciate greatly the comments from our students who saw earlier versions of the manuscript. We especially thank all the students and friends who shared their personal stories with us and now with the readers of this book.

Roxane Lulofs

Dudley (Lee) Cahn

Notes

1. See, for example, Erving Goffman, *The Presentation of Self in Everyday Life* (Garden City, NY: Doubleday, 1959).

2. For example, Joseph P. Folger and Marshall Scott Poole, *Working through Conflict,* 2nd Ed. (New York: HarperCollins, 1993).

3. Dudley Weeks, *The Eight Essential Steps to Conflict Resolution* (New York: G. P. Putnam's Sons, 1992).

I

Understanding the Nature of Conflict

Part I of this text consists of three chapters that define and describe how conflict works and what people bring to conflict processes. Some of the questions that are answered in this part of the text include:

What is the nature of conflict?

What functions or purposes does conflict serve?

What are the characteristics of productive and destructive conflict?

Why are conflicts often viewed negatively?

What are the attitudes, beliefs, and underlying values that affect how people approach and react in conflict situations?

What roles do culture and gender play in conflict situations?

These are important questions. Almost every definition of interpersonal conflict fails to capture the complexity of the subject. The term *interpersonal conflict* actually covers several forms of communication and miscommunication. So, in addition to defining the term, we need to realize that conflict is a complicated concept that may emerge in a variety of ways and may lead to productive or destructive outcomes. Conflict may be viewed positively or negatively. How we view conflict depends on the experiences we have in conflict situations. When conflicts seem to be uncontrolled, anger filled, and relationship threatening, it is hard for us to think of conflict in a positive way. But as we learn to deal with conflict and begin to accept it as a normal part of our lives, we come to think of it more productively, as this person suggests:

At the beginning of our marriage, it seemed like every conflict had the potential to cause divorce. It wasn't that we didn't love each other, but conflict was so frightening—we'd yell, storm around, and toss accusations at each other. It took us several years to work that stuff out of our systems and realize that we could have a conflict without all the ugly stuff that goes with it. We've been married twenty years, and we still have conflict, but I can't remember the last time we raised our voices or didn't stop ourselves when anger began to take over the conversation. I'm not afraid of it anymore.

1

1

Introduction to the Study of Conflict

Objectives

At the end of this chapter, you be able to

1. define interpersonal conflict and give examples of conflict situations.
2. explain why conflict is a fact of life.
3. explain why violence is *not* a fact of life.
4. explain the functions of conflict.
5. discuss how conflict has the potential to be productive and destructive.

Key Terms

conflict	destructive conflict	interpersonal violence
conflict functions	inevitability of conflict	productive conflict
conflict metaphors	interpersonal conflict	

Most of us are able to recognize when we are in a conflict. If a friend says, "We need to talk," we know that it is a situation quite different than one indicated by "I need to talk to you." If a friend needs to talk to us, we are to be a sounding board, or a source of advice, but when a friend says, "we need to talk," we usually know there's a problem, and the problem includes us.

In this chapter we first define interpersonal conflict and discuss some of the different ways people view it. We regard conflict as a fact of life, but we believe violence is not. Understanding what conflict is and the functions it serves are the objectives of this chapter.

A Perspective on Conflict

Defining Conflict

A first step in building conflict skills is to differentiate interpersonal conflict from other kinds of communication situations. Defining conflict has been a popular activity among researchers in and outside of the discipline of communication. One reason definitions are important is that the way something is defined will determine the judgments made about it. Some authors claim that conflict situations are tense, threatening, uncertain, and fragile; others argue that most conflicts can be viewed as bargaining situations in which there is an opportunity for one party to influence the other.[1]

Simons wrote almost twenty years ago that an establishment bias existed in approaches to the study of conflict, concentrating far more on learning means to reduce or control conflicts and not enough on means to escalate or exacerbate them.[2] That establishment bias has given way to a basic assumption that conflict is a natural and inevitable part of life, one that people must learn to manage through the acquisition of social skills.[3] Both positions result from the individual writers' definitions of **conflict:** At one end, conflict is seen as a disruption of the normal workings of a system; at the other, conflict is seen as a part of all relationships.

The two positions result from a dialectical tension experienced by those in conflict situations; that is, people expect (logically and intellectually) to experience conflict but want to get it over with as soon as possible so that things can get back to "normal." Interestingly, this tension between the positive and negative dimensions of conflict is reflected in the various Chinese characters used to symbolize conflict. As other writers about conflict have noted, the standard character consists of the characters representing "opportunity" and "danger." There are additional characters used to represent conflict situations consisting of such combinations as "to fight, to discuss," "to stand, to be against," and "collision-point." The character representing the concept of ambiguity (a condition of many conflict instances) is represented by three terms that indicate the "character" of "many" "righteousnesses."

In scholarly writing, a variety of conditions have been used as indicators of conflict situations.[4] Some definitions of conflict are quite simplistic, for example: Conflict is two or more competing responses to a single event, or differences between and among individuals, or mutual hostility between or among groups, or a problem to be solved.[5]

Most conflict definitions emphasize the role of perception in conflict; that is, conflicts arise when people perceive a "divergence of interest . . . a belief that [their] current aspirations cannot be achieved simultaneously,"[6] or that their activities or goals are incompatible with those of the other party. The idea of incompatibility awareness, or the perception that the other is frustrating one's attempts to achieve something, is central to definitions of conflict. Simons argued that conflicts are more serious than simple disagreements or differences of opinions because in conflict people believe that their interests are threatened by the actions of the other person.[7]

Competition for scarce rewards or resources is a common idea; less frequent is the notion that the end of such competition is to neutralize, injure, or eliminate one's rivals.[8] And although Simons discounted the idea that simple disagreements between people can be conflicts, sometimes what is called a "drawing room controversy" becomes a conflict, as when two people engage in a heated debate, which escalates and is observed by others.[9]

This narrator, for example, recounts a circumstance in which a controversy had the potential to erupt into a destructive conflict:

> One day at work a guy who is white was rambling on, releasing his thoughts about African Americans to a couple other coworkers who were black. It started out innocently enough but it was just that he was so persistent in what he believed and spoke of. He said that black people lived in a certain area of town where everyone is poor. He claimed that most of the people there were black. One black girl commented by saying that she lived in that development and she isn't poor. He went on asking other coworkers what they thought, trying to get them to back him up on this issue. I was so astonished because we worked in a grocery store in downtown Syracuse where most of the customers are black and the argument was so incredibly heated! I held my breath expecting them to somehow hurt one another. It was so loud and so intense and the fact that the evening supervisor was right there listening and didn't say anything for a long time made me nervous. I couldn't believe that a conflict rose to such a level and everyone just stood by and listened. I felt that the supervisor should have stepped in much earlier and stopped the conflict before it got to the level it actually did. Mainly, I felt that because we were at work, that the conflict was not occurring at the right place nor the right time. I was always told not to take your personal life to work with you and in this case, the guy shouldn't have been releasing his thoughts and beliefs while cashing people out at the checkout. Customers heard this conflict and it could've turned out much worse if some others began to join in the heated debate. This whole situation made me so incredibly nervous.

As a simple disagreement escalates into an argument and turns into a conflict, it gets more and more difficult to simply walk away from the situation. Driven by impression management issues, people want to appear that they know what they're talking about and will reiterate and escalate their arguments where there is no need to do so.

We may think that conflict revolves around the incompatibility of goals or activities, or arises from competition over scarce resources, but frequently what is at stake is the relationship itself and how the relationship is to be defined. In this case, it is difficult to characterize the conflict as incompatibility or competition—what seems to be at stake are the rules that define how people are to act toward one another. So, for example, although a mother could characterize her irritation at a teenaged daughter's unauthorized use of her makeup as "competition over scarce resources," it could also be seen as a privacy violation or a breaking of a relational rule.

In addition to the perception of conflict, the incompatibility of goals, the competition for scarce rewards or resources, and/or a recognition of rule violation, interpersonal conflict is almost always thought of as something that occurs between interdependent people or people who are mutually dependent on one another to meet their psychological and/or physical needs. If the people involved in the conflict don't have to compete with each other, if they can walk away and get what they need elsewhere, if maintaining the relationship is not a priority, then interpersonal conflict is probably not the best way to describe what is happening. A disagreement over who should be elected president becomes a conflict when it threatens our relationship. People can live with a disagreement without it significantly affecting their relationship, but an interpersonal conflict demands action and some kind of resolution. We can be irritated by the rudeness of a stranger, but the rudeness of a loved one is seldom tolerated. This story illustrates the difference between conflicts that must be addressed and disagreements that may be ignored:

I once sat quietly while the wife of one of my colleagues berated working mothers, claiming that they were harming their children and creating a generation of latchkey children and criminals. I surely did not agree with her, and staying quiet was very difficult. What profit would there have been, however, in arguing with her? I was not likely to change her mind. She can think what she wants about my working outside the home. She is not trying to prevent me from doing it. I do not need her approval, and I only have to see her about twice a year at faculty dinners. Much harder to ignore are my daughter's comments that "real moms make chocolate chip cookies without a mix," and "real moms don't put their kids into daycare." I want my child to understand that there are many different ways to be a mom and that "real moms" care enough to provide quality daycare for their children rather than letting them run wild after school.

The idea of interdependence is best understood when you consider how the outcomes of an interpersonal conflict are linked. When people are interdependent, the outcomes they seek or hope to obtain from the conflict depend on the other person. As one person makes choices, the choices of the other person are constrained; as you seek certain outcomes, you influence the options available to the other person.

These different views enable us to identify **interpersonal conflict** situations, which include these characteristics:

1. the people are interdependent;
2. the people perceive that they seek different outcomes or they favor different means to the same ends;
3. the conflict has the potential to negatively affect the relationship if not addressed; and
4. there is a sense of urgency about the need to resolve the issue.

This person's story illustrates these aspects of conflict:

> My boyfriend Billy is frequently late to things and often at the same time causes me to be late also. I place a high value on promptness. Billy knows I feel tense and angry when we are late to something. Being late appears to me as a lack of responsibility and lack of caring for the relationship, but I feel guilty asking Billy to change his behavior, even though I think it's in his best interest.

The definition we use distinguishes conflict from simple disagreements, bickering, physical aggression, or competition. This is not to say that disagreements, aggression, and competition are unrelated to conflict. They certainly can be. But these other kinds of behavior, although appearing to be conflicts, can be resolved more easily. People can sometimes shrug their shoulders and decide that they do not care or that agreement is not important. They can realize that their bickering is not over anything important. Physical aggression indicates that the people have moved well beyond incompatible goals or interests. And competition may or may not affect one's relationship with the other person. But interpersonal conflicts demand resolution: They concern issues that are important to a relationship; they are with people who are important; and they affect one another's self-concepts in important ways. Learning to differentiate interpersonal conflicts from other situations in which resolution is not as important is a first step in building interpersonal communication and conflict competence.

As the chapters of this book unfold, you will find that the majority of our examples reflect interpersonal conflict in a variety of relationships. You can experience interpersonal conflict with a friend, a classmate, a roommate, an intimate partner, a coworker, a supervisor, or a subordinate. There are many types of conflicts, which we will explain in the next chapter. What is important to understand is that interpersonal conflict occurs because of the relationships we have with others, and because of the things that relational partners in conflict regard as important. The fact that conflicting parties are also relational partners helps explain why interpersonal conflict is often viewed as something negative to be avoided.

Conflict Is Generally Viewed Negatively

Just because we are able to define conflict and recognize one when we are in the middle of it does not mean we have begun to think about conflict as something that is potentially helpful. What comes to mind when you think of interpersonal conflict? How would you complete this sentence?

> To me, conflict is like . . .

Would you describe conflict as being like a war, battle, or fight? Would you say it is more like a struggle, uphill climb, a contest of wills? Is it explosive, violent, an exploding bomb? Or do you think conflict is like being on trial, a day in court? Perhaps you see it as a game, match, or sport? Or would you describe it more as a communication breakdown, a barrier between you and another?

How or what do most people think of conflict generally? They usually agree with the statement, "Conflicts are an inevitable part of our interaction with others." That does not mean they feel confident about handling a conflict. A study asked people to describe conflicts they had experienced and found that overwhelmingly they used negative terms to describe their conflicts: It is like being in a sinking ship with no lifeboat, like a checkbook that won't balance, like being in a rowboat in a hurricane.[10] The conflicts recalled by those in the study were uniformly destructive or negative, suggesting that "if the interpersonal conflict was managed productively, respondents did not perceive it as a conflict at all."[11]

This perception of conflict as negative is underscored by one woman's description of her approach to conflict:

> As I began to analyze the way I approach conflict, I understood why I used to totally destroy and give up on relationships after major altercations. I was like a bulldozer—it took a lot to get me started but once I decided to conflict or move, I didn't leave anything retrievable behind.

You may have realized that being asked to say what conflict is like is an exercise in creating a **metaphor** because you are asked to compare one thing (conflict) with something else (struggle, exploding bombs, being on trial). Metaphors are not only figures of speech but also reflections of how we think.[12]

How we think about conflict creates an expectation as to what can happen, what will or should happen, and the sort of emotions and actions that might occur.[13] Because thoughts, feelings, and actions are intertwined, it is important to examine our attitudes, beliefs, emotional reactions, and behavior in conflict situations. If people describe conflict in negative terms and remember conflicts as unpleasant events, such thinking limits their action in new situations. The actions people choose are a result of the way they interpret situations. How they think about conflict in general terms affects how they see their current situation, how they see the conflict issue, what choices they think are available to them, and how they view the other person's actions. As people choose their responses, they affect the outcome of the conflict situation, and how they view the outcome of a conflict depends largely on their choices and their responses to the other(s) involved.

What do we learn from a collection of metaphors people give when asked what conflict is like to them? We learn at least two things. First, interestingly, not all people choose the same adjectives that you do when asked to describe what conflict means to them. Apparently people vary in which adjectives they choose to describe their perception of interpersonal conflict. These words reflect somewhat different views that are themselves in conflict. Quite often a person who sees conflict as a "battlefield with relationships being the casualties" does not feel like comparing it to being on trial or a day in court. Probably, neither person thinks of conflict as being like a basketball game, a tennis match, or some other sport. Second, we learn that, although people may vary in their perceptions of conflict, most seem to reject the idea that it is a positive, healthy, and fortunate event that should be welcomed. This common but negative attitude toward conflict hinders our learning how to better manage our conflicts. People often think that they may be able to improve the way they handle interpersonal conflicts by learning new communication skills, but they do not realize that their attitudes, beliefs, and emotional reactions may have to undergo change as well.

Part of the reason why many people dislike conflict is because they do not handle conflicts very well. Typical responses to conflict that are poorly managed often depend on the nature of the interpersonal relationship. One way to distinguish between different types of interpersonal relationships is to separate those that tend to be complementary from others that are more symmetrical. Both types can exist among friends, family, team members, coworkers, and other everyday relationships.

What are complementary relationships? In complementary relationships, one personality type is the opposite of the other—for example, dominate and subordinate, outgoing and shy, strong and weak. When conflicts occur in complementary relationships, typically one partner has been found to be more conflict engaging than the other who tends to withdraw more from the conflict.[14] This person's experience reflects a complementary relationship:

> My friend, Cory, likes to win as many arguments as possible. She'll argue over the most unimportant things you can imagine. I have learned to just give in and not make waves to avoid an argument I won't win anyway. If I were to confront her, she would just get defensive and not quit until she had the last word. One morning, she threw an extinguished cigarette butt in a wastepaper basket she keeps in her bedroom. She and I were in another room, when somehow the wastepaper caught fire and some of her clothes went up in flames before we could douse the fire with an extinguisher. She didn't apologize for putting our lives in danger but instead got angry at me for not being sympathetic when some of her clothes got ruined.

Management of conflict in complementary relationships has been found to be dissatisfying for many partners. If the complementary relationship is temporary, the way conflicts are handled may not always produce long-term effects, but for those complementary relationships that persist, partners' handling of conflict may do serious harm to the relationship.

What are symmetrical relationships? In symmetrical relationships, the two personalities are quite similar—for example, both partners are competitive, or both are shy. When conflicts occur in this type of relationship, the behaviors typically mirror each other. In the case of strong personalities that also may be characterized as competitive, dominant, and stubborn, the conflicts usually escalate, perhaps getting out of hand and becoming violent. In relationships consisting of such strong personalities, when one partner threatens, the other counters with a threat that is met by one of greater intensity, and so on.[15] In this example, the narrator has a complementary relationship with Augie and a symmetrical relationship with Brian, affecting the way conflict is played out with each person:

> This past summer, I worked with Brian and Augie in a house painting business. Not only did we work together every day but we also lived together. Augie and I got along quite well living and working together but Brian and I didn't. The conflict came when we were painting a house and we laid down a game plan as to how we would paint it. Brian didn't like it so he changed it. Augie and I didn't like it, so we tried to talk him out of his plan. He refused to change and said if he didn't do it his way he wouldn't work. We got into a shouting match and almost ended up in a fight.

Symmetrical relationships are not simply found in organizational contexts. People in romantic relationships can also be connected in a symmetrical way. When this occurs, conflict can take negative forms. Ting-Toomey found that partners in symmetrical long-term romantic relationships typically resort to attacking, complaining, and defending:

- Attacking directly criticizes, or negatively evaluates the other's feelings/ideas, and consists of loaded questions and direct rejection.
- Complaining discloses discontent and resentment through indirect strategies of blame aimed at the other and/or the situation.
- Defending persists in clarifying one's own position in spite of the other's feelings/ideas and involves justifying one's own actions, those of others, and/or the situation.[16]

Ting-Toomey concluded from her research that partners in long-term romantic relationships typically begin a conflict in a manner by directly attacking each other with criticism and negatively loaded statements, followed by attempts to justify oneself and blame the other. This common way of handling conflict potentially contributes to the disintegration of their relationship. Whereas some symmetrical relationships contain strong personalities, other relationships may consist of partners who are less engaging, more withdrawn, and more likely to avoid. In these cases, as issues continue to fester, each may wish that the other would do something. Each person may get more and more upset, frustrated, and withdrawn. As a result, the partners become so independent that the relationship becomes nonexistent over time.

Neither of these findings will give you particular confidence in approaching conflict situations. Although conflict is often handled differently in symmetrical and complementary relationships, parties typically handle the conflicts poorly in either case. Perhaps the mismanagement of conflict common to many of us has given the subject a bad name. It is possible through the learning of more constructive attitudes and more positive conflict management and resolution skills to become less apprehensive about engaging in conflict and more confident of a positive outcome.

APPLICATION 1.1

Overall, would you say you are a person who deals with conflict fairly easily or one who finds conflict difficult? What makes it difficult or easy? What prompted you to take a class in conflict management?

The Inevitability of Conflict

Conflict Is a Fact of Life

Whether we change our attitudes about it or not, conflict is a fact of life. We encounter it at home, at school, and at work. This person seems to have walked into a conflict on his first day on the job:

> I was recently hired as a daycare worker for a preschool. My co-worker has been in the field for a long time, and she has been at this particular center longer than anyone else, but the woman rules with a fist of iron! These little kids get told exactly what to do at all minutes of the day. I think little kids are best off just having fun and being taught something along the way. She seems to think that unless kids are forcibly disciplined that they'll walk all over her. I don't know how to bring this up to her, or whether I should talk to my supervisor about it. None of the parents are complaining, but the kids just seem miserable.

Think over years past and recall the conflicts, complaints, or grievances you had with these three types of people: (1) neighbors living a few houses away, (2) next-door neighbors, and (3) roommates (or teammate, close friend, or romantic partner). With the more distant neighbors, you may have been upset by the appearance of their home and yard, noise, or their pets and children trespassing on your property. As for your next-door neighbors, some people have encountered a number of serious problems. You may have experienced many of the same conflicts as you did with the distant neighbors and more—like disagreements over property lines, dropping in on you too often, borrowing tools and not returning them, unsightly fences, invasions of privacy, making noises far into the night, blinding lights, talking to you every time you go out into your yard (especially when sunbathing). What about your roommates? Here you could probably write a book. You may have had disagreements over study habits, sleeping habits, smoking, snoring, messiness, household chores, use of a car, friends who are noisy or sleep over, paying bills, buying furniture, television, tools, and borrowing clothes. If you substituted teammate, close friend, or romantic partner, you have likely accumulated a similar list of disagreements.

Undoubtedly, you can add many examples to these lists. The question is this: What happens to conflicts as relationships become closer, more personal, and more interdependent? If you compare the lists you created for the preceding three types of relationships, you probably found that as the relationship becomes closer and more interdependent (from a distant neighbor to a next-door neighbor and from a next-door neighbor to a roommate, teammate, close friend, or romantic partner):

- the more opportunities there are for conflict
- the more trivial (minor) complaints become significant ones
- the more intense the feelings

> Before I started keeping track of my conflicts, I didn't think that I was involved in many conflicts. Now, I see that I have a lot of conflicts, and that many of them could have been handled differently. There are acquaintances, outsiders, and strangers who make me angry, but I choose not to get into a verbal conflict with them. It just isn't worth the time or effort. Basically, I just walk away or change the topic. For example, when I asked a cashier a question in a store and she replied in a nasty and rude manner, I ignored her and proceeded to leave as if nothing had happened. I am more comfortable expressing my feelings to people who are closest to me. The other day I snapped at my mother in a way that I could never do to a bus driver or clerk. I know my mother realized that I wasn't disrespecting her.
>
>   With outsiders I feel anger, annoyance, confusion, and fear, but with those closest to me I still experience anger, annoyance, and confusion, but I feel more sorrow than fear. I also noted that I deal with my conflicts differently with people closest to me. It is always with the people that I care most about that I have the greatest difficulty reaching an agreement. I believe that beneath the surface of many of my conflicts with them is a basic lack of understanding.
>
>   It frustrates me when the people closest to me cannot understand how I feel. Such is the case with my father. He is home alone all day and does nothing to keep himself busy. In my opinion I think he enjoys getting into conflicts with me just to have something to do and to make me communicate with him. I find this ridiculous, annoying, and childish, but he says he doesn't do it intentionally. In conflicts with him, I feel a great deal of intensity. The topics of the conflicts with my father are basically trivial, but even so I think about them a lot and do not easily forget them. I think the reason our conflicts affect me so much is because deep down inside I know he is right, and I just don't want to admit it to myself. At the same time, he doesn't care enough about how I feel. Maybe I need to move away from home, and when I can afford to, I will.

As we go from our relationship with a distant neighbor to that of a roommate, we are physically closer, but we feel emotionally closer in that we care more about those people to whom we feel closest. In addition, the behavior of someone close to us usually has more consequences for us than the behavior of those more physically and emotionally distant. This interdependence means that the individuals involved can "potentially aid or interfere with each other. . . . In interpersonal relationships, parties depend on each other for a wide range of emotional, psychological, and material resources."[17]

Building on an idea which Foa and Foa originally devised, Rettig and Bubolz identified seven types of emotional, psychological, and material resources that produce satisfaction in long-term romantic relationships.[18] As you might have guessed, those things that provide satisfaction in relationships have the potential to create conflict when people perceive they are lacking. In order of importance, they are:

- love—nonverbal expressions of positive regard, warmth, or comfort
- status—verbal expressions of high or low prestige or esteem
- service—labor of one for another
- information—advice, opinions, instructions, or enlightenment

- goods—contributions of material goods
- money—financial contributions
- shared time—time spent together

The authors claim that the best kind of long-term romantic relationship seemed to be one in which partners felt that they got what they deserved. Although their research focused on romantic partners, many of these seven resources are relevant to other types of interpersonal relationships including roommates, neighbors, friends, coworkers, and family.

Getting from others what one feels one deserves in interpersonal relationships requires a great deal of cooperation by the parties involved. Because of this need for cooperation among interdependent people, conflicts are always characterized by a combination of incentives to compete and cooperate. Even when some communicators intend to cooperate, their words and actions often reflect only their own needs, which may make others think that they have to stick up for their own interests. As people think more in terms of themselves than as a family, couple, team, friends, or coworkers, the relationship is threatened, perhaps arousing strong feelings. Thus, the incentive to compete or cooperate is important in determining the direction the conflict interaction takes and the future of the interpersonal relationship.

Because we do become closer to and more interdependent with some people than with others, we can expect more conflict. The inevitability of conflict that exists in interpersonal relationships runs contrary to the idea that, if we look long and hard, we can find people with whom we can share our lives conflict free. The principle of the **inevitability of conflict** means that we should cease our efforts to find perfect people and learn how to manage the conflicts we are sure to have with those closest to us. We need to learn how to deal with minor as well as major conflicts, how to maintain our objectivity when engaged in conflict, and how to keep our self-control.

APPLICATION 1.2

Do you tend to cooperate or compete when you are involved in an interpersonal conflict? How could you learn to cooperate more frequently than you already do?

Interpersonal Violence Is Not a Fact of Life

If we were to ask you what is the *biggest problem* in interpersonal conflict, what would you say? What we are asking you to consider for a moment and then to answer to yourself is this: What is the biggest danger regarding interpersonal conflict? You might answer that you fear that conflicts will terminate your relationship. Later we will show you that conflicts may actually improve your interpersonal relationships.

We would hope you would answer that interpersonal conflicts are the biggest problem when they get out of hand and turn violent. **Interpersonal violence** is not difficult to recognize; it occurs when one person imposes his or her will on another through verbal or physical intimidation. Interpersonal violence is a violation of what is considered socially acceptable and is used to inflict pain on another person. Abusive behavior may be less intense, such as verbal attack, or more intense, such as physical attack. People may also be deliberate and plan their attack, or it may erupt spontaneously.[19] According to this view, interpersonal violence, physical aggression, and abusive relationships are a type of interpersonal conflict, albeit an extreme and unhealthy type.

We take this opportunity to introduce the concept of interpersonal violence because every interpersonal conflict carries with it the seeds of violent behavior, and violent behavior is becoming increasingly prevalent in American social life, making interpersonal conflict management and resolution essential social skills. By teaching nonviolent solutions to problems, setting an example in our daily lives, and raising our children to resolve interpersonal conflicts peacefully, we are helping to reduce a serious social problem. Thus, escalation of conflict into interpersonal violence is the most significant problem and learning to avoid escalation (i.e., de-escalation) is an important goal.

The idea that conflicts need not turn violent implies that we have some options for handling our differences with others. This is where interpersonal ethics enters in. The major determinant of whether our communication and conflict behaviors are ethical or unethical can be found in the notion of choice. Folger and Poole note that a person is acting unethically when his or her messages force another person "(1) to make choices he or she would not normally make, or (2) to decline to make choices he or she would normally make, or both."[20]

The notion of choice applies to interpersonal violence in two ways. First, when we turn violent or others use violence against us, we are using force to prevent others' freedom of choice. Second, the notion of choice should help us realize that we need not turn violent in the first place. We always have choices in conflict situations, we are all responsible for our own actions, and we can make a difference in our lives and in others' lives. Although conflict is inevitable, it need not, and should not, harm our relationships with others, get out of hand, and turn violent.

The Consequences of Conflict

Functions of Conflict

If we accept the inevitability of conflict in life, we should also accept that conflict serves important purposes in relationships. The purpose of this section is not reassurance, nor is it an attempt to establish the idea that conflict, like vitamins or exercise, is something that is "good for us." Rather, it is a reminder that conflict is not simply something visited upon us by a random or capricious environment. Conflict is at the root of social and personal change; it is a natural outgrowth of interactions with others and the choices made in those interactions. In this sense, conflict fulfills a **function,** which means that conflict serves a purpose. The purpose of conflict may be to bring about positive change, but if conflict is mismanaged, the opposite may occur. What purposes or functions does conflict fulfill?

> **APPLICATION 1.3**
>
> When you have had conflict in the past, what has it done for (or to) the relationships you had with the people involved? What kinds of conflicts have led to good outcomes? What kinds of conflicts have led to bad outcomes?

First, conflicts may help people find the boundaries of their relationships with others, or they may mark the termination of an existing relationship. For example, Lisa and Nathan are just friends and not ready yet for a romantic or intimate relationship. It is likely, though, that they will be more able to recognize that they are "just friends" if they have experienced a well-managed conflict over the inappropriateness of certain intimate behaviors rather than simply assuming that each knows what the other wants. If the conflict were handled poorly, or if the first experience of inappropriate behaviors led to the two of them distrusting each other's motives, conflict could just as easily lead to the end of the relationship.

Second, conflict from an external source may strengthen the cohesiveness of a group of people working together, or it may destroy a group's ability to think clearly and adapt productively to the situation. An external conflict may be seen as an opportunity for group members to rally together against a common enemy, or it may be seen as an opportunity to lay blame on others in order to save oneself.

Third, conflict within a working group may help the group clarify its goals and desires, or it may tear the group apart. A group of high school Girl Scouts, for example, may clarify goals by deciding what activities are feasible within the budget they have been given, but they may not survive as a group if they attack one another's ideas because of the person who happened to suggest it.

Fourth, conflict facilitates the reconciliation of people's legitimate interests, or it may keep them apart.[21] If people in a work group have different needs for different types of resources to do their job, they may work out, through a conflict, a priority list for obtaining the resources in an equitable manner. However, poorly managed conflict may reinforce competition for resources, resulting in no one obtaining what is needed.

Finally, at a personal level, the experience of conflict builds empathy because people begin to understand the feelings experienced by others in similar situations. When you are explaining a problem you are experiencing and your listener says, "Gosh, I know just how you feel," it is less irritating if that person has had similar circumstances. There is a feeling that another person has a sense of the problem you are facing. On the other hand, "Gosh, I know just how you feel" may contribute to defensiveness and misunderstanding if the other person really has no basis for saying so.

In extolling the virtues of conflict, we do not mean to reinforce what Sillars and Weisberg called a "strong cultural bias about openness in human relationships." In an important article on the communication skills associated with conflict management, Sillars and Weisberg point out that our society almost has a reverence for open communication, seeing it as a cure for conflict and other ills that assail us. In creating this expectation that a lack of open communication is at the root of our problems, we have downplayed the importance of "corresponding needs for privacy, mystery, and the occasional need to 'let sleeping dogs lie.'"[22] As they point out, sometimes conflicts are resolved without direct communication. And sometimes trying to talk about a conflict can create as many or more problems than the conflict entailed alone. Like Sillars and Weisberg, we advocate the management of conflict, which may or may not include the resolution of conflict, depending on the situation and best interests of the individuals and their interpersonal relationship.

Conflict Communication as Productive or Destructive

Conflict has the potential to be productive or destructive—actions and reactions to particular situations will determine the outcome. When conflict exists, there must be action to solve the problem, either through open confrontation or through indirect, tacit methods. How people think and feel about conflict affects the way they make choices in conflict situations. If one approaches conflict as a problem to be solved or an opportunity to persuade, more constructive choices are likely than if one views conflict as something to be feared. One woman reports her change in attitude toward conflict:

> The most valuable lesson I have learned is that conflict is not necessarily bad. Gaining all this knowledge and understanding of conflict skills did not help me change my behaviors overnight. It is still a conscious effort to analyze the conflicts that arise and it is difficult to direct my behaviors toward a productive and satisfying outcome. Usually, I understand what I have done after it happened less productively. Maybe one day soon I will be able to recognize and exercise the available resources naturally to produce a more satisfying outcome to conflict. One thing I have noticed is the change of my attitude toward conflict. I no longer see conflicts as the worst thing that can happen to relationships. My acceptance of conflicts as the result of relationships has helped minimize the discomfort I feel in conflict situations.

Conflict is destructive or dysfunctional when "the participants in it are dissatisfied with the outcomes and all feel that they have lost as a result of the conflict"; it is productive or serves a useful purpose when "the participants all are satisfied with their outcomes and feel that they have gained as a result of the conflict."[23] However, feelings about the outcome are not enough to determine the productivity of a conflict. Some conflicts, although uncomfortable in the short run, may serve the needs of those in the relationship in the long run, or may even serve others outside the parties' relationship or society at large.[24]

This makes sense, particularly for people who are uncomfortable experiencing conflict at the outset. If, for example, you have new roommate, and you find that almost immediately your personal habits are diametrically opposed, you might feel very uncomfortable as you initiate a conflict with your roommate in order to find some point of agreement on your habits. Because you do not know the other well, the conflict episode may seem strained and awkward. Afterward, you may feel you did not really say things in the best way possible. However, if over time it became clear that initiating the conflict had enabled you to tolerate each other's behavior better, then judging by the outcome, it was a productive conflict. Rather than judging the productivity of a conflict by people's feelings when it is over, it is more useful to consider people's actual behavior within the conflict itself.

In what way can conflict communication be viewed as negative and destructive? A conflict is destructive if partners are dissatisfied with the results and feel that they have lost as a consequence of the conflict. Conflict is dysfunctional when it harms the relationship because it is not managed or resolved in a way that is mutually satisfactory. When participants in the conflict lose sight of their original goals, when hostility becomes the norm, when conflict becomes a regular part of the interaction between people, it is destructive. **Destructive conflict** is characterized by a tendency to expand and escalate the conflict to the point where it often becomes separated from the initial cause and takes on a life of its own.[25]

Suppose Reshita wants to go shopping (as a couple) and Eddie would prefer to stay home and watch television. If they stay home, Reshita may be upset with Eddie. On the other hand, if they go shopping together, Eddie doesn't get to relax and watch his program. In either case, where one simply complies with the other without some kind of discussion, one person wins and the other loses. At a more subtle level, there is an implied inequality (my way is superior to yours), and attempts to manipulate the other person may dominate. This is called a win-lose situation, which is destructive for three reasons:

- it can provoke retaliation because it often results in anger, resentment, and the desire to get even
- it may not last because the losing party usually lacks commitment to the final outcome

- it may continue to fester emotionally because the parties may become entrenched in their own positions, feeling even more strongly that each is right.

The win-lose situation occurs because parties fear losing. Parties become difficult, argue, or fight because they fear losing one or more of the preceding types of emotional, psychological, or material resources. By failing to confront the problem in a constructive manner, over time Reshita and Eddie may disintegrate into separate, parallel lives (perhaps she goes shopping, eats out with friends, goes bar hopping, and he stays home to watch television)—heading down two roads that seldom intersect. In this case, the conflicts produce estrangement and the potential for bitterness. Consider this person's account of poorly handled conflicts:

> When in conflict with those closest to me, I experience a lot of frustration, anger, anxiety, irritation, and resentment, and I handle conflicts badly. I tend to "fly off the handle" a lot, not thinking first. Because I get upset, I yell, accuse, or become sarcastic. I usually don't look at the other person's point of view because I am too busy yelling or stomping around the room. For example, I gave one friend, Jason, an incorrect reason why another friend, Tim, was not going to have a drink. I told Jason that Tim had a problem with alcohol which wasn't really true. When Tim found out what I told Jason, he got upset (understandably) with me, and we had a nasty argument which continued to the following night. I remember yelling, swearing, flaying my arms in the air, kicking a chair, and accusing him of being from an alcoholic family (which wasn't true). I know I must have sounded ridiculous. Communication cannot be reversed. It is difficult to work out a solution to a problem after saying hurtful words to the other person. When I think back on my past conflicts, the majority were over trivial things and could have been handled differently.

Destructive conflict, as you can see, is characterized by expansion—of the issues, people, principles and precedents considered to be at stake, costs to the participants, and intensity of negative feelings. It is characterized by a desire to hurt the other person and to get even for past wrongs. Destructive conflict occurs when there is no de-escalation, even in the face of other options. Destructive conflict places heavy reliance on overt power and manipulative techniques.

Conflicts need not be destructive if managed properly. How, then, can conflict communication be constructive? A conflict is constructive if partners feel that they participated in making a decision that affects them, feel satisfied with the results, and think that they both have gained something as a consequence of the conflict. Suppose that in the preceding case, Reshita and Eddie discuss the matter, starting out on more equal footing and clearly stating their needs. Reshita explains the importance of shopping (perhaps for both partners) and Eddie talks about his work schedule in which he is more tired on some nights than on others. Because they create supportiveness and a willingness to cooperate, they come to an agreement in which both go shopping together at a time that is not a problem for Eddie. Knowing that they plan to shop on another night, Reshita does not object to relaxing and watching television that particular evening. When they go shopping, Eddie gets help on buying clothes, too. In this case, both partners may feel satisfied with the outcome. This is known as a win-win situation whereby the conflict is handled in a way that preserves or promotes:

- love; intense, positive feelings
- commitment; expectations that the relationship will continue
- expressions of affection, esteem, and recognition
- caring, concern, interest, fascination with the partner; orientation toward the partner

- desire to help the partner in material, tangible ways
- mutual interest and activities; continuing to enjoy being together, doing things together
- trust and disclosure; continuing to take the partner into one's confidence[26]

For Reshita and Eddie in a win-win situation, conflicts clear up misunderstandings and lead to more positive feelings toward each other.

> When engaged in conflict with my brother, Carl, we usually begin with a period of silence where we both contemplate our reasons for feeling as we do. Then comes the verbal argument (I prefer to call it a discussion). We try to be compromising and focus on the problem. We are supportive, encouraging, direct, and honest. We express positive feelings for each other to let him know that we care and want things to work out. We are careful about letting the other express himself while trying to understand his point of view. I would say we believe in equal power. Finally after we get everything off our chests and get the matter resolved, we poke fun at each other and feel like a weight has been lifted off our shoulders.

Some research has indicated that people who have similar values tend to engage in constructive conflict, as in the foregoing example, whereas relationships with low value similarity are more likely to experience destructive conflict.[27] In relationships with dissimilar others, how can productive conflict be created?

Productive conflict is characterized by flexibility, belief that all can achieve important goals, and balance between competitiveness and cooperation. Perhaps the most effective way to create productive conflict is to remain flexible in our own behavior and in our expectations of others' behavior.[28]

Everyone has preferred ways of doing things. Routines and rituals are useful because repetitive tasks can be performed without really thinking about them. But falling into a routine or resorting to comfortable behavior in a conflict is not necessarily the most adaptive response. For example, if your routine is to withdraw when faced with a conflict, it will occasionally be a useful strategy, but at times you will lose your input on a situation because you were not willing to become involved. In addition, flexibility in what you expect of others is important. People often expect others to behave essentially the same way today as they did yesterday. Change is often frightening and usually uncomfortable. Yet, if people have flexible expectations and tolerate others' behavior, conflicts may be managed productively.

A second key to productive conflict is the belief that all the parties involved can achieve important goals. The feeling that we must "win" a conflict leads to unnecessary escalation and expansion.[29] To implement this belief that all involved can achieve important goals, we need to learn to distinguish between outcomes we consider essential and outcomes we consider desirable. For example, when you go to purchase a car, you know there are certain things you must have: windshield wipers, tires, an engine, and so on. Other things are desirable but not essential: a compact disc player, variable speeds on your windshield wipers, air conditioning, and so forth. You decide what you can afford and pay for the extras that are within your budget. Balancing between essential and desirable outcomes in a conflict is similar. If you get your way in this conflict, will it affect your ability to negotiate with this particular person in the future? Will it adversely affect your relationship? If you fail to fight for what you want now, will you be unable to do so in the future? If you were the person telling this narrative, how would you resolve the conflict productively?

> There are three of us presently living together. The conflict is with a roommate who lived with two of us (I just transferred in) last semester. She moved out with a friend because it was

free room and board. Sometimes she decides she doesn't feel like driving the 12 miles home, so she stays the night with us. This went on just about every night last week. As a result, she wore my clothes every day (without asking first), slept on our couch (which gave us no place to study), ate our food, and used our personal items like shampoo and makeup. For me, it peaked when she walked by me after class wearing my brand new wool coat with the sleeves rolled up and said, "Hi! I'm wearing your coat!" As I looked over my shoulder to see her continue by, I noticed she also had on my shoes, pants (that were too small for her), and a sweater of mine. She is a wonderful sweet person and there never was any problem with her other than this. I don't mind if people borrow my clothes, but I prefer that they ask first and that I get them back in the condition I lent them. I also think I should wear my clothes more often than other people do. Also, I'd like it if she would plan when she is spending the night so she could bring her own clothes, makeup, and food. As the saying goes, "I love her but I can't afford to keep her!" I've asked her in the past not to stretch out my things and have made comments about the food being eaten, but she seems oblivious to the situation.

The difficulty in this narrative is that the person telling the story appears to genuinely like her friend but is bothered by the apparent disregard her friend has for rules about borrowing clothing and personal items. When the relationship is important to you, conflict becomes more problematic. In this case, the narrator wants to get the other person's attention without hurting the friendship.

A third characteristic of productive conflict is that it is characterized by a balance between competitiveness and cooperation. Cooperation aids in the creation of an open atmosphere and the exchange of information. It helps each side recognize the legitimacy of others' interests and goals, and, therefore, both sides are committed to finding a solution that meets the needs of all those involved. Cooperation helps to minimize differences between the parties in the conflict.[30]

Cooperation does not mean relinquishing one's own goals, however. It means that one recognizes that the others involved have goals that are equally important to them and that there should be an effort to fulfill both.

> **APPLICATION 1.4**
>
> Describe a recent conflict you experienced that you considered productive. Contrast it with one you experienced that you considered destructive. What made the difference for you? Why?

Although people in interpersonal relationships typically deal with conflicts by planning and engaging in negative and destructive communication practices, they could choose to learn conflict communication patterns that increase agreement and greater understanding of each other's perspectives, that produce more satisfying outcomes, that reduce stress, and that more frequently resolve problems. The benefits of a constructive approach, especially in cases where the interpersonal relationship is of importance, are obvious.

From Theory to Action

The subtitle of this book, *From Theory to Action*, describes the idea that competent behavior is based on an understanding of interpersonal conflict. The first step in moving from theories of conflict to better conflict management is to adopt a mind-set that embraces conflict as an opportunity while recognizing the risks involved in it. This mind-set recognizes the importance of personal responsibility for one's actions and encourages flexibility in oneself and in others within the conflict situation. The mind-set also recognizes that communication works no miracles but that it usually helps lead a conflict to management or resolution. Most important, this mind-set rejects easy solutions and recognizes the complexity of conflict situations and their outcomes. Adopting these new attitudes toward conflict is not an overnight process. It takes time, and it takes work. The important thing is for you to become aware of your behavior in conflict situations and to start to identify the way your thinking about conflict situations affects the outcomes you obtain. Self-awareness is the first step toward effective conflict behavior.

APPLICATION 1.5

Before reading this chapter, how did you feel about confronting others when a conflict arises? Did you feel positive or negative about it? How did that affect the way you handled past conflicts? Do you think you would be more successful if you felt more positively about conflict?

Often conflicts feel overwhelmingly large to us—there are many issues involved as we interact with someone and we are not sure where to begin. How would you handle this conflict if you were involved in it?

Case Study 1.1 ■ *Management Troubles*

I was involved in a particular conflict a couple years ago when I worked at a photography studio as the office manager. My employer was in the process of a very messy divorce, which not only left him without a wife, but without someone to run his business. He really just wanted to take the pictures and leave the administrative end to someone else. That is why I was hired. The pay was very good but, after awhile, it became very apparent that all the money in the world could not compensate for the misery I experienced as a result of our very conflicting personalities.

Although my boss said he wanted me to take charge and do things how I saw fit, I was constantly being interrogated as to what I was doing at every single moment and being second-guessed as to whether or not that was the most important thing to do at the time. When I tried to organize the office, which was a virtual pigsty, I was told that there were better things to be doing. I tried to explain to him that I simply couldn't concentrate on the work at hand, with all this clutter surrounding me. He could not appreciate this, and we constantly went head-to-head.

When I started to handle the bookkeeping, I met weekly with his accountants to try and make sense of things. They immediately told me that I was in over my head; rather than balance his checkbook, my boss would just call the bank every day and use the balance they gave him as the amount on which he could write checks. I had never seen anything so absurd in my life! He never took into account that there were countless checks that had not been cashed and would alter the amount that the bank was giving him. I also found out that he was delinquent on two years of income taxes. When I tried to approach him about this, he became very agitated and told me that the accountants were on his ex-wife's side and that they were trying to turn me against him. He told me not to do what they were telling me (which was to accurately report his income and correctly balance his accounts) and I resented the fact that he wanted me to cheat for him. I eventually told him I could no longer do the bookkeeping.

The last straw was when my paychecks started bouncing. Apparently, the IRS was beginning to take money directly out of his account to cover the back taxes. I first remedied this by going directly to his bank on payday and getting the cash right away. Then it got to the point where the bank would tell me there were insufficient funds, and I would be forced to either wait or, as I finally resorted to, demand that my boss get cash advances on his credit cards to pay me.

It was really awful. I finally ended up getting another job, one that paid four dollars an hour less, but at least I didn't have to put up with all that stress and insanity.

I'm still trying to figure out if this conflict could have been resolved. I'm not sure that it really ever could have, and I sense that leaving was really the only option I had.

Notes

1. Joseph Folger and Marshall Scott Poole, *Working Through Conflict* (Glenview, IL: Scott Foresman, 1984); J. T. Tedeschi, *The Social Influence Processes* (Chicago: Aldine Publishing, 1972). See also Thomas C. Schelling, *The Strategy of Conflict* (Cambridge, MA: Harvard University Press, 1980). Schelling characterized conflict situations as instances of bargaining, in which the ability of one person to attain his or her goals is dependent on the choices or decisions made by the other.

2. Herbert W. Simons, "Persuasion in Social Conflicts: A Critique of Prevailing Conceptions and a Framework for Future Research," *Speech Monographs* 39 (1972), 227–247.

3. Alan L. Sillars and Judith Weisberg, "Conflict as a Social Skill," in Michael E. Roloff and Gerald R. Miller (Eds.) *Interpersonal Processes: New Directions in Theory and Research* (Newbury Park, CA: Sage Publications, 1987), pp. 140–171.

4. For a complete discussion of the problems associated with definitions of conflict, see Clinton F. Fink, "Some Conceptual Difficulties in the Theory of Social Conflict," *Journal of Conflict Resolution* 12 (1968), 412–460.

5. These definitions come from (in the order presented): (1) H. Wayland Cummings, Larry W. Long, and Michael Lewis, *Managing Communication in Organizations,* 2nd Ed. (Scottsdale, AZ: Gorsuch Scarisbrick Publishers, 1987), p. 150; see also Clyde H. Coombs and George S. Avrunin, *The Structure of Conflict* (Hillsdale, NJ: Lawrence Erlbaum Associates, 1988), who define conflict as "the opposition of response (behavioral) tendencies, which may be within an individual or in different individuals" (p. 1). (2) Gary P. Cross, Jean H. Names, and Darrell Beck, *Conflict and Human Interaction* (Dubuque, IA: Kendall Hunt Publishing, 1979), p. v. (3) R. D. Nye, *Conflict among Humans* (New York: Spring Publishing, 1973). (4) Lynn Sandra Kahn, *Peacemaking: A Systems Approach to Conflict Management* (Lanham, MD: University Press of America, 1988), p. 3.

6. Dean G. Pruitt and Jeffrey Z. Rubin, *Social Conflict: Escalation, Stalemate, and Settlement* (New York: Random House, 1986), p. 4.

7. Herbert W. Simons, "The Carrot and the Stick as Handmaidens of Persuasion in Conflict Situations," in Gerald R. Miller and Herbert W. Simons (Eds.), *Perspectives on Communication in Social Conflict* (Englewood Cliffs, NJ: Prentice Hall, 1974), pp. 177–178.

8. Lewis Coser, *The Functions of Social Conflict* (New York: Free Press, 1956).

9. Simons, "Persuasion in Social Conflicts."

10. Suzanne McCorkle and Janet L. Mills, "Rowboat in a Hurricane: Metaphors of Interpersonal Conflict Management," *Communication Reports* 5 (1992), 57–66.

11. Ibid., p. 63.

12. S. I. Hayakawa, *Language in Thought and Action,* 4th Ed. (New York: Harcourt, Brace, Jovanovich, 1978).

13. McCorkle and Mills, "Rowboat in a Hurricane," pp. 57–66.

14. John M. Gottman and R. Krokoff, *Marital Interaction: A Longitudinal View* (Unpublished manuscript, University of Washington, Seattle, WA, 1989); Daniel Canary, E. M. Cunningham, and M. J. Cody, "Goal Types, Gender, and Locus of Control in Managing Interpersonal Conflict," *Communication Research* 15 (1988), 426–447; G. R. Pike and Alan L. Sillars, "Reciprocity of Marital Communication," *Journal of Social and Personal Relationships* 2 (1985), 303–324.

15. John M. Gottman, "Temporal Form: Toward a New Language for Describing Relationships," *Journal of Marriage and the Family* 44 (1982), 943–962; Stella Ting-Toomey, "An Analysis of Verbal Communication Patterns in High and Low Marital Adjustment Groups," *Human Communication Research* 9 (1983), 306–319.

16. Ting-Toomey, "An Analysis of Verbal Communication Patterns."

17. Joseph Folger, Marshall Scott Poole, and Randall K. Stutman, *Working Conflict,* 2nd Ed. (New York: Harper-Collins, 1993), pp. 5–7.

18. U. G. Foa and E. G. Foa, *Societal Structures of the Mind* (Springfield, IL: Thomas, 1974); K. D. Rettig and M. M Bubolz, "Interpersonal Resource Exchanges as Indicators of Quality of Marriage," *Journal of Marriage and the Family* 45 (1983), 497–509.

19. Dudley Cahn and Sally Lloyd (Eds.), *Family Violence from a Communication Perspective* (Thousand Oaks, CA: Sage, 1996), p. 6.

20. Joseph DeVito, *The Interpersonal Communication Book,* 6th Ed. (New York: HarperCollins, 1992), p. 77.

21. Pruitt and Rubin, *Social Conflict;* Morton Deutsch, "Conflicts: Productive or Destructive?" *Journal of Social Issues* 25 (1969), 7–41.

22. Sillars and Weisberg, "Conflict as a Social Skill," p. 146.

23. Deutsch, "Conflicts: Productive or Destructive?" p. 11.

24. Brent Ruben, "Communication and Conflict: A Systems Perspective," *Quarterly Journal of Speech* 64 (1978), 202–210.

25. Deutsch, "Conflicts: Productive or Destructive?" p. 11.

26. Dudley D. Cahn, *Intimates in Conflict* (Hillsdale, NJ: Erlbaum, 1990).

27. Lorel Scott and Robert Martin, "Value Similarity, Relationship Length, and Conflict Interaction in Dating Relationships: An Initial Investigation," paper presented at the Speech Communication Association Convention, Chicago, November 1986.

28. Folger and Poole, *Working Through Conflict,* pp. 6–7.

29. Deutsch, "Conflicts: Productive or Destructive?"

30. Ibid.

2

People in Conflict: Values, Attitudes, and Beliefs

Objectives

At the end of this chapter, you should be able to

1. explain how various attitudinal components such as rhetorical sensitivity, self-monitoring, interaction involvement, conversational sensitivity, willingness to communicate, and communication apprehension may affect interpersonal conflict behavior.

2. examine the functional beliefs for conflict, identify the ones with which you do *not* agree, and explain how they may affect the outcomes in conflict situations.

3. examine Filley's problem-solving beliefs, identify the ones with which you do *not* agree, and explain how they may affect problem-solving situations.

4. explain how, according to Filley, behavior is linked to attitude and belief.

Key Terms

attitudes	instrumental values	self-monitoring
beliefs	interaction involvement	socialization
communication apprehension	Noble Self	terminal values
communicator style	perception	values
conflict beliefs	Rhetorical Reflector	willingness to communicate
conversational sensitivity	Rhetorical Sensitive	
goals	rhetorical sensitivity	

One of the distinctive features of conflict is that, when people engage in conflict, they bring to the encounter their personalities and cultural identities. Frequently, unproductive behavior in conflict situations is the result of a lack of understanding of the role played by attitudes and beliefs in the conflict process. In addition, fundamental values we hold about the way the world works, often derived from our cultural background, can influence outcomes of conflict processes. **Beliefs** are thoughts and ideas we have about situations and people, which affect how we interpret behaviors and situational variables. **Attitudes** are positive or negative predispositions that affect the way we decide to behave toward others. **Values** are shared conceptions of desired ends and the means to reach them.[1]

In this chapter we highlight the role played by values, attitudes, and beliefs as we consider the effect of values, attitudes, and beliefs on conflict in general. We use *value* here in the sense of asking the question: What is important to you? To each and all of us, some people, places, principles, institutions, objects, and so on are more significant and worthwhile than others. How we evaluate them is indicated by our stated goals (purposes, aspirations), attitudes (interests, feelings), beliefs (convictions, thoughts), motives (social needs), concerns (worries, problems, perceived obstacles), and overt behavior (activities, actions). In the final portion of the chapter, we identify some alternative attitudes and beliefs, which constitute a mind-set that encourages productive conflict interactions.

> **APPLICATION 2.1**
>
> What do you value? How do you attach worth to different people, institutions, ways of doing things, and so on? How might your list be different from another person's?

Socialization and Conflict

Rokeach was among the first to distinguish between two major components of one's value system, instrumental and terminal values. **Instrumental values** are associated with means to ends and refer to "preferred modes of behavior." The code of Boy Scout behavior consists of instrumental values: trustworthy, loyal, helpful, friendly, courteous, kind, obedient, cheerful, thrifty, brave, clean, and reverent. **Terminal values** are associated with the ends themselves and refer to "preferred end states of existence" for which people strive. Many religions have adopted terminal values like peace, family, happiness, salvation, wisdom, and so on.[2] Interrelated instrumental and terminal values are combined into a value system.

One's value system is the result of socialization, which in turn teaches us how to behave. In the United States, **socialization** refers to the influence our family, schools, religious institutions, work experiences, mass media systems (and increasingly in the future, the Internet), political parties, and peer groups have on our upbringing. To an important extent, we are programmed because our values are learned and then expressed through the way we behave and communicate. Values prescribe the ends of our actions (terminal values) as well as the actions themselves (instrumental values). They help us determine what is good or bad, right or wrong.

From our standpoint, it is significant that our values also produce expectations about the behavior of others. This may not be a major problem for members of a culture who share the same value system because, among other things, our values function to reduce the chance of conflict within a single culture or ethnic group.[3] However, where values are not shared, conflict may arise over the values themselves or over the proper means of engaging in a conflict. In the next chapter, we will examine how the values of different cultures may affect the way in which conflict is played out. For right now, it is important to recognize that the way you judge the behaviors of others in conflict situations has a great deal to do with your socialization—what you were taught to value and what you were taught to devalue.

Attitudes toward Communication and Conflict

Along with values that place emphasis on different issues or different means of engaging in conflict, a person's motivation to avoid or engage in conflict with another person, coupled with his or her knowledge of conflict behaviors, is strongly related to positive conflict outcomes.[4] This motivational component may be found in the attitude a person holds toward communication in general.[5] One way of measuring these attitudes is through the concepts of rhetorical sensitivity and communicator style.

Rhetorical Sensitivity and Communicator Style

Rhetorical sensitivity measures a person's general attitudes toward communication and how those attitudes are manifested in one of three personality-like traits: noble self, rhetorical reflectiveness, and rhetorical sensitivity.[6] A **Noble Self** is a person who prefers to present a consistent, "true" self regardless of situational demands. Any variation from this true self is seen as hypocrisy and a denial of integrity. Any adaptation the Noble Self makes to a situation is a result of projecting the person's own frame of mind into it rather than seeing the situation from another person's point of view.[7] In addition, empirical research indicates that Noble Selves perceive more of a necessity to communicate in various situations than do Rhetorical Reflectors or Rhetorical Sensitives.[8] **Rhetorical Reflectors,** on the other hand, have no real self to call their own, preferring to meet the other person's needs and the needs of the situation rather than asserting themselves within it. Rhetorical Reflectors' flexibility stems in part from a need to please others and be liked by them.

Between the Noble Self and the Rhetorical Reflector is the **Rhetorical Sensitive,** characterized by five attitudes toward communication. The first attitude concerns the idea of self. Rhetorically sensitive people adapt to the demands of a situation by taking on different roles as needed, realizing that only part of the self is ever apparent at one time. Unlike Reflectors, who submerge any sense of self to the demands of the situation, Rhetorical Sensitives act in accordance with their sense of self, while being flexible. The second attitude held by Rhetorical Sensitives is inventional flexibility. What has worked in the past may or may not be effective in the here and now, so Rhetorical Sensitives' goal is to find effective behaviors for the situation at hand. Rhetorical Sensitives do not value consistency for consistency's sake. The third attitude concerns the treatment of ideas. Regardless of how well ideas are articulated, they are open for discussion. Rhetorical Sensitives, however, understand that at times nothing at all should be said regarding an idea. Related to this attitude is the fourth, which concerns the way in which things are said. Rhetorical Sensitives understand that ideas must be adapted to the audiences who hear them because "there are as many ways of making an idea clear as there are people."[9] The final attitude held by Rhetorical Sensitives concerns their consciousness of interaction. They believe it is important to balance their need to express themselves with consideration for the other person's feelings and ability to accept the message. The rhetorically sensitive person's behavior is characterized by "weighing the often inconsistent, contradictory motives one has in a conflict situation, and talking in a manner that is most appropriate for the situation."[10]

Research has been conducted on the association among rhetorical sensitivity, communication style, and communication competence. **Communicator style** is a measure of an individual's perception of his or her communication behaviors. These behaviors include the tendency to leave impressions (one's communication affects others) and to be contentious, open, dramatic, dominant, precise, relaxed, friendly, attentive, and animated; in addition, the measure provides an overall assessment of communication ability in a concept called *communicator image.*[11] When people become familiar with another person's style of communication, that knowledge helps them to interpret ambiguous messages. An example of a person apparently not displaying rhetorical sensitivity and apparently displaying an incongruent style with his audience is found in this narrative:

> We attended church services last Sunday and there happened to be a guest speaker. He was a chaplain from a local college and he was to give the message for the day. He started off with a very loud, booming voice despite the microphone and he spoke fast. He began by talking a little about himself and then by relaying stories and analogies to make his point. He began with an analogy about football and apologized to the women in the congregation for not perhaps being familiar with the sport. At this point I had a feeling that I was not going to like the way he was going to interpret the message. During his sermon he made several references regarding the makeup of the audience. Most of the congregation is of Asian descent (but not all) and in his attempt to connect with the audience he really turned us off. He said things such as "his last name was Smith . . . obviously not a Chinese name" and "we had some wonderful meals but of course nothing like sweet and sour pork . . . Chinese people really knew what they were doing." In addition the man was yelling at the audience. His voice was so loud and with his comments about Chinese people spread throughout his sermon, I couldn't help but feel that he thought we couldn't understand him so he had to yell.

APPLICATION 2.2

What kind of orientation would you say you have toward communication? Are you most interested in pleasing others? In pleasing yourself? Do you tend to adapt to different communication situations? How would you change if you wanted to?

Influences on Interpersonal Perception

In addition to rhetorical sensitivity, processes of perception can affect the way that we respond to conflict. A cognitive activity, **perception** is the process of assigning meaning to the things we see. A common assumption is that we all perceive differently. If you were to stop anyone on the street, he or she would probably be able to give you the textbook answer from a basic communication course on the effects of perception on communication. So why is this knowledge not put into practice?

One reason is that we tend to label others as we interact with them. These labels are another type of cognition that affects our behavior. Labels are unspoken inner stereotypes—what we think about the other person as he or she approaches, speaks, and so on. With strangers, we infer information from clothing and behavioral characteristics—the way the person walks, talks, and so on. But we also derive expectations from knowing what the other person does. How would you react to a high school football coach, a physician, a homemaker, an auto mechanic, a musician? The chances are that you have assumptions about the way each of them should act. Those assumptions, in turn, affect the way you behave toward them. Labels create expectations for behavior and limit the other person's possibilities for behavioral variety. Giving voice to our assumptions by using a label negatively (e.g., "what do you expect from a person who played football before they required helmets?") can damage the other's credibility, invite attack, dehumanize the other, and at the very least, make conversation difficult. Labels can create inaccurate perceptions and foster distrust among those who might have tried to accept or understand the other person before the label was applied. In addition, using labels against those who seem like outsiders may foster "groupiness" and narrow vision among those who think they have all the answers ("experts").

Other perceptual baggage interfering with the ability to act effectively includes knowing about a person's past or having had a negative interaction with the person in the past, as in the following example.

> A woman who lives down the street has a son a little younger than mine. I've heard her scream at him a lot, calling him stupid, threatening to spank him, and so on. One day she came to my door, absolutely irate, claiming that my son had pushed hers down and broken his new squirt gun after her son sprayed mine with water. I really had to work to stay calm, particularly when she asked me what kind of kid I was raising. I had my son apologize and offered to pay for the squirt gun, but she stomped away. "I just wanted you to know he did it," she said. I know it would be better if I would try to be nice to her, but frankly, it's all I can do to be civil.

Sometimes the experience is not with the other person directly but with someone like the other person and the similarity causes us to react negatively. An incident with a judgmental teacher in elementary school, for example, often gives children a negative attitude toward classroom experiences. We may have a personal dislike of the other that has no rational basis. Or we may simply cling to our notions or impressions of others because it is too much work to change the way we think. Whatever their source, our stereotypes and assumptions about others color our interpretation of their behavior.

APPLICATION 2.3

Go to a public place like a shopping mall or park. Pick out several people to observe, and write down the things that come to mind. As you go over your list for each person, distinguish between the statements that are purely descriptive and those that make a judgment about the other person. If you made a judgment, indicate why you did so.

Perceptual ability can be improved in a number of ways. Perhaps the most obvious way is to put yourself in the other person's place and try to see his or her view. Another method is to remember that just because you fear something does not mean the other person intends to do it. People have a tendency to project their feelings onto others rather than thinking about what the other might be feeling. Discussing how you and the other see the situation leads to a better understanding of goals and issues in the conflict. You can also look for opportunities to act inconsistently with the other person's perceptions, which can keep the other person from assuming things about you based on past interactions.[12]

Whereas some people ignore the uniqueness of people, others are more sensitive. Communication theories that attempt to explain differences in how people perceive themselves, others, and the situation include self-monitoring, interaction involvement, and conversational sensitivity. **Self-monitoring** is the tendency to rely on external or internal cues for the regulation of one's behavior in conflict situations. A high self-monitor is a person who relies on cues in the environment in order to make decisions about self-presentation strategies. The high self-monitor is very sensitive to situational demands and attempts to adapt to them, whereas low self-monitors are attuned to their own internal states rather than to contextual demands for action.[13]

Given the emphasis in competence research on the ability to adapt to situational constraints, the concept of self-monitoring would appear important in understanding the motivational component of competence. Self-monitoring can allow one to be more aware of what one says in a conflict situation and more aware of the effects of messages on the other person. Perhaps a high self-monitor is better able to anticipate the effects of ongoing behavior in creating or escalating conflicts.

One interesting aside on flexibility, however, is that it is not always the most useful approach to communication encounters. People exhibiting three styles of communication were tested on their ability to predict the behaviors of a person they encountered. Flexible people who focused on adaptation to the other and mutual satisfaction in the conversation, and dominant people, who imposed their will on the conversation, were less skilled at predicting the other's behavior than were those classified as "neutral responsives" who approach the conversation in a detached way but took the task of getting as much information as possible from the other more seriously than did those with the other two styles. Depending on the nature of the communication task, then, flexibility may not be as useful as withholding evaluation until all the information is in.[14]

Another communication predisposition that constitutes a portion of the motivational component of communication conflict is **interaction involvement,** the extent to which a person is actively aware of others in conflict situations.[15] Actively involved persons generally self-disclose more and are more aware of the immediate environment's impact on their conversation. Low involvement results in more self-focus and less awareness of the other and the immediate environment. Interaction involvement consists of three factors: (1) Perceptiveness is the ability to know what meanings the other person in the conversation has ascribed to oneself and the ability to integrate those meanings with one's own thoughts. (2) Other-oriented perceptiveness is a person's ability to know what meaning to ascribe to another's behavior. (3) Attentiveness is the ability to focus on what the other is saying. A moderate relationship between interaction involvement and the ability to elicit information from others has been demonstrated in research. Involved people are also more likely to recall details of a conversation they have recently experienced, and they feel more positive toward simulated negotiation situations than do people whose interaction involvement is low.[16] Interaction involvement probably has a positive effect on conflict behavior, with involved people better able to understand others' concerns.

We have all had the experience of trying to talk with another person who does not seem to focus on the conversation. Maybe you wanted to talk about something important, but the other person did not want to turn off the television or became distracted by objects in the room or other people in the area. Under these circumstances, it is easy to feel that the other is not truly listening. Interaction involvement is something that can be cultivated by improving one's listening skills and recognizing that what others have to say is important. And sometimes people give the appearance of being involved but are not, as this example illustrates:

> It was raining, and my daughter's coach had let them out early. Rather than call us, she stayed to talk with friends. Previous experiences with practices that had run over led me to think I could pick her up at the regular time. I had just enough time to run to the store to

get my son's birthday present before her pick-up time. I told my husband that I would run an errand and pick her up. He said, "Okay." I got to school to be informed by her that she had just called my husband, and he was on the way. We called again, but he had already left. We tried to wave him down on the way home, but he didn't see us. He apparently looked all over the school, and came home extremely angry. I reminded him that I had told him what was happening, and he said, "I don't remember that you said anything." So, what does "okay" mean then?

Related to the notion of interaction involvement is conversational sensitivity. Unlike the former, **conversational sensitivity** is a response to particular situations, which in this case involves conflict. People are more likely to become conversationally sensitive if personal topics are involved, the conversation violates expectations, or the conversation is unpredictable, interesting, and involving. Sensitivity is positively associated with variables such as self-monitoring, perceptiveness, self-esteem, assertiveness, empathy, and social skills, and it is negatively associated with communication apprehension to be discussed shortly. Like those who are involved in the conversation, people who become conversationally sensitive recall more of a conversation and make more accurate attributions about the other.[17] Because conflict situations typically involve personal topics, one would expect conversational sensitivity to increase during conflicts, making people more aware of the situation. On the other hand, whereas awareness and recall of the conversation might increase (demonstrated, for instance, by the ability of those recalling conflict stories in this book), emotional responses to the conflict topic might overshadow the positive effects of sensitivity.

Other dispositional attributes, or attitudes toward communication, that may affect conflict behavior are one's willingness to communicate, communication apprehension, and interaction involvement. A person's **willingness to communicate** is considered to be a traitlike predisposition to desire communication with others. Research has found this attribute to be negatively related to other attributes such as communication apprehension, introversion, anomie, and alienation and positively associated with self-esteem and self-rated communication competence. People with a high willingness to communicate were more likely to participate in class than those with a low willingness to communicate. It may be that subsequent research will find this attribute associated with decisions to confront a conflict.[18] One student felt it was strange that people in his class seemed to experience so many different kinds of conflicts and even more strange that they were willing to talk about those conflicts. He described himself as a conflict avoider—a person who would rather keep things inside than share his negative feelings with others. Unwillingness to communicate, then, is probably associated with conflict avoidance: Not only is conflict seen as something difficult to deal with, but the value placed on sharing feelings is low.

Another predisposition, **communication apprehension** reflects a person's anxiety about interacting in various communication contexts, which can be applied to conflict situations.[19] People who experience communication anxiety do so in response to specific situations requiring communication, and do so fairly consistently.[20] Especially threatening to the communication apprehensive person are situations seen as low in pleasure and high in emotional arousal—variables that can generally describe most conflict situations. Communication apprehension, like willingness to communicate, affects people's motivation to engage in conflict with others. In addition, some research suggests that different levels of communication apprehension are associated with various styles of conflict. However, people who experience high apprehension about dyadic interaction prefer accommodation (giving in to the other) as a conflict style. People experiencing high apprehension about group interactions prefer avoidance or, if conflict is unavoidable, competition (achieving their own goals even at the expense of the other) so as to end it quickly. Overall, however, the higher the communication apprehension, the less likely the person is to prefer an assertive style of conflict.[21]

APPLICATION 2.4

When has apprehension about a situation, or about simply talking to another person, kept you from engaging in a conflict? Was it a good decision to avoid the conflict? How might you have approached it in a way that could minimize your fear?

Functional Beliefs for Managing and Resolving Conflict

The way we think about conflict has a demonstrated effect on the conflict behaviors chosen and the amount of satisfaction experienced in relationships. Recent research examined the relationship between dysfunctional beliefs about conflict and relationships, the kind of behaviors chosen by people holding those beliefs, and the effect these beliefs had on the level of satisfaction people experienced in their interpersonal relationships. Dysfunctional beliefs included thinking that disagreement is destructive to a relationship, that partners are unable to change their behavior, and that one's partner should know what one wants. Yes, expecting others to be able to read one's mind is a dysfunctional belief. People holding dysfunctional beliefs were more likely to engage in destructive conflict behaviors to terminate their relationships when faced with conflicts and reported lower satisfaction with their relationships. Those who rejected these dysfunctional beliefs were more likely to engage in constructive conflict behaviors: discussion problems, compromising, seeking help from third parties, and changing the beliefs when necessary. People holding constructive conflict beliefs also experienced greater satisfaction in their interpersonal relationships.[22] **Conflict beliefs** guide the responses chosen in conflict situations and the way people feel about the conflicts once they are over. Creating more competent conflict behavior starts with the way people think about it (see Table 2.1).

Functional Belief One

People are responsible for how they feel, what they say, how they respond, and how they act in conflict situations. This is an easy belief to identify, and a very hard one to put into practice. In conflict situations, it seems much easier to say, "You make me so angry!" as opposed to "I am angry with you." The first statement shifts responsibility to the other person; the second owns it. Taking responsibility for thoughts and actions in conflict situations can be threatening at first, but it is ultimately freeing. I choose and, therefore, more actions are open to me than if I must simply respond to another's lead.

There is an important implication in this belief. When we acknowledge that we are responsible for the way we act and feel, we begin to realize that no conflict situation exists that we have not contributed to in some way.[23] By definition, conflict is the result of

TABLE 2.1   *New Assumptions for Conflict*

1. People are responsible for how they feel, what they say, how they respond, and how they act in conflict situations.
2. Both confrontation and avoidance are legitimate options, depending on the situation.
3. Communication will not necessarily make things better.
4. People in conflict situations respond to one another in terms of their perceptions.
5. The context of a conflict gives it meaning and creates expectations for behavior.
6. People are motivated both to cooperate and to compete in conflict situations.
7. People are guided by goals that may be nonexistent or ill-defined prior to enacting the conflict, and the goals may change in the course of the conflict.
8. Any action in a conflict situation affects future choices of action in the situation.
9. Not all conflicts are resolvable.

interdependence (*we are involved*); in practice, people have a tendency to shift the responsibility to others (it is *your* fault). Shifting responsibility to the other person can also have a negative impact on the outcome of conflict situations, as research demonstrates. People who attribute responsibility for the conflict to the other person are far more likely to use avoidance or competitive strategies (leading to avoidance and escalation cycles) and far less likely to use integrative or collaborative (win-win) strategies. When people accept responsibility for their thoughts and actions, they are far more likely to shift from blaming to information seeking in order to resolve or manage the conflict and far more likely to accept changes they may have to make to bring about resolution.[24]

This is illustrated with a simple example: Two women who share a dorm room are in conflict because one thinks the other interferes with her studying. The roommate who wants to study can shift the blame ("It's all your fault because you are always playing the radio or watching television when I am trying to study") or accept some of the responsibility ("Am I being unreasonable in the times I would like to have for studying? Is there a way my roommate can watch television, and I can get my studying in, too?"). If blame is shifted to the other person, the roommate wanting to study is far less likely to make any changes that would allow both people to get what they want out of the situation. We ourselves contribute to the conflicts we experience; understanding our own contribution will enable us to better choose modes of behavior.

Functional Belief Two

Both confrontation and avoidance are legitimate options, depending on the situation. Not all conflicts are worth the energy required for confrontation. This realization probably comes naturally to most people because evidence suggests that people have a natural desire to avoid conflict.[25] But just because there is a desire to avoid conflict does not mean people actually stop thinking about it.

The decision to confront a conflict starts with an internal assessment of its importance. Ask yourself these questions: Do I have a right to confront the other person? Is this issue important to me? Will not dealing with this issue affect my ability to deal with the other person? Am I likely to be resentful of the other person if I do not deal with this issue? And, perhaps most important, am I enabling another to be irresponsible or protecting that person from the consequences of thoughtless behavior by not confronting the issue? If the answers to these questions are affirmative, then you are going to have to deal with the conflict.

Research indicates that commitment to a relationship has an effect on willingness to confront the other.[26] As relationships increase in intimacy, people are more likely to think of confrontation as possibly rewarding,[27] although some evidence suggests that people will ignore minor conflicts with close friends if the threats to the relationship seem greater than the potential outcomes of conflict.[28] Most people make the decision to confront or avoid conflict based on their reaction to a number of variables: the nature of the relationship, the perceived urgency of the problem, their perceived responsibility to confront the other person, their perceptions of the other as approachable or defensive, their resources (e.g., energy, time, mood, confidence, etc.), the appropriateness of the timing and setting, and what they predict the outcomes will be. Perceived urgency has the greatest impact on whether or not a person will initiate a conflict.[29] Obviously, the decision to confront is not always an easy one to make.

Avoidance is a legitimate option if changing the other person is unlikely or if the issue is unimportant. A word of caution, though: It is typical in ongoing relationships to decide that issues are unimportant but to keep track of them. As issues mount up, the aggregate of conflicts seems to constitute a very important difference between basic values, and the past conflicts become ammunition for a major confrontation.[30] If an issue is not important enough to deal with, it should be *released.*

Avoidance is also the best option if you are not the right person to initiate the conflict. For example, you may frequently deal with an organizational representative who seems inappropriate in his or her telephone style. Teaching that person about telephone protocol isn't your responsibility—it is the responsibility of her supervisor. If the organization is not unhappy with her telephone skills, then your personal preferences are unimportant.

Another reason to avoid a conflict is when you are dealing with a "wookie." You may remember the classic *Star Wars* scene where R2D2, a droid, is playing a form of chess with Chewbacca, the wookie. Han Solo warns R2D2 not to irritate the wookie. C3P0 retorts that no one ever worries about irritating a droid. "That's because droids don't pull your arms out of their sockets when they lose." C3P0 advises R2D2 to "let the wookie win." It's not bad advice. There are some people who are used to bullying others around. They throw temper tantrums, make ultimatums, and generally make others' lives miserable until they get their way. By not confronting them directly, you can save your energy and use it in more constructive ways. Wookies are used to having people come at them in combat. They're not really sure what to do with someone who doesn't fight back.

Postponement of a conflict, a form of avoidance, delays dealing with a conflict until you can give full attention to it. Postponement, accompanied by a sincere desire to deal with the conflict at some point, is a good belief when you are too emotionally involved to think through the issue. Learning *when* conflict is best handled is an essential skill in conflict resolution.

Functional Belief Three

Communication will not necessarily make things better. People tend to see communication as a panacea.[31] One of the most serious indictments of the conflict literature is its tendency to assume that communication is a simple, linear process that will set relationships back on the right course if one simply follows the right steps.[32] More communication is not necessarily better. Sometimes more communication only clarifies how far apart people really are, and "bad" (i.e., manipulative, unloving, and/or untruthful) communication can certainly hurt a relationship.

In some cases, however, people in a relationship may experience a general feeling of dissatisfaction without really being able to identify the source of the feeling or the issue of the conflict. Rather than simply seizing on the first reasonable explanation, it might be better to engage in some "purposeful ambiguity" in order to allow all the issues behind the dissatisfaction to surface. Sometimes it takes ambiguity to resolve ambiguity; communicating in tentative rather than absolutist terms may be more useful in the long run.[33] An example of ambiguity that was helpful is found in Roxane's story:

> My colleague and I had returned from a convention on the same plane, and my husband, Ed, met me at the airport. At the luggage carousel, I was busy getting my bags, more than I usually carry. I struggled to get them off the luggage carousel while Ed waited on a bench nearby. My colleague kept glancing over at Ed, who did nothing to help me. I left with everything piled on a luggage cart and dragged it out to the car while Ed carried my coat. My colleague was apparently infuriated. Two days later, he approached me and started by saying he was not sure how to say what he wanted, but he thought Ed did not treat me very well. I asked him what led him to that conclusion, and he told me that he had been so angry he had thought of punching my husband for not carrying my luggage. I started to laugh and explained that since Ed had injured his back I did not allow him to lift anything at all.

In this case, conflicts between the colleague and Ed and between the colleague and Roxane were averted because the colleague started tentatively and in vague terms. The moral is, when you are not sure of all the facts, or even what the facts mean, being tentative about your conclusions may result in better conflict resolution than boldly stating your problem.

Functional Belief Four

People in conflict situations respond to one another in terms of their perceptions.[34] That is, we behave the way we do because of what we *think* we see. And what we see may or may not correspond to reality as the other person sees it. Although conflict is a process, with no clear beginning or end, people tend to *punctuate* the events of a conflict situation so that they point to particular (but different) triggers for the conflict or "red flags" to identify that the situation has progressed beyond a simple disagreement to something serious enough to warrant attention.

The classic example of the withdrawing husband–nagging wife syndrome illustrates this belief. The husband says he withdraws because his wife nags; the wife says she nags because her husband withdraws. Each sees the situation differently.[35] Or suppose a teacher has a student who receives consistently low scores on homework assignments. The student may think the teacher assigned the grade because of a personal dislike instead of looking at the homework fairly. Whether the teacher is prejudiced or not becomes immaterial at this point because the student is responding to the teacher as the student views the teacher. The teacher, in turn, begins to think that the student is acting in a hostile manner. In both situations, the people are punctuating the situation differently—they see a different starting point for the conflict cycle. There is a reality, but it exists only through the perceptions of the actors in the conflict situation. Even if those perceptions are wrong, they still guide behavior. Conflict interaction is like this. People are likely to see the event they say started the conflict in dissimilar ways.

Functional Belief Five

The context of a conflict gives it meaning and creates expectations for behavior. We act differently depending on where we find ourselves. When conflict occurs in a public place, people are more likely to constrain their actions or postpone the conflict to a later time. They feel more free to be themselves when in their own "territory" (e.g., their own office) than in someone else's territory (e.g., their boss's office). Consciously or not, people tend to adapt their behavior to their surroundings.

People also adapt their behavior to their relationships, usually in a more conscious way. They use different strategies and tactics with acquaintances and strangers than with people they know well. The power in the relationship affects what strategies and tactics will be used. For example, you might be stern with a child, allowing little room for negotiation; obviously, the same tactics will not work on your boss, and perhaps not even with a subordinate at work. Understanding conflict requires an understanding of the physical and social environment in which it occurs. Both are variables that affect the way people define the conflict and the way people respond to the conflict verbally and nonverbally.[36]

Functional Belief Six

People are motivated both to cooperate and to compete in conflict situations. That is, people are motivated to compete because they want to achieve their goals, but they are also motivated (usually) to cooperate because they want to maintain the relationship. By starting with cooperative behavior, one risks being taken advantage of and exploited. The risk implied by cooperative behavior makes it difficult for people to cooperate without some show of good faith from the other person. If a friend wants changes from you, the friend has to be willing to change also, but what happens if you do your part, and then your friend does not follow through? You will feel exploited in the situation.

The problem of mixed motives is an especially critical one in relationships in which conflict has been going on for a long time with little change, such as a turbulent marital relationship in which many issues are at stake. Perhaps change has been attempted before but has fallen through. Each person is suspicious of the other person: "How do I know you'll really do your part this time if all the other times you haven't followed through? Why shouldn't I just push to have things my way and be through with it? What will you give me as a symbol of your future cooperation?"

The implication is that you need to be aware of the background of the conflict. If the issue is not new, there are probably mixed motives in the conflict interaction—desires to cooperate and compete. Those in the conflict situation need to be made aware of these differing motives, so that they can work around them. They need to understand the various options open to them: What is the best thing that can happen if competition is chosen? If cooperation is chosen? How is the other likely to respond to cooperation? To competition? Understanding that fear of cooperation and a desire to compete may result in less than ideal circumstances may help them to risk cooperation and reject competition in their first attempts to resolve conflict.

Functional Belief Seven

People are guided by goals that may be nonexistent or ill-defined prior to enacting the conflict, and the goals may change in the course of the conflict. Not only do we respond to one another in terms of our perceptions and act on the basis of these beliefs, but we often seek outcomes to a conflict situation based on goals we have for the future. A **goal** is what a person hopes to achieve from engaging in a conflict.

Ideally, people should enter communication situations with an idea of what will happen and what they want out of the situation; when they do so, they are most likely to act in communicatively competent ways. Realistically, particularly in conflict situations, people may enter the situation without a clear idea of what the issue is or what they hope to accomplish. For example, if Chris believes there is a conflict, and has thought about the conflict, but Dana is hearing about it for the first time, Chris will probably have goals. Dana probably will not.

Hocker and Wilmot have identified four types of goals that are important in interpersonal conflict.[37]

1. content goals: What do we want?
2. relational goals: What sort of relationship do we want?
3. identity goals: Who do we want to be?
4. process goals: What process do we want to use to manage or resolve the conflict?

The goals people develop for their conflict interaction are largely dependent on how they define the conflict or how they identify the central issue of the conflict. Although most authors write about goal development and the need for goal clarity in conflict, the simple fact is that people often enter a conflict without a clear idea of the conflict issue or the goals they have regarding it. Whether or not a person has time to reflect on a conflict also affects whether goals are formulated—conflicts that arise suddenly and are dealt with immediately may give those involved no real chance to think about what they will do to bring the conflict to resolution.

Hocker and Wilmot also say that clarifying goals is a key step in conflict management.[38] It is important to clarify goals for the following reasons:

1. Solutions go unrecognized if you do not know what you want.
2. Only clear goals can be shared.
3. Clear goals can be altered more easily than vague goals.
4. Clear goals are reached more often than unclear goals.

Even when there is time to formulate goals, they frequently change when additional information concerning them is received. Suppose, for example, a couple has been arguing about money a great deal, and the husband thinks that the conflict would be resolved if the wife changed to a different job that would provide a higher salary. His goal in initiating the conflict would be to convince his wife to change jobs. During the conflict, however, the husband might realize how much his wife likes her job and how much more pressure she might experience if she changed to a new one. His goal might be revised to examining the family budget to determine how they can better live within their means, or he might decide that he ought to change jobs himself. If he simply sticks to his original goal, both people are going to wind up unhappy. And, if his wife does not allow him the flexibility to change his goals, if she accuses him of not knowing what he wants instead of realizing that they are exploring optimum solutions to the money problem, they will get bogged down on the issue of "Can't you make up your mind?" instead of working on "How do we deal with this money problem?"

It is important to realize when going into a conflict situation that goals are subject to change. Moreover, people must realize that the other person also has goals that might change. Flexibility is essential in working toward conflict resolution and management.

Functional Belief Eight

Any action in a conflict situation affects future choices of action in the situation. Put simply, what is done now affects what happens later. An employee constantly under the threat of demotion, penalty, or firing soon learns to ignore those unfulfilled threats. Failure to follow through on threats *and* promises destroys credibility and makes future interaction uncertain.[39] A refusal to discuss certain issues makes future discussion of those issues more unlikely. Conversely, a history of openness to the management of conflict makes the future management of it more possible.

Furthermore, certain actions within a conflict situation constrict future actions. Taking a nonnegotiable stance early in a conflict (e.g., either I get my way or I leave) sets up few possibilities for resolution of the conflict. This has been found to be a major cause of failed negotiations in businesses.[40] The maintenance of flexibility is important not only with respect to goals in the conflict, but also in terms of the possible solutions verbalized.

Functional Belief Nine

Not all conflicts are resolvable. Resolution of a conflict means that the participants have come to an agreement about what they will do and that they have put the issue behind them. This is not always possible. Sometimes we must simply agree to disagree, and live with the fact that our goals are fundamentally opposed to one another. Such a situation is illustrated by the following account:

> I was involved in a school program where I was to be a leader of a small group. During the two weeks of leadership training, one of my supervisors and I had a few conflicts. Joan was a very controlling woman and very detail oriented. If things did not go her way she became very irate. My style of leadership is more flexible and my personality is quite different from Joan's and that was what sparked our conflicts. During the training, Joan fostered ill feelings in me both directly and indirectly. Directly in that she snapped at me with personal remarks, apparently because she thought I was threatening her authority, when all I did was ask questions and express my opinion. Joan hurt me indirectly by venting to others her tainted opinion of me, which I saw as unjustified as well as undermining to my integrity. What made things even more complicated was that Joan was a peer, and I saw her actions as evidence that she was on a "power trip."
>
> I refused to confront Joan because I believed that if anyone was going to bring up the problem it should be her. After all, I had stayed quite rational over the incident. Joan never apologized. Several weeks passed, and when it was time to fill out an evaluation of our training experience, I answered honestly. Although I did not mention her specifically in my evaluation, Joan confronted me a week later to express her indignation over some of my

comments. I replied that I wrote them very carefully, meaning that what she read was exactly what I meant to say. Joan spent a few minutes expressing her view and though it was time for me to go to class, we did get some things out in the open that had been pent up. I do not feel the conflict was completely resolved because I expected more of an apology from Joan, but it was enough for me to be satisfied. We will maintain a professional relationship, but I foresee the friendship gone, which is fine. I do not believe it is a priority for either of us.

The ideal for many conflict situations is resolution, but, realistically, we must understand that some conflicts may only be controlled and managed rather than eliminated. The narrator of the preceding must continue to work in a difficult situation in which, although major differences have at least been discussed, it is unlikely that any rapprochement will occur in the near future. More likely, especially as this is a short-lived college position, is that those involved will simply live with their differences and go their separate ways when no longer forced to work together. Although this is not an ideal way to deal with conflict, sometimes it is the best option available.

Attitudes Fostering Conflict Resolution

A final note on motivation comes from various authors' advice for successful conflict resolution. Most identify mind-sets that will foster productive conflict interaction. One representative list comes from Filley who argued that successful conflict interaction occurs when there is:

1. belief in the availability of a mutually acceptable solution. (If conflicting parties are willing to expend the time and effort, they can usually find a mutually acceptable solution.)
2. belief in the desirability of a mutually acceptable solution. (One must realize that joint decisions are more likely to be supported, followed, and lived up to than are imposed decisions.)
3. belief in cooperation rather than competition. (Cooperative groups are said to be more satisfied, more interested in the task, more productive, and better organized than competitive groups.)
4. belief that everyone is of equal value. (Rather than see differences among people as good or bad, see them as resources to draw upon for better solutions to problems.)
5. belief in the views of others as legitimate statements of their position. (Strive to understand the views of others, which does not mean that you must agree with them.)
6. belief that differences of opinion are helpful. (Disagreement can lead to creativity in solving problems.)
7. belief in the trustworthiness of other members. (Trust begets trust; distrust begets distrust.)
8. belief that the other party can compete but chooses to cooperate. (Cooperation occurs when both parties believe that the other chooses to cooperate rather than compete.)[41]

Whereas this chapter discusses values, attitudes, and beliefs, the significance of such cognition is tied to behavior. Filley emphasizes the link between beliefs and behavior by calling attention to the many ways in which we strive to maintain consistency between our hidden thoughts and our observable behavior. He claims that our need for consistency is so strong that differences between our thoughts and behavior motivate us to change one or the other to restore consistency. If we think it is a bad idea to confront someone, we are more likely to avoid her or him. If we believe that the other party is out to get us, we tend to not engage in open, honest communication. If we expect the other to compete rather than cooperate, we probably will engage in competitive behavior.

Although the basic thrust of this section on beliefs suggests that the motivational aspect of conflict management and resolution is disposition oriented rather than a behavioral response to a situation, this need not be a discouragement. Knowing your attitudes toward communication, communicator style, and so on can help you become aware of your basic beliefs toward conflict, so that you can change them if you wish.

APPLICATION 2.5

How difficult or easy is it for you to accept the functional assumptions about conflict? Do you think they are always applicable to your situations? To which ones do you take exception?

APPLICATION 2.6

Assessing Your Conflict Attitudes

Instructions: Answer each question as to the extent you think, believe, or feel the statement is true: always, usually, occasionally, seldom, or never true.

1. Do you believe that in every conflict situation mutually acceptable solutions exist or are available?
2. Do you feel that in each conflict situation, mutually acceptable solutions are a desirable thing?
3. Do you favor cooperation with all others in your everyday activities and disfavor competition with them?
4. Do you believe all people, regardless of age, race, religion, culture, or sex, are of equal value?
5. Do you feel that the views of others are legitimate (genuine, accurate, true) expressions of their positions?
6. Do you believe that differences of opinion are helpful and beneficial?
7. Do you feel that others are worthy of your trust?
8. Do you believe that others can compete, but they can also choose to cooperate?
9. Do you believe that how one feels and thinks are factors in deciding how to behave?

How you answer these questions will give you insight into how you will behave in conflict situations.

From Theory to Action

An important step in moving from theories of conflict to better conflict management is to adopt a mind-set that embraces conflict as an opportunity while recognizing the risks involved in it. This mind-set recognizes the importance of personal responsibility for one's actions and encourages flexibility in oneself and in others involved in the conflict situation. The mind-set also recognizes that communication works no miracles but that it usually helps to lead a conflict to management or resolution. Most important, this mind-set rejects easy solution and recognizes the complexity of conflict situations and their outcomes.

Becoming a more competent communicator in conflict situations, therefore, requires actively cultivating habits of thinking about conflict that lead to better outcomes. We need to understand that there will be times when we know what we should do but cannot quite accomplish it. There will be other times when we achieve our goals but at a cost to the relationship. And finally, there will be times when we feel we have acted competently in a conflict situation, meeting our own needs and those of the other. At these times of accomplishment, we should be self-reflective, assessing what we did right in the hope of accomplishing the same results in the future.

For many people, adopting these new attitudes and beliefs toward conflict is not an overnight process. It takes time and it takes work. The important thing is for you to become aware of your behavior in conflict situations and to start to identify the way your thinking about conflict situations affects the outcomes you obtain. Self-awareness is the first step toward more effective conflict behavior.

Notes

1. Milton Rokeach, *Beliefs, Attitudes, and Values* (San Francisco, CA: Jossey-Bass, 1969).

2. Ibid.

3. Richard E. Porter and Larry A. Samovar, "Basic Principles of Intercultural Communication," in Larry A. Samovar and Richard E. Porter (Eds.), *Intercultural Communication: A Reader,* 6th Ed. (Belmont, CA: Wadsworth, 1991), pp. 5–21.

4. Brian H. Spitzberg and Claire C. Brunner, "Toward a Theoretical Integration of Context and Competence Inference Research," *Western Journal of Speech Communication* 55 (1991), 28–46.

5. Terence L. Chmielewski, "Communicator Orientations: Attitudes Underlying the Rhetorical Sensitivity Archetypes," paper presented at the International Communication Association Convention, San Francisco, May 1984.

6. Roderick P. Hart and Don M. Burks, "Rhetorical Sensitivity and Social Interaction," *Speech Monographs* 39 (1972), 75–91; Roderick P. Hart, Robert E. Carlson, and William F. Eadie, "Attitudes Toward Communication and the Assessment of Rhetorical Sensitivity," *Communication Monographs* 47 (1980), 1–22.

7. Donald K. Darnell and Wayne Brockriede, *Persons Communicating* (Englewood Cliffs, NJ: Prentice-Hall, 1976).

8. William F. Eadie, "Influence of Attitudes Toward Communication and Relational Factors on Rhetorical Force," paper presented at the Western Speech Communication Association Convention, Albuquerque, February 1983.

9. Hart et al., "Attitudes Toward Communication," p. 2.

10. Chmielewski, "Communicator Orientations," p. 4.

11. Robert W. Norton, "Foundations of a Communicator Style Construct," *Human Communication Research* 4 (1978), 99–112.

12. Roger Fisher and William Ury, *Getting to Yes: Negotiating Agreement Without Giving In* (Boston: Houghton Mifflin, 1981).

13. M. Snyder, "Self-Monitoring of Expressive Behavior," *Journal of Personality and Social Psychology* 30 (1974), 526–537; "Self-Monitoring Processes," in Leonard Berkowitz (Ed.), *Advances in Experimental Social Psychology,* Vol. 12 (New York: Academic Press, 1979), pp. 85–128.

14. Jim D. Hughey, "Interpersonal Sensitivity, Communication Encounters, Communication Responsiveness, and Gender," paper presented at the Speech Communication Association Convention, Washington, DC, November 1983.

15. Donald J. Cegala, "Interaction Involvement: A Cognitive Dimension of Communicative Competence," *Communication Education* 30 (1981), 109–121.

16. Donald J. Cegala, "Affective and Cognitive Manifestations of Interaction Involvement During Unstructured and Competitive Interactions," *Communication Monographs* 51 (1984), 320–338.

17. John A. Daly, Anita L. Vangelisti, and Suzanne M. Daughton, "The Nature and Correlates of Conversational Sensitivity," *Human Communication Research* 14 (1987), 167–202.

18. Walter R. Azakahi and James C. McCroskey, "Willingness to Communicate: A Potentially Confounding Variable in Communication Research," *Communication Reports* 2 (1989), 96–104.

19. James C. McCroskey, "Oral Communication Apprehension: A Summary of Recent Theory and Research," *Human Communication Research* 4 (1977), 78–96.

20. Thompson Biggers and John T. Masterson, "Communication Apprehension as a Personality Trait: An Emotional Defense of a Concept," *Communication Monographs* 51 (1984), 381–390.

21. Pamela S. Shockley-Zalabak and Donald D. Morley, "An Exploratory Study of Relationships Between Preferences for Conflict Styles and Communication Apprehension," *Journal of Language and Social Psychology* 3 (1984), 213–218.

22. Sandra Metts and William R. Cupach, "The Influence of Relationship Beliefs and Problem-Solving Responses on Satisfaction in Romantic Relationships," *Human Communication Research* 17 (1990), 170–185.

23. Walter Isard and Christine Smith, *Conflict Analysis and Practical Conflict Management* (Cambridge, MA: Ballinger Publishing, 1982), p. xxxiv.

24. Alan L. Sillars, "The Sequential and Distributional Structure of Conflict Interactions as a Function of Attributions Concerning the Locus of Responsibility and Stability of Conflicts," in Dan Nimmo (Ed.), *Communication Yearbook* 4 (New Brunswick, NJ: Transaction Books, 1980), 217–235.

25. Candida C. Peterson and James L. Peterson, "Fight or Flight—Factors Influencing Children's and Adult's Decisions to Avoid or Confront Conflict," *Journal of Genetic Psychology* 151 (1990), 451–471.

26. Lorel Scott and Robert Martin, "Value Similarity, Relationship Length, and Conflict Interaction in Dating Relationships: An Initial Investigation," paper presented at the Speech Communication Association Convention, Chicago, November 1986.

27. Sara E. Newell and Randall K. Stutman, "A Qualitative Approach to Social Confrontation: Identifying Constraints and Facilitators," paper presented at the Speech Communication Association Convention, Louisville, KY, November 1982.

28. Kowk Leung, "Some Determinants of Conflict Avoidance," *Journal of Cross Cultural Psychology* 19 (1988), 125–136.

29. Leung argued that the severity of the issue is one of the main factors in our decision to pursue conflict; see also Sara E. Newell and Randall K. Stutman, "The Episodic Nature of Social Confrontation," in James A. Anderson, *Communication Yearbook* 14 (Newbury Park, CA: Sage Publications, 1991), 359–392.

30. Irving Altman and D. Taylor, *Social Penetration: The Development of Interpersonal Relationships* (Chicago: Holt, Rinehart and Winston, 1973).

31. Roxane Salyer, "Communication: A Resource, Not a Panacea," *Southern California Business,* August 13, 1980, p. 23.

32. Alan L. Sillars and Judith Weisberg, "Conflict as a Social Skill."

33. Karl Weick, *The Social Psychology of Organizing,* 2nd Ed. (New York: Addison-Wesley Publishing, 1979). See also Eric Eisenberg, "Ambiguity as a Strategy in Organizational Communication," *Communication Monographs* 51 (1984), 227–242.

34. See R. J. Rummel, *Understanding Conflict and War: The Conflict Helix,* Vol. 2 (Beverly Hills, CA: Sage, 1976), chapters 5–7; Morton Deutsch, "Toward an Understanding of Conflict," *International Journal of Group Tensions* 1 (1971), 42–54.

35. Paul Watzlawick, Janet Beavin, and Don D. Jackson, *Pragmatics of Human Communication* (New York: Norton, 1967).

36. Deutsch, "Toward an Understanding of Conflict."

37. William W. Wilmot and Joyce L. Hocker, *Interpersonal Conflict,* 5th ed. (Boston: McGraw-Hill, 1998), p. 56.

38. Ibid., p. 77.

39. Barry R. Schlenker, B. Helm, and J. T. Tedeschi, "The Effects of Personality and Situational Variables on Behavioral Trust," *Journal of Personality and Social Psychology* 32 (1973), 664–670.

40. Max Bazerman, "Why Negotiations Go Wrong," *Psychology Today* (June 1986), 54–58.

41. Alan C. Filley, *Interpersonal Conflict Resolution* (New York: HarperCollins Publishers, 1975), pp. 60–69.

3

Culture and Gender in Conflict

Objectives

At the end of this chapter, you should be able to

1. describe the hierarchical model of cultural understanding.
2. explain how the three levels of the hierarchical model apply to a given culture.
3. explain how people from different cultures may better communicate by transcending their cultural constraints.
4. list the steps to successful collaboration in intercultural conflict situations.
5. describe some of the differences in male and female styles of conflict.

Key Terms

cultural perspective	hierarchical model	monochronic time
culture	high context culture	polychronic time
ethnocentrism	intercultural communication	sex
face	intercultural conflict	socialization
gender	low context culture	

When people engage in conflict, they bring to the encounter their personalities, gender, and cultural identity. In Chapter 2, we learned that these personalities are made up of traits and values. Along with attitudes, beliefs, and goals, values play an important role in cognition. As we indicated earlier, conflicts over values are often difficult to resolve because the values held by the participants give them the feeling that "truth" is on their side and to compromise would be to give up that truth. Thus, we sometimes deal with cultural diversity by insisting that things be done "our way" (because we feel that "our way" is best).

The "our way" phenomenon is also referred to as **ethnocentrism,** which may be defined as "the view of things in which one's own group is the center of everything, and all others are scaled and rated with reference to it."[1] Ethnocentrism frames the way we view our culture and that of others.

> Although we often rely on the knowledge of our own cultural approach, rhythms, norms, and styles to explain the behavior of other people from our culture, the same criteria may not be applicable to another culture. Being unfamiliar with the other party's cultural norms creates problems that can exacerbate an already tense intercultural conflict episode. An examination of such problems is a natural extension of the discussion on differences in conflict styles.[2]

One of the difficulties in identifying the basic attitudes and beliefs that different cultures bring to the conflict situation is that so many of them reside below the surface of conscious thought. That is, we are aware of differences such as language, clothing, or food preferences, but people do not articulate their beliefs about conflict very readily. Thus, it may be confusing for us as we try to understand the conflict and the way the other person is acting within it.[3] To manage and resolve conflicts competently in intercultural communication, we must come to grips with our own as well as others' ethnocentric views.

The importance of values is highlighted when we turn to the subject of intercultural communication. **Intercultural communication** "occurs whenever a message produced in one culture must be processed in another culture."[4] But what is culture? "**Culture** refers to a group-level construct that embodies a distinctive system of traditions, beliefs, values, norms, rituals, symbols, and meanings that is shared by a majority of interacting individuals in a community."[5] The values and other cultural concepts by which communicators function as active participants in their respective cultures or ethnic groups are unique to that culture and ethnic group.

There are many differences between cultures, but the question arises, when does a difference really make a difference? There are at least two answers to this question. First, languages and nonverbal differences may make communication difficult if not impossible for those who don't know the language at all. Unlike traffic signs that are universally accepted in many countries, there are many other linguistic signs and symbols that are arbitrary. In the United States waving a hand signifies "good-bye" but in Japan a similar gesture represents a request to "come here." Such differences in the meanings of messages often contribute to miscommunication. Usually, miscommunication due to lack of knowledge about the different verbal and nonverbal codes is quickly corrected with few ill feelings by simply sharing information. This narrative illustrates a conflict based on misperception of nonverbal behaviors.

> My young daughter was waiting to use the restroom on a plane, and apparently was getting kind of desperate. She started a little dance, saying "ooo" and "aah" and rushed into the restroom after the previous occupant left. Later, we were standing at the baggage claim, and the woman, an Asian, came up to my daughter and demanded to know what those sounds meant. My daughter was embarrassed and said she was just saying "hello." The woman then said she didn't think that's what it meant and that she was offended by hearing the "ooo" and "aah." My daughter apologized, and the woman left angrily.

Second, there are differences in **cultural perspectives,** which are shaped by unique value systems shared by a group of people that contribute to important behavior differences including communication behavior. If we have one set of values and you have another, we may expect you to behave or communicate in a certain fashion that runs contrary to your value system. In intercultural communication, the participants, if they are to understand and establish an interpersonal relationship with one another, must come to grips with understanding their own and the other's culture.

Mastering the interpersonal conflict process is difficult enough when the parties are from the same culture but becomes more complicated when cultural differences are added in. Ting-Toomey defines **intercultural conflict** as the "perceived incompatibility of values, norms, processes, or goals between a minimum of two cultural parties over identity, relational, and/or substantive issues."[6] Based on Ting-Toomey's definition, we can expect a great deal of conflict in intercultural communication because the participants are from different cultures.

Why is this so? The more similar the **socialization** processes, say, for example, between Americans and Canadians, the greater the likelihood that the symbols of different cultures share common interpretation. This makes it easier for similar cultures to communicate, resulting in less likelihood of miscommunication and misunderstanding. In cases where conflicts due to cultural differences occur, the resolution of conflict may depend on competition, compromise, or accommodation because the differences between the cultures are not great.

Conversely, the less similar the socialization processes, say, between Japanese and Americans, the wider the gap confronting intercultural communicators. In situations involving major cultural differences, members of one culture may be obliged to adopt the values, roles, and rules of the dominant cultural group, as in the case of immigrants assimilating into a new culture where they wish to go to school, do business, or perhaps marry and raise a family. This has been a traditional way of resolving intercultural conflicts. However, as specific cultural and ethnic groups gain political and economic influence in a country, unsurprisingly they find the traditional approach less desirable and become more assertive of their own cultural heritage. Then the resolution of conflict becomes more dependent on integrative and collaborative approaches that must strive to satisfy the interests, needs, and goals of the parties involved.

Although cultural differences appear to represent significant barriers to communication, they may be overcome. According to Cushman and Cahn, "We can bring to consciousness our own cultural tendencies and those of others, define the conventions that link what is perceived with what is communicated, and then exert some control over the process of cross-cultural communication."[7] Because we are spending more and more time in interaction with people from other cultures, we must become aware of our cultural inclinations and their social pressures if we are to successfully communicate interculturally.

APPLICATION 3.1

When conflict arises, do you normally look for "personal" causes of the conflict, or do you consider whether cultural perspective has something to do with the conflict that is occurring? How can you become more aware of the role of culture in the various conflicts that you experience?

The subject of intercultural conflict strikes us as especially important today in a country like the United States that continues to march toward diversity. Classrooms, neighborhoods, workplaces, showrooms, and places of worship are becoming increasingly more open to members of different ethnic and cultural groups. When one considers the number of intercultural friendships, working relationships, marriages, and families, it becomes apparent that many people spend at least some of their time in interaction with members of other ethnic and cultural groups.

Moreover, the principles applicable to intercultural communication and conflict have wider applicability in the sense that they apply to encounters between subgroups in the same country (i.e., different ethnic, racial, religious groups, gender, generations, classes, different regions of the same country, etc.). According to Ting-Toomey, ". . . the general concepts (regarding intercultural conflict differences) . . . should serve as a working basis in managing any kind of group-based difference in conflict. Both general and specific knowledge of other cultures and ethnic groups can increase our motivation and skill in dealing with people who are culturally and ethnically different."[8]

A Hierarchical Model of Cultural Understanding

To understand intercultural communication, we must begin with the way values influence communication within a culture. Traditionally, the role of cultural influence in communication and, hence, conflict processes is described by a **hierarchical model** of cultural understanding. In this model, the meaning or interpretation of the significance and value of objects, symbols, and behaviors is dependent upon the higher-order identification of its context.[9] The elements of the communication situation are arranged in a hierarchy, with elements at the top of the hierarchy influencing elements lower in the hierarchy (see Figure 3.1).[10]

At the highest level of the model lies the cultural perspective, or "world view," which consists of a culture's general orientation toward life. As Skow and Samovar have explained, a person's world view affects the way he or she thinks about central ideas such as God, his or her place in the universe, death and afterlife, nature, and so on. A person's world view "influences nearly every action in which an individual engages."[11] A world view, or cultural perspective, is a person's model for perceiving, relating, and interpreting.[12] As a frame of reference, a world view, or what we will refer to now as a cultural perspective, is characteristically referred to as common sense by members of that culture.

Values are the evaluative aspect of this cultural perspective.[13] A cultural perspective is linked to the lower levels of the model because it includes a value system which ". . . rep-

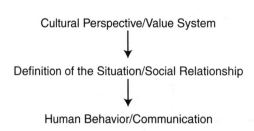

FIGURE 3.1   *Hierarchical Model of Culture and Communication*

resents what is expected or hoped for, required or forbidden. It is not a report of actual conduct but is the system of criteria by which conduct is judged and sanctions applied."[14] These standards are used to evaluate the desirability of people, actions, and objects. By examining the various values that make up this cultural perspective, one may better understand how members of a culture define situations and why they communicate or behave as they do.

At the next lower level, the definition of the situation or relationship consists of one's perception or understanding of a recurring social setting with particular roles, rules, spatial arrangements, and a purpose or goal.[15] Situations or social contexts that have common definitions in American culture range from highly ritualized, special, formal occasions such as funerals, weddings, trials, birthdays, job interviews, and sporting events to more informal, everyday "nonoccasions" such as meetings, meal times, social get-togethers, dating, and courtship.

If values represent a collective view of what is important and unimportant, good and bad, rules link values to thoughts and actions. Rules allow people to "engage spontaneously in everyday social behavior without continually having to 'guess' what other people are going to do."[16] They function as criteria for choice among mental and behavioral alternatives, and serve as constraints on the range of options a person may have for any particular situation. Although rules are social conventions that can be violated or changed by individuals or groups, when people know the rules they tend to conform to them. For example, consider the situation in which a customer enters a small store and finds the clerk on the telephone. If the clerk looks up, smiles, and holds up a hand to indicate that he or she will be available in a moment, the customer will generally interpret this as a positive behavior and will be willing to wait. If the clerk looks up, scowls, and goes back to the telephone conversation with no apparent desire to end the conversation, the customer will generally interpret this behavior negatively, and may even leave the store to seek help elsewhere. However, these rules are applicable only to American culture. They may not be applicable in other countries.

At the lowest level of the model lies human behavior. Our most significant behavior is learned through experience as we are positively or negatively reinforced for performing it. When children are confronted with a novel situation, they often engage in random behavior. However, if that random behavior leads to a favorable consequence, the behavior is reinforced and the child may repeat it for a similar situation in the future. So, for example, children generally receive positive reinforcement for sharing their toys and negative reinforcement for refusing to share. According to our model, given a particular cultural perspective complete with a value system, we learn our cultural rules as our behavior is rewarded. If no consequences result, the behavior is not reinforced and therefore abandoned. When unfavorable consequences result, the tendency to avoid the punished behavior is reinforced.

The most significant learned behavior of interest to us is communication. When people communicate, they share a system of sounds, gestures, and symbols for the expression and comprehension of thoughts and feelings.[17] Consisting of both verbal and nonverbal communication behaviors, the system includes linguistic rules unique to a language and its culture. Depending on a culture's definition of a situation or social relationship, people who are competent communicators realize the appropriateness and potential effectiveness of particular actions. By examining cultural perspectives and definitions of situations or social relationships, we are better able to identify and understand communication behavior in a particular culture.

> **APPLICATION 3.2**
>
> Use the hierarchical model to analyze a recent conflict you have experienced. What differences and similarities existed between you and the other person? Does the model help you better understand your behavior in this situation?

The Hierarchical Model and Cultural Variability

There are many ways that different cultures vary in their perspective, values, definitions of recurring social situations, rules, and appropriate communication behavior. Several core values, which are expressed differently among various cultural groups, may cause conflict. These core values include the perception of how people should relate to nature, religion and the role people believe it should play in government, the social obligation of a culture's members to one another, the importance of the social context in determining what one should do, face and facework, and the use of time. Some short examples of how such values cause conflict include:

• Harmony with Nature: Kluckholn and Leighton have argued that traditionally members of the Navaho Native American culture ascribe to the view that "nature is more powerful than (humankind)" and that "nature will take care of (people) if they behave as they should and do as she directs."[18] This is a statement of a set of values that make up the Navaho view of humankind and its harmonious relationship to nature. Traditionally, when a Navaho suffers an illness, a diviner must be consulted to determine the appropriate ritual for warding off evil. The diviner knows the rules to do the proper ritual. This makes sense to a Navaho who values harmony, views the illness as a disturbance in the harmonious balance between nature and humans, and believes that the appropriate ritual is needed to restore the proper balance. However, it may make no sense to someone outside of that particular culture.

• Religion: Unlike the United States (where there is a constitutional separation of church and state), in many Muslim cultures religion and government are practically one and the same. Moreover, in the United States, many rules for human behavior are believed to be rationally derived to facilitate individual needs and aspirations. In India, on the other hand, individual and social behaviors are thought to be manifestations and expressions of a deeper reality. The dharma is a code of conduct that prescribes right living in accordance with the "double objectives of happiness on earth and salvation."[19] Because the dharma links a strong sense of morality to human behavior, everyone is encouraged to follow his or her dharma. In the United States, the lack of religious backing for various claims that people make about right and wrong actions may be confusing to people who do not make private and public distinctions in their religious beliefs.

• Social Obligation: Confucian philosophy, which views relationships as complementary and reciprocally obligatory, has greatly influenced the behavior of many Asians. According to Yum,

> In a sense, a person is forever indebted to others, who in turn are constrained by other debts. Under this system of reciprocity, the individual does not calculate what he or she gives and receives. To calculate would be to think about

immediate personal profits, which is the opposite of the principle of mutual faithfulness. . . . The practice of basing relationships on complementary obligations creates warm, lasting human relationships but also the necessity to accept the obligations accompanying such relationships.[20]

The high individuality of the U.S. culture stands in direct contrast to the Asian notion of social obligation, and differences in orientation may create or exacerbate conflicts.

• High/Low Context: According to Swanson and Delia, the interpretation appropriate for a particular message is meaningless apart from a message receiver's definition of the situation.[21] That is, we cannot give meaning to a message we have just heard without hearing the message within a particular context. However, the role played by the situation or context may vary across cultures. For example, compared to others, some cultures place greater significance on the second level—the situation—and, therefore, ascribe more meaning in its definition. This distinction has resulted in cultures being classified along a continuum ranging from high context to low. At the high end of the continuum (**high context,** HC), a culture is said to place less of the information needed to understand a message in the verbal language and more in the nonverbal cues as well as physical and social context. At the low end of the continuum (**low context,** LC), a culture places most of the information needed to understand a message in the verbal language itself.

One implication of this distinction between high and low context cultures is that different communication and conflict resolution styles emerge. Members from LC cultures tend to talk more, seem more direct, aggressive, discourteous of other's feelings, rely more on written documents, and make explicit more warnings, rules, and explanations than do members of HC cultures. In addition, they are likely to place the responsibility for communicating a complaint on the one who has the complaint. Conversely, members of HC cultures may place greater value on silence, seem more indirect, ambiguous, and evasive, rely more on social relationships than verbal agreements, and know how to behave without explicit written instructions in many social settings than do members of LC cultures. Moreover, they tend to expect others to discern from the context the reason for a subtly expressed complaint. When engaged in conflict, members of LC cultures may say everything they think with no restraints. They may be direct, to the point, highly self-disclosing of their feelings, and unconscious of their face-threatening messages. In contrast, members of HC cultures may respond by not directly expressing their concerns because they want to save face and maintain their relationships. Instead, they express only indirect hints and subtle nonverbal cues to get across their point.

• Face/Facework: The notion of face is more important in some cultural perspectives than in others. In stark contrast to the United States, the Chinese concept of **face** (mien-tzu), or the impression that a person maintains for others, is central to a Chinese view of their social life.

When we say in Chinese that one loses face, we mean that he (or she) loses prestige, he (or she) has been insulted or has been made to feel embarrassment before a group. When we say that a man wants a face, we mean that he wants to be given honor, prestige, praise, flattery, or concession, whether or not these are merited. Face is really a personal psychological satisfaction, a social esteem accorded by others.[22]

According to Chang and Holt, social situations are defined in terms of facework.

> Social others, whether specific individuals or the society at large, have a stake in the individual's maintenance of protection of mien-tzu. Mien-tzu is said to be distributed among all interactants in a situation, as reflected in the common phrase, "everybody gets mien-tzu," meaning that matters are handled in such a way that everyone shares the honor of looking good. . . . Interactants are expected to know how to respect the mien-tzu of others in order to ensure smooth social interaction.[23]

As these expressions show, the Chinese have developed a detailed set of communication behaviors that are dictated by their cultural perspective and compatible with their definition of social situations. But the Chinese are not the only ones concerned with face and facework. Other cultures have expectations for the way in which people should act toward one another in order to give respect, as this narrative illustrates:

> I learned very early shopping in the Quetzelon market in Lima, Peru, that one does not simply see an item to be purchased and ask the price. Shopkeepers are people who expect respect and relationship. As one enters the store, one should say "Buenos Dias"—good day—as a greeting. One should smile and look around at the various items, and praise the selection. Only after these amenities have been observed should one ask the price. And asking the price is simply the beginning, as most of the shopkeepers are willing to bargain (and seem to expect it). Failure to observe such rules results in paying much more for an item than someone who does.

Because face and facework are important factors in interpersonal conflict, we will return to this subject in Chapter 15 when we discuss impression management.

• Time: Cultural perspectives also have different views of "time," resulting in different definitions of how time functions in social situations and different codes for time-related behaviors. Hall distinguishes between two extremes: monochronic (M-time) and polychronic (P-time) treatments of time.[24] The dominant groups in American culture are said to be **monochronic** in their approach to time—they see time as lineal and segmented (i.e., the time it takes to play quarters and halves of a sport like football or basketball). As parents they will teach their children to "take one day at a time." Time is often treated as money and usually as something one shouldn't waste. In an M-time culture, people prefer orderly scheduling of appointments and are often very distressed by interruptions. Condon points out that the treatment of time in the United States may be somewhat unique on a worldwide scale.[25] The dominant groups in Mexican culture appear to be more **polychronic** than people in the United States in their approach to time—they view time in a nonlineal, nonsegmented fashion as many things happening at once. Interruptions are expected and permitted. According to Condon, U.S. citizens express special irritation when Mexicans seem to give them less than their undivided attention.[26] When a young woman bank teller, awaiting her superior's approval for a check to be cashed, files her nails and talks on the phone to her boyfriend, or when one's taxi driver stops en route to pick up a friend who seems to be going in the same direction, U.S. citizens become very upset. They interpret such behavior as showing a lack of respect and a lack of "professionalism," but the reason may lie more in the culturally different treatment of time.

According to Ting-Toomey, different orientations toward time may contribute to friction in a conflict situation. Not surprisingly, people who view time as monochronic don't want to waste time, but are eager to get to conflict resolution quickly. People who view time as polychronic may focus more on the relationship and the situation itself, building trust and commitment, before moving onto resolution of the particular conflict.[27]

An implication of the hierarchical model for intercultural communication and the resolution of conflict is that communicators must learn more about another culture's perspective, values, definition of recurring social situations, rules, and appropriate communication behavior. As Barnlund argues:

> As we move or are driven toward a global village and increasingly frequent cultural contact, we need more than simply greater factual knowledge of each other. We need, more specifically, to identify what might be called the "rule books of meaning" that distinguish one culture from another. For to grasp the way in which other cultures perceive the world, and the assumptions and values that are the foundation of these perceptions is to gain access to the experience of other human beings. Access to the world view and the communicative style of other cultures may not only enlarge our own way of experiencing the world but enable us to maintain constructive relationships with societies that operate according to a different logic than our own.[28]

APPLICATION 3.3

Compare your culture and the culture of a friend you know fairly well across the various values discussed in this section. On which are you similar? Which of these values is likely to cause conflict between you and your friend?

The Challenge of Diversity

Intercultural conflict may actually be more manageable when our differences are very apparent because those differences seem to stare us in the face and draw our attention to them. Issues of diversity (e.g., gender, sexual orientation, ethnic identity, socioeconomic status, disabilities, etc.), however, are not so obvious, and may also present problems in conflict resolution. Within the United States, we may only speak of a "dominant culture"—one represented through the media. But there are thousands of subcultures here, many of which do not share ideas about the best way to solve conflicts.

On the other hand, we may run the risk of confusing a person with his or her indigenous culture and, thus, complicate conflict through our assumptions about the other. Adler argues that we are increasingly multicultural people, people whose orientation transcends the culture into which they are born:

> [It is] a person whose essential identity is inclusive of life patterns different from his own and who has psychologically and socially come to grips with a multiplicity of realities. . . . The identity of multicultural man is based, not on

a "belongingness" which implies either owning or being owned by culture, but on a style of self-consciousness that is capable of negotiating ever new formations of reality. . . . He is neither totally *a part of* or *apart from* his culture; he lives, instead, on the boundary.[29]

In contrast to Adler, Schwarz (writing in the same book) argues that pluralism and tolerance are a myth that the United States has tried to export and impose on other countries:

> After four centuries we are nagged by the facts that we do not "all get along" and that the apparent success of our own multiethnic and multicultural experiment might have been engendered not by tolerance but by hegemony. Without the dominance that once dictated, however ethnocentrically, what it meant to be an American, we are left only with tolerance and pluralism to hold us together. Unfortunately, the evidence from Los Angeles to New York, from Miami to Milwaukee, shows that such principles are not so powerful as we had believed and hoped.[30]

Where do such extreme opinions leave us? At the risk of making an ethnocentric pronouncement, we believe that the best communication style is one that is adaptive to the situation while maintaining consistency with personal values. This balance is a hard one to maintain, and yet we believe that conflicts with diverse people may be more manageable if we can maintain this balance in our approach.

Sex, Gender, and Conflict

Walk into any bookstore and head for the self-help section. You are likely to find a number of different books purporting to explain differences between women and men. People use **sex** (i.e., what a person is biologically) to explain a great deal of behavior. In addition, research has investigated the relationship between **gender** (a person's psychological orientation toward femininity, masculinity, or androgyny) and conflict. Whereas some authors claim that men and women have biologically different brains that create startlingly different behavior,[31] others minimize biological differences between men and women and argue that our similarities are far greater than our differences.[32] This debate continues to be played out in communication and conflict literature as well as in the popular press, as Turner and Sterk note:

> Essentialists are those theorists who . . . argue that there is something essentially female (and, for many theorists, superior) about all women that contrasts sharply with men's essentially male nature. Opponents of this position . . . opine that women [and men] are too diverse a group to possess an essential nature, and other concepts such as race, ethnicity, and status, for example, play a much larger role than gender in shaping people's behavior. Further, these theorists maintain that the essentialist views cause more problems than they solve by obscuring the real differences among women [and men] and rendering women [and men] of color invisible.[33]

Given this brief introduction to the politics of gender and sex differences and similarities in communication and conflict research, we will highlight a few of the findings. According to some studies linking biological sex to conflict behavior, women tend to be more accommodating and more compromising than men. Women also learn how to avoid conflict situations; when in conflict, women express more support and exhibit more facilitative behaviors than men. Men tend to be more dominant in conversation and more verbally aggressive than women.[34]

Some studies indicate that women are more likely than men to employ strategies that focus on reasoning or understanding and are more likely to internalize the conflict. Women are more likely than men to use personal criticism and anger strategies, whereas males are more likely to use denial tactics.[35] Burggraf and Sillars's review of previous research indicated that studies conducted in the 1970s had found some systematic differences in the ways men and women behave in conflicts.[36] It was assumed, for example, that women would be more accommodating and expressive and men would be more dominant and instrumental (task oriented) in conflict situations. Earlier research tended to bear out these findings, although more recent research found few sex-related differences, particularly in marital communication.

On the other hand, some studies have found no difference in how men and women do conflict.[37] One such study, based on observations of interaction between dyads, concluded that the power and the sex of the "opponent" was a better predictor of strategy use than biological sex or psychological gender of the actor. Men and women choose strategies not because of who they are but because of the nature of their opponent. Women supervising men, for instance, use assertiveness more than do men supervising men, who use more than men supervising women. Male supervisors use assertiveness less with female than with male subordinates. And female supervisors tend to report coming to agreement more readily than male supervisors.[38]

Conrad, however, concluded that the results of research examining the effect of gender on the selection of conflict strategies can be grouped into three categories of approximately equal size:

> (1) those which found no significant [sex] effect on parties' cooperativeness and competitiveness . . . (2) those which found that males are more cooperative than females . . . and (3) those which found that females are more cooperative than males.[39]

In addition, an analysis of the data from a number of different communication studies examining differences due to biological sex found that knowing the sex of the person behaving could only predict communication behavior about 1 percent of the time.[40] Those are not very strong predictions.

Some research suggests that men and women use talk to accomplish different things, and the differences (and difficulties) they experience may be explained by these different goals. Ivy and Backlund, for example, argue that men *primarily* use conversation to impart information, whereas women *primarily* use conversation to understand the relationship. This doesn't mean that there is never a relational aspect to men's talk or an informational aspect to women's talk; all talk has both an informational/content dimension (what is being said) and a relationship dimension (who are we to one another as a result of this conversation). They report some preliminary findings indicating that when men and women view videotapes of conversation and ascribe motives to those communicating, women more frequently believe the purpose of a conversation is to accomplish a relational goal (e.g., get to know the other better), whereas men more frequently believe the purpose of the conversation is information (e.g., to see if she is available for a date).[41]

APPLICATION 3.4

If the research demonstrates that men and women aren't all that different in their manner of conflict engagement, why do we see so much talk about it in the popular press? Do you tend to think of a conflict as being caused by the sex of the participants?

Regardless of whom you would like to believe (the essentialists or their opponents), it is evident to us that, at the least, men and women have different expectations of male and female roles and the way those roles should be enacted. "Sex roles are behaviors that traditionally are labeled masculine or feminine. These behaviors are stereotypically associated with (biological sex) males and females . . . for example, women are viewed stereotypically as less assertive than men."[42]

Gender stereotypes affect expectations of conflict behavior for men and women. Some think that women accommodate more in order to be social and that they compete only as a last resort. Men are seen as preferring competition and women as preferring compromise. When men engaged in conflict with other men, they were more goal oriented. In one study, women engaged in conflict with other women concluded their conflicts with bargaining sequences so that both would achieve at least part of their goal.[43] Research concerning assessments of the appropriateness of various conflict strategies found that sex role identity affected reactions to the strategies: Feminine persons were far less approving of competitive conflict strategies than masculine or androgynous persons.[44]

Some research has examined the effects of sex differences in perceptions of communication competence. One study asked respondents to describe the best and the worst communicators they knew and to provide at least three adjectives or short phrases for each person they described. Table 3.1 shows the various descriptors used by men and women in rating communication competence.

TABLE 3.1 *Gender Differences in Perceptions of Competent Communication Ratings*

Best Communicator		Worst Communicator	
According to Females	*According to Males*	*According to Females*	*According to Males*
Direct eye contact	Knowledgeable	Lacks eye contact	Avoids talking; is shy
Listens	Intelligent	Inattentive	Opinionated
Attentive	Relaxed	Interrupts	Nervous
Caring and concerned	Sense of humor	Unclear	Not knowledgeable
Gestures	Objective	Inappropriate nonverbal	Unresponsive
Perceptive	Honest and sincere	behavior	Does not listen
Interested		Preoccupied	Inappropriate topic
Understands me		Speech problems	changes
Interesting		Self-centered	Uninteresting

Women tend to value other-oriented behaviors, such as listening and attentiveness, which can be expressed nonverbally through the use of direct eye contact. [M]en place value upon an individual attribute, knowledgeability, which may be interpreted as a concern for the content (rather than the form) of interpersonal communication.[45]

Clearly, what men and women deem as competent communication behavior differs, and this will have important consequences for conflict behavior. Whereas a woman will expect competence in the form of attentiveness and other "personal" behaviors, a man might expect attention to the issue of conflict. Both are likely to be disappointed in opposite-sex conflicts. An example of such disappointment is contained in the following account.

On Sunday, my boyfriend and I decided he would wait for me at my place and cook dinner. I was exhausted, having had surgery the previous Thursday and having been involved in too many group projects at school. I was also dealing with the stress of his leaving in two days on Tuesday. I arrived frazzled and stressed about my overdue projects. I walked through the door, and the apartment was spotless. The lights were dim, and there were purple roses and purple orchids in every room. The scent of a great dinner filled the apartment. Dinner relaxed me, and my boyfriend's company both soothed and mellowed me. Who would have thought we were about to have the biggest conflict of our relationship?

We had talked about both of us going to work in Chicago on a movie. We had decided that he would go and that I would stay and finish school. It wasn't that I didn't want to work on another movie. The reason I didn't want to go was that finishing school means my complete freedom from my parents. My dad can no longer say I'm nothing because I don't have a degree, and I am able to support myself through my education. Not to mention that I feel better about myself and I feel educated. I thought my boyfriend understood me when I expressed all these emotions to him, and was not prepared for his one last plea.

After dinner, he asked me one last time if I would reconsider and go with him to Chicago. His complete disregard for my feelings blew me away. It was hard enough dealing with our separation. It was also hard for me to make the decision to stay and not go work on another movie. I was so disappointed in Dan. I felt like I could not even trust him with my feelings. I wanted to revert back to my usual handling of a conflict and scream at him all my hurt and frustration. I didn't, only because I love him so much and I want us to work it out. I tried to talk with him through my tears, but something inside me feels totally torn apart. My heart feels heavy and crushed. I don't think I can trust Dan like I used to and that made me want to talk with him until all the hurt went away, but that didn't work, the feelings of hurt and distrust remained.

The woman involved in this conflict interpreted from the positive cues surrounding her dinner that her boyfriend really understood her feelings about taking a break from school and that this wonderful dinner was a temporary "good-bye" as they parted for a time. The boyfriend, on the other hand, appears to have set up the dinner as one last way of persuading her to go to Chicago with him. His focus was on the issue of them being together; her focus was on her feelings about finishing school and becoming independent. Both were communicating in ways they thought were effective but found themselves at cross-purposes.

For example, the woman considers her boyfriend's attention to her frazzled feelings and his attempts to soothe her as competent, not his goal-directed attempts to persuade her to go to Chicago. Even if he were to achieve his goal by persuading her through manipulation, pleading, or reasoning, such behaviors would probably not be viewed as competent by the woman involved because she sees them as inappropriate to the situation given her previously stated feelings on the subject.

From Theory to Action

Although the content of the cultural model's three levels may vary across cultures, the model of cultural understanding is hierarchical in that each level governs what is appropriate and defines the level below. First, the cultural perspective governs one's understanding or definition of recurring social situations, activities, or events. Given a particular cultural perspective, only certain social situations are required, expected, or hoped for and others are forbidden by socially prescribed rules, and the significance of the social situation is determined by the appropriate cultural perspective. Thus, there are certain recurring social activities that dominate in a particular culture due to its unique perspective. By determining the value system characteristic of a particular culture, one may identify rules that define these recurring social situations and govern human behavior in them.

Second, one's understanding or definition of the situation or social relationship governs what verbal and nonverbal communication behaviors are appropriate. Many communication behaviors such as vocabulary choice, sentence construction, word speed, tone of voice, volume, and accompanying use of the body and hands are regulated by the situation or interpersonal relationship as defined culturally.

Recent years have witnessed a redistribution of political and economic power among nations and among ethnic groups within the United States producing greater interdependence among cultural groups. Today, one's interests and goals can only be achieved through the cooperation of these diverse groups. Our interdependence as Americans requires that we take account of others who frequently view the world in a different way than we do. Our failure to take into account people of different ethnicity or nationality leads to withdrawal and the inability of achieving goals. Therefore, a contemporary approach to intercultural communication seeks to bridge the cultural gap by collaborating and discovering the common ground or integrative solution that exists between members of different cultural groups.

In addition, we need to be alert to issues of diversity within our own communities. We cannot simply assume that others think like us, or will want to resolve a conflict in a manner similar to the way we have chosen. Questioning our expectations of others' behavior, being adaptive to the situation, and remaining alert to what we perceive the other's expectations to be will help us to act more competently in conflict situations.

Notes

1. W. Sumner, *Folkways* (Boston: Ginn, 1940), p. 13.
2. Stella Ting-Toomey, "Intercultural Conflict Competence," in William R. Cupach and Daniel J. Canary (Eds.), *Competence in Interpersonal Conflict* (New York: McGraw-Hill, 1997), p. 139.

3. Gary R. Weaver, "Contrasting and Comparing Cultures," in Gary R. Weaver (Ed.), *Culture, Communication and Conflict: Readings in Intercultural Relations,* 2nd Ed. (Needham Heights, MA: Simon and Schuster, 1998).

4. Ibid., p. 6.

5. Ting-Toomey, "Intercultural Conflict Competence," p. 124. (Italics ours)

6. Ibid., p. 122. (Italics ours)

7. D. Cushman and D. Cahn, *Communication in Interpersonal Relationships* (Albany, NY: SUNY, 1985), p. 145.

8. Ting-Toomey, "Intercultural Conflict Competence," p. 142.

9. Alfred Whitehead and Bertrand Russell, *Principia Mathematica,* III, 2nd Ed. (Cambridge: Cambridge University, 1910–13); G. Bateson, *Steps to an Ecology of Mind* (New York: Ballantine Books, 1972).

10. W. Barnett Pearce, Vernon Cronen, and F. Conklin, "A Hierarchical Model of Interpersonal Communication," paper presented at the annual meeting of the International Communication Association, Berlin, 1977.

11. Lisa Skow and Larry Samovar, "Cultural Patterns of the Maasai," in Larry A. Samovar and Richard E. Porter (Eds.), *Intercultural Communication: A Reader,* 6th Ed. (Belmont, CA: Wadsworth, 1991), p. 91.

12. Richard Wiseman, "Towards a Rules Perspective of Intercultural Communication," *Communication* 9, (1980), 30–38.

13. Donald W. Klopf and Myung-Seok Park, *Korean Communicative Behavior* (Seoul, Korea: The Communication Association of Korea, 1994), p. 21.

14. E. Albert, "Values Systems," in *International Encyclopedia of the Social Sciences* (New York: Macmillan, 1968), p. 287.

15. P. Brown and C. Grazer, "Speech as a Marker of Situation," in K. Scherer and H. Giles (Eds.), *Social Markets in Speech* (Cambridge: Cambridge University, 1979.)

16. William B. Gudykunst and Young Yun Kim, *Communicating with Strangers: An Approach to Intercultural Communication* (New York: McGraw-Hill, 1997), p. 47.

17. D. Swanson and Jesse Delia, *The Nature of Human Communication* (Palo Alto, CA: SRA, 1976).

18. C. Kluckhohn and D. Leighton, *The Navaho* (Cambridge, MA: Harvard University Press, 1946), pp. 227–228.

19. Nemi C. Jain, "World View and Cultural Patterns of India," in Larry A. Samovar and Richard E. Porter (Eds.), *Intercultural Communication: A Reader,* 6th Ed. (Belmont, CA: Wadsworth, 1991), p. 82.

20. June Ock Yum, "The Impact of Confucianism on Interpersonal Relationships and Communication Patterns in East Asia," in Larry A. Samovar and Richard E. Porter (Eds.), *Intercultural Communication: A Reader,* 6th Ed. (Belmont, CA: Wadsworth, 1991), pp. 69–70.

21. Swanson and Delia, *The Nature of Human Communication.*

22. M. C. Yang Yang, *A Chinese Village* (New York: Columbia University Press, 1945), p. 167.

23. Hui-Ching Chang and G. Richard Holt, "A Chinese Perspective on Face as Inter-Relational Concern," in Stella Ting-Toomey (Ed.), *The Challenge of Facework: Cross-Cultural and Interpersonal Issues* (Albany, NY: SUNY, 1994), p. 101.

24. Edward T. Hall, *The Silent Language* (New York: Anchor, 1973).

25. John Condon, ". . . So Near the United States: Notes on Communication between Mexicans and North Americans," in Larry A. Samovar and Richard E. Porter (Eds.), *Intercultural Communication: A Reader,* 6th Ed. (Belmont, CA: Wadsworth, 1991), pp. 106–112.

26. Ibid., p. 111.

27. Ting-Toomey, "Intercultural Conflict Competence," p. 135.

28. Dean C. Barnlund, *Public and Private Self in Japan and the United States* (Tokyo: Simul, 1975).

29. Peter S. Adler, "Beyond Cultural Identity: Reflections of Cultural and Multicultural Man," in Gary R. Weaver (Ed.), *Culture, Communication and Conflict: Readings in Intercultural Relations,* 2nd Ed. (Needham Heights, MA: Simon and Schuster, 1998), pp. 251–252.

30. Benjamin Schwarz, "The Diversity Myth: American's Leading Export," in Gary R. Weaver, (Ed.), *Culture, Communication and Conflict: Readings in Intercultural Relations,* 2nd Ed. (Needham Heights, MA: Simon and Schuster, 1998), p. 480.

31. Robert L. Nadeua, *S/he Brain* (Westport, CT: Praeger, 1996).

32. Carol Tavris, *The Mismeasure of Woman* (New York: Simon and Schuster, 1990).

33. Lynn H. Turner and Helen M. Sterk, "Introduction: Examining 'Difference,' " in Lynn H. Turner and Helen M. Sterk (Eds.), *Differences That Make a Difference: Examining the Assumptions in Gender Research* (Westport, CT: Bergin & Garvey, 1994), p. xiii.

34. See, for example, Elizabeth M. Georing, "Context, Definition, and Sex of Actor as Variables in Conflict Management Style," paper presented to the Speech Communication Association Convention, Chicago, November 1986; Joyce Frost and William Wilmot, *Interpersonal Conflict* (Dubuque, IA: Wm. C. Brown, 1978); J. M. Bardwick, *Psychology of Women: A Study of Biocultural Conflicts* (New York: Harper & Row, 1971); L. Strodtbeck and R. Mann, "Sex-Role Differentiation in Jury Deliberation," *Sociometry* 19 (1956), 3–11; D. H. Zimmerman and C. West, "Sex-Roles, Interruptions, and Silences in Conversation," in B. Thorne and N. Henley (Eds.), *Language and Sex: Differences and Dominances* (Rowely, MA: Newbury House, 1975), pp. 105–129; J. Sears, E. Maccoby, and H. Levin, *Patterns of Childrearing* (Evanston, IL: Row Peterson, 1957).

35. Michael E. Roloff, "The Impact of Socialization on Sex Differences in Conflict Resolution," paper presented at the International Communication Association

Convention, Acapulco, Mexico, May 1980; Daniel J. Canary, Ellen M. Cunningham, and Michael J. Cody, "Goal Types, Gender and Locus of Control in Managing Interpersonal Conflict," *Communication Research* 15 (1988), 426–446.

36. Charles T. Brown, Paul Yelsma, and Paul W. Keller, "Communication-Conflict Predispositions: Development of a Theory and Instrument," *Human Relations* 34 (1981), 1103–1117.

37. H. Rausch, W. Barry, R. Hertel, and M. Swain, *Communication, Conflict, and Marriage* (San Francisco: Jossey-Bass, 1974); Lynn H. Turner, "Women, Men and Conflict Management: When Do the Differences Make a Difference?" paper presented at the Speech Communication Association Convention, Louisville, KY, November 1982; Lynn H. Turner and S. A. Henzl, "Influence Attempts in Organizational Conflict: The Effects of Biological Sex, Psychological Gender, and Power Position," paper presented at the Speech Communication Association Convention, Boston, November 1987; N. L. Harper and Randy Y. Hirokawa, "A Comparison of Persuasive Strategies Used by Female and Male Managers," *Communication Quarterly* 36 (1988), 157–168.

38. Lynn H. Turner and S. A. Henzl, "Influence Attempts in Organizational Conflicts: The Effects of Biological Sex, Psychological Gender, and Power Position," paper presented at the Speech Communication Association Convention, Boston, November 1987.

39. Charles Conrad, "Gender, Interactional Sensitivity, and Communication in Conflict: Assumptions and Interpretations," paper presented to the Speech Communication Association Convention, Denver, CO, November 1985, p. 1.

40. Daniel J. Canary and Kimberly Hause, "Is There Any Reason to Research Sex Differences in Communication?" *Communication Quarterly* 41 (1993), 129–144.

41. Diana K. Ivy and Phil Backlund, *Exploring GenderSpeak: Personal Effectiveness in Gender Communication* (New York: McGraw-Hill, 1994).

42. R. J. Burke, "Methods of Resolving Superior-Subordinate Conflict: The Constructive Use of the Subordinate Differences and Disagreements," *Organizational Behavior and Performance* 5 (1970), 393–411.

43. Michael J. Papa and Elizabeth J. Natelle, "Gender, Strategy Selection and Discussion Satisfaction in Interpersonal Conflict," *Western Journal of Speech Communication* 53 (1989), 260–272.

44. Leslie A. Baxter and Tara L. Shepherd, "Sex-Role Identity, Sex of Other and Affective Relationship as Determinants of Interpersonal Conflict Management Styles," *Sex Roles* 6 (1978), 813–825.

45. Claire C. Brunner and Judy C. Pearson, "Sex Differences in Perceptions of Interpersonal Communication Competence," paper presented at the Speech Communication Association Convention, Chicago, November 1984, p. 12.

Part II

Understanding How Conflict Works

In Part II, we move from understanding what people have brought into the conflict situation via their attitudes, beliefs, values, ethnic identity, and so on, to an understanding of the way conflict generally works. Some of the questions that are answered in this part of the text include:

What are the various behaviors that people call conflict?

How does conflict repeat itself?

What does it mean to view conflict as a process?

What are the stages through which a successfully resolved conflict evolves?

When are conflicts better managed than resolved?

What kinds of styles and strategies may be employed in the conflict situation?

There are times when I think I must be stuck in some kind of time warp, reliving the same event again and again. These happen when I get into the same conflict with the same person, and it's like the 1000th time we've tried to resolve it. Isn't there some way to stop fighting over the same issue?

Whether productive or destructive, and whether it is the first time or the hundredth time an issue has been discussed, conflict serves a variety of functions. In the extreme, it may include verbal abuse or even turn physically violent. Our goal is to help people avert that possibility by helping them recognize various types of conflict situations so that they can choose productive responses to them. Generally, we know that successfully resolved conflicts typically go through particular stages, even though some conflicts are better off managed than resolved. We also know that conflict has the potential to get bogged down in avoidance or competitive cycles that make resolution difficult to achieve. Understanding the types of situations conflict encompasses, the processes that characterize conflict, and the various styles and strategies people use within conflict situations are all important steps in creating competent behavior in conflict situations.

4

Types of Conflict

Objectives _____

At the end of this chapter, you should be able to

1. compare and contrast real and unreal conflicts.
2. compare and contrast different types of unreal conflicts.
3. compare and contrast substantive and nonsubstantive conflicts.
4. compare and contrast different types of nonsubstantive conflicts.
5. compare and contrast mere disagreements and interpersonal conflicts.
6. differentiate among behavioral, normative, and personality conflicts.

Key Terms _____

argument	mere disagreements	real conflicts
behavioral conflict	misplaced conflicts	relationship conflicts
bickering	moral conflict	substantive conflicts
competition	nonsubstantive conflicts	unreal conflicts
displaced conflict	normative conflicts	verbal abuse
false conflict	personality conflicts	verbal aggression
issues	physical aggression	

In Chapter 1, we defined interpersonal conflict as any situation in which the people are interdependent, they seek different outcomes or perceive the other as interfering with each one's outcomes, the issue has the ability to adversely affect the relationship between those involved in the conflict, and there is a sense of urgency about the need to resolve the issue. And whether productive or destructive, conflicts come in many different shapes and sizes. It is important for us to understand the kind of conflict in which we are engaged because different types of conflicts call for different methods of management or resolution. This chapter presents different ways of classifying conflicts, based on the extent to which they meet the conditions for interpersonal conflict as listed earlier. The terms presented in this chapter are designed to help you understand what kind of conflict you are involved in so that you can choose strategies and tactics that are most appropriate for the conflict.

Types of Conflict

The English language is filled with terms for different types of conflict: *confrontation, verbal argument, disagreement, differences of opinion, avoidance of confrontation, avoiding others, changing the topic, problem-solving discussion, interpersonal violence, physical abuse, sexual abuse, verbal abuse, silent treatment, stonewalling, glaring at one another, making obscene gestures, expressions of anger, hostile reactions, ignoring the other, unhappy relationships, simply giving in, accommodating, going along reluctantly, not making waves, competition, negotiation, bargaining, mediation, disputing, quarreling, threatening,* and *insulting.* Even though it's a long list, probably it is not complete. Table 4.1 summarizes different types of conflict. The difficulty of identifying different types of

TABLE 4.1   *Types of Conflict*

Type of Conflict	*Definition*	*Manifested In*
Unreal Conflicts	Conflicts that are perceived by one person but which really don't exist, or conflicts that actually exist but are misperceived by the participants.	False Conflicts Displaced Conflicts Misplaced Conflicts
Nonsubstantive Conflicts	Conflicts in which there is no real issue involved.	Bickering Verbal Abuse Physical Aggression Competition
Mere Disagreements	May occur with significant others over issues that are not central to the relationship.	Arguments
Real and Substantive Conflicts	Conflicts that occur between interdependent people, which focus on an issue that has the potential to harm the relationship if it is not addressed.	Issues that are central to the relationship: resources, boundaries, beliefs, values, etc.

conflict is that people often don't even like to use the word *conflict* to describe their experiences, as this narrative demonstrates:

> I don't have conflicts, because to me, a conflict is when you have no place left to go. I'm right, you're wrong, so let's forget it. Up to that point, I bargain or argue, but I don't have conflicts.

The most important step in understanding different types of interpersonal conflict is to underscore the fact that they occur with people who are important to us. We may argue with a stranger, have a difficult time returning a defective product to a store, or endure the bad driving habits of another on the road, but these are not examples of interpersonal conflict because there's no established relationship involved. Some of the skills involved with arguments with strangers overlap the skills taught in this book. If you have to return a product to a store, for example, and you expect that it will be difficult, explaining the situation carefully using the skills outlined in later chapters will probably boost your chances of success. However, we don't need to be every stranger's potential friend, lover, or spouse. Although this doesn't give us permission to act irresponsibly, it frees us from thinking that we have to worry about our relationship with a person we don't know, as this narrative illustrates:

> I accidentally locked my baby in the car. It was so stupid—I realized just as the door latched that my purse was on the seat and my keys were in the purse. I panicked, but a kind person called the fire department, which will come and open a car under those conditions. A crowd gathered round the car while they were trying to find the "Slim Jim" to unlock it, and this couple parked nearby. They approached the crowd, looked in my car, and said "There's a baby in there!" Then the woman looked up at me and said, "Someone ought to kick you in the ass!" and walked away. I was dumbfounded. All I could say was, "That was unnecessary." The fireman working on my car patted me on the shoulder and told me to ignore them—that everyone made mistakes. But it still hurt to have someone attack me like that.

Because the writer is unlikely to have anything to do with the woman in the future, there is an option to ignore her comments and walk away. But imagine if it is a good friend or a relative who says that she ought to be ashamed for doing something. It is a great deal more likely that she will feel a need to address the other's judgment.

APPLICATION 4.1

Have there been times when you paid more attention to a critical comment from a stranger than necessary? How did you free yourself of the negative feelings it aroused? Did you feel competent in the way you dealt with the situation?

Real versus Unreal Conflicts

Conflicts may be real or unreal. **Real conflicts** actually exist in fact and are perceived accurately; **unreal conflicts** either don't exist in reality but are thought to exist in someone's mind, or do exist in reality but are misperceived. Dealing with unreal conflicts often costs us unnecessary time and energy because we have not judged the situation accurately. Although some may feel as though discussion of this topic is not warranted because unreal conflicts do not exist anyway, the simple fact is that we encounter them frequently and expend unnecessary energy worrying about them. Understanding that unreal conflicts exist may help us to stop, step back, and consider whether we are indeed experiencing a conflict before attempting to analyze our situation.

The unreal conflicts consist of three types. One of these is **false conflict,**[1] in which at least one person in an interdependent relationship thinks that there is a conflict but, after talking to the other(s) involved, finds there is no conflict. This narrative demonstrates a false conflict:

> Generally, it doesn't take much for my daughter and me to get into a conflict. If I say something about her room, and ask her to clean it up, it's a conflict. If I remind her that her shoes are in the living room still, it's a conflict. If I forget to remind her of something she is supposed to remember herself, it's a conflict. So, imagine my trepidation when I accidentally hurt her kitten. I was hanging curtains in my daughter's room, and it was pulling at the material, so I picked the kitten up and put it behind me without looking. I should have known better—there were things all over the floor and apparently it landed on something the wrong way. I heard a meow-spit-hiss, and turned around to see it favoring one leg. Horrified, I picked it up and rushed it to the vet to find that its leg was broken.
>
> When I picked my daughter up from school, I tried to find some way to explain gently that it was my fault her kitten was injured. She simply looked at me and asked, "Is Sheba okay?" I replied that she was, although she would wear a cast for four weeks. My daughter said, "Well, accidents happen, Mom. You didn't mean to hurt her." I thought I would drive the car onto the sidewalk in amazement. I expected fireworks, and all that happened was a fizzle.

Here is another example of a false conflict: Jamie had worked at an exclusive dress shop for several years while attending college. During her time there, her hourly wages had risen as she took on a variety of duties, including the ordering of clothing lines. During the middle of her senior year, a new salesperson was hired and was given many of the hours Jamie worked. She worried that she had done something to offend the owner, who was not regular in his feedback concerning performance and who tended to be defensive when asked about his reasoning concerning organizational decisions. Jamie stewed about it for some time, wondering if it was worthwhile to ask her employer because she had only a few weeks left before she would move on to a new position. When she finally did ask, Jamie was told that business had been quite slow and that her employer had been able to hire the new salesperson at a lower hourly rate. Because Jamie had not been needed to perform many of the duties that justified her higher wage, he had cut back her hours to save money. It had nothing to do with her performance, only with the conditions of the shop; thus, she was in a false conflict, perceiving one where none really existed.

False conflicts are generally resolved with sufficient information—we presume that we are in a conflict because of the limited knowledge we have. Asking and being answered leads to resolution fairly easily. Other false conflicts have to do with what people think that the other person might have done before they get their facts straight. Conflicts concerning beliefs, facts, or perceptions generally arise from a lack of information or from distorted information, as this narrative suggests:

> My third-grade daughter is assigned homework every night. Generally, it isn't too taxing and is not meant to take more than one hour; the goal is simply to develop the habit of completing homework. Over a week's time, she seemed to bring more and more home, until one

afternoon it took five hours to finish the work. My daughter made it sound as though it had all been assigned that day. To sit with her that long after I had worked all day anyway was outrageous. I talked to the teacher and found that the students could leave school each day with no homework, depending on how quickly they worked during study time. Unfortunately, my daughter is more interested in reading, talking to other students, and fantasizing than she is in homework. Our marathon had been the result of her putting it off and putting it off. My conflict with the teacher was easy to resolve. The conflict between my daughter and me goes on, requiring me to be skeptical when she sweetly looks me in the eye and says, "But Mom, I don't have any homework today."

Imagine thinking you are in conflict with someone only to find that you are not. This is one reason why it is so important to talk to the other parties. Otherwise, you may fret for nothing. Clearing up false conflicts is one goal of Chapter 12.

A second kind of conflict related to interpersonal conflicts is **displaced conflict,** which occurs when people direct a conflict toward the wrong person, generally using a relatively unimportant issue as a focal point. This narrative illustrates a displaced conflict:

I had been having a really bad day. I was so stressed out and overburdened by homework and job responsibilities, and to top it off, I had a huge paper I was working on that was due in two days, which I had barely even started. Mary chose this particular time to enter the room and discuss the positioning of our bathroom towels on the rack. She seemed frustrated that the four of us, who were sharing the apartment, had taken to haphazardly pushing and stuffing our towels through the narrow metal rods, thus having them all scrunched up together, which did not allow them to dry properly. I felt that this was such an inane discussion, so I told her to do whatever she wanted with my towels; I really did not care. Mary then felt miffed at my apparent disregard of her and her problem, so she continued to talk about the situation in hopes of eliciting some cooperation from me, only this time I could see that she was beginning to get annoyed. I, on the other hand, was so stressed out from the day, and was frantically trying to finish my paper, that I could not bear to hear her analretentive lament about the placement of our towels on the bathroom rack! I basically told her how asinine I felt this conversation was; we bickered for about 5 more minutes, and then she left the room. The next day, I was able to apologize to Mary for my short temper. I explained how I was not really angry with her, but with the stressful situation I was in that day, and she was the one on whom I chose to take out my aggressions.

Although the towels might be a conflict issue to be discussed rationally at some point, in this displaced conflict they have served as a way for the person trying to study to release her frustration about her lack of progress. Dispaced conflicts almost always happen with people with whom we have an interpersonal relationship, whom we think of as a "safe target" for our frustration, and whom we may even expect to sympathetically listen to us as we rant and rave. Displaced conflicts are often resolved when the person who has done the ranting and raving apologizes, usually making some excuse for the untoward behavior (e.g., "I was stressed out") that the target of the conflict accepts as a reasonable excuse. Generally, we allow those close to us to occasionally engage in displaced conflicts, but we create a real conflict when we reject the other person's excuse for his or her behavior or decide that we have had enough of another's need to take his or her frustration out on us.

Disagreements over habits such as leaving dishes in the sink, how office practices might be accomplished, squeezing the toothpaste in the middle, and so on tend to be small but annoying conflicts. Like mushrooms that grow in the dark, these conflicts may add up and become blown out of proportion because they are generally suppressed rather than addressed.[2] When they are finally addressed, they may become the trigger for a displaced conflict, with a great deal of aggression being directed toward a relatively small matter. Altman and Taylor argue that a simple disagreement over a small item probably will not adversely affect the relationship between two people. Over time, however, little conflicts can build up to an explosion, and in retrospect, the people involved may recognize that the little conflicts were symptoms of something deeper that was not being addressed in the relationship.[3] Understanding how little issues affect us, especially when we displace or misplace them, can help us avoid the huge blowups that hurt relationships. We will return to the subject of displaced conflicts later in Chapter 7.

APPLICATION 4.2

How do you make amends after you have engaged in a displaced conflict with someone close to you? What can you do to avoid such displaced conflicts in the future?

Misplaced conflicts occur when people argue about issues other than the ones at the heart of the conflict.[4] The following story, told by a wife about her marriage, is an example of misplaced conflict with serious implications for the relationship:

> We've been seeing the marriage counselor for several weeks now, and we deal with all sorts of things like my husband's problem with the way I do the housework (even though I work full-time) and my concern that he doesn't put enough time and energy into his business. But I feel like we're just putting out little brushfires when the forest is burning down. The heat of the real conflict is so intense we keep going around it. I think the real problem is that he treats me more coldly and cruelly than he would treat a stranger. He never touches me or shows me any kind of affection. He belittles me in front of our children and will tell them they can't do something after I've said they could. All I am asking for is respect and kindness, and what I get is sarcasm and insults.

Whereas displaced conflicts involve directing frustration toward a "safe" *person,* misplaced conflicts involve "safe" *issues* that people are more willing to talk about than the issues that underlie them. In the preceding example, concern over the housework or the effort put into the business are legitimate issues. The real issues, however, are masked by these "safer" issues. The wife uses the housework as a weapon against a husband who emotionally abuses her: It bothers him to have the house messy, so she just cannot seem to get around to doing it. It helps that she works outside the home. She can say, with some legitimacy, that there is not enough time to do everything. She does not really want to deal with his lack of respect, so talking about his lack of business efforts is a safer issue. Because they keep dealing with the small, visible conflicts instead of looking at the pattern of their conflict behavior, the small conflicts will continue to multiply until one or the other leaves or until they learn how to deal with the conflicts. Deutsch argued that manifest or overt conflict is difficult, if not impossible, to resolve unless the underlying conflict has been dealt with in some way or unless the overt conflict is separated from the underlying conflict and treated in isolation.[5]

Because misplaced conflicts revolve around "safe" rather than "real" issues, they can be difficult to diagnose. A conflict issue that comes up repeatedly may be a mask for a deeper issue between those involved. However, it is important to understand that, where conflicts are managed rather than resolved, the same issues may arise frequently that have no other underlying meaning. For example, if you are a person of tidy habits rooming with a messy person, the issue of cleanliness is likely to arise often. But it probably does not mask a deeper issue other than the fact that you have different habits. Misplaced conflicts concern relational issues such as power sharing, expectations for behavior, respect, ways of showing affection, and so on. Because these issues are central to the way people relate to one another, people often find it easier to focus on visible issues, such as money or work habits, where any difference in action would be observable.

Substantive versus Nonsubstantive Conflicts

In addition to being real or unreal, conflicts may be substantive or nonsubstantive. In interpersonal conflicts, **substantive conflicts** focus on issues or problems that potentially could harm the relationship and possible solutions. The **nonsubstantive conflicts,** in which no real issue is involved include bickering, verbal aggression, nonverbal (physical) aggression, and competition.

We've all been around people who like to bicker. Unlike **argument,** in which people generally make claims about something and provide some sort of evidence or support for their claim, **bickering** takes on a "yes, it is" "no, it's not" kind of format. Most of the characters on *Seinfeld* engage in bickering during every episode. Their bickering is a form of aggression toward one another, manifested verbally.

Bickering may give way to **verbal abuse,** when "yes, it is" and "no, it's not" turn into personal insults.[6] Although the witty put-down is an important piece of dialogue in many situation comedies, most people do not appreciate such a put-down when they are engaged in what they believe to be a conflict. If the issue is important, insults will cause a degeneration of the conflict quickly and may, in turn, lead to further escalation of the conflict. We will have more to say about verbal abuse in Chapter 11, but for now we want to say that, in some cases, verbal abuse may escalate into **physical aggression.** Bickering, verbal abuse, and physical abuse are all nonsubstantive conflicts.[7]

A substantive conflict (i.e., one in which people are interdependent and focused on an important issue, problem, or solution) may turn into a nonsubstantive conflict in which the emphasis is more on releasing **verbal aggression** than on dealing with particular issues. Or, when people get bogged down in trying to make their point, they may resort to bickering, verbal abuse, or physical abuse because they are unable to resolve the conflict and because they do not take a time-out from the situation. Likewise, playful aggression not intended to be taken in a hostile manner can create a conflict, as the following account indicates:

> I rushed to work with a hat on one day, knowing my wet hair would dry matted to my head. I worked at the front door of the cafeteria, letting in the students and answering many people's questions. After I finished, I was exhausted and very tense. I was standing in the back of the kitchen surrounded by other student workers when a new employee I barely know grabbed my hat off my head because he could not tell if it was really me. He stood there with my hat in his hand, exposing my swirled, matted mess of hair and said, "No, can't be you? You usually look different." I yelled at him to give me my hat; then, at the top of my lungs, I lost all control and screamed, "Give me my hat!," grabbed him by the shoulders and

shook him so hard he went into shock. I yanked my hat out of his hands and, and I stomped away. After apologizing to each other profusely a few minutes later, we tried to make amends, but to this day our relationship is practically nonexistent, and he doesn't look me in the eye.

APPLICATION 4.3

How has a substantive conflict turned into bickering or verbal abuse in your past? How do you distinguish between verbal aggression and situations that require some resolution between you and the other person?

Another kind of nonsubstantive conflict is **competition.** We may be competitive with those with whom we have relationships, but we need not let the competition become an issue in our relationship. In a formal sense, as Mack and Snyder point out:

> Competition . . . involves striving for scarce objects (a prize or resource usually "awarded" by a third party) according to established rules which strictly limit what the competitors can do to each other in the course of striving; the chief objective is the scarce object, not the injury or destruction of an opponent per se.[8]

In less formal circumstances interpersonal behavior resembles a competitive game. Nicole's account of her desire to do well in a class explains the idea of competition:

> I find that I sometimes fall into this trap many times with my friends and acquaintances with whom I'm in class. For instance, my roommate, Jen, and I, both highly competitive people, decided to take the same class together. Every time I noticed Jen reading her text for the class, I felt myself become agitated because I did not want her to get ahead of me while I lagged behind. Therefore, I would drop whatever homework I had been working on in order to read our assignment also. If I saw her studying for a class, I'd anxiously ask her what class she was studying for, and if it was our class, I'd soon be studying my notes too. I noticed Jen doing the same with me, glancing to see what I was working on, and whipping out her notes if it was our class that she saw me studying for. My goal with Jen was not an intent to "beat her" to get a better grade than her; I simply wanted to be considered a good student and not have her think of me as an "incompetent dimwit." I wanted to receive an "A" alongside of her, not come in second with merely a "B" and be less of a student.

Competition of this sort has the potential to affect the relationship if either roommate finds the competition upsetting. But a competition does not necessarily have to turn into a conflict requiring confrontation. It depends on whether or not those involved have an interpersonal relationship worth preserving.

> I like to play Ping-Pong, and I often win. One friend keeps challenging me to see if eventually he will win (no conflict), but the other was offended after a couple of games (conflict). He said, "It's no use playing against you, you always win." So, if we are to preserve a friendship, we shouldn't play Ping-Pong, or I'll have to take it easy and (not too obviously) lose sometimes.

APPLICATION 4.4

When does the urge to compete affect your relationships? How do you make sure that both you and the other person understand that the competition is "friendly" rather than something to be taken seriously?

Real and Substantive Conflicts

Real and substantive conflicts occur when people accurately perceive that they have incompatible goals or activities and perceive that the other person is somehow interfering with their wishes and desires. They also occur when at least one person in a relationship perceives that the other has broken an important relational rule and has failed to adequately explain why the rule was broken. This narrative illustrates a real and substantive conflict:

> I came home from work and my wife was sitting near the door waiting for me. She said she had to talk to me about something she got in the mail. I realized that she had opened the credit card bill and I knew we were going to have a BIG problem. I hadn't told her the truth about how much money I had been spending, and she's a person who thinks we shouldn't even have credit cards. It's no wonder when I can't seem to control myself.

The narrated incident has all the elements of real and substantive conflict. First, an important rule of the relationship has been broken: Purchases have been made that were unknown to the other person, and those purchases are evidently very large. There is also an apparent disagreement over the way money should be spent, and it will need to be resolved.

Real and substantive conflicts may be over small matters or large, but they are those that become problematic for a relationship if they are not addressed. Frequently, they do begin as small issues and become larger ones as a behavior that we thought was a momentary aberration becomes a habitual action that bothers us over time. For example, if a person in your organization calls you by the wrong name, it is annoying but probably not worth more effort than it takes to say your correct name. However, if a teacher continues to call you the wrong name, even after having been corrected several times, you may begin to wonder if that person is displeased with your work, or considers you unimportant. The teacher's behavior may start a conflict. This narrative shows how grievances may build up over time and become a large conflict that almost seems unmanageable:

> Irritated with me, my husband went to the other room and began to complain about me to our eldest daughter, Kim. But my husband's complaints served as a triggering device for my daughter's own conflict with her father. Kim had been trying to approach him with reasons why she should be able to get married this summer, before her graduation from medical school next year, only to be rebuffed each time without a thorough hearing. When she heard her father showing yet more insensitivity to a person's feelings by complaining about me, she finally and suddenly—entirely out of character with her gentle nature—exploded.
>
> Hearing a noise in the other room, along with Kim's scream, I rushed right in assuming he had hit her. I was ready for a fight—like the proverbial tigress defending her young. We were really in a state of bedlam for a few minutes—both Kim and her sister Lisa were crying, Larry was staring in shock at Kim, and I was demanding of everyone if he had struck Kim.
>
> Kim herself finally defused the situation by saying she had created the noise by screaming and throwing her book across the room in breaking-point frustration with her fa-

ther. His complaints about me had finally allowed her the ability to stand up to him. The crack in the dam of Kim's feelings flowed that night until the wee hours of the morning. She was finally able to be honest about years' worth of quietly swallowing her grievances, which she suppressed in order to keep peace with her father. And he finally had to listen.

As this narrative demonstrates, such conflicts that are not addressed often become huge and unwieldy as people add more and more complaints to their list. Addressing real and substantive conflicts as they arise can help to make conflict management less frightening and overwhelming. Another conflict that built up from small issues into large ones is this:

> My husband must have gotten up on the wrong side of the bed that day. He was acting like a jerk, complaining that no one but him does chores around the house (not true at all). And every time he gets pissed, he takes a privilege away from our son, especially things our son really values like student activities. This time, he thought Aaron wasn't doing enough chores, so he yells, "I don't care what he wants, he's never going to drive!" That did it. Aaron marched in and began to have words with his father. Lots of words. I was trying to bang the dishes around in the sink and run the water so I wouldn't hear. I was so afraid my husband would kick Aaron out of the house. Instead, I heard little bits of the conversation like, "You never say you care about me. Mom does. Sis does. I need to hear it from you. Don't you ever approve of me?" I was so astonished at my son, and even more astonished when they calmed down and apologized to each other.

Mere Disagreements versus Interpersonal Conflicts

Recall from Chapter 1 that for something to be an interpersonal conflict, these conditions must be met:

- the people are interdependent;
- the people perceive that they seek different outcomes or they favor different means to the same ends;
- the conflict has the potential to negatively affect the relationship if not addressed; and
- there is a sense of urgency about the need to resolve the issue.

Some conflicts may be interpersonal in nature or they may be **mere disagreements,** which do not have to affect the relationship between those involved, but they do have the potential to turn into relationship-threatening issues. Mere disagreements may occur over issues that are peripheral to the relationship, although people often can become quite agitated and excited when they find themselves disagreeing with another person. One woman reports the argument she had with her sister:

> She mentioned that she and her husband were no longer speaking to her father-in-law. Her mother-in-law had just recently died after many years as an invalid, and her father-in-law had given the appearance of being a faithful caretaker for her in their home. However, he had been seen in a restaurant hugging and kissing a woman just two weeks after his late wife's funeral; his neighbors "reported" that this woman had also been staying at his home overnight, even while his wife was in her final days in the hospital. My sister and her husband were outraged, not only at the apparent lack of mourning, but also because this man was a pillar of his community and should uphold higher standards. I told her that I thought she was overreacting and

shouldn't cut off her relationship on the basis of hearsay. Even though we disagreed, our different beliefs did not affect our relationship. She didn't change her mind, and I still think she's wrong, but having said that, it's not my place to say anything further.

Although the woman reporting this conflict was quite perturbed with her sister, she made a conscious decision to not let her anger affect their relationship. This issue certainly could have, if she had decided that her sister's behavior was so uncharitable that she didn't want to have anything to do with her sister anymore. Recognizing when an issue is not central to the relationship helps us to know that we are in a mere disagreement that does not require a great deal of energy on our part. It is largely resolved when one person decides to agree with the other, or when both "agree to disagree" because the relationship is more important than the issue.

Issues as Indicators of Real and Substantive Conflicts

Often, people are more comfortable with the idea of typing conflict according to the issue that the conflict involves. **Issues** are the focal point of the real and substantive conflict, the things that people point to when they are asked what the conflict was about (see Table 4.2).

Several authors have made an effort to identify the causes of the conflict, or the issues people point to when asked why a conflict is occurring. The kind of issue identified by the people in the conflict affects how they enact and resolve the conflict. Table 4.2 summarizes the issue types proposed by various authors. Braiker and Kelley's broad categories of behavioral, normative, and personality issues help us to understand different types of conflicts.[9]

Behavioral Conflicts

Braiker and Kelley's category of **behavioral conflicts** includes what others call issues concerning control over resources, tangible issues, and interest-based issues, and also what others have called belief-based issues, facts-based issues, or issues concerning perceptions and preferences and nuisances. Generally speaking, these issues concern behaviors we can observe.

TABLE 4.2 *Types of Issues in Conflict*

Braiker and Kelley	Deutsch	Wehr	Harvey and Drolet
Behavioral	Control over resources	Interests based	Tangible
	Preferences and nuisances	Nonrealistic	Perceptual
		Facts based	
	Beliefs		
Normative	Relationship		Interpersonal
			Boundary
Dispositions and Values	Values	Values based	Values

Tangible, resource, or interest-based issues generally are conflicts over things that are countable and divisible, such as how we behave regarding the handling of money, time, space, and so on. Tangible issues are most susceptible to win-lose thinking and present a challenge for those who would create win-win outcomes. A married couple, for example, may be trying to decide how to spend their vacation. She likes the fact that they "always go to the East Coast to visit her parents," but this time he wants to go to Hawaii. They do not have enough money to do both. A solution that would feel like "winning" to both of them might be to find a vacation package in the Caribbean that would allow them a stop on the East Coast. People in conflicts over tangible resources often have a difficult time seeing the other person's perspective, and the production of win-win outcomes will be time consuming. This narrative describes a behavioral conflict based on tangible issues:

> I had just my frosh year here and it was wonderful. Yes, I was a long way from home, but I had made a lot of friends with people in my dorm and was excited about getting into my major. I had obtained a leadership position on campus. But my parents wanted me to come back and attend school near them next year. My mom said she missed me and wanted me to go to school nearby so that I could commute from my parents' house. They're having a hard time letting me go. They tell me they can't afford this college, but the one they want me to attend is just as expensive. I work 30 hours a week and would pay for my own school on my own if I could take out more loans. There is so much tension in my family over this. I grew up in this state—my parents are the ones who moved. There's nothing for me there and I don't want to leave here.

Tangible, resource-based issue conflicts are almost always real and substantive conflicts: They occur between interdependent people arguing over issues and possible solutions that could potentially affect their relationship.

Normative Conflicts—Issues of Relationships

A second category of conflict issue has to do with the "oughts" people define for their relationships with others. Some of these "oughts" are minor, but a lack of desire to address them may lead to a **relationship conflict**—one in which we are concerned that we cannot receive from the other what we believe is due us. Relationship issues are often involved in misplaced conflicts in which the participants focus on a safe issue rather than one that is more threatening. For example, a student may wish to challenge a grade in a class. Perhaps the student has been to see the instructor several times and in class has tended to be disruptive or uninvolved. Although the grade, a tangible issue, may serve as a focus for the conflict, the underlying conflict (for the instructor) is about the relationship between the teacher and student—such as whether the instructor meets the student's expectations for the class. Until the underlying relationship issue is addressed, the surface issue of grades can continue to be an annoyance to both parties. This narrative demonstrates a relationally based conflict:

> A recent conflict I had with my girlfriend of seven months goes as follows. She wants me to be verbally open with her all the time and when I'm silent it tends to intimidate her and make her nervous. I am, by nature, a person who needs silence because in those times I can grab the space I need to have to think, and so on. She, on the other hand, is more of an even-keel person and is pretty much always happy and bubbly. I have my times when I am the opposite of that and it intimidates her and she feels I'm not being considerate of her feelings. She feels left out in the cold. In my struggles and times I really need to think, I have

to think first about how it will affect our relationship and how to act around her so as not to upset her.

Another way people might describe a relationally based conflict is to say that it is about boundaries. Boundary conflicts concern both penetration and expansion—when someone intrudes on what you think is your territory, either physically or psychologically, or when someone expects more of you than you believe you should have to deliver. For example, a department head may think it her right to select a secretary, but an overzealous personnel officer might intrude on that right, sending over a person he has already hired. Or a wife might expect some "tender loving care" from her husband when she is sick, but her husband might see this as an unreasonable expectation. Normative conflicts like relationship conflicts and boundary conflicts concern the rules of the relationship that two people have and disagreements over what those rules should be.

Personality Conflicts—Dispositions and Values

Personality conflicts can range from our irritation over the way another person simply is—that is, their personality traits and quirks—up to deep-seated conflicts over values and what should be. We tend to reduce such conflicts to an attitude of simply not liking the other. A personality-based conflict is related by this woman:

> My older sister and I are the best of friends, but there are just some things that she does that I don't agree with. For instance, she had been wanting to get a tattoo. I had been trying to talk her out of it, explaining that she would regret it at some point in her life. And then she got one—a brightly colored sun on her lower back. Yes, it can only be seen when she wears midriffs or a bathing suit, but Mom and Dad will flip. I'm angry because she used money they sent her for food to get the tattoo. I think that was really disrespectful.

Conflicts over values may "involve convictions held on faith, independent of evidence or logic. They may evolve from the history of the individual or the experiences of the group."[10] Conflicts over values are difficult to resolve because the issue is generally ego-involving to the participants, who tend to feel that "truth" is on their side and that to compromise would be to give up that truth. The conflicts occurring in higher education today, for example, over the content of general education and the response of general education to the demands of multiculturalism are largely over values: What values should be taught? What values are most important? What are the basic values that bind us together as a culture? How can we be more sensitive to underrepresented viewpoints in the educational process?

Questions such as those concerned with general education are usually answered in a civilized way. But sometimes people get so caught up in their vision of what is right and what is wrong that they find it difficult to communicate rationally with those who do not share their beliefs. Often, value conflicts spill into other types of conflicts, such as those involving relational issues, as this narrative suggests:

> My older brother is very different from me when it comes to fashion, money, and priorities. He likes to buy expensive stuff and I tend not to buy anything at all unless I need it. I have worked hard to get out of the neighborhood and get into college. He just lives for the moment. He likes going out to clubs, expensive restaurants, the movies, and any place where people hang out. I am very good at saving my money and I tend to spend on my family and

give more to them than I spend on myself. About two months ago, my brother asked me if he could borrow $500. The next two months after I let him borrow the money he bought an $800 suit, $200 shoes, a couple of shirts, and has consistently gone out on the weekends to the movies and expensive restaurants. I confronted him and told him that he needed to pay me back. He was very offended and said that we're family and that he will never ask for a favor from me again. He said he did not have the money and that he will pay me when he can. I brought up the things that he has been buying and he said that he needs those things. I felt like he was using my money for his entertainment while I am at school working hard trying to make ends meet with my bills.

When people become highly ego-involved in their vision of what is right and are prepared to try to convert all who cross their path, the stage for moral conflict has been set.

Moral Conflict

There are times in interpersonal conflict when the issue takes on moral overtones. Those in the conflict become embroiled in sometimes unanswerable questions about the right or wrong way to do things. In such a situation, how should one behave? An area of conflict research that has arisen recently can help you to understand how moral dimensions of issues can create gridlock in conflict resolution. Whereas *moral conflict* is a term originally meant to refer to conflicts that happen in a social area between groups representing different ideologies, it also can be applied to interpersonal conflict situations.

Because of the inability of participants to agree on how to resolve their differences, moral conflicts are persistent: They "fuel themselves and are therefore self-sustaining. Often the original issue becomes superfluous. . . . Participants in a moral conflict tend to treat each other as mad, bad, sick, or stupid, and they experience a crisis of rationality, feeling that they cannot reason with people "like that.' "[11] An example of this inability to communicate is found in the abortion controversy. A person who believes that a woman has the right to control her body finds no common ground with a person who believes that a fetus is an unborn human being with rights independent of its mother.

In addition to being self-sustaining, moral conflicts may take on a pattern that is something other than what any of the participants wanted or expected. Like the unwanted repetitive patterns that will be discussed in Chapter 5, each side is hard-pressed to understand why its best efforts to communicate are not understood by the other side. As each party in the conflict ignores what the other has to say, or disregards the arguments of the other, the conflict becomes more entrenched and more institutionalized. The pattern of discourse in moral conflict moves from persuasion to schism—from each side believing the other capable of understanding if it were only able to hear the arguments to each side treating the other as crazy and unworthy of communication. When moral conflicts become entrenched, participants on one side have nothing to say to those on the other side: They are subhuman, perverts, infidels.[12]

Various patterns are possible in the schism stage of moral conflict. Figure 4.1 illustrates position based on two factors—the degree of excitement about the issue and the equality of power between those in the moral conflict. Where excitement is high and power is equal between those involved, reciprocated diatribe is the pattern of communication. Each side flings epithets back and forth, but little happens as a result. The exchanges between one partner who is a member of the New Christian Right and another who is a

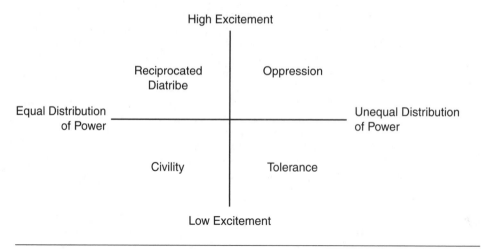

FIGURE 4.1   *Types of Discourse in Moral Conflicts*

humanist and a member of a group like People for the American Way is an example of reciprocated diatribe. Where excitement is high but power is unequal, oppression occurs as the one with more power tells a member of a subjugated group that she or he deserves to be pushed down. Faludi argued that the backlash to the women's movement has done just that:

> In 1975, The New Assertive Woman issued an "Everywoman's Bill of Rights" that called for the "right to be treated with respect" and the "right to be listened to and taken seriously." The 80s advice writers, by contrast, seemed to go out of their way to urge women to *stop* challenging social constraints and to keep their thoughts to themselves—to learn to fit the mold rather than break it. . . . [Women were to] get "power" by "surrendering" and "submitting" to [their] man's every whim.[13]

Where excitement is low and power is equal, communication about moral conflict is characterized by civility; low excitement and unequal power brings tolerance.

As the conflict becomes more entrenched, the discourse in the conflict becomes more simplified and shallow. It no longer reflects the richness of reasoning that first characterized the conflict; instead, slogans and simple answers substitute for arguments and reasoning as each side despairs of winning the other to its way of thinking. When a person on one side in the moral conflict addresses those who think like her, discourse continues to be eloquent and elaborated; in addressing outsiders, discourse becomes simplified and defensive. As discourse fails, violence becomes more likely; "as a response to moral conflict, force becomes a self-sealing pattern. Each side views the other as aggressor or oppressor, and violence is viewed as necessary for self-protection."[14]

Moral conflict becomes part of an interpersonal conflict situation when those involved not only do not agree on their goals, or see their activities as incompatible, or feel as though relational rules have been broken, but when those involved become so entrenched in the discussion of who is right and who is wrong that they are unable to get past the issue. Although those involved may have started the conflict by trying to persuade each other to their point of view, the conflict begins to repeat itself over and over as those involved fail to change the other and, thus, begin to see the other as someone who is unable to understand reason. An example of a moral conflict in an interpersonal relationship is given in this narrative:

> For years, we have struggled with the fact that our child was noisier and more energetic than most. We resisted using Retalin to control his behavior. We kept thinking that all we had to do was be better parents, to be more consistent, to work harder and that he would eventually settle down. But as the years went by, he began to suffer in his schoolwork because he just couldn't concentrate. We tried behavioral modification and tried teaching him ways to control himself. He just couldn't. It was like an itch that had to be scratched. We finally consented to medication. He is happier, more in control, and doing better in school. But the crap I get from my sister-in-law is almost too much to bear. It started with comments like "Funny, neither of our kids have that problem. We just tell them they can't act that way," or "Don't you worry about him becoming a drug addict later on?" I can't be around her without her making some remark about my irresponsibility in "drugging" my child. I'm tired of her stupid remarks—she has never listened to us when we said we did it for our child's good. She's just convinced that people who drug their kids do it for their own sake because they're lazy parents. It's gotten to the point where I don't even want to be around her.

Moral conflicts are often resolved when people can accept the fact that differences can exist between them without resolving or agreeing on those issues. An example of a moral conflict handled in a way that transcended the entrenchment of issues is found in Case Study 4.1. The person telling the story is faced with a situation in which ideological values hit reality: If you think abortion is wrong and you are counseling a woman with an unwanted pregnancy, how will you help her to make the decision best for *her* and how will you support that decision? From the conflict account, it would seem that moral conflict was averted.

Case Study 4.1 ■ *Morality and Reality*

When I was a sophomore in college, I got pregnant and had an abortion. It was soon after *Roe* v. *Wade* had been decided. I went to Planned Parenthood, and when I blurted out that I wanted an abortion, no one tried to dissuade me or offer me any alternatives. I felt trapped. I didn't know that there were places I could go and have the baby and give it up for adoption. All I could think of was my high school friend who had to drop out of school when she got pregnant and carried the baby to term. I didn't want to do that. So I had the abortion. It was probably the most horrifying experience of my life. I know that some women have abortions and never feel any qualms about it. I went under the anesthetic screaming and came out weeping. It took a long time for me to forgive myself for what I had done. I felt I had taken the coward's way out of my situation. I'm married

and have children and I love them to death, but I still think about that one baby and who it might have been. Well, one of my employees came to me and told me she had to have some time off. She hadn't been with us very long and I asked her if it could wait until Easter because we'd be closed. She said no, that it couldn't. I asked her if something was wrong and she just said that she had to have time off. She looked nervous and upset, and it seemed like she wanted to talk to me but was afraid, so I just asked her point blank, "Are you pregnant?" At first she looked away and said she didn't want to talk about it, and then she burst into tears and said, "How did you know?" Having been down that road myself, it wasn't all that hard for me to figure out.

I talked to her and she said she was scheduled to have an abortion. I asked her if that's what she really wanted to do, and she said she thought it was all she could do. I'm not a person who would ever work to outlaw abortion because I don't think that really addresses the real issue, which is keeping people from getting pregnant to begin with. But I knew that I wanted to save her baby if I could, and I thought if she just knew that there were people who would support her and that there were alternatives that maybe she wouldn't have the abortion. We took off from work and talked all afternoon. I told her about my experiences, and why I wanted so much for her not to make the same mistake I made. I took her to my doctor and paid for the examination, because all she had taken was a urine test and she hadn't had a physical exam yet. We went to a pregnancy counseling center where she saw *The Silent Scream.* That was probably a bit heavy-handed, but I really believe that abortion is murder and if you're going to do it, you ought to do it with your eyes open. We talked; she talked to friends. As she was wavering in her decision, she confided to me that she didn't want to have an abortion but that she was afraid to tell her parents about her problem. She was afraid they'd disown her.

She delayed the abortion a week, and during that time I found five couples who were interested in being prospective parents. None of them knew who she was, but I told her about them. There were two families who volunteered to have her stay with them during her pregnancy. One family offered to help her with her medical bills. I lined up all these people willing to help her, hoping to make her see that she wouldn't have to deal with the problem alone. Unfortunately, what mattered to her was whether she had support at least from the baby's father or from her parents. The father had taken off for parts unknown after urging her to have an abortion. She still hadn't told her parents and was afraid if she did she would lose them too.

I told her that as much as I wanted her to have the baby, and as much as I deplored abortion as a choice, that I would love her, accept her, and support her regardless of the decision she made. She decided on the abortion, and believe me, it was hard for me to live up to my promise. The important thing is that she came to me afterward and said that all the talking we did helped, because she realized that she made a choice. No one forced her to do what she did; she decided to do what she did because of the circumstances, but she does recognize her responsibility in the situation. And that's good. She still works for me, and we talk, and I do like her. I have urged her to go to counseling so that she won't suffer the way I did. I guess that if I helped her to make a decision in a more informed way that I did some good. I would rather have saved the baby.

Ultimately, the study of moral conflict has implications for interpersonal settings. When we find ourselves in conflict with another person, and that conflict becomes part of the interaction pattern between us, the conflict can easily take on dimensions of a moral conflict as can conflict over public issues between large groups. If we devalue the thinking of the other, think the other unworthy of our arguments and past persuasion, value our own position so highly that we are unable to see the position of the other, then moral conflict defines our relationship with the other and makes reconciliation unlikely. It is important that we be self-reflective when we feel moral smugness or superiority toward another. Such attitudes lead to entrenchment of conflict rather than to rewarding relationships with others.

APPLICATION 4.5

On what issues are you likely to find yourself embroiled in a moral conflict? What happens when you argue with people who believe they have absolute truth and will not even listen to what you have to say? How can you learn to listen to the other side of issues that are very important to you?

From Theory to Action

This chapter has focused on the different types of conflicts people experience. In what ways can this information be useful? First, understanding the nature of real and substantive conflict and the situations that are unreal or nonsubstantive will help you to handle these difficult situations. You can get caught up in arguments, competition, or bickering with someone and begin to believe you are in a conflict with that person. When possible, you should take the time to step back, and ask yourself whether the issue truly involves behaviors, whether a relationship rule has really been broken, or whether the issue is one of personality. Realizing, for example, that a person likes to play "one-up" games with you can be a freeing experience; even more so is the realization that it is within your power to control the situation by not playing the game. When you recognize that a particular issue surfaces on a regular basis in one of your relationships, you may be able to identify previously unaddressed underlying issues. Taking time to differentiate conflict from nonconflict situations can keep you from acting foolishly and harming your interpersonal relationships.

In the following chapter, we will examine the process of conflict—how it tends to get started, how it unfolds, and how it moves to some sort of resolution. In addition, we have identified three repetitive and destructive cycles in which conflict participants can get embroiled. By understanding the type of conflict, and by being aware of the ways in which you can get trapped in destructive conflict patterns, you will be on your way to more productive conflict management.

Notes

1. Morton Deutsch, *The Resolution of Conflict* (New Haven, CT: Yale University Press, 1973).

2. Thomas R. Harvey and Bonita Drolet, *Building Teams, Building People: Expanding the Fifth Resource* (La Verne, CA: Department of Educational Management, University of La Verne 1992), p. 94.

3. Irving Altman and D. Taylor, *Social Penetration: The Development of Interpersonal Relationships* (Chicago: Holt, Rinehart & Winston, 1973), p. 171.

4. Ibid.

5. Morton Deutsch, "Conflicts: Productive or Destructive?" *Journal of Social Issues* 25 (1969), 7–41.

6. Dominic A. Infante and C. J. Wigley, "Verbal Aggressiveness: An Interpersonal Model and Measure," *Communication Monographs* 53 (1986), 61–69.

7. Shinobu Suzuki and Andrew S. Rancer, "Argumentativeness and Verbal Aggressiveness: Testing for Conceptual and Measurement Equivalence Across Cultures," *Communication Monographs* 61 (1994), 256–279.

8. Raymond W. Mack and Richard C. Snyder, "The Analysis of Social Conflict: Toward an Overview and Synthesis," in Fred E. Jandt (Ed.), *Conflict Resolution through Communication* (New York: Harper and Row, 1973), p. 34.

9. H. Braiker and H. Kelley, "Conflict in the Development of Close Relationships," in R. Burgess and T. Huston (Eds.), *Social Exchange in Developing Relationships* (New York: Academic Press, 1979), pp. 135–168.

10. Harvey and Drolet, *Building Teams, Building People,* p. 99.

11. Ibid., p. 315.

12. W. Barnett Pearce, "Keynote Address: Communication Theory," Institute for Faculty Development: Communication Theory and Research, Hope College, Holland, MI, July 1992.

13. Susan Faludi, *Backlash: The Undeclared War Against American Women* (New York: Crown Publishers, 1991), p. 338.

14. Sally A. Freeman, Stephen W. Littlejohn, and Barnett W. Pearce, "Communication and Moral Conflict," *Western Journal of Communication* 56 (1992), 319.

5

The Process of Conflict: Phases and Cycles

Objectives

At the end of this chapter, you should be able to

1. explain the phases of conflict according to any one of the phase theories.
2. explain the steps in avoidance, chilling effect, and competition conflict cycles.
3. identify a triggering event in a conflict that you have experienced.
4. explain the four steps in successful conflict resolution.
5. explain how the strategies you used in a conflict situation led to the outcomes you achieved.

Key Terms

chilling effect	cycle of behavior	resolution phase
competitive conflict escalation cycle	differentiation phase	schismogenesis
conflict avoidance cycle	initiation phase	scripted events
conflict management	phase theory	triggering event
conflict phase	prelude to conflict	undesired repetitive pattern (URP)
conflict resolution	process model of conflict	

In Chapter 4 we described the different types of conflict. Although conflict may take on different forms depending on your relationship with the other person, the issue involved, the importance of the issue, your goals, and so on, many writers argue that conflicts proceed through fairly recognizable stages. In this chapter, we explore phase theory and the process model of conflict, and demonstrate how choices made in different stages of the conflict may contribute to productive or destructive outcomes. A **conflict phase** is a portion of conflict, or a stage in the interaction, that tends to be similar across various conflicts. For example, as we mentioned in Chapter 1, most people understand that the statement "we need to talk" is an invitation to conflict, creating the first stage of interaction called the initiation phase. Our purpose here is not only to identify the stages through which many conflicts progress, but also to suggest some of the behaviors that contribute to successful resolution of conflict and others that either go nowhere or get out of hand and perhaps turn violent.

Phase Theories of Conflict

You may have noticed that your conflicts are often alike in the way they are played out: You have a complaint about another person, you point it out to that person, the other responds, the two of you go back and forth for a while, and then find a way to work things out. **Phase theory** starts with this assumption: Conflict unfolds in fairly predictable ways over a period of time and progresses through recognizable stages of interaction. When behaviors are fairly predictable, moving through various stages and creating the possibility of new movement through similar stages, we say that they are cyclic. A **cycle of behavior** exists when people get a sense of repetitiveness in the way it happens. The academic school year is a cycle—you begin in August or September, work through the fall semester or quarter, take exams around Christmas break, get a few days off, begin classes again, and end May or June for the summer. It starts all over again the next year. It is also a process—because it is dynamic, changeable, and moves toward some end. Similarly, we usually know when conflict begins—we hear the words, "we need to talk," and we usually know when a conflict ends—such as when people reach an agreement. In Chapter 2, we learned that resolving conflict, however much we might want it to be the case, does not end conflict for us forever. We're going to have to engage in conflict again and again, and we have a pretty good idea how these conflicts will unfold.

In presenting some of the phases of conflict, we will begin with the simple and move to the complex. The simplest phase model was created by Walton, who identified only two stages in the conflict process—differentiation and integration.[1] An event brings a conflict to the participants' attention, and they make their different positions known and argue for them until it seems pointless to continue. At that point, participants work toward a solution through integrating their various needs and desires.

Ellis and Fisher have added a third phase based on their observations of conflict during decision making in small groups.[2] In their research, small groups first engaged in conflict over the differences among the members themselves rather than over the issues the group had generated. In the second phase, interaction centered around the advantages and disadvantages of the proposals themselves. Then in the third stage members looked for ways to agree with the final outcome as the conflict de-escalated.

Kriegsberg provided a little more complicated model that adds the notion of circularity in the process of conflict:

- There is an awareness of conflict,
- strategies and tactics are used to address the conflict in some way,
- the conflict escalates and then de-escalates,
- some termination to the conflict is seen,
- and then the outcome of the present conflict affects the way future conflicts are enacted.[3]

Other authors have developed even more elaborate models of conflict. Rummel, for example, viewed conflict as a "potentiality" arising from dispositions and powers within a "conflict space."[4] When opposing powers attempt to expand or balance out one another, conflict ensues. He identified five stages of conflict:

1. latent conflict phase, in which the possibility of conflict is inherent in people's different meanings, values, norms, status, and class;
2. initiation phase, in which some event acts as a "trigger" for the conflict;
3. balancing of power phase, in which participants assess each other's power and act in order to bring about some resolution to the conflict;
4. balance of power phase, in which those in the conflict accept the resolution and live with the consequences of the resolution; and
5. disruption phase, in which those in the conflict realize that the stage is set for a new conflict.

An interesting claim about triggering events is that the same kind of action may be a trigger in one situation but not in another, depending on the context of the action. That is, you might find it aggravating that your coworker borrows your office supplies, but say nothing most of the time. On a day when it is urgent that you complete a project and you once again reach for supplies that have been borrowed, a conflict may be triggered.

Phase theories of conflict are useful for a number of reasons. Although they can be seen as overly simplistic in their depiction of conflict, they do suggest that conflicts have a cyclic pattern: They arise, are dealt with in some way, and then die out, only to set the stage for the next conflict. Furthermore, phase theories point out that conflicts have triggering events, actions seen by participants as initiating the conflict and bringing it to their attention. Phase theories also indicate that conflicts often involve a "testing period" before they are enacted, during which participants assess their strengths and weaknesses and try to determine conflict outcomes before taking any action.[5] Phase theories focus on conflict as interaction over time, as something that unfolds as people interact with one another.

APPLICATION 5.1

How have your conflicts typically played themselves out? Do you sense that there are patterns in your conflicts that are repeated?

Patterns and Cycles in Conflict

Another way to look at conflicts from a process view is to describe the cycles characteristic of certain types of conflict. Many activities are repetitive. You probably get up at the same time each day, have a breakfast similar to the one from the day before, put on your clothes in the same order, and walk or drive to classes using the same route as always. Sometimes routines are nearly unconscious behaviors. Routinized events are **scripted** and are performed with little deviation. People repeat similar behaviors each time they encounter the event. Without scripted events, it would be difficult getting through the day. Imagine having to make a new decision for each thing that you did!

A major disadvantage of scripted behavior is what Cronen, Pearce, and Snavely called an **undesired repetitive pattern (URP)**[6]: the feeling of being trapped in a set of circumstances beyond one's control. Those involved in URPs can have automatic, "knee-jerk" responses to one another: Something one of them says triggers an automatic response in the other, and the episode quickly escalates out of control. It happens when those involved have a pretty good idea of what the other will say next, or at least they think they do. URPs are recurrent, unwanted, and generally occur regardless of the topic or situation. Those in the URP have a feeling that the pattern is hard, if not impossible, to avoid.

URPs sometime have an escalation effect, in which each exchange between those involved gets increasingly intense. **Schismogenesis** (the escalation of the cycle) occurs when the behaviors of one person intensify the behaviors of another person.[7] Schismogenesis can be complementary, with the exchanges corresponding to each other (e.g., as one person becomes more dominant, the other becomes more submissive; as one person shows off, the other becomes more admiring, which leads to more exhibitionism, and so on). Schismogenesis can also be symmetrical, with each person trying to outdo the other's behavior. Seeking revenge can often lead to schismogenesis, as blood feuds escalate through retaliation after retaliation.

The belief that conflicts are cyclical is widespread in the conflict literature. It is not that conflict occurs frequently within a relationship that makes it dysfunctional; it is rather the repetitive, unchanging, and negative way in which it recurs that creates dysfunctional conflict. When people are locked in a set of behaviors and seem unable or unwilling to change those behaviors, and when issues are not resolved in some way, conflict can become a destructive element in the relationship. Productive conflict behavior is flexible and varied; these destructive cycles are inflexible and unchanging.

Three dysfunctional conflict cycles are common: the **conflict avoidance cycle** (conflict is avoided), which generally occurs intrapersonally when we try to get out of dealing with our conflicts; the **chilling effect,** a "de-escalatory cycle," (communication is diminished), which occurs when people do not tell each other about conflicts because they fear the effect it will have on the relationship or because they do not think the relationship warrants the energy a conflict will entail; and the **competitive conflict escalation cycle** (conflict intensifies, issues are unresolved), which occurs between people who carry unresolved issues forward into each of their conflicts. All of these three cycles stem, in large part, from the attitudes people have about conflict and from the way those attitudes are validated by their conflict behavior.

The Conflict Avoidance Cycle

The conflict avoidance cycle is characteristic of a relationship between people whose first impulse is to avoid initiating conflict or to quickly withdraw when conflicts arise. This is not the same as avoiding particular topics within a relationship;[8] an avoidance involves delaying the confrontation of an important issue. Hocker and Wilmot identified several misassumptions about conflict.[9] Taken together, these create a series of behaviors that can be identified as a conflict avoidance cycle.

Probably the most widespread misassumption about conflict, and the one that has the greatest chance of creating a conflict avoidance cycle, is the notion that conflict is abnormal. People who experience conflict want to get it over as soon as possible so that things can "get back to normal"—harmony being the norm. The truth is that both excessive conflict and excessive harmony are abnormal. Harmony and conflict are processes in life; people move back and forth between them. Harmony in a relationship is desirable, but it does not allow growth because it does not allow change. Rummel noted that "the desire to eradicate conflict, the hope for harmony and universal cooperation, is the wish for a frozen, unchanging world with all relationships fixed in their patterns—with all in balance."[10] This misassumption affects the way people approach the study of **conflict management.** They are motivated to learn about conflict so they can do it better, and faster; their motivation is not to gain a true understanding of the process while they are in it.

Related to the notion that conflicts are abnormal is the idea that conflicts are pathological: They are symptoms of a system that is functioning incorrectly. Some conflicts are indeed pathological. We have all had the experience of observing people who continued a conflict long after it made any sense to do so. For the most part, though, conflict is a sign that a system (an interpersonal relationship, a task group, or an organization) is functioning well and testing itself to make sure the boundaries are clear and understandable to those involved.

A second misassumption people hold is that conflicts and disagreements are the same or that a conflict can be reduced to a disagreement by saying, "We only have a difference of opinion." A disagreement may concern favorite colors, but a conflict arises if two people want their (different) favorite colors painted on the same walls. Conflicts have a structure: People want different things; they depend on one another to get these things, and they cannot both get what they want at the same time. At some point conflict demands attention, but a disagreement can be postponed indefinitely. By labeling a conflict a simple disagreement, people are more likely to postpone or avoid the conflict rather than doing something about it.

A third misassumption, perpetuated by numerous popular writings on conflict management, focuses on reducing or avoiding conflict rather than initiating or escalating it. The belief is that starting or escalating a conflict is bad. Some people avoid conflict as long as they can and, therefore, the problem continues. At the risk of oversimplification, one could identify two basic approaches to conflict interaction—confronting and avoiding—although people may do both in different relationships. When dealing with an avoider, one may have to heighten the avoider's awareness of the conflict so that it is impossible to ignore. For example, a newly married couple may have different expectations about how to account for their whereabouts to the other. The wife may frequently leave the house without indicating a destination or return time. The more conscientious husband indicates that such behavior is worrisome but gets little response from his wife. Were he to copy his wife's behavior for a few days, she might realize how inconsiderate her behavior is. Communicating one's needs to the other may not be the most effective way to initiate conflict management if the other does not understand the negative aspects of the behavior involved.

When conflict is viewed as negative and as something to be avoided, when people think conflict can be postponed indefinitely, or when they fear initiating a conflict, then a cycle of avoidance behavior is likely to be created. (See Figure 5.1.) Thinking about conflict negatively creates anxiety about a particular conflict being experienced. Because people feel anxious, they put off dealing with conflict as long as possible—until something must be done. Unfortunately, the longer conflict is delayed, the harder it is to resolve. If a confrontation occurs too late in the cycle, the conflict may get out of control; the situation is handled poorly; and people's negative views of conflict are confirmed—creating a per-

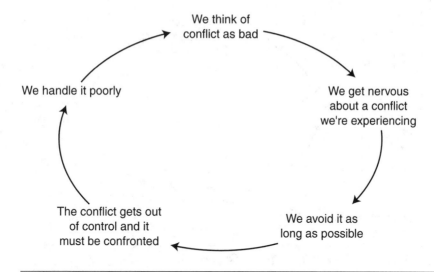

FIGURE 5.1 *The Conflict Avoidance Cycle*
The cycle generally begins with a belief that conflict is something that we would rather avoid if at all possible. Because we would like to avoid conflict, experiencing one makes us nervous. Generally, something that makes us nervous is something we put off. Unfortunately, most conflicts get worse when left alone, so the conflict gets to the point at which it must be confronted. Our anxiety causes us to handle the conflict badly, and so perceptions of conflict as something that is bad are confirmed, and the cycle starts again.

petual conflict avoidance cycle. Because some people avoid or put off a confrontation until it is too late, their fear of conflict is confirmed ("see, I never should have said anything"). This cycle may be confined to a particular relationship or may be characteristic of many relationships.

> **APPLICATION 5.2**
>
> Compare two conflicts in which avoidance worked in different ways—one conflict you avoided that turned out to be resolved anyway, and another you avoided that got out of hand and worsened because you put it off.

The Chilling Effect: A Diminished Communication Cycle

No matter how you view conflict, the simple fact is that it takes time and energy to deal with it constructively. Research indicates that conflict avoidance is related to the amount of commitment in the relationship: People are likely to avoid conflict in low-commitment relationships, whereas in strong, committed relationships, conflict is more spontaneous and emotional.[11] Over time, people may lose the desire to conflict with each other—to work through important issues. Thinking "it doesn't matter" or "it's not worth it," they tell each other nothing is wrong and, in doing so, may pull away from each other.[12] (See Figure 5.2.) The pattern of reducing communication creates a chilling effect in which one person in a relationship withholds grievances from the other, usually due to fear of the other person's

FIGURE 5.2 *The Chilling Effect in Conflict*
The chilling effect begins with the perception that conflict will have negative effects on the relationship. Because of that fear, there is an additional perception that conflict is not worth the effort it would take to enact. When conflicts are avoided, however, other types of communication in the relationship tend to decrease. A decrease in communication often leads to a decrease in a commitment to the relationship. After several cycles of decreased communication and decreased commitment, a person may simply cycle out of the relationship altogether.

reaction.[13] The chilling effect focuses on the negative aspects about the other person that irritate or anger the withholder. These negative aspects become areas of perceived incompatibility and evolve into ongoing conflicts. Sometimes the withholder describes the conflict to friends or other third parties but does not confront the irritating person; therefore, the conflicts remain unexpressed. Generally, the withholder does not confront the other because of fear of damaging the relationship.

Research indicates that a chilling effect is most likely to occur when the other person appears to have attractive alternatives to the relationship with the withholder and when the other's commitment to the withholder seems weak. If you are worried that your friend does not care very much about you and that your friend could easily leave the relationship, you are not likely to tell your friend when you have a grievance. Conversely, if you are not worried about my leaving because I have no alternatives and care very much about you, you are more likely to express your dislikes and desires. You have nothing to fear from conflict.[14]

The chilling effect occurs in its greatest degree when the other person is dating outside the relationship and shows little commitment to the withholder because the withholder fears abandonment if the other is irritated. The negative effects of the chilling effect include ending the relationship, but the fear of ending the relationship due to conflict is what leads to the chilling effect in the first place.

If ending the relationship is ultimately what is desired, then the chilling effect is a way to disengage from the other. It could be used as easily in an organizational relationship (no longer caring about office functions, putting less time and energy into the work) as in an interpersonal one. However, a chilling effect is negative in desirable, ongoing relationships because it puts barriers between those involved.

The Competitive Conflict Escalation Cycle

I already knew where my favorite blouse was—it was in my sister's room. She seems to have this habit of borrowing whatever she wants without my permission. I went into her room and stuffed under her bed was my blouse. I was so angry that I had KILL written on my forehead. I went searching for my sister throughout the house, like a lion searches for its prey. When I found her, I brought up all the past times that she had taken things from me without permission, and then I called her a kleptomaniac. Neither of us tried to de-escalate the conflict. I left her room because I was afraid that I would say more damaging things that I would regret later on. It was a lose-lose situation for both of us.

The third conflict cycle is probably the most common of the three. The pattern is that people rehash the same issues repeatedly, focusing on past grievances as well as present ones, without finding mutually satisfactory solutions. Several authors have noted that once a conflict is initiated, the greatest pressures are toward escalation rather than toward containment and management.[15] Competition, biased perceptions, and commitment to one's original position may all push a conflict into an escalating cycle.

When people deal with conflict by contending, each trying to do well at the other's expense, a set of moves and countermoves tends to result that drives conflict to increase in intensity. . . . The escalation of conflict is accompanied by a number of transformations, each of which is difficult—though not impossible—to reverse. First, relatively light, friendly, and inoffensive contentious tactics tend to give way to heavier moves. . . . Second, the number of issues in conflict tends to increase. . . . Third, a focus on specifics gives way to more global, all-encompassing concerns. . . . Fourth, motivation in escalating conflict shifts from an initial interest in doing well for oneself to beating the other side and (eventually) to making sure that the other is hurt more than oneself. Finally, the number of parties to the conflict tends to increase. . . . Once conflict begins to escalate, the preceding transformations make it increasingly difficult for de-escalation to occur.[16]

Three models have been developed to explain conflict escalation. The first is the *aggressor-defender model,* in which the aggressor has a goal or set of goals that places him or her in conflict with the defender. The aggressor starts with small tactics and escalates to heavier ones until the goals are attained or the value of goal attainment is outweighed by the anticipated cost of continued escalation. Throughout this process, the defender merely reacts to the actions taken by the aggressor, and escalation continues until the aggressor wins or gives up trying. An illustration of this kind of conflict cycle is found in a reported divorce battle, in which the husband was trying to get custody of the children. He harassed his ex-wife in a number of ways, going so far as to bribe a police officer into arresting his ex-wife the night before the custody hearing so that she would appear unsuitable for custody. The ex-wife spent so much time defending herself from the barrage of conflict tactics that she had no time to counterattack with any of her own.

The second model is the *conflict spiral,* or *schismogenesis,* which asserts that escalation results from a vicious circle of action and reaction. It is a retaliatory spiral, in which each party punishes the other for actions that it finds aversive, as when an argument escalates from insults into a shouting match and finally into a fist fight. Conflicts can quickly become spirals when the response to an opening problem statement is another problem statement (He says: "It bothers me when you leave the dishes in the sink"; she responds, "Well, you leave your dirty clothes on the floor"). Various problems and complaints are raised by both parties without either admitting any fault, as illustrated by the following account:

> Our neighbor came over around 9:00 P.M. to ask us if we would please turn down our music as they were trying to study. It was a reasonable request, considering we could hardly hear her speak. One of my roommates retorted with "As long as you won't bang on the walls and break my picture frames, sure." The conversation was heated because they had banged on the walls in the past, breaking one picture frame. The result of this encounter is that we aren't speaking anymore and really resent each other.

A variant of the conflict spiral is the *defensive spiral,* wherein each party reacts to protect itself from a threat it finds in the other's self-protective actions. The arms race is an example of a defensive spiral. Defensive spirals escalate when the reactions are more severe than the action they follow.

The third model is the *structural change model,* in which the conflict and the tactics used to pursue it produce *residues* in the form of changes in the parties and the communities to which the parties belong. These residues then encourage further contentious behavior, at an equal or still more escalated level, and diminish efforts at conflict resolution. As in the preceding example, you and your neighbor may have had a conflict concerning the amount of noise that is tolerable on a weekday night. The particular tactics used to resolve that conflict will affect how new conflicts arise and how you and your neighbor handle them. Banging on the wall every time there is noise or calling the police to lodge a complaint differs significantly from talking to your neighbor calmly and explaining why you need more quiet than you are getting. Negative feelings from previous encounters spill over into the current conflict, affecting the way the conflict is defined and enacted.

Structural changes can be psychological, such as negative attitudes and negative perceptions of the adversary, zero-sum thinking, and diminished capacity for empathy. Changes in groups and other collectives may occur when these psychological reactions become collective norms, and changes in the community surrounding the parties can occur through polarization, siding with one of the contenders, and so on. Psychological changes, in particular, become a self-fulfilling prophecy.[17] An example of the impact that negative feelings and residues can have on community relations was the outburst of violence and destruction following the 1992 announcement of the verdict in the trial of the white police officers accused of beating Rodney King, an African American, in Los Angeles. Prior to the announcement of the verdict, another verdict had been handed down concerning the shooting of an African American teenage girl by a Korean American grocer. Although the girl was killed, the grocer was only sentenced to probation, creating many negative feelings between African Americans and Korean Americans. When the predominantly white jury (selected from Simi Valley residents because of a change of venue in the trial) for the Rodney King trial declared three of the four police officers innocent of any charges of excessive force, violence erupted throughout south central Los Angeles. In riots worse than the Watts Riots of 1965, over fifty-five people were killed, and the damage to property, particularly that owned by Korean Americans, was numbered in the hundreds of millions. Local officials claimed that the area never fully recovered from the 1965 Watts Riots, and that it would take years to undo the damage. Did the announcement of the verdict cause the riots? Most officials agree that the verdict was simply the trigger that unleashed years of bitterness and anger. The point is that conflict residues can occur at any level of relationship. That is, a person may have negative feelings toward you and your intentions, and, although you do nothing to encourage those feelings, you also do nothing to discourage them—leading to increased hostility and conflict escalation.[18] Case Study 5.1 is another example of a structural change conflict in which each encounter feeds the next encounter, intensifying the conflict.

Case Study 5.1 ■ *The Ongoing Battle*

Since I began school, my father and I haven't spoken to one another. I was having dinner with my parents and a visiting cousin. When the topic of politics arose, I made a negative comment about the president. My father called me an idiot. I always feel my dad devalues what I say by insulting me. Here was another example. I felt my dad wasn't even listening to my story but rather looking for ways to criticize me. I told him that he wasn't listening and that he never listens to me. This in turn angered him and he told me that I'm someone impossible to carry on a conversation with. I told him that he was regressing to the way he treated me when I was a child and, as usual, not giving me a fair chance.

I'm tired of apologizing, listening to my dad insult and demean my behavior and my character, and then just "patching things up." We never really solve any problems. I wanted to talk about our ongoing battle with a mediator present. I apologized to my dad and suggested we see a counselor to work out our problem. My dad said that he didn't have a problem and that I was the one who needs to work on myself. He also said counseling didn't work. Nothing between us was resolved; my apology came with the stipulation that more was needed to work things out and this was unacceptable to my dad.

I didn't even want to apologize this last time, but my mom's birthday wish was for the family to be together. So in order to please my mom, once again I tried to talk with my dad. He said, "Fine, but when is your attitude going to change? Are you going to grow up?" I told him I was trying but felt that he was too demanding in his expectations of my maturity. Dad doesn't feel he is too demanding but that I am immature and need to grow up. I told him that this is why we should talk about the conflict with a third party. "Oh, that again." He said, "If you can't grow up and change and accept responsibility for your actions, then we don't have a relationship."

What we have termed the *competitive conflict escalation cycle* is similar to the structural change model but also considers the impact of "face" on the conflict (see Figure 5.3). The concept of face is adapted from the work of Goffman.[19] He argued that all of us have an image of ourselves that we work to maintain in our interactions with others. Generally, people cooperate with one another in the projection and maintenance of face. When face is threatened, they will respond with face-saving strategies to restore the impression others have of them. In conflict, the introduction of face issues can be extremely threatening. Introducing face issues decreases flexibility in conflicts and decreases the likelihood of reaching resolution because, once a face issue is introduced, the participants in the conflict may focus on it to the exclusion of the original issue.[20] A fundamental assumption of this text is that people work to maintain favorable impressions of themselves in their relationships. If they feel that impression is threatened, face becomes an issue in the conflict situation.

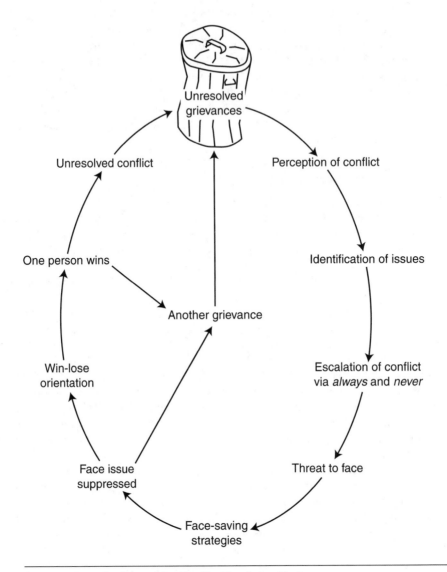

FIGURE 5.3   *The Competitive Conflict Escalation Cycle*
The cycle begins with a trash can full of unresolved grievances from the past. Past grievances color the present perception of conflict, and make it easy for us to identify this as a repetitive issue. The cycle is made possible when people use conflict messages that include absolutist terms such as *always* and *never,* which create a threat to the other person's self-image. Generally, when our face is threatened, we move to face-saving strategies leaving behind the original issue. The face issue is generally suppressed rather than cleared up in this kind of conflict, and the suppressed face issue becomes another unresolved grievance. As the face issue is suppressed, we move to a win-lose orientation. If one person wins, the other loses and wants to get even the next time (another grievance for the trash can). And so the cycle continues on and on.

An idea related to the notion of face and impression management is the tendency to take conflict personally. Hample and Dallinger suggest that although people have a trait-like tendency to personalize conflict, elements in the conflict situation may also promote the personalization of conflict. When a person has begun to take a conflict personally, face overwhelms any substantive issue. This reaction is "more likely when the conflict is stressful . . . or because of the interpersonal interplays it contains. . . . TCP [Taking Conflict Personally] is contagious: it can manifest itself as aggression or avoidance, and can challenge or frustrate others into reciprocal TCP reactions."[21] The phenomenon of taking conflict personally is characterized by hurt, persecution feelings, stress reactions, and perceptions of the effect of the conflict on the relationship. Clearly, the tendency to personalize conflict will help fuel a competitive conflict escalation cycle.

The cycle begins with a perception of conflict, which is colored by past issues that may not have been satisfactorily resolved. We carry these around with us in a "trash can," allowing us to introduce them when convenient. This "trash can" of unresolved issues leads us to a win-lose orientation in the conflict. Because so many issues remain from previous conflicts, we want to be on top when this one is over. When a conflict is perceived, issues are identified and the conflict is initiated. In the beginning of the conflict and during the identification of the issues, several words have a negative impact: *always, never, can't,* and the like.

> "You never think about me when you take on these extra assignments."
> "You're always late."
> "You can't do anything right."

The effect of messages containing these words is to attack the other personally, to threaten the other's face or self-image. Immediately trying to defend oneself, as in "Yes, I do think about you" or "No, I'm not always late" does little to contain the conflict. A request for information, such as "I don't understand why you feel that way" may encourage the other person to be more specific in his or her complaint rather than making a global complaint that creates immediate defensiveness.

APPLICATION 5.3

What kind of issues are in your "trash can" of unresolved grievances? How can you avoid making them part of your conflicts with others?

In conflicts, though, particularly conflicts between people who have experienced conflict together before, a threat to face is something that becomes part of an ongoing interaction in which the individual does not feel accepted by the other. For example, a husband thinks of himself as hard-working, a good provider for his family. He thinks of himself as a man who cares about his family, who is willing to take on overtime assignments to better provide for them. His wife, angry over the amount of time he is spending at work, says, "You never think about me when you take on these extra assignments." Suddenly, his concept of himself is threatened—his wife does not see that the very reason he takes the extra assignments is that he does think about his family. He feels a need to restore his projected image and may defend himself or counterattack: "Why can't you see that I'm doing this for you and the family?" In Case Study 5.1, despite apologies to one another, the woman and her father cannot seem to end their conflict because an apology is almost always followed with a statement of why the conflict is not over. She is not responding as a "good daughter," he is being a "good father."

The problem with face issues in conflict situations is that once they are introduced, they add a new issue to the conflict that people must deal with in addition to the original point of contention. If the issue is whether or not taking overtime assignments negatively affects the family, then attacking the husband's concern for his family keeps the couple from dealing with the original issue of whether overtime assignments should be accepted. The face issue is as real as the issue of overtime assignments, but the pressing concern—whether the assignment should be turned down—is not dealt with as rapidly as it should be.

As the face issue is dealt with, then, in the conflict cycle the original issue is frequently suppressed, adding another grievance to a "trash can" full of unresolved conflicts. Generally, such conflicts result in win-lose outcomes. When one person does "win," a new conflict is created because, when people lose, they usually want to "get even." And so the issue is remembered and added to the trash can. The next time a conflict arises between the participants, everything in the trash can will affect their perceptions of the new conflict.

As in the conflict avoidance cycle, the competitive conflict escalation cycle is exacerbated by misassumptions. People often think that conflict results from personality problems of people who just cannot get along. That implies that the people are helpless to do anything about conflict. It also leads to a blaming tendency: "The only reason we're having conflict is because we just don't get along very well" or "It's your fault because you're so stubborn about this issue."

Blaming the other person is a convenient way to ignore the actual issue of the conflict.[22] Rather than focusing on the problem, people focus on one another, creating face issues and distracting from the original issue. "Since blame presupposes that the accused know the evil they do, blamers often fill out the picture with appropriate motives and corresponding character traits."[23] Blaming the other and holding oneself blameless is an almost guaranteed way to turn a conflict into an escalation cycle.

A misassumption that is especially effective at bringing about conflict escalation cycles is the feeling that compromise is impossible. Some people act as though each conflict has a critical impact on their lives: If they do not get their way this time they never will again; if they give in on one point, they will lose everything at stake in this particular conflict. Flexibility is a characteristic or productive conflict interaction; inflexibility may lead a person into an escalation cycle.

When people are unwilling to work with each other, it is often because they believe there is no way that they can both benefit from a conflict situation. Although some conflicts do have lose-lose outcomes (in which everyone walks away unsatisfied), going into a conflict thinking that both people cannot benefit makes reaching a mutually satisfying outcome difficult. Conflict solutions that suit both people take work and take time. People who do not believe win-win outcomes are possible rarely find them; it becomes a self-fulfilling prophecy.

Another misassumption that can lead to conflict escalation cycles is the notion that conflict issues cannot be separated from one another. In escalation cycles, the tendency is to address too many issues at one time. For example, if a couple is trying to set a budget for this year, bringing up instances of poor spending habits in the past or arguing about the way one of them spends money will only block agreement about the issue at hand—this year's budget.

A related aspect of this misassumption is the counterattack. One person brings up an issue, relatively focused, and the other person ignores it, issuing a counterattack. For example, a wife overreacts when she steps on a toy while not wearing any shoes. She yells at the kids and threatens to throw away all their toys if they do not keep them picked up. The husband says, "I don't think it was necessary to yell at the kids that way," and the wife replies, "Well, you're always yelling at them." Dealing with a person who favors counterattacks is especially difficult because they rarely acknowledge the original issue. One may be tempted to "up the ante" by bringing up a second issue also. Then the other person introduces yet another issue, and so forth, until everything either person has ever done is part of the conflict. Counterarguing is an effective way to start a conflict escalation cycle. Moreover, research indicates that counterarguing leads to less and less satisfying communication between people in relationships, until they become unable to resolve the original conflict.[24]

A final misassumption that leads to escalation cycles is the idea that other people cannot be trusted to be honest and fair. Certainly, some people do not appear to deserve trust, but in ongoing relationships one needs to be willing to give the other person a chance. Mistrust creates escalation cycles, and too much trust can cause one to be badly hurt; but somewhere in the middle is an attitude that allows two people to work toward an outcome that will benefit both of them.

Conflict as a Process

As described earlier in this chapter, a process is a dynamic, ever changing, progressive event. Processes don't sit still; they grow, develop, progress toward some end. A **process model of conflict** suggests that conflict moves through a series of four recognizable stages, steps, or phases. These stages are the **prelude to conflict** (known as the frustration or latent stage in some theories), the **triggering event** (a behavior that at least one person in the conflict points to as the "beginning" of the problem), the **initiation phase** (in which at least one person makes known to the other the presence of a felt conflict), the **differentiation phase** (in which the participants work out the problem using various strategies and tactics), and the **resolution phase** (in which those involved agree to some outcome to the conflict). From this perspective, an unsuccessful conflict is one that becomes mired down in one of the first three stages. Such a model is, as Thomas argued, "concerned with the influence of each event upon the following events."[25] This section describes the sequences of events in conflict and discusses research that views conflict as a process.

In examining the process model of conflict, it is important to understand that the event we term *conflict* has been recast as a process or a series of steps or stages from beginning to end in order to examine it in more detail. Conflicts may follow this sequence of events quickly or slowly, and the distribution of time within the model can be uneven. For example, the prelude to conflict may be a matter of months and the actual overt manifestations of conflict a matter of minutes, or the opposite may occur. A conflict may begin to cycle through the phases and stop, or it may return to a previous stage when new issues are introduced and added to the conflict. As in examining any communication event, the model may illuminate, but may also distort the process. The sequence is used for explanation and analysis, not as a Procrustean bed into which all conflicts must fit.[26]

The Prelude to Conflict

The prelude consists of the variables that make conflict possible between those involved. The prelude comprises four variables:

- the participants in the conflict situation (number, age, sex, etc.)
- the relationship between them (which may vary in closeness and distribution of power) and their conflict history
- other interested parties to the conflict (including bystanders)
- the physical and social environment of the conflict situation.

In the prelude to conflict, the potential for manifest conflict exists because of the people involved and the other social and physical factors that define the situation. Like the first block in a line of dominoes, these variables affect the course of conflict.

The Participants.   As we saw through the examination of values, attitudes, and beliefs in Chapter 2, the people involved in the conflict have the greatest influence on whether a conflict will arise and on how it will be played out. Participants vary in their temperament, attitudes, and outlook; they also vary in the amount of anticipation they experience concerning a conflict.[27] Nye pointed out that both individual characteristics such as defensiveness and frustration as well as interaction patterns such as competition create a potential for conflicts,[28] and Hample and Dallinger argue that those who take conflict personally often propel others into the same behavior.[29] When others are cooperative, we tend to be so. When they are hostile or suspicious, it is difficult to cooperate with them.

Age of the conflicting parties may also be a contributing factor. Among married couples, younger parties in conflict seem to react differently to one another than do their older counterparts. In comparison to retired and middle-aged couples, younger couples have a comparatively intense engagement style of interaction, characterized by alternation between analytic confrontation and humorous remarks.[30] Of course, factors other than age may also contribute to differences in conflict behavior between younger and older married couples.

In addition to the ages of the people involved in the conflict, the number of people involved may also affect the way the conflict unfolds. Mack and Snyder offered three tentative conclusions about the number of people involved in a conflict:

1. The larger the number of parties, the more difficult it will be to discover a common solution in which all parties can achieve at least some gain over previous power positions.
2. The larger the number of parties, the less intense will be the nonrealistic components of the conflict relationship.
3. There is a persistent tendency to reduce multiple-party conflict to two-party conflict via coalitions and blocs.[31]

The Relationship.   The relationship between the conflict participants affects the way they perceive and react to a conflict. Are the participants in a hierarchical or equal relationship? How well do they know each other, both in breadth and depth of knowledge? Does one tend to dominate the other? How have they done conflict in the past?

The variable with the greatest effect on the enactment of conflict in a situation is the conflict history of the participants—how have they resolved the conflicts in the past? Conflicts in a new relationship may be threatening because of high levels of uncertainty. The relationship may not be able to withstand scrutiny under the microscope of conflict analysis. If the participants have engaged in unsatisfactory conflict before, they may expect that the current conflict will also be difficult, polluting the conflict situation with unresolved issues from the past. To the extent that conflict participants can approach the conflict in the "here and now," rather than dwell on what happened in the past, conflict history will not realize its negative potential. One woman reports a conflict in which history had a negative effect on the outcome:

> For the first time in about two weeks, my dad, stepmother, brother, and I were all in the same place at the same time. We went to dinner together, giving us our first chance in weeks to talk together. Pop is just learning how to relate to my brother and me about things beyond grades, so it has been fun this year telling him about things going on in my life and how I really feel. We had just ordered dinner when the inevitable question came up. What am I going to do after I graduate? I'm not used to sharing details about my life with him because he was never around when I was growing up to take part in my life. I thought I had been more than fair all along in telling him about my plans. When the question came up this time, I had an answer. I told him about the progress I had made in job contacts and other possibilities I was considering. I especially want to travel during the summer with a sports team as a sports information director, but I had made no specific plans. Pop asked if I had sent in my application yet. I said that I hadn't. My brother, Stuart, chimed in that I'd better do it soon. This is when the conflict started. The tone in Stuart's voice was what set me off. He was using a condescending attitude toward me, which I hate. I told him that it was none of his business, that he didn't need to tell me what to do. Stuart got mad, as usual, and stormed away from the table. Pop then told me that I was interpreting the situation incorrectly. He basically told me that I shouldn't be feeling the way I was because they were only showing that they care. This rubbed me the wrong way because I've had enough of people telling me how I should feel. I tried to explain how I felt but was interrupted several times with the response that I was wrong. I told them—actually Pop because Susan, his wife, was surprisingly quiet that night—that I thought I was being more than fair in telling them my plans and feelings. I didn't have to tell them anything, and if I was going to be continually shot down, then that was what I would do. I was trying to be honest with my feelings and include my dad in my life by telling him about them. It really hurt that he kept telling me that I was wrong, that my feelings were wrong. I said I didn't plan on living off of him for the rest of my life if that was what he was worried about and would find a job. I'm sure I overreacted in this situation but only because it sounded so "déjà vu." I feel like every time I tell my dad about my plans for the future, he finds something wrong with them. I told him this and that I wasn't looking for his approval, just informing him. It's not that I don't listen to his advice or occasionally seek it, but I was looking for support, not criticism. If this was going to be the lecture on how terrible I am and how I'm not doing anything right, then I wasn't going to share anything that would again bring this on. This conflict was not resolved, only dropped for the moment. I was sure that I had a right to my own feelings, and Pop and Stuart were convinced that my feelings were wrong.

Some research suggests that value similarity and relationship length affect the way people engage in conflict. Relationships with high value similarity are more likely to produce constructive (i.e., collaborative) conflict, whereas low value similarity is associated with destructive conflict. In addition, strongly committed relationships are more prone to spontaneous and emotional handling of conflict, whereas less committed relationships are more likely to produce conflict avoidance.[32]

Interested Third Parties.   Sometimes outsiders happen to be present when conflicts occur. This occurs when some bystanders egg people on, hoping that the conflict will escalate and turn into a brawl. "You tell him, Nick." "Don't let her say that to you, Joy Ann." "You go, girl." At other times, they may be asked to participate by the conflict parties. Morrill and Thomas found that conflicting parties were more likely to seek outside assistance in resolving the conflict if they had a less involved relationship.[33] Perhaps more strongly involved persons should seek assistance from outsiders more often because they can be important in moving a conflict to some resolution, as Mack and Snyder claimed: "The pressure for liquidation or control of social conflict from disinterested but affected bystanders is one of the primary limits on its duration, extension, and intensity."[34]

Third parties may not be immediately present in order to affect the outcomes of a conflict situation. In most decision-making situations, there are people who have an interest in the decision made. For example, if parents are deliberating over when an older child may have some privilege, the younger child has an interest in the decision because it will affect when he or she is allowed the same privilege. A teacher making a decision to change a grade for one student has as interested parties the rest of the students in the class. If flexible time is awarded to one employee, other employees have an interest in the decision. So, often when people are working out a conflict, they are doing so with respect to what they think others will think of the decision they make, regardless of whether those third parties are physically present.

Some evidence suggests that, at least at the interpersonal level, how third parties perceive the behavior of those in conflict depends on their own aggressive tendencies. Results of one study indicated that generally, aggressive people interpret other's behavior as aggressive. However, knowing why a person is acting aggressively reduces impressions of aggressiveness. The research also indicated that people who shun communication see verbally aggressive persons as powerful.[35] Thus, the personality of the third party may influence how she or he views an interpersonal conflict and determine the constructive or destructive role that person plays.

The Physical and Social Environment.   Surprisingly little has been written about the effects of the physical environment on how a conflict is played out. Where a conflict is initiated can certainly affect the way it is enacted because the place could be public or private, owned or shared, comfortable or uncomfortable, and so on. This narrative reports an observed conflict:

> I couldn't help but eavesdrop on the couple in the booth next to us in the coffee shop. They were trying to negotiate the details of their divorce. It seemed like they had chosen a public spot to try to control themselves, but as the hour went on they got more and more heated. Now and then one would say, "Okay, let's not shout at each other here." I really felt sorry for them.

Filley reported several studies that measured the impact of the physical environment, particularly the dimensions of space, on conflict interactions.[36]

The social environment, which is often tied directly to the physical setting, can also affect how people enact conflict episodes. Deutsch noted that any group of people tends to develop techniques, values, symbols, and rules for interacting with one another.[37] A social system has a purpose, determines what it means to be a member of that system, what behaviors are appropriate and inappropriate within the system, and what behaviors will occur within the system. For example, a couple that thinks of conflict as normal probably engages in conflict in a fairly open manner in which their children can observe the conflict and see how mom and dad work their way to an agreement, whereas a couple who thinks of it as abnormal may do their conflict in hushed tones behind closed doors because they are afraid to let the children see them fight. People develop a sense of *where* it is appropriate or inappropriate to engage in conflict and *when* it is appropriate or inappropriate to do conflict. Thus, whether or not a conflict occurs and how it may occur are determined to some extent by the nature of the social system itself. To understand how conflict is played out, then, we need to have some understanding of the rules and procedures the people involved have created for dealing with conflicts.

The Triggering Event

Recent research by Witteman examined the relationship between situational perceptions that creates an awareness of conflict and affects the way people perceive the triggering event (often a behavior important enough to create the perception of conflict) for the conflict. Five situational variables affect the way people assess the presence and severity of a conflict: the frequency of the problem's occurrence, the degree to which they believe the other will allow them to achieve goals, the uncertainty associated with achieving goals, the degree to which they believe the other is responsible for the problem, and the degree of negative feelings held toward the other. As these five variables interact, the triggering event is perceived when the person experiencing the conflict (Person A) observes one of the following behaviors (in Person B):

- *rebuff.* Person A asks Person B for a desired behavior and Person B fails to respond as hoped. For example, you ask your roommate to take a message for you while you are out and your roommate says no.
- *illegitimate demand.* Person B places or imposes his or her wants, needs, desires, or demands on Person A. For example, you find that your roommate has borrowed your new leather jacket without permission.
- *criticism.* Person B criticizes or finds fault with what Person A is doing, saying, or feeling without demanding or asking that Person A do something different. For example, your roommate tells you that the paper you about to turn in is not even close to what the professor wants.
- *non-cumulative annoyance.* Person A realizes a difference in attitude, lifestyle, and/or opinion between him/her and Person B. For example, you are disturbed by a new political attitude expressed by your roommate and your roommate's efforts to change your thinking about the issue.
- *cumulative annoyance.* Person A realizes a difference in attitude, lifestyle, and/or opinion between him/her and Person B and also realizes that it occurred more than once. For example, you realize that it really bothers you

when your roommate gets drunk every Friday night and passes out on the couch in the living room.

- *mutual cumulative annoyance.* Person A and Person B are mutually or interactively involved in the creation of a cumulative annoyance. For example, you and your roommate are purposely bothering each other—not taking each other's messages, bad-mouthing each other to friends, and so on.[38]

The Initiation of Conflict

The initiation phase, in which the parties realize that a conflict exists over some issue, constitutes the first portion of the enacted conflict. Generally, both people in the conflict will recognize that a conflict has been initiated, although they may not agree on precisely the same starting point. Because people interpret the same event differently, they may not identify the same one as the triggering event, but sometimes they will agree on what started the conflict. Conflict moves into the initiation phase when at least one conflict participant observes a triggering event, such as those discussed previously. Those whose awareness has been raised by the triggering event will, if time allows, assess the issue and try to determine "the primary concerns of the two parties—the party's own frustrated concern and his perception of the concern which led the other party to perform the frustrating action."[39] The participants' issue assessment depends on their definition of the issue, and how they define the issue may depend on whether they define it solely in terms of their own concerns or mutual concerns, whether they see how the issue is tied to others, and how large they perceive the issue to be.[40]

Given their assessment of the issue and the time and opportunity necessary to reflect, the persons observing the triggering event then choose to confront or avoid the conflict. The choice is the fulcrum of a dilemma: Conflict is necessary to clarify issues, but conflict is feared because of the feelings of vulnerability and frustration it can arouse.[41]

It is in this choice-making portion of the initiation stage that people often get stuck in an avoidance or chilling effect cycle. When conflict is feared and seen as something to avoid, it is easy to decide that the current conflict should be avoided. If the conflict really needs to be addressed, the person caught in an avoidance cycle will have his or her negative perceptions reinforced when conflict is finally addressed after it has gotten beyond the stage in which productive engagement is possible. Similarly, a person might enter a chilling effect cycle as he or she thinks that engaging in a conflict may have harmful consequences on the relationship and avoids conflict.

Chapter 1 noted that the bulk of conflict resolution advice is slanted toward conflict engagement as an inherent good and does not discuss the times when it might be better to avoid conflict. Not every conflict should be confronted. Some spouses have learned in their marriages that they are better off avoiding some conflicts, as in Bill's case:

> This is a second marriage for both of us, and my wife brought three kids with her. Her oldest daughter seems really wacky to me, but I have learned not to criticize her to my wife. She gets real defensive and angry with me. I have learned to overlook her daughter's nutty behavior and not comment on it. My wife has so many other good points, it is not worth fighting over her daughter, especially now that she is in college, and doesn't live with us anymore.

However, if any participant in the conflict feels that leaving the issue unresolved is more costly than confrontation, avoidance is potentially destructive.[42]

Once a person decides to confront or avoid conflict (assuming that sufficient time is allowed to make this decision, which is not always the case), the conflict is ignored, suppressed, or engaged. Prior to engagement, in the best of circumstances, those involved may be able to identify and analyze the issue, set some preliminary goals, and think about their strategy choices and the other's probable responses. Thus, the initiation stage is mental, mostly involving the decision whether one should confront the other, avoid the issue, or take other actions. When one or more of the participants initiates communication about the conflict, it moves into the differentiation stage.

APPLICATION 5.4

Describe a conflict situation in which the same behavior could be a triggering event or just another event in your life. For example, a person at work is always borrowing your materials without permission. One time it leads to conflict. Why did it happen that time and not another?

The Differentiation of Conflict

The differentiation phase, in which the parties reveal their differences, calls attention to the fact that conflict exists. Lasting anywhere from a few minutes to days or even weeks, this is the stage in which the conflict becomes quite obvious. Although for the parties this may be "the conflict" as they openly disagree, argue, or quarrel, from a communication point of view, the revelation of differences is the third phase in the interpersonal conflict process. During this phase, a number of factors may be added to those that occur at earlier stages to help determine whether the conflict is eventually resolved.

This phase serves a useful purpose by allowing both parties to explain how they see the situation giving rise to conflict and what they want to happen as a result of the conflict. Sometimes only one participant wants to address the conflict; the other person may be avoiding conflict. The relationship, the conflict history of the participants, and their preferred styles in doing conflict all affect how the conflict escalates and how the other person views the escalation behavior. The type of issue involved often affects the way the conflict is approached and the means used to bring the conflict to resolution. Research indicates that the most successful conflict resolution occurs when conflict participants focus on substantive issues rather than on the people involved (affective conflict).[43] Folger and Poole explained that two extreme and opposite ends of the conflict continuum are avoidance and hostile escalation. Differentiation, according to the authors, is so stressful that sometimes people will simply cling to rigid behaviors that may have served them in the past but do not serve them well in the present.[44]

There are several sources of rigidity in a conflict: personalization of the conflict, in which the conflict is seen as the result of who is involved instead of what is involved; stress of acknowledging opposing stands or hostile or emotional statements; uncertainty about the outcomes of conflict; and the heightened awareness of the consequences of not reaching a conclusion. In established relationships, the decision-making history and established ways of resolving conflict may heighten the problem of escalation, particularly when a conflict is resolved by forced compromise, resulting in clearly identified winners and losers. Early public commitment to inflexible positions may also create destructive differentiation as the middle ground between conflicting parties disappears. All these sources of rigidity may serve to create a competitive escalation cycle, when participants enter the conflict with a win-lose orientation, create threats to the other person's face, and suppress issues rather than resolving them.

When conflicts involve more than two people, formation of coalitions may also be a destructive element in the differentiation phase. Gamson argued that a full-fledged coalition situation is one in which the following conditions are present: There are more than two social units in the conflict, no single solution will maximize the payoff to everyone involved, no single party has sufficient resources to control the decision, and no party has the power to veto solutions singularly. Predicting the composition of coalitions requires knowledge of how resources are initially distributed, what the payoff is for each coalition, and how inclined parties would be to join with each other regardless of their resources. People joining in a coalition will demand from it a share of the payoff proportional to the amount of resources they contribute.[45] Coalitions are frequent when three or more roommates live together, in class projects in which the grade will be shared by all the participants, in organizations in which people depend on one another to get their work done, and so on. Whenever possible, coalition formation should be avoided because it tends to lead to a win-lose, us versus them mentality that makes resolution of the conflict difficult.

As conflict progresses, Thomas argued, a number of different dynamics may occur. The participants may reevaluate their positions in the conflict; rather than giving in, they change their minds about the issue. Self-fulfilling prophecies may guide the conflict as participants react to what they think the other is doing. That is, if one person distrusts the other and expects the other to act in ways that are not mutually beneficial, the first person will interpret behaviors in light of that suspicion and react in accordance to them, thus confirming what the person suspected in the beginning. In addition, biases in perception occur, causing people to see their own behavior as reasonable while viewing the other's as arbitrary. This can result in both participants underestimating their commonalties and missing the other's cooperative overtures or other signs of goodwill in the conflict. Cognitive simplification can also lead to black and white, win or lose thinking and away from the search for mutually satisfactory outcomes.

On the other hand, listening to the other may cause people to reevaluate their own position and revise stereotypes. Conversely, distortion in communication enables both participants to develop and maintain their distorted views of each other and feed their mutual hostility, and as hostility and distrust increase, tactics tend to become more coercive. After competing with the other person to satisfy an initial concern, participants may lose sight of that initial concern and simply compete with the other for the sake of competition. Competition may then spread to other issues. As competitiveness spreads, accompanied by cognitive simplification, one person may perceive that the participants' concerns are incompatible, which may lead to the idea that the relationship cannot be continued. To complete the differentiation stage successfully when this level of hostility and cognitive simplification exist, the participants must ventilate their feelings to each other and state the issues that divide them before they can begin to seek an integrative solution.[46]

Differentiation of the conflict is achieved through the use of strategies—(broad-based plans of engagement) and tactics (specific behaviors used to advance a strategy). Recent research by Alberts and Driscoll focused on the pattern of interaction in conflict episodes that leads to escalation of the conflict to containment. The authors studied 40 married couples, whose responses to a marital satisfaction scale were used to classify them as satisfied, dissatisfied, or mixed (one satisfied partner, one unsatisfied partner). The couples were videotaped as they discussed issues identified on their questionnaire as points of difference between them. Alberts and Driscoll found six patterns couples used to make complaints to the other person. Two in particular were found to escalate the conflict and make an agreement difficult to reach.

In the unresponsiveness pattern, one person makes a complaint, the other person tries to justify the behavior, the justification is denied, and then the discussion is abruptly terminated. This might happen, for example, if Maria tells her husband Raul that she thinks he could have put more effort into painting a door, and he responds that he did the best he could. Maria might say, "Well, it wasn't good enough," and walk away. The conflict never really escalates, but the issue doesn't get resolved either. When partners in conflict are underresponsive to one another, it may lead to the creation of a chilling effect, where one or both of those involved begin to think that conflict is simply not worth the effort required to engage in it.

The escalation pattern is similar to unresponsiveness, except that a countercomplaint is made after denying the justification. Escalation is a series of charges and countercharges, basically a "well, you . . . " kind of pattern, with no real engagement of issues but only a series of complaints. This narrative demonstrates how countercomplaint can rapidly escalate a conflict:

> In our house we have an agreement: All of us do our dishes after using them and clean up our mess after making it. When I came home on Wednesday, there was a mess in the kitchen. I am the roommate who likes to keep things clean, and the rest of the guys do not follow our agreement very consistently. Usually, I do not do conflict over a messy kitchen because I do not think it is worth it. This time it was really messy and I wanted to prepare a meal but there was no room to do so. I talked to the roommate I believed to be responsible for the mess. I made a big mistake—I used a phrase that included one of the vulgar words of conflict: "This kitchen is always a mess!" My roommate took offense and we began to argue about past times when the kitchen was clean and when it was not. We never did resolve the conflict.

Patterns that lead to conflict containment and agreement were labeled:

1. passed (the complaint is ignored and then dropped). For example, a wife ignores her husband's mutterings about something that displeases him, even though she can hear them. She refuses to allow the conflict to emerge.
2. refocused (the complaint is made but then is put onto a third party or an object outside of the relationship). For example, a husband tells his wife that he is really unhappy about her coming home late from work again, and she tells him that she was unable to leave a meeting even though she really wanted to do so.
3. mitigated (the complaint is made but steadily watered down as the couple talks about the issue). For example, a spouse who believes in having dinner together every day might settle for three to four times a week because of the work schedules each spouse must fulfill.
4. responsive (the participants listen to and validate each other during the interactions and respond to the complaint as a legitimate concern).

This narrative demonstrates how agreement can be reached quickly when partners are responsive to complaints:

> Our daughter is not a morning person. My husband is one, but I am usually the one who drags her out of bed for school. The other morning I was having a hard time waking up, and I didn't worry too much about it because my husband was up and I didn't have to be anywhere early. I finally got up just before my daughter had to leave, and my husband remarked "I got Jenny up for you." That really irritated me—when he says that it sounds like taking care of our daughter is a favor he does me instead of an obligation we both have. When I was awake enough, I remarked that it really bothered me when he put things like that. He immediately apologized and said he knew it was wrong the minute it came out. He was just trying to reassure me that I didn't have to worry about getting Jenny to school. I told him I appreciated being reassured but really needed to feel as though we were in this together. He agreed, and we dropped it.

Not surprisingly, the authors found that complaints focused on behaviors (e.g., "I don't like it when you leave your dirty socks on the floor") were more likely to lead to conflict resolution or management than complaints focused on personal characteristics (e.g., "I think you're a slob"). Although the study was limited, it confirms the commonsense idea that conflict management is easier if cross-complaining does not take place and if there is a genuine engagement of the issues.[47]

Throughout the differentiation phase, participants may undergo goal revision as they examine whatever goals they came into the conflict with in light of the other person's response and decide whether it is still fruitful to pursue those goals. The number of issues being dealt with in the conflict may expand or, it is hoped, become more focused. Those in the conflict start to search for solutions, and once solutions are the focus of discussion, the conflict moves into the resolution stage.

The Resolution of Conflict

A successful conflict results in a win-win outcome, but at any point along the way, it can turn into lose-lose or win-lose outcomes. It can also end in one of two orientations: resolution (the participants will never have to deal with the issue again) and management (the issue has been dealt with for now but not really to the satisfaction of all parties involved and will probably have to be addressed again in the future). Resolution is a probable outcome when the conflict can be resolved to the satisfaction of all concerned; management is more likely when only one or neither party can be satisfied.[48]

In **conflict resolution** a decision has been made by the parties to end the disagreement, and they are both satisfied with the outcome. When people are able to bring their conflicts to successful resolution, it reinforces positive thinking about conflict. Each successful conflict we engage in increases the chances that future conflicts will be productive because we learn that conflict isn't dreadful and something to be avoided. Later Part III presents various methods of creating optimum outcomes to conflict management, which, it is hoped, will reduce the frustration that results in future conflict. For now, the important thing to remember is that conflict is a cyclical process: In ongoing relationships, outcomes from one conflict will affect the way conflict is enacted in the future. Although short-term gains may be appealing, the future implications of the mode of conflict resolution must be considered.

From Theory to Action

In this chapter, we described the process of conflict and different ways conflict unfolds as people begin to voice their complaints to one another. Conflicts are not always predictable. They are governed by the rule of equifinality—meaning that one cannot always predict the end state of a conflict by knowing the initial conditions.

The key to effective conflict management is an understanding of both the things that give rise to conflict (what we have termed the *prelude to conflict*) and the things that occur at different stages in the process of conflict. The way we view our relationship with the other person, our past successes and failures in enacting conflict with the other, how we identify an issue, how we assign blame, and how we voice our complaint will affect the pattern of interaction. Somewhere in the maze of options, including avoidance, chilling, and competitive cycles, is potentially productive conflict behavior. Similarly, in each stage of productive conflict, there are opportunities to spin off into the avoidance, chilling, and competitive cycles. As with the destructive cycles, productive conflict behavior stems from attitudes about conflict and from what is assumed to be true.

When we see conflict as something that is a normal part of relationships, when we are willing to hear and be heard, when we are realistic about our expectations for the outcome of the conflict, we are less likely to get locked into destructive conflict cycles. Becoming aware of behavior and ways of thinking about conflict can help us; the more aware we are of behaviors at each stage of a conflict, the more successful we are likely to be in dealing with the conflicts in our lives.

Notes

1. Richard E. Walton, *Managing Conflict: Interpersonal Dialogue and Third-Party Roles,* 2nd Ed. (Reading, MA: Addison Wesley, 1987).

2. Donald Ellis and B. Aubrey Fisher, "Phases of Conflict in Small Group Development," *Human Communication Research* 1 (1975), 195–212.

3. Louis Kriegsberg, *The Sociology of Social Conflicts* (Englewood Cliffs, NJ: Prentice Hall, 1973).

4. R. J. Rummel, *Understanding Conflict and War: The Conflict Helix,* Vol. 2 (Beverly Hills, CA: Sage Publications, 1976); "A Catastrophe Theory Model of the Conflict Helix, with Tests," Behavioral Science 32 (1987), 241–266.

5. Joseph Folger and Marshal Scott Poole, *Working Through Conflict* (Glenview, IL: Scott Foresman, 1984), pp. 21–22.

6. Vernon E. Cronen, W. Barnett Pearce, and Lonna M. Snavely, "A Theory of Rule-Structure and Types of Episodes and a Study of Perceived Enmeshment in Undesired Repetitive Pattern ('URPs')," in Dan Nimmo (Ed.), *Communication Yearbook 3* (New Brunswick, NJ: Transaction Books, 1979), pp. 225–240.

7. Gregory Bateson, *Naven,* 2nd Ed. (Stanford, CA: Stanford University Press, 1958).

8. See, for example, Laura K. Guerrero and Walid A. Afifi, "Some Things Are Better Left Unsaid: Topic Avoidance in Family Relationships," *Communication Quarterly* 43 (1995), 276–296.

9. William W. Wilmot and Joyce L. Hocker, *Interpersonal Conflict,* 5th Ed. (Dubuque: Wm. C. Brown, 1998), pp. 9–11.

10. Rummel, *Understanding Conflict and War,* p. 238.

11. Lorel Scott and Robert Martin, "Value Similarity, Relationship Length, and Conflict Interaction in Dating Relationships: An Initial Investigation," paper presented at the annual meeting of the Speech Communication Association, Chicago, November 1986.

12. Irvin Altman and D. Taylor, *Social Penetration: The Development of Interpersonal Relationships* (Chicago: Holt, Rinehart, & Winston, 1973); Denise H. Cloven and Michael E. Roloff, "Sense-Making Activities and Interpersonal Conflict, II: The Effects of Communicative Intentions on Internal Dialogue," *Western Journal of Communication* 57 (1993), 309–329.

13. Michael E. Roloff and Denise H. Cloven, "The Chilling Effect in Interpersonal Relationships: The Reluctance to Speak One's Mind," in Dudley D. Cahn (Ed.), *Inmates in Conflict: A Communication Perspective*

(Hillside, NJ: Lawrence Erlbaum Associates, 1990), pp. 49–76.

14. Ibid.

15. Morton Deutsch, "Conflicts: Productive or Destructive?" *Journal of Social Issues* 25 (1969), 7–41; Kriegsberg, *The Sociology of Social Conflicts;* Dean G. Pruitt and Jeffrey Z. Rubin, *Social Conflict: Escalation, Stalemate, and Settlement* (New York: Random House, 1986); R. D. Nye, *Conflict Among Humans* (New York: Spring Publishing, 1973).

16. Pruitt and Rubin, 1986, pp. 7–8.

17. Ibid.

18. Ibid. See also R. C. North, R. A. Brody, O. R. Holsti, "Some Empirical Data on the Conflict Spiral," *Peace Research Society (International) Papers 1* (1964), 1–14; Charles Osgood, *An Alternative to War or Surrender* (Urbana: University of Illinois Press, 1962); Charles E. Osgood, *Perspective in Foreign Policy,* 2nd Ed. (Palo Alto, CA: Pacific Books, 1966).

19. Erving Goffman, *The Presentation of Self in Everyday Life* (Garden City, NY: Doubleday Books, 1959); "On Face Work," in Erving Goffman (Ed.), *Interaction Ritual* (New York: Anchor Books, 1967), pp. 5–45.

20. Folger and Poole, *Working Through Conflict,* see especially pp. 153–154.

21. Dale Hample and Judith M. Dallinger, "A Lewinian Perspective on Taking Conflict Personally: Revision, Refinement, and Validation of the Instrument," *Communication Quarterly* 43 (1995), 306.

22. Virginia Satir lists blaming as an unhealthy communication behavior in her book *Peoplemaking* (Palo Alto, CA: Science and Behavior Books, 1972). Other unhealthy responses include placating (so the other does not get mad), acting like a computer (using large words that convey a sense of impartiality), and distracting the other through ignoring the threat and hoping it will go away.

23. Giles Milhaven, *Good Anger* (Kansas City: Sheed and Ward, 1989), p. 5.

24. Paul Watzlawick, J. H. Weakland, and R. Fisch, *Change* (New York: W. W. Norton, 1974).

25. Kenneth W. Thomas, "Conflict and Conflict Management," in M. D. Dunnett (Ed.), *The Handbook of Industrial and Organizational Psychology* (Chicago: Rand McNally, 1976), p. 893.

26. In Greek mythology, Procrustes was an innkeeper with only one bed. If his guest was too short for the bed, he stretched the guest to fit; if the guest was too long, he cut off the guest's legs to fit.

27. Denise Haunani Cloven and Michael E. Roloff, "Cognitive Turning Effects of Anticipating Communication on Thought about an Interpersonal Conflict," *Communication Reports* 8 (1995), 1–9.

28. R. D. Nye, *Conflict Among Humans,* p. 94.

29. Hample and Dallinger, "A Lewinian Perspective."

30. P. Zietlow and A. Sillars, "Life-Stage Differences in Communication During Marital Conflicts," *Journal of Social and Personal Relationships* 5 (1988), 223–245.

31. Raymond W. Mack and Richard C. Snyder, "Cooperators and Competitors in Conflict: A Test of the 'Triangle' Model," *Journal of Conflict Resolution* 22 (1978), 393–410.

32. Scott and Martin, "Value Similarity, Relationship Length, and Conflict Interaction."

33. Calvin Morrill and Cheryl King Thomas, "Organizational Conflict Management as a Disputing Process: The Problem of Social Escalation," *Human Communication Research* 18 (1992), 400–429.

34. Mack and Snyder, "Cooperators and Competitors in Conflict," p. 49.

35. David L. Alloway and Janis F. Andersen, "Individual Differences of the Perceptions of Verbal Aggression," paper presented at the Western Speech Communication Association Convention, San Diego, February 1988.

36. Alan C. Filley, *Interpersonal Conflict Resolution* (New York: HarperCollins, 1975).

37. Deutsch, "Conflicts: Productive or Destructive?" p. 8.

38. Hal Witteman, "Analyzing Interpersonal Conflict: Nature of Awareness, Type of Initiating Event, Situational Perceptions, and Management Styles," *Western Journal of Communication* 56 (1992), p. 264.

39. Thomas, "Conflict and Conflict Management," p. 896.

40. Ibid.

41. Folger and Poole, *Working Through Conflict,* p. 60.

42. Ibid., pp. 57–58.

43. H. Guetzkow and J. Gyr, "An Analysis of Conflict in Decision-Making Groups," *Human Relations* 7 (1954), 367–381.

44. Folger and Poole, *Working Through Conflict,* p. 63.

45. William A. Gamson, "A Theory of Coalition Formation," in Claggett C. Smith (Ed.), *Conflict Resolution: Contributions of the Behavioral Sciences* (Notre Dame, IN: University of Notre Dame Press, 1971), pp. 146–156.

46. Thomas, "Conflict and Conflict Management," pp. 905–907.

47. Jess K. Alberts and Gillian Driscoll, "Containment vs. Escalation: The Trajectory of Couples' Conversational Complaints," *Western Journal of Communication* 56 (1992), 394–412.

48. Thomas, "Conflict and Conflict Management," p. 895.

6

Conflict Styles, Strategies, and Tactics

Objectives

At the end of this chapter, you should be able to

1. identify five communication styles used in conflict situations and their two underlying factors that have been investigated by communication researchers.

2. explain how personality measures and rhetorical sensitivity relate to the five communication styles.

3. explain the outcomes researchers have linked to the three conflict strategies used in conflict situations that have been investigated by communication researchers.

4. describe the sequence of cognitive strategies that partners progress through as dissatisfaction in a relationship grows.

5. explain the advantages and phases of collaboration.

Key Terms

accommodation	conflict style	relationship stress
avoidance	distributive strategy	strategy
avoidance strategy	exit	styles theory
behaviors	integrative strategy	tactic
collaboration	loyalty	voice
competition	neglect	
compromise	personal stress	

In this chapter, we focus on the behaviors that people may use in order to bring a conflict to some kind of resolution. This discussion is based largely on what is termed *styles theory*. **Styles theory** suggests that people have preferred means of dealing with conflict situations and will generally use those preferred means whenever possible. This theory has intuitive appeal, as it provides a means for people to easily assess their own behavior and to see a connection between theory and action.

Have you done something you didn't want to do or intend to do? We probably all have at least once in our lives. On the other hand, have you done things you wanted or intended to do? Of course, we all have. There are times we make plans and carry them out. When we don't enact the plan, it is because we forget, change our minds, are convinced that we should not carry it out, or simply are not allowed to by someone. The same is true for conflict in which strategies and stylistic preferences often play a role. People tend to respond to conflict situations based on their **conflict style,** or their preferred mode of dealing with conflicts. When people deal with conflicts, they employ both strategies and tactics. A **strategy** is an overall plan for dealing with conflicts generally.[1] In contrast, a **tactic** is a specific observable action that moves a conflict in a particular direction in line with the strategy.

In this chapter, we will be discussing styles, strategies, and tactics of conflict. One way to conceptualize these three terms is to think of *strategies* and *tactics* as the general ways in which people behave within conflict situations, whereas *conflict style* is a general way of thinking about conflict and getting ready to act within the situation. We begin our discussion with an examination of conflict styles, which, as rhetorical sensitivity and communicator style, reflect the way people think about conflict and begin to select strategies and tactics for conflict engagement.

Conflict Styles, Strategies, and Tactics

As we stated previously, a conflict style is a preferred approach to handling conflict situations. Just as tactics may conform to a strategy, **behaviors** are manifestations of one's style. Table 6.1 lists conflict styles originally identified by Blake and Mouton and relabled by Kilmann and Thomas and Rahim.[2]

Although a style may be dominant in a person's actions for a while, it may be abandoned and replaced by another. An assumption underlying styles theory is that individuals maintain a particular conflict style throughout a conflict situation, but actual research shows that individuals may switch from one style to another as a conflict progresses.[3]

Originally, the five styles were identified on the basis of how much concern a person had for the relationship with the other person and for attaining his or her personal goal. One can have little concern for either of these things, or a high concern for both of them,

TABLE 6.1   *Five Common Conflict Styles*

Blake and Mouton	*Kilmann and Thomas*	*Rahim*
Avoiding	Avoiding	Avoiding
Smoothing	Accommodating	Obliging
Forcing	Competing	Dominating
Compromising	Compromising	Compromising
Confronting	Collaborating	Integrating

or some other combination in between. Rahim later labeled these two basic dimensions underlying the five styles as concern for self (or one's personal goal) and concern for others (or the relationship).[4] As shown in Table 6.2, the five styles differ in the way they maximize or minimize one's own or the other's outcomes (winning versus losing).

Avoidance is a preference for not addressing a conflict at all. People who avoid conflict may understand intuitively that confronting others might bring about better results, but they are not sufficiently concerned about getting those results to risk doing the conflict. In addition, they do not care enough about their relationship with the other to use conflict to improve or clarify it. People who favor the avoidance style may use procedures and routines to circumvent conflict situations by insisting that the rules be followed. By referring to rules or procedures, people can remove themselves from personal involvement in the situation (e.g., "I'm just doing my job—this is what is supposed to happen"). Behaviors indicative of this style include choosing to withdraw, being physically absent, avoiding issues, or remaining silent.

Accommodation is a preference for smoothing over conflicts, obliging others, and not making waves because one has a high concern for others and a low concern for results. Those using this approach prefer to maintain the illusion of harmony. As a result, conflict issues are often suppressed or postponed because those choosing this style do not want to risk ill feelings by clarifying and resolving problems. A style of acquiescence, one gives up personal gains for the benefit of one's partner. An "accommodator" is one so concerned about the relationship and the other person that he or she suppresses personal needs, interests, and goals, and, thus, does not "make waves." Although the "accommodator's" partner may derive considerable personal growth and satisfaction, actually the two are pursuing divergent paths because the "accommodator" is not deriving the same benefits from the relationship.

Competition is a preference for dominating and forcing one's decision on others. Those who use a competitive style are not necessarily uncaring about others, but they value their self-interests or getting the job done more than they value how other people feel about the situation. In situations of crisis, a competitive style can be useful, but over the long term, those who are subjected to it are likely to feel disenfranchised from decision making. Because the objective is "win-lose" in favor of oneself, one gains at the other's expense (zero-sum game). As defined here, those who choose the style of competition appear to others as argumentative, selfish, and confrontational. They beg and borrow excessively from their friends, steal from and cheat their colleagues and neighbors, and use coercive communication.

TABLE 6.2 *Five Conflict Styles, Their Definitions, Objectives, and Behaviors*

Conflict Style	Definition	Objective	Behavior
Avoidance	withdrawal	lose-lose	physically absent or silent
Accommodation	acquiescence	lose-win	give in; don't make waves
Competition	aggression	win-lose	selfish, argumentative
Compromise	trade-offs	win and lose	wheeler-dealer
Collaboration	mutual satisfaction	win-win	supportive of self and other

A middle-of-the-road approach is **compromise,** which is a preference for making sure that no one totally wins or loses. People who prefer compromise as a conflict style are interested in finding workable rather than optimal solutions. Compromise can contribute positively to the outcomes in a conflict situation, especially in situations in which all parties cannot get exactly what they want. However, compromise can also contribute negatively to the outcomes if all parties exchange offers and make concessions but walk away from the conflict unsatisfied and feeling that little was accomplished. As a style favoring trade-offs involving "give and take," it is designed to be a realistic attempt to seek an acceptable (but not necessarily preferred) solution of gains and losses for everyone involved. This style is not ideal because, regardless of the initial objective, in the end neither party may win using it—both lose at least some of what they had hoped to achieve.

Collaboration is a preference for solving problems and developing mutually satisfying agreements. Under this approach, "disagreement is valued as an inevitable result of the fact that strong-minded people have convictions about what is right."[5] Collaboration is a style of win-win in which one's attempts to satisfy personal concerns and the other's concerns and one's motivation regarding trust of others are also maximized. The collaborator has self-interests but respects the other's interests, needs, and goals. Although it may involve confronting differences, collaboration requires a problem-solving attitude and includes sharing information about everyone's needs, goals, and interests.

In class, Lee asked the students to fill out a conflict strategy questionnaire.[6] Although he found that some students ended up preferring each of the five strategies as predicted by styles theory, most selected either avoidance or compromise. When he grouped together students who preferred the same strategy and assigned them conflict scenarios to discuss and resolve, each group produced suggestions in line with their preferred strategy. Avoiders said "they would wait and not say anything, because most problems take care of themselves." Accommodators said they would try to please the other, stay out of the limelight, and try to facilitate the relationship. Competitors said they would dominate the other and do most of the talking. (One even said he would get physical if necessary to get his way.) Compromisers said they wanted to be fair and treat everyone equally. Finally, Collaborators said they would first listen to all sides and strive for a mutual understanding. The teacher was impressed with how the students created solutions in line with their strategy.

Research on styles of conflict has found that they are related to rhetorical sensitivity. Figure 6.1 illustrates the overlap of the two concepts. The high concern for both self and the other, coupled with high flexibility, would put a person classified as Ambivalent into the collaboration style. The Noble Self's high concern for self and moderate concern for the other, coupled with rigidity, would probably fit the competing or compromising styles better than the others. And the Rhetorical Reflector's focus on the other, with little focus on self, is most reflective of the accommodating and avoidance styles. These three general attitudes suggest that the person chooses a conflict style without regard to the uniqueness of a conflict situation. The Rhetorical Sensitive, on the other hand, who has high concern for self and moderately low concern for the other, coupled with flexibility, would select different conflict styles depending on the conflict situation. One study, which tested relationships between a number of variables, among them rhetorical sensitivity and conflict styles when in conflicts, found that, in general, people with high Noble Self scores preferred a compromise style, whereas people with high Rhetorical Reflector scores preferred avoidance. However, the effect of rhetorical sensitivity was confounded by sex differences, and finding a clear pattern was, therefore, difficult.[7] It would seem, though, that

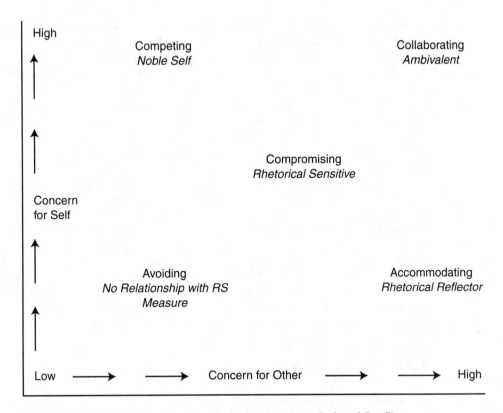

FIGURE 6.1 *The Relationship of Rhetorical Sensitivity to Styles of Conflict*

this study lends credence to the associations between rhetorical sensitivity and conflict style made here.

As Lee discovered in his class, researchers have found that different people seem to prefer different strategies.[8] Meanwhile, individuals have been found to be quite consistent in their conflict styles across different types of conflict situations, and the style could be predicted quite well from knowledge of certain intellectual and personality characteristics.[9] It is the case that a person might succeed at work with one communication style that would fail at home.

> My husband, Peter, is a doctor who works in a hospital emergency room. He is used to making the decisions and giving orders. When he gets impatient, he turns red and yells at the nurses and orderlies. So much of what goes on there is life and death where seconds really matter. The problem is that he can't leave his "dominant personality" at work when he comes home. He'll snap at me and the kids and even yells at us when he loses his patience. I tell him that we are not an emergency medical unit, just a family. He didn't always act like this, but years at the hospital have turned him into a tyrant.

Personality variables have been linked to the conflict styles of collaboration, accommodation, and competition. The extent of a person's motivation to achieve things has been positively linked to collaboration, and aggression has been linked to competition.[10]

Likewise, accommodation was linked to positive personality tendencies such as the need for affiliation, succorance, and nurturing but not to Machiavellianism (a tendency to be manipulative in order to achieve one's goals). Somewhat unexpectedly, collaboration was linked to dogmatism (the tendency to be rigid in one's beliefs) and to Machiavellianism.[11]

It should be noted, however, that although personality measures continued to correlate with the conflict style, little association was found between preference for particular styles and actual observed conflict behavior.[12] When people are asked to choose styles from a list, they tend to indicate the use of different styles than when they are asked to write out the way they would do the conflict. This is because people are generally able to recognize what might be good to use in a conflict when the list is in front of them, but when actually faced with a conflict, apprehension tends to constrain their range of choices.[13] In addition, Conrad found only a moderate relationship between a person's reported style preference and his or her actual behavior. Regardless of their reported conflict style, supervisors reported the use of collaborative-type strategies more often than any other approach, but their behavior showed a consistent preference for the use of coercive tactics with noncompliant subordinates. Collaborative strategies are seen as socially desirable and are, therefore, reflected in what people say they do. When compliance is vital, however, most people use stronger tactics.[14] Overall, the evidence on conflict style indicates that people have a preferred method of doing conflict, which they may or may not be able to use in actual conflict situations, and people's preferred style affects the way they perceive the other in the conflict situation.

Conflict Strategies and Tactics

Collaboration, Competition, and Avoidance

Although a number of different conflict strategies have been investigated by communication researchers,[15] three—collaborative/integrative, competitive/distributive, and avoidance—have received the most attention, each associated with a number of conflict tactics.[16]

For example, if your roommate is playing the stereo too loudly while you have to study for a test, you may choose the competitive/distributive strategy and enact that strategy by choosing the tactics of shouting, demanding, and threatening your roommate. In addition, you may choose one strategy initially but change to another later. The three basic conflict strategies and their associated tactics are listed in Table 6.3.

How do people determine which style they will use? Pruitt and Rubin argued that making a choice among the various strategies is "a matter of perceived feasibility—the extent to which the strategy seems capable of achieving the concerns that give rise to it and the cost that is anticipated from enacting each strategy."[17] They argued that

- a collaborative/**integrative strategy** is more feasible if the person making the conflict choice perceives a common ground between the parties and, therefore, believes there is a likelihood of finding an alternative that suits both people. Faith in one's own ability to solve problems, success in using problem solving, and a perception that the other is ready to focus on solving the problem also contribute to choice of a collaborative style.
- a competitive/**distributive strategy** is more likely if the other shows some resistance to the situation or "if the other's aspirations (however high they may be) seem relatively easy to dislodge."[18]

TABLE 6.3 *Strategies and Tactics Most Frequently Identified for Conflict Situations*

Conflict Strategy	Conflict Tactics
Collaborative/integrative strategy	Involves a cooperative mutual orientation, seeking areas of agreement, expressing trust, seeking mutually beneficial solutions, showing concern
Competitive/distributive strategy	Involves competing, insulting, threatening, using sarcasm, shouting, demanding
Avoidance strategy	Involves minimizing discussion, avoiding issues, shying away from a topic

The most important factor in the choice of competition appears to be the perceived cost associated with its use.

We would add that the **avoidance strategy** is preferred:

- when the problems of confronting the issue outweigh the problems of avoidance,
- when it is simply not worth the effort to engage the other in conflict,
- when postponement to another time would be more advantageous,
- when one's communication skills are not equal to the task of confronting the other person, or
- when there will be sufficient time to deal with a problem later when conditions are more conducive.

Clearly, most people in long-term relationships would prefer to resolve their conflicts rather than provoke their partners into more destructive behavior. Competitive behaviors focus on one's own interests without regard to those of the other person (see Table 6.4). They reflect a win-lose orientation, a belief that allowing the other person to gain something will come only at one's own expense.

Competitive behaviors tend to place blame on the other person and focus on the people involved in the conflict rather than on the issues. Labeling the other person's behavior ("that's childish" or "that's irresponsible"), threatening the other, expanding the issue, forming coalitions within groups, and breaking relational rules (e.g., bring up past problems that the parties agreed not to talk about anymore) all are instances of competitive escalation behaviors. Denying responsibility, hostile jokes, hostile questions, and presumptions (e.g., "You're really angry about something else, not this") also serve to escalate a conflict competitively. As mentioned before, use of these strategies is more likely in tense situations, but their use can exacerbate the problems already present. In addition, use of competitive behaviors can escalate a conflict situation from verbal exchanges into physical violence. (More will be said on the relationship of conflict to violence in later chapters.)

Collaborative or integrative behaviors are designed to resolve conflict (see Table 6.5). They are analytic, conciliatory, and problem solving in focus. They attempt to clarify the issues and facilitate mutual resolution of the problem. Analytic behaviors describe behavior, disclose feelings, ask for disclosure from the other person, ask for criticism from the other person, and qualify the nature of the problem (e.g., "The only time your music bothers me is when I am trying to study" versus "I can't stand your music at all").

TABLE 6.4 *Tactics Used to Enact a Strategy of Competition*

Faulting	Statements that directly criticize the characteristics of the partner
Rejection	Statements in response to the partner's previous statement that indicate personal antagonism toward the partner as well as disagreement
Hostile questioning	Directive or leading questions that fault the partner
Hostile joking	Joking or teasing that faults the partner
Presumptive attribution	Statements that attribute thoughts, feelings, intentions, or motivations to the partner that the partner does not acknowledge
Avoiding responsibility	Statements that minimize or deny personal responsibility for conflict
Prescription	Requests, demands, arguments, threats, or other prescriptive statements that seek a specified change in the partner's behavior in order to resolve a conflict

Source: Alan L. Sillars, Stephen F. Coletti, Doug Parry, and Mark A. Rogers, "Coding Verbal Tactics: Nonverbal and Perceptual Correlates of the 'Avoidance-Distributive-Integrative' Distinction," *Human Communication Research* 9 (1982), pp. 83–95, copyright © 1982 by Sage Publications, Inc. Reprinted by permission of Sage Publications, Inc.

Conciliatory behaviors support the disclosures or observations the other person has made (e.g., "I didn't know you felt so strongly about that") and accept responsibility for one's part in the conflict.

The strategies and tactics that people use in resolving their conflicts are associated with perceptions of competence. The conflict strategies have a well-demonstrated relationship with people's perceptions.[19] When perceptions are compared across partners, individuals generally see their conflict behavior as more effective and more appropriate than their partners do. Both people in the conflict recall the distributive strategy with the greatest agreement and demonstrate the least agreement in recalling the integrative strategy (for example, "I thought I was trying to be integrative; you don't think so"). Canary and Spitzberg found that the integrative communication strategy was positively related to scores on a perceived communication competence questionnaire, whereas the distributive and avoidance conflict strategies were negatively associated with communication competence.[20] Researchers have linked the competent use of strategies to relational outcomes like communication satisfaction and interpersonal attraction.

The use of conflict strategies is defined as competent when those using the strategies have been able to maintain impressions of appropriateness and effectiveness; that is, they acted in accordance with social expectations and achieved their goals. Researchers have also identified tactics for each communication strategy usage that are associated with marital unhappiness, as well as with labor-management dyads who are at an impasse. In both instances, there is heavy reliance on a distributive strategy enacted by a repeating pattern of attack-attack or defend-defend tactics.[21] "Distressed marital couples match their opponent's distributive tactic by engaging in one-upmanship behaviors; that is, they lock into negative affect cycles."[22] These behaviors indicate that incompetent conflict actors may choose a distributive strategy and use destructive tactics. Thus, what distinguishes compe-

TABLE 6.5 *Tactics Used to Enact a Strategy of Collaboration*

Description	Nonevaluative statements about observable events related to conflict
Qualification	Statements that explicitly qualify the nature and extent of conflict
Disclosure	Nonevaluative statements about events related to conflict that the partner cannot observe, such as thoughts, feelings, intentions, motivations, and past history
Soliciting disclosure	Soliciting information from the partner about events related to the conflict that one cannot observe
Negative inquiry	Soliciting complaints about oneself
Empathy or support	Statements that express understanding, acceptance, or positive regard for the partner (despite acknowledgment of a conflict)
Emphasizing commonalties	Statements that comment on shared interests, goals, or compatibilities with the partner (despite acknowledgment of a conflict)
Accepting responsibility	Statements that attribute responsibility for conflicts to self or to both parties
Initiating problem solving	Statements that initiate mutual consideration of solutions to conflict

Source: Alan L. Sillars, Stephen F. Coletti, Doug Parry, and Mark A. Rogers, "Coding Verbal Tactics: Nonverbal and Perceptual Correlates of the 'Avoidance-Distributive-Integrative' Distinction," *Human Communication Research* 9 (1982), pp. 83–95, copyright © 1982 by Sage Publications, Inc. Reprinted by permission of Sage Publications, Inc.

tent from incompetent conflict participants is their reliance on integrative conflict strategies and tactics rather than distributive and avoidance conflict strategies.

APPLICATION 6.1

Which of the three strategies (integrative, distributive, or avoidant) are you most likely to use first? What difference does the relationship in which the conflict is occurring make on your choice of strategy?

Other Strategies and Tactics

Social scientists have examined people's cognitive strategies in conflict situations and found that the three strategies of collaboration, competition, and avoidance are not the only options available to relational partners. A comprehensive research program on strategies in conflict situations undertaken by Rusbult and her colleagues has identified four options (see Table 6.6).[23]

These strategies vary in destructiveness.[24] **Exit** (leaving the relationship) and **neglect** (ignoring the problem and its effect on the relationship) are destructive, whereas **voice** (saying something about the problem) and **loyalty** (diminishing the problem's importance in

TABLE 6.6   *Strategies and Tactics Used by Relational Partners*

Strategy	Tactics
Exit	Divorce, breakup, a separation
Voice	Attempts to change the relationship, discuss problems, compromise, work things out, and engage in problem solving
Loyalty	Accepting of minor problems, highly committed to maintaining the relationship, and assuming that conditions will improve
Neglect	Ignore the partner, show that you don't care about the relationship, and allow conditions to worsen

light of the various good things in the relationship) are considered to be more constructive. Rusbult and her colleagues found that women were more likely than men to choose strategies of voice and loyalty and less likely than men to choose neglect as a strategy. Where partners are committed to their relationship (i.e., the rewards outweigh the costs), partners prefer loyalty or voice as alternative cognitive strategies in conflict situations. The greater the commitment to a relationship, the more likely they will choose voice rather than loyalty as a strategy. However, where partners are not committed to remain in the relationship, partners prefer neglect or exit from the relationship as alternative cognitive strategies in conflict situations. The less the commitment, the more likely they will choose exit rather than neglect as a strategy. This narrative shows a progression from neglect to voice to exit.

> I finally confronted my former best friend about trying to steal my boyfriend from me. Because it took me four months to confront this conflict, I was hoping for a resolution, but not expecting one. Pam and I started growing apart a year ago as we became different people with different views. At first I wanted to blame Pam for the conflict, but I realized that I was to blame because I waited to confront her, I ignored her when she confronted me, and because I purposely distanced myself from her. In a letter, I told her that I forgave her and realized most of what happened was my fault. Pam wrote back and basically attacked me for everything I have done wrong since I met her. She also critiqued my letter! I am so frustrated because I tried to be the good person by carefully handling the conflict and forgiving Pam, and all I got in return was bitterness. We just can't be friends any longer.

Building on Rusbult's typology of conflict strategies in conflict situations, Healey and Bell argue that partners may cognitively progress through different strategies as dissatisfaction in a relationship grows.[25] At first, they might prefer loyalty as a strategy, hoping that things will get better soon. They may turn to the strategy of voice when the situation does not improve, then decide on neglect, and eventually choose exit as the preferred strategy. It might be argued that newly formed romantic couples would prefer loyalty because they fear losing their partner who is not yet fully committed to the relationship. However, after commitment takes place such as engagement or marriage, they prefer the strategy of voice, but if conditions worsen, then they change mentally to neglect. Finally, when superior alternatives appear, they prefer exit as a strategy.

More recently, Fritz has examined which of the four strategies people are likely to use when faced with unpleasant work relationships.[26] Her results indicated that the choice of strategy depended on one's position in the organization as well as perceptions of the problem. People were most likely to use exit when the problem was with superiors or peers; voice and loyalty were more likely responses with subordinates. Neglect was likely to be chosen when a person did not believe the problem could be solved and had little desire to try. Loyalty was associated with a desire for the problem to be solved, but the strategy of voice required that a person had a desire to solve the problem, a belief that it could be solved, a belief that the other wanted to solve the problem, and a belief that the problem inconvenienced the other person involved. It would seem that, at least in organizations, people do not want to engage in conflict without a reasonable chance of having something change as a result.

APPLICATION 6.2

When you have been faced with a conflict, which of the strategies discussed previously have you used? What differences exist among relationships in which you have used voice, loyalty, neglect, and exit?

Collaboration: The Preferred Style

In theory, Blake and Mouton favored the collaboration style in conflict situations. As a general rule, we also advocate a collaboration style because it contributes less toward long-term personal and relationship stress and most toward personal and relationship growth and satisfaction. Although a person can adopt a collaborative *strategy* for a particular conflict, changing one's *style* to collaboration will require a change of attitudes toward conflict. It requires that a person believe that the concerns of the other person are as important as one's own. Adopting a collaborative style generally results in less stress in conflict situations.

Low Personal and Relationship Stress

In general, stress is defined as "the tension generated from an event which is unmanaged at that point in time."[27] Stress may be either personal or relationship in nature or a combination of both. The five behavioral orientations may be arrayed along both types of stress, each ranging from low (0) to high (10) as illustrated in Figure 6.2.

Personal stress occurs within a person and refers to wear and tear on one emotionally and physically. Although a little stress may be positive and pleasurable as when one experiences an uplifting associated with falling in love, seeing a great performance, or watching an exciting athletic event, other stressors such as strong feelings of anxiety, frustration, and anger, which are associated with life crises such as a death of a family member, a divorce, a marriage, a new job, or a change in one's location, may contribute to ulcers, heart disease, hypertension, migraine headaches, and even suicide. Loneliness is also stress producing. Psychologists have long argued that stress improves performance, but only up to a point at which efficiency drops off sharply.

Relationship stress occurs outside the individual and refers to wear and tear on a relationship. Whereas personal stress goes on within the individual, relationship stress goes on between two or more persons. In opposite-sex, long-term relationships, "new social roles of the sexes" is frequently mentioned as a relationship stress producer. Because of

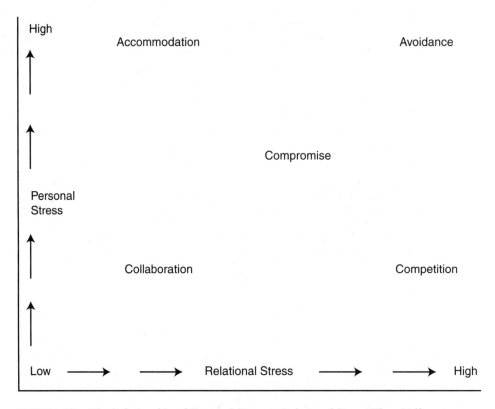

FIGURE 6.2   *The Relationship of Personal Stress to Relational Stress When Different Conflict Styles Are Used*

the omnipresence of interpersonal conflict, a little relationship stress is normal and unavoidable, but in the extreme, relationship stress results in relationship dissatisfaction and deterioration, which eventually may result in social disengagement such as breaking up, getting a divorce, or losing a job.

As displayed in Table 6.7, the five alternative communication/conflict styles vary in the degree and/or nature of type of stress underlying them. Again, collaboration is the most advantageous alternative because it alone reduces one's emotional and physical stress as well as the stress on the relationship.

High Personal and Relationship Growth and Satisfaction

As depicted in Table 6.8, a comparison of the five styles reveals that, if enacted, they differ in their contributions to personal and relationship growth and satisfaction. By failing to include one's self-interests, both avoidance and accommodation create conditions characterized by low feelings of self-worth and relationship satisfaction, and no opportunities for personal or relationship growth. By considering one's self-interests (but at the expense of

TABLE 6.7 *Degrees of Stress Underlying Five Conflict Styles*

Conflict Style	Degrees of Stress
Avoidance	High personal stress/high relationship stress
Accommodation	High personal stress/low relationship stress
Competition	Low personal stress/high relationship stress
Compromise	Moderate levels of both types of stress
Collaboration	Low personal stress/low relationship stress

Reprinted from *Letting Go,* by Dudley D. Cahn, by permission of the State University of New York Press. © 1987, State University of New York. All rights reserved.

others, too), competition creates conditions one may describe as high in personal growth, feelings of self-worth, and relationship satisfaction for the competitor but low in personal and relationship growth for the other person. Thus, it may happen that accommodators and competitors are attracted to each other initially, but find that the stress and strain on the relationship as they grow apart often lead to relationship dissatisfaction for the accommodator and eventual disengagement. By gaining some and losing some of one's interests, needs, and goals, compromise as a style contributes to moderate feelings of self-worth and relationship satisfaction, and moderate personal and relationship growth. Finally, by allowing for self-interests, encouraging effective listening, and promoting an integrative approach to problem solving, collaboration, if enacted, is the only style that contributes to high feelings of self-worth and relationship satisfaction for both partners and maximum personal and relationship growth.

    Derr offers support for the collaborative style when he argues that it promotes authentic interpersonal relations, is used as a creative force for innovation and improvement, enhances feedback and information flow, and increases feelings of integrity and trust.[28]

TABLE 6.8 *Conflict Styles and Effect on Relationship and Personal Growth*

Conflict Style	Personal/Relationship Growth
Avoidance	Low feelings of self-worth and relationship satisfaction; no personal/relationship growth
Accommodation	Low feelings of self-worth and relationship satisfaction; no personal growth; partners grow apart (high growth only for partner)
Competition	High feelings of self-worth and relationship satisfaction; high personal growth for self; partners grow apart (no growth for partner)
Compromise	Moderate feelings of self-worth and relationship satisfaction; moderate personal/relationship growth
Collaboration	High feelings of self-worth and relationship satisfaction; maximum personal/relationship growth

Reprinted from *Letting Go,* by Dudley D. Cahn, by permission of the State University of New York Press. © 1987, State University of New York. All rights reserved.

When successfully utilized as a mode for resolving interpersonal conflict aimed at developing an integrated consensus through argumentation and perspective taking, collaboration not only ends conflict but modifies the perspective of the individuals involved to a consensus framework that respects individual differences.

Meanwhile, Blake and Mouton argue that an improved quality of life and more efficient interpersonal relations result when the collaboration style of communication is used in conflict situations. Evidence exists that their judgment is shared. One study found that across types of relationships and issues of conflict, respondents approve of collaboration strategies for conflict resolution over the other orientations.[29] Without training in conflict resolution, many people see the concern for the other and concern for one's own goals as competing and believe that being self-oriented and getting things done while at the same time demonstrating concern for others is difficult to do if not impossible.

Collaboration is necessary for genuine and mutual understanding. With training people can adopt a style of collaboration and find ways to develop mutually satisfying solutions to conflicts.

Phases of Collaboration

Given our emphasis on the desirability of collaboration, this section will demonstrate how one might accomplish a collaborative process. We use an extended example to illustrate it.

Clarification of Perspectives.   First, communicators need to clarify their points of view for the understanding of others. Collaboration calls for understanding the other as well as one's own position and respecting one another. It also calls upon one to be aware of his or her own needs for confirmation and to be alert to the other's use of unfair tactics against one.

To illustrate the first and the following phases of collaboration, the following extended example is offered. Suppose Oganna and Adrian were married soon after graduation four years ago and each has been employed since that time. Suppose further that Oganna and Adrian do not resort to unfair communication techniques to cloud differences of opinion that exist between them. In the first phase of collaboration, interpersonal communication between Oganna and Adrian reveals that Oganna wants to take a year off from work and use a $20,000 inheritance (left to both of them) for a year of schooling, whereas Adrian is against her taking a year off from work and favors banking the inheritance instead. Both indicate that these differences of opinion must be resolved because they are creating a strain on their marriage.

Rigid Goals but Flexible Means.   Collaborators are rigid in terms of goals but are flexible with respect to the means for achieving them. They are committed to a particular outcome but are able to devise alternative ways to resolve their differences. Thus, they accept only high personal gains for themselves and their partners and tend to pursue many alternative paths in an effort to achieve a mutually satisfying outcome.

In the extended example just introduced, Oganna states that she wants to take a year off from work to attend a local university to acquire a Master's degree in business administration, which she says will advance her career in the long run. Adrian, who is very satisfied with his job, is adamantly opposed to her taking a leave of absence because after four years of their paying off debts for an automobile and furniture for their apartment, he would like to put the money in a bank to earn interest. Adrian and Oganna say that a completely satisfactory understanding must not break up their marriage, but at the same time not result in one or the other having to give up one's ambitions, needs, and goals. Moreover, it must enable Oganna to advance in her career; yet it must provide greater financial security for Adrian. Thus, whereas Adrian and Oganna appear to be rigid with respect to goals, they report that they are willing to entertain a wide variety of means for attaining them.

Developing Mutual Understanding. To resolve differences in opinion or points of view in a manner that is mutually advantageous to everyone involved usually requires first that partners increase their range of perspectives, solutions, or alternatives. After identifying the differences in interests, goals, and needs of the partners, each person must try to think of their positions as end points on a continuum with many intermediate views. For example, Oganna could earn her degree on a full-time basis, on a part-time status, or not return to college at all and do something else instead. Adrian, meanwhile, could bank all $20,000, or $10,000, or $5,000, or none at all. At this point, however, a premature understanding that consisted solely of Oganna agreeing to return to school on a part-time basis and Adrian banking $10,000 would result in a compromise with both people getting less than they desired.

In addition to increasing the range of perspectives, the partners would benefit by trying to discover new perspectives, solutions, or alternatives that are related to the matter at hand, such as time, money, interests, security, and status or other factors that were not considered at first. Perhaps, in the case of Oganna and Adrian, a time dimension could be introduced in at least two ways. Oganna could attempt to complete the degree in one year or spread it out over two years or more. Adrian could invest the entire inheritance for an indefinite period or invest some of it now and some of it later. Moreover, because Oganna expressed a desire to get away from it all, she could consider getting away from some aspect of her work that is especially bothersome to her. Perhaps a vacation or a change in her job situation such as a different task, new coworkers, or a different department (or even a new job) would satisfy her need for a change.

Another technique for generating mutual understanding involves reordering the partners' views on the matter at hand, or helping the other person to see that the problem might be defined differently than his or her first impression of it. Such a shift creates an entirely new perspective. Realizing that there are other possible solutions to the problem, each person must take a new look at the matter. For example, in Oganna and Adrian's case, each one's interest in preserving the relationship deserves mention. Presumably, Oganna is interested in working most of the time, which contributes financially to the marriage. In fact, she states that obtaining a Master's degree may make her more valuable to her employer and better guarantee her tenure and advancement in the long run. Adrian's concern about savings reflects his interest also in long-term financial security for the couple. They need to realize that neither Oganna's desire for time off nor Adrian's desire for financial security may be achieved in the event of a marital breakdown, especially if it means divorce. The threat of severe financial loss at this time, which neither party wants, may motivate the couple to see the value of the newly discovered alternatives to the problem, to realize that there may be a way to reach mutual understanding, and to make an even greater effort to achieve it.

Using the acceptable elements of the possible alternative opinions, points of view, and solutions, the partners work together to find a choice that meets the needs of everyone involved. In the case of Oganna and Adrian, an example of an understanding that is mutually advantageous might be as follows. As soon as possible, they could take a three-week camping trip that they both want. Oganna could return to her job after the vacation and enroll part-time at the university for one year, after which she could request a leave of absence to attend to her studies full-time, and after that any remaining credits could be obtained on a part-time basis. In the meantime, most of the inheritance could be banked to draw interest for one year, after which half could be spent on Oganna's education and the remainder could stay in the bank indefinitely. This solution has the potential of completely satisfying both Oganna and Adrian because while on a vacation with Adrian, Oganna is "getting away for a while," upon return she commences work on her degree and looks forward to a semester of full-time graduate student status next year, while Adrian gets to bank most of the money for one year and half after that. Although other agreements are possible, this is an example of an understanding that both parties may find mutually satisfying and may enhance their interpersonal relationship.

Implementation of a Mutual Understanding.   Whereas the discovery of a mutual understanding is often a challenging task, all the time and effort spent on its pursuit are wasted if appropriate measures are not taken to put the solution into effect. As a result of the preceding phases in the collaboration process, Oganna and Adrian have a greater understanding of each other's needs, desires, and beliefs. Each may feel that his or her position has a valuable contribution to make to their relationship in the long run, and that each one's ideas are to be taken into account in any decision the couple reaches. They may take pride in the fact that they asserted themselves and participated in the process of reaching a mutual understanding. The partners may need to reinforce these attitudes during the next few months to guarantee the successful implementation of the mutual understanding.

Case Studies of Cultural Differences in Conflict Resolution Styles

The description of alternative conflict resolution styles suggests that all exist in a particular culture. In fact, one style tends to dominate in some cultures whereas other styles dominate in others. In this section, we will use case studies that describe the dominant styles that exist in three diverse cultures: Japan, the United States, and the former Yugoslavia. These cultures have been chosen for analysis because each one views interpersonal conflict quite differently from the others and acts differently according to those views. These three views represent extremes: accommodation, competition, and compromise. In the section following this one, we will argue that all three cultures could benefit by relying more on collaboration.

Case Study 6.1 ■ *Interpersonal Conflict Resolution in Japan* ————————————

The dominant conflict resolution style in Japan is accommodation. Although there are many features characteristic of the Japanese cultural perspective, this section deals with the Japanese values associated with group harmony. For many Japanese, accomplishments are viewed in terms of a group effort involving a dependence on others. Japanese are expected to be aware of others, their social status, and contribution to group harmony. One should not stand out as individuals, manifest selfish delusions of independent grandeur, or separate themselves from the group. This perspective governs and defines recurring social activities, events, and situations in Japan.

The manner in which many Japanese resolve interpersonal conflicts is a recurring social activity found in business, government, education, and the family. Due to their particular cultural perspective, the Japanese have a culture-specific perception of the resolution of interpersonal conflict. In Japan, the national values of harmony, collective achievement, and maintenance of public face lead many Japanese to define interpersonal conflict resolution as accommodation. The interpersonal conflict situation is viewed as one in which Japanese tend to sacrifice individual needs, goals, and interests for the good of the relationship, family, organization, or culture as a whole. Because the resolution of a conflict frequently requires sacrificing one's own self-interests for those of others, Japanese seek to avoid conflicts or withdraw when confronted.

Because Japanese tend to perceive that interpersonal conflict threatens harmonious interpersonal relations, they include in their communication system specific codes or communication behaviors for avoiding confrontation, which are *nemawashi* and the use of go-betweens.

Nemawashi is a method for involving all relevant parties in the decision. *Nemawashi,* which literally means "root building," refers to one-on-one consultation before taking action. This allows each individual or group time to become aware of the emerging consensus and adjust to it, understand the goals and rationale for the decision, and allow for modification before it is made. Through this method of behind-the-scene negotiation, the group is placed in a position to support the final solution in an open meeting. Go-betweens are sought to avoid confrontation. In delicate interactions a neutral person seeks out the positions of both sides in a conflict and attempts to resolve differences or terminate discussion without loss of face on either side. *Nemawashi* and the use of go-betweens may appear strange to Americans visiting Japan, but they make sense given the Japanese cultural

perspective that values group harmony and a definition of the conflict situation that favors avoidance of conflict or accommodation.[30]

The Japanese value system reduces conflict among members of its own culture: Conflict is far less common in Japanese society for a number of reasons. First, the emphasis on the group instead of the individual reduces interpersonal friction. Second, an elaborate set of standards emphasizes "obligations" over "rights," what one owes to others rather than desires for oneself. Third, the value attached to harmony cultivates skill in the use of ambiguity, circumlocution, euphemism, and silence in blunting incipient disputes. The ability to assimilate differences and to engineer consensus is valued above a talent for argument.[31] Meanwhile, the same value system may produce conflict when Japanese communicate and relate to members of other cultures.

My friend, Roger, called to say that he wanted to talk something over with me. When he arrived, he immediately showed signs of frustration. It all started yesterday, he said, when he met a young, pretty Japanese tourist on the beach. He said that he thought that they had really "hit it off" and agreed to go out for dinner later that evening. He went home to shower and change for dinner, but when he knocked on her hotel room door last night, no one answered. He thought he had been stood up, but he called her this morning and found her in. In a matter-of-fact way, she told him that members of her tour group decided to go out for dinner, and she "had to go with them." He said he got angry with her, and said he didn't believe her. Why would she go with them? She said it was the thing to do. He accused her of standing him up. All she would say was that she was sorry, but the tour group was very important to her. This really upset him, so he called me right away because he remembered that I used to live in Japan. I told him that actually I was not surprised by her behavior, and that intercultural dating was sometimes very difficult. I explained how many Japanese appeared more susceptible to group pressure than we Americans. The Japanese are very concerned about their responsibilities and obligations to their social groups. I advised him that if he wanted to date someone from another culture like Japan, he would have to accept the cultural baggage each person brings to the encounter. In this case, he might suggest

that he join her with the group. In fact, this might be the only way he will be able to see her, at least until the group decides not to spend some time together. Roger never called her back.

Case Study 6.2 ■ *Interpersonal Conflict Resolution in the United States* ————————

The dominant conflict resolution style in the United States is competition. Although Japan and the United States both have a centralized government, representative democracy at national, state, and local levels, and a high standard of living as modern industrial giants, the homogeneity of the Japanese stands in stark contrast to the pluralistic society of the United States made up of successive waves of immigrants in search of individual freedom and economic opportunity. The key attractions that brought these people to American shores have become the values that make up the U.S. cultural perspective. What are these values?

The ideal of individual freedom is institutionalized in the Bill of Rights. The dominant U.S. culture values the pursuit of individual economic opportunity made possible in a capitalistic economy and laissez-faire or competitive work ethic. Many U.S. citizens value religious and political freedom as embodied in the doctrine separating church from state. In the United States, the dominant cultural values of individual freedom, competition, and opportunity are favored over group harmony and collective action or consensus and provide for a cultural perspective that governs and defines interpersonal conflict.

Because the dominant culture in the United States values individual freedom and opportunity over group harmony and collective action, it tends to view interpersonal conflicts as a competition where one wins the satisfaction of his or her needs, interests, and goals or loses them to the satisfaction of others. Whereas the Japanese may fail to understand how a U.S. citizen can stand up against a group, disgrace one's family name, and strike or file a grievance against one's employer, U.S. citizens view such actions as an

assertion of one's interests, rights, or concerns to freely seize upon such opportunities to compete with the interests of others.

The competitive, self-oriented manner in which many U.S. citizens attempt to force others into giving in to their demands may be found in empirical research on interpersonal conflict. Researchers have found that U.S. couples often display aversive behavior,[32] express criticisms, blame, and accusations, and are less responsive to the other party.[33] Gottman has observed that couples in conflict are likely to use cross-complaining and countercomplaints.[34] Ting-Toomey discovered that couples are likely to begin a conflict by directly attacking one another with criticism and negatively loaded statements,[35] followed by attempts to justify oneself and blame the other.[36]

When U.S. citizens can't get what they want in interpersonal confrontation, they are encouraged to go to court. Adjudication starts out as a form of competition and remains so, or gets worse.[37] According to the American Bar Association's 1981 Moral Code of Professional Responsibility, the attorney is required to represent only his or her client because the assumption is that the other partner is represented by opposing legal counsel.[38] Initially, the parties retain the services of attorneys who are trained in the adversary role. The attorneys structure and organize the information to convince the judge that their party's position is the right one. Due to the adversarial nature of the process, Girdner claims that court-imposed decisions may actually perpetuate conflict between the parties.[39] Kaslow adds, "Sometimes the battle becomes hostile and demeaning, resulting in prolonged bitterness and anguish into which relatives and friends are drawn; children are traumatized by the continuing strife . . . , and everyone involved suffers a long-term loss of self-esteem and confidence."[40] Adjudication like compulsory arbitration allows the conflicting parties to seek a strictly competitive solution to their differences (with the idea that one will lose and the other win) by interjecting a neutral, objective third party into the conflict to decide who wins.

In sum, interpersonal conflict occurs with great frequency in U.S. society for a number of reasons. First, the emphasis on the individual instead of the group increases interpersonal friction.

Second, an elaborate set of standards emphasizes one's "rights" over one's "obligations," what one desires for oneself rather than what one owes to others. Third, the value attached to competition and individual accomplishment cultivates skill in aggressiveness, directness, and accomplishment in promoting disputes. The ability to emphasize differences, to promote one's individual goals, and to argue one's position is valued above a talent for assimilating differences and engineering consensus.[41]

Case Study 6.3 ■ *Interpersonal Conflict Resolution in the Former Federal Republic of Yugoslavia*

The dominant conflict resolution style in the former Federal Republic of Yugoslavia was compromise. Some think that the best way to maintain interpersonal relationships and resolve conflicts is through compromise. Although it may be appropriate on some occasions, we would like to argue that it may not be a good idea as a general conflict resolution style, especially where differences in values are great. Whereas one should be cautioned against speculating on the causes of war in a country like the former Republic of Yugoslavia, at least one can claim that attempts to compromise as a general rule did not resolve some of the most important prewar issues in that country. The following description of a prewar "Yugoslav" cultural perspective, definition of the situation, and communication behavior is based on Lee's experience.

Although there were many values, attitudes, and beliefs characteristic of the Yugoslav people prior to the recent war over "ethnic cleansing," many Yugoslavs valued worker self-management. This term symbolized a unique form of socialism as a "human experiment" created when Yugoslavia broke off with Russia in 1948. As part of its cultural heritage, Yugoslavia was made up of several strong ethnic groups— Serbs, Croats, Slovenes, Macedonians, Magyars, Italians, and others. Many were Greek Orthodox, Roman Catholic, or Moslem. In 1963, the Yugoslav constitution extended self-management to the governmental assemblies of the six republics, two autonomous provinces, and the Yugoslav Federation.[42] Although members of a variety of ethnic groups integrated the various states, each state remained dominated by an ethnic group with its own language and traditions.

The manner in which prewar Yugoslav workers made decisions regarding disputes was characteristic of its diverse culture. In Yugoslavia, the national values emphasizing direct democracy and commitment to political and economic equality among individuals and groups led the nationals to define conflict situations as compromise. For example, the running of the government was viewed as a compromise. All national positions in government including the nation's office of president were rotated with the leaders of each state (and, hence, each dominant ethnic group) taking a turn at running the nation. A direct democracy with collective ownership of property, Yugoslavia kept political and economic power at the local level. Travelers to Yugoslavia recognized immediately that the most widely used language, Servo-Croatian, itself was a compromise between two dominant ethnic groups, Serbs and Croats. Because Yugoslavs viewed conflict as a compromising activity, all parties had a right to receive an equal share.[43]

Criticisms of the Japanese, American, and Yugoslav Approaches to Conflict Resolution

The Japanese, American, and Yugoslav approaches to conflict resolution contain destructive elements that limit the usefulness of each approach in settling intercultural communication conflicts. The Japanese view of conflict as processes of avoidance and accommodation results in considerable loss of needs, interests, or goals for at least some parties in the conflict. Because the resolution of conflict frequently requires sacrificing one's own self-interests for those of others, Japanese seek to avoid conflict, withdraw when confronted by conflict, or accommodate when unable to withdraw. The key resolution mechanism is maximizing the other's satisfaction. Because accommodation leads to the sacrifice of one's own interests, the Japanese procedure is unacceptable to those conflicting parties who fail to appreciate the value of losing at the benefit of others.

The American approach to conflict, which is typically competitive in nature, results in either winning or losing. Acting in terms of their own self-interests, competitors employ strategies and tactics designed to better one's power position, so that in the end, a settlement maximizes one's own self-interests. Characterized as efficient, this style of conflict resolution frequently relies on secrecy or distortion (to keep the opposition at a disadvantage). The key resolution mechanism is the realization of maximum self-interest. Because competition leads to the domination of one party over the other, the American procedure is unacceptable to those who fail to appreciate losing a conflict or the destruction of their interpersonal relationship.

Whereas avoidance, accommodation, and competition are problematic, the prewar Yugoslav approach to conflict, which favored compromise over the long run, was no more effective because it resulted in partial winning and losing. They employed strategies and tactics designed to better their own power position and pursued goals of mutual benefit or loss. Information was shared strategically, and the key resolution mechanism was to trade off on positions to which there was apparent commitment. However, although compromise may have been useful on occasion, it was often difficult to determine equal outcomes when the parties saw different issues as important and wanted different outcomes. In addition, compromise by definition meant that no one was entirely satisfied by the outcome leaving some conflicts essentially unresolved at least in the minds of the parties. Like Japan and the United States, the former Republic of Yugoslavia would have benefited more from a collaboration approach to conflict resolution.

From Theory to Action

Styles and *strategies* are two terms for general cognitive orientations that are often used to explain the different tactics and behaviors enacted to deal with conflicts. Assuming one decides to do something about the conflict, there are different conflict strategies and styles that vary in their outcomes. If both of you are willing to try, collaboration is the best way to resolve interpersonal conflicts because it produces less personal and relationship stress and the most personal and relationship growth. To collaborate effectively, you need to include your interests, feelings, and needs. Then you need to listen to the other's interests, feelings, and needs to see if you can support them in future interaction. Finally, you need to see if the other is willing to collaborate and invest the time and effort to develop understandings that are mutually advantageous, or does the other prefer to avoid, accommodate, or compete? Although compromising may be preferable on some occasions, is the other willing to go the extra distance to collaborate where possible? We will conclude this chapter with the reminder that you cannot collaborate by yourself.

Notes

1. Alan L. Sillars, Stephen F. Coletti, D. Parry, and Mark A. Rogers, "Coding Verbal Conflict Tactics: Nonverbal and Perceptual Correlates of the 'Avoidance-Distributive-Integrative' Distinction," *Human Communication Research* 9 (1982), 83–95.

2. Robert R. Blake and Jane Srygley Mouton, "The Fifth Achievement," in Fred E. Jandt (Ed.), *Conflict Resolution through Communication* (New York: Harper & Row, 1973); R. H. Kilmann and K. W. Thomas, "Developing a Forced-Choice Measure of Conflict-Handling Behavior: The Mode Instrument," *Educational and Psychological Measurement* 37 (1977), 309–325; M. A. Rahim, "A Measure of Styles of Handling Interpersonal Conflict," *Academy of Management Journal* 26 (1983), 368–376.

3. A. Nicotera (Ed.), *Conflict and Organizations: Communicative Processes* (Albany, NY: SUNY 1995), p. 26.

4. M. A. Rahim, "A Measure of Styles of Handling Interpersonal Conflict," *Academy of Management Journal* 26 (1983), 368–376.

5. Blake and Mouton, "The Fifth Achievement," p. 96.

6. K. Thomas and R. Kilmann, *Conflict Mode Instrument* (Tuxedo, NY: XICOM, Inc., 1974).

7. Charles Conrad, "Gender, Interactional Sensitivity and Communication in Conflict: Assumptions and Interpretations," paper presented at the Speech Communication Association Convention, Denver, November 1985.

8. R. J. Sternberg and D. M. Dobson, "Resolving Interpersonal Conflicts: An Analysis of Stylistic Consistency," *Journal of Personality and Social Psychology* 52 (1987), 794–812.

9. R. J. Sternberg and L. J. Soriano, "Styles of Conflict Resolution," *Journal of Personal and Social Psychology* 47 (1984), 115–126.

10. E. C. Bell and R. N. Blakeney, "Personality Correlates of Conflict Resolution Modes," *Human Relations* 30 (1977), 849–857.

11. R. Jones and B. Melcher, "Personality and the Preference for Modes of Conflict Resolution," *Human Relations* 35 (1982), 649–658.

12. B. Kabanoff, "Predictive Validity of the MODE Conflict Instrument," *Journal of Applied Psychology* 72 (1987), 160–163.

13. Barbara Mae Gayle, "Sex Equity in Workplace Conflict Management," *Journal of Applied Communication Research* 19 (1991), 152–169.

14. Charles Conrad, "Communication in Conflict: Style-Strategy Relationships," *Communication Monographs* 58 (1991), 135–155.

15. Hal Witteman, "Interpersonal Problem Solving: Problem Conceptualization and Communication Use," *Communication Monographs* 55 (1988), 336–359.

16. Daniel J. Canary and William R. Cupach, "Relationship and Episodic Characteristics Associated with Conflict Tactics," *Journal of Social and Personal Relationships* 5 (1988), 305–325.

17. Dean G. Pruitt and Jeffrey Z. Rubin, *Social Conflict: Escalation, Stalemate, and Settlement* (New York: Random House, 1986), pp. 35.

18. Ibid., p. 39.

19. See, for example, William R. Cupach, "Perceived Communication Competence and Choice of Interpersonal Conflict Message Strategies," paper presented at the Western Speech Communication Association Convention, Denver, February 1982; Daniel J. Canary and William R. Cupach, "Relational and Episodic Characteristics Associated with Conflict Tactics," paper presented at the Western Speech Communication Association Convention, Fresno, February 1985; Daniel J. Canary and Brian H. Spitzberg, "Appropriateness and Effectiveness in the Perception of Conflict Strategies," *Human Communication Research* 14 (1987), 93–118; Daniel J. Canary and Brian H. Spitzberg, "A Model of the Perceived Competence of Conflict Strategies," *Human Communication Research* 15 (1989), 630–649.

20. Canary and Spitzberg, "A Model of the Perceived Competence of Conflict Strategies."

21. Linda L. Putnam and Joseph P. Folger, "Communication, Conflict, and Dispute Resolution: The Study of Interaction and the Development of Conflict Theory," *Communication Research* 15 (1988), 349–359.

22. Ibid., p. 351.

23. C. E. Rusbult and I. M. Zembrodt, "Responses to Dissatisfaction in Romantic Involvements: A Multidimensional Scaling Analysis" *Journal of Experimental Social Psychology* 19 (1983), 274–293.

24. C. E. Rusbult, D. J. Johnson, and G. D. Morrow, "Determinants and Consequences of Exit, Voice, Loyalty, and Neglect: Responses to Dissatisfaction in Adult Romantic Involvements," *Human Relations* 39 (1986), 45–63.

25. J. G. Healey and R. A. Bell, "Assessing Alternate Responses to Conflicts in Friendship," in D. D. Cahn

(Ed.), *Intimates in Conflict: A Communication Perspective* (Hillsdale, NJ: Erlbaum, 1990), pp. 25–48.

26. Janie M. Harden Fritz, "Responses to Unpleasant Work Relationships," *Communication Research Reports* 14 (1997), 302–311.

27. C. Cole and R. Ackerman, "A Change Model for Resolution of Stress," *Alternative Lifestyles* 4 (1981), 135.

28. C. Derr, "Managing Organizational Conflict," *California Management Review* 21 (1978), 76–83.

29. Tara L. Shepherd, "Content and Relationship Dimensions of a Conflict Encounter: An Investigation of Their Impact on Perceived Rules," paper presented to the Speech Communication Association Convention, Anaheim, CA, November 1982.

30. Dudley Cahn, "Communication Competence in the Resolution of Intercultural Conflict," *World Communication* 14(2) (1985), 85–94.

31. Dean C. Barnlund, *Communicative Styles of Japanese and Americans: Images and Realities* (Belmont, CA: Wadsworth, 1989), p. 39.

32. G. R. Birchler, R. L. Weiss, and J. P. Vincent, "Multimethod Analysis of Social Reinforcement Exchange Between Maritally Distressed and Nondistressed Spouse and Stranger Dyads," *Journal of Personality and Social Psychology* 31 (1975), 349–360.

33. P. Koren, K. Carlton, and D. Shaw, "Marital Conflict: Relations Among Behaviors, Outcomes, and Distress," *Journal of Consulting and Clinical Psychology* 48 (1980), 460–468.

34. J. M. Gottman, *Marital Interaction: Experimental Investigations* (New York: Academic Press, 1979); J. M. Gottman, H. Markman, and C. Notarius, "The Topography of Marital Conflict: A Sequential Analysis of Verbal and Nonverbal Behavior," *Journal of Marriage and the Family* 39 (1977), 461–477.

35. Stella Ting-Toomey, "Coding Conversation Between Intimates: A Validation Study of the Intimate Negotiation Coding System (INCS)," *Communication Quarterly* 31 (1983), 68–77.

36. Stella Ting-Toomey, "An Analysis of Verbal Communication Patterns in High and Low Marital Adjustment Groups," *Human Communication Research* 9 (1983), 306–319.

37. B. L. Werner, "I Want the Kids! Parents' Conversational Strategies During Child Custody Mediation." Paper presented at the annual meeting of the Speech Communication Association, Chicago, IL, November 1990.

38. F. W. Kaslow, "Divorce Mediation and Its Emotional Impact on the Couple and Their Children," *American Journal of Family Therapy* 12 (1984), 58–66.

39. L. K. Girdner, "Adjudication and Mediation: A Comparison of Custody Decision-Making Processes Involving Third Parties," *Journal of Divorce* 8 (1985), 33–47.

40. Kaslow, "Divorce Mediation," p. 62.

41. Cahn, "Communication Competence," 1985.

42. Dudley Cahn, "Communication and Self-Management in Yugoslavia," *World Communication* 18(2) (1989), 1–22.

43. Ibid.

Part III

Analyzing Conflict: Theory and Research in Interpersonal Conflict

Living with a close friend can be difficult because you assume many things about the relationship. One of my friends likes to borrow my things: my Walkman, tapes, and even clothes. I don't mind that he uses my things because I am very blessed and I didn't buy the things myself anyway. But I am very sensitive to treating other people with respect and taking care of others as well as their possessions. If I borrow something, I will put it back when I am done with it and I take good care of it. When my friend borrows my things, very rarely do I find them in my room. I usually will have to look for them in his room. I was late to an appointment and wanted to wear a certain belt, but it wasn't where I keep them. Later, I found it in his room. I confronted him about it and told him that if he borrows something to put it back when he is done. He agreed with what I had to say but was very sarcastic about it and tried to give me a guilt trip because I brought it up. He still uses my things, but he always makes a dramatic scene when he returns them. For example, "Here's the Walkman that I used and I'm putting it back because I just got done using it!" Now I don't know if I should just tell him that he can't use my things anymore.

In the previous section, we learned about conflict situations: what constitutes conflict and what is not conflict. In this section of the book, explanations of conflict behavior are the focus. Some explanations emphasize the individual; some emphasize relationships. Other explanations emphasize the role of communication in the enactment of conflict episodes. In addition, various researchers have looked at conflict in intimate and marital relationships. Both conflict theory and its application in different research settings are the focus of this section.

Studying conflict theory is important because simply acquiring skills for conflict management is not enough. Skills are limited in their application. Sometimes they work, and sometimes they do not. Theories help us understand when particular conflict skills can be used and when they are not appropriate. Theories explain conflicts and allow us to choose appropriate behavior within conflict situations.

Understanding the relationship between theories and skills is like understanding the relationship between *playing a game* and *mastering a game*.[1] Playing a game requires that we know the rules and that we understand and can produce the skills necessary to play it. Playing chess requires that you know how pieces are to move: A pawn can only go forward one space, except on the first move, but takes another piece by going diagonally. No wonder chess is not a real popular game; there are five other pieces for which to remember moves! But simply knowing how the pieces move will not make you a good player—you have to understand strategy and responses to the other person. Or, to use a different metaphor, the difference between skills and theory is like the difference between being a cook and a chef. A cook follows the recipe, but a chef creates it and tries new combinations of foods. If you were only to learn the skills involved in conflict, you would have a difficult time understanding when they do not work, and you would probably have a difficult time adapting when a new situation arose. Theory helps us get to the level of game mastery.

The body of conflict theory has grown rapidly in the last twenty years. Chapter 7 covers traditional theories of conflict, largely derived from the social-psychological literature. Chapter 8 presents what we call an emerging communication perspective on conflict behavior. Chapter 9 is concerned with various areas of conflict research that have provided interesting findings to guide effective behavior in those situations.

An understanding of conflict and communication behavior theories and a knowledge of conflict situations will enable you to better analyze conflict situations and to respond more competently in your conflicts. Unlike the person who wonders whether he should confront his roommate and tell him not to borrow his things anymore, you will have an understanding of conflict situations that will allow you to make these kinds of choices confidently.

---

[1]W. Barnett Pearce, *Interpersonal Communication: Making Social Worlds* (New York: HarperCollins College Publishers, 1994).

7

Social-Psychological Perspectives of Conflict

Objectives

At the end of this chapter, you should be able to

1. explain the key concepts and assumptions that identify factors that play an important role in interpersonal conflict according to each theory.
2. explain key principles that describe how conflicts develop according to each theory.
3. show how one should manage or resolve interpersonal conflicts according to each theory.

Key Terms

attribution theory
game theory
power
psychodynamic theory

social exchange theory
structural theory
structured situation
systems theory

theory
trust
uncertainty

In this portion of the text, we turn to the various theories that have been created to explain why people behave the way they do in conflict situations. There are many reasons for including theories when studying interpersonal conflict. They are discussed here because such theories call our attention to key concepts, assumptions, and principles that will lay the groundwork for developing techniques for the management and resolution of conflict that will receive greater treatment in later chapters.

There are a number of different conflict theories, which have generally been classified on the basis of the assumptions they make about human behavior. A **theory** is a means of explaining how something works. The way we explain conflict determines how we interpret it and choose our responses. If we think conflict is best explained by knowing the personal characteristics of those involved, for example, we are much more likely to focus on individual variables than if we think conflict is best explained by looking at the process that those in the conflict have enacted. The focus of a theory's explanation directs attention to that part of the conflict and assigns causes at the point of its focus.

Whereas communication can be the cause as well as the effect of interpersonal conflict, other factors derived from the study of social psychology also contribute to the creation, management, and resolution of conflict. This may seem surprising to you if you are taking this class as a communication major. Although these theories are not message centered and do not give us an understanding of communication behavior within conflict situations per se, they introduce us to additional factors that must be considered if one is to have a comprehensive view of interpersonal conflict. These social-psychological theories emphasize the role of the individual and her or his perceptual processes, the nature of the relationship that binds the conflicting parties, and the structures that shape conflict behavior in a relationship. In Chapter 8, we will discuss communication-based theories that examine interaction within the conflict situation.

Psychodynamic and Attribution Theories

Conflict theories generated by researchers in the area of psychology have focused on what individuals bring to the conflict situation, and how that impacts the conflict process. *The key concept that unifies these theories is their assumption that the way people act in conflict situations is due, in large part, to their individual dispositions and ways of thinking.* The theories remind us that the individuals in the conflict play no small part in determining the direction that the conflict will take.

Psychodynamic Theory

Stemming from one of the most historically significant psychological theories, based on the work of Sigmund Freud and his followers, **psychodynamic theory** says that people experience conflict because of their intrapersonal states. Both nonsubstantive conflict (in which there is a need to release tension unrelated to the other person in the situation) and misplaced or displaced conflict (in which the conflict is acted out with the wrong person or over the wrong issue) are largely psychodynamic in origin. This narrative illustrates a displaced conflict driven by psychodynamic tension:

> When I'm going to leave for an extended trip, I often wind up fighting with my husband before I go over some insignificant but overblown issue. This time I was really aware of the tendency, and we had avoided any major blowups. It took a toll, though, in my response to a neighbor's irritating comments at the shared swimming pool. Normally I simply would have left the situation, but I wound up telling him off in no uncertain terms. I was really embarrassed that I blew up—not only was the issue simply not worth the anger I felt, but I didn't even know this person before and now I feel like I have to avoid him.

Several aspects of Freud's theory can be used to explain how conflict occurs for the individual.[1] Freud conceived of the mind as a body of psychic energy that is channeled into various activities. Not only is the psychic energy channeled, but it must be channeled into appropriate or inappropriate places. For the person in the preceding narrative, the tension created by trying not to fight before leaving on a trip gets channeled onto a "safe person," a stranger. People often will displace or misplace conflict when they feel that dealing with the other person directly is not possible or that it will only make things worse.

Three aspects of the human mind affect the way in which frustration or, more generally, psychic energy, is released. The principal component of the mind is the *id,* the unconscious aspect that "contains everything that is inherited, present at birth, or fixed in the constitution."[2] The id contains the *libido,* the source of instinctual energy, which demands discharge though various channels. The id operates on the "pleasure principle," a tension-reduction process in which tension from a bodily need is translated into a psychological wish in order to reduce the tension. The id seeks pleasure and avoids pain; it seeks only to satisfy its needs without regard for the cost of doing so.

Opposing the id is what Freud called the *superego,* containing both the ego ideal and the conscience. The ego ideal is an internalized idea of what a person would like to be. The conscience contains morals and other judgments concerning correct and incorrect behavior. As a parent does, it tries to punish a person for "immoral" behavior and reward a person for "moral" behavior through feelings like guilt or pride.

Mediating between the id and the superego is the *ego,* which is governed by the "reality principle" that attempts to "postpone the discharge of energy until the actual object that will satisfy the need has been discovered or produced."[3] The ego, in mediating between the id and the superego, plays a significant role in conflict situations—it tries to reconcile the desires of the id ("I want it all, and I want it right now") with the constraints of the superego ("Nice people don't throw temper tantrums"). The ego must constrain aggressive impulses and control the level of anxiety conflict creates.

The ego deals with aggressive impulses by suppressing them or redirecting them through a process of displacement. In displacement, the aggressive impulse is often redirected "toward a more vulnerable or socially acceptable target than the actual source of frustration. . . . Displacement is more likely when the true source of frustration is powerful or particularly valuable to the individual."[4] Coser argued that the process of scapegoating in groups may be the result of displaced aggression, used when people are afraid to blame the entire group for a situation.[5]

Anxiety is an additional product of frustration and tension, occurring when people perceive danger in a situation. People can become anxious when they think that someone will interfere with their goals, when they fear their own impulses in a situation, or when they disapprove of their own actions. The major impact of anxiety on a conflict situation is the rigidity and inflexibility it causes in people's responses to the situation.[6]

Psychodynamic theory explains how individuals respond to conflict situations, particularly in light of their aggressive impulses and their anxieties. The theory points out that people are not always aware of the motivations that drive their behavior. When diagnosing conflict situations, an understanding of the foundations of psychodynamic theory will remind you that the first task is to determine who is involved in the conflict.

APPLICATION 7.1

Are there situations in your life in which you are more likely to displace your anger or conflict with the other person than to deal with it directly? What characterizes those situations?

Attribution Theory

Sillars argued that in a conflict situation one makes conclusions about the other person's behavior and that those conclusions lead to theories to explain the conflict.[7] **Attribution theory** states that people act as they do in conflict situations because of the conclusions they draw about the other. Conclusions about the other are based on attributions about that person or on inferences about the meanings, causes, or outcomes of conflict events. Attributions may be internal, related to the person's general personality, or external, related to the other person's circumstances. As you might suspect, attribution theory accounts for unreal conflicts—when we are assuming we are in conflict due to insufficient information or because of faulty conclusions we have drawn about the other person's behavior.

Sillars claimed attributions affect the way people define conflicts, interpret the other's behavior, and choose strategies to achieve their goals effectively within conflict situations. Furthermore, the process of making attributions about the other may discourage the selection of integrative or collaborative conflict strategies because the process of attribution may shift the blame from oneself to the other. This reciprocal relationship between making attributions and the escalation of a conflict also can affect international conflict: The tendency to maintain attributional consistency (i.e., to generate an explanation of the other's behavior and stick to it) and consequent misinterpretation of information increases the likelihood of escalating conflict and prolonged hostilities in international conflict.[8]

People are most likely to perceive the other as aggressive and respond with anger and retribution when three conditions are met. First, the action the other person has taken is seen as a constraint to one's own alternatives or outcomes. Person A cannot act in the way A wishes because of B's actions. Second, the action taken by the other appears to have been done intentionally to do harm. Not only has B taken action that constrains A, but B appears to have done so in order to intentionally harm A. Third, the action taken by the other is seen as abnormal or illegitimate. A sees no action on A's part that might have provoked B into acting as B did. Anger or retribution are less likely on A's part if B is seen as having acted without choice and because forces moved B in the direction taken. Anger and retribution are more likely if A sees B's action as arbitrary or whimsical.[9]

In a slightly different approach, Louis explained conflict by examining how people conceptualize it and attribute it to various causes.[10] According to her approach, conflict is a series of affective, cognitive, and behavioral phases. The perception of conflict arises when a person feels some frustration, thinks about the source of the frustration, and then acts in response to it. Frustration is, thus, the stimulus initiating a conflict episode. The person in this narrative allowed her frustration to build three years before saying anything about the conflict:

> Before I was hired at my parish church, there had been no young women working in the office for over thirty years. I could tell that Monsignor was hesitant about hiring us three girls but he seemed to get more enthusiastic about it after we started working there. He gave us pet names and always had something nice to say. Then three weeks into the new schedule, he called a meeting. He told us that one of the parishioners had said we wore our skirts too short. Monsignor had defended us, though, and everything seemed fine. Then six months into the job, I was working alone when a man came in and asked to speak to a priest. He needed money. While we were waiting for the priest to come, he began to make sexually suggestive remarks about me. I asked him to leave, and he did before the priest could arrive. I reported this the next day, and they added some security measures like a button to

call the police directly. But when I came back to work, Monsignor was cold and professional toward me. This lasted three years, until I finally decided to write him a note and tell him that I was hurt about the way he was treating me. He wrote back and said he had felt bad that he wasn't there to protect me. So we had a conflict for three years because both of us thought we knew what the other one was thinking.

The context surrounding the frustration can reduce or enhance the interpretation of a stimulus as frustrating, depending on the importance of the context characteristic. If you are trying to study, for example, and your neighbor is making a great deal of noise, you probably will be frustrated. However, if it is Saturday night, and people generally socialize and make a great deal of noise on Saturday nights, you may not feel as frustrated as you would be if it were the middle of finals week. Once you analyze the other person's behavior and make attributions about it, you decide on the choices that are available to you to reduce the source of the frustration.

One shortcoming in Louis's model is the assumption of rationality on the part of the individual. The explanation of the process of analyzing the source of a conflict and choosing responses is insightful, but it is unlikely that people will always choose or be able to act in such a rational manner when responding to conflicts. Some conflicts occur rapidly, with no time for thought or reflection. For conflicts that occur over a period of time, this model may illustrate how people decide they are experiencing a conflict; at the least, it is a reminder that the way that people judge the conflict situation and the other person's behavior affects the way that they choose their own behavior.

APPLICATION 7.2

When have false attributions you have made about another exacerbated a conflict situation? Have there been times when making accurate attributions about the other has helped you?

APPLICATION 7.3

To correctly label the following statements, select either internal attributions or external attributions.

1. If you say that "he did this to me because he wants to get even," are you making an internal or an external attribution about his retaliatory behavior?
   a. internal   b. external
2. If you say that "she did this to me because she hates my guts," are you making an internal or an external attribution?
   a. internal   b. external
3. If you say that "he did poorly because his parents expect the worst from him, so he delivers accordingly," are you making an internal or external attribution about his behavior?
   a. internal   b. external
4. If you say that "he didn't show for the test because he is probably afraid he will fail," are you making an internal or an external attribution about his behavior?
   a. internal   b. external

5. If you say "he made the test too hard, so I flunked it," are you making an internal or an external attribution about your test grade?
   a. internal   b. external

6. If you say, "Of course, she didn't return the laptop. She is an idiot. What do you expect from an imbecile?" are you making an internal or an external attribution about her behavior?
   a. internal   b. external

7. If you say, "They keep tearing up the parking lots and that is why I was late to class," are you making an internal or an external attribution about your behavior?
   a. internal   b. external

8. If you say, "I've been in a slump, which is why I am not doing well these days," are you making an internal or an external attribution about your behavior?
   a. internal   b. external

9. If you say to a male friend, "She's immoral and only wants you for your money," are you making an internal or an external attribution about her behavior toward him?
   a. internal   b. external

10. If you say, "He treats you badly because you are so tall. He has a rotten attitude toward others taller than he is," are you making an internal or an external attribution about his bad treatment of others?
    a. internal   b. external

11. If you say, "Luck is against me. Maybe next time I will get lucky," are you making an internal or an external attribution about losing money in a card game?
    a. internal   b. external

Answers: I, I, E, I, E, I, E, E, I, I, E

APPLICATION 7.4

Indicate with a "yes" those statements that contain attributions that are most likely to lead to successful conflict resolution.

1. Maybe our relationship can't handle this pressure.
   a. yes   b. no

2. Why is she so stubborn about this problem?
   a. yes   b. no

3. Why didn't I tell her how I felt about her problem?
   a. yes   b. no

4. He just doesn't understand me.
   a. yes   b. no

5. I guess my parents taught me to avoid conflict too much.
   a. yes   b. no

6. My reaction was probably uncalled for.
   a. yes   b. no

7. I guess she just doesn't care about me.
   a. yes   b. no

8. I forced the confrontation, but he overreacted.
   a. yes   b. no
9. Was my timing bad in confronting this problem?
   a. yes   b. no
10. I can get pretty angry at times.
    a. yes   b. no

Answers: 1, 3, 6, 9, 10 should be yes.

From William A. Donohue and Robert Kolt, *Managing Interpersonal Conflict* (Newbury Park: Sage, 1992), p. 57.

Relationship Theories

Whereas the theories in the first section focused on the individual as a key element in conflict, this section considers theories of *how the relationship between the people involved in a conflict affects the way the conflict is enacted and resolved.* The two dominant theories of this type are social exchange theory and system theory.

Social Exchange Theory

Developed by Kelley and Thibault, **social exchange theory** states that people evaluate their interpersonal relationships in terms of their value, which is created by the costs and rewards associated with the relationship.[11] A person's feelings about a relationship, according to this theory, depend on assessments of the amount of effort put into the relationship (costs) compared to what is received as a result of the relationship (rewards). People assess the costs and rewards associated with their relationships through what is termed the *comparison level* (CL) and the *comparison level of alternatives* (CL_{alt}). People enter into conflict when they believe that the rewards they are receiving are too little in comparison with the costs they must pay in the relationship.

CL and CL_{alt} emphasize the role of relationship satisfaction and commitment in interpersonal conflict. The CL is a standard with which people determine how satisfactory or attractive a relationship is. This standard reflects what people feel they deserve. If the rewards of a relationship compared to its cost fall above the CL, then a person considers the relationship satisfying; if the outcome falls below the CL, the person will probably be dissatisfied with the relationship. A person's CL is created by considering all the possible outcomes a relationship might have, either from direct experience in the relationship or by observation of other relationships. Outcomes considered to be more attainable will be more important in calculating the CL. This narrative illustrates how a person begins to make changes in a relationship through a consideration of the rewards and costs:

> My mother graduated from high school early in order to marry my biological father and move with him to Germany, where he was stationed in the service. I was born a year later, and they divorced a few months after I was born. My mom then married Harry when I was about two. For the next fourteen years, I lived with my mom and Harry, seeing my dad on the weekends. I felt like I lived two separate lives. Home was where Mom and Harry were—in fact, I didn't call him my stepfather, I called him "Dad." My biological father didn't like that.

My relationship with my biological father got worse over the years. I never enjoyed spending time with him and I even dreaded seeing him because he bad-mouthed my mom and Harry. My biological father resented the relationship I had with Harry and he kept trying to make me think Harry was a bad guy. He would use gifts as a way of making me visit him. He bought me lots of toys, took me fun places, and as I got older the gifts got more expensive—a television, a stereo, the promise of a car. I accepted these gifts with a clear conscience because I figured he "owed" me for the miserable weekends I spent with him.

When I was sixteen, my biological father and I had a major confrontation over this pattern we had developed. I basically stood up to him and told him how I hated the way he bad-mouthed my mom and how I didn't want to spend any more time with him if he was going to be like that. My father comes from a culture where you don't argue with your parents, so when I stood up to him, he got upset and told me never to come back to his house. That was five years ago, and I have never spoken to him since that time.

The narrator in this conflict has a clear comparison level when she evaluates the relationship she has with her biological father. She has a good relationship with her stepfather, and wants only one family, not two. Her father appeared to be satisfied with the relationship they had, but her dissatisfaction grew as the expensive gifts no longer were enough to make up for the unpleasantness of each weekend visit.

This conflict also illustrates the idea of CL_{alt}, which is the lowest level of outcomes a person will accept in a current relationship in light of available opportunities in other relationships. The more the outcomes in a relationship exceed the CL_{alt}, the more committed a person will be to the current relationship, and the more dependent that person will be on the relationship for psychological rewards. As time wears on, the rewards of the narrator's relationship with her father are too low for her to accept. The emotional cost of staying in the relationship is higher than the value of any gift her father can give her.[12]

Social exchange theory assumes that people choose their behaviors due to self-interest and a desire to maximize rewards while minimizing costs. However, choices are made with respect to rules of fairness: People expect rewards to be proportionate to contributions they make to the relationship, based on their perceptions of the rewards and costs involved.[13] So, even if a relationship is unsatisfactory at a particular point in time, if people feel that it was a good relationship in the past and think it might be satisfactory in the future, they do not immediately abandon the relationship when things are rough.

From a social exchange point of view, *conflict arises when one person in the relationship feels that the outcomes are too low and perceives that the other will resist any attempt to raise the outcomes.*[14] This is precisely what happened in the narrative. It is possible that the narrator could have convinced her father that continuing to bad-mouth her mother (particularly sixteen years after the divorce) was not appropriate. Such an outcome would have been the result of what social exchange theory terms *cooperative joint action* in which both people agree together to make changes in the relationship. Through independent action, the narrator could simply have continued her relationship with her biological father without expecting him to change, although this was unlikely as his behavior really bothered her. The actual outcome of the conflict was imposed joint action, where the narrator's father discontinued their relationship.

How people choose to alter their outcomes depends on the power held by each person in the relationship. Kelly and Thibault argued that the dependence of person A on person B constitutes person B's power, and vice versa. A person may have "fate control" over the other, the ability to affect the other's behavior regardless of what the other does, or may have "mutual fate control" over the other, the ability to make it desirable for the other to behave as the person wants.

Overall, social exchange theory leads to four insights about conflict behavior. First, the theory recognizes that people are often quite purposeful about the way they do conflict, calculating the costs of various options and weighing those costs against the potential rewards the options might bring. This strategic calculation is illustrated by the following conflict account:

> The other night my mom called me to ask me what I was doing for the weekend. I told her I was going to come home because I had some plans with friends. She wondered if I could do something around the house so that I could spend some time with my brother. I was upset because she knew I had already made plans, and she was going out also. I felt like I was being pushed to cancel my plans because my brother wasn't doing anything. I was very hurt and angry because she was not even thinking about canceling her plans with her new boyfriend. I thought the request was very unfair. Because my mom had started dating again, I was feeling pressure in our relationship because I felt like it was changing. Most of her free time was spent in this new relationship, and I felt like she was only thinking of herself and failing to see how hard it would be for me to adjust to the change. As a result of the negative feelings, we didn't hang up the phone on a very positive note. I feel very upset when there are negative feelings between my mom and me, but I felt the situation was not approached fairly. However, I must communicate my feelings to my mom in order to understand her motives and actions.

The preceding account also illustrates a second concept emphasized by social exchange theory: the interdependence of those in the conflict. Moves on the part of one person lead to countermoves on the part of the other. It is not possible, according to social exchange theory, to take steps to resolve a conflict without reactions from the other person involved.

The third social exchange theory concept is that conflict is a situation in which moves and countermoves take place. This aspect of conflict is further developed in phase and episodic theories of conflict. The fourth concept of social exchange theory is that people in conflicts choose actions based not only on their particular outcomes but also on their costs for the relationship.[15]

Although some people initially react to social exchange theory negatively, thinking it is wrong to use an economic model to explain relationships, social exchange theory does make sense. We don't like feeling as though we put more into a relationship than we receive. If we have hope of staying in the relationship, we will work to increase our rewards relative to our costs. On the other hand, if the costs continue to rise without some increase in rewards, people tend to cycle out of the relationship in a way similar to the chilling effect—as they see conflict as creating too high a "cost" with respect to the "reward" they might receive, they do not communicate their concerns and eventually do not communicate at all.

APPLICATION 7.5

What conflicts can you identify that were motivated by a desire to increase your rewards or to decrease your costs in a relationship? Were you successful? Why or why not?

Game Theory

Like social exchange theory, **game theory** assumes that people act in conflict situations from a position of self-interest and that moves and countermoves are chosen to maximize rewards and minimize costs. Games are conflict situations in which people must make choices while the other person is also making choices and in which both parties know that the combination of choices will determine the outcome. "Real life consists of bluffing, of little acts of deception, of asking yourself what the other man is going to think I mean to do."[16] A game approach is illustrated by one person's description of a conflict:

> I always feel like part of a chess game when doing conflict with Mother. She moves carefully, then sits back waiting for you to fall into her trap. Sometimes I see the bad move, sometimes I don't, but it seems as though she is happiest when someone falls into the trap.

Tedeschi, Schlenker, and Bonoma described the character of interaction in a "conflict game":

> The person's purpose in such games in both normal and abnormal interactions is to maneuver another person into a vulnerable position or to elicit from him behavior that will benefit the manipulator. . . . Each individual attempts to fathom the other's behaviors, and employs deception to achieve a pre-planned and expected outcome. Further, each is probably aware of the other's plans, and each devises counterplans and tactics based on his awareness. It is this calculated failure to communicate each other's intentions, the unwillingness to accept at face value the statements and proposals made, and the interconnectedness of social outcomes that gives the interaction the character of a game.[17]

Game theory has four primary assumptions. The first assumption is that of *interdependence,* meaning that the outcomes achieved by one person depend on one's own choices as well as the choices of the other person. It is not possible to act independently in a game theory model. Second is the assumption of *quantification*—game theory assumes that it is possible actually to calculate the value of the positive or negative outcomes that result from choices within the situation. Third, game theory assumes *exhaustiveness,* that every possible outcome that could result from any choice in the situation is known to those within the situation. Finally, game theory assumes *maximization,* or that each party seeks to act in such a way to gain the best possible rewards for its own interests.[18]

Game theory's detractors appear to outnumber its adherents. Few practical problems fit into a game theory "if this, then this" format. However, game theory has contributed a rich and extensive body of research to the understanding of conflict behavior. Although the role of communication has tended to be minimized within this tradition, game theory demonstrates how interdependent actions and estimations of the effects of moves and countermoves within a conflict situation affect the movement of a conflict toward resolution.

Considerable conflict research has used a game theory approach, most of it using the Prisoner's Dilemma (PD) paradigm.[19] PD is a game based on a familiar situation: Two people are caught burglarizing a building and are brought separately to the police station. If both of them remain silent, they will both go free, but there is an incentive to speak—if only one confesses, the one confessing will receive a reward and go free and the other will go to jail. If both confess, they both will go to jail. In order to benefit, then, they must trust each other to cooperate and act in each other's best interest. However, to cooperate first (by remaining silent), if the other chooses not to cooperate, will result in the worst outcome for the person acting first. This is called a mixed motive situation because those involved have incentives to both cooperate and compete.

In Chapter 2 we outlined a set of beliefs for effective conflict management that views cooperation as the highest value. One way for students enrolled in an interpersonal conflict course to experience the way basic beliefs derive from cooperation and trust is to engage in the PD game. Whether or not one "wins" the game depends on the choice to cooperate or compete. The best outcomes occur when both people cooperate; the worst occur if both people compete. When only one competes, the outcomes are mixed. If we think that you will try to maximize your gains at our expense, we will distrust you and choose to compete. However, the PD game reveals that people who choose to compete do not fare as well as those who choose to cooperate. To cooperate, we must think that you will not take advantage of us. Then we will trust you and choose to cooperate with you. When played in class, some students get very upset and angry when others choose to compete. They say that the others can't be trusted and accuse them of ruining the game. Discussion following such an exercise can be emotionally intense and lively.

Criticisms of the PD paradigm have been widespread. Perhaps the most serious concerns the artificial and limited conditions under which communication can take place in PD simulations. Those involved are rarely allowed to communicate freely with one another. Nemeth concluded that the paradigm did not represent a real example of conflict because there appears to be no real solution from the participant's point of view. Furthermore, even if a solution existed, there is no way to communicate it to the other person.[20] The lack of social interaction prior to the game and the lack of interaction during the game create a situation of "beating" the other person, rather than one of searching for an optimal solution. Pruitt and Kimmel argue that this need not be the case. When people think of long-term rather than short-term results, they are likely to be more cooperative. This is especially true if those involved understand that they depend on one another, that exploiting one another is not likely to achieve a good outcome, and that cooperating with the other will probably generate cooperation.[21]

Systems Theory

A number of authors have written about conflict behavior from a systems perspective, which has generally assumed that conflict represents a breakdown in communication from the normal, harmonic state of affairs. **Systems theory** is best summarized by Ruben, who took issue with the idea of equating conflict with breakdowns. Rather, he argued, if human relationships are thought of as systems, *communication and, therefore, conflict are not only inevitable but also continual.*

> There are no "breakdowns in communication," there is no option not to be in communication with the environment so long as a system is alive. Secondly, it is through this communication process . . . that the system adapts to . . . its environment. . . . Discrepancies between the needs and capacities of the system and those in the environment emerge, and the system, acting on the discrepancy,

strives to close the gap. From a systems perspective, it is such discrepancies between the demands and capacities of an environment and the demands and capabilities of a living system that may be termed conflict.[22]

Ruben's view of conflict within a system turns to an entirely different assumption from previous theories: Conflict, rather than being a disruption in the normal state of affairs, is the normal state of affairs within any system. Conflict is necessary for the growth and adaptation of a system; in fact, conflict becomes a system's primary defense against stagnation and decay. As a system's means of adapting to its environment, then, the major defining condition of conflict is the process of reducing alternatives as the system adapts to changes and demands in the environment.[23]

From a practical point of view, conflict occurs within a relationship (a system) because a person in that relationship needs to adapt to demands of the other person or to demands in the environment surrounding the relationship. Families in which parents have divorced can create systemic conflicts for the children involved, as Case Study 7.1 indicates.

Case Study 7.1 ■ *Whose Daughter Am I?*

Family conflicts are my specialty. No one drives me nuts the way they do, but I guess that's normal for all of us. My mom asked me several weeks ago if my father and his wife, Susan, were going to have a get-together at their house for me after graduation. She used her usual snide tone that is always there when she talks about my father doing something for or with me. I had only thought briefly about actual plans for graduation, such as who was coming, dinner plans, and so on. I said I hadn't asked him about doing anything after graduation. I told her that I thought it would be better if "we," meaning my mom's family and I, just went to dinner at a restaurant afterward. Mom's response was a dejected "okay." She was not pleased.

This conflict has caused me a lot of grief because things have been uptight in my family ever since Mom remarried last November, telling me only the week before and not telling my brother at all until after it was over. My brother and Mom aren't speaking, and I'm the only one who has met Ron, my mom's husband. I don't really want to have a big get-together because the tension will be tremendous. Everyone in the family keeps telling me that this is my day, and it should be the way I want it. Well, I can't imagine

the day being very pleasant if some people aren't talking to others.

I think Mom is mad at me because finally, ten years after the divorce and Dad's remarriage, she has remarried. This was her chance to show off her "catch," and I wasn't giving her the opportunity. I didn't want the hassle of having everyone together, and she knew it.

Things got worse when I stopped by my brother's house on the way home from classes. I was tired but I knew I had to get it over with. When I asked him if he was going to dinner with Mom and Ron and me after graduation, he asked who was going. I told him. He said, "Guess?" I played along and said, "Great! Where should we go?" I figured if I had to guess, I'd guess my way. He corrected me with a loud "Wrong!" and said he wasn't going. I was so tired I didn't feel I could say the right things. I walked out rather than say the wrong thing.

At home, I thought about how I should have explained how important it was to me that he go with us. My brother is really hurting from the situation with Mom and not being told. He really needs to deal with the problem, but I didn't know how to say it at the time.

Three assumptions guide thinking about conflict within systems. First, if growth and decay are simultaneous in a system, conflict (or competition) and cooperation (or collaboration) must also be simultaneous. And because cooperation and competition are simultaneous, judging a specific behavior as cooperative or competitive depends on which process is dominant in the system: In a cooperative system, a behavior is likely to be judged cooperative and vice versa. Given the various issues going on in the family situation just narrated, the brother sees his mother's failure to tell him about the remarriage as a competitive act, and he responds competitively by refusing to attend a family dinner.

A second assumption of systems theory concerns the purpose of conflict. In the systems perspective, conflict is predominantly a process of reducing alternatives as one adapts to the environment; that is, conflict occurs so that people can examine the available options and reduce their number so as not to be overwhelmed. Thus, interactions between people are seen as conflict processes if people are eliminating alternatives and assigning new values to the remaining alternatives. It is a conflict when one person tells another, "These are the only options available to you," or "This option is more desirable than other options." Cooperation processes are dominant when alternatives are increasing and values are being redistributed to accommodate additional choices. Interaction is more cooperative when people say, "Well, you could do *x, y,* or *z,* depending on what suits you best." The brother's refusal to attend the dinner is narrowing the alternatives to only one and, thus, feeds a competitive process.

The third assumption concerning conflict in systems centers on the interconnectedness of processes within a system. Processes within a system are interrelated and, therefore, changes in competition or cooperation will be accompanied by changes in relationships among the other processes. If conflict is accepted as an inevitable part of a system, then the study of conflict management becomes a study of ways in which to work with the regularly occurring conflict so that it happens on a minor, rather than major, level.

When thinking of conflict as a system event, one must identify the particular system in which conflict is thought to be occurring. The preceding narrator is part of two family systems that affect one another but which also compete against one another for her time and affection. Both systems have a vested interest in being part of her graduation activities, and yet the competitive nature of the two systems makes the prospect fairly unpleasant for the narrator. However, any decision she makes about her graduation plans will affect both systems, in addition to affecting her future relationships with both.

Mack and Snyder argued that the goal of conflict management should be to use the natural limitations on conflict that occur inside and outside of the system to limit the severity of the conflict. Internal factors that can limit the intensity or severity of a conflict include the nature of the relationship between those in the conflict, institutionalized norms and procedures that relate to the conflict, the need of those in conflict to continue to communicate with one another, the cost of the conflict, the availability and cost of different solutions to the conflict, inertia or inefficiency of those in the conflict, ignorance or misunderstanding, and conflict avoidance taboos.[24] Factors external to the system that may help limit the conflict include transcendent cultural or social values that can neutralize or dominate conflicting values, institutional sanctions against uncontrolled conflict, third parties' interest in control or resolution, other conflict systems that prevent a particular system getting out of control, and "cross-pressures" that create ambivalence with parties.[25]

Perhaps the most important contribution of systems theory to theories of conflict and its management has been the idea that conflict is a normal part of interaction. Rather than seeing conflict as a disruption that occurs within an otherwise healthy and normally functioning relationship, systems theorists see conflict as an important part of a system that allows change and adaptation to various demands.

Structural Theory

In Chapter 5 we talked about the process of conflict—how it unfolded over fairly recognizable stages and progressed toward some sort of resolution. People recognize the patterns of conflict. They often know when a conflict is building up. And although conflict is a process, with no clear beginning or end, people tend to "punctuate" the events of a conflict situation so that they point to particular triggers for the conflict or "red flags" to identify that the situation has progressed beyond a simple disagreement to a more serious type of conflict.

A conflict is also a **structured situation:** It takes its shape from the conditions that make joint interaction possible between the people involved. Thomas argued that both models of conflict are important for understanding the nature of conflict interaction:

> The *process model* focuses on the *sequence of events within a conflict episode,* and is intended to be of use when intervening directly into the stream of events of an ongoing episode. The *structural* model focuses upon the *conditions which shape conflict* behavior in a relationship, and is intended to help in restructuring a situation to facilitate various behavior patterns.[26]

Whereas psychological approaches such as psychodynamic theory and attribution theory ask how people are thinking about the conflict, and relational theories ask how interdependent are the people involved in the conflict, **structural theory** focuses on the conflict situation and asks how different variables in the situation are impacting behavior. Structural theory asks questions like:

1. Who is involved? Are they predisposed to act in particular ways toward each other?
2. Do they trust one another?
3. How well do the people involved know one another? Do they feel a high or low level of uncertainty when conflict occurs in the relationship?
4. Is either party acting as a representative for someone else? Is there pressure from behind this person to achieve a particular outcome?
5. How much power does each person have in the situation?
6. Who has a stake in the outcome of this conflict beyond the immediate participants?
7. Are there constraints in the situation that will lead to particular outcomes and make other outcomes impossible?

Structural theory, then, examines conflict as something that results from the conditions that characterize relationships and that make interaction possible between the people in the relationship. In particular, three factors—trust, uncertainty, and power—help to determine the choices people make in conflict situations and the way they behave with respect to one another. Structural theory's ability to explain conflict arises not only from understanding trust, uncertainty, and power, but in understanding how they work together in conflict situations.

Trust

The variable with the greatest effect on the other conditions of conflict is the amount of trust we have in the other person. The more we trust the other, the less uncertain we will feel about the other's motives in the conflict. We are more likely to think the other has our best interests at heart and will not use power in ways that will hurt us. Most authors define **trust** as the belief that another is benevolent or honest toward the trusting individual, believing that the other person's caring transcends any direct benefits the other receives as a result of caring.[27] Trust is defined by Deutsch as an instance in which

> the person who has to choose whether to trust is faced with the possibility that, if he trusts, something detrimental may happen to him. That is, the choice to trust may lead either to benefit or to harm, depending upon whether or not one's trust is fulfilled. It may also be noted that the harm that may befall the trusting individual if trust is unfulfilled is not a trivial harm in relation to the amount of benefit to be received from trusting and having his trust fulfilled.[28]

Trust grows out of a dialectic of hope and fear in which the desire for closeness raises the fear of giving more and being more dependent. Trust reflects "people's abstract positive expectations that they can count on partners to care for them and be responsive to their needs, now and in the future."[29] Within each relationship, trust develops depending on the actions of those involved, but still a leap of faith is required.[30] Most people will go ahead and act as though a sense of security about the other was justified because evidence for trustworthiness can never be conclusive. The feeling that the other is benevolent toward oneself allows a person to move forward on the assumption that the other is trustworthy.[31]

The tendency to be trusting, according to Holmes and Rempel, is seen as a "contingency rule," a preferred way of acting within a relationship if the characteristics of the relationship warrant it:

> If we think in terms of readiness to trust, we also avoid creating an unrealistic caricature of a trusting individual as a blind optimist. If anything, there is some evidence to suggest that distrusting individuals react less effectively to the features of particular relationships than do trusting individuals. People who distrust the motives of others tend to have more rigid and narrow expectations and to provoke the very reactions they fear.[32]

Healthy trust can be distinguished from pathological trust or suspicion. Deutsch argued that what characterizes healthy trust (or suspicion) is flexibility and responsiveness to changing situations. Pathological trust or suspicion is typically inflexible, rigid, and consistent in actions toward others, without regard for the situation.[33] Those who trust pathologically have a tendency to confuse risk-taking and trusting situations, overestimating the probability of getting what they want or underestimating the negative consequences of not getting what they want. Pathological trusters may also overestimate the benevolence of the trusted person or overestimate their power to affect the trusted person's behavior.

Pathologically suspicious persons make opposite assumptions. Either extreme makes it difficult to act effectively with respect to others. An example of pathological trust is illustrated by the following conflict between two roommates living in Los Angeles:

> I own a great deal of expensive photography equipment, which I keep at my apartment because I often do my studio work there. My roommate has this weird idea that the world is safe—he leaves doors and windows unlocked all the time. He comes from the Midwest, where "people are decent" and he never locked a door in his life.
>
> This conflict used to arise when I would come home in the afternoon and find the apartment wide open. Sometimes, if he went next door he would leave the door standing open, but most of the time he would be at work and everything would be unlocked and the windows would be open. If I confronted him, he would fall back on the fact that if God wanted us to have our material possessions, then He would be sure they were not stolen (since everything is God's and He will let us keep them or take them away). I, on the other hand, have all this equipment and this is the only way I pay the rent, buy food, and so on. I also would try to explain to him that he was in L.A. now and that there were a lot of crooks around. I would even point out that people in our own building had been recently robbed, but it made no impact.
>
> After many confrontations, he did decide it would be better to lock the doors. But this only happened after I loaned my television to a friend and he came home early to an unlocked apartment only to find the set missing. Well, he panicked and called the police and had them looking our apartment over until I came home and straightened everything out. This taught him just how he would react in a real robbery situation and that he should be more cautious in securing the apartment.

APPLICATION 7.6

How had your trust of another person affected the way you behaved in a conflict with him or her? Describe two situations: one in which you trusted and one in which you did not.

What direct effect does trusting have on conflict situations? Research seems to indicate that, to begin with, trusting individuals are more likely to assume positive implications of behaviors than are distrusting individuals. Although they do not deny the negative elements in their relationships, they limit the implications negative events have for the relationship, but distrusting individuals overemphasize the importance of negative events. Trusting individuals tend to see negative events in a larger time frame stabilizing perceptions and making conflict less threatening.[34]

This tendency to see events in the larger time frame was tested with married couples. Prior to the videotaped discussion of a difficult issue in a couple's relationship, researchers measured the trust couples had toward one another by having the couples respond to semantic differential items concerning their expectations of each other's behaviors. After the discussion, the researchers had the couples watch the videotaped discussion and had each partner independently rate any behaviors of the other that had positive or negative effects on them. After viewing the tape, the couples again completed semantic differential scales, which asked for perceptions of the partner's actual behavior during the interaction, then for their inferences for why their partner was acting that way.

The results were very interesting. Couples who trusted one another were more optimistic, and they tended to report that their partner's motives were positive, even to the extent of saying that the other person's motives were more positive than their own. People who had high trust for their partners did not change their opinions of the other person's behavior very often. The authors

> . . . speculated that the confidence and clarity of the core attitudes held by trusting individuals lead them to react affectively to the partner's behavior in a relatively automatic, positive way and that little consideration of its meaning typically takes place. The potential cost of this process is that acts of caring may be taken for granted if the implications of events are not elaborated.[35]

Uncertainty

Uncertainty can be discussed at two levels. Conflict creates uncertainty within the *relationship* in which it occurs, and uncertainty also exists to different degrees within the particular conflict *episode*. **Uncertainty** in the conflict situation occurs when we have insufficient information to understand another's motives, goals, or behaviors or when we do not understand how another is responding to us.

Many events are capable of creating uncertainty in relationships: changes in the other person's behavior, the breaking of a confidence, a friend breaking off contact, a dating partner going out with someone else. Interestingly, nearly all the events recalled as those causing uncertainty can be classified as conflict episodes.[36] Most people cannot recall anything that might have been a clue to events causing uncertainty, or they can recognize clues only in retrospect. Uncertainty in relationships does lead to increased communication with the other person, and when people communicate about events causing uncertainty, they tend to be more satisfied. Those who do not talk about uncertainty-causing events generally express regret about avoiding the issue. As time passes, feelings about uncertainty-causing events become less negative.[37] Communication with the other, "doing" the conflict, is generally the best way to reduce uncertainty within a relationship. But there is a deeper level of uncertainty—that within the conflict itself.

Conflicts are inherently messy and filled with ambiguity. "The characteristic of conflict that is most difficult to capture in research is the chaos that pervades a heated argument or a long-simmering conflict."[38] There are three sources of ambiguity and disorder in conflict: the source of the conflict, the organizational complexity of conflict patterns, and the embeddedness of conflict in daily activities.

Issues in conflict are rarely singular or straightforward. Rational views of conflict assume that both people are able to identify the issue, develop straightforward goals about it, and move toward resolution through compromise or collaboration. However, the real case is that people may not share the same perception about the issue or may not agree on the conflict issue at all. They may think the conflict has arisen due to different causes; they may interpret the other's behavior differently than the other intends; and so on. Furthermore, conflicts may exist simultaneously at different levels—superficial issues may also involve deeper relational implications. Mild conflicts generally reflect agreement concerning the deeper relational issues involved; in bitter and destructive conflicts, relational issues are entangled and difficult to resolve.

The complexity of conflict may also affect the level of ambiguity present. Whereas casual conversation is characterized by adherence to a set of cooperative principles, these principles are often violated in conflict because it may not be in one's best interest to be truthful, succinct, relevant, and orderly in one's conversation. In addition, patterns in conflict (beyond the broad stages of prelude, initiation, differentiation, and resolution) are difficult to identify. Most conversation shows a reciprocal pattern, in which message types are generally followed by similar types, but "conflicts often have a dynamic quality characterized by oscillation between aggression and withdrawal."[39] Furthermore, participants in conflicts often introduce, drop, reintroduce, and expand topics in an unpredictable pattern, making it difficult for the other person to know where the conversation might lead.

A final source for the situations of uncertainty created by conflicts is the embeddedness of conflict in our everyday lives.

> Conflicts occur at all hours of the day and night, on any occasion, during any activity, for any number of reasons. There is often a large surprise element in conflict for both parties involved; neither person necessarily anticipates having conflict at a particular moment and conflict may not be recognized as such until after it has occurred.[40]

How do people react to uncertainty in conflict situations? One study found that uncertain individuals tended to make more negative attributions about the other and fewer positive attributional statements. In addition, uncertain individuals made fewer specific and more frequent global attributions for very negative events, seeing particular instances as indicative of character. They also had a lower threshold for perceiving threats than promises. In short, uncertain individuals construct a social reality that mirrors their fears but frustrates their hopes.[41]

In addition to making negative attributions, those in uncertain relationships may go so far as to test whether their partner cares about them and is responsive to their needs.

> They will be relatively vigilant and monitor behavior for any diagnostic signs . . . the emotional investment of uncertain individuals leads them to be hopeful, primed to detect clear evidence of positive behavior and code it for its relevance to larger issues. On the other hand, their hopes are constrained by feelings of vulnerability that lead them to consider the possibility that negative behavior is, in fact, the result of the partner's lack of concern for them. This elaboration process will amplify the reactions they have to events in their relationship, because they will be reacting not only to the behavior itself, but to the symbolic content it is perceived to convey.[42]

People reduce uncertainty in conflict situations in one of three ways. First, they may choose to trust the other, although the ability to trust does depend on past behaviors. Second, they may reduce uncertainty by taking the perspective of the other person. And third, they may reduce uncertainty by engaging in "imagined interactions," or thoughts about what they might say and what the other might do in a conflict situation.[43]

Power

Power frequently receives bad press in popular writing about conflict. Many people think of power and the use of power as negative. This negative view of power is derived from understanding it as something a person has over another, as in the power to compel another person to act in a particular way. But **power** can also be thought of as the ability to get things done by accessing resources. In addition, as Folger and Poole pointed out, the use of power is necessary to move a conflict to productive management.[44] Along with the amount of uncertainty present in the situation and the trust people have for the other, the power people have available influences the way they analyze the issues of the conflict and set goals for themselves within it. Because of the attribution process, people will view each other as having used power strategies, so there is really no option not to use power in a conflict situation. We can only choose the type of power to use and whether to use it in productive or destructive ways.

Traditional Views of Power.   The concept of power has been presented in a number of ways. The most common view of power sees it as something held over the other person, as in the power to compel someone to do something. Winter, for example, defined power as "the ability or capacity of O to produce (consciously or unconsciously) intended effects on the behavior or emotions of another person P."[45] Thibault and Kelley distinguished between "fate control," in which one person can determine the outcomes another may achieve regardless of the behaviors the other enacts, and "behavior control," in which the variations in one person's behavior make it desirable for the other to vary his or her behavior also. In their view, then, power is determined by the extent to which one partner is dependent on the other for his or her outcomes.[46]

Thus, the traditional view speaks of the bases of power, the source of people's ability to compel others to action. Several authors, such as French and Raven among others,[47] identified these power bases in various ways, but a combination of their typologies reveals at least fifteen bases of power. Wheeless, Barraclough, and Stewart found three categories that subsume the various bases of power, which are summarized in Table 7.1.[48]

The traditional view offers several insights on how to assess and use power in conflict situations. Authors writing from this approach point out that power is not a finite quantity but something produced by human transactions.[49] The power people have in a relationship is a function of the type of relationship they have with each other. People do not have reward or punishment power over another unless the other person perceives that they have those rewards and punishments. Power is also a function of dependency: It depends on others to the extent that others can affect one's goals, and to the extent that others have resources one needs to accomplish one's goals.

People also have power to the extent that they have access to resources that can be used to persuade or convince others, change the group's or relationship's course of action, or prevent others from moving toward their goals in conflict situations. Anything that enables participants to move toward their own goals or interferes with another's actions is a resource that can be used in conflict.

Assessing Power.   Some authors have argued that the person who brings the most resources to the relationship has the most power.[50] Other authors have claimed that people get power in a relationship through access to the symbols of power (e.g., status) and control over resources that others need to do their work.[51] Clearly, the power one has in a conflict situation is partially based on the resources at one's disposal, as illustrated by the following conflict interaction:

> Being an assistant cook is no easy job. I have a manager and five cooks over me telling me what to do. Because of my friendly nature and the amount of time I spend with them, I thought I had achieved a peer status with them. After dinner, I said to one of the cooks, "Let's clean up." (I was already cleaning a pot and he was surveying the dining room.)

TABLE 7.1   *Dimensions of Power*

This table suggests three bases for power: the ability to show people what the outcome of a particular action will be, the ability to use the relationship as a basis for requesting action, and the ability to link particular values to a desired behavior. Within each power base are several strategies that can be used to activate the power base.

Power Base	Statement
Preview Expectations/Consequences	
Reward	Comply because you will benefit.
Coercive	Comply or you will be punished.
Remunerative	Comply because you are being paid to do so.
Compliance	Comply because I am watching you.
Inducement	Comply because I have badgered you into it.
Deterrence	Comply to avoid negative outcomes.
Invoke Relationships/Identification	
Expert	Comply because I know more than you.
Referent	Comply because I am a good role model.
Social	Comply because you want to continue our relationship.
Identification	Comply because you want to be like me.
Summon Values/Obligations	
Legitimate	Comply because my position allows me to ask you.
Pure Normative	Comply because it is the right thing to do.
Internalization	Comply because you have accepted the values of the decision.
Persuasion	Comply because I have convinced you to do so.
Activation of Commitments	Comply because you owe it to me.

Source: Lawrence R. Wheeless, Robert Barraclough, and Robert Steward, "Compliance-Gaining Power in Persuasion," in Robert N. Bostrum (ed.), *Communication Yearbook 7*, pp. 105–145, copyright © 1983 by Sage Publications, Inc. Reprinted by permission of Sage Publications, Inc.

He looked at me a second and said, "You want to play hardball? I'll play hardball." Being the sincere and naive person, I asked, "Hardball?"

He said, "I am the boss. I tell you what to do. Do you pay for your meals here on the weekend? Are your snacks paid for? You are not a full-time cook here, you do not get the benefits. I am being nice in letting you have all those things."

It all hit me kind of hard. I wasn't prepared for this. I said, "Thank you for not playing hardball with me." And then to lighten up the atmosphere I asked, "So, can you keep playing softball?" He raised his eyebrows again, and I thought I saw him crack a smile on the corner of his mouth.

Power may also be assessed by examining the pattern of accommodation in the relationship. The "principle of least interest" dictates that the person with the least interest in continuing the relationship has more power within it because that person is less dependent on the relationship for psychological rewards.[52] One can also assess power by asking who accommodates the most in the relationship, what the possibilities are for change, and who labels the conflict. Generally, people with less power accommodate more and are asked to change more radically than those with more power. Powerful people accommodate less, have the opportunity to label the conflict or define its parameters, and have the least interest in ensuring that the resolution of the conflict meets the needs of all involved.

A final way of assessing power is to examine the way in which people use speech. What is powerful and powerless speech? Powerful speech refers to verbal and nonverbal messages used to dominate and control others or to "talk down" to them, whereas powerless speech includes those messages that set one up to be dominated, controlled, or to "talk up" to others. Powerful speech can occur in different degrees. At one level it includes interrupting others, speaking loudly, controlling the topic of conversation, and sounding like one is very confident in being right (implying that the other is wrong). At another level it also includes put-downs, efforts to belittle others, interrupting the other, talking through the other, and talking louder than the other. At the extreme it includes verbal threats, swearing, name calling while shouting, standing up to or over the other accompanied with menacing facial expressions, nasty looks, and so on.

Powerless speech includes the nonassertive use of language, making requests, speaking softly, and sounding tentative, uncertain, or unsure of oneself. One is exercising powerless speech when accommodating others. Powerful speech is often used by people employing a competitive style of conflict. Erickson and his colleagues identified some differences between powerful and powerless speech. Powerful speakers used more intensifiers (e.g., "very"), fewer hedges (e.g., "I guess"), especially formal grammar, fewer hesitation forms (e.g., "uh, you know"), more controlled gestures, fewer questioning forms (e.g., rising intonation at the end of a declarative sentence), and fewer polite forms when addressing others.

The question arises as to whether there is a neutral form of speech that is neither powerful or powerless. Most communication researchers would have trouble identifying that form. Even in cases in which communicators rely on objective language, there tends to be a power differential. For example, if a male simply asks a male friend what time it is and he provides the answer, he is using powerless speech to a very mild degree because he is asking a question. The male friend is using more powerful speech, again to a very mild degree, because he shows that he knows the answer.

Another question is whether it is bad to use powerful or powerless speech. We believe that normally people switch back and forth. This reinforces the idea of our always having a choice. There are times in one's job or as a parent when one must rely on (mild) forms of powerful speech to exercise control. Meanwhile we must also acquiesce to others on some legitimate occasions. The problem comes when one tends to rely for the most part on one form of speech more than the other. Some people rely too heavily on either the powerful or the powerless speech patterns making them too dominant (and sometimes harming others) or too submissive (and sometimes harming themselves).

Power has been called "the architect of conflict" because it enables people to use the resources available to them and to communicate the power that moves a conflict along to its end. Power shapes the perceptions people have of their choices and their estimations of the other's behavior in conflict situations. It is, however, situated in a matrix of variables, along with trust and uncertainty. The trust one has of another affects the power moves one makes in a conflict. The way people view the other's use of power affects their trust level. Uncertainty results from trust and affects the degree to which people feel the need to make explicit power moves in a conflict. All of these, in turn, affect how issues are defined in a conflict and how goals are generated to address these issues.

APPLICATION 7.7

Power is frequently seen as something based on resources. Describe a conflict event you have observed (in your life or in fiction) in which power was gained through communication strategies rather than through resources. For example, can you think of a time when a person distorted the facts of a situation in order to look better and gain power where the person had none before?

From Theory to Action

This chapter examined three major areas of theoretical development in the study of conflict: theories emphasizing the role of the individual participants in the conflict, theories emphasizing the role of the relationship between those in the conflict, and theories emphasizing the structure of conflict. The people involved in the conflict, how they view the conflict, and how they are related to one another all affect the way in which the conflict is managed or resolved.

Clearly, the means we use to explain a conflict influence how we react to it and how we choose behaviors within it. If we see conflict as something that occurs because of the people who are involved, we will tend to have a fatalistic attitude about it. "That person is always avoiding, how can I get her to see the point?" or "He is always trying to have his way" are attitudes we may adopt when we see another person's conflict style as fixed. Similarly, we are likely to excuse ourselves for untoward behavior if we see our mistakes as the result of too much pressure: "I was having a really bad day and didn't mean to take it out on you." Such excuses may absolve us from blame but do not address the problem well.

When we view conflicts as the result of relationships, we begin to see how our behavior is linked to others. Two individuals do not have a conflict separately. They are in conflict together, and conflict has occurred because of the way they have acted toward one another. Toward the end of *The Lion in Winter,* a classic movie about the tempestuous relationship between Henry II of England and his wife Eleanor of Aquitaine, Eleanor asks how they came to be at such odds. He replies, "Step by step, Madam." Recognizing that the actions we take have consequences for others and are themselves affected by the actions of others is the first step toward understanding our mutual interdependence. Where there is no interdependence, there is little basis for conflict.

Understanding the assumptions of these various theories can help us to better understand our behavior, as illustrated by Case Study 7.2, which was written by a woman who experienced numerous conflicts with her father. She wrote it as an exercise in connecting theory to action. It demonstrates the effects of theory on thinking.

Case Study 7.2 ■ *It's More Than Theory* ─────────────────────

It was Saturday afternoon and I stopped by my parent's home to drop off my father's gift. I realized that our lack of communication needed to come to an end. I mustered a "Hi, Dad . . . happy birthday." He turned and flashed half a smile. It became clear that in order to better understand the process of conflict (which we were definitely experiencing) it was essential that my dad and I try to better understand the theories of conflict.

"Dad, we need to talk. I really think that if we look at the process or the way in which we engage in conflict, we might be able to discover some common assumptions that will help us to resolve our conflict."

"What are you talking about?" he asked.

"All I'm trying to say is that theories help explain how processes work. In understanding communication and theories of conflict, we should be able to interpret our conflicts better and act in more constructive ways."

"Why would I want to do that?" he complained.

"Because, Dad," I said, defending myself, "conflict theories help us to learn about conflict behavior. Research even suggests that all conflicts have much in common."

Dad thought to himself for a minute and said, matter of factly, "How can looking at research theories help us? It's not like I have a problem."

"I'm not saying either one of us has a problem. What I am saying is that there are several ways we can try to understand our conflicts and that this could help us with our relationship."

"Like what?"

"Well, in our disagreements we continually follow a series of actions and reactions. We also have specific ways of communicating with one another. We need to realize that how we perceive our communication influences the type of opinions we form and these perceptions affect how we act toward each other in terms of reaching our goals."

I could tell by my dad's expression that he was finally interested in what I was saying. "How can I use these theories to better understand our conflict?"

"First off, it is helpful to understand the role of individuals participating in the conflict. There are four theories that look at the role of individuals. Psychodynamic theory concludes that conflict is experienced by us based on our intrapersonal states."

"What do you mean by that?"

I explained that Freud believed that conflict is within ourselves and that the conflicts we engage in can be nonrealistic because they are just a release of tension unrelated to the other person involved. Or they can be misplaced because we don't look at the real issue.

"I can see how conflict can be based on our aggressive impulses and anxieties," Dad replied. "But how can I use this theory in our entanglements?"

"Well, we can use it to try to understand the various things that motivate us in a conflict. Maybe we are making things worse because of unrelated issues. Another theory discussing the role of the individual is attribution theory. This is when we draw conclusions about each other's behavior in order to explain the conflict."

"I think I may do that to you," said Dad.

"You see, we're only halfway through the theories and already you can apply them to your own behavior. Attribution theory goes on to say that we have ideas about each other's character. This information can help us see how our choices of actions are made."

"Boy, you just gave me a lot of information about individual roles in conflict, but what about how our relationship affects the way our conflict will be handled or resolved?"

"Dad, you are so on top of it. The role of relationship between those in conflict is what the next three theories are all about. The social exchange theory says we evaluate our relationships in terms of the value of the costs and rewards created by having it. We have comparison levels (CL), which are standards we use to determine if the relationship is satisfactory. Our CL_{alt} is the lowest level acceptable to continue the relationship. The social exchange theory shows us that we use strategy to handle conflict. Conflict becomes a situation of moves and countermoves leading to particular outcomes. Because there is interdependency in conflict we choose actions based on our self-interest."

"Won't we try to maximize benefits and minimize our losses in this conflict?" Dad asked.

"Of course, Dad, but with a level of fairness. We can act independently, or we can engage in cooperative joint action, where we agree on a conflict resolution path. Or we can act through an imposed joint action, where one of us imposes a threat to get his way."

"Do you feel that is how we handle our conflicts?" asked Dad.

"Sometimes. But I think the point here is that we choose our actions in regard for a particular outcome in conflict situations, or we choose our actions based on the cost of the relationship."

"Why can't we just learn to communicate the right way and avoid all this conflict stuff?"

"Good point, Dad, and one that brings to me a last theory based on relationships—it's called systems theory. It states that not only are breakdowns in communication inevitable, they are normal. We need to compete and collaborate constructively and realize that these differences of opinion are a normal process for growth and adaptation."

"So let me get this straight. You're telling me that the system theory helps us to see the importance of conflict in order to change and fit into our 'system' during periods of conflict."

"Exactly, Dad, and to put this all together, a final theory emphasizes the structural aspects of conflict. When one of us fails to trust the other, the less certain we are about the other's intentions. When we are unsure about the other's motives, we resort to power moves and try to force each other to do what we want. Now can you see the importance of understanding these theories and their assumptions in order to engage in constructive conflict?"

"Absolutely. By recognizing who is involved, how they view conflict, how they are related to one another, and at what stage the conflict is viewed, we can see how these factors affect the way in which the conflict will be managed and resolved."

"Right on, Dad."

Notes

1. C. S. Hall, *A Primer of Freudian Psychology,* 2nd Ed. (New York: World, 1979), p. 28.

2. Ibid.

3. Ibid.

4. Ibid., p. 14.

5. Lewis Coser, *The Functions of Social Conflict* (New York: Free Press, 1956).

6. Joseph Folger and Marshal Scott Poole, *Working Through Conflict* (Glenview, IL: Scott Foresman, 1984), p. 15.

7. Alan L. Sillars, "Attributions and Communication in Roommate Conflicts," *Communication Monographs* 47 (1980), 180–200; "The Sequential and Distributional Structure of Conflict Interactions as a Function of Attributions Concerning the Locus of Responsibility and Stability of Conflicts," in Dan Nimmo (Ed.), *Communication Yearbook* 4 (New Brunswick, NJ: Transaction Books, 1980), pp. 217–235.

8. Shawn W. Rosenberg and Gary Wolsfeld, "International Conflict and the Problem of Attribution," *Journal of Conflict Resolution* 21 (1977), 75–103.

9. Ibid., p. 1093.

10. Meryl Reis Louis, "How Individuals Conceptualize Conflict: Identification of Steps in the Process and the Role of Personal/Development Factors," *Human Relations* 30 (1977), 451–467.

11. John W. Thibault and Harold H. Kelley, *The Social Psychology of Groups* (New York: John Wiley, 1959); Harold H. Kelley and John W. Thibault, *Interpersonal Relations: A Theory of Interdependence* (New York: John Wiley & Sons, 1978).

12. Kelley and Thibault, *Interpersonal Relations,* pp. 8–9.

13. This concept of fairness is called "distributive justice" in G. C. Homans, *Social Behavior: Its Elementary Forms* (New York: Harcourt Brace Jovanovich, 1961); it is called "equity" in E. Walster, G. W. Walster, and E. Berscheid, *Equity Theory and Research* (Boston: Allyn and Bacon, 1978).

14. Folger and Poole, *Working Through Conflict,* p. 24.

15. Ibid., pp. 36–37.

16. William Poundstone, *Prisoner's Dilemma* (New York: Doubleday, 1992), p. 6.

17. James T. Tedeschi, Barry R. Schlenker, and T. V. Bonoma, *Conflict, Power & Games: The Experimental Study of Interpersonal Relations* (Chicago: Aldine Publishing 1973), p. 1.

18. James A. Schellenberg, *The Science of Conflict* (New York: Oxford University Press, 1982).

19. An estimated 1,000 studies were reviewed in Dean G. Pruitt and Melvin J. Kimmel, "Twenty Years of Ex-

perimental Gaming: Critique, Synthesis and Suggestions for the Future," *Annual Review of Psychology* 28 (1977), 363–392.

20. Charlan Nemeth, "A Critical Analysis of Research Utilizing the Prisoner's Dilmma Paradigm for the Study of Bargaining," in Leonard Berkowitz (Ed.), *Advances in Experimental Social Psychology,* Vol. 6 (New York: Academic Press, 1982).

21. Pruitt and Kimmel, "Twenty Years of Experimental Gaming."

22. Brent D. Ruben, "Communication and Conflict: A System-Theoretic Perspective," *Quarterly Journal of Speech* 64 (1978), 205–206.

23. Delmar M. Hilyard, "Research Models and Designs for the Study of Conflict," in Fred E. Jandt (Ed.), *Conflict Resolution Through Communication* (New York: Harper & Row, 1972), pp. 439–451.

24. Raymond W. Mack and Richard C. Snyder, "The Analysis of Social Conflict: Toward an Overview and Synthesis," in Fred E. Jandt (Ed.), *Conflict Resolution Through Communication* (New York: Harper and Row, 1972), p. 82.

25. Ibid., p. 83.

26. Kenneth Thomas, "Conflict and Conflict Management," in M. D. Dunnett (Ed.), *The Handbook of Industrial and Organizational Psychology* (Chicago: Rand McNally, 1976), p. 889.

27. R. Larzalere and T. L. Huston, "The Dyadic Trust Scale: Toward Understanding Interpersonal Trust in Close Relationships," *Journal of Marriage and the Family* 42 (1980), 595–604; John G. Holmes and John K. Rempel, "Trust in Close Relationships," in Clyde Hendrick (Ed.), *Close Relationships* (Newbury Park, CA: Sage, 1989), pp. 187–220.

28. Morton Deutsch, *The Resolution of Conflict* (New Haven, CT: Yale University Press, 1973), pp. 144–145; see also "Trust and Suspicion," *Journal of Conflict Resolution* 2 (1958), 265–279.

29. Holmes and Rempel, "Trust in Close Relationships," p. 18.

30. John K. Rempel, John G. Holmes, and M. P. Zanna, "Trust in Close Relationships," *Journal of Personality and Social Psychology* 49 (1985), 95–112.

31. Larzalere and Huston, "The Dyadic Trust Scale," p. 596.

32. Holmes and Rempel, "Trust in Close Relationships," p. 190.

33. Deutsch, *The Resolution of Conflict,* pp. 170–175.

34. John Holmes, "The Exchange Process in Close Relationships: Microbehavior and Macromotives," in M. J. Lerner and S. C. Lerner (Eds.), *The Justice Motive in Social Behavior* (New York: Plenum, 1981), 261–284; John K. Rempel, "Trust and Attributions in Close Relationships," unpublished doctoral dissertation, University of Waterloo, Ontario, 1987.

35. Holmes and Rempel, "Trust in Close Relationships," p. 205.

36. Sally Planalp and James M. Honeycutt, "Events That Increase Uncertainty in Personal Relationships," *Human Communication Research* 11 (1985), 593–604.

37. Sally Planalp, Diane K. Rutherford, and James M. Honeycutt, "Events That Increase Uncertainty in Personal Relationships II," *Human Communication Research* 14 (1988), 516–547.

38. Allan L. Sillars and Judith Weisberg, "Conflict as a Social Skill," in Michael E. Roloff and Gerald R. Miller (Eds.), *Interpersonal Processes: New Directions in Theory and Research* (Newbury Park, CA: Sage, 1987), p. 148.

39. Ibid., p. 153.

40. Ibid., p. 157.

41. Rempel, "Trust and Attributions in Close Relationships," 1987.

42. Holmes and Rempel, "Trust in Close Relationships," p. 210.

43. James M. Honeycutt, Kenneth S. Zagacki, and Renee Edwards, "Imagined Interaction and Interpersonal Communication," *Communication Reports* 3 (1990), 1–8.

44. Folger and Poole, *Working Through Conflict.*

45. D. G. Winter, *The Power Motive* (New York: Free Press, 1973), p. 5.

46. Thibault and Kelley, *The Social Psychology of Groups,* 1959.

47. John R. P. French and Bertram Raven, "The Basis of Social Power," in Dorwin Cartwright and A. Sander (Eds.), *Group Dynamics,* 2nd Ed. (New York: Harper and Row, 1960); Herbert C. Kelman, "Compliance, Identification and Internalization: Three Processes of Attitude Change," *Journal of Conflict Resolution* 2 (1958), 51–60; Amatai Etzioni, *A Comparative Analysis of Complex Organizations* (New York: Free Press, 1961); Talcott Parsons, "On the Concept of Influence," *Public Opinion Quarterly* 27 (1963), 37–62; Joyce L. Hocker and William W. Wilmot, *Interpersonal Conflict,* 3rd Ed. (Dubuque, IA: Wm. C. Brown, 1991).

48. Lawrence R. Wheeless, Robert Barraclough, and Robert Stewart, "Compliance-Gaining and Power in Persuasion," in Robert Bostrum (Ed.), *Communication Yearbook* 7 (Beverly Hills, CA: Sage, 1983), pp. 105–145.

49. Andrew King, *Power and Communication* (Prospect Heights, IL: Waveland Press, 1987), p. 138; see also Hocker and Wilmot, *Interpersonal Conflict.*

50. R. O. Blood and D. M. Wolfe, *Husbands and Wives: The Dynamics of Married Living* (New York: Free Press, 1960).

51. Charles Conrad, *Strategic Organizational Communication,* 2nd Ed. (Fort Worth, TX: Holt, Rinehart & Winston, 1990).

52. W. Waller and R. Hill, *The Family: A Dynamic Interpretation* (New York: Dryden, 1951).

8

A Communication Perspective on Conflict Behavior

Objectives

At the end of this chapter, you should be able to

1. describe the difference between the linear view of communication and the transactional view of communication.

2. articulate the rules that people are using to bring a conflict to resolution.

3. explain how dialectical tensions concerning competence have affected a conflict you experienced in the past.

4. identify the goals and issues in a particular conflict.

Key Terms

appropriateness	fidelity	regulative rules
communication competence	goal	relational goal
definitional rules	identity goal	rule
dialectical tension	instrumental goal	transactional model
effectiveness	issue	
evidence	linear model	

In the previous chapter, we examined social-psychological views of the conflict situation. These views have in common the idea that the people involved in the conflict, the way in which they relate to one another, and the structure of the situation are the driving forces behind conflict situations. The communication theories of conflict presented in this chapter assume not only that the people involved in the conflict, and their relationship to one another, create conflict situations, but that people create conflict situations through their communication or message behavior. From this perspective, *communication is viewed as both the cause and the effect of conflict situations.* This perspective arises from three assumptions about the role of communication in conflict:

1. "It is through communicative action that persons initiate, define, maintain, and terminate their social bonds."[1]
2. Much of our interpersonal communication is conflict related in that it is intended to prevent conflicts from occurring, may be used to manage or resolve them when they do occur, and is employed to repair relationships after experiencing a conflict.
3. It can provide people with the proper knowledge, attitudes, and skills for constructive conflict management and resolution.

To take a communication perspective on conflict, one must realize that communication ranges from extremely positive forms of interaction (e.g., lovemaking, gift giving, expressions of affection) to extremely negative (e.g., intimidation, harassment, threats, verbal abuse, conflict, and fighting). This statement may come as a surprise to someone who sees communication solely as a positive, constructive activity. Another way to put this is to say that conflict, despite the potential for growth that it presents to people, often lies on the "dark side" of interpersonal communication.[2]

What is a communication perspective? There are probably as many answers to that question as there are people who would answer it.[3] Typically, the field of communication has embraced a wide variety of perspectives. In this chapter we'll introduce two of those perspectives, and demonstrate how looking at communication in that manner affects the way we define and perceive conflict.

Linear versus Transactional Views of Communication and Conflict

The Linear Model: Message Senders and Receivers

A way in which communication researchers have traditionally viewed communication is to define it as a process of sending and receiving messages. Some communication studies have focused primarily on the sending or encoding of messages and how people in certain situations tend to engage in certain kinds of message production behaviors. These studies raised questions related to goals, purposes, and intentions of message senders. Other communication studies have examined the receiving or decoding of messages and how people are likely to respond to messages. These latter studies raised questions related to the effects of messages on receivers.

Focusing on message senders or message receivers is a way of studying communication. This orientation to communication has been called the **linear model,** because it focuses on the sequential production of messages with either the senders as the starting point or the receivers as the end point. For the most part, it has focused on issues of **fidelity;** that is, is what was "received" the same meaning as what was "sent"? A visual metaphor for the linear model of communication is a conveyor belt that runs back and forth between two people. The sender puts a message on the belt, sends it to the receiver, who then does something to the message and sends it back to the receiver. Along the way, the message may be sent via one channel or another and may be distorted by external sources, or noise.

Although this approach has helped communication scholars to focus on important issues such as phrasing conflict messages "correctly" (e.g., using "I" language) and listening with empathy to others in the conflict situation, it has largely ignored the fact that conflict is something that people do together. All the empathic listening in the world will probably not bring a conflict to resolution if the other person is determined to yell and scream until the conflict tilts in his or her favor. Similarly, responsible communication is difficult to maintain in the face of one who will not listen. In addition, using a linear model to explain conflict often results in trying to fix the "blame" of the conflict situation on one person or another, not recognizing that both people in a conflict situation contribute to the emergence of the conflict. These kinds of shortcomings have led most in the field of communication to embrace the transactional model of communication.

The Transactional Model: People Communicating Together

Although researchers have commonly referred to senders and receivers of messages in the past, it is more common today to talk about communication as a process by which people make or create meaning together. This is commonly called the **transactional model** of communication. Such an approach recognizes that communication (and by extension, conflict) isn't something we do *to* one another, but something we do *with* one another (like teamwork). A conflict is not seen as something that happens when one person sends a message to another indicating that he or she is unhappy with some behavior performed by the other. That is a traditional view of communication and conflict. Rather conflict is seen as the behaviors of each person, in response to one another, conjointly creating an understanding in which both people perceive themselves as being in conflict with one another. The transactional view emphasizes the process of communicating, whereas the linear view emphasizes the end product of communicating. Some other differences between the linear and transactional views of communication are:

1. The linear view focuses on how an individual's behaviors are followed by another's responses to them, whereas the transactional view emphasizes what people do together. Thus, the transactional view highlights the *inter* in interpersonal communication and conflict: how people collaborate, cooperate, and work together to negotiate and renegotiate an understanding, agreement, or consensus.
2. The linear view treats people as though they have set identities before, during, and after communication or conflict, whereas the transactional view includes the idea that whenever we are in communication with others, we are negotiating and renegotiating who we are—our definitions of ourselves and the impressions we make on others.
3. The linear view also treats relationships as fixed entities that do not change (once friends, always friends; once enemies, always enemies), whereas the transactional view acknowledges that, whenever we are in communication with others, we are negotiating and renegotiating our understanding of our relationship.

The advantage of this latter view is that we begin to recognize the importance of both people's behavior in the conflict situation. One person acting competently in a conflict situation, using good communication skills, usually cannot bring the conflict to some resolution. It takes two people to make the conflict, and it takes two people to manage or resolve it. The way people talk about the conflict together, the way they express messages in response to one another, the way they "read" each other's nonverbal messages as the conflict is being enacted all create the conflict situation as well as manage it or move it to resolution.

In this transactional view of communication and conflict, communication is seen as something that surrounds us. We are not even aware of all the things we do that are communicative in nature. We act within the confines of our culture, our expectations for a particular situation, our expectations for the relationship we are in, and our expectations for our own behavior, and at the same time, we affect our cultural view, our view of the situation, our view of the relationship, and our view of ourselves. The primary difference between the linear and transactional focus in communication may be seen in the visual metaphors we might use to explain each. Whereas the primary visual metaphor for the linear model is a conveyor belt, in the transactional model, communication (and, hence, conflict as a type of communication) is seen more as a dance that two people do together.

APPLICATION 8.1

How can you understand conflict better by explaining it from a linear model or a transactional model? Which one makes more sense to you? Why?

As we examine a communication perspective on conflict, we see that it has the potential to incorporate many of the traditional notions about conflict derived from social-psychological theories, as well as examining meaning-making behavior in conflict situations. Three areas of research take a communication perspective: (1) research that examines communication and conflict as rule-regulated behavior; (2) research that examines the communication competence of those involved in the conflict situation; and (3) research that examines the goals and effects of communication as they relate to the messages that people choose in conflict situations.

Rules and Conflict Communication

> This conflict happened two years ago, when I was still in language school. I had conflicts with several people who were also from Taiwan. They thought I was a snob and didn't want to stay with them. When I had come to the United States, there were several Taiwanese students who had already been here. They usually spent time together and talked together. The reason I spent a lot of money to come here is because I wanted to study in English, in order to make American friends. So, I spent more time with my American friends than with the other students from Taiwan, because I wanted to practice my English. They didn't understand, and spread the rumor that I thought I was too good for them. Eventually, the conflict was gone because they understood my point of view.

Perhaps the easiest kind of conflict to recognize is the kind in which we believe that someone important to us has broken some kind of "rule" about the way people should behave. In the preceding example, the international student was accused of not following the norms for international students—hang around with others like yourself. Stick together.

The student thought it was more important for him to learn English because he had spent so much money in order to come here. When the other students recognized that he was not being standoffish, but only trying to achieve his goals, they were less judgmental about his behavior.

Shiminoff described a communication **rule** as a "followable prescription that indicates what behavior is obligated, preferred, or prohibited in certain contexts."[4] Rules tell us what we must say, what we should say, and what we better not say in different situations. In addition, rules not only tell us what we should and should not do together, but also how we create meaning together.

Rules are of two types, regulative (sometimes called procedural) and definitional (sometimes called constitutive). **Regulative rules** influence our actions or behavioral choices. We generally know that a regulative rule exists largely when we have broken it and face some sort of sanction. For example, at a friend's wedding, it is customary to congratulate the groom and convey best wishes to the bride. Saying "congratulations" to the bride is considered to be in poor taste, and if you do so, you may get a disapproving look from someone. This is a regulative rule, governing what behavior we should choose. The rule is there, but it is not a very strong one—it is a preferred rule. On the other hand, laughing at a funeral is almost unheard of. It is prohibited behavior, and anyone who breaks the rule would probably be escorted out of the room.

We encounter regulative rules when we feel social pressures that encourage us to act one way or another in a given situation. For example, regulative rules tell us that we should indicate we are listening to another person on the telephone by inserting nonverbal phrases like "uh-huh." When we don't do so, the other person may ask if we are still listening. Thus, regulative rules tell us how we should act in particular situations.

On the other hand, **definitional rules** tell us how to interpret what is happening in various situations. In a long-term relationship like a marriage, you may come to understand that when your spouse comes home, enters the house without speaking, and sits in a favorite chair staring off into space, that he or she has had a stressful day and needs some time to calm down. Using particular words within an ongoing relationship may signal a deeper meaning without having to use many words to activate the meaning. For example, one student reported that in his family, they use the word *hernia* to indicate any kind of mistake from one of the members. It's a meaning limited to the family, and simply saying "hernia" is like saying "Gosh, that was dumb. What are you going to do about it?"

We learn rules from experience, through teaching, and when watching others. When we first meet another person, the rules that generally apply to any relationship govern the way we communicate. As the relationship develops, rules become more idiosyncratic, applying to a particular relationship but not to other relationships. For example, when you first met the person whom you currently consider your best friend, you probably talked about things in a pretty general way. There wasn't much difference between the way you spoke with that person and anyone else. As you have come to know each other, though, you know that there are certain things your friend will and will not talk about, and you know the best way to approach any particular topic. You have gone from using general rules to idiosyncratic rules—rules that apply only to this friendship.

The study of rules has important implications for conflict communication. As we observe conflicts, we can see that many of them seem to arise because one person thinks the other has broken some important rule in the relationship. Some of the rules are "common sense" or "common courtesy" rules, as when roommates conflict over cleanliness habits. Rules about keeping the house clean are rarely discussed before a violation occurs. We assume that others know how to clean up after themselves. It is only when we find out differently that we feel a need to discuss the rules. Other rules have been either tacitly or explicitly discussed by people in a close relationship. When you begin to date someone exclusively, for example, you generally agree with the other person that this is what you will do. Accepting a date with another person would violate the rule of exclusivity. Understanding that broken rules may be at the heart of a conflict, however, helps us to recognize what we should do in order to resolve the conflict.

Communication Competence and Conflict Behavior

One way of thinking about how people understand the rules of conflict situations is to examine their behavior as competent or incompetent. People described as competent are often better able to understand both the explicit and implicit rules of relationships, and adjust to expectations accordingly. **Communication competence** "is best conceived as an impression or attribution formed about others. Just as with source credibility, communication competence is attributed to a communicator on the basis of behaviors perceived and judged by others."[5] An extensive study of interpersonal communication competence concluded that these impressions of competent behavior are derived from two perceptions of the other's behavior: **appropriateness** (or, you can follow the rules and fit in) and **effectiveness** (you can use the rules to achieve your goals).[6]

Appropriateness has to do with how well one's behavior fits situational expectations. For example, it would be inappropriate for you to say to your supervisor at work, "If you loved me, you'd give me different hours." Effectiveness concerns whether or not one achieves one's goals in a particular communication situation. For example, if you used intimidating tactics with your supervisor and got your way, you would be considered effective in your communication, although you might ruin your chances for future influence. Together, appropriateness and effectiveness are indicators of behavioral flexibility, or one's ability to adapt to the constraints of a situation.[7]

People judging the communication competence of others are influenced far more by appropriateness than by effectiveness. One can be effective without being appropriate, but others will judge such communication as less competent than communication that is appropriate without being effective. In addition, a strong link exists between appropriateness within the situation and the task and social attractiveness of the actor.[8] Moreover, competence is a communication outcome in its own right. The more successfully people manage or resolve their conflicts, the more competent they appear to each other and to other people.[9] To create competent communication behavior, and by extension competent conflict behavior, requires that motivation, knowledge, context, skills, and outcomes be considered.[10]

APPLICATION 8.2

What seems like appropriate and effective conflict behavior to you? Describe a conflict episode you recently experienced, and list some behaviors that seemed appropriate, inappropriate, effective, and ineffective within it.

Additional characteristics of competent behavior have been suggested by other authors: adaptability, flexibility, supportiveness, ability to take the other person's perspective, ability to see an issue in all its complexity instead of black-and-white extremes, sensitivity to the other person, awareness of one's own behavior, timing of the conflict, and listening to the other person.[11] Some of these characteristics concern the way we think about conflict, and others are actual behaviors within the conflict, lending at least anecdotal support to the idea that competence has several dimensions.

A final point about competent communication behavior comes from Spitzberg, a frequent writer on the subject. He argued that competence is a complex phenomenon and there are value-laden ideas about the positive relationship between competent behavior and desirable outcomes. However, to the extent that people in communication situations, particularly conflict situations, face ambiguous or incompatible personal goals, they will face a number of tensions in the selection of competent behavior. These **dialectical tensions,** as Spitzberg called them, are composed of opposite ideas. Just as a person wishing to bring up a conflict is sometimes torn between the fear of offending the other and the desire to clarify an issue, these tension points demand some sort of balance or resolution; sometimes that resolution favors one demand over the other. The most competent behavior results from paying attention to both of the competing demands so that they are both somehow satisfied.

The most important of these tensions is the appropriateness-effectiveness dialectic. What combination of these two demands constitutes competence? People often assume that ineffective and inappropriate behavior is incompetent, but research indicates that appropriateness alone may generate perceptions of competence, or vice versa, as this narrative indicates:

> I was at a home improvement store on a Friday evening, and there were only three cashiers working (where fifteen could be). It was really busy, and it got worse when one of the cashiers closed. A man hadn't seen the closed sign, and came up carrying two big pots of flowers. He started yelling, "Where's the damn manager? What makes you think you can make all of us wait? Who do you think you are?" He was really angry. It didn't matter that he pretty much said what the rest of us were thinking. We hadn't said it because it didn't look like it would do any good. We all just sort of edged away from him and tried not to look at him.

Within the appropriateness-effectiveness dialectic are five other tensions:

1. *Politeness versus assertiveness:* Assertive people often get what they wish, but others sometimes do not like the way they achieve their goals. Consider this narrative of assertive behavior (at least, from the actor's point of view):

> I went to the student employment office to get information about how my student worker would be paid and asked about her papers. The person who answered me started off with a disclaimer that she knew nothing about student employment and that those who did would not be in until the following day, and then she proceeded with irrelevant information. I stopped her mid-sentence, thanked her, and said I would come back when the person who did know the information was there. I thought I was being assertive—I did not really wish to hear someone's speculation when it was unfounded. She thought I was very impolite and complained to her supervisor about me, who asked if I could be "more gentle" with student workers. My lack of "politeness" (not allowing the student to finish) resulted in her perception that I was communicatively incompetent and cruel.

2. *Social competence* (in general) *versus relational competence* (with respect to another person): People have habits that work in general, and they also develop habits that work with particular people. A problem arises in using general competence behaviors with a person who does not respond to that particular style or in using a particular style suited to limited relationships in general encounters. In the preceding encounter with the student worker, for instance, the narrator used a style that creates no difficulties in dealing with people who know the speaker well and who understand the hurried communication that results when that person is pressed to accomplish some task. What the narrator forgot was that the small campus where she works prides itself on its "friendly atmosphere" and has many people who expect more elaborate forms of address and longer interactions.

3. *Communality* (focusing on group or relational interests) *versus instrumentality* (focusing on individual interests): There is often a tension between what will benefit the relationship and what might benefit only one of the individuals within the relationship. One person writes:

> I have rarely taken a real vacation with my wife. When we have vacation time and money, she wants to visit her family in Costa Rica. I would rather go someplace different. We have generally wound up visiting her family, but this year, I put my foot down and said that I want to go to England. I have saved for this vacation for three years, and I don't want to go somewhere I have been before. So, she said, "Fine, go alone." I want to spend time with my wife, but it's just not relaxing for me to be with her family. This isn't the outcome I wanted—what I really wanted was for her to come to England with me. But it's not going to cause a divorce either, so we'll go our separate ways this year.

4. *Adaptation versus control:* In order to achieve goals in a situation, people need to have some control over the interaction. Too much control, however, can cause others to feel that they have no say in the way the encounter unfolds. Furthermore, too much planning or controlling can diminish the flexibility needed to change direction when a first strategy fails. Consider this example:

> I am currently enrolled in a conflict management class, and my supervisor took the same class from the same instructor. Sometimes what we know really gets in the way! I plan out my "good" messages, and since he knows where we have to wind up, he "cuts to the chase" and asks me what I want to have happen. Both of us know what we're supposed to do, but sometimes we're trying so hard to control things that we don't get anywhere at all.

5. *Competence versus incompetence:* Sometimes people appear incompetent in a particular situation even though they generally handle conflict in a competent manner. One person's experiences with a parent of a member of her troop underscores this tension:

> My Junior Girl Scout Troop (ages 9–12) meets with a Brownie Troop (ages 7–8) to have enough adults to supervise the girls. Because I had been a leader previously and the Brownie leader had not, I did all the organizational and task items. One day I had a confrontation with one of the mothers of a troop member. The confrontation was over a craft we made where we had to use hot-glue guns. I did not allow her seven-year-old daughter to assemble the craft. We leaders did most of the work. I did allow an eleven-year-old to use a glue gun. She complained that the craft "wasn't special" because all her daughter got to do was

> pick out the pieces for assembly. She then complained about everything else we had done since the start of the troop, comparing our troop to others and claiming that we were doing an inadequate job. I reflected her concerns, pointed out that I had erred on the side of safety with the hot-glue guns, pointed out that we were a combined troop and so were accommodating the needs of a diverse population, and so on. As the confrontation progressed, control became increasingly difficult. I suggested that if she were unhappy, there were other troops her daughter could join. When she got up to the sixth complaint, I became testy and said, "Could we do a reality check here? I am a volunteer. I don't do this full time, I don't get paid, and I'm not actually the Brownie leader—Mrs. P. is. You'll need to direct the rest of your complaints to her." And I walked away.

The narrator's behavior was competent up to a point, but the encounter underscores the notion of relational competence: It is extremely hard to keep following the rules of good conflict management and containment when the other person keeps escalating the conflict and introducing new issues.

The other dialectics of competence include short-term versus long-term objectives, openness/intimacy versus closedness/autonomy, and consistency versus flexibility.[12] In the Girl Scout confrontation, achieving a short-term pleasure by telling off the mother would do nothing to establish a positive long-term relationship with her.

> The Brownie leader helped by explaining how our troop worked and pointing out my efforts. My next encounter with the mother (over planning of a camping trip) was actually polite. Being open about our plans and desires for the troop helped clear the air, particularly with the Brownie leader's intervention. I also started a weekly letter to the parents (one of her complaints was the lack of communication about troop plans). Being consistent in communication appears to be more important than flexibility to this mother; she did not like our occasional spontaneity in meetings, for example, when plans fell through.

The dynamics of competence are complicated, and perceptions of competence may depend on a variety of decisions made in communication situations. We may know what to do yet find it difficult to create competent behavior in real life. Knowledge makes doing possible but does not ensure success. We need to learn how to create competent behavior without having to stop and figure out what to do each time we need to do it.

The goal of instruction in creating competent communication was best explained by Reardon. She argued that some communication behaviors may be classified as spontaneous—unplanned, subconscious, and unmonitored. For example, if you drop a heavy object on your foot, you are likely to say "ouch" and, depending on your level of pain, any number of obscenities (or euphemisms you substitute for them). Other behaviors are categorized as scripted and culture specific; they are learned through socialization, and the planning and monitoring needed to produce them become automatic as time passes. In the United States, if you want the attention of a clerk in a store, you might say, "Excuse me," or "Pardon me," prior to placing your request to get the clerk's attention. You do not have to think consciously about how to make the request. The third kind of communication behaviors are classified as contrived. They involve conscious planning and monitoring in the interaction. Conflict interaction is often contrived in that the participants are more or less aware of their own and the other person's behaviors. In teaching people to behave more competently in communication situations, then, one goal is to move behaviors that previously took monitoring and concentration into the scripted area so that good communication skills become a habit rather than an effort.[13]

> **APPLICATION 8.3**
>
> What part of competent communication behavior comes easily to you? What do you have to struggle to create in a conflict situation? How might you improve your behavior in the long run?

Examining Goals and Effects in Conflict Situations

Still another line of research in conflict and communication has to do with the goals that people have as they enter a conflict and the effects that having such a goal may create, whether intended or not. The goals people develop for their conflict interaction are largely dependent on how they define the conflict or how they identify the central issue of the conflict. In Chapter 2 we argued that in everyday interactions, people often don't think about their goals, or are unable to articulate them well prior to engaging in a conflict. Ideally (and this is a theory chapter), people act best in conflicts when they have clear goals, recognize that the other person has goals, and are flexible enough to find ways to satisfy both person's goals. In theory, one can best understand the focal points of conflict by examining the issues that give rise to it and—by understanding those issues—can begin to comprehend the role of issues and goals in an actual conflict. The **issue** is the focal point of the conflict, the thing that people point to when they are asked what the conflict is about. The topic of issues will be discussed in the next chapter. We define a **goal** as what a person hopes to achieve from engaging in a conflict.

Communication scholars Clark and Delia argue that communicators produce messages to attain one or more of the following three goals:

1. **instrumental goals** that concern solving problems or accomplishing tasks (such as discussing what to do today and deciding to go biking in the mountains)
2. **relationship goals** that concern creating and preserving a particular relationship between interactants (such as discussing your relationship and deciding to be just friends)
3. **identity goals** that concern establishing or maintaining a desired image of the communicator with others (such as saying something that one hopes makes a good impression on the other person).[14]

It is easy to see how such goals become part of conflict situations. An instrumental goal may be the main impetus to a conflict, as when you approach your supervisor to work out your hours when you have been scheduled at times that overlap your other commitments. You may have a relationship goal in mind when you and your dating partner discuss the frequency with which you see each other. Or, you may have an identity goal in mind when you ask someone, whose behavior toward you has changed for the worse recently, whether you have done something to offend him or her.

In addition to having conflict goals that reflect one of these three areas, Benoit and Cahn point out that a conflict message has potential effects on others in the situation in these three same areas, whether or not intended by the person creating the message:

1. **instrumental effects** that result in the solving of problems or in accomplishing tasks (such as discussing what to do today and deciding to go biking in the mountains)
2. **relationship effects** that create or preserve a particular relationship between interactants (such as discussing your relationship and deciding to be just friends)
3. **identity effects** consisting of a certain impression (such as actually impressing others because you appear to know what you are talking about)[15]

In interpersonal relationships, conflicting parties may have similar or different goals and experience similar or different effects. As noted earlier in this chapter, focusing on either the message sender's goals or the message's effects on the receiver is characteristic of the linear view of the communication process. Those communication scholars, who transcend the sender or receiver orientation, may view the process as a whole in which the interaction between communicators is seen as joint ventures and meaning as jointly created. For example, if someone is offended or provoked, communication has occurred whether or not the communicator intended to be abusive. This is important to realize because part of the communication that takes place during a conflict consists of the message sender's behaviors and their effects on the message receiver (for which some communicators do not want to take responsibility).

For example, a male member of a team of coworkers may have uttered a remark that offends his female coworkers. When confronted, the offender may not want to take responsibility for making the remark by claiming that he did not intend to offend the others and accuse them of being "too sensitive." The fact is that the others were offended by his remarks, and he needs to apologize to them. Part of learning how to improve our conflict communication skills involves our taking responsibility for the effects of our messages whether or not these effects were intended.

APPLICATION 8.4

Describe a conflict where the participants had instrumental, relational, and identity goals within the conflict. Which goal was achieved most easily? Which was the hardest to achieve?

Instrumental Goals and Effects of Communication in Conflict

The first goal/effect of communication in interpersonal conflict is instrumental, task accomplishing, goal attaining, problem solving, or issue resolving. For example, Zietlow and Sillars report marital conflicts over the following problem areas: housing, irritability, criticism of the partner, leisure time activities, household duties, and lack of communication, affection, or money.[16] This roommate conflict is one with instrumental goals/effects:

> Basically this problem deals with my roommate, Leslie, who likes to borrow my car. The problem is that she uses my gas and doesn't return it with a full tank. I get angry at her but she doesn't do anything about it.

Essentially, the **instrumental goal** or effect in a conflict is to *convince* someone that you are right. Most writing on the subject of convincing others concerns argumentation and how to improve one's skill in making arguments. Much of the research on the effectiveness of arguments has been conducted in public speaking situations rather than interpersonal; nevertheless, the ability to make a cogent argument in a conflict situation about what you feel and why you feel that way will undoubtedly affect the type of outcome you are able to reach.

One line of research on instrumental goals and effects has to do with the use of evidence in argumentation. Reinard suggests, "Perhaps on no other area of argumentation has so much attention been focused as on the persuasive function of evidence."[17] **Evidence** is whatever another will accept as proof of some claim. In formal argumentation, evidence consists of examples, statistics, and expert testimony from others. In a conflict situation, evidence may be examples of behavior that demonstrate the point the communicator is trying to make (e.g., Noriko shows her roommate the gas gauge as evidence that she has not refilled the tank). According to Rieke and Sillars, "most decision makers are influenced by evidence."[18] Unsurprisingly, research has found that arguments supported by strong evidence are more effective than those employing weak evidence,[19] and new evidence (i.e., previously unknown to the hearer) is frequently more persuasive than familiar information.[20]

Thus, research on message reception indicates positive relationships between argument strength and effectiveness. However, many questions remain unanswered, such as at what point do people abandon arguments in favor of less reasonable tactics, to what extent are people expected to use arguments when in a conflict, and how effective are arguments.

Relational Goals and Effects of Communication in a Conflict

The second goal/effect concerns the establishment, maintenance, and repair of relationships. The **relational goals** and effects of communication in a conflict focus on the degree of commitment to a premarital or marital relationship, love and emotional involvement, jealousy, the influence of friends and relatives, interpersonal trust, separation/breakup/divorce, compatibility, frequency of sex in marriage, satisfaction with sexual relations, and balance of power. Regarding this goal/effect of communication, there are two ways in which it emerges in interpersonal conflict. First, relational issues may be the focus of a conflict. For example, couples may argue about the depth of or commitment to their relationship. Jason's conflict with his housemate over her new boyfriend is one with relationship goals/effects.

> Jennifer, my housemate, and I have been friends since the eighth grade, about seven years. We have gone through life together, thus far, and just recently a problem has cropped up in our relationship. She met a man, with whom she has become quite close, and has been neglecting the friendship we have worked on for so long. I don't want our relationship to suffer because of this man in her life, so I decided to take a stand and tell her how I felt about the matter. This isn't about twenty dollars she owes me or a sweater she borrowed. It's about a lifelong friendship, and the attention deficit I am feeling. My pursuit was tampered with by Jennifer's new friend. We were more or less in battle for her attention.

Second, and possibly more commonly, conflicts over instrumental concerns may have unintended effects on the relationship (e.g., a conflict over a task could lead to relationship dissatisfaction).

Several scholars discuss how our relationships are negotiated or renegotiated in interaction with others. Here "an individual's goals involve defining the relationship in a particular way, and arguments erupt when the partner's acts impede that goal or are expressions of competing goals."[21] Thus, at times conflicts address relationship issues. Given the analysis that suggests that communication is a goal-directed activity, that one goal of communication concerns relationships with others, and that conflict is a form of communication, the claim that people argue over relationship concerns is reasonable.

At least one study shows how relationship goals influence message production. Canary, Cunningham, and Cody found that integrative tactics were used more than competition or avoidance when the person's goal was to change the nature of a relationship.[22] That finding makes sense—if you want to improve your relationship with the other person, you'll get a lot farther by emphasizing what you have in common than by emphasizing your differences or by walking around the situation.

Others have researched indirect effects of conflict on relationships using both survey (questionnaire) and subject diaries to discover what people believe about their conflict practices.[23] This research indicates that people in general believe that some of their conflicts do have effects on their relationships. Many conflicts in the diary data (72 percent) did not affect the relationship, but in the remainder the effects on the relationship were mixed (some positive, some negative). Although it is important to realize that relationships are of different types, communication researchers have repeatedly identified three relational themes that occur in conflicts and are affected by conflict: affect (or the expression of emotion toward the other), control, and longevity.

Some studies examine affect or the emotional effect of conflict by comparing the conflict behavior of relationally satisfied partners with those who are dissatisfied. Usually, it is assumed that conflict has contributed in some way to the partners' reported satisfaction or dissatisfaction with their relationship. For example, after participants rated their marital satisfaction, Canary, Brossmann, Sillars, and Lovette had participants rate their marital satisfaction, and then observed the types of arguments they used. They found that satisfied couples produced different argument sequences from dissatisfied couples. Satisfied couples had a greater proportion of developed argument structures over undeveloped arguables than did dissatisfied couples.

Of the argument structures, satisfied couples engaged in a greater proportion of simple structures, and tended to enact a greater proportion of convergent arguments.[24] Similarly, Canary, Weger, and Stafford discovered that relationship dissatisfaction was associated with reciprocation of diverging sequences (i.e., disagreement statements),[25] whereas Canary and Sillars reported that relationship satisfaction was associated with convergent arguments (i.e., agreement statements).[26]

Other studies pay less attention to what is said than how it is said to show the emotional impact of conflict on relationship satisfaction or dissatisfaction. This line of research becomes especially important in everyday conflict when one considers that marital and engaged couples claim that their partners appear more rational when they avoid getting angry and raising their voices.[27]

Based on the claim that verbal communicative acts are key determinants of marital satisfaction, Ting-Toomey coded verbal disagreements and focused on three types of verbal behavior: integrative (confirming, coaxing, compromising, and agreeing), disintegra-tive, (confronting, complaining, defending, and disagreeing), and descriptive (socioemo-tional description and questions, task-oriented descriptions and questions). Ideally, partners who value their relationship should argue in a way that contributes to integration of the relationship and avoid statements that lead to disintegration, but unfortunately the latter course is the more common. According to Ting-Toomey, marital partners typically begin a conflict in a manner directly attacking one another with criticism and negatively loaded statements, followed by attempts to justify oneself and blame the other. Given the natural inclination of people to act in ways that don't benefit the relationship, it is no sur-prise that we need courses in conflict management.[28]

On a more positive note, Alberts found that the verbal communication of nondis-tressed couples complained more about their partner's behavior (rather than personality), made more agreement responses, and expressed more positive affect than did distressed cou-ples. Distressed couples complained more about their partner's personality characteristics, offered more countercomplaints, and expressed more negative affect than did nondistressed couples. Interestingly, the two groups of couples did not differ in the number of complaints made, but rather in the way they were made.[29] In addition, Alberts found that well-adjusted couples are twice as likely to engage in types of complaint behavior designated as effective as maladjusted couples. Moreover, less effective complaint behavior occurred more often in maladjusted than well-adjusted couples.[30] Moreover, Newton and Burgoon found that use of supportive strategies in a disagreement was directly related to a partner's satisfaction, whereas use of accusation was negatively correlated with a partner's satisfaction.[31]

Some studies have examined the issues of control, power, and dominance. Roloff and Cloven found that people who feel less powerful than their partners avoid conflicts with them. Therefore, to create conditions conducive to conflicts, both partners must perceive that they have mutual control.[32] Meanwhile, Canary, Weger, and Stafford found that con-trol mutuality (i.e., who influences whom in the relationship) was associated positively with convergent statements (e.g., agreement) and the extent to which points were devel-oped (e.g., elaboration, amplification, and justification).[33]

Finally, relationship longevity may also influence the production of conflicts. Canary and Weger found that the longer the relationship, the more partners structured arguments as convergence sequences (i.e., agreement statements).[34] Similarly, Canary, Weger, and Stafford again discovered that converging arguments were linked positively to the length of the relationship.[35]

Thus, conflict may alter relationships directly when relationship issues are discussed and may produce unintended effects when instrumental or identity goals are being pursued. Although communication researchers have related everyday conflicts to affect, control, and relationship longevity, conflict's effect on other relationship characteristics needs to be ex-amined (e.g., emotional and physical intimacy, trust, commitment, and attitudinal similarity).

Identity Goals and Effects of Communication in Conflict

The third goal/effect of communication and conflict concerns identity management. **Iden-tity goals** and effects of communication include self-esteem, sexual esteem, a male's man-hood or masculinity, a female's womanhood or femininity, impression formation and management, egocentrism, appearing to be in control of others, perceptions of oneself, and traditional stereotypes regarding sex roles. As with the relational goal/effect, the identity goal/effect emerges in a conflict in two ways. First, identity issues may be the focus of a conflict. Alice's conflict with her boyfriend's sister is one with identify goals/effects.

> I am having a problem with my boyfriend's sister. I have been avoiding this situation for over a year and a half. I do not want to stir things up between his family and myself. His sister knows a lot more about me than a boyfriend's family should. Every time my boyfriend and his sister fight, she brings up some fact from my past, in front of their parents. I don't know if she realizes that her comments are hurting me and not her brother. But more importantly, I don't like the feeling of being betrayed and humiliated.
>
> I approached her and said: "Something has been bothering me. Are you free to talk with me for a minute or should I wait until later?" She said: "NO! I am in a hurry to see Danielle." But she stopped a minute and realized she could not wait until later that night to hear what I had to say. She decided to call Danielle and tell her that she would be late. Once you get someone's interest, it is very hard for that person to wait to hear what you have to say.
>
> I told her that something has been bothering me for quite a while. "While in the heat of an argument with your brother, you tend to blurt out unnecessary things about my past in front of your parents. It makes me look bad. At first I thought you were doing it to hurt your brother, but now I am beginning to think that you're doing it to hurt me, or at least to make your parents think that I have flaws, and that I am not good enough for your brother. I would like to find out why you do it, and if by any chance you would reconsider saying anything."

Second, and possibly more commonly, conflicts over instrumental concerns may have unintended effects on the identities of the arguers. For example, two roommates might want to watch different television programs. One could switch channels and tell the other to get lost. The conflict should be over the fair use of the television set, but instead it turns into name calling, put-downs, and personal attacks.

Essentially, the identity goal or effect in a conflict refers to our attempts to negotiate or renegotiate the definition of who we are—our definition of ourselves and the impressions we make on others. Some conflicts directly address the "face of arguers," or the impression they have of themselves. As we will return to this idea later in the chapter on impression management, we'll simply introduce you to some of the research related to identity goals and effects here.

There is, for example, a variety of face-saving strategies that can be used to change how others may perceive your actions and to smooth out negative effects in the relationship. One face-saving strategy is the use of accounts, defined as linguistic devices that serve to change for the better situations that could turn worse and to "repair" one's identity after a personal attack.[36] In essence, accounts explain our behavior to others. For example, accounts are often given as reasons for not complying with a request, rejecting offers, and an inability to answer questions. In all such cases, accounts function to transform what might initially be seen as reproachable behavior to an action seen as justifiable or understandable.

Buttny provides an intensive analysis of one couple's use of blames, criticism, and accounts in marital therapy. Couple therapy is often characterized by recurring instances of partner criticism or blame. Repeated blaming suggests the salience or importance of an underlying issue over which partners disagree. Buttny suggests that recurring blames and criticism may give rise to accounts as a way to defend against the implied change.[37]

Moreover, some writers have argued that conflict can be usefully viewed as a response to threats to one's image, face, or identity. Benoit and Benoit, in their discussion of conflict openings, suggest that aggravating utterances, which potentially threaten the face of interactants, consistently signal the beginning of a conflict.[38] For example, if you initiate a conflict by insulting the other person (e.g., saying "You're such a slob!" to your roommate), you may threaten the other person's self-image and provoke his or her defensiveness. Consistent with this analysis, Benoit and Benoit also found that three of the four ways conflicts closed tended to repair face.

Research on the role of conflict in identity development has led O'Keefe and Shepherd to claim that identity effects are best viewed as "by-products" of interactions.[39] Canary, Cunningham, and Cody report that competitive strategies were used more when defending oneself (identity management).[40] In addition, Canary and Spitzberg showed that communicators are perceived to be most competent when using positive conflict strategies, whereas their use of avoidance and competitive strategies was negatively linked to perceptions of their competence.[41] Finally, Canary and Spitzberg separated perceptions of self from perceptions of other to show that people perceived themselves as more competent and appropriate than partners judge them. They were most similar to one another for competitive tactics (behaviors) than avoidance as a conflict strategy, and then integration (problem solving) as a strategy.[42]

Our explanation for this finding is that arguers may be more focused on achieving what they want in the conflict situation (their instrumental goal pursuits) than other outcomes, but the people hearing the argument are more sensitive to the impact of conflict tactics on their impressions of the other as a person. Thus, conflict may alter identity directly when identity issues are the subject of discussion and may produce unintended effects when other nonidentity goals (instrumental or relationship) are being pursued. Specifically, the research shows that accounts play a role in conflict to save face and that conflicts themselves may enhance or harm one's identity characteristics such as credibility, persuasiveness, and competence.

Interrelationship of the Three Types of Goals and Effects

Some research addresses the interrelationships among the three types of goals/effects of communication in conflict. Dillard, Segrin, and Hardin suggest that primary or influence goals (instrumental) induce attempts to persuade or influence another person, whereas secondary goals (including relational and identity concerns) modify the message.[43] Similarly, O'Keefe and Shepherd argue that "identity communication is subordinated to some other task."[44] Thus, it appears that although there are three key potential goals (instrumental, relationship, and identity), some communication researchers view the instrumental goals as most important.

Although we would agree that the instrumental goals are often (perhaps even usually) foremost in arguers' concerns, the work on accounts cited earlier demonstrates clearly that identity concerns are often key features of messages. Furthermore, an interesting anecdotal example occurred in Benoit and Benoit's data.[45] One female participant wanted her male partner to tell her something. Eventually he did as she requested, but nonetheless she reported that she lost the argument because her partner became angry. Here the relational consequences of the conflict were more salient to her than the instrumental effect. Thus, we argue that although instrumental concerns may be primary in general, relational and identity concerns occasionally predominate. Because few studies interrelate the three types of goals/effects, and others emphasize the importance of a single goal/effect, it is important to remain aware of the potential importance of all three types. It appears that the three types are interrelated and vary in importance depending on the social context in which they occur. In the following case study, the tension between instrumental goals, relational goals, and identity goals is resolved in favor of instrumental goals for one person in the conflict, but the other person had hoped for greater attention to relational and identity goals.

Case Study 8.1 ■ *A Conflict about a Conflict*

My boyfriend, Chris, doesn't think that he can express something important without getting, or at least acting, angry. I, on the other hand, would rather let something slip by and ignore it before I would get angry. We both try to work on skills to balance this out. I try to be more assertive in situations and he tries to stay level-headed and not get angry. With that said, here's the story.

We went to the homecoming football game on Saturday night. Chris is an alum and a former football player, so he assumed that it would be free for him to go to the game. We arrived at the game and it was $5 if you weren't a student. I told them that he was an alum. Chris complicated things when he said rather heatedly, "I am not going to pay to get into this game!" The person working the gate asked if he had an alumni ribbon to prove that he was an alum. Chris told them he did not. Then they asked if he had registered with the alumni house. Chris again told them he had not. He was already getting angry when they directed us over to the alumni table to pick up the ribbon that he needed to come into the game. At that table we realized that he had not sent in the correct form to register as an alum. He marched back to the table as I asked him to please not get mad at the people working as they were simply doing their jobs and following the rules. He didn't listen to me, but told them that he was not going to pay to get into the game. So they said, "Okay, see you later." He asserted that he would watch this game and asked who he could talk to

in order to get into the game. All this time I was very embarrassed. He was angry for no reason and his approach was getting him nowhere.

Finally, someone known to the alumni staff walked up and asked if he could vouch for Chris. The staff wouldn't allow that either, but said that we could simply enter through another gate. We went there and got into the game. The problem was that I became upset with Chris for the way he acted in that situation. I was embarrassed and I was wondering if he even tried to control his anger at all.

My conflict with Chris occurred during the game when he made the mistake of asking how I thought he had dealt with that situation. I was planning to save that conversation until after the game, but he asked so I told him that I was embarrassed and that I didn't think he needed to get so angry. This got us into a big discussion, but it was a productive conflict. I admitted that even though he hadn't followed the proper rules, he did have the right to go to his homecoming game for free, especially because the only purpose of preregistering was so the alumni staff could brag about how many alumni had attended. He had, after all, played on the football team for three years. But I told him that no matter what his rights were, he wasn't going to get that much accomplished with his behavior. We resolved it with him agreeing to work harder to control his temper and with me agreeing to give him the benefit of the doubt when it comes to his "rights."

From Theory to Action

Why study interpersonal conflict from a communication perspective? Many communication scholars place their discipline in the liberal arts. A liberal education serves to free the individual. It informs individuals so that they are free to exercise choice, empowers them to respond in responsible and constructive ways, and shows them how to apply newly acquired knowledge in everyday life. The study of conflict from a communication perspective fits nicely with the ideals of a liberal education. When faced with a problem to be solved, an interpersonal conflict, or legal dispute, many people are constrained by self-defeating conflict behavior patterns, imprisoned by negative conflict attitudes, and respond in ways that may be described as reactive or ignorant. Conflicting parties need to realize that they have options and are free to make choices that vary in social value and that can affect the quality of their interpersonal relationships. To free the individual, both on an attitudinal level as well as on a behavioral level, people need to learn certain values and attitudes and specific communication skills that encourage constructive problem solving and effective resolution of interpersonal conflicts.

This chapter has focused on how communicators behave in conflict, and the way in which various message behaviors move the conflict to resolution more easily, or make it more difficult for those involved to reach agreement. It is hard to explain conflict using only one explanation—how people think affects how they behave. How others behave toward them affects the kinds of behaviors they will respond with, and also affects the way they are thinking about the conflict. We need to understand both to begin to produce competent behavior in conflict situations.

In Chapter 9, the final chapter of this part on conflict theory, we will explore various lines of research concerning interpersonal conflict, particularly in intimate relationships. Through your understanding of the various conflict theories, and how those theories have led communication researchers to various conclusions, you will better understand why certain attitudes and skills are vital in creating competent conflict behavior.

Notes

1. Leslie A. Baxter, "Accomplishing Relationship Disengagement," in Steven Duck and D. Perlman (Eds.), *Understanding Personal Relationships: An Interdisciplinary Approach* (London: Sage, 1985), p. 245.

2. This is a term coined by William R. Cupach and Brian H. Spitzberg (Eds.), *The Dark Side of Interpersonal Communication* (Hillsdale, NJ: Lawrence Erlbaum, 1994).

3. See, for example, the discussion on pp. 27–32 in Lawrence R. Frey, Carl H. Botan, Paul G. Friedman, and Gary L. Kreps, *Investigating Communication: An Introduction to Research Methods* (Englewood Cliffs, NJ: Prentice Hall, 1991).

4. Susan Shiminoff, *Communication Rules: Theory and Context* (Beverly Hills, CA: Sage Publications, 1980), p. 57.

5. Rebecca R. Rubin, "Communication Competence," in Gerald M. Phillips and Julia T. Wood (Eds.), *Speech Communication: Essays to Commemorate the 75th Anniversary of the Speech Communication Association* (Carbondale, IL: SIU Press, 1990), pp. 94–129.

6. Brian H. Spitzberg and William R. Cupach, *Interpersonal Communication Competence* (Beverly Hills, CA: Sage, 1984). Also, a study of perceptions of the competence of others suggests that those perceptions are based on the exhibited behavior's response to the situation rather than knowledge about the person (Larry Haight and Charles Pavitt, "Implicit Theories of Communication Competence 1: Traits, Behaviors, and Situation Differences," paper presented to the Speech Communication Association Convention, Louisville, November 1982).

7. Rubin, "Communication Competence."

8. Daniel J. Canary and Brian H. Spitzberg, "Appropriateness and Effectiveness in the Perception of Conflict Strategies," paper presented at the Speech Communication Association Convention, Denver, November 1985.

9. Brian H. Spitzberg, Daniel Canary, and William R. Cupach, "A Competence-Based Approach to the Study of Interpersonal Conflict," in Dudley D. Cahn (Ed.), *Conflict in Personal Relationships* (Hillside, NJ: Lawrence Erlbaum Associates, 1994).

10. Brian H. Spitzberg, "Cans of Worms in the Study of Communicative Competence," paper presented at the International Communication Association Convention, Honolulu, May 1985. Judy C. Pearson and Tom D. Daniels, in comparing Spitzberg's list to others in the literature, reduced this list to knowledge, motivation, and behavior; however, the impact of the context on the

judgment of the competence of any communication behavior is established in the literature. "Oh, What Tangled Webs We Weave: Concerns About Current Conceptualizations of Communication Competence," *Communication Reports* 1 (1988), 95–100.

11. William S. Howell, *The Empathic Communicator* (Belmont, CA: Wadsworth Publishing, 1982); Mark L. Knapp, *Interpersonal Communication and Human Relationships* (Boston: Allyn and Bacon, 1984); B. Aubrey Fisher, *Interpersonal Communication: Pragmatics of Human Relationships* (New York: Random House, 1987).

12. Brian H. Spitzberg, "The Dialectics of (In)Competence," paper presented at the Western Speech Communication Association Convention, Phoenix, February 1991.

13. Kathleen Kelly Reardon, *Interpersonal Communication: Where Minds Meet* (Belmont, CA: Wadsworth, 1987).

14. Ruth Anne Clark and Jesse G. Delia, "Topoi and Rhetorical Competence," *Quarterly Journal of Speech* 65 (1979), 187–206.

15. William L. Benoit and Dudley D. Cahn, "A Communication Approach to Everyday Argument," In D. D. Cahn (Ed.), *Conflict in Personal Relationships* (Hillsdale, NJ: Erlbaum, 1994).

16. P. H. Zietlow and Alan L. Sillars, "Life Stage Differences in Communication During Marital Conflicts," *Journal of Social and Personal Relationships* 5 (1988), 223–245.

17. John C. Reinard, *Foundations of Argument: Effective Communication for Critical Thinking* (Dubuque: William C. Brown, 1991), p. 105.

18. Richard D. Rieke and Malcolm O. Sillars, *Argumentation and Critical Decision-Making,* 3rd Ed. (New York: HarperCollins, 1993), p. 110.

19. B. L. Brilhart, "Relationships of Speaker-Message Perception to Perceptual Field Dependence," *Journal of Communication* 20 (1970), 153–166.

20. D. Hample, "Predicting Immediate Belief Change and Adherence to Argument Claims," *Communication Monographs* 45 (1978), 219–228.

21. P. J. Benoit, "Relationship Arguments: An Interactionist Elaboration of Speech Acts," *Argumentation* 3 (1989), 430.

22. Daniel J. Canary, E. M. Cunningham, and Michael J. Cody, "Goal Types, Gender, and Locus of Control in Managing Interpersonal Conflict," *Communication Research* 15 (1988), 426–446.

23. W. L. Benoit and P. J. Benoit, "Everyday Argument Practices of Naive Social Actors," in J. W. Wenzel (Ed.), *Argumentation and Critical Practices* (Annandale, VA: SCA, 1987).

24. Daniel J. Canary, B. G. Brossmann, Alan L. Sillars, and S. Lovette, "Married Couples Argument Structures and Sequences: A Comparison of Satisfied and Dissatisfied Dyads," in J. W. Wenzel (Ed.), *Argument and Critical Practices* (Annandale, VA: Speech Communication Association, 1987).

25. Daniel J. Canary, H. Weger, and Laura Stafford, "Couples' Argument Sequences and Their Associations with Relational Characteristics," *Western Journal of Speech Communication* 55 (1991), 159–179.

26. Daniel J. Canary and Alan L. Sillars, "Argument in Satisfied and Dissatisfied Married Couples," in W. L. Benoit, D. Hample, and P. J. Benoit (Eds.), *Readings in Argumentation* (Dordrecht: Foris, 1992).

27. J. M. Honeycutt, B. L. Woods, and K. Fontenot, "The Endorsement of Communication Conflict Rules as a Function of Engagement, Marriage and Marital Ideology," *Journal of Social and Personal Relationships* 10 (1993), 285–304.

28. S. Ting-Toomey, "An Analysis of Verbal Communication Patterns in High and Low Marital Adjustment Groups," *Human Communication Research* 9 (1983), 306–319.

29. J. K. Alberts, "An Analysis of Couples' Conversational Complaints," *Communication Monographs* 55, (1988), 184–197.

30. J. K. Alberts, "Perceived Effectiveness of Couples' Conversational Complaints," *Communication Studies* 40 (1989), 280–291.

31. D. A. Newton and J. K. Burgoon, "Nonverbal Conflict Behaviors: Functions, Strategies, and Tactics," in D. D. Cahn (Ed.), *Intimates in Conflict: A Communication Perspective* (Hillsdale, NJ: Erlbaum, 1990).

32. M. E. Roloff and D. H. Cloven, "The Chilling Effect in Interpersonal Relationships: The Reluctance to Speak One's Mind," in D. D. Cahn (Ed.), *Intimates in Conflict: A Communication Perspective* (Hillsdale, NJ: Erlbaum, 1990).

33. Ibid.

34. D. J. Canary and H. Weger, "The Relationship of Interpersonal Argument to Control Mutuality: An Observational Analysis of Romantic Couple's Conversations," in B. E. Gronbeck (Ed.), *Spheres of Argument* (Annandale, VA: Speech Communication Association, 1989).

35. Ibid.

36. R. Buttny, "Blame-Account Sequences in Therapy: The Negotiation of Relational Meanings," *Semiotica* 78 (1990), 219–247.

37. Ibid.

38. P. J. Benoit and W. L. Benoit, "To Argue or Not to Argue: How Real People Get into and Out of Interpersonal Arguments," in R. Trapp and J. Schuetz (Eds.), *Perspectives on Argument: Essays in Honor of Wayne Brockriede* (Prospect Heights, IL: Waveland, 1990).

39. B. J. O'Keefe and G. J. Shepherd, "The Communication of Identity During Face-to-Face Persuasive Interactions: Effects of Perceiver's Construct Differentiation and Target's Message Strategies," *Communication Research* 16 (1989), 375–404.

40. D. J. Canary, E. M. Cunningham, and M. J. Cody, "Goal Types, Gender, and Locus of Control in Managing Interpersonal Conflict," *Communication Research* 15 (1988), 426–446.

41. D. J. Canary and B. H. Spitzberg, "A Model of the Perceived Competence of Conflict Strategies," *Human Communication Research* 15 (1989), 630–649.

42. D. J. Canary and B. H. Spitzberg, "Attribution Biases and Associations Between Conflict Strategies and Competence Outcomes," *Communication Monographs* 57 (1990), 139–151.

43. J. P. Dillard, C. Segrin, and J. M. Harden, "Primary and Secondary Goals in the Production of Interpersonal Influence Messages," *Communication Monographs* 56 (1989), 19–38.

44. O'Keefe and Shepherd, "The Communication of Identity," p. 376.

45. W. L. Benoit and P. J. Benoit, "Accounts of Failures and Claims of Successes in Arguments," in B. E. Gronbeck (Ed.), *Spheres of Argument* (Annandale, VA: Speech Communication Association, 1989).

9

Research on Intimacy and Conflict

Objectives

At the end of this chapter, you should be able to

1. relate Mead's twenty-nine marital complaints to Gottman's five general categories of conflict issues.

2. describe the conditions under which developmental changes significantly impact on intimate and marital relationships.

3. recommend a list of resources that a couple can turn to when they experience relational conflict.

4. determine the best way for a couple to respond to life crises.

5. explain how romantic involvement, life cycle, couple type, marital distress, couple complaints, individual differences, and family strengths can influence a couple's conflict style.

Key Terms

couple type	external resources	issues
cross-complaining	Independents	problematic behaviors
developmental changes	individual differences	Separates
distressed couples	internal resources	Traditionals

One writer suggested that "the last time married couples agree about anything is when they say 'I do.'"[1] Before you jump to conclusions that we are against marriage, let us hasten to add that each of us authors is married and has a family. We would be among the first to say that the positive side of being married definitely outweighs the negative. In Chapter 1, we learned that conflict is an inevitable part of everyone's life, and that is even more true for those who live together in dating, intimate, and marital relationships.

The fact that conflict inevitably exists in intimate and marital relationships is not what differentiates functional and dysfunctional couples. Instead what makes relationships healthy or unhealthy is the way in which conflict occurs and how it is managed or resolved.[2] Different families have different rules for conflict and how it is to be handled in interpersonal relationships, and difficulties arise when people whose families' conflict rules differ widely get married to one another and mix their conflict styles. People establishing a relationship together bring expectations from their family of origin that may not be shared by the other person. For example,

> My father was very skilled in carpentry and other home-improvement skills, although he was an engineer by profession. I assumed that my husband would not only possess similar skills but have a desire to do home-improvement projects around the house as they needed to be done. His lack of desire to engage in these activities was a real source of conflict for us early in our marriage—until I changed my expectations of his role. I decided that because I was the one who thought these projects were important, I should be the one to do them. I occasionally hire people to help me paint or wallpaper, and I contract out important jobs like plumbing and tiling, but I can say with some satisfaction that I have developed skills I never thought I would. I can use a circular saw and still have my fingers left, and I have built things like cupboards and closets.

Consider this account of how two people had to come to terms with different conflict styles:

> I come from a family of screamers. You don't have to guess where you stand in my family —we tell you. I remember when I was little and my parents had a big fight, I asked my mom if they were going to get a divorce. She told me not to worry—it was when she and Daddy stopped yelling that things would be bad. My husband, on the other hand, comes from a family of snipers. They shoot and run. There's no real engagement. One person will say something snide. Then the other will respond anywhere from minutes to hours later. The conflict can go on for days. I've never seen anyone but his mother apologize, and I think she just does it to smooth things over because most of the time she has nothing to apologize for. When we were first married, my husband would get mad and wouldn't tell me—I was supposed to just know and take care of it. I, on the other hand, would tell him just exactly how I felt and not pull any punches at all. We've sort of met in the middle over the years. He is much better at telling me what bothers him, and I have gotten more calm in my approach when I am upset about something. I guess what is really important is that we don't have any more of those scary kinds of fights when I wasn't sure if we'd be married the next day. I know that, at least with the everyday stuff, we take care of it as it goes and nothing is building up to an explosion.

Styles of doing conflict differ, views of conflict differ, and attributions about the cause of conflict differ. Before people are married, for example, they tend to see conflicts as situational, but after marriage they tend to see conflict as resulting from their partner's personality.[3] The implication of this change in perception is that people are more likely to see a conflict as resolvable before being married because they feel as though they can change situations. When people see conflicts as the result of another's personality, they are more likely to be pessimistic about the hope of resolving the situation.

APPLICATION 9.1

When have you observed conflict due to the differing expectations people had in an intimate relationship? How were those involved able to resolve their differences?

A great deal of research has been done on conflict in courtship and marriage. Many intimate couples share to some degree the physical and emotional closeness experienced by many spouses, which sets the stage for intense conflicts. The way marital couples often handle such conflicts consist of styles they developed when dating and proceeding through stages of increasing intimacy. Because the frequency and impact of these conflicts on marriage are viewed as an important social problem (i.e., high divorce rates), it is the purpose of this chapter to identify many of the issues that frequently arise in intimate and marital relationships and to describe common conflict patterns or styles associated with key variables such as romantic involvement, life cycle, couple type, marital distress, couple complaints, individual differences, and family strengths. Studying research on conflict style in intimacy and marriage helps us identify key factors that enable us to better understand and analyze the process of interpersonal conflict. This understanding reveals some of the constructive ways couples can manage and resolve their conflicts.

Before examining the factors that contribute to couples' conflict style, we will discuss the issues common to interpersonal conflicts as reported in the conflict research literature.

Intimate and Marital Conflict Issues

As defined in Chapter 4, **issues** are the focal point of a conflict, the things that people point to when they are asked what the conflict is about. Wilmot argued that there are different combinations of agreement between people on content issues and relationship issues, and that these differing degrees of agreement generate conflict between people.[4] Possible causes of conflict include the following:

1. They agree and mutually understand each other on the content issue, but they still have a relationship conflict. For example, you believe it is important for you and your spouse to tell each other about a destination and return time when you leave the house. Your spouse understands that it is important to you, yet still leaves the house occasionally without telling you a destination or return time. You interpret this behavior as a lack of concern for your feelings.

2. They agree on the content issue, but one or both participants misunderstand the other's position. A couple both want what is best for their children, but they don't know that and instead see the other as selfish and unwilling to make sacrifices for their children.

3. They disagree on the content issue and understand that they do. For example, a couple may have different attitudes toward spending and saving. The couple may try to accommodate each other's desires, but conflict may arise when a large expenditure needs to be made.

4. They disagree on the content issue, and on top of that, one or both misunderstand the other's position. Caring for a sick child is often a problem for working parents. One parent may believe it is important for each to take turns staying home to care for the child, but the other may feel that it is not primarily his or her obligation because his or her job pays more and is more demanding. Furthermore, if the person who does not feel an obligation to take turns also does not understand why the other person does feel that way, there is both a content issue and a misunderstanding of positions.

5. They agree and mutually understand each other on the relationship dimension, but they still have a content conflict. For example, a couple may agree on the importance of disciplining their children and on the importance of backing each other up, but they may disagree over what misbehavior calls for corporal punishment. One may think that spanking is the first alternative ("Spare the rod and spoil the child"), and the other may think it is the punishment to choose only when all other alternatives have failed.

6. They are in relational agreement, but they misunderstand that they are. For instance, they may misperceive each other's relational stance. O'Henry's classic tale "The Gift of the Magi" illustrates this problem. A young man and woman married against the wishes of their parents and struggled financially through their first year of marriage. Christmas came, and, although neither wanted a present from the other or thought it was important, both believed that they should give a gift to the other. The woman sold her hair to buy a chain for her husband's watch; the man sold his watch to buy combs for her hair. Had they simply talked about Christmas and gifts, they would have known that receiving a gift was unimportant to the other.

7. They disagree relationally (both wish to control the relationship) and understand that they do. For example, a couple known to one of the authors has a blended family. They both have a child from a previous marriage, and they have a baby from their marriage as well. A frequent source of conflict is fairness in how the older children are treated. The children from previous marriages are three years apart. He believes their privileges should be equal (his child is the younger); she believes that their privileges should be different. They often disagree about what privileges the children will have, and they recognize this as a source of conflict and are working to resolve the issue.

8. They disagree relationally and, in addition, misperceive the other's relational stance. The spouses in the previous example moved from disagreeing relationally and misperceiving each other's stance to disagreeing and understanding that they do. In the early years of their marriage, the conflict was even more pronounced, and the attributions being made were "He undermines my authority with his child," and "She gets angry when I attempt to discipline her son in any way." Both felt the other did not understand how they were responding to the issue.

APPLICATION 9.2

For each of the eight possible causes of conflict listed here, find an example of a conflict that you have observed that illustrates the relationship between understanding of and disagreement over issues.

What specific issues come up in an intimate or marital relationship? To answer this question, John Gottman interviewed sixty married couples who produced 180 descriptions that were reviewed and reduced to five general areas:[5]

1. communication, which included spending time together, conversations, sharing feelings, recreation, and lifestyle.
2. sex, which dealt specifically with physical affection, including manner, style, and frequency.
3. jealousy, which occurred when a partner attended to other people of either sex.
4. in-laws, which included spouse differences in relating to in-laws.
5. chores, which included household maintenance, errands, management of children, and financial behavior.

Gottman found that these five areas contained many issues that were important to married couples generally and were especially problematic for unhappily married couples.

Mead, Vatcher, Wyne, and Roberts continued efforts to determine the behaviors that partners find objectionable.[6] They assessed marital complaints and created a list of twenty-nine topic areas including many **problematic behaviors** or potential conflict issues that are relevant to many unhappily married couples:

Communication	Physical Abuse
Affection	Addiction
Sex	Power Struggles
Problem Solving	Finances
Health	Roles
Children	Individual Problems
Affairs	Household Duties
In-Laws/Relatives	Conventionality
Jealousy	Employment
Leisure Time	Alcoholism
Prior Marriage	Psychosomatic Illness
Friends	Loving Feelings
Personal Habits	Values
Religion	Expectations
Incest	

APPLICATION 9.3

How are Mead's twenty-nine issues related to Gottman's list of five issues in intimate conflict? Which don't match up?

In truth, determining the issues that lead to conflict is made complicated by the fact that couples also face **developmental changes,** or changes that occur with the passage of time and the addition of family members, in the relationship. Belsky, Lang, and Rovine examined marital quality and found that it declines especially over the first six months after the wedding ceremony.[7] Swensen, Eskew, and Kohlhepp investigated changes in love and marital problems and found that younger married couples appeared to have more marriage problems than older couples.[8] The change in the relationship from intimate dating to day-to-day living has an effect on behavior and expectations, most of which will become less conflicting as the marriage progresses. The changes in the relationship are illustrated by this narrative:

> A couple who used to live across the street from me said that they wished they had never gotten married. Apparently they had lived together for three years, given birth to Wendy, and then decided to marry. They said that what they used to perceive as voluntary behavior now struck them as expected, and they didn't like that. In addition, their lives had settled into a rut. After four years, they decided to call it quits and get a divorce. Unfortunately, they did not seek marital counseling to discover their beliefs and attitudes about marriage. Without changing how they think, they will again be unhappy if either one marries again. I think if they had worked on changing their expectations, they could have saved their marriage. I think most people realize that marriage carries with it responsibility and obligations. However, they should be able to talk these over to make sure that they are fair and reasonable.

One gains insight into the developmental changes that often occur in marriage by examining Pearson's eight-stage model of family development:

1. selecting a mate and developing the unmarried relationship;
2. beginning marriage (couples married fewer than seven years and having no children);
3. childbearing and preschool stage;
4. school-aged children;
5. adolescent stage;
6. launching stage (when children are leaving home);
7. families in middle years; and
8. families in older years.[9]

The kinds of conflict issues that arise in families differ for each stage. In the early stages of marriage, for example, couples concern themselves with "three basic tasks: (1) separating further from the families of origin; (2) negotiating roles, rules, and relationships; and (3) investing in a new relationship."[10] The conflict pattern established in the first two years of marriage tends to be perpetuated throughout the rest of the marriage,[11] although people can learn new ways of relating to one another and more constructive ways to manage and resolve conflicts if they are willing.

In what way does the addition of children into a family change the dynamics and create a new set of stressors? In various studies, children were shown to interfere with couples' companionship activities and reduce marital satisfaction. This was especially true in the case of two working parents. Others have also reported that increased work hours for wives and the presence of school-aged children in the family contributed significantly to marital instability, problems, and disagreements. Researchers reported, however, that the trend toward greater problems and decreasing marital satisfaction reverses itself in later years.[12]

Couples are also affected by "their views on parental responsibilities and restrictions, on how gratifying child-rearing can be for them as a couple, and on their own marital intimacy."[13] Couples may have different views on involvement in the birth process as well as the degree of involvement expected with an infant. As children grow, new coalitions are possible within the family, and one parent and child may side against the other parent. As children leave home, couples need to reestablish their relationship. And the natural processes of aging bring their own problems.

In spite of a large literature that demonstrates correlations between the presence of children, marital problems, and relationship dissatisfaction, some researchers have found that the transition to parenthood does not seem to affect marital happiness, interaction, disagreements, or number of marital problems.[14] The effects of children and working parents may depend more on the attitudes, needs, and goals of a couple. Some couples may find the presence of children or a working wife an added asset to the couple's relationship satisfaction, whereas others do not.

In addition to conflicts that arise from developmental stages, families often face conflicts due to crisis situations: an unplanned pregnancy, loss of a job, loss of a child, and so on. Case Study 9.1 concerns a family who faced the loss of the husband's job due to alcohol problems. Interestingly, when one author asked the husband and wife if she could interview them about the conflict they experienced, they insisted that they had not experienced a conflict. They had a problem and they faced it as a family, and that was all there was to it. One reason they had been so successful in weathering the crisis was that they came together to fight against a common foe—the alcohol problem—instead of turning on each other and blaming each other for what had happened. Like the boys in Sherif's classic studies, in which hostility between groups was reduced by having them fight against a common enemy, the spouses in this case chose to treat the alcohol problem as a common enemy that they could fight together, thus working to overcome any difficulties the alcohol created between them.[15]

Case Study 9.1 ■ *Overcoming a Problem of Alcohol Abuse*

This case study comes from a tape-recorded interview with a couple who are close friends of Roxane's. As an observer, she thought they had a crisis situation when the husband was fired from his job as an intensive care unit nurse because he was under the influence of alcohol at work. Not only was he fired, but in order not to lose his license he had to enter a rehabilitation program and still cannot work particular shifts or do particular kinds of nursing more than a year and a half after entering rehabilitation. However, when interviewed, they had a very different perspective of their crisis situation. (W-wife; H-husband; A-author clarifications.)

W: The crisis didn't actually start when he got home from work. I can't actually say when it started, when I said, "Oops, this is a problem." We would run into these problems with anger, or disappointment, or whatever you want to call it. I would say it started after Dave was born, after we became parents.

H: I look at it as I hadn't really learned to be unselfish enough, to take care of something as absolutely dependent on me as an infant. I'd always been very well taken care of. I think it really comes down to a problem of being self-centered. Children are just demanding, by their very nature. First there was one, and then another, and another, and another, and I just never learned how to. I just never grew up. The alcohol abuse, it just exacerbated a problem that was there. It just got in the way of any kind of maturing process I could have done.

A: So you don't see your alcohol problem as the central thing so much as simply being a person who wasn't ready to be a parent.

H: I didn't know how. I started drinking when I was fifteen. It pretty much became a lifestyle after that. Some of my colleagues say you just stop growing when you start drinking. Like, you're stuck in that teenage mind-set—it's absolutely egocentric, a child in a man's body.

But definitely, the abuse of alcohol was a symptom of not knowing how to handle life. In the big book of AA, he says alcohol was not only a crutch to get through life but an escape from it, and that sentence is absolutely me. I identify with it totally. I didn't get sober by my own will. This is something I know was a divine intervention, and the occupational health services that administer the program for the board of registered nurses—they told me exactly what to do: You will not work for ninety days, you will go to ninety meetings in ninety days, and so on.

W: I didn't realize how bad it [the alcohol problem] was.

H: Well, you said you thought I was getting better that last year before I lost my job.

W: Yeah, it was.

H: It was getting better; it felt easier. But still, I know I was drinking more than I'd ever done, on a much more daily basis. But yet living with me was not getting worse.

W: Yeah, the anger, the horrible, irrational anger wasn't a problem. You fell into deeper depression.

A: So you didn't have the energy to be angry anymore?

W: I didn't think he thought anything could ever get better. And that's where I had been a year before he went for counseling for anger. I had thought . . . and I know that it's different now, I know that we're doing well now, and I know that we'll continue to grow and that there'll be good days and bad days. It's different from what I felt just before he went into AA. I know then I thought to myself, "Well, at least it's not horrible, it's just not agony, but there's still something missing and I can't put my finger on it. It's not quite right. I know there's supposed to be more to this, or is there?" And so I was beginning to think, "Maybe there isn't. Gee, how disappointing that this is as good as it gets." Because he wasn't irrationally angry anymore. But way back in the back of my head I'd think, "Why

does he drink so much, then?" But at least he wasn't irrationally angry.

A: So, let me get the chronology straight. In 1989 you [the wife] were feeling very depressed about the marriage and about his anger.

W: Anger, self-centeredness, immaturity—and that was during the time that I did what they call emotional detachment. I called it emotionally divorcing myself from him, saying, "That's it, I've had it with you. I'm not going to go down this deep, dark hole with you. Go by yourself. I will stay here, and we'll see what happens." Then he went to counseling; the anger got better; he started to deal with his anger. By June 1990 he had his last (that I know of) burst of horrible, irrational anger, and the reason I remember it was because that was the only day I have ever had an outburst of irrational anger where I hit the wall because I wanted to hit him so badly. And I ran around here screaming at the top of my lungs. And that was the one day . . . and when it was all over and I realized a month later that he had not had a day of irrational anger, I thought, "That's all I needed a day where I yelled so he'd know how stupid it looks." And since then—I remember the date after that—in June 1991 I said to him, "Gee honey, it's been a year since you got really angry." At that time, I thought, "Wow, it's a whole year, an anniversary. Why aren't things quite right?"

A: And that's when you still felt like "is this all there is?"

W: Right, that's when I began to think, "Even though we've gotten rid of the anger, if this is all there is, then it's just not what I thought it was going to be and this is really disappointing."

A: And then right after that he lost his job.

W: It was August 1991 when he lost his job and this whole recovery started. But through the years he has always had some part of him that recognized that there was something wrong, that he was doing something wrong. He's the one. If, as you say, we were able to keep the conflict outside us and hold together, it's because I would confront him and say, "You did this, this, and this wrong." And he would say, "Yes, it was." He would readily admit that. Even when I would bitch and complain, I would say to myself, "He's a jerk, but at least he admits it." And that's probably where both of us were able to say, "You've got this really dark side to you," whereas if it was anybody else, that might not have happened.

A: So, how do you feel about it now? Where are you now?

H: It's good. This whole thing, AA and all the twelve-step programs, they're spiritual programs. The greatest gift that you just put your finger on is that I feel like I actually have me. Actually, for the first time in my life, I feel entirely myself. I don't have to assume any other persona, or wear any other mask or facade, or . . . I actually feel like I can just be me and be comfortable in that skin. From taking responsibility for my life no one else can make me feel any way. It's always my response to what comes at me, and what other people think of me is none of my business. What I think of them is my business. I have no control over anything but my own thoughts and my own responses. That has just been the key. One of the major things we do in any twelve-step program is to make a thorough inventory of our own self—the positive and the negative. And then we share it with God and another human being. It's absolutely essential that those other two be involved. It's a form of housekeeping; it's a cleansing activity of testimony and confession. It doesn't exist anymore. You make amends to those you have hurt in the past. The depression I went into was something that extended over years and also culminated in a flash point of my intervention and losing the job, and going to AA, that was a culmination of a process that had been going on for years. We were just going through the physiological motions of being alive. But what was missing was the joy of living. Somehow or other, I had gotten out of step with God. My journal entries . . . I would remark so much time has passed and I haven't made any progress. I remember, like this one journal—there's more than ten years in the same volume—and I look over it and see the same entries over and over again. I had not made any kind of progress. I don't have any explanation for it except that I wasn't willing to give up my defects of character. What I've learned in the twelve-step program is about total surrender. You have to give God everything. Don't keep the illusion of control. I think that's why we're doing so well now.

W: Well, you know, I think—I know it affected us, but I never felt like there was a conflict with us, him and me. I always felt that if he and I were stranded on a desert island, we'd do just great; we could really well. It was outside intervention, which included our own children. Yeah, there was a lot of anger and resentment and problems that came with life in general, which would be accentuated by his problem. I always felt that he and I were a good couple, we had a good marriage, we were meant to be together. Even when it was horrible, horrible, and I was so angry I wanted to hit him, I still thought that he and I were still good. But it's so neat now, because we're a family now, where we weren't before. We can actually sit at the dinner table and have fun. We could never do that before. Before, everything he did, everywhere he went, there was always that dark cloud looming over: "Something might tick off Dad and the whole day will be ruined." And it would be. He had absolute, utter control of our lives. Which was really pathetic and really made me angry. So I would try to step away from it, but even though I could do that I couldn't make my kids do that. How can I tell them: "Emotionally divorce your daddy today"? They couldn't get that. But now we don't have to anymore and it feels like a family. And that's why I think it's really neat. It's normal. It's functional.

The ability of this family to cope with its crisis illustrates the resources Olson and McCubbin identified as those that can help families.[16] **Internal resources** are attitudes and behaviors that are part of the family's normal methods of coping with different events, and include redefining the stressful event so that it is more manageable and attempting to view the stressful event as less important by determining a positive response to it. In this family's case, the crisis of losing a job was redefined as an opportunity to seek help for the alcohol problem that had been previously recognized but not addressed. A positive response to the crisis was created when the wife, who is also a nurse and had only been working occasional shifts, realized that she would be able to pick up the slack when finances were jeopardized by the husband's loss of his job. She felt competent to make up the difference, so their lifestyle was not financially disrupted as much as it could have been. The family also availed themselves of **external resources,** or support systems outside of the family. They had a great deal of social support from family and friends, particularly because they were very open about the problem and what they were doing to address it; they are active members of a church and find a great deal of support in their church community; and, because the husband was required to go into a rehabilitation program, many social services became available and were used to get past the crisis. As a side note to the foregoing case study, the couple experienced the loss of their oldest child to illness four years later. Despite research that suggests the death of a child frequently leads to marital breakup, this couple again pulled together and called upon outside resources to survive the blow to their family. Although they grieve, they haven't fallen back into the crisis situation they had before.

Other factors that affect how couples respond to stress were identified by Sarason: (1) the nature of the stressor event; (2) the skills or resources available to deal with the crisis; (3) the individuals' personality characteristics; (4) the individuals' history of stress-arousing experiences; and (5) the available social support.[17] Pearson offers the following conclusions:

> Few studies have examined family coping skills, but two conclusions seem warranted. First, the family may be better able to cope with a stressful situation if they perceive it as less rather than more severe. . . . The meaning the family attaches to the event is critical in determining how they will experience it and how they will cope with it. Second, discussing the stressful situation in order to gain a shared social meaning may render it more understandable and solvable.[18]

APPLICATION 9.4

In your own family, how has the presence or absence of external resources and the ability to understand a stressful event affected your family's ability to cope with the event?

Additional research on intimate and marital conflict has been mainly in how romantic involvement, a couple's life cycle, the kind of relationship a couple has, marital distress, couple complaints, individual differences, and family strengths affect the way the couple does conflict—their conflict styles. The following briefly reviews some of the research in each of these areas.

Relationship Life Cycle, Aging, and Conflict Style

Not only do issues change as couples age, so does their conflict style. For example, research suggests that intimate partners may confront or avoid conflict at different stages in their marriages. According to Zietlow and Sillars:[19]

> *Young couples* tend to utilize an engagement style in which conflict issues are alternatively fought over, analyzed, and joked about. Younger partners are more likely to use a more direct and expressive style of communication than are older couples.
>
> *Middle-aged couples* are avoiders. Occasionally, they are more similar to the younger couples when the discussion topics represent salient issues and frequently they are more similar to the older, retired couples when the issues are not salient. Suggesting low risk and disclosure, they have a noncommittal style of discussion that includes abstract remarks, irrelevant statements, and questions lacking focus.
>
> *Retired couples* typically have a less expressive style for communication about sources of marital conflict than do young couples.

Couple Type and Conflict Styles

In her research on marital communication, Fitzpatrick developed a typology of relationships evidenced by couples in marriage, which accounts for differences in styles of communication and conflict.[20] **Couple type** refers to the assumptions a married couple has about things that affect the marriage, such as communication, the "proper" way to do conflict, gender roles, the household tasks that should be assigned to each person, and so on. She suggested three basic couple types: Independents, Separates, and Traditionals, in addition to the possibility of mixed types (in which couples don't define their relationship in the same way).

    Independents are couples who "are the most committed to an ideology of uncertainty and change."[21] They tend to reject traditional values and roles (e.g., a homemaker-breadwinner division of labor). They have a relationship characterized by autonomy. Independents engage in moderate amounts of sharing, do not set many boundaries on their physical and emotional space, and do not try to avoid conflict in their relationship. An example of an independent couple is Al and Tipper Gore. They both have careers to which they are committed, they appear to engage in occasional conflict without feeling threatened by it, and they appear to share at a moderate level.

    Separates "are defined by very little sharing and a high degree of conflict avoidance."[22] They tend to define their emotional and physical space very clearly. They do not feel autonomous from one another, but they report very little sense of togetherness. They tend to be very frank and almost combative in their communication. An example of a separate couple is the Bundys on *Married with Children*.

    Traditionals are couples who tend to follow established belief systems. They are more likely to adopt the homemaker-breadwinner role relationship. If the wife works outside the home, her job is considered to be less important than the husband's. They prefer regularity and pattern in their lives. They have few boundaries on their use of space and are not autonomous, engaging in a high degree of sharing. They prefer to engage in conflict rather than avoid it, but they are more socially restrained than Independents. Former President George Bush and his wife Barbara are an example of a traditional couple.

Extending Fitzpatrick's work, Sillars, Pike, Jones, and Redmon examined the patterns of communication and conflict evidenced by various couple types:

1. There was a pronounced difference between the communication of more and less satisfied Separates. In general, Separates maintained a neutral emotional climate and kept discussion of conflict to a minimum. However, these tendencies were much greater among the more satisfied Separates. Separates expressed the lowest marital satisfaction on the average.

2. There was very little difference in the (nonverbal) expression of feelings by more and less satisfied Independents. Both groups expressed negative feelings frequently. The distinctive difference between these groups was that more satisfied Independents engaged in more informational acts, such as self-disclosure, description and qualification of conflict, and questions eliciting disclosure.

3. There was very little difference in the types of statements made by more and less satisfied Traditionals. In terms of paralinguistic affect, more satisfied Traditionals were more positive and less negative, but these differences were typical of the entire sample [all types of couples].

4. The relationship between nonverbal affect and marital satisfaction was more consistent across couple types than the relationship between verbal communication and satisfaction. Irrespective of couple type, more satisfied spouses were (nonverbal) more positive and less negative than less satisfied spouses. More satisfied spouses also made fewer direct distributive statements. In no other respect was the difference in verbal communication between more and less satisfied spouses consistent across all three couple types.[23]

Further research by Witteman and Fitzpatrick examined the effect of couple type on the use of power strategies in marital communication. The authors identified three bases of power in marital relationships: referencing expectancies (e.g., talking about the possible consequences of taking or failing to take the requested action); invocation of identification/relationship (e.g., asking the other to comply because of who the couple is to each other—"If you loved me, you'd . . ."); and appeals to values or obligations (e.g., "a good spouse would do this"). Traditional couples, because of their shared conventional ideas and relative openness in communication, are more likely to discuss the positive and negative outcomes of a course of action in order to persuade the other. They also are likely to use the relationship as a source of power in gaining compliance from the other. Separates "tend to focus on the negative consequences of noncompliance. The messages of the Separates are blatant attempts to constrain the behavior, and in some cases even the internal states of their spouses."[24] Independents use all three power bases when seeking compliance from their spouse.

One study compared fourteen couples who exhibited complementary traditional sex roles (traditional male-traditional female) with fourteen couples in which both partners were identified as androgynous (having psychological characteristics associated with both masculinity and femininity, such as assertiveness and sensitivity). The couples were asked to identify issues that created conflict between them and were videotaped as they discussed one issue and attempted to resolve it. No differences were found between the two groups in how they discussed the conflict issues, but the conflict issues did differ between the groups. Androgynous couples identified lack of time together, free time, and religion as issues creating conflict between them; traditional couples identified communication, finances, and household chores as conflict-provoking issues. Traditional wives were more likely than androgynous wives to identify household chores as a conflict issue, and androgynous husbands identified free time more frequently as a conflict issue than did traditional husbands.[25]

A final study of interest was conducted by Burggraf and Sillars who analyzed data from questionnaires (completed by spouses separately) concerning the relevance of ten conflict topics to the couples' marriage and from the relational dimensions instrument measuring the couples' type.[26] Couples then audio-taped their discussion of the ten conflict topics, skipping any they felt were too personal or threatening, and talking about each topic until they felt they had exhausted it. The audiotapes were transcribed and coded into avoidance, confrontive, analytic (giving and receiving of information), and conciliatory acts. In accordance with the researchers' expectations, biological sex alone did not predict communication behavior about the conflict topics. However, couple type did predict the use of different strategies: Traditionals frequently used avoidance and conciliatory strategies and infrequently used confrontive strategies. Separates used more confrontive strategies and fewer avoidance strategies than did other couple types. Mixed couples did not evidence any strong patterns of conflict behavior. (There were no data reported for Independents because the sample was too small for analysis.) In addition to the effects of couple type on behavior, the authors found a strong tendency for the type of strategy to be reciprocated: Avoidance followed avoidance, confrontive strategies followed confrontive, analytic followed analytic, and conciliatory followed conciliatory.

The research on the effects of **individual differences** (or personality characteristics that each person has prior to entering the marriage) on marital conflict communication would suggest that individual differences are insufficient to explain why people choose the conflict strategies they do; rather, marital couples develop patterns of interaction together that predict how they will resolve conflicts.

The kind of relationship established by marital couples affects the way they feel about conflict, how they approach it, and the kinds of strategies they choose to use. The next section examines research that differentiates between satisfied and dissatisfied couples.

Distressed and Nondistressed Couples and Conflict Styles

Much of the research on destructive interpersonal conflict relies on couples seeking counseling—known as **distressed couples.** Such couples are usually functioning at low levels; they are often unhappy, dissatisfied, maladjusted, or unstable.

Distressed couples are more defensive than nondistressed. They tend to engage in fewer positive's and more negatives during casual conversation and problem solving than did nondistressed couples. They are more likely to begin a discussion by **cross-complaining** (i.e., returning a complaint in response to a complaint instead of acknowledging what the other person said), followed by negative exchanges and less problem solving.[27] Low marital adjustment interaction was mainly characterized by unique reciprocal patterns of confront → confront, confront → defend, complain → defend, and defend → complain verbal interactions.[28]

Gottman argued that it is possible to tell the difference between distressed and nondistressed couples in each phase of a conflict. In the first stage, for example, distressed couples are more likely to use cross-complaining, but nondistressed couples are more likely to respond with a validation of what the other says through messages such as "yeah," "oh," "mmm-hmmm," and so on. In the second phase, distressed couples are more likely to exchange proposals and counterproposals, but nondistressed couples are more likely to engage in a contracting sequence. That is, if one person in a distressed marriage suggests some kind of action, the other will offer an alternative instead. In nondistressed couples, there is some acceptance of the proposal offered before any alternative is mentioned. Another pattern found in the second stage of distressed couples is excessive metacommunication, or talking about the way they communicate. Gottman offered this example of a distressed couple's metacommunication:

Husband: You're interrupting me.

Wife: I wouldn't have to if I could get a word in edgewise.

Husband: Oh, now I talk too much. Maybe you'd like me never to say anything.

Wife: Be nice for a change.

Husband: Then you'd never have to listen to me, which you never do anyway.

Wife: If you'd say something instead of jabbering all the time maybe I would listen.[29]

In addition to excessive metacommunication, distressed couples also engage in "mind-reading" sequences, in which they make attributions concerning emotions, states of mind, attitudes, and so on, about the other person. Interestingly, nondistressed couples are more likely to interpret such statements about their emotions as a "reality check"—as the other's attempt to understand their feelings—whereas distressed couples are more likely to interpret the statement as an argument to counter.

In the final phase, nondistressed couples are more likely to express direct agreement with the other's statements, through messages like "yes, you're right" or "I agree," creating a climate of cooperation and agreement. Assent, if given by distressed couples, comes grudgingly and reluctantly.

Other researchers have also examined patterns of interaction differentiating distressed and nondistressed marital couples. Vincent, Weiss, and Birchler found that distressed couples made significantly greater numbers of negative problem-solving statements and a significantly smaller number of positive problem-solving statements than nondistressed couples did.[30] Syna found not only that nondistressed couples were more likely to use problem solving over win-lose strategies to deal with conflict, but also that they were more likely to take responsibility for problems experienced. Distressed couples were more likely to engage in win-lose strategies and to assign blame for their problems to each other.[31]

APPLICATION 9.5

When have you found yourself "arguing about arguing" with another person? How did you end the conflict? How could you avoid engaging in too much metacommunication in the future?

Couple Complaints and Conflict Style

Alberts created a research program to investigate the patterns associated with the way in which couples make complaints to one another. She identified five kinds of complaints and five kinds of responses to complaints, which are listed in Table 9.1.

In her preliminary work, Alberts found that behavioral complaints were the most frequently occurring kind, constituting 72 percent of couple complaints, and that these behavioral complaints were most frequently met with justification responses. The second most frequent complaint concerned personal characteristics (17 percent), which were most frequently responded to with denials. Men and women did not differ significantly in their reported complaint types, response types, or responses given to particular forms of complaints. In addition, Alberts found no differences between well-adjusted and maladjusted couples in use of complaints and complaint responses, although she pointed out that the finding is suspect because of a small sample size and because it was based on self-report data.[32]

In subsequent research, Alberts analyzed videotaped conversations of couples in complaint episodes. Using a larger sample size, she found that well-adjusted couples were more likely to make behavioral complaints with positive nonverbal affect, and to respond with agreement in their complaint sequences. Distressed or maladjusted couples were more likely to make personal characteristic complaints with negative nonverbal affect and to re-

TABLE 9.1   *Types of Complaints and Responses to Complaints Made by Marital Couples*

Complaint Types	*Response Types*
Behavioral—Actions that were not performed by the partner ("You didn't go to the bank and make that deposit.")	Justification—Respondent gives a reason for the criticized behavior or characteristic ("I'm sorry I didn't get to the bank; I got a phone call that I had to take and I just didn't get out of the office on time.")
Personal Characteristic—Complaints that concern the whole person: personality, attitudes, emotional or belief system ("You are always forgetting to do the things I ask you to do.")	Denial—Respondent says the complaint is not true ("I did too get to the bank.")
Performance—Complaints about how an action was performed ("I wish you had gotten to the bank before noon so the deposit would be counted today instead of tomorrow.")	Agree—Respondent says the other person is right ("You're right, I should have gotten there on time.")
Complaining—Complaints about the other person complaining ("You're the one who is always telling me I run the bank account too close to zero.")	Counterclaim—Respondent makes a complaint in response to the complaint ("If it's so important to get to the bank, you just better do it yourself instead of making me take time out of my day to go.")
Personal Appearance—Complaints about the other's grooming or dress ("I really dislike it when you perm your hair. It makes you look stupid.")	Pass—Respondent ignores or fails to respond to the complaint verbally ("So, what's for dinner?")

spond with countercomplaints. Alberts concluded that, for this sample, marital adjustment was a better predictor of responses to complaints than was the type of complaint made.[33]

In another study examining the effects of the nonverbal delivery of complaints, Alberts found that negative nonverbal affect in a relationship has a stronger influence on marital satisfaction than does positive affect, so that decreasing negative affect is a better strategy for improving marital satisfaction than increasing positive affect. Couples reporting on the kind of complaint behavior they would like to receive indicated that style is important: They prefer to hear a rational, calm, specific, and constructive complaint. Their least desired complaint is one about personal characteristics or appearance, particularly if delivered in a teasing manner. Desired responses to complaints are acknowledgment or agreement with the complaint, with the other remaining calm and evidencing a desire to work toward a solution. In addition, couples desire that the other be understanding and stay on the original issue when responding. The least desired response to a complaint is to pass or ignore the complaint or to yell and argue about it.[34] Alberts's work is important because it examines interaction and ties complaint sequences to the theoretical work on remediation and accounting sequences (a body of research explored in Chapter 15).

Clearly, the way in which a couple engages in conflict has an important impact on marital satisfaction. Putnam and Folger noted that both distressed and nondistressed couples are able to use and even reciprocate positive behaviors at various times, but it is the containment of negative behaviors, such as cross-complaining and attack-defend cycles, that typifies the conflict interaction of nondistressed couples. "This principle suggests that disputants need to be trained in how to balance attack-defend patterns in confrontation and how to use negative affect statements appropriately, in addition to developing integrative problem-solving skills. . . . [D]isputants need training in effective ways of fighting."[35]

Family Strengths and Conflict Style

Due to lack of family strengths, some couples are ill prepared to deal with conflicts. They report less satisfaction with their marriage, poorer communication, more unresolved conflicts, lack of sexual relations, and other problems.[36] Because some couples can draw upon family strengths, they feel better prepared to deal with sources of conflict, and they are more likely than others to confront problems. Greater prior satisfaction with a relationship and greater investment of resources are associated with stronger tendencies to actively engage in problem solving. Similarly, intimate partners who are more satisfied with their family and quality of life are more likely to discuss their differences. Finally, more securely attached dating partners report higher relational satisfaction and are more likely to engage in constructive problem-solving strategies.[37]

From Theory to Action

How do you take this information and make it work for you? If nothing else, the materials in this chapter underscore the ubiquity of conflict in our lives. Regardless of the relationships in which we find ourselves, we will experience conflict. Some conflicts will be difficult, and some will not. Some will cut to the core of our identities, and some will be peripheral. To prepare ourselves better for conflict, we must accept that it is a natural part of our lives.

Beyond this assumption are important implications in the kind of research you have read here. Intimate and marital communication research demonstrates clearly that conflicts are much more likely to escalate out of control and cause negative feelings and dissatisfaction when people do not really listen to what others have to say. The phenomenon of cross-complaining arises from an inability or unwillingness to listen to others and hear them out. A person who cross-complains essentially dehumanizes the other by making the complaint seem unworthy of attention. People have preferred ways of hearing complaints from others: They want to know what behaviors are bothering the other person, and they want to hear the complaint in a calm and rational manner. It is easy to feel defensive and helpless to do anything to better the situation when you hear a "you're-ugly-and-your-momma-dresses-you-funny" kind of complaint from another person. We need to focus our conflict behaviors on things that can be changed and let other things go by.

Couples' conflicts and crises are more manageable when people avail themselves of the internal and external resources available. Couples are successful in dealing with conflict when they can take the conflict and put it outside the relationship, making it something to be fought together, or when they can redefine the conflict as something manageable. Couples are also more successful when they take advantage of the external resources available to them: other family members, friends, churches or other significant groups, and social agencies.

Notes

1. B. Lansky, *Mother Murphy's Second Law: Love, Sex, Marriage and Other Disasters* (New York: Simon & Schuster, 1986), p. 81.

2. Kathleen M. Galvin, "Communication and Well-Functioning Families," paper presented at the Western Speech Communication Association Convention, Fresno, CA, February 1985; John M. Gottman, "Emotional Responsiveness in Marital Conversations," *Journal of Communication* 32 (1982), 108–133; John Gottman, Howard Markham, and Cliff Notarius, "The Topography of Marital Conflict: A Sequential Analysis of Verbal and Nonverbal Behavior," *Journal of Marriage and the Family* 39 (1977), 461–477.

3. Judy Pearson, *Communication in the Family: Seeking Satisfaction in Changing Times* (New York: Harper & Row, 1989); see also J. H. Harvey, A. L. Weber, K. L. Yarkin, and B. E. Stewart, "An Attributional Approach to Relationship Breakdown and Resolution," in Steven Duck (Ed.), *Personal Relationships 4: Dissolving Personal Relationships* (New York: Academic Press, 1982); C. Kelly, T. L. Huston, and R. M. Cate, "Premarital Relationship Correlates of the Erosion of Satisfaction in Marriage," *Journal of Personal and Social Relationships* 2 (1985), 167–178.

4. William W. Wilmot, *Dyadic Communication: A Transactional Perspective* (Reading, MA: Addison-Wesley, 1979), p. 95.

5. John M. Gottman, *Marital Interaction: Experimental Investigations* (New York: Academic, 1979).

6. D. E. Mead, G. M. Vatcher, B. A. Wyne, and S. L. Roberts, "The Comprehensive Areas of Change Questionnaire: Assessing Marital Couples' Presenting Complaints," *American Journal of Family Therapy* 18 (1990), 65–79.

7. J. Belsky, M. E. Lang, and M. Rovine, "Stability and Change in Marriage Across the Transition to Parenthood: A Second Study," *Journal of Marriage and the Family* 47 (1985), 855–865.

8. C. H. Swensen, R. W. Eskew, and K. A. Kohlhepp, "Five Factors in Long-Term Marriages," *Lifestyles* 7 (1984), 94–106.

9. Pearson, *Communication in the Family,* generated this model from the writings of Evelyn M. Duvall, *Family Development,* 2nd Ed. (New York: Lippincott, 1962); Boyd C. Rollins and Harold Feldman, "Marital Satisfaction over the Family Life Cycle: A Re-Evaluation," *Journal of Marriage and the Family* 32 (1970), 20–27; M. McGoldrick and E. A. Carter, "The Family Life Cycle," in F. Walsh (Ed.), *Normal Family Processes* (New York: Guilford Press, 1982), pp. 167–195; and Stephen A. Anderson, Candace J. Russell, and Walter R. Schuman, "Perceived Marital Quality and Family Life Cycle: A Further Analysis," *Journal of Marriage and the Family* 45 (1983), 127–139.

10. Kathleen M. Galvin and Bernard J. Brommel, *Family Communication: Cohesion and Change,* 2nd Ed. (Glenview, IL: Scott Foresman, 1986), pp. 201–202.

11. H. L. Raush, W. A. Barry, R. K. Hertel, and M. A. Swain, *Communication, Conflict and Marriage* (San Fran-

cisco: Jossey Bass, 1974); Marcia Lasswell and Thomas Lasswell (Eds.), *Love, Marriage, Family: A Developmental Approach* (Glenview, IL: Scott Foresman, 1973).

12. Dudley D. Cahn, *Intimates in Conflict* (Hillsdale, NJ: Erlbaum, 1990), p. 14.

13. Galvin and Brommel, *Family Communication,* p. 204.

14. L. K. White and A. Booth, "The Transition to Parenthood and Marital Quality," *Journal of Family Issues* 6 (1985), 435–449.

15. Mustafer Sherif, *In Common Predicament* (Boston: Houghton Mifflin, 1966).

16. David H. Olson and Hamilton McCubbin, *Families: What Makes Them Work?* (Beverly Hills: Sage, 1983).

17. I. Sarason, "Life Stress, Self-Preoccupation, and Social Supports," in I. G. Sarason and C. D. Speilberger (Eds.), *Stress and Anxiety,* Vol. 7 (Washington, DC: Hemisphere, 1980).

18. Pearson, *Communication in the Family,* p. 347.

19. P. H. Zietlow and Alan L. Sillars, "Life Stage Differences in Communication During Marital Conflicts," *Journal of Social and Personal Relationships* 5 (1988), 223–245.

20. Mary Anne Fitzpatrick, "A Typological Approach to Communication in Relationships," in Dan Nimmo (Ed.), *Communication Yearbook* 1 (New Brunswick, NJ: Transaction Books, 1977), pp. 263–275.

21. Ibid., p. 273.

22. Ibid.

23. Alan L. Sillars, Gary R. Pike, Tricia S. Jones, and Kathleen Redmon, "Communication and Conflict in Marriage," in Robert N. Bostrum (Ed.), *Communication Yearbook* 7 (Newbury Park, CA: Sage, 1983), p. 426.

24. Hal Witteman and Mary Anne Fitzpatrick, "Compliance-Gaining in Marital Interaction: Power Bases, Processes and Outcomes," *Communication Monographs* 53 (1986), 140.

25. Mary Helen Nowak, "Conflict Resolution and Power Seeking Behavior of Androgynous and Traditional Married Couples (Sex Roles)," Doctoral dissertation, Michigan State University, 1984.

26. Cynthia S. Burggraf and Alan L. Sillars, "A Critical Examination of Sex Differences in Marital Communication," *Communication Monographs* 54 (1987), 276–294.

27. Dudley D. Cahn, *Intimates in Conflict* (Hillsdale, NJ: Erlbaum, 1990), pp. 11–12.

28. Stella Ting-Toomey, "An Analysis of Verbal Communication Patterns in High and Low Marital Adjustment Groups," *Human Communication Research* 9 (1983), 306–319.

29. Gottman, "Emotional Responsiveness in Marital Conversations," p. 112.

30. John P. Vincent, Robert L. Weiss, and Gary R. Birchler, "A Behavioral Analysis of Problem Solving in Distressed and Nondistressed Married and Stranger Dyads," *Behavior Therapy* 6 (1975), 475–487. These findings are duplicated by Andrew Billings, "Conflict Resolution in Distressed and Nondistressed Married Couples," *Journal of Consulting and Clinical Psychology* 47 (1979), 368–376; and Gary R. Birchler, Robert L. Weiss, and John P. Vincent, "Multimethod Analysis of Social Reinforcement Exchange Between Maritally Distressed and Nondistressed Spouse and Stranger Dyads," *Journal of Personality and Social Psychology* 31 (1975), 349–360.

31. Helena Syna, "Couples in Conflict: Conflict Resolution Strategies, Perceptions About Sources of Conflict, and Relationship Adjustment," Doctoral dissertation, State University of New York at Buffalo, 1984; see also Shula Shichman, "Constructive and Destructive Resolution of Conflict in Marriage," Doctoral dissertation, Columbia University, 1982, who found essentially the same results.

32. J. K. Alberts, "A Descriptive Taxonomy of Couples' Conversational Complaints," paper presented at the Western Speech Communication Association Convention, Salt Lake City, February 1987.

33. J. K. Alberts, "An Analysis of Couples' Conversational Complaints," *Communication Monographs* 55 (1988), 184–197.

34. J. K. Alberts, "A Descriptive Taxonomy of Couples' Complaint Interactions," *Southern Speech Communication Journal* 54 (1989), 125–143.

35. Charmaine E. Wilson, "The Influence of Message Direction on Perceived Conflict Behaviors," paper presented at the Western Speech Communication Association Convention, Denver, CO, February 1982.

36. Dudley D. Cahn, *Intimates in Conflict* (Hillsdale, NJ: Erlbaum, 1990), p. 15.

37. Dudley D. Cahn, *Conflict in Intimate Relationships* (New York: Guilford, 1992), pp. 103–104.

Part IV

Effective Communication Behavior

In Part IV we turn to the idea of behavior in conflict situations. Although some would like to skip right to this section, we need to realize that our behavior in conflict situations depends largely on (1) how we think about conflict in general and (2) what we think about this conflict in particular. Consider, for example, the challenges faced by one woman who has a new roommate after a succession of unsatisfactory experiences with sharing housing:

> This conflict started when I was doing dishes. My roommate had left for the weekend, and it was my turn. I started washing out cups when I realized that one had gum stuck to the bottom. The gum had been in there at least two days because I had not had the chance to do dishes in that amount of time. The gum got all over my dish sponge, and I could not get it out. I had to use nail polish remover in order to get it off, and this scored the bottom of my cup. My first reaction was to yell out, "How can there be so many stupid people in this world?" My previous roommate situation had been a nightmare, and I was afraid that this one might also turn out to be the same. Well, I did not bring it up when she got home because it only happened once, and she is really nice and we get along fine, so I did not feel like rocking the boat.
>
> Well, last weekend, she was gone again, and I started to clean the apartment. As I began to sweep the kitchen floor, I found, yes, yet *another* gooey, gross glob of gum stuck next to the trash can on *my* nice, relatively clean (I had mopped not too long before) kitchen floor! I must say that it was a good thing she was not at home because I was so angry. I am not a total neat-freak or anything, but I do like a relatively clean house, and gum is one of those things that just grosses me out.
>
> My problem is that she and I have been living together for only a month and a half, and this will be our first conflict. I really do not want to bring up this issue because it really does seem minor. She is a good roommate otherwise, we have no troubles sharing cleaning and dish-washing duties, and she pays me her share of the utilities promptly. So I am very reluctant to make waves, yet the gum issue *does* bug me.

For the woman involved in this conflict, there are a number of decisions to be made: Is the issue important enough to confront? Will not confronting it lead to it becoming an additional issue in an unrelated conflict later on? Does she want to risk a conflict in the early stages of a relatively good roommate situation? All these questions can be answered and appropriate strategies of engagement (or avoidance) chosen through the S-TLC model presented in this section.

S-TLC—Stop, Think, Listen, and Communicate. Strategies for slowing down our responses to conflict, thinking about or analyzing the conflict, and listening to the other are the focus of Chapter 10. Chapter 11 introduces various communication options for framing competent conflict messages, and Chapter 12 provides examples of how those options will sound when you are actually in a conflict situation. And as Chapter 13 explains, in some conflicts, the presence of tangible, resource-based issues may lead to a win-lose orientation on the part of those in the conflict. Good communication skills alone may not be enough—we need to know how to look for creative solutions to these conflicts. This chapter also contains information on bargaining and negotiating situations, and suggests ways in which the strategies and tactics used by professional negotiators may also be employed in interpersonal conflict.

10

Using the S-TLC System

Objectives

At the end of this chapter, you should be able to

1. briefly explain the S-TLC system for dealing with conflict situations.
2. explain in depth different ways to think about a conflict.
3. offer constructive advice to someone who doesn't listen very well.

Key Terms

analysis	conflict traps	preferences over principles
chaining approach	last tags complex	S-TLC
competitive climate	listening	trained incapacity
conflict dimensions	mushroom syndrome	
conflict pollutants	overblown expectations	

In Chapter 8 we learned to talk about communication as a process by which people make or create meaning together. In this transactional view of communication, conflict is created through the behaviors of each person as they respond to one another.

The transactional view recognizes the importance of both people's behavior in the conflict situation. It takes two people to make the conflict, and it takes two people to manage or resolve it. The way people talk about the conflict together, the way they express messages in response to one another, the way they "read" each other's nonverbal messages as the conflict is being enacted all create the conflict situation as well as manage it or move it to resolution.

Chapter 8 also discussed communication competence, which is knowledge that relates theories about conflict into thinking about conflict, allowing people to communicate well in conflict situations. This chapter discusses the skills associated with thinking about the conflict so that you will be more effective as you speak within it. Our goal is to connect skills associated with thinking about conflicts with those skills associated with acting in conflicts so as to choose the most effective behaviors possible.

> Often I think of what I should have done or said after my conflict is over, but every now and then I actually say what I want at the time I'm with the other person. The other day, I telephoned a person who had left several messages saying she was interested in submitting a bid to my company. The particular person who had called me wasn't there, and the person answering the call said, "She'll be in tomorrow. Why don't you call back then?" Normally, I'd just hang up and never return the call. I don't have to seek out bids right now. But I'd also be irritated—why should a person trying to get my business continue to annoy me with messages and then expect me to do the work? So I just said, "Well, she was the one who wanted my business. Perhaps you could take the details of the bid down and she can submit the bid if she wants to." He apparently decided it was worth his time because he listened to the details I gave him. I felt that the call had been resolved better than it would have been if I had just hung up.

In previous chapters, we have discussed views of conflict: how conflict can be examined through various theories, and how those theories help us explain conflict situations and the behavior of people within them. The subtitle of this book is *From Theory to Action;* theories are excellent means for understanding conflict, and good theories suggest skills for addressing the conflicts we experience. Beginning in this chapter, we turn our attention to various means of resolving conflict—actions that you can take to address conflict issues and maintain your relationships. The following system is designed to help people in conflict to create a mutual understanding.

The S-TLC System

The **S-TLC** system is an acronym for Stop, Think, Listen, and Communicate. We use the hyphen in S-TLC to help you recall the system because we all need a little TLC in our lives; so we thought S-TLC would be easier to remember. Note, however, that our TLC stands for something different from tender, loving care. By following these four steps, one can often resolve interpersonal conflicts through basic communication skills such as assertiveness. Each of these steps consists of several relevant factors that should be considered.

Stop

When you realize that a conflict exists, begin by saying: *Stop*! Take a time out! Try to get your mental faculties in order. Exit temporarily if necessary to get hold of yourself. Don't get so upset that you start to lose control of yourself. Instead, try to calm down and cool off. For many people this is not too difficult. For others, acquiring skills for slowing down the conflict is imperative. One way you can slow down your response to the other is to get a glass of water or some other beverage and take sips of the beverage before you respond to the other person. Counting backward from 100 can also help calm you down.

Think

Think before you act! Try not to take things personally. Avoid jumping to conclusions. Try to go lightly on yourself and on the other person. Don't make mountains out of molehills.

If possible, find some humor in the situation. Remember to take things a step at a time. Tell yourself that you can handle the situation.

Think about your options. Ask yourself, "What do I want to accomplish?" Think both about the problem and about your relationship with the other person. You could react with violence or not. What are the outcomes if you react violently? What would happen if you don't? You could respond by communicating in a destructive way such as aggressive speech. You could respond by avoiding the conflict altogether or simply by giving in. You could respond by communicating in other ways taught later in this chapter. Think about the pluses and minuses for each of these alternatives.

In the next chapter, four communication options for dealing with conflict will be presented. Throughout this textbook, numerous additional techniques are discussed. At this point in the conflict, now is the time to think about your alternatives and determine which is most appropriate for a particular conflict situation.

Listen

Listen before you say anything. The tendency of most people is to justify themselves the moment they hear criticism, rather than really listening to what the other person is saying. We believe that as important as what we say in a conflict is the ability to truly hear what the other person is saying. Most popular advice on conflict emphasizes speaking skills: Say it this way, at this time; assert yourself. But communication is the interaction of two or more people, and conflict occurs because the people have unmet needs and goals. No one likes to hear "I can't believe you feel that way," or "You're wrong," when he or she is trying to explain feelings.

To concentrate on one's own goals is to misunderstand the nature of conflict. More importantly, though, listening is a way to affirm the value and worth of others. One author wrote that the feeling of being truly heard is so close to the feeling of being loved that most people cannot tell the difference.[1]

Communicate

Decide how to *communicate* and do it! We hope you will choose to react nonviolently unless in self-defense and when violence is the only option. Remember that some people believe that violence is never an option. They claim that if you put your mind to it there is always a nonviolent solution to be found. At least, we strongly encourage you to try communication first. The skills learned in communicating feelings and active listening are relevant here.

APPLICATION 10.1

As you consider the S-TLC approach to conflict, how hard is it for you to stop a conflict? How do you usually think about a conflict? How do you usually communicate in a conflict situation?

This chapter focuses in depth with the T and L portions of S-TLC, and provides specific means for thinking about conflict and listening to others in conflict. We will discuss various options for communication in the next chapter where they are explained in detail.

Thinking about Conflict:
Analyzing Conflict Situations

The thinking step is very important because you may talk yourself out of confronting people for the wrong reasons. Expectations and fears may intervene in the conflict resolution process to deter you from making an intelligent decision and taking appropriate action.[2] In established relationships, patterns of conflict become part of the way in which people relate to one another. Because of these patterns, people may feel they do not need to be analytical in conflicts with the other person: They understand how the other person expresses desires and know automatically how to respond, as this narrative indicates:

> My sister and I will argue about a lot of things. When I think she's got something wrong, I'll tell her. She listens to what I have to say, and sometimes she changes her mind. The point is that she listens, and I do too. With my brother, I don't even try. He is so used to talking all the time, and he is right about everything (at least he thinks he is). With him, I've learned to just say things like "Really?" and "You don't say?" I mean, how else am I supposed to respond when he says crazy things like "You're fat because you eat off blue dishes. Blue slows your metabolism." He can't even imagine anyone would have something worthwhile saying, so I don't even bother.

The situational knowledge that the preceding narrator demonstrates is a foundational skill for acting effectively in conflict situations. In the introduction to their test of a three-component model of competent conflict behavior (consisting of motivation, knowledge, and skills), Spitzberg and Hecht claimed:

> The more knowledgeable a person is about the specific context, specific other, and specific topics discussed, the more likely this person is to possess the requisite information, experience, and repertoire to act competently in this situation.[3]

The authors studied naturally occurring conversations, in malls, at the beach, in waiting lines, and so on, which were interrupted to request completion of the questionnaire. Their study demonstrated strong relationships between communication motivation and skills and outcomes such as communication satisfaction and perceptions of competence. However, they failed to demonstrate any strong effect of knowledge on conversational outcomes. Knowledge was assessed with questions such as, "I knew the other person very well," "The conversation was similar to other conversations I have had before," and "I was (un)familiar with the topic of the conversation." The authors concluded that, because the majority of the conversations they studied occurred between people who knew each other well, the knowledge component was not as important. It may be that the knowledge the people had of one another had become more implicit than explicit, guiding behavior in covert rather than overt ways. "Knowledge of conversational forms, other, and topic may be more important in novel situations that tax a person's creativity in assimilating information from prior communicative experience."[4]

Despite its generally poor showing in predicting the outcomes of conversations, having knowledge of conflict situations in general (and of specific conflicts) is likely to result in more satisfying outcomes than if one goes into a conflict without thinking about it ahead of time. The purpose of this section, then, is to increase your ability to understand and analyze conflict situations, so that you can choose the most effective conflict behavior. Several authors have proposed models for analyzing the conditions of a conflict, and the rest of this chapter presents various research areas that impact understanding of conflict situations.

The Goal of Analysis

The most important goal in conflict **analysis** is the determination of whether the conflict is worth investing the necessary time and effort. Chapter 2 discusses various demands that make confronting conflict necessary: When the situation is likely to get worse if the conflict is not confronted or when the others involved feel a need to deal with the issue, then one must engage in conflict interaction.

What are the possible goals when a conflict presents itself? One can have as a goal changing the behavior of the other(s) involved in the conflict, one can have a goal of trying to change the structure of the conflict, or one can make it a goal to change her or his own behavior.[5] The problem with wanting to try to change the other person's behavior is that the other person most likely wants to try to do the same in return. It is nearly impossible to change another person's behavior unless the person cooperates. Wanting to change the structure of the conflict means wanting to change the conditions that give rise to it; this includes increasing resources, changing the way resources are distributed, changing the nature of an interdependent relationship, changing goals, and so on. This option is often possible if the full array of information about a problem has been previously unexamined. In the course of exploring various options in a conflict, the structure of the conflict may be changed, or one can change oneself. Hocker and Wilmot noted the following:

> This is usually the most difficult and, paradoxically, the most successful way to alter a conflict. A true change in your orientation to the other, your interpretation of the issues, reaction to power, or alterations in your own conflict process will have profound effects on the conflictual elements in the relationship . . . recognition of what you are gaining from the ongoing conflict may free you up for change.[6]

People do not always realize that in spite of being in the middle of what seems to be an emotionally draining situation, there are payoffs to continuing a conflict. One such gain is that the relationship with the other person continues, even though it may be destructive. Another gain is the delight people feel when they can prove how wrong the other person is and how right they are about the issue. In addition, the opportunity to exert power over the other person through conflict interaction may perpetuate a conflict situation. Later in this chapter we will provide you two models for analyzing conflict situations and deciding how to act within them. As a preliminary exercise, you can ask yourself the following questions to determine whether a conflict engagement is necessary:

1. Is this really a conflict? Chapter 4 discussed a number of communication situations that appear to be a real conflict but are not—bickering, competition, arguments. Is there a true incompatibility of goals or of the means needed to achieve goals? Can you get what you want elsewhere? Is it really necessary to have things your way?
2. If this is really a conflict, is it important enough to justify a confrontation? Life is full of small annoyances and things we do not like. Is this issue really important to you?

3. What role do you play in the conflict? How have you helped to bring the conflict about? What behavior is the other person likely to identify as a conflict when telling his or her side of the story?

4. What do you gain from the present pattern? Despite the fact that conflict is generally regarded as unpleasant, people often have vested interests in continuing a conflict. Are you continuing a conflict because the rewards, however negative, outweigh the costs of resolving the issue?

5. Is it reasonable to ask the other to change? What will you ask the other to give up? Will your request essentially demand that the other person change in ways that do not really benefit him or her? Ask yourself: Even if the other person would change because you asked, is it really your right to ask?

6. Finally, is this the right time to do the conflict? When the other person is going out the door or is tired, or when you are tired is not the best time to discuss important issues. You need to find a time when both of you can give the conflict your full attention.

APPLICATION 10.2

Think of three conflicts: one in which you felt it was the other person's duty to change, one in which you were able to change the conditions of the conflict, and one in which you decided it was best simply to change yourself. Was the decision to change yourself actually the easiest one to implement?

APPLICATION 10.3

Watch your favorite situation comedy. What kinds of conflicts tend to arise? Are they spontaneous or planned? Compare the conflicts in the comedy to conflicts in a soap opera or dramatic series. How do they differ? If the treatment of conflicts is different, what does that say about how the characters on each show view conflict and its role in their lives?

Dimensions of the Conflict Situation

As we consider the **conflict dimensions** and how to analyze them, we will examine this case study based on a new teacher's experience as she entered the teaching profession.

Case Study 10.1 ■ *A Change in Status*

This conflict occurred over a two-year period, beginning in January, when I began my student teaching at a high school in the Southwest. I had previously become acquainted with the journalism advisor there and had specifically requested this high school for my supervised teaching experience because of the rapport we had developed. I felt I could learn a great deal from Frank, who was not only a recognized instructor in yearbook journalism but also an excellent classroom manager and motivator. We worked well together, and over the course of the semester I was allowed to teach several units unassisted, making it a highly practical experience.

After interviewing at several schools over the summer, I decided there was no place I'd rather teach than with Frank. As it turned out, Frank's coworker, the photojournalism teacher, was leaving. I interviewed for the position with Frank's strong recommendation that I be hired. In fact, I was specifically hired because of my proven ability to work with Frank. The previous teacher had failed to do so, and the stress from their clashes of personality had forced her to seek work elsewhere. However, I was buoyed by the excitement of being hired and by Frank's reassurances. I felt confident that we would have a dynamic, effective, and enjoyable working relationship.

From my first week as a "real teacher," things began to go wrong. There were the normal stresses for a first-year teacher, but things weren't right between Frank and me either. He was often "too busy" for our regular meeting, or even for informal discussions. More than once, he barged into my classroom with some petty grievance while I was lecturing. This not only startled and angered me, it shook the confidence of my students in their new teacher. He also scheduled my classroom for use by the portrait photographer when I had already set it up for something else, even though his stood empty during that time. Though I made repeated attempts to communicate with Frank, the situation only worsened. I found he criticized me to students and administrators in a ridiculing manner that was not intended to be taken constructively.

Now that my standing was as an equal, Frank seemed threatened, though I tried to make it clear that I intended to work in a support capacity and was willing to take directions from him. But this failed to please him. He had been used to performing a highly successful "one-man show" and had received a great deal of recognition for his efforts. He was not inclined to become a team player so that any credit for success would have to be shared.

It was obvious that Frank and I approached conflict differently. I tend to collaborate and on occasion am willing to even accommodate in conflict; Frank was quite competitive. In addition, we didn't share any of the same assumptions about working together. My assumption on being hired was that Frank wanted a coworker and that we shared a common vision for the improvement of the journalism department. However, it seems more probable that Frank was forced to accept a coworker because of the way his department had been organized by the administration. His choice of coworker appeared to be influenced by the amount of control he could exert in the relationship. As his former student teacher, I was an ideal choice.

Frank exercised the power of his position, his seniority, and his relationships with administrators to damage my credibility. There was never any doubt in my mind that should administration get word of our troubles, fault would be found with me and not with Frank. I made it a priority to minimize the conflict and not discuss it with anyone. I had very little power over Frank, but I realized I could decrease his power by reducing my dependence on him. Also, I had some power of internalization, in that, by remaining calm and courteous during one of his tirades, I could appeal to his sense of decency and usually evoke an apology. I also kept careful records of our meetings and our conflict encounters. If nothing else, they showed that I had repeatedly set up meetings to discuss our work and that he had routinely failed to attend.

He evaded my attempts to discuss matters. I wrote him a letter detailing our working relationship and the change since my student teaching experience, describing the problem as I saw it and proposing several measures for improvement. I requested his feedback and cooperation in resolving the conflict. By this time, however, I had devised several methods for coping and was able to contain the situation and keep it from worsening. When I left my job to move on to another career, I felt Frank had come to respect me somewhat. I had no desire to stay in that job but had stuck with it long enough to call my initial teaching experience a success overall, and I had made great progress with my students.

Chapter 7 identified conflict structure, the situational conditions that give rise to conflict interaction: trust, uncertainty, and power. These three variables are affected by the relationship between the people involved, the social or organizational context of the conflict, the apparent issue of the conflict, and interested parties to the conflict (i.e., people not involved directly in the conflict who nonetheless have a stake in the outcome).

The first step in conflict analysis is to examine these situational variables affecting trust, uncertainty, and power. What kind of relationship existed between Ann and Frank? She was originally his student; she became his colleague. This shift in relationship caused power difficulties, as we will see later. The conflict occurred in the context of a high school situation in which there are rules for teacher conduct and expectations about how colleagues should act with respect to one another. The apparent issue was about sharing resources in the journalism program. Interested parties to the conflict included the students who witnessed some of the interactions and were affected by the decisions reached by those in charge.

The second step in analysis is to examine trust, power, and uncertainty. How much do the conflict participants trust one another? What basis do they have for their trust or distrust of one another? What power bases are present in the situation? What kind of power is demonstrated by those in the conflict? In Case Study 10.1, trust is a dynamic factor that changes over the course of the conflict. Whereas the author (Ann) trusted Frank at the beginning of her regular teaching assignment, based on her previous relationship with him, that trust quickly turned to distrust when she found the relationship had changed. Ann had looked forward to being a part of Frank's team, but found that he did not really want her, or anyone, on it. The distrust in their relationship was exacerbated by her feelings of uncertainty concerning her position and her belief that should the conflict become public, she would be seen as the instigator. The trust level between Ann and Frank diminished to the point where she kept records of their interactions. Such a level of distrust can become a self-fulfilling prophecy because a person who distrusts looks for evidence that the other is unworthy of trust, and usually finds it.

Power is an important variable in the case study. Clearly, the shift in their relationship is uncomfortable for Frank. Ann noted the following in her analysis:

> In terms of control, we had gone from student/teacher relationship, in which I could be managed like any other of his students, to that of an equal, whom he could not control overtly but could either assist to become more competent or undermine to maintain his superiority. Frank was playing a game that transactional analysis refers to as "yes, but," in which the manager responds affirmatively to suggestions, implying receptivity, then quickly finds a way to avoid actually implementing the idea. Frank consistently agreed that we needed to spend more time building our relationship and discussing the work ("yes"), but something would nearly always come up to prevent the meeting from happening. In this way, Frank established himself as the greater power or controller.

The central issue in Case Study 10.1 was one of power and relationship, but the issue was frequently masked by problems over classroom use, timing of complaints, complaints about Ann's students, and so on. The various issues involved created conflict pollutants, an idea discussed in the next section.

Conflict Pollutants

Conflict pollutants are "factors that clog and choke the climate for effective conflict management. They are elements that are not inherent in the conflict itself, but that distract from and complicate the resolution process."[7] Pollutants may obscure the nature of the problem, which makes focusing on the real issues difficult.

The first pollutant is **preferences over principles,** in which conflict occurs over style-oriented options rather than imperatives. That is, those involved think that having the conflict go according to the way they prefer things is more important than establishing some lasting means of resolving conflicts. It becomes a pollutant when preference issues are added to central problems and distract attention from the more important issues.

A second pollutant is **overblown expectations**—expecting too much change too quickly. Overblown expectations create a climate for failure and can become an issue in and of themselves in future conflicts. Poor feedback skills are also a pollutant in conflicts when people confuse the conflict issue with the person. A message like "You don't care about this job, do you?" is not as specific as "You've been late three times this week." The first message makes the listener guess at the nature of the problem; the second one makes it clear.

Other pollutants include negativism and joylessness, which can lead to **conflict traps.** Traps occur when circumstances predispose people to overreact to triggering events, usually displacing the original conflict with one that can generate more energy. Harvey and Drolet's example makes the point:

> I get up in the morning and discover that I have an awful cold. I realize that my alarm has failed to go off, making me 30 minutes late. . . . I rush to the office, but the traffic is terrible. . . . I get to work, only to find files stacked all over my desk. . . . I am a time bomb waiting to happen. I am sure I will get into a fight with the first person through the door. . . . [I]t will not be over the issue of the moment . . . and my efforts to resolve the conflict will meet with only limited success because they will focus on the apparent, surface problem.[8]

Another kind of pollutant is the **mushroom syndrome** in which unresolved conflicts have been left to grow in the dark until they become large and unmanageable. Poor problem ownership can also be a conflict pollutant when people get involved in conflicts that are not their own or when they involve others who really do not need to be involved in the conflict.

Solving conflicts before getting all the information acts as a conflict pollutant, too. Such behavior is the opposite of conflict avoidance. On hearing of a problem, the person offers an immediate solution without really knowing the whole situation. Premature solutions to conflict can be as damaging as letting conflicts build up because the failure of the premature solution must be dealt with, as well as additional problems when the conflict is finally confronted.

The last conflict pollutant is called the **last tags complex,** or the need to have the last word in a confrontation. We have all known someone who has done what we did before we did it, better than we did it—or who suffered more while doing it than we did. The need to have the final say in a conflict situation can prolong it far beyond its expected end.

Ann had several conflict pollutants in her situation, most notably overblown expectations. For many people, the transition from student teacher to colleague is difficult, even for those willing to take the lead from the other. The teacher has graded the student, examined the student's work, and evaluated the student. To drop that role and move into one based on cooperation rather than control is not easy. In addition, the number of conflicts Ann experienced with Frank, few of which were ever resolved to her satisfaction, created a competitive conflict escalation cycle, even as she struggled to remain calm and deal with issues in the present rather than focusing on past issues. As you analyze your conflicts, look for influences that may affect the way you interpret and react to them.[9] Eliminating extraneous influences and focusing on the essential will help you move toward conflict resolution.

APPLICATION 10.4

What means can you use to identify and eliminate conflict pollutants in your conflicts? Which pollutants most frequently occur in your conflicts?

Cooperation versus Competition

When engaged in communication with others, we commonly speak of a *climate* as an atmosphere or context that is conducive or harmful to communication. Two types of climates that affect how we relate and interact with others are competitive and cooperative climates. Similarly, in conflict situations, the communication processes can be predominantly cooperative or competitive, with a cooperative stance preferable.

The primary determinant of cooperative processes is the quality of the communication process. A cooperative climate is characterized by the open and honest communication of relevant information between those involved, whereas a **competitive climate** is characterized by distorted or absent communication. When communication processes lead to perceived cooperation rather than competition, participants have an increased sensitivity to similarities and common interests rather than a focus on differences or threats. Cooperation generally increases levels of trust and the willingness of parties to respond to each other's needs. And, when processes are cooperative rather than competitive, conflict becomes a matter of mutuality, a problem to be solved rather than a win-lose situation.[10]

How does one create a cooperative climate within conflict situations? A focus on the issue involved, an emphasis on the need to reach some agreement about it, and an emphasis on mutuality will help. Often creating a cooperative climate is a matter of risk, stemming from a willingness to act cooperatively even when unsure of how the other person will respond. Deutsch noted that conflict over negatives (e.g., I want you to stop something) is more difficult to resolve cooperatively than conflict over positives (e.g., I want you to do something). Large issues are more difficult to resolve cooperatively than small ones, and issues that threaten the self-esteem of the parties in the conflict are more difficult to resolve cooperatively than nonthreatening issues. Deutsch concluded by arguing that some conflicts are "inherently pathological and can best be handled by preventing their occurrence."[11]

From Ann's description of the conflict it is clear that although she expected a cooperative climate and tried to establish a cooperative relationship, the situation was largely competitive and Frank reacted as though he lost as a result of any success Ann experienced. As each issue arose and was dealt with in a win-lose manner, the competitive climate became more entrenched until it was almost impossible to create a cooperative climate. The best Ann could hope for, and what she did do, was to change her own behavior and position in the conflict: to lessen her dependence on Frank, to control her own behavior and act calmly even if she was not calm, to increase her competence, and to keep quiet about the conflict and not express her feelings to others in the organization.

Although Ann may seem improbably saintlike in these interactions, one author's observations of her confirm her ability to do these things: She is a soft-spoken person who does not anger easily. Her personality is probably the reason that she lasted longer than her predecessor and left on her own terms. She kept the conflict contained; she minimized its effect on her relationships with students and other faculty; and she eventually bartered a truce of sorts with her coworker.

Trained Incapacities

A dimension of the situation that may distort how people approach conflict management or that might limit their ability to choose among options is the presence of trained incapacities. A **trained incapacity** occurs when a person's abilities and talents actually limit the person's thinking.[12] Because the behavior has become generally beneficial (in non-conflict situations), the person expects it to work in conflict situations, where it may not be appropriate. Four such trained incapacities are goal centeredness, destructive redefinition, evaluative tendency, and using standards.

On the one hand, goal centeredness is generally positive: People identify the end point they hope to reach and then take the necessary steps to get there. It can function as a trained incapacity, however, when people are so eager to get to the end point that they do not adequately address all the dynamics of a situation. The following narrative illustrates this desire to resolve a conflict too quickly without examining all the options that could be taken:

> An interesting situation is occurring with another tenant and my roommate and myself in our apartment building. We have assigned parking spaces, and the tenant who parks next to my roommate has a tendency to pull his car in and park it in half of her space. She has asked him to pull over because it is hard for her to get her door open. He gets upset because his car gets wet by the sprinklers located on the other side of his car. Two nights ago when we came home, he was over his line and into our space. My roommate parked very close to his car because she thought it might make him realize how close he was parking. However, he got angry and left a nasty note on her car. Both parties are not happy and something has to be done. I see the situation as petty, and I think that some kind of agreement needs to be worked out instead of exchanging unpleasant words or notes.

Redefinition is the ability to adapt to situations as they change: As new elements enter a situation, people change their thinking to accommodate them. Redefinition can help move a conflict to resolution if participants stop defining the conflict in their own terms and start defining it in terms of mutuality. Destructive redefinition may occur, however, when participants decide that winning the issue or beating the other person is their major goal. Consider how one person shifted from making a pass to being obnoxious about it:

> My friends and I went out for a beer after a football game. One of the customers became belligerent. Nothing new. Except that he turned his affections toward Kate, one of my friends. As I have said before, one way to get my attention is to be disrespectful to one of my friends. Well, I couldn't let this boy get by without a talking to. Which is all that I wanted to do, just talk to the guy and let him know that his actions and words were not appreciated and they would not be tolerated. Well, as I walked away, he used colorful words and imagery to tell me how he felt, which I don't mind. But, he insisted on continuing and again approached my friend. Well, I went over to him again and asked him to be polite to the lady. At this point he took a swing at me. I have learned self-defense over the years and reacted instinctively to his punch, which landed him on the floor. I didn't worry about him after that because his friends came over and dragged him away.

Have you ever gotten so mad at someone that you could only think about getting even or seeking revenge? We hope you now realize that this is no way to resolve a conflict.

Evaluative ability is beneficial when it generates critical thinking about a topic and allows more complete discussion of an issue. However, it can be overused to where no solution seems feasible and the flaws overwhelm their usefulness, or it can stifle the introduction of issues, leading to situations in which conformity is more important than the examination of issues. Sometimes this trained incapacity is seen where people feel they have "talked a problem to death" without really coming up with any kind of solution for it. An instance of a person's evaluative ability getting in the way of initially solving a problem (although a solution was reached shortly after this narrative was written) is found in this account:

> We have a $31,000 piece of equipment that is not functioning properly. Because of some serious budget problems a year ago, we had to let the person go who had been maintaining this equipment as part of her lab chores. There was a big pall over the lab because of this money crunch, and a lot was being asked of everyone since the boss had asked me to come up with a solution to the budget problem. I began implementing a proactive budget recovery program that required everyone's serious participation. I didn't have the heart to ask anyone to accept the additional chore of maintaining the equipment, so I took it on myself, although my skills weren't really up to it. I wanted to straighten out a few organizational aspects of this chore, and get the facility organized before I asked anyone to do it. We hired a new person, but I didn't want to dump it on her immediately. Since the equipment is down so much, we got permission to use an identical piece in another lab, and now our equipment has become an expensive paperweight. This is very hard on lab relations, but I cannot seem to find a plan that I think will work.

A final kind of trained incapacity is the use of objective standards or expectations for behavior. Established standards may be useful as guidelines for decision making and interaction but can be a problem when parties in the conflict believe there is one right answer and refuse to compromise that position. When applying the rules, rather than finding an optimum solution, becomes the basis for managing the conflict, a trained incapacity is evident. An example of objective standards applied in a way that makes it difficult for people to reach an agreement is found in this narrative:

> Before I even considered enrolling in the accelerated Master's of Management program, I made sure that our educational reimbursement policy considered it an acceptable one for our employees. They reimburse 80 percent of the tuition of programs that are job-related, and pay 60 percent of the materials costs. I have taken classes before with no problems. Prior to the beginning of the class, I filled out the paperwork. Three weeks went by and I started to get nervous. I had already attended two of the classes without approval. I went in to check on it, and found a new person in charge. Despite the fact that the proper signatures were on the form, she told me that the company would not reimburse me at the full amount and that it would be a taxable benefit. She said it was because I am a buyer, and the program is in management. I told her there weren't any graduate programs for buyers. I am in a business management portion of the organization, so it should be applicable. Then she started to question every class in the program, like how a marketing class would help me do my job better. It's a whole program—I can't pick and choose what I am going to take. And I don't want to be a buyer forever. I realized I wasn't going to get anywhere with her, so I went back to my own supervisor to let him handle it. She'll listen to him.

Models for Analysis

A skill that is useful in conflict situations is the ability to think about the conflict and its various implications. One way to analyze conflict is to create a conflict map that identifies the elements in the conflict's structure and process. To create a conflict map, it helps to first create a narrative that describes the conflict as thoroughly as possible. Write out the conflict as though you were telling someone else about it. As you do so, try to recall everything that has happened until this time. After writing out your narrative, answering the questions in Table 10.1 can help clarify the conflict situation for you.

For people who think in terms of cause-effect relationships, the questions in Table 10.1 can be helpful guides. However, emotions and level of anxiety about a conflict can sometimes block discursive thinking. When a conflict is hard to analyze, however, an alternative "right-brain" approach might work. Take a piece of paper, and begin to chain out some thoughts by jotting down the various aspects to the problem that come to mind. You can start with any thought you have about the conflict. For example, suppose you are the person in the following situation:

> This conflict has been an ongoing thing with my mother and father for two months now. My parents are very protective of me and they tend to smother me at times. They don't think of what would be best for me and my life, only what would make them feel better. For example, I want to go to Italy this summer, but my parents don't want me to go because it's too far. I would completely pay for the trip, but instead of them thinking this would be a great opportunity for me to visit relatives I've never met, they don't want me to go because they can't let go and let me grow up. I love to travel anywhere that's new, and they keep holding me back. Another example would be the fact that I want to move out and be on my own and be more independent. But then when the idea comes up, my mother starts crying and gets very upset.

Figure 10.1 illustrates a **chaining approach** to the problem. The woman describing the conflict might start with the idea that her parents are very protective. She would write this down on the paper and circle it. Related to being protective is her parent's lack of enthusiasm for travel to Italy or moving out of the house. These ideas are written down, circled, and connected to the central idea of protectiveness. An issue related to traveling to Italy is the fact that the woman is willing to pay for the trip herself, so that idea would be written and connected to the Italy trip. As issues that are related to other issues are thought of, they are written down, circled, and connected to the various other aspects of the conflict. The chaining technique is most useful when people are not really sure about all the issues that might be involved in a conflict or when they are dissatisfied with a situation but not exactly sure why. It is a good tool for identifying issues.

Once the issues are identified, the person experiencing the conflict can begin to prioritize them: What is the most important issue here? What issues are beyond my control? In the preceding example, the parents' feelings about her moving out or traveling alone are beyond the control of the student. However, she can demonstrate her ability to do these things by saving money for the trip or for her moving costs, making the arrangements, and so on.

The chaining technique shows how many issues are really present in a conflict and how they affect each other, at least from the one person's point of view. The young woman

TABLE 10.1 *Questions for Analyzing a Conflict*

I. Analyze the background of the conflict.
   A. What set off the conflict? That is, what made you think that you were having a conflict with the other person?
   B. Explain the conflict from your perspective.
   C. Explain the conflict from the other person's perspective. How would that person describe the conflict?
   D. What kinds of feelings does the conflict arouse in you—anger, frustration, and so on? Why do you think you feel the way you do about the conflict?
   E. To whom does this conflict seem apparent?
   F. Who will be the first to notice if this conflict is resolved in some way? Who else will notice?
II. Analyze the situation.
   A. What kind of relationship do you have with the other person?
   B. What is the organizational or social context of the conflict? Where is the conflict occurring?
   C. Who are interested parties to the conflict? Who else has a stake in the way this conflict will be resolved?
   D. How much do you trust the other person?
   E. What kinds of power are available to you in this situation? What kinds of power are available to the other person in the situation?
   F. How certain or uncertain are you about the other person's motives?
   G. How has the situation that gave rise to the conflict been altered as a result of the conflict occurring? That is, has your relationship with the other person changed? Has trust decreased? Have power relations shifted?
III. Analyze your choices.
   A. What are your instrumental, relational, and identity goals in the conflict?
   B. What can you do to achieve your goals?
   C. How do you think the other person will respond to your goal-seeking behavior?
   D. What is the very least you need from the other person in order to say that the conflict is over?
   E. What kind of person will you be if you achieve your goal?
   F. What kind of relationship will you have with the other person if you achieve your goal?
   G. Do you want to be the kind of person or have the kind of relationship that is likely to result from achieving your goal in the conflict situation?
IV. Plan the conflict.
   A. How could you bring the conflict up to the other person (assuming you haven't done so already)? What can you say to the other person?
   B. What do you think the other person would say about the conflict if he or she was initiating it?

in the example, however, has apparently made little effort to see things from her parents' point of view; the chaining process could be used to try to describe the issues as her parents see them. In a conflict, you need to S-TLC: Stop, think, listen, and communicate. Thinking about the conflict means that you bring your skills of analysis to the situation. In the next section, we discuss some means for improving your listening.

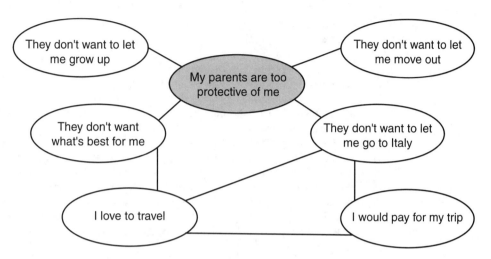

FIGURE 10.1   *Chaining Approach to Identifying Conflict Issues and Goals*

Listening in Conflict Situations

Listening is a desire to pay attention to the other person, openness to the other person's views, willingness to suspend judgment during the discussion, patience to hear the other out, an empathic response to the other person, and a commitment to listen to all the other person has to say.[13] Listening does not come naturally. Rogers noted the following:

> Our first reaction to most of the statements which we hear from other people is an immediate evaluation or judgment, rather than an understanding of it. When someone expresses some feeling or attitude or belief, our tendency is, almost immediately, to feel, "That's right"; or "That's stupid"; "That's not nice." Very rarely do we permit ourselves to understand precisely what the meaning of his statement is to him. I believe this is because understanding is risky. If I let myself really understand another person, I might be changed by that understanding. And we all fear change.[14]

We typically feel defensive when others have something critical to say about us. We do not want to know that we are not doing well or not doing the things we are supposed to do. We want to think everything is fine. Defensiveness is "a somewhat hostile, emotional state which causes people to either partially or totally reject incoming messages and other stimuli which they perceive as being incorrect or contradictory to their point of view. . . . [It] affects both our perception and our subsequent behavior."[15]

Defensiveness arises from the interaction of people in a situation and occurs when people have a perceived flaw, which they do not want to admit, and a sensitivity to that flaw. When sensitive people believe that another has attacked their flaw, they respond to defend themselves. Certain behaviors do foster defensiveness, but they do so because people tend to react defensively with regard to certain topics.[16]

> My friend and I both struggle with a lot of psychological and emotional problems. Lately, we have both been working on areas in our lives. She is trying to be more assertive, and I am to the point where I cannot take any more advice on how to run my life. I need to start thinking about what I want to be, not what everyone else tells me I should be. Unfortunately, these two areas have run into each other. She feels she needs to tell me how she feels about everything, including how I act. For example, she told me the other day that I should just say, "I can't go with you today," instead of giving a long explanation. She told me when I give a long explanation it seems that I am trying to make up an excuse and that I just don't want to go with her. I told her I really couldn't handle that kind of criticism right now, and she said "no problem." Two days later, we got into it again when she got mad at me for something that wasn't my fault. She still believes she should be assertive and tell me exactly what is on her mind, and I still cannot handle it right now. It's a stalemate.

There are several skills associated with listening to the other person. Some of these may seem obvious to you, and others may seem new. This list, although not exhaustive, can help to make you a better listener in conflicts.

First, stop whatever you are doing and give your attention to the other person. It's frustrating to feel as though one's message isn't worthy of full attention. One student, for example, reported that whenever she has a meeting with her boss, he continues to read and answer his e-mail as she is talking to him about issues in the office that must be addressed. She rarely walks out feeling as though he knows what is happening in the office and what she is doing about it.

Second, look at the other person. It's harder to let your mind wander when you are making eye contact. You need to make sure that you blink, though, because you may otherwise wind up staring blankly and disengaging yourself mentally from what is happening.

Third, engage in positive nonverbal feedback. Head nods, vocalizations such as "uh-huh," and forward lean toward the other all indicate interest. Make an effort not to engage in what are called adaptive behaviors (e.g., chewing on your nails, examining your skin or clothing carefully, etc.). These tell the other person you are not listening, even when you may be.

Fourth, work on understanding the other person's feelings, not on arguing with the other person. Indicate that you are following the other person's train of thought or not, but avoid saying things that diminish the importance of the other person's feelings or assert that the feelings are invalid.

From Theory to Action

We need to stop, think, listen, and communicate with the other person. *Stop* means that we don't react blindly to the other person. We consider our options in a conflict situation, and try to exercise them rationally. *Think* means we analyze the situation to try to know what is really happening within it. *Listen* means that we consider the other person's opinion important, and that we try to hear and understand it before we make a point of saying what's on our mind. Finally, we *communicate,* purposefully and empathically. In the next chapter, we'll explore various communication options.

Notes

1. David Augsburger, *Caring Enough to Hear and Be Heard* (Ventura, CA: Regal Books, 1982).

2. Denise H. Cloven and Michael E. Roloff, "The Chilling Effect of Aggressive Potential on the Expression of Complaints in Intimate Relationships," *Communication Monographs* 60 (1993), 199–219.

3. Brian H. Spitzberg and Michael L. Hecht, "A Component Model of Relational Competence," *Human Communication Research* 10 (1984), 577.

4. Meira Likerman, "The Function of Anger in Human Conflict," *International Review of Psychoanalysis* 14 (1987), 152.

5. Carles Speilberg, Susan S. Krasner, and Eldra P. Solomon, "The Experience, Expression, and Control of Anger," in M. P. Janisse (Ed.), *Health Psychology: Individual Differences and Stress* (New York: Springer-Verlag, 1988), pp. 89–108.

6. Joyce L. Hocker and William W. Wilmot, *Interpersonal Conflict,* 3rd Ed. (Dubuque, IA: Wm. C. Brown, 1991), pp. 180–181.

7. Thomas R. Harvey and Bonita Drolet, *Building Teams, Building People: Expanding the Fifth Resource* (La Verne, CA: Department of Educational Management, University of La Verne, 1992), p. 84; see also Marc Roberts, *Managing Conflict from the Inside Out* (San Diego: Learning Concepts, 1982).

8. Harvey and Drolet, *Building Teams, Building People,* p. 93.

9. For a discussion of the importance of situational variables in conflict, see Daniel Druckman, "The Importance of the Situation in Interparty Conflict," *Journal of Conflict Resolution* 15 (1971), 523–554.

10. Morton Deutsch, "Conflict and Its Resolution," in Clagett G. Smith (Ed.), *Conflict Resolution: Contributions of the Behavioral Sciences* (Notre Dame, IN: University of Notre Dame Press, 1971), pp. 39–40.

11. Ibid., p. 44.

12. The idea of trained incapacities was generated by Kenneth Burke, *Permanence and Change* (Indianapolis: Bobbs Merrill, 1954) and developed by Folger and Poole.

13. William H. Baker, "Defensiveness in Communication: Its Causes, Effects and Cures," *Journal of Business Communication* 17 (1980), 33–43.

14. Carl R. Rogers, *On Becoming a Person* (Cambridge, MA: The Riverside Press, 1961), p. 18.

15. Baker, "Defensiveness in Communication," pp. 33, 35.

16. Glen H. Stamp, Anita L. Vengelisti, and John A. Daly, "The Creation of Defensiveness in Social Interaction," *Communication Quarterly* 40 (1992), 177–190.

11

Choosing among the Communication Options in Conflict Situations

Objectives

At the end of this chapter, you should be able to

1. compare and contrast the four communication options for dealing with conflicts.
2. describe the primary communication considerations that should influence your choice of a communication option.

Key Terms

accommodation	gunny-sacking	rights
aggressive communication	interpersonal violence	sexism
assertive communication	nonassertive communication	stereotypes
communication options	passive-aggressive communication	verbal aggression
communication rights	racism	

Stop, think, listen, and communicate! But what are your **communication options** in conflict situations? When a conflict occurs, both parties may choose to be nonassertive, aggressive, passive-aggressive, or assertive. The following sections explore some of the implications and factors that are relevant when considering each of these conflict options based on the assumption that with some instruction and practice many people are able to modify their behavior to better adapt to their circumstances.

This is not to be taken as an exercise in labeling people as personality types such as nonassertive or aggressive personalities. Nor is this to be taken as a psychological approach that digs for deep emotional problems that account for personality disorders. Our goal is to identify certain conflict communication behaviors that are viewed as good or bad habits or behaviors learned from good or poor models. Quite often the destructive behaviors are done without knowledge of their impact (not realizing the harm they do to others). The important point about this approach to conflict is that if the behaviors are learned, they can be unlearned. The change may not be easy, but it is possible without solving all our early psychological problems.

Conflict Communication Options

Nonassertive Communication (Avoidance or Accommodation) as an Option

I notice that when I am physically and emotionally close to someone like my boyfriend, I am nonassertive. Sometimes I don't want to say anything because I don't want to hurt him. I feel the need to protect him, so I try to ignore the problem or talk to a third person about it. Although it seems unproductive, it is the only way I know to try to keep him from suffering. At other times, I start out being nonassertive, but I don't always stay that way. I have avoided confronting some conflicts until I am so upset that I become furious and can no longer hold back. Then I explode!

Nonassertive communication may be defined as the ability to avoid a conflict altogether or accommodate (by simply giving in) to the desires of the other person through the use of verbal and/or nonverbal acts that conceal one's opinions and feelings. When people decide to use nonassertive communication, they fail to speak up for their interests, concerns, or rights. There are different ways in which such people may fail to speak up for their interests.

- They may do it in only one situation for a particular reason. Perhaps they let someone choose a movie to see that does not interest them because on that occasion it happens to be their friend's birthday.
- People may also choose to avoid conflict in certain types of situations or relationships. In this case, they may think that they should never argue with their father, boss, or aging grandparent.
- Finally, some may choose to avoid conflict altogether regardless of the situation. This happens when individuals do not feel that others would or should take their needs into consideration.

Nonassertive communication comes in two forms: conflict avoidance and **accommodation.** Nonassertive communicators tend to allow themselves to be interrupted, subordinated, and "used as a doormat to be walked on." They often have poor eye contact, poor posture, and a defeated air about them. We may recognize the nonassertive communicator by her or his indecisiveness. People complain that when they confront someone who responds in a nonassertive way, the other often apologizes too quickly, refuses to take the conflict seriously, becomes evasive, stonewalls (avoids or ignores them), or walks out. A nonassertive communication may sound sarcastic, but when confronted the person denies that there is anything wrong. We would classify as nonassertive statements like these:

> "I don't dare say anything."
> "I want to avoid creating unpleasantness for myself."
> "What good would it do to speak up?"
> "I went along because I didn't want to offend anybody."
> "I don't want to make waves."
> "It's okay for you to take advantage of me. I don't mind."
> "I don't want to say anything that will make you uncomfortable, upset, or angry."
> "Whatever you decide is okay with me."

The concept of nonassertiveness is similar to communication apprehension.[1] Both terms describe people's failure to engage in conflict with others. For example, people who describe themselves as high in communication apprehension in interpersonal relationships prefer accommodation as a conflict style. However, in a group of people, they tend to prefer conflict avoidance, but if a conflict is unavoidable, they prefer to compete in an effort to end the conflict quickly. In any case, people high in communication apprehension find it difficult to use the assertive style when in conflict.[2]

When they avoid dealing with the problems that plague them, people who choose nonassertive communication behavior and their partners both lose. If they accommodate by giving in, their partners may win the fight, but the accommodators lose it. In fact, it may be argued that over time, the losing partner will eventually "have enough" and leave the relationship, so both end up losing in the long run.

APPLICATION 11.1

In what kinds of situations are you most likely to be nonassertive? When has this been a disadvantage for you? Under what conditions, if any, might this be an advantage to you?

Aggressive Communication as an Option

> When I started to keep track of my conflicts, I saw that I could have handled many of them differently. Because I was frustrated and angry, I often handled them in an aggressive way. Looking back on them now, I can see that I wasted a lot of energy, and the conflicts were basically unnecessary. Now the majority of them seem trivial, and in some situations could have been avoided. I could have stopped the conflicts before they started. I find it funny now to look back at the situations where I got bent out of shape. I had almost forgotten that I even experienced some of the conflicts. In most cases I became defensive especially when there was a romantic interest involved, probably because I felt more vulnerable and insecure. I now see the pattern and my tendency to take out on others problems with myself.

From a communication perspective, aggression may be defined as the ability to impose one's will (i.e., wants, needs, or desires) on another person through the use of verbal and/or nonverbal acts done in a way that violates socially acceptable standards and carried out with the intention or the perceived intention of inflicting physical and/or psychological pain, injury, or suffering. When people decide to force others to give them what they demand, they advance their interests, concerns, or rights in a way that interferes with the interests or infringes on the rights of others. Their communication behavior reminds us of bullies when we were in grade school.

Aggressive communication behaviors are practically synonymous with conflict because they range from mild forms of verbal intimidation to more severe beatings to extremely violent rapes and homicides. Aggression ranges from carefully planned attacks to sudden emotional outbursts inflicting injury on other persons. There are different ways in which people use aggressive communication to get what they want at the expense of others.

- They may choose to be aggressive in only one situation for a particular reason. Perhaps they take advantage of another person because that person has hurt them in the past.
- They may also choose to pressure others into submission but only in certain types of situations or relationships. For example, one may dominate a spouse, employees at work, or other members of a fraternity, but not other people. In this case, he or she may think that it is okay to put down a spouse, employee, or lower-level classmate.
- Finally, some may try to dominate everyone she or he encounters regardless of the situation. This happens when people get too high an opinion of themselves, have little respect for other people, and feel that it is a sign of weakness to take into consideration the other's needs.

What communication behaviors are given off by an aggressive communicator? Aggressive communication may take two forms: physical and verbal aggression. Aggressive communicators tend to interrupt, subordinate, and stereotype others. If nonassertive people feel "used as a door mat to be walked on," probably the ones who walked all over them used aggressive communication behavior. When engaged in aggressive communication, people are often poor listeners or offend others by ignoring them. They engage in intense, glaring eye contact, put forward an invading posture as they bear down on others, and emit an arrogant air about them. They try to dominate others by being loud, abrasive, blaming, intimidating, and sarcastic. We would call the following statements aggressive:

> "I have never lost an argument."
> "His stereo was so loud, I had to go over and pull the plug out of the wall. Then he got the message."
> "I try to make others look bad, so that I look good. I try to get my way at all costs."
> "I am the boss. I know what's best."
> "I don't care what you think."

If they don't start a fight by getting physical, they react with violence the instant the other party "provokes them." Aggressive communication often gets nasty in an argument by "hitting below the belt" (using intimate knowledge against the other), bringing up unrelated issues, making promises they don't intend to keep, using other people (attacking through friends or family), and demanding more.

People who resort to aggressive communication often win conflicts at the expense of their partners. Other people may fear those who turn aggressive. Aggressive communication gives the impression that one does not respect or care about other people, which earns little respect or care in return. As noted earlier, it may be argued that over time the losing partner will eventually "get fed up" and leave a relationship with one who is aggressive, so both end up losing in the long run.

APPLICATION 11.2

In what kinds of situations are you most likely to be aggressive? When has this been a disadvantage for you? Under what conditions, if any, might this be an advantage to you?

Nonverbal Aggression (Physical Violence) as an Option

My father was a person who hit first and asked questions later when he was angry. I learned early in my life how to appease him so that I wouldn't get punished as frequently. But it took me a long time to realize that my husband wouldn't hit me because he was angry. I guess I just kept waiting for him to be like my father.

The realization that communication plays a role in physical violence has resulted in a new field of study that focuses on **interpersonal violence,** which studies both verbal and nonverbal aggression.[3] Research shows that men are more likely to be the perpetrators of physical violence toward their female partners who are more likely to be the victims. Bograd reports that "wives suffer significantly more physical injuries than do husbands."[4] According to Marshall, males are more likely to hit or kick a wall, door, or furniture; drive dangerously; act like a bully; hold and pin; shake or roughly handle; grab; and twist an arm, whereas more females sustain these acts.[5] As Dobash and Dobash state, "Certainly, there is a vast body of evidence confirming the existence of persistent, systematic, severe, and intimidating force men use against their wives . . . (that) does warrant the use of terms such as wife beating or battered woman."[6]

More than half of all women homicide victims are killed by former or current boyfriends or husbands, usually after they are separated.[7] Research also shows that women and children are more likely than male partners and fathers to be harmed by physical force in the family.[8]

Noting that abusers are more likely to use violence in the home where they expect the costs of abuse to be less than the rewards, Margolin argues that women suffer greater penalties than do men for domestic violence.[9] If abusive behavior is more "costly" to women, men are more likely than women to beat or abuse their partners and children who love them. Furthermore, if violence committed by men is more likely to avoid sanctions such as police intervention, loss of status, and public humiliation, men's violence toward family members is less subject to social control. Finally, due to their greater size and economic-social status, men may abuse family members with less fear of reprisal. When one combines the privacy of the home with the lack of stigma, lack of social sanctions, and lack of social control, getting his way whenever he wants it may outweigh the cost of a man's being violent.

APPLICATION 11.3

Sometimes abusive parents say they merely teach stick discipline. What do you think is the difference between punishing and disciplining a child? When do people overstep their parental authority to punish their children?

Verbal Aggression as an Option

Defining Verbal Aggression.   In communication research, **verbal aggression** is defined as a person's predisposition to attack the self-concept of another person in order to cause psychological pain for the other.[10] It is a synonym for emotional maltreatment and psychological abuse. The concept of verbal aggression extends beyond the simple notion of a person achieving goals at the expense of others. It is considered to be a personality trait (an enduring characteristic of a person) that manifests itself in fairly predictable communication patterns. Verbal aggression takes the form of character attacks, insults, ridicule, profanity, and threats. Interestingly, whereas verbal aggression can consist of many descriptive statements about what is said in terms of verbal messages (insults, criticism, telling people when they are unreasonable, etc.), it also includes how something is said in terms of nonverbal messages (tone of voice such as yelling and screaming). Verbal aggression also includes stereotypical and prejudicial remarks.[11]

Stereotyping as Verbal Aggression.   Stereotyping refers to statements that suggest a fixed impression of a group of people (teachers, plumbers, police, etc.). For many years, stereotyping was seen as a mental ability that helped people know how to respond to individuals. By recognizing someone's group identification, one might be able to predict that the individual would manifest certain behaviors, attitudes, needs, or values. Today, however, members of various groups rightfully resent being stereotyped. "**Stereotypes** distort accurate perception. They prevent you from seeing an individual as an individual rather than as a member of a group . . . (and) fail to benefit from the special contributions each individual can bring to an encounter."[12]

Now it is recognized that stereotypes, like first impressions, often are barriers to be overcome. For example, in sex role stereotyping, some people will make the faulty assumption that doctors are men, nurses and secretaries are women, and department heads are men. Older people are becoming increasingly sensitive to the stereotypes reflected in such statements as "You can't teach an old dog new tricks," suggesting that older people are less willing to accept change and adapt to the needs of a changing environment.

Many courses in interpersonal communication attempt to teach people how to get past stereotypes and first impressions and perceive people as unique human beings with individual worth. We need to use our communication to get to know others better and "personalize our interpersonal messages." As Stewart wrote in his basic interpersonal communication textbook, communicators need "to highlight in their speaking and listening aspects of their own and the other's 'personness.'"[13]

Racism and Sexism as Verbal Aggression.   **Racism** and **sexism** are stereotypes with prejudice. When uttered as statements, they defame members of another race and opposite sex. Racist or sexist jokes can be most harmful. In addition to limiting individuals' progress, racism and sexism are emotionally negative terms, statements, and jokes that greatly offend members of racial groups and members of the opposite sex. Racist or sexist language serves no constructive purpose. Instead, it creates barriers to interpersonal communication by making a communicator appear insulting, ignorant, prejudiced, and threatening, and by causing the offended listener to stop listening.

There is no need to list here specific examples of racial remarks because they are well known and clearly offensive terms. What are some sexist expressions to avoid?

- Generic Man—Common man, mankind, caveman, chairman, ombudsman, sportsmanship, craftsmanship, repairman. Use instead—humanity, people, cave dwellers, chairperson or chair, ombudsperson, a good sport, a talented person, a person who repairs.
- Generic He/His—When a baby cries, he may make a great deal of noise. Use instead she or he; still better, use the plural forms (they, them, their) to avoid problems.

Women are not the only ones offended by sexist remarks. Many men may be offended when women say such things as: "All men are jerks." "All men want is only one thing (or all men want is sex)." "Men are insensitive." "Men are financially responsible for their family." Expressions like these need to be avoided, too.

Reasons for Verbal Aggression.   Research conducted in the area of verbal aggression has examined the reasons for verbal aggression, the situations that encourage verbal aggression, the kinds of messages that are seen as aggressive, and the factors that distinguish verbal aggression in a person. People are verbally aggressive toward others for a variety of reasons. One reason stems from psychopathology; that is, I might attack you verbally because you remind me of another person who caused me some kind of hurt that I have been unable to resolve. Most of us have had the experience of meeting someone we did not particularly like, and frequently it was because the person reminded us of someone we had disliked previously. Another reason for verbal aggression is disdain for someone or expressing extreme dislike for someone. Verbal aggression may be the result of social learning, as when someone models aggressive behavior performed by another person. Situation comedies like *Married with Children, Seinfeld,* and *The Simpsons* get laughs out of people being nasty toward one another. Seeing the behavior work for others (even in a fictional mode) may influence people to adopt it for themselves.

Verbal aggression may also result from argumentative skill deficiency, which is another way of saying that people sometimes verbally attack the other person because they cannot think of a counterargument to the person's claims.[14] This inability to think of a response may result in verbal aggression or the "well, you" retort:

> ***Worker One:***   "You know, I really wish that you would give me a little more notice when you have an urgent job for me to do."
>
> ***Worker Two:***   "Oh, up yours."

Or

> ***Worker One:***   "You know, I really wish that you would give me a little more notice when you have an urgent job for me to do."
>
> ***Worker Two:***   "Yeah, well, if you'd move at the same speed as the rest of us it wouldn't be a problem."

For most people, an occasional lapse into verbal aggression is not enough to brand them as a verbally deficient arguer. However, a response that indicates listening, rather than a counterattack, will generally be more helpful in problem solving, as this response indicates:

> *Worker One:*   "You know, I really wish that you would give me a little more notice when you have an urgent job for me to do."
>
> *Worker Two:*   "I didn't realize it was causing a problem. How much of a lead time did you have in mind?"

Some situations may encourage a person to be verbally aggressive. For example, if Worker One had said something like, "Can't you get your act together enough to give me some time to do this work," Worker Two probably would feel justified in making an aggressive response. Anticipating a positive outcome as a result of being aggressive, being frustrated by the situation, having aggression cues present in the situation, and verbal aggression on the part of the other may all prompt people to become verbally aggressive themselves. On the other hand, anticipated punishment for aggression, feelings toward the other that are incompatible with aggression, being an easy-going other person, and the other's use of nonhostile language all tend to discourage verbal aggression.[15]

Verbal aggression takes a number of different forms. Attacks on the character or competence of the other person, attacks on the background (ethnic, racial, etc.) and gender of the other person, attacks on the other's physical appearance, maledictions (i.e., expressing a hope that something bad will happen to the other person), teasing, ridicule, threats, swearing, and nonverbal emblems (e.g., giving the other person "the finger") all have been associated with verbal aggression.[16] The model of verbal aggression developed by Infante and his associates suggests that people with this trait both send and receive more self-concept-attacking messages and that, because of their exposure to the attacking messages, they are not bothered by the hurt they produce.

A recent study compared people who scored high on the trait of verbal aggression with those whose scores were low. People high in verbal aggression created messages with competence attacks, teasing, nonverbal emblems, and swearing much more frequently than did those who were low in this trait. In addition, people high in verbal aggression viewed threats, competence attacks, and physical appearance attacks as less hurtful than did people who were low in verbal aggression. People high in aggression used aggressive messages to appear tough to the other, to be mean to the other, to express disdain for the other, or to fight with the other when a rational discussion had degenerated. The authors noted that teasing may be a method verbally aggressive people use to appear humorous or to soften the effects of their verbal aggression by indicating that the attack does not have to be taken seriously. It also may be a way to keep the other person guessing about their intentions.[17]

Other research demonstrates the importance of avoiding verbal aggression. College students describing patterns of aggression in their homes demonstrated the link between verbal and physical aggression. As the frequency of verbal aggression between their parents increased, so did the incidence of physical aggression. Parents who attempted to solve conflicts through rational means (i.e., talking it over) were much less likely to engage in physical aggression during conflict episodes.[18] One final point: Verbal aggression often plays a role in conflicts that get out of hand. In actuality, physical (nonverbal) and verbal abuse often occur together, sequentially or simultaneously. Although not all verbal aggression leads to violence, many violent episodes begin with verbal aggression.

> ### APPLICATION 11.4
>
> In what kinds of situations are you most likely to be verbally aggressive? When has this been a disadvantage for you? Under what conditions, if any, might this be an advantage to you?

Passive-Aggressive Communication as an Option

> When I didn't like the way my team at work felt about something, I would go directly to the boss and win her over to my position. That way, it would look like the boss didn't like the group's idea. Admittedly, I did get nasty sometimes when I would tell her what was going on behind her back. She was always interested and would probe me whenever I was in her office. I know that members of my team suspected what I was up to. None of us liked each other very much.

At first glance, passive-aggressive communication behavior may appear to be a type of aggressive behavior. However, the passive-aggressive communicator (seemingly like the conflict avoider or accommodator) does not openly and directly stand up for her or his interests, concerns, or rights. Instead, one might argue that passive-aggressive communication behavior is a type of nonassertive behavior. The problem with that claim is that this individual is not really avoiding or accommodating. The passive-aggressive communication behavior is a type of its own with some characteristics from both the nonassertive and the aggressive types.

Passive-aggressive communication may be defined as the ability to impose one's will on others through the use of verbal and/or nonverbal acts that appear to avoid an open conflict or accommodate the desires of others but in actuality are carried out with the intention (or perceived intention) of inflicting physical and/or psychological pain, injury, or suffering. When people engage in passive-aggressive communication, they do not openly and directly stand up for their interests, concerns, or rights but attempt to get what they want by underhanded means.

There are different ways in which such people get what they want at the expense of others.

- They may do it in only one situation for a particular reason. Perhaps they take advantage of another person because that person has hurt them in the past.
- Passive-aggressive people may also choose to pressure others into submission but only in certain types of situations or relationships. For example, one may attempt to do harm to other employees at work, or other members of a fraternity, but not his or her friends or romantic partners. In this case, one may think that it is okay to take indirect actions against some people, but not others.
- Finally, some may take passive-aggressive action against everyone they encounter regardless of the situation. This happens when people have too little respect for other people and for themselves.

What communication behaviors are given off by passive-aggressive communicators?

- They may spy on others or stalk them without their knowledge.
- They may withhold something the other person wants, such as approval, affection, or sex, in order to get what they want.

- They may operate behind the scenes in an attempt to undermine others or to motivate outsiders to act against their adversaries.
- They may spread lies behind their adversary's back and engage in backstabbing.
- They may disclose some personal information to people they shouldn't after it was told to them in confidence.
- They might encourage attacks from outsiders.
- They may simply refuse to defend the adversary when she or he is being attacked by others.
- They may give away to others something of value to their adversary to make them think that they are perceived as friends when they are not.
- They may also deny to one's face that there is a problem but at the same time fail to cooperate.

Scholars have compiled the following list of passive-aggressive behavior,[19] to which we have added a few of our own:

- Forgetting promises, agreements, and appointments.
- Making unkind statements, then quickly apologizing.
- Playing a stereo too loudly, slamming doors, banging objects.
- Not doing their chores.
- Taking more time than usual to get ready.
- Getting confused, sarcastic, helpless, or tearful without saying why.
- Getting sick when they've promised to do something.
- Scheduling too many things at once.
- Evading meetings so that others are inconvenienced.

On occasion, we all get sick, make noises, fail to do a chore, or overschedule activities, but the passive-aggressive communication behavior is done with malicious intent. We would place the following statements in the passive-aggressive category:

"I don't think this is true but have heard that Dave . . ."
"I couldn't do my part of the project as I promised because I was sick" (when really I didn't to upset you or get you into trouble).
"You should know that Mary was the one who probably told the teacher that you cheated on the exam."
"Am I being too noisy? I am sorry. I didn't know I was bothering you" (when really I am glad to know you are irritated).
"Don't look at me; she's no friend of mine just because we hang out together."
"She thinks that you are not her type."

Initially, passive-aggressive communication behavior is of the win-lose variety. It may result in one getting what he or she wants while "doing in" the other. Eventually, however, the situation may turn into the lose-lose type because when the victimized individual discovers the truth, he or she may end the relationship and have nothing more to do with the abuser.

> **APPLICATION 11.5**
>
> In what kinds of situations are you most likely to be passive-aggressive? When has this been a disadvantage for you? Under what conditions, if any, might this be an advantage to you?

Assertive Communication as an Option

Using the preceding discussion of verbal aggression makes identifying assertiveness easier. Assertiveness is a concept that became very popular in the 1970s through various programs that trained people how to say "no" to others in interpersonal confrontations.

> I can be assertive with my daughter. When the issues are important (dating, car rides, new boundaries), I am an active and empathic listener. I allow her to focus her thoughts and views so I can understand and address them. Our arguments aren't loud or upsetting. I am calm and never raise my voice. I always try to use reason to try to find a solution. Resolutions to conflicts come about through compromise and collaboration.

A way of confronting others in conflict situations, **assertive communication** may be defined as the ability to speak up for one's interests, concerns, or rights in a way that does not interfere with the interests or infringe on the rights of others.[20] It also means being able to "communicate your own feelings, beliefs, and desires honestly and directly while allowing others to communicate their own feelings, beliefs, and desires."[21] Assertiveness is seen as a middle ground between nonassertiveness, which is failing to stand up for your personal rights or doing so in a dysfunctional way, and aggressiveness, which is standing up for your personal rights without regard for others. In conflict style terms, assertiveness is similar to collaboration, the style that combines a high regard for the other with a high regard for one's personal goals. Assertiveness is a concept linked to communication competence: The skillful use of it, rather than its mere use, is an indicator of competence.

What are some rights, concerns, or interests common to all of us as communicators? The following list is a sample of our basic communication **rights** as adults. You have the right to:

1. be listened to and taken seriously.
2. say no, refuse requests, and turn down invitations without feeling guilty or being accused of selfishness.
3. be treated as an adult with respect and consideration.
4. expect that others will not talk to you in a condescending way.
5. not feel what others want you to feel, not to see the world as they would have you perceive it, or not to adopt their values as your own.
6. your own feelings and opinions as long as you express them in a way that doesn't violate the rights of others.
7. have and express your interests, needs, and concerns as long as you do so in a responsible manner.
8. change your opinions, feelings, needs, and behaviors.
9. meet other people and talk to them.
10. to privacy—to keep confidential or personal things to yourself.

11. to be alone if you wish.
12. to ask others to listen to your ideas.
13. to ask for help or information from experts and professionals, especially when you are paying for it.
14. not assert yourself, confront someone, or resolve a conflict.
15. to ask others to change their behavior when it continues to violate your rights.

You can add to this list. Do some of these items surprise you? Are you violating the rights of others? With these rights comes responsibility. For example, in the next section, we will present some communication considerations that may cause you to choose to be nonassertive when it is appropriate. Moreover, to be treated fairly, you must also respect the **communication rights** of others and treat them as you yourself would like to be treated. In fact, "A person's individual rights in any relationship are the same rights he (or she) enjoyed before he (or she) even knew the other person existed. Rights are not to be bargained for. They simply exist. A relationship's task is to recognize and protect the rights of both parties."[22]

Assertiveness is the appropriate expression of one's point of view. Such messages reflect the premise that all persons should communicate in a manner that does not violate self-worth; the needs and goals of both persons have equal value. The outcomes of assertive behavior may be accomplishment of goals, reinforcement of the self-concept, and perhaps relational development or maintenance.[23] There are different ways in which such people may speak up for their interests.

- They may do it in only one situation for a particular reason. Perhaps they state a preference regarding the selection of a movie for that night's entertainment.
- People may also choose to assert themselves in certain types of situations or relationships. In this case, they may think that it is proper to only assert themselves around their friends, brothers or sisters, or romantic partners, but not with others such as their fathers, bosses, or aging grandparents.
- Finally, some may choose to assert themselves in all cases regardless of the type of interpersonal relationship. This happens when one feels strongly that she or he must always be open and honest with everyone and tell the truth no matter what the outcome.

Four defining features set assertive people off from other types. They are:

- open in that they do not withhold information, opinions, and feelings.
- contentious in that they take positions and define issues clearly.
- not anxious in that they are not afraid to initiate relationships or conversations.
- not intimidated in that they choose to confront others rather than avoid them or simply give in to avoid "making waves."

One study comparing communication behaviors and assertiveness found that assertive people see themselves as talkative, precise, not easily persuadable, and contentious. They also experience low anxiety about communication situations and are likely to impress others.[24]

Behaviorally, assertiveness can be contrasted with aggressiveness, in which one's own needs are preeminent, and passivity, in which one's needs are underemphasized. Writers in the area of assertiveness claim that it promotes more caring and honest relationships with others,[25] and they associate the concept with flexibility of response, arguing that assertiveness includes the ability to determine when not communicating one's rights is the best course.[26] Although most early writers associated assertiveness with flexibility of response,[27] it is now associated more with saying what one thinks in order to achieve one's own goals, although not at the expense of the other person. Lane described an assertive individual as one who "emphasizes his/her ideas by a change in tone of voice, exhibits dominant statements, makes statements more often than asks questions, and lets others know of his/her needs and wants."[28] Is Amanda being assertive in the following interchange?

> The three of us have our own houses and families, and so my sisters and I have tried to take the burden of holiday dinners off our mom because it tires her out so. Audrey and I really enjoy the cooking and entertaining, even though it's a lot of work, but Amanda doesn't. We were planning the year, figuring out who would take what holidays, when Amanda said, "I really don't care to cook any more holiday dinners. I'd rather visit with people and enjoy myself." Audrey and I were really irritated by that. I mean, who doesn't want to sit and visit with people on holidays rather than cook? But we got to thinking about it—frankly, Amanda's dinners aren't all that great anyway. The food isn't burnt, but she just doesn't take the time to make things as good as they can be. If she doesn't enjoy it, why put a burden on her when Audrey and I like to do it? We decided that if she could keep the kids from running wild and keep the outer room under control it would be a fair exchange.

Amanda is being assertive in stating her dislike for holiday dinner preparation. However, the fact that the other two sisters have to work out the meaning of the message and decide on a way to resolve the conflict means that the conflict could have been handled better. An assertive message would take into account not only personal wants ("I don't want to cook anymore") as well as the needs of others who have to do the cooking. If Amanda had also said, "I'd be happy to keep the kids in line and help set up or clean up if you two will do the cooking," it would have reflected assertive and collaborative behavior. On the other hand, Audrey and her sister were also not assertive because they did not respond immediately to Amanda's statement. Instead, they worked out the problem by themselves. An ideal handling of the conflict would have been for Amanda to have offered something in place of the cooking the sisters had previously agreed to share. In the absence of such an offer, Audrey and her sister should have immediately asked Amanda why she felt it was fair simply to exclude herself from the holiday work.

To be an assertive person, you must show respect for both yourself and others. You are encouraged to use the first-person singular pronoun (I, me, my) because you are a fellow human being and your needs are as important to you as others' needs are to them. You should have self-confidence and manifest it in the way you talk, walk, and carry yourself generally. It should not bother you when others talk in the first person because you recognize that their needs are as important to them as yours are to you. You do not need to like or agree with the ideas of others, but you need to respect how they feel and their right to say what's on their mind as long as they respect your rights, too.

What communication behaviors are given off by an assertive person? Of course, assertive communication does not include the behaviors described earlier as nonassertive, aggressive, or passive-aggressive. Instead, assertive communicators tend to state their feelings, wants, and needs directly and in a responsible manner. Assertive communication includes good eye contact, straight posture, and an air of competence. People are assertive when they are able to disclose their feelings (both positive and negative), offer their opinions, and provide information as needed. Assertive communications consist of spontaneous expressions of warmth, humor, caring, and cooperation. To be assertive, people must also try to be effective listeners, which requires that they determine how deeply the other feels about an issue and restate the other's feelings in their own words. We would consider the following statements as assertive:

> "I try to satisfy the other person and myself."
> "I like to consult others before I act."
> "I try to get everything immediately out in the open."
> "I'll tell you what I think, and I want you to tell me your ideas."
> "I am concerned about everyone. I don't want anyone left out."

When people choose not to engage in nonassertive or aggressive communication, and instead speak up about their concerns, interests, and needs, they and their partners may both win. Assertive communication behavior gives others a chance, which is a good idea when a relationship is important to you. She or he says what the problem is so that the other may choose to do something about it. The other person may not respond in a manner that the assertive person would prefer, but at least the other is given a chance to do so.

Moreover, by asserting themselves, people may avoid storing up hurts and anger until it is too late to save a relationship or they explode. Bach and Wyden call this harmful strategy **gunny-sacking** because "when . . . complaints are toted along quietly in a gunny sack for any length of time they make a dreadful mess when the sack finally bursts."[29] By not gunny-sacking, assertiveness may prevent a relationship from turning sour. All too often, I have heard people say, "If only he (or she) had said something. I never knew there was a problem." We shouldn't wait until it is too late or lose our self-control. It isn't fair to ourselves or our partners. By getting troubles off our chests, we can monitor one another, adapt as needed, and avoid little problems turning into bigger ones. The relationship between assertive partners has the most opportunity for mutual satisfaction and growth.

Some research has examined how assertiveness differs across cultural groups. In her comparison of men and women across four groups (Anglos, Asian Americans, African Americans, and Mexican Americans), Collier found differences in male and female rankings of the importance of assertiveness only within the Mexican American culture, where men rated it as more important than did women. Anglos ranked the importance of assertive behavior the highest, followed by African Americans, Mexican Americans, and Asian Americans. Culture also predicted the extent of assertive behavior recalled in a conversation: Asian Americans viewed the other person as less assertive than did respondents in other groups. Cultural and gender differences in ratings of the appropriateness of the assertive behavior were minimal: "Assertiveness is viewed as competent behavior for conversations among acquaintances, but culture/ethnicity and gender do mediate perceptions of how appropriate the behavior is."[30]

Lane argued that both empathy and assertiveness are part of communication competence. It is possible, she argued, to be empathically assertive—to maintain a sympathetic orientation toward the other while pursuing one's own goals.[31] As discussed previously, this orientation is associated with collaborating, or exhibiting a high regard for both the relationship and for the issue at hand. Empathy is a sympathetic orientation toward the other, and is associated with the ability to take the other's perspective and assess the other's definition of the situation, by being attentive and sensitive to cues in the situation.[32]

The degree to which a person's behavior is labeled aggressive or assertive often depends on the observer. It also depends on who is performing the behavior. Generally speaking, a man and a woman can behave the same way in conflict and yet be perceived differently: He is assertive; she is aggressive. Consider this example:

> I was trying to teach a class when a student came in to remove some audio visual equipment. He didn't explain why he was there. I had to ask him. I then asked him if it could wait until the end of the class. He said no. I said "Okay," rather reluctantly. He left, then came back about five minutes later. I said nothing. When he came back the third time (all the while making noise and making it difficult for me to continue the class discussion), I finally said (in a level voice), "You are disturbing my class and I must ask you to stop coming in. This really bothers me." He replied, "I'm having a bad day." My female students thought the student should have initially apologized for the disruption, explaining his actions to begin with, and should have responded more adequately at the least. My male students said that I "went nuclear" on the student!

Despite sex differences in the way people are perceived, we can differentiate, at least on a general level, between aggressiveness and assertiveness in conflict situations. Assertiveness in communication behaviors is a skill that can be learned, unlike verbal aggressiveness, which is a trait that must be overcome. Assertiveness starts with an assumption of responsibility for one's own behavior and feelings in a conflict and is reflected in messages created during the conflict. In the next chapter, specific conflict messages that reflect assertiveness are discussed.

APPLICATION 11.6

In what kinds of situations are you most likely to be assertive? When, if ever, has this been a disadvantage for you? Under what conditions will being assertive be an advantage to you?

Communication Considerations: Which Conflict Communication Option Is Best?

Respond to each of the following statements according to this scale:

A = Always true
B = May or may not be true (it depends)
C = Never true

1. The first thing that comes to mind is the best thing to say. _____
2. You should do what your boss or supervisor tells you to do. _____
3. You should be nice to those who love you. _____
4. When you're sure you're right, you should press your point until you win the argument. _____
5. You should keep quiet rather than say something that will alienate others. _____

As you look over your answers to the preceding questions, keep in mind the basic principle, "It depends." For each question, what is called for in one situation may be inappropriate in another. This implies that one has to also be flexible. Hart and his colleagues stress the importance of flexibility in interpersonal encounters by identifying "B" as the preferred answer to all such statements.[33] Answer "B" reflects what we called rhetorical sensitivity in Chapter 2.

Whereas many advocates of nonviolence claim that physical aggression is never an appropriate response, it would seem that in a few specific cases (involving self-defense) it might be justified. However, we are unable to imagine a situation in which a verbally aggressive or a passive-aggressive response is appropriate. Effective communicators are assertive when it is appropriate and nonassertive when the situation justifies it. When might it be appropriate for us to engage in assertive or nonassertive communication behavior? At least three factors should be considered when choosing a particular conflict communication option: the occasion, the other person, and your needs.

The Occasion (Including Time and Location)

Here the occasion, time, and location of a (potential) conflict are important considerations. One behaves differently in class, in the library, and at a birthday party. What might call for an assertive response in one situation may not in another. Whereas the occasion might discourage us from being assertive, we could consider if there is a better time and place to be assertive. If the immediate situation is not one in which a conflict can be addressed, bringing up the situation soon after it is over (when both people are able to give their attention to the problem) is a good way to be assertive and yet sensitive to the situation.

The Other Person

Those who will be parties to the conflict and affected by your behavior should be taken into account. We treat our parents, grandparents, romantic partners, siblings, children, employers, employees, and friends differently simply because of who they are and what they mean to us. We may find it more appropriate to be more assertive in one type of interpersonal relationship than another. Moreover, if we choose to be assertive, we need to consider the needs of the other person.

Your Needs

We will also want to consider how we have prioritized our needs. Not all our needs constitute a life or death situation. Some needs must be satisfied if we want to live a satisfactory life, but others can be put off or reduced to a less prominent position. Generally, we are more assertive on matters that make an important difference in our lives. In some instances, less important concerns may be overlooked. Consider assertive communication:

- when a conflict is over something that is important to you.
- if you will "hate yourself" later for not letting your feelings, ideas, or opinions be known.
- when a long-term relationship between you and the other person is important.

- when the other person can handle your assertiveness without responding with aggression or passive-aggression.
- when the other person will take advantage of you if you let him or her.
- when a win-win solution to a problem is possible.

Consider nonassertive communication:

- when you think you may be wrong or have a poor idea.
- when the emotional hurt offsets any benefits that might result.
- when something has occurred that is more important to the others than it is to you.
- when a long-term relationship between you and the other person is important.

Consider aggressive communication:

- when you have exhausted the other options, and you are in a physically threatening situation in which you must defend yourself to avoid being seriously injured or killed. Even then, use the minimum force necessary to overcome the threat.
- when a physically threatening situation exists for others and you choose to intervene on their behalf.

Lisa is an older student, a single mother with a teenage son. One day she confided to me that her son had beaten her on occasion. She said that she had tried to get her son to realize the harm in his behavior, but he wasn't listening to her. I was shocked and hastily informed her that I'd read that abusers continue to beat their victims as long as they can get away with it. I encouraged her to go to the police and report her son. She was shocked at the idea. She kept saying that she couldn't do anything that really would hurt her son. Some time later, she told me that her son had beaten her again, but this time she went to the police. She said it was so disheartening to see the police arrest her son, handcuff him, and forcefully drag him to a police car. However, she said that when she visited her son in jail, she was surprised at the difference in his demeanor. He suddenly treated her with a whole new respect. He told his mother that he never believed that she would have him arrested. He apologized to her for the first time and promised to never hit her again. When she said that she would do it again if he ever laid a hand on her, he said that now he believed she would do it. He is home now and things are really different. She told me that turning her own son into the police was the most difficult decision she had ever made, but now she was glad she did it.

Lisa felt that she had tried everything else, but now she had to meet force with force. No one would call her behavior excessive, but there came a time when she realized that only by creating an uncrossable boundary ("You will no longer hit me or you will not live here") would she be able to change her son's behavior.

From Theory to Action

This chapter has provided practical advice and strategies for working through conflict situations. As a continuation of the last chapter on the S-TLC system (stop, think, listen, and communicate), in this chapter we discussed four communication options in conflict situations in which you may choose to be nonassertive, aggressive, passive-aggressive, or assertive.

When communicating nonassertively, you avoid a conflict altogether or accommodate (by simply giving in) to the desires of the other person. When communicating aggressively, you impose your will (i.e., wants, needs, or desires) on another person in a way that violates socially acceptable standards. You can also choose to communicate in a passive-aggressive manner by imposing your will on others through the use of verbal and/or nonverbal acts that appear to avoid an open conflict or accommodate to the desires of others, but in actuality are carried out with the intention (or perceived intention) of inflicting physical and /or psychological pain, injury, or suffering. Finally, you can choose to communicate assertively by speaking up for your interests, concerns, or rights in a way that does not interfere with the interests or infringe on the rights of others. Whereas it would seem that aggressive communication behavior is seldom if ever warranted and passive-aggressive behavior should be avoided, effective communicators are assertive or nonassertive depending on the occasion, time, and location, the other person, and their own needs.

Probably the most important factor that will affect your ability to put the advice in this chapter into effect is to remember that you always have choices in conflict situations. Even when you feel that things are happening too fast or that you must deal with problems that arise suddenly, you still have choices as to how you act or react with respect to the other person. Your first response is not necessarily the best one. Slow down, think about the situation, and then respond to the other, using the skills discussed here. Learn from your mistakes, and move on. The only way you will develop conflict skills is to use them in conflict situations.

Because assertiveness is so important in conflict situations, in the next chapter we will explain how one can create effective assertive messages.

Notes

1. James C. McCroskey, "Oral Communication Apprehension: A Summary of Recent Theory and Research," *Human Communication Research* 4 (1977), 78–96.

2. Pamela S. Shockley-Zalabak and D. D. Morley, "An Exploratory Study of Relationships Between Preferences for Conflict Styles and Communication Apprehension," *Journal of Language and Social Psychology* 3 (1984), 213–218.

3. Sally Floyd and Beth Emery, "Physically Aggressive Conflict in Romantic Relationships," in Dudley D. Cahn (Ed.), *Conflict in Personal Relationships* (Hillsdale, NJ: Lawrence Erlbaum Associates, 1994). For more information on the relationship of verbal to nonverbal aggression, see Michael E. Roloff, "The Catalyst Hypothesis: Conditions Under Which Coercive Communication Leads to Physical Aggression," in Dudley D. Cahn and Sally A. Lloyd, *Family Violence from a Communication Perspective* (Thousand Oaks, CA: Sage Publications, 1996) and Colleen M. Carey and Paul A. Mongeau, "Communication and Violence in Courtship Relationships," in Dudley D. Cahn and Sally A. Lloyd, *Family Violence from a Communication Perspective* (Thousand Oaks, CA: Sage Publications, 1996).

4. M. Bograd, "Why We Need Gender to Understand Human Violence," *Journal of Interpersonal Violence* 5 (1990), 133.

5. L. L. Marshall, "Physical and Psychological Abuse," in W. R. Cupach and B. H. Spitzberg (Eds.), *The Dark Side of Interpersonal Communication* (Hillsdale, NJ: Erlbaum, 1994).

6. R. Dobash and R. Dobash, "Research as Social Action: The Struggle for Battered Women," in K. Yllo and M. Bograd (Eds.), *Feminist Perspectives on Wife Abuse* (Newbury Park, CA: Sage, 1988), p. 60.

7. L. Walker, "Psychology and Violence Against Women," *American Psychologist* 44 (1989), 695–702.

8. Marshall, "Physical and Psychological Abuse."

9. L. Margolin, "Beyond Maternal Blame: Physical Child Abuse as a Phenomenon of Gender," *Journal of Family Issues* 13 (1992), 410–423.

10. Dominic A. Infante and C. J. Wigley, "Verbal Aggressiveness: An Interpersonal Model and Measure," *Communication Monographs* 53 (1986), 61–69.

11. Teresa Chandler Sabourin adapts verbal aggression to the instrumental, relational, and identity goals discussed in Chapter 8 ["The Role of Communication in

Verbal Abuse between Spouses," in Dudley D. Cahn and Sally A. Lloyd, *Family Violence from a Communication Perspective* (Thousand Oaks, CA: Sage Publications, 1996)]. See also Yvonne Vissing and Walter Baily, "Parent-to-Child Verbal Aggression," in Dudley D. Cahn and Sally A. Lloyd, *Family Violence from a Communication Perspective* (Thousand Oaks, CA: Sage Publications, 1996).

12. J. DeVito, *The Interpersonal Communication Book,* 6th Ed. (New York: HarperCollins, 1992), p. 60.

13. J. Stewart, *Bridges Not Walls: A Book About Interpersonal Communication* (New York: Random House, 1986), p. vii.

14. Dominic A. Infante, J. D. Trebing, P. E. Shepherd, and D. E. Seeds, "The Relationship of Argumentativeness to Verbal Aggression," *Southern Speech Communication Journal* 50 (1984), 67–77.

15. Dominic A. Infante, Bruce L. Riddle, Carl L. Horvath, and S. A. Tumlin, "Verbal Aggressiveness: Messages and Reasons," *Communication Quarterly* 40 (1992), 116–126.

16. Dominic A. Infante, Teresa Chandler Sabourin, Jill E. Rudd, and Elizabeth A. Shannon, "Verbal Aggression in Violent and Nonviolent Marital Disputes," *Communication Quarterly* 38 (1990), 361–371.

17. Ibid.

18. M. A. Strauss, "A General Systems Theory Approach to a Theory of Violence Between Family Members," *Social Science Information* 12 (1973), 103–123.

19. Joyce L. Hocker and William W. Wilmot, *Interpersonal Conflict,* 4th Ed. (Dubuque, IA: William C. Brown, 1995); G. R. Bach and H. Goldberg, *Creative Aggression: The Art of Assertive Living* (New York: Avon Books, 1974).

20. R. E. Alberti and M. L. Emmons, *Your Perfect Right: A Guide to Assertive Behavior* (San Luis Obispo, CA: Impact, 1970).

21. Judy C. Pearson, *Interpersonal Communication: Clarity, Confidence, Concern* (Glenview, IL: Scott Foresman, 1983), p. 130.

22. D. Viscott, *Risking* (New York: Pocket Books, 1977).

23. Mary Jane Collier, "Culture and Gender: Effects on Assertive Behavior and Communication Competence," in Margaret L. McLaughlin (Ed.), *Communication Yearbook* 9 (Beverly Hills, CA: Sage, 1986), p. 578.

24. Robert Norton and Barbara Warnick, "Assertiveness as a Communication Construct," *Human Communication Research* 3 (1976), 62–66.

25. P. Jakubowski and A. Lange, *The Assertive Option: Your Rights and Responsibilities* (Champaign, IL: Research Press, 1978).

26. Alberti and Emmons, *Your Perfect Right.*

27. See, for example, Ronald B. Adler, *Confidence in Communication: A Guide to Assertive and Social Skills* (New York: Holt, Rinehart & Winston, 1977).

28. Shelley D. Lane, "Empathy and Assertive Communication," paper presented at the Western Speech Communication Association Convention, San Jose, CA, February 1981, p. 10.

29. G. R. Bach and P. Wyden, *The Intimate Enemy: How to Fight Fair in Love and Marriage* (New York: Avon, 1969), p. 19.

30. Collier, "Culture and Gender," p. 591.

31. Lane, "Empathy and Assertive Communication," p. 11.

32. Eugene A. Weinstein, "The Development of Interpersonal Competence," in D. A. Goslin (Ed.), *Handbook of Socialization Theory and Research* (Chicago: Rand McNally, 1969), pp. 753–775; see also James B. Stiff, James Price Dillard, Lilnabeth Somera, Hyun Kim, and Carra Sleight, "Empathy, Communication, and Prosocial Behavior," *Communication Monographs* 55 (1988), 198–213.

33. Roderick P. Hart and Donald M. Burks, "Rhetorical Sensitivity and Social Interaction," *Speech Monographs* 39 (1972), 75–91; Roderick P. Hart, Robert E. Carlson, and William F. Eadie, "Attitudes Toward Communication and the Assessment of Rhetorical Sensitivity," *Communication Monographs* 47 (1980), 1–22.

12

Effectively Confronting Others

Objectives

At the end of this chapter, you should be able to

1. explain what it means to say that communication is a skill.
2. list the six steps to confronting interpersonal problems.
3. explain how to prepare for a confrontation and to make a "date" to sit down and talk.
4. list the four parts of an effective I-statement.
5. explain how you might consider your partner's point of view during a conflict.
6. explain how to make a mutually satisfying agreement and what it means to follow up on it.

Key Terms

communication skill
confrontation
confrontation steps
consequences statement
difficult people

feelings statement
game
goal statement
I-statements
personalized communication

problematic behavior statement
responsibility
self-talk

It would be nice if we all could be spontaneously assertive in our everyday conversations and let people know right off when there is a problem or when we have a feeling to express. If that were the case, there would be little need for a textbook such as this, and people would probably not use such negative metaphors to describe conflict. The fact is that we just don't handle all of our conflicts as they arise. Because of this, there are times when we have to make a special effort to confront others, creating a unique situation that has to be handled with care. How to do this is the focus of this chapter.

According to Remer and de Mesquita, ". . . **confrontation** is viewed as an interpersonal invitation to identify self-defeating and harmful defenses . . . (interpersonal discrepancies, distortions, games, and smoke screens) and to achieve a sense of self-understanding resulting in a functional change in behavior."[1] Because of the potential benefits, we need to know how to effectively confront others about conflicts that eat away at our relationship.

Many of our everyday conflicts can be handled with little "pomp and circumstance." If you are able to address a problem as it happens, a simple, "You know, it bothers me when you do that" may be sufficient to draw the other person's attention to the behavior and work out an agreement to stop or modify it.

However, we don't always confront problems as they arise, and often they become bigger because we have not dealt with them in a timely way. When problems are large, people often ask us: "How do you actually go about confronting someone when there is a big problem? My boyfriend is often late, my girlfriend wears a perfume that bothers me, my parents won't let me drive their car, my roommates leave their clothes all over the place, my neighbor plays the stereo too loudly late at night, so what should I say to them?" In this chapter we will help you answer this important question.

In Chapter 8 we introduced the idea of communication competence, which is knowledge that relates theories about conflict into thinking about conflict, allowing people to communicate well in conflict situations. In this chapter, we will apply this idea to conflict situations by describing communication skills that are useful in conflict situations. A learned behavior, a **communication skill** is "the successful performance of a communicative behavior . . . [and] the ability to repeat such a behavior."[2] Because some communication skills are useful in conflict situations, we can also call them conflict communication skills.

Conflict communication skills are not innate; they are learned. We develop them through experience. The only way you learn how to handle conflict situations more competently is to work through the conflicts you encounter, trying to practice your new skills. No one rides a bicycle the first time they get on it. They fall off. Sometimes they get lucky and stop without hurting themselves. Soon, with a great deal of concentration, riding a bike is manageable, and then it becomes something that is almost second nature. The problem is that most of us are more willing to learn how to ride bicycles than we are to learn conflict communication skills. Communication competence takes knowledge about the way conflict works, knowledge of the skills that can be used in conflict situations, and practice. This chapter discusses the skills associated with framing messages in conflict situations—specific message behaviors that have proven effective in various kinds of conflicts. The goal is to connect thinking about conflicts with acting in conflicts so as to choose the most effective behaviors possible.

APPLICATION 12.1

Think of a time when you felt that you handled a conflict well. What did you do that seemed competent to you? How do those behaviors contrast with a time when you felt you handled a conflict poorly?

The Interpersonal Conflict Ritual: Six Steps to Successful Confrontation

There are six **confrontation steps** to move through as you confront another person. They are:

1. Preparation: Identify your problem, needs, and issues.
2. Make a "date" to sit down and talk.
3. Interpersonal confrontation: Talk to the other person about your problem.

4. Consider your partner's point of view: Listen, empathize, and respond with understanding.

5. Resolve the problem: Make a mutually satisfying agreement.

6. Follow up on the solution: Set a time limit for reevaluation.

Although we would like to avoid giving the impression that all conflicts, large and small, can be resolved by following six easy steps, it helps to know what to do and what not to do when confronting someone with whom you disagree. Also, keep in mind that when stopped at one step, it may be advisable to backtrack one or more steps to allow for a more thorough discussion before attempting to move forward.

Preparation: Identify Your Problem, Needs, and Issues

"Preparation is the most extensive and, in many ways, the most important stage of the confrontation process."[3] This process is the stop and think portion of the S-TLC model. At this stage, self-talk is important. **Self-talk,** as you can guess, is verbalizing, either out loud or to ourselves, inner messages. People can talk themselves out of confronting others, they can talk themselves into it, or they can talk themselves into handling confrontations in negative, destructive ways. In Chapter 1, we noted that many people prefer to avoid conflicts, but this is not a good idea when the continuation of problems and unmet needs will do damage to a relationship. Asking yourself, "who, what, where, when, how," it is important to examine all aspects of a situation to determine what the problem is, how it impacts on you and the relationship, and how you feel about it. You need to determine what you want (goal). Ask yourself what will happen if you don't get what you want or what will happen to the relationship if you do. Once you have determined that you should confront the other person, you should try to think positively and encourage yourself to go through with it.

A way to prepare is through what is termed an *imagined interaction,* which is a form of intrapersonal communication in which you think about what you might say and another might say in response to you in a particular conversation.[4] Imagined interactions serve as a planning function. People who imagine interactions with others do not actually think about the interaction as they expect it to occur. Rather, they think about the interaction in an "if-then" kind of way: If he says "x," I will tell him "y"; if she says "a," I will say "b." In this sense, imagined interactions are very much like cartoon strips. They are both visual and verbal, they happen sequentially, and the imaginer can rewrite the script if desired. Imaginers also have powers similar to comic strip characters: The conversation can be controlled to their satisfaction, they can read the minds of other characters, and they can travel through time or back up action if they want to replay it.[5]

There is a downside to imagined interactions. When people are asked about thoughts they have concerning conflict situations, only 1 percent report thinking about the other person's view in the conflict situation.[6] People do try to make sense of conflict situations, however, by answering two questions: Who or what is responsible for the conflict? How serious is the conflict? Unfortunately, thinking about a conflict often makes it worse. People who think a great deal about a particular conflict will place the blame on the other person involved and overestimate the seriousness of it.[7] It is important not simply to think about the conflict, but to think about what the other person might say about it, what you would like to say, and to do so in a competent way. That is, you don't want to practice negative or aggressive messages as you are imagining the conflict—you will find a way to say them. Imagining yourself acting competently in the conflict situation is most likely to result in your actual behavior being competent.

Make a "Date" to Sit Down and Talk

Tell the other person that you want to meet and talk about something. Personally, we think it is a good idea to provide a little bit about the subject so that the other person has some idea about the topic to be discussed. You should pick a time and place that are appropriate, but usually not over twenty-four hours from the time when you ask the other person to meet and talk. Working spouses, for example, usually don't want to get into a serious discussion when they first arrive home from a hard day's work. Supervisors generally like to have some warning that a problem is afoot, and usually have less busy times when they can meet with employees about problem areas. The point is this—try to anticipate the other person's schedule so that the time to talk doesn't become one more crisis in a day full of them.

Pick a place that is relatively private and free of distractions. It's usually not a good idea to try to talk with children, roommates, or others around or with the television set on. They can be distracting. An example of a way to ask for a meeting is: "I want us to talk about what happened last night. I know that now is not a good time, so can we discuss it tomorrow after your Modern World class? We could go for a ride and talk."

Interpersonal Confrontation: Talk to the Other about Your Problem

Collaboration is necessary for genuine and mutual understanding. To collaborate successfully, you and your partner must try to establish an atmosphere of support that encourages openness, trust, and cooperation. The atmosphere or communication climate may appear threatening and defensive or unthreatening and supportive. In a seminal article, Gibb identified factors differentiating defensive and supportive climates (see Table 12.1).[8] These climates either encourage people to become closed and hostile toward one another or encourage them toward greater openness and trust.

An evaluation consisting of praise and blame immediately arouses one's defenses, whereas a nonjudgmental description may be worded in a way that does not ask the other to change behaviors or attitudes. Control refers to attempts to dominate another's behavior, whereas a problem orientation implies a desire for collaboration. Whereas strategy in-

TABLE 12.1   *Defensive versus Supportive Climates*

Defensiveness Arises From	Supportiveness Arises From
Evaluation	Description
Control	Problem Orientation
Strategy	Spontaneity
Neutrality	Empathy
Superiority	Equality
Certainty	Provisionalism

volves hidden motives and agendas, spontaneity is straightforward and free of deception. Neutrality, as defined by Gibb, refers to a lack of concern for the welfare of others, whereas empathy includes an expression of respect for the worth of others. Superiority tends to arouse feelings of inadequacy in others, whereas equality expresses a willingness to enter into participative planning with mutual trust and respect. Finally, certainty appears dogmatic, whereas provisionalism suggests tentativeness, a desire to withhold one's judgment until all the facts are in.

Although the preceding list of defensive and supportive characteristics of communication climates may appear in an "either-or" format, typically climates exist somewhere in between such extremes. The more supportive the communication climate, the more interpersonal trust and openness, thus reducing the need to avoid, accommodate, or compete. As defenses are reduced, communicators can more easily concentrate on one another's perceptions and achieve mutual understanding.

Mutual understanding requires that communicators participate in the decisions, agreements, solutions to problems, and resolution of conflicts that affect them. To the extent that they feel safe enough to assert their interests, needs, and goals, listen to the expression of others, and cooperate in the process of achieving an understanding, communicators perceive that they are understood. This perception, if mutual, contributes to personal and interpersonal growth and satisfaction. As we confront another, it is important to express needs and feelings. Expressing needs or feelings is difficult to do because it makes a person in a conflict situation vulnerable. Many of us would prefer that our loved ones realize what we need before we ask, that they should be so observant they can anticipate our desires. It is not a fair expectation. Statements about your problem and needs

- tell the other person why the conflict situation is important to you.
- disclose your emotional reactions to the situation at hand.
- form the basis for the action requested in a conflict situation.

To illustrate an interpersonal confrontation, we use an extended example. The two characters in the conflict are a dating couple: Jerry and Elaine. Jerry tends to be a conflict avoider or accommodating. He likes to smooth things over rather than confront them directly. Elaine, on the other hand, is more of a confronter, although she tends to want to please others. They have been dating for over a year and share many activities together. Their roles are fairly well defined. Lately, they have been spending more evenings at Elaine's house, where she cooks dinner and they watch a movie on the VCR. Elaine wants Jerry to realize that she is not satisfied with the way they are spending time together. On this particular evening, after dinner, she asks him to talk instead of watching television.

> ***Elaine begins by saying:***   You know, we seem to be spending a lot of time at my place lately.
>
> ***Jerry:***   Oh?
>
> ***Elaine:***   This is the third time this week you've come over for dinner and a movie.
>
> ***Jerry:***   Well, I really like being with you.

From the exchange, Elaine has also learned that Jerry appears to like the way things are. It is also important for both parties not to be sarcastic or threatening in their vocal tone.

If they use the right words but speak in a sarcastic tone, their nonverbal expression can change the meaning completely.

> *Elaine:*   I really like to be with you, too, but I feel as though I am putting more effort into our time together than you are. I buy the groceries, cook the dinner, and rent the movie.
>
> *Jerry:*   You're right. I haven't brought anything the last few times I was over here.

Expressions of feelings go beyond what is observed. If Elaine had simply started with "I think I am putting more effort into this relationship than you are," Jerry might have been confused about the issue of the conflict. Elaine goes on to say:

> *Elaine:*   I guess I feel as though you're taking advantage of me.
>
> *Jerry:*   I really don't want to take advantage of you. What do you want to do?
>
> *Elaine:*   I need to feel that I am special to you. I feel special because we're comfortable together, but I like to go out now and then.
>
> *Jerry:*   But you know that I don't have a lot of money after school takes its cut. What kinds of things are you talking about?

Despite a false state with a vague need, Elaine is getting around to something specific. She probably does not mind fixing dinner as long as it is not the only thing that she and Jerry do together. If they pursue the issue, they might find some low-cost entertainment that they can enjoy. Needs have to be as specific as possible. Elaine could be even more open in her statement of needs:

> *Elaine:*   But that's the point. We're both in school and on limited budgets. To be honest, I feel like you're taking advantage of me when you don't contribute anything to the evening. I don't think it's fair for me to buy everything.
>
> *Jerry:*   I don't expect you to buy everything. I haven't this week, and I'm sorry. I really didn't think about it.

To express feelings constructively, our disclosures should be relationship directed and proportional to the importance of the relationship. They should be gradual and reflect caring for the other. Like observations, they should be personalized and well timed. They also should be as specific as possible—"I'm upset" is not as helpful a message as "I'm upset because I am being taken advantage of."

We also need to express our wants in a conflict situation. Wants are specific actions requested of the other person to resolve the conflict. Telling the other person that you are dissatisfied with a situation is not enough. You must specify what you would like as a solution. A number of attitudinal barriers interfere with the ability to express wants. We often believe that the other person understands us, or should understand us, sufficiently to know what we want in a situation. Expecting others to be mind readers increases the likelihood of our being disappointed.

To express wants constructively, we must focus on desired actions rather than our feelings, state the desired behavior explicitly, tell the other person when we expect the behavior to be performed, and choose a want that the other person is capable of delivering.

We should also speak of wants instead of "not wants"—stating our desires in positive rather than negative terms.

At this point, Elaine needs to express some specific wants to see if Jerry is willing to resolve the conflict in a way that will benefit them both.

> *Elaine:* I had an idea for next week. Tuesday is dollar night at the movies, and we could go for ice cream afterwards. Or you could surprise me—I really like it when you plan something. It doesn't have to be big—you could make dinner. We could go miniature golfing, or bowling, or take a walk. I want to be with you, but I guess I don't want to have to do the planning and all the work.
>
> *Jerry:* That seems fair. But does this mean no more dinners?
>
> *Elaine:* No, it just means that I want something besides our dinners. Okay?

A great deal was *not* addressed by this exchange. If Elaine feels ambivalent about her relationship with Jerry, she probably received little that would clarify it, except that he did seem willing to take more responsibility for their dating activities and did not seem to realize that his actions could be viewed as taking advantage of her. However, conflicts are best dealt with in small pieces. If this issue has been clarified, then Elaine is better off waiting until later to deal with the issue of where the relationship is headed.

Elaine also has to realize how important her part is in changing Jerry's behavior. If she simply states her conflict and Jerry agrees that it is a problem but then goes back to the same pattern of fixing dinner for him, nothing has changed.

There are three principles demonstrated in the preceding conflicts. First, any requested change must be specific, both in the action requested and in the amount of change desired. One cannot just say, "I want you to change your attitude." What is an attitude? What does it look like? How much change is involved in producing a better attitude? Second, the wants have to be something that the other person can do, which must be assessed as realistically as possible. We need to ask whether we have correctly assessed the other person's ability to do whatever we ask. And third, the request needs to be reasonable. If Elaine had wanted Jerry to take her out to dinner twice a week, the request may be unreasonable considering his student status. Wants need to sound reasonable from the other person's point of view. Test your recognition of legitimate and effectively stated "want statements" in Application 12.2.

APPLICATION 12.2

Recognizing Wants

Look at the following statements. Which statements clearly express specific wants? Circle the ones that do.

1. Let's get together for lunch.
2. I want us to spend more time together with the kids.
3. I want you to attend this class with me.
4. I wish we could play different kinds of music around here instead of yours all the time.
5. I want to stop feeling overwhelmed.

6. I don't want your pity!
7. I wish you'd get off my case!
8. I would like us to have one night a week just for ourselves.
9. I want you to exercise more.
10. I want you to put your dirty clothes in the laundry instead of on the floor.

Statements 3, 8, and 10 describe specific wants. Statement 1 is too vague—when should we get together? Statements 2 and 9 suffer from the same problem—how much is "more"? The want is not quantified. Statement 4 can create defensiveness by implying that the other "always" gets his or her way. Statement 5 does not suggest a solution. Statements 6 and 7 are statements we often say, but they do not really communicate. In the heat of a conflict, almost anything sympathetic may be construed as pity, and almost any constructive criticism may be interpreted as overly demanding.

Consider Your Partner's Point of View

Put yourself in the other's position and ask yourself how you would feel if requested to make the same change. Would you resent it? Would you think it is a reasonable request? If you do not think it is, chances are the other will not either.

Assertiveness sounds self-oriented, but it is both self- and other-oriented. Self-orientation is standing up for your rights, interests, and concerns as discussed in the previous chapter. Other orientation is the tendency to be attentive to, adaptive toward, and interested in others participating in a conversation. Other orientation is seen in expressions of empathy and concern about the other's feelings, listening well, providing relevant feedback to the other, and the tendency to support and accept what the other is saying as a true representation of whom the other person is. Lane argued that both empathy and assertiveness are part of communication competence. It is possible, she argued, to be empathetically assertive—to maintain an orientation toward the other while pursuing one's own goals.[9] As discussed previously, this orientation is associated with collaborating, or exhibiting a high regard for both the relationship and for the issue at hand. Empathy is an orientation toward the other and is associated with the ability to take the other's perspective and assess the other's definition of the situation, for example, by being attentive and sensitive to cues in the situation.[10]

There are four skills for responding. You can rephrase. Another way of responding is simply to ask the other person what he or she means. Or you can provide a possible reason for the statement and see if it is correct. Finally, you can use an unfinished question and let the other person fill in the rest. In responding, it is important to keep your temper under control. Act; don't react. You do not have to accept what the other person says if it is incorrect.

When we listen to another's feelings, sensitivity is important. Perhaps the most disconfirming thing we can do to others is to tell them that they have no right to feel the way they do. It is more useful to focus on why others feel the way they do and what role those feelings play in the conflict than to argue about the legitimacy of the feeling. If Jerry had challenged Elaine, for example, when she said, "I feel like you are taking advantage of our relations," by disparaging the feeling, she would have been less likely to continue the conflict episode to a mutually satisfactory ending. She more likely would have shut down and said, "Never mind. It doesn't matter," leaving both people feeling that the issue is unresolved.

Sometimes, one person in the conflict has a hard time framing wants so that the conflict can come to some sort of resolution. Frequently, people are better able to say what they don't want or what they should want rather than what they do want. Moreover, when a person has difficulty framing their desires in a conflict, the tendency is for the listener to start suggesting solutions. If what the listener suggests is unacceptable to the speaker, the exchange can quickly degenerate into a "yes, but" scenario, with one person suggesting solutions and the other person vetoing each one as unacceptable. How can the listener help the speaker frame different alternatives without taking over the responsibility of creating the solution?

Resolve the Problem: Make an Agreement

An important step in resolving or managing conflict is coming to agreement about what can be done to change things. Requested action needs to be specific. The reason the action is being requested is shown in the expression of needs. Through the expression of specific wants, Elaine and Jerry may bring their conflict to resolution.

Follow Up on the Solution: Set a Time Limit for Reevaluation

It is one thing to resolve a conflict, it is another for you to actually carry out an agreement. We suggest that you set a date with the other to return to the issue at hand to evaluate the progress made, reward yourselves if successful, or to revise your agreement if not. Give yourselves a few weeks and then discuss whether the necessary changes are being made.

Key to the whole confrontation is the ability for the grieving individual to use effectively worded I-statements. In the following section, we will try to help you improve this important conflict communication skill.

Doing Conflict Messages: Using I-Statements

An interesting research finding indicates that as a conflict progresses, people tend to repeat what they have said previously and/or use a more restricted vocabulary in describing their problems. In addition, they use fewer words that overtly connect sentence parts with each other, making their communication more abbreviated and harder for the other to understand. The researcher concluded that

> As participants move from simple disagreement to conflict, their levels of anxiety increase and apparently their perspective-taking skills decrease. . . . [T]he speaker begins to use talk that is habitual and comfortable to the speaker, with less thought to the impact the words have on the other(s). Instead of "How can I say this so s/he will understand (or be persuaded)?" the response is to repeat what was just said with even less elaboration.[11]

Clearly the way we state problems in a conflict situation affects the other person's response. If we respond in kind with accusations or retaliation, we contribute to the competitive conflict escalation cycle described in Chapter 5. On the other hand, if we respond assertively with well-worded statements, we interrupt the cycle and switch to a more constructive one.

Assertive behavior reflects both our rights as a communicator (to express our feelings) as well as our responsibilities (to communicate those feelings in a way that reflects ownership of them). Probably the most important skill in conflict is the ability to use **I-statements** that personalize the conflict by owning up to our feelings rather than to make them the responsibility of the other person. Saying "I feel" and "I think" is far less threatening to the other person than saying "you make me feel" and "most people think." Unfortunately, we sometimes want to put the blame on the other person ("you make me") or to have the weight of a group's opinion ("most people think") rather than simply to express our feelings as our own. The ability to personalize communication comes from a basic assumption:

> If I experience myself as free, I am more likely to personalize my messages. If I am not free, I will not own my feelings. The two skills involved are (a) explicitly signifying that I am the one possessing the feelings, wants, and beliefs when that is what I mean and (b) refraining from holding others responsible for what is going on. Depersonalized communication is characterized by words like "they," "one," "it," and "people"; such words duck responsibility for what is going on and assign it to someone else.[12]

Central to the notion of assertiveness is responsibility—for our actions, for our feelings, for our words, and for the consequences of all of them. We must take **responsibility** for what we say in a conflict: We must own our feelings and try to state them as clearly as possible. In the previous chapter in which we made the point that we have options and can choose to be assertive when it is appropriate, we explained how people are *responsible* for what they do and how they feel in conflict situations. This suggests that when we take responsibility for how we feel and act, we start to realize that in every conflict situation we have contributed to it in some way.[13] Interpersonal conflicts occur because we are interdependent (involved). As Folger and Poole say, "the key to resolving almost any conflict lies in gaining a perspective on how we ourselves contributed to it."[14] However, instead of owning what they say and how they feel, people often tend to express themselves in impersonal or generalized language or blame someone else for their feelings and behaviors. As the following examples in Table 12.2 show, when you own up to your statements and feelings, you take responsibility for them.

A common type of responsibility avoidance is the use of you-language. We often resort to blaming the other person for our behavior and feelings, but again we should be more truthful and accurate and take responsibility, as you can see in the difference between the statements in Table 12.3.

Assertive behavior is characterized by **personalized communication**—language using I-statements (i.e., "I think, I feel") versus you-language or depersonalized statements (i.e., "you always, most people think").

It is not easy to learn assertive behavior and I-statements. Two misassumptions about others lead us to prefer depersonalized communication over communication that owns our feelings. We tend to confuse our perceptions of the other person with their qualities. Suppose, for example, your roommate frequently leaves a wet towel on the bathroom floor and

TABLE 12.2   *Statements Demonstrating Responsibility*

Escaping Responsibility	Taking Responsibility
He made me do it.	I did it.
She upset me . . . she made me angry . . . she got me all riled up.	I was angry.
The professor is too hard and insensitive.	I think that the professor is . . .
That was a great movie!	I liked the movie a lot.
Everyone knows that isn't true.	I don't believe it.
Adults don't behave like that.	I don't approve of your behavior.
Nobody likes her.	I don't like her.
Anyone with any sense at all would not . . .	I don't understand why you would not . . .
This is the way it has always been.	I don't want to change it.

TABLE 12.3   *Statements Demonstrating Responsibility*

Escaping Responsibility	Taking Responsibility
You are too hard and insensitive.	I think that you are . . .
Your hair, hat, shoes is (are) terrible.	I don't like your hair, hat, etc.
You have a warped sense of humor.	I don't think you're being funny.
You're too sarcastic.	I don't like sarcasm.

hair in the sink after bathing. Which are you more likely to say to the other person (be honest!): "You're such a slob," or "It bothers me when you leave your towel on the floor and hair in the sink." The first statement puts all the blame on your roommate. With the second statement, you run the risk that your roommate will not care if it bothers you. And so the first statement seems less risky, but that is an illusion. Say to your roommate, "You're such a slob," and unless you have a pretty good relationship that permits occasional joking insults, you create defensiveness. Defensiveness, in turn, causes people to tune out your ideas.

Another misassumption that seduces us into depersonalized communication is thinking that others do not change much, and so we can predict their behavior. We can make some educated guesses about the way others react, and the better we know them, the better those guesses become. But making sweeping statements about the other person's behavior to make him or her "pay attention" belittles the other and indicates a lack of trust. We can say only that people respond to situational demands; we can estimate how they might perceive those demands and respond to them.

We need to overcome these misassumptions. Accepting responsibility linguistically is less likely to result in defensiveness from the other person. Inferences or feelings about the situation should be as specific as possible and should be linked to behavior in some way. Only then is the other person likely to understand what is meant. Even if you first state the observation that your roommate left towels on the bathroom floor before declaring, "You're a slob," the statement is not owned by the speaker. Poorly stated inferences often project judgments on the other without being personalized (e.g., "we think you're acting like a child"); are phrased in absolute, certain, or dogmatic language; or lack a context for the description (e.g., "she's so defensive").

Components of I-Statements

To make effective I-statements, we have devised the following form to guide you:

I feel . . . when I . . . because I (think, believe) . . . I'd like (want, wish) . . .

Table 12.4 contains four types of descriptive statements:

1. **feelings statement:** a description of your feelings (such as feeling angry, neglected, offended, surprised, depressed, unhappy, etc.).
2. **problematic behavior statement:** a description of the offensive, upsetting, incorrect, selfish, problem-producing behavior (such as the other saying something insulting, nasty, sarcastic, or leaving clothes all over the room, or forgetting an important date, etc.).
3. **consequences statement:** a description of the consequences the problematic behavior has for you or others (wastes your time, you have to expend the effort, you could lose friends, your parents may get angry, etc.). The statement contains the word *because.*
4. **goal statement:** a description of what you want specifically. (One may want the other to be on time in the future or call if delayed, etc.) It states what you want, would like, prefer, hope for, expect, ask (avoid using words like *demand, require, or else*). A major challenge is identifying what it is you really want and stating your position in a clear way that specifically describes what it will take to satisfy you.

Notice that every part includes "I," and ideally, none contains "you." Although in theory the best I-statements do not contain "you," it is often very difficult in reality to avoid saying "you" when describing the problem. Test your recognition of specific need/feeling statements in the following application.

TABLE 12.4 *Examples of I-Statements*

Feelings Statement	*Problem Behaviors*	*Consequences*	*Goals*
I feel annoyed	when I have to put gas in my car after you use it	because I end up having to take the time to get gas.	I'd like you to get gas after you use my car.
I feel depressed	when I hear about all the fun others are having	because the doctor says I have to remain inactive.	I'd prefer to talk about other topics.
I feel frustrated	when I study but still get a poor grade on a test	because this could hurt my grade in this course.	I would like to go over the chapters with you.

APPLICATION 12.3

Recognizing Needs and Feelings
Look at the following statements. Which are correctly stated needs or feeling statements? Circle the correct statements.

1. I feel disappointed that you are backing out of this show after you agreed to help me with it.
2. You really irritate me when you don't show up for a date with me.
3. I need to be told I am loved in a language I understand.
4. I need to be able to see where a class is going so that I can get excited about it.
5. I feel like a single parent around here.
6. You don't seem to contribute anything to our group project.
7. I feel frustrated when it seems that I have sole responsibility for planning our dates.
8. I feel like I am going crazy.
9. I feel insecure when we don't have at least the equivalent of a month's salary in the bank.
10. I am not the only person who's having trouble in your class.

Statements 1, 3, 4, 7, and 9 are correctly stated because they link the feeling to a current or desired behavior. Statement 2 is incorrect because the focus is on the other person creating the feeling rather than on the speaker owning the feeling. Statement 5 states a feeling but it is vague—what would eliminate the feeling? Statement 6 denies responsibility for the feeling—it is the other person's fault. Statement 8 is probably a legitimate feeling but does not tell the other why the feeling is there. Statement 10 uses "mob appeal" (a type of logical fallacy) to validate the feeling rather than personally owning it.

We should point out that the form of the I-statement may not be as short as the preceding examples. You may choose to talk for a while about how you feel. Then discuss what it was that made you feel this way and why. It may take a while before you eventually get around to saying what it is you want. The present form is presented only to ensure that you address all four components when presenting your side of the conflict.

Finally, I-statements won't work unless they are accompanied by a calm, nonthreatening tone of voice and facial expression. If one is to avoid being perceived as judgmental, she or he must sound nonjudgmental in both *what is said* and *how it is said*. Otherwise, even the best worded I-statements won't work because they are accompanied by upset and anger, which contradict your words.

APPLICATION 12.4

Fill in the blanks with words that will complete the sentence using the formula:
     I feel . . . when . . . because . . . I want

1. I feel (   ) when I have to wait and wait because I hate waiting around and wasting time. I want to be able to leave at the time we agreed on.
2. I feel frustrated when (   ) because I don't know what is expected of me. I would like some help on how to improve my grades.

3. I feel angry at myself when we stay out too late and drink too much because (   ). I want to get more sleep and cut down on my drinking.
4. I feel frustrated when I am the only one who cleans up this place because it's not fair to me. I want (   ).

Create your own I-statements:

5. I feel afraid when (   ) because (   ). I want (   ).
6. I feel (   ) when (   ) because (   ). I want (   ).

General Tips on Being Assertive

When you want to be assertive, the following list of suggestions can be useful.

- Stand tall, or if sitting, lean slightly forward, but don't crowd the other person—keep at least a couple of feet between you both.
- Look at the person, but don't stare (suggestion: focus on her or his forehead).
- Look serious, but don't frown, glare, and appear menacing.
- Speak firmly, calmly, slowly, and don't allow yourself to become verbally aggressive.
- Use open gestures, and avoid any threatening gestures such as arm waving, pointing, standing up, or making a fist.
- State your own point of view in terms of your needs, wants, interests, and concerns, but find something on which you both agree.
- Use techniques for communicating emotion and active listening. Don't expect that effective communication will always resolve a conflict; however, when an interpersonal relationship is at stake, it is worth a try.

Advantages of Using I-Statements

By asserting yourself in this way, you provide much needed information, demonstrate honesty, and reduce defensiveness in others.

- You provide necessary information because the other person doesn't need to "read your mind" to determine what you are thinking, feeling, and wanting.
- You reveal your honesty by telling others what is on your mind, what you prefer, or what is upsetting you.
- You reduce defensiveness in others because you are not assigning blame or blurting out accusations.

APPLICATION 12.5

When does assertiveness become aggressiveness? What guidelines do you need to develop for yourself in order to create assertive rather than aggressive statements?

Challenges Associated with I-Statements

Two challenges are commonly associated with I-statements:

"I get too mad to be nice."

Aggressive communication laden with blame, anger, and accusations may seem warranted in a particular conflict situation, but such communication behavior will only make matters worse. If you value your interpersonal relationship, you owe it to yourself and the other person to resolve the problem in a constructive and positive way. I-statements allow one to be assertive without producing ill feelings and provoking retaliatory behavior.

Moreover, recall the S-TLC system presented in Chapter 10. You may need to stop and wait a few minutes, hours, or days until after you have cooled down. Then you may find it okay to express yourself using I-statements rather than abusive language.

"It doesn't sound right or normal for me to talk that way."

Many people have bad habits; they avoid, simply give in, or respond to conflict in aggressive ways. Meanwhile, what is learned can be unlearned. The problem is that these habits have become "normal" for them, and any new behaviors seem artificial at first and require effort to learn as new habits. As you see the effect of using I-statements on others, you will be motivated to use them even more often. You should give them a try and see how they improve your interpersonal relationships.

> **APPLICATION 12.6**
>
> What habits do you have that interfere with creating a positive conflict experience? How can you begin to overcome them?

Dealing with People Who Play Games

Some people play games in conflict situations. This is an idea separate from formal game theory, which we discussed in Chapter 7. We discuss "games people play" because assertiveness and I-statements may be applied to encounters with game players, too. A **game** is "an ongoing series of ulterior transactions progressing toward a well-defined, predictable outcome. . . . [It is] a series of moves with a snare. . . . Every game is basically dishonest, and the outcome has a dramatic, as distinct from merely exciting, quality."[15] There is a joke, for example, where the speaker shows the following three words one at a time and asks the listener how to pronounce *twa, twi,* and *two.* The responder usually answers by pronouncing the *w* in all three, although (as we all know the rest of the time) the *w* is silent in *two.* This is a "gotcha" situation, in which the responder knows he or she has been had as soon as the last word is pronounced.

In more serious games, however, people initiate conflicts to seek a well-defined payoff that hurts the other person. These games have a common structure and have been identified by authors such as Harris and Berne: "If It Weren't for You," which is used to blame others for one's own problems; "I'm Only Trying to Help," in which the initiator brings up some problem of the listener so that the initiator can be seen as a savior to the other; "NIGYSOB," in which the initiator maneuvers the other into a position of vulnerability so that the other can be punished; "Yes, But," in which a person asks for advice and then rejects all suggestions as not useful (proving that his or her problem is more serious than anything anyone could imagine); or "Wooden Leg," in which people respond to the conflict concerns of others by using a variety of excuses to show that the responder cannot meet the expectations or requests of the person making the request.[16]

The problem with game playing in conflict is that the game player does not work toward a mutually satisfactory outcome. Rather, game players' goals are to attain the payoffs that allow them to remain in control of the other person. Where choices are limited or where players cannot leave the situation, the game can become destructive to the relationship.

The solution to game playing is easy to state but hard to perform: Refuse to provide the payoff. Consider the following "If It Weren't for You" game between two roommates:

> *Dana:*   You cashed my rent check too soon! I told you not to cash it until Monday. Now three of my checks have bounced, I got charged $30.00, and I can't pay my part of the phone bill!
>
> *Chris:*   You didn't say anything about holding the check.
>
> *Dana:*   Why do I have to tell you everything! You always do this to me. I can't believe how much my bank account gets screwed up because you don't wait to cash my checks until I tell you to.
>
> *Chris:*   We both have to pay the same amount of rent, at the same time, every month. It's your responsibility to make sure you have enough money to cover your share. It's not my responsibility to make sure it's okay to cash your check before I go to the bank.

The important thing in this exchange is for Chris to be assertive and call attention to the fact that the other is playing a game. You can note such phases as "You always do this to me . . . because you . . ." as being indicative of the "If It Weren't for You" game. By so doing, you refuse to play. If Chris becomes defensive about cashing Dana's check, Dana can continue to play the "If It Weren't for You" game and find even more problems for which Chris is responsible. It is important that we make it clear to game players that we will not play their games.

Confronting Difficult People

Unfortunately, some people can be impossible or at least difficult! We have all met someone we think is extremely rude, hostile, pushy, underhanded, manipulative, self-centered, obstinate, or critical. Many popular publications will tell you how to deal with difficult people.[17] Solomon categorized people as hostile/angry, pushy/presumptuous, deceitful/underhanded, shrewd/manipulative, rude/abrasive, egotistical/self-centered, procrastinating/vacillating, rigid/obstinate, tight-lipped/taciturn, or complaining/critical. Within each category are subcategories, making a total of one hundred different types of difficult people. Interestingly, Solomon never defined what a difficult person is in general. Others define **difficult people** simply as those who do not respond to "rational attempts at conflict resolution,"[18] or, more narrowly, "people who drive us crazy, but whom we can't ignore or leave—co-workers, neighbors, relatives, friends."[19] Facetiously, we might say that, for many of us, a difficult person is someone who does not agree with us.

We certainly would not dispute that everyone displays angry, pushy, or whatever characteristics at one time or another. What surprises us is that, in an age when none of us would presume to assign a racial or ethnic insult to another person, we feel free to label people as "difficult." There is a giant leap between "I don't like what you're doing right now" and "I think you are doing this because you are a. . . ." Ury responsibly argued that there are often reasons for why people are "difficult":

> Behind your opponent's attacks may lie anger and hostility . . . fear and distrust. Convinced that he is right and you are wrong, he may refuse to listen. . . . [Y]our opponent may dig in and attack, not because he is unreasonable but because he knows no other way to negotiate. . . . Even if he is aware of the possibility of cooperative negotiation, he may spurn it because he does not see how it will benefit him. . . . he regards negotiation as a win-lose proposition, he will be determined to come out the winner.[20]

The way to handle such people is not to respond in the aggressive way they have started the conflict, but rather surprise the person by responding in an unexpected way. Assertive communication in the form of I-statements may disarm the other person, throw him or her off balance, and make it hard for a difficult person to mistreat you (other suggestions appear toward the end of this chapter).

Although I-statements are designed to avoid or reduce defensiveness in others, they do not always succeed. In such cases, they do not make matters worse (than blame and accusations), and they provide an opportunity for more positive and constructive communication.

However, suppose when we have used all the "correct" conflict management skills—we have responded empathically, we have paraphrased, we have stayed calm—the other person has not. One of the best pieces of advice is to remember that a "difficult person speaks only for the difficult person."[21] Suppose, for example, that you have been assigned to a group project. As is often the case, one member of your six-person group has missed a number of meetings and has failed to complete the work assigned. The deadline is approaching, and you need her to finish her part of the group project. You go to her apartment to talk about the project. When confronted, she says things such as, "It was a stupid idea for a group project anyway. I don't like it, and neither does anyone else. They're just doing their part because they don't want to tell you it's dumb. You're the only one who cares about this." As she talks, you may well have a crisis of confidence and wonder if everyone else hates the project. Focus on the complaints of the person in front of you and remember that she speaks only for herself. Other useful techniques include the out-of-body experience, that is, pretending that you are a third-party observer to the situation. Listen to the other person's complaints as if you had no stake in the outcome of the conflict. How would someone else hear the complaints?

> Ultimately, dealing effectively with "difficult" people is a matter of acting counterintuitively: When your opponent stonewalls or attacks you, you feel like responding in kind. When he insists on his own position, you want to reject it and assert your own. When he exerts pressure, you are inclined to retaliate with

direct counterpressure. But in trying to break down your opponent's resistance, you usually only increase it.[22]

Roxane has the following story to tell:

I'm not at all inclined to create a bunch of labels for people who seem difficult. Frankly, I see only two kinds that really test my skills in a conflict area. Because the home video of *Star Wars* has just been rereleased (and because my kids watch it on tape all the time), I have drawn two difficult types from that movie: Wookies and C3POs.

Wookies are a little easier to understand. They want their way, they want it now, and their only means of negotiation are growling and making life miserable for you until you give in. Like C3PO, I usually think it's better to let the Wookie win, or at least let the Wookie *think* he or she has won.

In various areas, the Wookie uses a high level of energy to force his or her way. Threats are a common means of manipulation, but they also throw temper tantrums to bully people around. Let me shift metaphors a little here. When I'm dealing with a Wookie, I often feel as though I'm in the surf at the beach. The waves can be really strong there. When I was little, I tried to avoid the waves by staying near the shore in shallow water. As I got bigger, I learned to dive under the waves so that I could go farther out. When I was a teenager, I learned to body surf and use the wave's energy to serve my purposes. The point is that the waves are always going to be there.

So how can you use the Wookie's energy to serve your purposes? There are times when it makes more sense to dive under it. Diving under includes being conciliatory, reassuring the Wookie he or she is important, and so on. When I feel in control of this behavior, I am likely to call it "strategic groveling." I realize that it serves a purpose. I can do it because I have a strong sense of who I am and what I want to accomplish. And I can do it because I don't compromise my core values when I make the other person feel important.

There are times, though, that simply diving under the energy isn't going to accomplish what needs to happen. Diving may compromise your values or let an issue be decided in a way that you don't think you can live with. In this case, you have to use the Wookie's energy. This means determining what the Wookie is really bellowing about. A lot of people become Wookies because they have learned that pushing people around works. So what you need to do is find out what the Wookies are really concerned with, how you can grant part of their issue without giving up your own, and how you can put their energy into creating the solution. For example, in a volunteer group where I served, we had a new member who kept complaining about the way things were done. She'd often throw temper tantrums when things were done without her input, so we gave the task to her to do. When she brought it back to the group, we put the finishing touches on it together, and she finally calmed down (at least about that issue). We only have a few hundred issues more to go. The rather depressing fact is that it's hard to change a Wookie. Generally, they change themselves (if at all) after some life-impacting event.

A difficult person of the C3PO type is more subtle. This is the kind of person who finds fault with everything that is being done, but he or she is generally very polite about it. Often, this person plays the game Eric Berne called "Yes, But." "Yes, that's a good idea, but I really couldn't do that because . . .". I have had a lot of experience with this type of person in faculty governance here at APU. We'll create a new university-wide requirement, and they'll be the ones pointing out that their majors could not possibly participate in such a program because the major requirements are far more important than anything general studies could demand. We just don't understand the special circumstances they face.

There are two ways that the C3PO makes life difficult. One is to "yes, but" you. I don't know if you recall the Uncle Remus stories, but one involves Brer Rabbit meeting up with a statue made of tar. He greets the statue politely, and when it doesn't respond, socks it in the mouth. His hand gets stuck in the tar. He gets angry, and strikes the tar again, getting his second hand stuck. He kicks it once, twice, and soon is completely trapped, allowing Brer Fox to capture him.

C3POs are like tar babies. Every "yes, but" traps you. How do you avoid getting trapped? Try to avoid posing solutions for the other person. Each time you do, you're getting a hand or foot caught in the tar. Encourage the other person to generate his or her own ideas (and don't "yes, but" him or her).

The C3POs also can wear down your resistance by repeating their objections so often (but politely) that you finally say, "Fine, whatever you want, just go away." And they win. So if the issue is important, you need to very politely express your position. And repeat it, politely, with few variations. For example, if you are a person working the return desk, and you simply cannot offer a refund to someone who is insisting that you do so, you repeat the rules. Politely. You repeat them again. Politely. You offer to call your manager. Politely. But you don't let yourself get worn down.

As a last resort, you can walk away from a conflict. If you find yourself overwhelmed by the situation, unable to remain in control of your emotions, and unwilling to listen to the other, tell her you need to leave but that you still want to talk about the situation. Walking away is not wrong if the alternative is losing control of yourself and ruining any chance to bring the conflict to resolution. Also consider the possibility of bringing in a third party to help, using the processes described in Part V.

From Theory to Action

Competent communication behavior in conflict situations occurs when people have the knowledge to behave skillfully, are able to apply that knowledge in a particular situation, and are able to repeat their performance in similar situations. Competent conflict behavior is a matter of learning skills of analysis and skills of communication and then applying them in conflict situations. One success does not mean you have achieved competency any more than one failure means that you will not achieve it.

Because people are responsible for what they do and how they feel in conflict situations, we are competent to the extent that we take responsibility for how we feel and act. However, instead of owning what they say and how they feel, people often tend to express themselves in impersonal or generalized language. Another common type of responsibility avoidance is the use of you-language. We often resort to blaming the other person for our behavior and feelings, but again we should be more truthful and accurate and take responsibility.

In Chapter 5 we discussed the competitive conflict escalation cycle, which occurs because previously unresolved conflict and face issues cloud the current conflict issue. Other behaviors that can fuel competitive escalation are the "don'ts" in conflict: Don't complain, don't be glib or intolerant, don't assume you know what the other is thinking, don't tell the other person how to feel, don't label the other person (as childish, neurotic, incompetent, etc.), don't be sarcastic, and don't talk about the past—stick with the here and now.[23] This last don't is particularly important. When conflicts accumulate over a long time, a big bag of grievances results. Eight months ago, you lost the Acme account; last week you offended another client; and so on. What matters most of all is right here, right now. The most threatening thing a person can do to another is hit the person with a bagful of complaints saved over a period of time.

People also tend to assume they know what others are thinking. They can work through a conflict, get to the resolution stage, and then ruin things by saying something like, "Well, you won't like my solution anyway" or "You're just doing this because you have to." We all know it is frustrating to have another person tell us what we think or what we plan to do, particularly if we have not decided yet.

Related to the assumption process is the response many people make when listening to others: "I know exactly how you feel." This is one I-message that does not belong in our conflict language. It may be an appropriate comment toward someone close to you when you're sharing an excited exchange or discovering mutual interests. But in conflict, it is a belittling statement. It negates the uniqueness of the listener's experience, and, in essence, it is a play for power—"I know how you feel." The emphasis is on "I" (my wants, needs, desires, importance) not on "you" (your wants, needs, desires, importance). If you tell me how angry you are with me because I was on the phone when you expected an important call and I say, "I know just how you feel. Last week I didn't get an important call, either," whose feelings become the focus of attention? Mine do. How is it different if I respond, "I didn't realize that you were expecting a call" or "You're really angry, aren't you?" I make your feelings the focus of my attention and, in doing so, acknowledge my responsibility in the conflict and my willingness to make amends.

Another temptation is to hit the other person where it hurts. This option seems particularly tempting when the other person has already hurt us. The nature of relationships, regardless of their setting, provides information that can embarrass or hurt the other person. When we are hurt, we are tempted to pull out this "albatross" and drape it around the other's neck. The communication process has a funny dimension to it: It is irreversible. Or, as Omar Khayyam put it, "The Moving Finger writes; and having writ, Moves on: nor all your Piety nor Wit shall lure it back to cancel half a Line, Not all your Tears wash out a Word of it" (*The Rubiyat,* verse 71). Owning your feelings, using the words *I think, I feel,* and *I want* will minimize the possibility of regret over what is said.

I-statements can be an effective way to take responsibility for yourself and be assertive if they take the following form: "I feel . . . (feeling statement) when I . . . (problematic behavior statement) because I (consequences statement) . . . . I'd like (goals statement) . . . ." By asserting yourself in this way, you provide much needed information, demonstrate honesty, and reduce defensiveness in others.

I-statements do not always succeed. However, in cases in which you value your interpersonal relationship, you owe it to yourself and the other person to resolve the problem in a constructive and positive way. I-statements allow one to be assertive without producing ill feelings in others and encouraging retaliatory behavior. Any new behaviors seem artificial at first and require effort to learn as new habits. As you see the effect of using I-statements on others, you will be motivated to use them often.

Notes

1. R. Remer and P. de Mesquita, "Teaching and Learning the Skills of Interpersonal Confrontation," in D. Cahn (Ed.), *Intimates in Conflict: A Communication Perspective* (Hillsdale, NJ: Lawrence Erlbaum Associates, 1990), p. 225.

2. Brian H. Spitzberg and Michael L. Hecht, "A Component Model of Relational Competence," *Human Communication Research* 10 (1984), 577.

3. Remer and de Mesquita, "Teaching and Learning the Skills of Interpersonal Confrontation," p. 229.

4. James M. Honeycutt, Kenneth S. Zagacki, and Renee Edwards, "Imagined Interaction and Interpersonal Communication," *Communication Reports* 3 (1990), 1–8.

5. Renee Edwards, James M. Honeycutt, and Kenneth S. Zagacki, "Imagined Interaction as an Element of Social Cognition," *Western Journal of Speech Communication* 52 (1988), 23–45.

6. Denise H. Cloven, "Relational Effects of Interpersonal Conflict: The Role of Cognition, Satisfaction, and Anticipated Communication," Master's thesis, Northwestern University, Evanston, IL, 1990.

7. Denise H. Cloven and Michael E. Roloff, "Sense-Making Activities and Interpersonal Conflict: Communication Cures for the Mulling Blues," *Western Journal of Speech Communication* 55 (1991), 134–158.

8. Jack Gibb, "Defensive Communication," *Journal of Communication* (September 1961), 141–168.

9. Shelley D. Lane, "Empathy and Assertive Communication," paper presented at the Western Speech Communication Association Convention, San Jose, CA, February 1981, p. 11.

10. Eugene A. Weinstein, "The Development of Interpersonal Competence," in D. A. Goslin (Ed.), *Handbook of Socialization and Theory and Research* (Chicago: Rand McNally, 1969), pp. 753–775; see also James B. Stiff, James Price Dillard, Lilnabeth Somera, Hyun Kim, and Carra Sleight, "Empathy, Communication, and Prosocial Behavior," *Communication Monographs* 55 (1988), 199–213.

11. Mae Arnold Bell, "A Research Note: The Relationship of Conflict and Linguistic Diversity in Small Groups," *Central States Speech Journal* 34 (1983), 128–133.

12. Herbert J. Hess and Charles O. Tucker, *Talking About Relationships,* 2nd Ed. (Prospect Heights, IL: Waveland Press, 1980).

13. Walter Isard and Christine Smith, *Conflict Analysis and Practical Conflict Management* (Cambridge, MA: Ballinger Publishing, 1982).

14. Joseph P. Folger and Marshall Scott Poole, *Working through Conflict,* 2nd Ed. (Glenview, IL: Scott Foresman, 1993), p. 56.

15. Eric Berne, *Games People Play* (New York: Ballantine Books, 1964), p. 48.

16. Berne, *Games People Play;* Thomas A. Harris, *I'm Okay, You're Okay* (New York: Avon Books, 1967).

17. See, for example, Muriel Solomon, *Working with Difficult People* (Englewood Cliffs, NJ: Prentice Hall, 1990), who offers "hundreds of office-proven strategies and techniques to get cooperation and respect from tyrants, connivers, badmouthers and other difficult people you must work with every day." See also William Ury, *Getting Past No: Negotiating with Difficult People* (New York: Bantam Books, 1991).

18. Thomas R. Harvey and Bonita Drolet, *Building Teams, Building People: Expanding the Fifth Resource* (La Verne, CA: University of La Verne, Department of Educational Management, 1992), p. 139.

19. Carol Tavris, *Anger: The Misunderstood Emotion* (New York: Touchstone, through Simon and Schuster, 1989), p. 294.

20. Ury, *Getting Past No,* p. 7.

21. Ibid., p. 149.

22. Ibid., p. 9.

23. G. R. Bach and R. M. Deutsch, *Pairing* (New York: Peter H. Wyden, 1970).

13

Cooperative Negotiation in Win-Lose Conflicts

Objectives

At the end of this chapter, you should be able to

1. explain the difference between a tangible and an intangible conflict issue.
2. summarize research on bargaining in formal organizational negotiations.
3. summarize research on bargaining in interpersonal negotiations.
4. list the four principles of reconciliation.
5. describe four ways to generate more options.
6. explain how one converts a potentially competitive negotiation into a cooperative one.

Key Terms

BATNA	intangible issues	negotiation
bridging	interests	positions
compensation	language of cooperation	tangible issues
cost cutting	logrolling	*thromise*

Earlier in this text, we made the point that conflicts involve a variety of issues. Some conflicts, when examined, turn out to be unreal conflicts—false conflicts, displaced conflicts, misplaced conflicts. These are conflicts that either are perceived but are not actually occurring, as in a false conflict, conflicts in which there is no real issue, as in a displaced conflict that simply releases the other's aggression, and conflicts in which the issue raised within the conversation masks a deeper one, as in a misplaced conflict. We also distinguished between substantive conflicts, those focused on a particular issue, and nonsubstantive conflicts, or those that do not involve an actual issue or that involve issues not relevant to the relationship.

Real and substantive conflicts consist of issues perceived by all involved in the conflict as relevant to the relationships of those involved. They can be of two types of issues or resources, and the type of resource involved will determine how we go about addressing the conflict. People have a tendency to see real and substantive conflicts as win-lose situations, as this narrative seems to indicate:

> This is an ongoing conflict that has occurred every Christmas since we got married. What always sets off the conflict is that I want to be able to send gifts especially to my parents, and to our children and grandchildren. My husband hates that Christmas has become so commercialized and that people expect to receive gifts. He'd rather just give gifts on an ordinary day. He "allows" me to buy gifts for my parents, but tells me not to buy other gifts. This really frustrates me when I am not allowed to buy Christmas presents if I want to when our money is mine, too. It seems that if I do the things that make me happy during the Christmas season, my husband will be unhappy. And if I try to make him happy, I am miserable.

Conflicts that people have a tendency to consider as win-lose are generally over resources.

Conflicts over Two Types of Resources

Conflicts may be over two types of resources, intangible or tangible. Intangible resources include love, attention, cooperative and beneficial behaviors, respect, power, self-esteem, and caring. Although these later resources may be perceived as scarce, this is a misperception because they can be shared. Where resources are not scarce, people do not have to gain at the other person's expense. Conflicts involving resources that are not scarce are often resolved through interpersonal communication (as discussed in Chapters 10, 11, and 12). Sometimes, though, people perceive that the conflict is over scarce resources when in fact it is not. This conflict, for example, appears to be a conflict over scarce resources:

> This has been an ongoing conflict for about three years. It is between a friend and me over cheating. It started when we both changed our majors to the same one and began taking classes together. My friend would expect me to give her my answers to study guides for tests. When I did not, the conflict began. Then just this last week we had a midterm in one of our classes. The week before the midterm we had been given a study guide. My friend was not in class, and I forgot to get a guide for her (she hadn't asked me to do so). She waited until the night before the test to ask me if she could photocopy my copy of the study guide, which was a list of vocabulary words. At that point I had already looked up all the page numbers for the words, had looked up the words themselves, and had written the information on the study guide. She knew this, so I had to figure out a way to give her the study guide without giving her all the answers. I went to the professor's office to ask him for a study guide, but he did not have any more of them. After spending some time trying to figure out what to do, I finally just marked out the answers and photocopied the study guide. The problem with my solution was that there were three essay questions on the other side of the page as part of the take-home exam. The marker went through the paper and made it a little difficult to read. When I gave it to her she was rude, began to make fun of me for not giving her the answers, and was upset with me because the back was difficult to read. Then she told her roommate to come over and look at the paper, and they both laughed about the way I marked out the answers just so she could not have them. I finally handed her the essay part of the study guide, and then she got mad and said, "Cindy, I cannot read this. How am I supposed to do

the essay?" I said, "Yes, you can. You just have to look at it carefully and you can understand it." Then she said, "I can't believe this, Serious Cindy!" I was getting so mad that I wanted to scream at her, but instead I said, "Well, I have to go home. See you later." To top it off my roommate was standing there the whole time and did not stick up for me or say anything in my support. That made it even worse. I walked home crying.

What makes me so mad is that she has no right treating me like that. I was the one doing her a favor. I did not have to give her a copy of my study guide. She is just very lazy and she procrastinates. She waited until the last moment and then expected me to help her. I do not think it is right for me to give her the work that I spent hours doing. It was not like she had been working on it all weekend and needed help. She just wanted the answers so that she did not have to do the work herself. She cheats on papers and tests all the time, and I do not think that is right.

Information, and the work required to attain it, may be considered a scarce resource. Even more significant, however, is the question of relational boundaries in this situation. The narrator admits that the conflict has been three years in the making. Her friend has been taking advantage of her ability to stay on top of assignments for quite a while. Information seems like a scarce resource, but anyone can attain it if he or she is willing to look for it. It is not a zero-sum situation. On the other hand, the narrator feels as though her work efforts are appropriated by another without any kind of compensation. In a very real sense, her friend is "stealing" from her—time, effort, and information—because she is not giving anything in return (in addition to the fact that it is wrong to cheat). In this situation, if the use of competent communication and conflict skills cannot help the narrator to establish boundaries, it may be that the relationship is not worth preserving. At the very least, the narrator has the right to say, "I will no longer feed you the answers, and if that costs us our friendship, so be it."

Conflicts over **intangible issues,** which do not involve truly scarce resources (even though conflicting parties may think otherwise), include situations like these:

- one partner has not been paying enough attention to the other (ignoring her or him).
- one person offends another by using sexist, racist, stereotyped, offensive language.
- one person's behaviors, habits, or actions annoy or upset another person.
- one partner needs time to be alone or time out with friends.

Note that the common feature of these examples is that they all involve nonmaterial issues. There are few situations in which someone who has been asked to spend more time with his or her partner will see that as a loss for himself or herself. Being aware of the effects of one's behavior on others need not be a win-lose situation. Asking one's relational partner to allow time for other friends or to be alone should not be something that threatens the partner or that takes away from the relationship. When one is involved in situations like these, careful diagnosis of the conflict should allow the implementation of the interpersonal communication and conflict skills discussed in Chapters 10 through 12.

At other times the resources may be tangible and scarce because there are not enough to go around. **Tangible issues** involve one's personal property, money, land, grades, promotions, water, food, or air supply, natural resources (oil, timber, precious metals), awards or rewards, jobs, and so on. When tangible resources are scarce, conflicts involving them take more than interpersonal communication to resolve; they require more advanced problem-solving techniques that will be discussed later in this chapter. Some examples of conflicts involving scarce resources include:

- another person asks to move in with you and your roommate in an apartment or room designed for only two occupants.
- you and another must share only one car.
- there is not enough money for both of you to buy what you each want.
- both parents want full custody of the children.
- an ex-spouse believes that she or he cannot maintain her or his standard of living and at the same time pay alimony to the ex-partner.

Note that these situations all involve tangible resources—things that can be divided, subtracted, or alternatively, added and multiplied. In this chapter, we will learn how to resolve conflicts even when they are over scarce (tangible) resources. One way to do so is through bargaining and negotiation.

APPLICATION 13.1

Identify which conflict situations involve scarce resources (true) and which ones do not (false).

1. There is not enough time to divide between friends, partner, and children. Here, time is a scarce resource.
   a. true　　　　　　　b. false
2. Your roommate didn't return a book or rental video as promised or returned the item late incurring a fine.
   a. true　　　　　　　b. false
3. Both sets of parents want their married children to spend the holidays with them.
   a. true　　　　　　　b. false
4. Borrowed items weren't returned to you as promised.
   a. true　　　　　　　b. false
5. One partner is private and closed and won't open up to the other partner.
   a. true　　　　　　　b. false
6. Your parent received a job transfer, which necessitates moving, leaving friends, changing schools, and so on.
   a. true　　　　　　　b. false
7. Two people are interested in the same person as a romantic partner.
   a. true　　　　　　　b. false
8. Showing disrespect, inconsideration of the other and her or his possessions, borrowing without asking, and returning things in an unsatisfactory condition are scarce resource conflicts.
   a. true　　　　　　　b. false
9. Your roommate fails to share domestic tasks and to take turns with chores.
   a. true　　　　　　　b. false
10. One partner always blames the other for all problems experienced. One always criticizes the other for personal inadequacies.
   a. true　　　　　　　b. false
11. One person needs assistance, help, or cooperation but isn't getting it where it could be provided.
   a. true　　　　　　　b. false

12. Partners share only one television set, but they want to watch different channels at the same time.
    a. true   b. false
13. Two roommates share one shower, kitchen, study room, or living room, but both want to use one or the other at the same time.
    a. true   b. false
14. One partner does not appreciate the other's efforts and time spent on both their behalf.
    a. true   b. false
15. Two siblings share one car, and they both want to use it at the same time.
    a. true   b. false

Answers: 1, 3, 6, 7, 12, 13, and 15 are all true (conflicts over scarce resources).

Bargaining and Negotiation

Putnam defines **negotiation** as "a particular type of conflict management—one characterized by an exchange of proposals and counter proposals as a means of reaching a satisfactory settlement."[1]

> Nothing could be simpler or broader in scope than negotiation. Every desire that demands satisfaction—and every need to be met—is at least potentially an occasion to initiate the negotiation process. Whenever people exchange ideas with the intention of changing relationships, whenever they confer for agreement, they are negotiating.[2]

By agreeing to negotiate, people are agreeing (1) to engage in the conflict rather than avoid it and (2) to try find an outcome that is mutually acceptable to all those involved in the conflict by exploring various options in the conflict.[3]

The terms *bargaining* and *negotiation* are often used in place of each other. Unions might bargain for their new contract; two people contemplating marriage might negotiate how they will handle various household tasks. Authors in this area of research claim that bargaining and negotiation are essentially interchangeable.[4] Both terms describe people in a conflict situation agreeing to common rules to manage their conflicts.[5] For this discussion, formal negotiation will be used for reporting research conducted in organizational settings and informal negotiation for research in interpersonal relationships.

The Nature of Bargaining in Formal Situations

Formal negotiation is a process in which interdependent people who have different goals exchange information in an attempt to produce a joint decision.[6] Bargaining may occur in a variety of organizational settings: between a buyer and a seller, between management and labor, between a superior and a subordinate, and so on. This section considers situations in which bargaining is relatively formal; that is, the bargainers may represent others in organizational situations that are fairly structured.

Several aspects of the formal bargaining situation are significant. The parties are interdependent, which means that neither one can get what he or she wants without the help of the other. The outcome must be mutually agreeable because both parties will have to adhere to the decision. And there is usually a difference between what the parties want and what they will settle for in order to reach agreement. Moreover, the bargaining situation is highly structured, and the moves and countermoves of the people involved have a direct impact on the outcomes of the bargaining situation.

Four aspects of the formal negotiation situation are important to the development of a joint decision. Both parties start bargaining with an aspiration level (their preferred option). Both parties also have a resistance point, which is an identifiable maximum amount that they are willing to concede to the other person. Between both parties exists a bargaining range, which is the difference between the resistance points of the involved parties. And finally, both parties have a status quo point, the point to which they will return if no agreement is reached.[7]

> The following example of the bargaining process comes from my experience as a yearbook advisor. Each year I negotiated the university's contract with the yearbook company representative. It was the most enjoyable thing I did as advisor. I loved the give and take of the bargaining situation and playing the various representatives against one another to get the best deal. The various bargaining points might be as shown in Table 13.1.
>
> Actually, the gap between our resistance points was usually not too big. However, that would not become apparent if we did not present our sides in a way that facilitated the achievement of a mutually satisfying outcome. If the final offer the yearbook company made did not emphasize the importance of spot color (adding one color like blue or red to a black and white page to liven it up) and how spot color can make black and white pages look better at a more reasonable price, they might have lost the bid. In my six years as advisor, though, companies always seemed willing to give something to obtain the bid. One year, I got the company to provide a free trip for the editor and me to travel to the plant and see the printing process. What really made the difference in signing a contract with a company the next year was the level of service we had received in the preceding year. If the service was not satisfactory, it did not really matter what they promised me.

The two different approaches to negotiation are competitive (win-lose) versus cooperative (mutual gain). The foregoing negotiation as described is primarily competitive: Concessions made by one side benefit the other. The goal in competitive bargaining is to learn as much as possible about the other person's position without giving away one's own position. For example, when taking bids for the yearbook, the speaker had the prospective company detail every possible charge it could make when printing a yearbook (having learned the hard way in the first year that one should know exactly what can be charged for any particular graphic effect before using it in the design). The competitive bargaining

TABLE 13.1 *Elements of a Formal Bargaining Situation*

	University	*Yearbook Company*
Aspiration Level	Full-color cover, 32 pages of full color inside, 208 pages—all included in base bid	Base bid for a 208-page black-and-white book; all color billed separately
Resistance Point	32 pages of color must be included in base bid	Free spot color
Status Quo Point	Go with another company	Lose bid

communication pattern is an exchange in which one must start high, concede slowly, exaggerate the value of one's concessions, conceal information, argue forcefully, and be willing to outwait the other.[8] It is also important not to show weakness in one's position or to offer concessions too soon.[9]

If you decide to adopt this style of bargaining, the decision should be based on the demands of the situation. It is an appropriate style of bargaining for situations that truly are win-lose. The university, for example, expected the yearbook advisor to negotiate the best contract with the most concessions she could obtain because the university would have to pay for any yearbooks it did not sell.

The disadvantages of competitive bargaining are found in the climate it fosters between those in the bargaining situation. Competitive bargaining is confrontive rather than collaborative—it is "me versus you" rather than "both of us." Because of its win-lose nature, competitive bargaining can lead to an impasse and prevent agreement. The emphasis on secrecy makes it difficult to predict the responses of the other person. Still, because we sometimes are in situations of competitive bargaining, we should not simply reject it as a possibility, but choose it purposefully as needed.

APPLICATION 13.2

What kind of competitive bargaining are you likely to do in your lifetime? When are you more likely to engage in integrative bargaining?

Research on Formal Bargaining

The majority of research on bargaining has been conducted from the perspective of game theory, introduced in Chapter 7, which is a mathematical model used to explain and predict strategic behavior, based on the economics of the system. It assumes that people act in rational ways. In some forms, the outcome is determined by splitting the difference between what the first person offers and what the second person offers. In other forms, the format is zero-sum—what is achieved by one person is lost by the other. The assumption behind negotiation in game theory is that people will try to minimize their losses and maximize their gains—the minimax principle. For the yearbook example, anything they concede to me, such as color or special effects, is technically a loss for them because they must pay someone extra to create the special effect or must absorb the cost of the color ink.

In early research, the predominant paradigm was competitive—bargainers strive to gain as much as possible at the expense of the other person. Later research introduced the notion of mixed-motive situations in which bargainers have varying incentives to cooperate and compete with the other person. In a mixed-motive situation, cooperation brings the greatest rewards for both participants.

Some research examined the effect of information on bargaining situations. Schelling argued that having information about one's opponent can weaken one's personal position and that ignorance functions as a source of strength[10] because the purpose of disclosing information in competitive bargaining situations is to mask objectives, distort messages, reduce the other person's options, or manipulate how the other person views the costs of reaching a settlement.[11] "Bargainers who know their opponent's limitations will behave more altruistically in making concessions whereas uninformed negotiators will choose to maximize self-gain without concern for their opponents."[12] Researchers investigated

Schelling's claim by examining how knowledge of the opponent's cumulative wins and losses affected the settlements to which negotiators came. One set of studies supporting Schelling's claim concluded that "bargainers who knew each other's payoffs made smaller initial bids . . . employed less overall interaction . . . showed more profit equity . . . used softer bargaining tactics . . . presented more reasonable demands . . . and were more cooperative when receiving demands than uninformed negotiators."[13] On the other hand, several studies came to opposite conclusions: Where one bargainer was informed about the other person and one bargainer was ignorant, informed bargainers "exploited the ignorance of their opponents by making higher initial offers, fewer concessions, and higher profits than did their competitors."[14]

Bargainers can also feel they have too much information. One study indicated that too much information, particularly for people who were low in cognitive complexity, made it difficult for the bargainers to process information effectively for the bargaining situation.[15] Bargainers with a low tolerance for ambiguity were also more likely to behave competitively when they had incomplete information.[16]

Both the competitive and the mixed-motive games labored under assumptions that may or may not hold true in real-life situations. Perhaps the most damning assumption is that people act rationally and make logical, rather than emotional, choices of strategy. Consider, for example, the odds of the gaming table. The odds are always in the favor of the gambling establishment. Yet a gambler will invest time after time, convinced that the odds will turn in his or her favor given enough time, even though the odds are randomly determined. Or consider the situation of negotiating a contract with a supplier of service. If you do not like the other person with whom you are bargaining and if accepting the offer means that you will have to work with that person, you will probably look for reasons to reject the offer and go with an offer from a person who seems more friendly.

Another assumption that may not hold true is that bargainers have complete information concerning the choices and the value of those choices for everyone involved. If complete information is available, then the whole idea of bargaining seems superfluous—people would simply make their final offers and be done with it. Furthermore, research indicates that bargainers who are informed of the aspiration level and resistance point of the other person negotiate less successfully than those without knowledge.[17] This is probably because, knowing both the highest the other hopes to achieve and the lowest the other will accept, the bargainers make little effort during negotiations to discover new information that might change the resistance point and the aspiration point of the other or even for themselves.

A further assumption of game theory is that neither party will accept a solution that is not mutually satisfactory. But clearly, many bargainers are willing to achieve as much as possible at the expense of the other person. Other assumptions of game theory include the mathematics of the model and need not be discussed here. The point is that, although game theory provides a simple model, real-life situations may or may not adhere to game theory assumptions. Despite its limitations, game theory has brought about considerable research on the moves and countermoves in bargaining that lead to cooperative or competitive behavior. The findings concerning moves and countermoves are discussed in the next section on getting to agreement.

Researchers have examined the motives and thought processes of people involved in bargaining situations, along with contextual features that may affect the outcomes of bargaining. Sereno and Mortenson found that ego involvement in the situation affected the ability of dyads to come to public agreement. Those who were slightly ego involved reached public agreement with greater frequency than those who were highly ego involved.[18] Personality characteristics, the role the person plays within the organization, and the political and economic climate in which the bargaining takes place are all variables that have been found to affect the bargaining process. In fact, one author argued that the outcomes of bargaining are more strongly determined by the personalities and perceptions of the bargainers than by the use of mutual persuasion.[19]

Communication-related research has been conducted most clearly by authors such as Donohue and his associates, who devised a coding system to categorize the messages used by bargainers in negotiation with each other.[20] Messages may be either cues (introducing a new subject) or responses (to the cues) and may attack the other, defend one's own position, or attempt to integrate one's own and the other's position. By examining the actual content of the messages, more information can be gained than by looking only at the level of cooperation displayed within a game theory format.

Informal Negotiation

In the field of communication, interest has shifted from competitive bargaining situations to cooperative ones that encompass both formal and informal negotiation. Lax and Sebenius argued that negotiation is at the heart of a manager's job:

> Virtually everyone accepts the importance of bargaining to sell a building, resolve a toxic waste dispute, acquire a small exploration company, or handle like situations. Yet negotiation goes well beyond such encounters and their most familiar images: smoke-filled rooms, firm proposals, urgent calls to headquarters, midnight deadlines, and binding contracts. Though far less recognized, much the same process is involved when managers deal with their superiors, boards of directors, even legislators. Managers negotiate with those whom they cannot command but whose cooperation is vital, including peers, and others outside the chain of command or beyond the organization. Managers even negotiate with subordinates who often have their own interests, understandings, sources of support, and areas of discretion.
>
> In a static world, agreements once made generally endure. Yet change calls on organizations to adapt. And rapid changes call for new arrangements to be envisioned, negotiated, and renegotiated among those who know the situation best and will have to work with the results.[21]

Given the various ways in which bargaining can be studied, what findings can help us understand how bargainers reach mutual agreement through integrative behaviors in negotiation situations? Pruitt argued that integrative solutions occur when people are rigid in the goals they are pursuing but flexible in means they adopt for those goals. In addition, Pruitt claimed that information exchange leads to integrative agreements only when bargainers believe that the other is truly concerned with both their own needs and the other person's needs.[22] Research supports Pruitt's claims.[23]

Research on Tactics and Strategies in the Negotiation Situation

Findings generated through game theory and study of simulated interactions by researchers in social psychology suggest that, in general, bargainers who make concessions are more likely to elicit cooperative behavior from the other than are those who make demands or who make no concessions at all.[24] However, the person making concessions may also be exploited. People who made concessions quickly were exploited by other players who retaliated with a competitive strategy.[25] The greatest cooperation was found when a bargainer was slow to compete and slow to cooperate in reciprocating the other's behavior. The pattern of cooperation and competition also appears to affect the behavior of the other person. In another study, starting at a low level of cooperation and shifting to greater cooperativeness induced more cooperation in the other person than did shifts from high to low cooperativeness.[26] Other research has confirmed the utility of starting tough and becoming more cooperative later. However, recent research in the field of communication conducted by Tutzauer and Roloff indicates that toughness should be used in moderation: If combined with pressure tactics, it can create a perception of competition between bargainers and reduce the likelihood of integrative agreements.[27] As Bostrum pointed out, making concessions and acting cooperatively reveals information about a person's interests in the bargaining situation:

> A bargainer who makes frequent concessions will probably be viewed as willing to settle for less than one who makes concessions only occasionally. Also, a person who concedes up to a certain point and then refuses to move beyond this point will probably be seen as being close to some cut-off point below which he or she will leave the relationship rather than settle. . . . If a person systematically refuses to concede, we might arrive at the conclusion that we are not as important in the value systems as we would like to be. . . . The individual who finds making concessions highly upsetting is probably expressing a particular outlook on life. This pattern may be highly revealing to the other person in the interaction.[28]

How people behave in a bargaining situation affects the way they are viewed by the other. Who the people are and what roles they play also affect bargaining behavior. Research has demonstrated that bargainers who are representing others besides themselves, and are thus accountable to those others, are less likely to engage in compromise or concession than bargainers who are not accountable to their constituency.[29] Throughout all the research on bargaining is the assumption that bargaining is a communicative behavior, and as such, the actual messages exchanged by people in a bargaining situation are of interest. Perhaps the greatest attention has been paid to the role of threats and promises in the bargaining situation.

More than anything else, the consistency with which a person acts in regard to threats or promises made has the greatest effect on outcomes of the bargaining situation. If a person makes threats but fails to carry them out when compliance is not obtained, or makes promises that remain unfulfilled, then the person is unlikely to affect the outcome of the bargaining situation through the use of them.[30] A person who consistently carries through on threats gains greater cooperation than a person who does not follow through, and consistency in the fulfillment of promises lends greater credibility to both threats and promises. However, consistency in carrying out one's threats does not create greater believability for one's promises. Obviously, one must also have the credibility to carry out a threat or fulfill a promise; that is, the fulfillment of the threat or the promise must be within one's power. In addition, the bargainer may use a *thromise*—a message that sounds like a promise (i.e., if you do *x,* you will receive *y*) but operates like a threat because it is the noncompliance that will hurt the recipient, not simply failing to receive a benefit.[31]

Another aspect of the bargaining process concerns the explicitness with which promises, threats, and commitments are made. The major reason for failed negotiations is the tendency of negotiators to make early, firm commitments from which they cannot retreat without losing face.[32] Tentativeness, such as the use of qualifiers (e.g., "that could work"), allows for more give and take in the situation until a final solution is reached. When one party firmly commits to a position, the other party has no choice but to concede or escalate the conflict.

Strategies for Tangible-Issue Conflicts

Many of the strategies devised by negotiators are useful for resolving interpersonal conflicts, particularly when resources are scarce. If you were this person, how might you have handled the conflict he describes?

> Last week I met with the division chief for right of way (I am division chief of planning) to discuss our mutual need to staff a receptionist position on the eighth floor of a new office building we will occupy beginning next month. She will have about eighty employees working on this floor, whereas staff will total around forty.
>
> For security and customer service reasons we need to place a receptionist at a cubicle opposite the elevator where visitors can be greeted, screened, and directed as they enter the floor. We do not currently have this problem in our existing building because the organization has a guard hired to check visitors in and out of the one public entrance to the building.
>
> Because the right of way division has twice the number of employees and many more visitors than we do in Planning, I attempted to convince her to agree to staff the position out of her budget. I have had some previous history negotiating with this division chief and have found her difficult to work with. This meeting was no exception. I tried to convince her that equity demanded she pay for the position or at least two-thirds of the costs. She refused, arguing that I should pay the entire cost because her budget had been reduced this fiscal year.
>
> After posturing for some time, it was clear that she was not going to budge in her negotiating position. I had more important issues on my plate that day and also I did not want to take this issue to our mutual boss, the district director, to resolve. In light of this, I proposed that we split the costs fifty-fifty, which she agreed to almost immediately. The problem I have is that this really is not a fair decision for my division and is another example in which I should have been more aggressive in sticking to my position, instead of looking for resolution through a compromise.

In a win-lose situation, we generally have three options: We can try to change the other person, we can try to change the situation, or we can try to change ourselves.[33] The division chief tried to change the other person and was only moderately successful. He is not happy about the decision to split the costs down the middle, and although he could change his mind about that, there is still a lingering feeling of inequity in the situation, given the larger number of employees in the other section and their higher need for the screening of visitors. The division chief did not want to take the problem to their mutual supervisor, but that might have created a sense of equity in the situation, as whatever option was chosen would have been out of his hands. It might have been easier to cope with the situation knowing that it was imposed on him by a superior rather than negotiated between peers. Furthermore, it is possible that their mutual supervisor might have had additional funds or other ideas about how this situation could be managed.

Sometimes a conflict is over scarce resources but one or both parties see it as one over something less tangible such as power, authority, and status:

> I had just bought a new computer and was in the process of getting it all set up. Space is a precious commodity in university housing. My roommate has had a laptop computer for over a year that obviously requires less space to operate than does a full-sized computer like mine. He also has a printer that is about half the size of mine. Prior to my computer being shipped, we realized we would need another desk in the room. We were able to find one that barely fit in our room, and we moved it in. The new desk was half again as big as the one already in the room, and he started using it first.
>
> Once I got my computer partially set up, I realized that it was going to be a tight fit to squeeze all the equipment into the available space, and I asked my roommate if we could switch desks. He quickly and firmly replied "no." I asked why not, because my computer took up so much more space, and it was already cramped in the corner where my desk is, without even having all the equipment set up. He replied that he simply liked the bigger desk so that he could spread out more. I half jokingly said I would pay him to switch, and he said, "This isn't a barter system, and you can't bid on this desk." At that point, I could tell he was getting more serious, so I just said "whatever" and let it go at that. My computer is now set up, and the situation is workable, but it is not the most comfortable set-up for me, and I think that it would have worked fine the other way, especially because he has used the smaller desk for a year and a half without any problems whatsoever.

In this conflict, the space is too limited to consider trying to obtain two desks of the same size. And the roommate who refuses to change desks is apparently not convinced that the size of the desk should be based on space needs rather than on his desires for a particularly sized desk. What are the options available in such a situation? In the interest of exploring a variety of solutions, we will list all those that occurred to us, both negative and positive.

1. The narrator (let's call him Henry) could simply give up on the idea of a larger desk.
2. Henry could pretend to give up the idea of having a larger desk, but could do sneaky things like changing the preferences on his roommate's (let's call him Matt) computer, or hiding his mouse, and so on.
3. Henry could pretend to give up the idea of having the larger desk, but complain vociferously each time he was forced to use his computer in such limited space.
4. Henry could suffer in silence and hope that Matt would perceive how difficult the situation is over time and will be moved to make the change out of consideration for the narrator.
5. Henry could try to find something of value to Matt and offer it in trade for the desk (other than money, as that did not seem to work the first time).
6. Henry could change his work habits by using the desk only when using his computer, switching to the dining room table to do other work, or doing other written work in a place like the library. The disadvantage of this option is that it may be inconvenient to complete class assignments when using two different locations.
7. Henry could buy a desk with a different configuration, such as one of the specialized computer desks for limited space.
8. Henry could find another roommate in a larger room.
9. Henry could trade in his desktop computer for a laptop that takes up less space.
10. They could work out a deal in which they both use Henry's computer on the larger desk and Matt's laptop on the smaller desk.

Given our emphasis on collaborative and cooperative behavior in conflicts, you are probably able to see that options 1–4, while a possibility, would probably not create the outcomes he sought. Options 5–7 are more positive ways of addressing the problem, and option 8 is a way of avoiding it (although at great cost to oneself). If they could do option 9 or 10, Henry might also find advantages to having access to a laptop. Jandt argues that it is important to consider all the various options that occur to us, both positive and negative, so that we can be reminded of one simple fact: The relationship should always receive serious consideration because it may be more important than the conflict itself.[34]

One might argue in response that a person need not care deeply about his or her roommate, and may very well want to insist that he or she achieves only his or her goal when dealing with an organizational entity such as a department store. However, Jandt reminds us that we cannot simply terminate relationships when we do not achieve our goals; we will run out of people and organizations with which to have relationships. A college may let you change roommates once, but we doubt that it will be as responsive to your complaints the second or third time around. Given this constraint, how do we go about identifying the various options in a win-lose conflict over scarce resources?

We suggest several steps of analysis. Jandt, for example, provides these points to remember as we approach a conflict over scarce resources:

- Power grows out of someone else's dependency. If you can give someone something that he desires, you have power over that person—no matter who he is or what it is that you can give him. You also have power if you are able to withhold something that someone desires. In this case, Matt has power over Henry, because Matt has something that Henry wants, and it is apparently something Henry doesn't think he can get elsewhere.
- Understanding what people want is not always simple. You must make judgments about what a person really wants, and this may be something entirely different from what he says he wants. It is possible that in this situation Matt's desire for the larger desk has more to do with how he sees himself than with actual need. It is also possible that Matt wants the larger desk because he feels he has given in to Henry's demands in the past.
- The key to gaining power is to identify what you and other people really desire. Assess whether you are striving for what you really want or for merely a symbol of what you really want.
- When you've decided that you want something, look at the bigger picture. More specifically, make a list of what you want in your current situation and also in the foreseeable future. Critically assess those wants. Do you want them for what they are, or do you want them for what they represent? If they represent something, what do they represent to you? Is there a better way to acquire what they represent?
- Rank your wants in order of importance. Recognize that you may have to sacrifice the less important to gain the more important.
- Determine who controls what you want and who or what stands in your way of getting it. Keep in mind that the better you understand what you want and why you want it, the better your chances will be of acquiring it. Explore alternative ways to get what you want; they may be much more effective—and easy—than what at first appeared to be the only way.
- Identify the resources that you control and the people who want those resources.

How does Jandt's method of analysis add to our understanding of the conflict between Henry and Matt over the desk? One consideration is that the roommates are located in university housing in which much of the furniture is provided by the university. Henry could try approaching the person who controls the storage room to find out if there are two desks of medium size in storage that might replace the one large and one small desk Henry and Matt currently have in their room. Or, Henry could simply put his computer out in the living room of their apartment, with access limited by password. Henry could offer the use of his computer to Matt in exchange for having it on the larger desk, a move that might be appreciated if Matt would rather work with a bigger screen and keyboard.

Here is another conflict over a tangible issue. How would you recommend that the people in the conflict follow Jandt's advice?

> We were given a small amount of money by my husband's parents. When they sent it, they indicated that they intended for us to use it for improvements around the house. They knew we needed to replace a crumbling wall and that our windows weren't much good on bad weather days. However, they made the check out to my husband, and he thinks that because it came from his parents, he should have the larger say in how the money is spent. That wouldn't bother me too much, except that he wants to buy an expensive "toy" with it that only he will use. Any kind of work we do on the house benefits both of us—we improve its value, we lower utility bills, and all that. This seems really unfair to me, but I don't know how to talk to him about it without both of us getting angry.

What are the various options open to this couple?

1. They could send the money back because it is causing a conflict between them.
2. They could split the money evenly between them.
3. They could make a list of the various things they want to do around the house, and decide that the most important would be done before he gets to spend money on his "toy."
4. They could spend the money on the house and take out a loan for his "toy" that he pays for with overtime work.
5. They could invest the money and wait until it had increased enough to both complete the work on the house and buy the "toy."
6. They could do nothing at all with the money.
7. They could donate the entire amount to charity.
8. They could seek the counsel of a friend and abide by the friend's decision about how the money should be spent.
9. They could ask his parents what the money should be spent for and abide by that decision.

You might be able to add to this list. The point of creating it is to show that spending or splitting the money is not the only option the couple has, even though it might be the first thing they think to do.

Some conflicts seem intractable. And it may be that, for right now, a mutually acceptable alternative is not available. In that case, you must consider your **BATNA,** the acronym Fisher and Ury have given to the idea of one's best alternative to a negotiated agreement. If you cannot come to some understanding with the other person, what is the next best thing to do? Your BATNA can be determined on a number of levels. For example, if you can't come to an agreement today with the other person, what's the next best thing? If you can't come to an agreement with this person in the foreseeable future, what are your other alternatives?

In addition to calculating a BATNA, people in the conflict may also engage in fractionation in order to work through the problem.[35] Fractionation is a matter of breaking the problem down into its smallest pieces, and then dealing with each piece one at a time. There are not a lot of ways to fractionate the conflict over the size of the desk, but the people in the next narrative appeared to solve their problem equitably by looking at the various pieces of the situation and dealing with them:

> This conflict occurred on Super Bowl Sunday. We attend church about twenty-five minutes from our home. Because I work with the high school students, I have to be at church for a Sunday night activity, as well as needing to be there in the mornings. So it is a weekly dilemma whether we stay out there all day (at my parents' house), or if we come home and then I go back later on. On this particular Sunday, we had planned to go straight home after church. My wife had some things to do, and I was planning to go to the library. I was able to get the things I needed from the library at church instead, so I no longer had a reason to go home. My entire family was going to watch the Super Bowl that afternoon at my parents' house. So I, having got my stuff done, decided that I would watch the game with my family instead of watching it at home. Once I realized that I didn't have to go to the library, I didn't see any problems in our staying at my parents' house. What I failed to realize was that my wife had already made plans to be at home that afternoon. It wasn't that she didn't want to be with my family, but she had things to do elsewhere.
>
> Knowing that my wife would rather go home and be able to get the things accomplished that she needed to do, we decided to have a "meeting." Before our conflict occurred, we set some ground rules and decided we were just going to discuss our options and stick to the topic at hand. My goal was to come to a decision that would satisfy both of us, and an important part of achieving my goal was the fact that I didn't talk about it in front of my parents. We went into another room to discuss the issue without even alluding to the fact that we were thinking about changing plans. At first, I offered to let her take the car home and I would get a ride halfway home after church. She'd just have to meet me. But she didn't like the idea of waiting up for me to be done when my leaving would depend on someone else. We decided to run home and get most of the things done, and then come back to watch the Super Bowl before going to church together. I promised not to hang around after the evening service talking with people because she was tired and wanted to get to bed early. We both felt satisfied with the outcome.

There were several pieces to this conflict. The wife had already planned to be home and accomplish a number of chores, none of which she would be able to do if she stayed at her in-laws' house all day and went to church in the evening. She also did not want to have to drive back to get her husband after church. He wanted to spend some time with his parents, especially because he had already accomplished what he had planned to do in the way of chores for the weekend. However, he was unwilling to let his wife feel as though she were working alone while he was playing. There was also the problem of the distance of their house from the place where he wanted and needed to be. By considering all the components, they were able to address the problem and come to a solution that pleased both of them.

It's important to note that, in this conflict, the offered compromise (you take the car and do what you want, and I'll do what I want) doesn't work. One reason is that the relationship is important. As newlyweds, they have a desire to be together, and as a committed married couple, they have a desire to be equitable in the completion of chores around the house. For her to go home and get chores done while he watched the game did not seem equitable, and he was open to discussion about how they could both achieve what they wanted. This was a fairly simple conflict. Both of the win-lose conflicts we have presented in this chapter point to several pieces of advice concerning the resolution of tangible-issue conflicts. These concern both principles of reconciliation and skills in converting competition into cooperation.

Principles of Reconciliation

Fisher and Ury, who headed the Harvard Negotiation Project, developed a method they called principled negotiation, which consists of four points:

People: Separate the people from the problem.
Interests: Focus on interests, not positions.
Options: Generate a variety of possibilities before deciding what to do.
Criteria: Insist that the result be based on some objective standard.[36]

In order to understand the various principles of reconciliation and skills for turning competition into collaboration, we present a case study of a conflict that spun out of control. Whereas it is easy for us to play "Monday Morning Quarterback" and assess the problems in the conflict, we hope that by studying this situation, you can see the various points at which alternative behaviors might have led to alternative outcomes.

Case Study 13.1 ■ *Being Nice Can Get You Sued* ─────────────────────

I was holding an open house in February at one of my listings, and some people came through who seemed quite nice. I hit it off with Mark and Kathy right away. They kind of liked the house that I was showing, but not too much. It wasn't quite what they needed. A lot of times when you have a good rapport with people you can get a good idea of what they want in a house instead of having to guess and show them a bunch of houses to see what they like.

I'd just taken a listing two days previously on another house on Shadow Lane. That one instantly came to mind as being perfect for them from what they described; so I closed the open house a little early and took them right over to that house. They spent a lot of time there and they really liked it. I was holding an open house there the following day and they came over again to see it and spent about three hours talking about all the things they could do to it. It was perfect for them. So we made an appointment for two days later to go over to their house and list it for sale and to take an offer on the Shadow Lane house, contin-

gent upon their home selling. I got all my facts and figures together, did a little research, looked at other houses in their area to get an idea of how things were selling, and got ready for my appointment with them.

I went up to their home, and we got along even better. I met their dog, met their cat, met their bunny, got along great with them. There shouldn't have been anything that went wrong with this. So the appointment went fine, I wrote up the offer, I took their listing, and I presented the offer to the Shadow Lane owners, Bill and Ethel. They countered the offer, we finally settled on a price, everything was fine, and we were ready to open escrow.

Now, when an offer is contingent, it means that they cannot perform and are not obligated to perform unless their house sells. It also means that if the seller gets another offer that is not contingent, the contingent buyers have so many hours, in this case it was forty-eight hours, to say "I can perform" or "I can't perform." So they have first rights of refusal on the house. If they can't perform, the second offer is taken.

So everything was fine, but we did not open escrow yet. I had their check in hand with their permission to hold it. I got everything rolling on their listing; they had no reason to believe that I wouldn't sell their house quickly. Within a week of taking their offer on the Shadow Lane house, a noncontingent offer came in before we opened escrow (although it wouldn't have made a difference if I had opened escrow because the seller has the right to accept a noncontingent offer over a contingent one). Mark and Kathy loved the house, we were getting along great, and my nature is to be protective and motherly. All I thought when this new offer came in was how hurt they were going to be that they weren't going to get their dream home. From our conversations when I listed their house, there was nothing said that would possibly indicate that they could buy the house without selling theirs. Nothing was said about any other way they could buy it. I had no reason to believe they could possibly perform on the contract. If their house didn't sell, that was it.

So the offer came in and my duty, both to Bill and Ethel as the seller and to Mark and Kathy as the buyer, was to get the form out that says, "We're giving you forty-eight hours to perform or quit the offer." Thinking that they couldn't perform, I didn't tell them. I figured what I would do is find them a perfect replacement house and be able to give them "good news, bad news." The second offer was great. It was noncontingent, it was for more money, and Bill and Ethel wanted to take it. They asked me what would happen with Mark and Kathy, and I told them they would not be able to perform. I did not tell Bill and Ethel that I was not giving Mark and Kathy the forty-eight-hour notice.

So, Bill and Ethel accepted the offer, which they really didn't have a right to do because the notice wasn't given. The agent who presented the offer for the second buyer, Susan, made a lot of mistakes in the contract she wrote up. In my counteroffer, I had to catch a lot of her mistakes, and because I was thinking about that and also thinking at the back of my mind, "Mark and Kathy can't get the house and I feel sorry for them," I failed to write in the counteroffer: "Seller's acceptance subject to buyer #1's nonperformance."

The other agent had been told there was another offer but that they couldn't perform. She had knowledge of it, but when everything hit the fan she lied and said she didn't know about the first offer. But nowhere in the contract was it referenced. So we accepted Susan's offer and no notification was given to Mark and Kathy. Escrow opened on Susan's offer and things proceeded as if she was the buyer. I looked at tons of houses and found a couple that were suitable and one that would really work, and it was less than the one on Shadow Lane.

Some background on Mark and Kathy: They were feeling victimized by his ex-wife. She'd been hammering them, and her most recent move had been to say, "I'm moving to Las Vegas—take the kids," which was why they were moving. So what happened with this house was like one more thing in their lives, and I think they overreacted because of it.

I called them up, and the time had passed for notification. The forty-eight hours was up by an extra twenty-four hours, and they had never been notified. I called them up and said, "I have some good news and some bad news," and I started telling them about all the houses. Mark said, "I assume that because you're telling me about other houses a noncontingent offer has been made on Shadow Lane." I said yes, and the seller wants to take it (I did not tell him the seller had already taken it). He held the phone sort of away from his mouth and said to his wife, "Well, I guess we could go into our 401K and pull out the money from there to make it work." My jaw was hanging on the ground. He'd never given me any reason to think that they could perform on the contract. I was dumbfounded, like "Oh, my God, what have I done?" And he asked me how much time they had, and like an idiot I said, "The clock is ticking," instead of saying right then, "I'm sorry. I screwed up. I had no idea you had 401K. I had no idea you could buy the house." He asked how much time they had, and I don't know how I even came up with what I replied.

So we went out looking at the other houses, and they did like the one I thought they'd like, and they made an offer for less than the offer on Shadow Lane. Mark was a licensed real estate agent who didn't practice but was pretty savvy on deals. He made a really good offer, but the seller was a real jerk, and very manipulative, and would only take full price. Ultimately, he took less, but that's a different story. So when I called Mark back to tell him about the offer-counteroffer process, he said it just confirmed that the Shadow Lane property was the one for them. So they were planning to call their financial advisor the next day to make it work. I was thinking, "I have buried myself on this one."

Several things were supposed to be happening with the second buyer, Susan, that didn't. She was supposed to deliver a letter from her bank indicating that she had been approved for a loan. She didn't do that in a timely manner. She also bounced her deposit check, which is a major no-no. I called the other agent to tell her about it. Susan replaced the check the same day. I shouldn't have taken it. It was coming to the day that Mark and Kathy thought they were going to open escrow.

All of this was undermined by the poor relationship I had with my broker, Dick. He was really an incompetent agent who could mess up a deal beyond belief. I had finally gotten him to the point where he left me alone—I handed him checks and he stayed out of my deals, and that's the way I liked it. So I wasn't likely to go to him and tell him I have a problem. And I should have, even though he's an idiot.

I sat down with Bill and Ethel and told them everything I had done—I had screwed up; I apologized. I told them what their options were. I told them it was my mistake, and I would really appreciate it if they would help me out, but they had to make their own decision about what to do. I told them that Mark and Kathy were more qualified, that Susan had bounced a check, which showed bad faith. They didn't really like Susan because she was always complaining about the house, and they were really concerned that she would prove difficult. They decided that they would rather sell the house to Mark and Kathy. I had legitimate reasons to cancel out on Susan's offer. So I called the other agent and told her that the offer was canceled.

The other agent went nuclear on me. She threatened to sue; she threatened to cloud the title

on the property. She said she had the letter and I should come get it. Because I was feeling wrong and guilty, I let her manipulate me. I went to her office and picked up the letter, and she deemed it as acceptance. The next morning we had a physical inspection scheduled for Susan, which would imply a contract and an escrow. She was all set to show up in the morning. I called the sellers; they said they wouldn't fix anything anyway. It could be construed as a legitimate contract if the inspection went through, so I got there early enough to keep the inspection from happening. Bill and Ethel didn't want her to come anyway. The other agent showed up for the inspection and again went nuclear. I stayed calm; I kept saying, "We don't have an escrow. You'd better leave."

At this point, I knew she was going to call Dick; so I figured I'd better get to him first. He was really upset that I hadn't told him earlier about the problems. He came in; we discussed it more. The other agent called and screamed. He somewhat supported my position even though I'd made some mistakes, but he's a reed in the wind. We told the other agent that the sellers decided to reject the offer and go with the first offer. Finally, I got everyone to settle down and said, "Let's talk to our attorneys because we're all screaming lawsuit." By a day later, my boss had flip-flopped and was supporting the other agent. He told me to go "blow off" Mark and Kathy who were his clients too. I was to tell them that it just wasn't going to work out, that Bill and Ethel wanted the second offer.

I went and talked to Mark and Kathy and told them the whole story. They were pretty mad. I told them I was sorry that I had let them down, that I felt like I had been looking out for their best interests, that I knew how much they liked the house, and everything I had thought. What they figured out was that the only reason that my broker wasn't accepting their offer was that they weren't screaming loudly enough.

A couple of conversations took place with Dick, which I wasn't privy to, but Dick thought they accepted an offer of having $4,000 rebated to them from commission. By the time Mark came down to the office two days later, he was completely worked up. The house was under market and was a good buy. To get the same house in the same condition would have cost him $10,000 more. I guess they talked to an attorney or someone who told them they should get some money out of this.

I was out running errands. I got paged that Mark was coming in at 4:00 to meet with Dick and me. From where I was when I got the page, 4:00 was really pushing it, and I pulled up at 4:07. Mark and Dick were in the parking lot screaming at each other. Dick was by the front door of the office, and Mark was just in the parking lot. I went in and tried to talk to Dick. He was completely unreasonable, saying Mark was trying to hold him up. Dick's mentality is that before he has the money, he feels it can be used. In this business, until an escrow closes and you have a check in your hand, you don't have any money. But for him, the minute it goes into escrow you can take the money away for him. It was just worthless to talk to him.

He chose the attorney that had sued and beat him in a lawsuit three years earlier, assuming that the nice guy won, he must be good. The guy wasn't really all that great. We talked to him about the case, and he said it could be construed as fraud because I willfully withheld knowledge from two sets of clients, even though I did it with good intentions. Even though there was no malice of intent to defraud, I withheld knowledge. Mark was asking for $25,000 in damages. Letters went back and forth. I offered to sell Mark and Kathy's home for no commission and find them a new home for no commission. Every time we got close to settling something Dick would put the skids on it. It went back and forth so much that I got to the point where I didn't want to deal with it anymore. I wanted to make sure that Mark and Kathy understood that any money paid would come out of my pocket and not Dick's, and that they'd realize that it was Dick who had been such a jerk and not me. But that didn't go. And I started to get defensive and hurt because the whole cause was me being too concerned about their feelings. I got to the point where even if they'd accepted the offer of me working for free I wouldn't want to do it.

We started going for a cash settlement instead. They were threatening to file an actual lawsuit, which they hadn't done yet, and to cloud the title on the Shadow Lane house, which would endanger the seller. All this time, there was conflict with Bill and Ethel because they were afraid of being sued, and Dick treated them badly. In the meantime, Susan's escrow closed, and so Mark and Kathy wouldn't be able to do anything to Bill and Ethel.

My conflict with Dick also got completely out of control. Every time he talked to me he lost his temper and told me what an idiot I was. We were so close to settlement, and every time we got to the point where we could, he would mess it up again. The lawyer kept calling Dick and talking to him instead of me, even though I was paying the bill. I asked him not to run up my bill talking to Dick. I felt like I was a puppet and everyone was pulling my strings except me.

We were in an office meeting. The lawyer called again, and we came up with an offer to settle. Dick started in again about how I had messed up, and I said it wouldn't do any good to go down that path again. I told him I had never failed to admit that I was the cause of the problem. But I said he wouldn't accept the fact that he made it worse by blowing up at Mark. He started cussing me out. I said, "You know, just because I started a fire didn't mean you had to throw gasoline on it." He exploded and told me to clean out my desk and get the _____ out of the office.

I stood up and said, "You know, that's a hell of a way to talk to someone who put $25,000 in your pocket last year." He told me to "f— off." I practically ripped the door off the hinges as I went out. It was 92 degrees that day and I had a cast up to my knee, but I didn't stop moving until my desk was packed and I was out of there. I had already been talking to other offices because I knew once this was settled I wanted out. I was employed the same day by a different office and I am really happy there.

I called the lawyer and told him it was essential that we settle immediately because I was no longer working for Dick. We finally settled this in May, three months after it all started. I paid a $3,500 attorney bill and $7,000 to the client because I tried to be nice.

Separate People from the Problem

One of the most important things we need to do in a win-lose conflict is to keep our perceptions about the other person separated from our perceptions about the problem. It is easy in a conflict to confuse how we feel about the issue with how we feel about the person involved with it. This can work in both positive or negative ways—both our like or dislike of a person can cloud our decision-making processes.

The person in this situation tried to avert a win-lose situation because she cared about the couple and didn't want to hurt their feelings by telling them that they would have to change their offer. Her personal feelings got in the way of good decision making. Whether we like or dislike the other, we need to focus on the issue. Instead, this conflict ends up with Dick calling the realtor an idiot. He accuses her of messing up rather than focusing on the problem. He curses at her. Of course, Dick takes the easy way out and fires his realtor, as though she were entirely to blame for the whole business (she may have made an error in judgment initially but Dick was the one who "threw gasoline on the fire"). As is often the case in conflict, it gets out of hand when people shift to an attack on the parties involved rather than focusing on the problem.

An example of focusing on the problem rather than those involved is found in this narrative:

> As a driver of a school bus, I occasionally have conflicts with students, and sometimes these spill over to conflicts with their parents. That is usually when the principal, Bob, gets involved. Recently, parents complained that they felt I had falsely accused their son, Rick, of misbehaving on the bus. They saw the "referral for misbehaving" as an attack on their child by me. When the meeting occurred in the principal's office, they immediately began by attacking me and questioning my judgment as though I had something personal against their son. Bob really did a good job of separating their son and me (as people) from the problem, which was really Rick's behavior.

Focus on Interests Rather Than Positions

What is the difference between interests and positions? Think of **positions** as the final part of an I-statement (the goal part of the statement—what you want). For example, Ray wants to buy a particular car for $10,000. Now suppose that Jamie wants to buy the same car that Ray wants. Both have the same position: They both want that car and cannot share it. **Interests** are needs that may be satisfied by both positions. For example, Ray really needs sharp transportation, but he can only pay $10,000 for it. If the car sales rep can show him another sharp car for $10,000, and he decides to buy it, then the interests of both can be satisfied. Ray got what he wanted, and Jamie got a car that satisfies her interest or need. People will change their positions, if you show them how to meet their interests or needs. Thus, a good way to resolve conflict (when over scarce resources) is to shift from positions (in which we really want the same thing) to interests (in which different positions or wants may satisfy our needs).

Positions become clear as conflicting parties describe their wants. Interests may be clarified by asking people why they want something. For example:
"I want to use the car tonight."
"Why?"
"I have to go to Phil's to study for an exam."
"Couldn't he come here?"
"Yes, I think he will if I ask him to."

When a conflict is first identified and people begin to make their opinions about the matter known, it is easier to identify the various positions people have taken than it is to identify the interests each party has in resolving the conflict. In the case study, two different couples wanted to buy the same house.

The realtor did realize what interests were behind Mark and Kathy's position and tried to find them an alternative house (new position) that would satisfy their interests. She might have succeeded had they not been able to perform on the first house. The realtor was on the right track as far as conflict resolution is concerned, but unfortunately she made an error in not telling Mark and Kathy initially.

APPLICATION 13.3

For each of the following situations, identify and write out each person's position and interest that caused them to take that position.

1. Jennifer wants the computer so that she can research her paper. Cheryl wants to surf the Internet.
   Jennifer's position: She wants to use the computer.
   Cheryl's position:
   Jennifer's interest: She needs to do research for a paper.
   Cheryl's interest:

2. Dan wants the car to get groceries. Scott wants it to "get out and go somewhere."
   Dan's position:
   Scott's position:
   Dan's interest:
   Scott's interest:

3. Maria wants to cook dinner to try out a new recipe. Larry wants to go out to eat because he is hungry.
   Maria's position:
   Larry's position:
   Maria's interest:
   Larry's interest:

4. Rob wants to have his friends visit homecoming weekend (and stay in their small apartment). Diane, his roommate, wants to have her friends the same weekend.
   Rob's position:
   Diane's position:
   Rob's interest:
   Diane's interest:

Generate More Options

As we learned earlier, it is important to identify both positions and interests in conflicts over scarce resources. Moving from positions (wants) to interests (needs) automatically expands your options for resolving a conflict in a more mutually satisfying manner.

You are probably aware that the first solution that occurs to you is not necessarily the best one. But how do you get beyond your first solution? Brainstorming is a process that requires you to list all possible solutions, irrespective of their initial feasibility. Our lists of options for Henry and Matt and their desk problem, as well as the couple with the inheritance to spend, were examples of brainstorming lists. Not all the options are workable, but when you have examined all the possible solutions you can think of, it is easier to focus on one. In our case study, very little brainstorming was going on. After the original move to look at interests by finding another house for Mark and Kathy, the situation stalled. An account of the results of successful brainstorming is related by this person:

> At the car dealership I work for, the service manager frequently finds himself in conflict with unhappy customers. He normally comes up with several remedies and presents them for the customers to decide what would make them the happiest or the most satisfied with the situation. The customers generally feel like he is concerned about them and solving the problem. I've witnessed very few times when he had been unable to solve the conflict in a positive way for both sides of the issue.

There are other ways to generate more solutions in a situation involving conflict over scarce resources. Pruitt offers four techniques for increasing such options.

Cost Cutting: "The other will sometimes cut his or her own costs, so as to more easily accept and live with unavoidable decisions that benefit the source."[37] This technique was demonstrated when the realtor in Case Study 13.1 offered to sell Mark and Kathy's house for no commission and to find them a new home for no commission. Realtors know a variety of ways to reduce the costs for home buyers to help them close a deal. Another example of cost cutting is found in this narrative:

> My boyfriend is Scott. His family was planning a two-week vacation to St. Martin and wanted us both to go with them. I was busy with school and he was overloaded with work. We both really needed to take a vacation, but for financial reasons, Scott couldn't afford to take two weeks vacation from work. After some discussion, we came up with the idea that I would leave a week early with his family and he would join us the second week. This worked great because I not only got the time to get away, which I really needed, but we also had a wonderful time together the second week. He really enjoyed the much-needed vacation, and he didn't have to take the full two weeks from work.

Compensation: "The other party is indemnified for the losses that result from the actor's costly demands."[38] In the case study, apparently Dick offered Mark and Kathy a $4,000 rebate from the realtor's commission. However, later, Mark and Kathy sued for $25,000. Normally, the earlier a deal involving compensation can be reached, the less expensive it will be in the long run.

Logrolling: Each side grants to the other those issues that are given top priority by each other. Both parties make concessions, but not on those issues to which they give top priority. Logrolling did not occur in the case study, but does in this narrative:

> I wanted to help with finishing an installation job on a van, but my fellow worker Trish wanted to go to lunch before I did that same day. We discussed the matter and decided that Trish could help me first with the van and then she could go to lunch early while I would cover for her. Each of us had our main concern dealt with. We gave into the other on something that was low priority for ourselves but high for the other.

And in this one:

> Recently, I visited a stereo store to buy a new FM tuner. I also needed a pair of surround speakers to make the whole system work like it should. During the discussion over FM tuners and prices, it became clear that the sales rep did not want to reduce the price of the stereo receiver, but he discovered that I needed speakers. At that point, he threw in a pair of new

surround sound speakers, which resolved the negotiation over price. I got what I wanted—the receiver and speakers. The seller got what he wanted—the regular price.

Bridging: "occurs when a new option is developed that satisfies both parties' most significant needs."[39]

Bridging could be a minor or a major new option. A renter may be hesitant about renting a particular apartment because she wants to have a home office but there is no telephone jack in the second bedroom. The landlord may bridge the deal by offering to pay for the installation of another telephone jack. Whereas that could be a simple bridge, a more complicated one occurred in our case study. There the realtor had the right idea when she went out of her way to find another home that was equally appealing and available for less money. That probably would have settled the deal had it not been for other problems that interfered with the home sale. Although this option did not successfully occur in the case study, it is illustrated in the following narrative:

> Yesterday my roommate and I discussed our plans for the weekend. I wanted my sisters to come and stay with me, and she wanted her two friends to come and to stay, too. The problem is that there isn't enough room for everyone, and this was the only weekend that everyone could come. Luckily, we did talk about other options and came upon a good idea. We decided that her friends would come up on Friday, stay over, and on Saturday they would all go to visit another friend of theirs in a city not far from here. Because they would be staying elsewhere until Sunday, there would be room for my sisters on Saturday. So my roommate and I would both get what we wanted.

Base Decisions on Objective Criteria

We do this often in everyday situations when decisions are made on the basis of trade-offs, sharing, and turn taking, for example:

- women before men.
- it's my turn this time and you can go first next time.
- the majority rules.
- let's toss a coin or draw straws to see who gets it.
- he needs it more than she does.

These are common objective criteria we all use on occasion to settle everyday conflicts over scarce resources.

How do you know when the solution you have decided on is the best one for all concerned? One way is to try to base the decision on objective criteria. Objective criteria were available to the real estate agent. Had she played the sale "by the book" and if she had tried, at the same time, to explain the situation to Mark and Kathy, much of the conflict might have been averted. At the very least, even if Mark and Kathy had been unable to buy the house, they would know that they had been given the chance and would not feel as though they were cheated out of something.

Converting Competition into Cooperation

The principles of creating win-win outcomes are found in the separation of people from the problem, focusing on interests, brainstorming, and finding objective criteria on which to base decisions. These principles need to be translated into action.

Mind-Set: Seeking Commonalties. When you look at a half glass of water, do you see the glass as half full or half empty? A half-full glass may make you feel happy, whereas a half-empty glass may be depressing. Your point of view makes a difference. We know, for example, that it is difficult to cooperate and collaborate with others if you disagree with them. That disagreement may produce distrust and competition. If instead you focus on areas of agreement, you are more likely to trust and cooperate, as this narrative demonstrates:

> I once had a professor who divided his discussion class into two groups, which he assigned to different classrooms. He then gave each group different instructions, initially. He told one group that they would receive a group grade and to cooperate and work together to solve a problem. That group did end up working together and quickly solved the problem. Although he gave the same problem to the other group, he told the group members that they were in competition with each other. He said he would give each student a separate grade based on his or her individual contributions to the group. That group had a tough time working together and found it difficult to come to a consensus.

The Language of Cooperation. Unlike some of the conflict messages we wrote of earlier that take responsibility for feelings and wants, the **language of cooperation** is "we based." We both want this. We both think this. This is important to everyone concerned. Cooperative language is also tentative—"What would you say if . . ." or "Do you think that's a good idea?" It leaves space for people so that they don't feel backed into corners.

Consulting before Acting. Clearly, this skill was not followed in Case Study 13.1. The real estate agent made assumptions about her buyers, and acted without asking them about what she should do. Her broker made things worse by acting on her behalf without consulting her, and muddying the waters. This skill is of paramount importance. Don't assume that you know what the other wants. Don't assume that you know what is best for the other person. Instead, check your statements to make sure they are right, or even more conservatively, ask what the other person wants before tendering an offer.

Increased Frequency of Communication. As conflicts escalate, people have a tendency to shut down communication. They become entrenched in their positions and conclude that because nothing apparently can be done, nothing apparently should be said. One difficulty in Case Study 13.1 is the real estate agent's lack of communication with her broker. Because she had concluded he was worthless in this situation, he was not kept abreast of developments, and his ignorance of the situation's nuances helped to make everything worse. Although communication is not a magic cure-all for conflict, frequent and nonhostile communication keeps those in the conflict from making too many unchallenged assumptions about the other.

Control the Process, Not the People. In a tangible-issue conflict, we need to remember that we cannot be responsible for how others react to the situation at hand. We can only be responsible for our own responses. What this means in terms of control is that we may be faced with people who do not share the same feelings about the situation as we do and who may even want to sabotage the efforts we are making. We cannot control their emotional responses, but we can keep a lid on the process. In Case Study 13.1, for example, the late arrival of the real estate agent in the meeting of her broker and the disgruntled parties helped to intensify the conflict. Whether she intended it or not, her absence communicated a lack of concern, and coupled with her broker's irresponsible communication, the disaffected buyers left the situation even more unhappy than when they had entered it.

Be Positive in Attitude and Behavior.   People often resemble the characters in the children's book *Winnie the Pooh*. Some people are Rabbits, compulsive about everything, wanting to control all events. Others are like Piglet, worried that the sky might fall in. Some are happy-go-lucky Poohs, content to take life as it comes. And then there are the Eeyores. They're pretty easy to recognize. They say the equivalent of things such as, "I didn't get invited to the party, but I wouldn't have had fun anyway." Eeyores are not positive people. And their pessimism can really make it difficult for others to feel as though they are making progress. Eeyores are the ones who shoot down all the solutions during a brainstorming session, who don't believe any objective criteria can be generated to judge a problem, and who don't think any mutual interests exist when people are in conflict. Don't be an Eeyore!

From Theory to Action

Given the variety of research on bargaining and negotiation, what is the best way to enter a bargaining situation? First, understanding how goals affect behavior in negotiations is important. Putnam and Wilson argued that people pursue instrumental, relational, and identity goals in negotiation, some of which are generated ahead of time and some of which arise during the course of interaction. These goals may be ill defined, may emerge during interaction, or may change as interaction progresses. Understanding the dynamic nature of goals (see Chapter 8) can help you to be more open to possibilities in bargaining situations.

Instrumental goals are those that require the opponent to "remove a specific obstacle blocking completion of a task."[40] If you want a professor to change a grade, for instance, your instrumental goal is the actual changing of the grade as a result of your interaction with the professor. Relational goals involve attempts to gain power and to establish trust as the relationship between the bargainers is established. Relational goals would include establishing your right to question the grade you received while not infringing on the professor's power. Identity goals concern how bargainers view each other in the situation. Not only are people motivated to maintain and support each other's facework, but they sometimes desire to attack the face of the other in a bargaining situation. "Bargainers may adopt face-attack goals when they perceive their opponent as (a) attacking, (b) resisting a warranted persuasive appeal, especially in the face of constituents, (c) violating an organizational or relational obligation, or (d) failing to make reciprocal concessions or bargain in good faith."[41] In questioning a grade, for example, you would want to make sure that you do not attack the professor's face; comments such as "your grades are unfair" or "you never give consideration to what I say" would be face attacks. More face-supportive comments would be "I guess I met the requirements because. . . ."

Second, bargainers should resist the temptation to make their final offer too soon. Neither person in the bargaining situation is likely to have full information on what the other's most desired position is. It will take some time to figure out the bargaining range involved.

Third, bargainers should make implicit, rather than explicit, commitments until the final details of the negotiation are settled. Promises and threats should also be implicit whenever possible to allow the bargainer to back away from the promise or threat should it become untenable.

Fourth, whether explicit or implicit, threats are a last-resort measure. A threat clearly defines one's resistance point—the point at which one will concede no further. Use a threat only when you are amply prepared to carry it through and have clearly thought out the consequences. In particular, if you are negotiating with your employer, threatening to quit has been found to be one of the worst bargaining options because it gives the employer a feeling of having no choice in dealing with you.

There are other considerations besides how offers and counteroffers are made. In bargaining situations, people often confuse the problem at hand with the people involved. Keeping these things separated will help you focus on issues rather than on personalities. In addition, you should focus on the interests of the people involved rather than on their articulated positions.

By focusing on interests, you may find areas of overlap, which is likely to happen if you focus just on the people's positions. When looking for areas of overlap, try to find solutions that allow both of you to gain from the situation. Many that appear to be win-lose situations are not. Only through careful definition of the situation can a mutually satisfactory solution be negotiated.

Finally, as a last-resort measure, find the best possible alternative outside the system you are in. That is, if you want a promotion to a new position or a transfer to a different department within your organization, determine the possibilities of getting what you want from a different company. This knowledge of alternatives can prevent poor decisions, such as accepting a less than satisfactory offer or rejecting a good offer.

In this chapter, we have looked at ways of addressing conflicts that by their involvement with tangible resources have a tendency to be approached in a win-lose manner. Successful resolution of these conflicts depends on our ability to assess the situation and decide how important it is to achieve our initial goal in the situation. There are times when we will decide to back off the conflict, giving more importance to the relationship. At other times, we will need to be more forceful. In most cases, though, finding a solution may be a matter of learning how to "color outside the lines."

Notes

1. Linda L. Putnam, "Bargaining as Organizational Communication," in Robert D. McPhee and Phillip K. Tompkins (Eds.), *Organizational Communication: Traditional Themes and New Directions* (Newbury Park: Sage, 1985), p. 129.

2. Gerald I. Nierenberg, *The Complete Negotiator* (New York: Nierenberg & Zeif Publishers, 1986), p. 16.

3. Joyce L. Hocker and William L. Wilmot, *Interpersonal Conflict,* 3rd Ed. (Dubuque, IA: Wm. C. Brown Publishers, Inc., 1991).

4. Linda L. Putnam and Trisha S. Jones, "The Role of Communication in Bargaining," *Human Communication Research* 8 (1992), 262–280.

5. Linda L. Putnam and M. Scott Poole, "Conflict and Negotiation," in Fred M. Jablin, Linda L. Putnam, Karlene H. Roberts, and Lyman W. Porter, *Handbook of Organizational Communication: An Interdisciplinary Approach* (Newbury Park, CA: Sage, 1987), pp. 549–599.

6. Erwin P. Bettinghaus and Michael J. Cody, *Persuasive Communication,* 4th Ed. (New York: Holt, Rinehart & Winston, 1987).

7. James T. Tedeschi and Paul Rosenfeld, "Communication in Bargaining and Negotiation," in Michael R. Roloff and Gerald R. Miller (Eds.), *Persuasion: New Directions in Theory and Research* (Beverly Hills, CA: Sage, 1980), pp. 225–248.

8. David A. Lax and James K. Sebenius, *The Manager as Negotiator* (New York: Free Press, 1986), p. 32.

9. J. A. Wall, *Negotiation: Theory and Practice* (Glenview, IL: Scott Foresman, 1985).

10. Thomas C. Schelling, *The Strategy of Conflict* (Cambridge: Harvard University Press, 1960).

11. R. J. Lewicki, "Lying and Deception: A Behavioral Model," in Max Bazerman and R. J. Lewicki (Eds.), *Negotiation in Organizations* (Newbury Park, CA: Sage, 1983), pp. 68–90.

12. Putnam and Jones, "The Role of Communication in Bargaining," p. 267.

13. Ibid.

14. Ibid.

15. T. A. Saine, "Perceiving Communication Conflict," *Speech Monographs* 41 (1974), 49–56.

16. L. Davis, "An Experimental Investigation of Tolerance of Ambiguity and Information in Interpersonal Bargaining," *Dissertation Abstracts International* 2 (1975), 970-B.

17. L. L. Cummings and D. L. Harnett, "Bargaining Behavior in a Symmetric Bargaining Triad," *Review of Economic Studies* 36 (1969), 485–501.

18. Kenneth K. Sereno and C. David Mortenson, "The Effects of Ego-Involved Attitudes on Conflict Negotiation in Dyads," in Fred E. Jandt (Ed.), *Conflict Resolution through Communication* (New York: Harper and Row, 1973), pp. 145–152.

19. Bertram Spector, "Negotiation as a Psychological Process," *Journal of Conflict Resolution* 21 (1977), 607–618.

20. William A. Donohue, "Analyzing Negotiation Tactics and Development of a Negotiation Interact System," *Human Communication Research* 7 (1981), 273–287; see also William A. Donohue, Mary E. Diez, and Mark Hamilton, "Coding Naturalistic Interaction," *Human Communication Research* 10 (1984), 403–425.

21. Lax and Sebenius, *The Manager as Negotiator,* p. 2.

22. Dean G. Pruitt, *Negotiation Behavior* (New York: Academic Press, 1981).

23. See, for example, M. J. Kimmel, Dean G. Pruitt, J. M. Magenau, E. Konar Goldband, and P. J. D. Carnevale, "Effects of Trust, Aspiration and Gender on Negotiation Tactics," *Journal of Personality and Social Psychology* 38 (1980), 9–22; Dean G. Pruitt and S. A. Lewis, "Development of Integrative Solutions in Bilateral Negotiation," *Journal of Personality and Social Psychology* 31 (1975), 621–633; P. J. D. Carnevale, Dean G. Pruitt, and S. Seilheimer, "Looking and Competing: Accountability and Visual Access in Integrative Bargaining," *Journal of Personality and Social Psychology* 28 (1973), 12–20.

24. V. Bixenstein and K. Wilson, "Effects of Level of Cooperative Choice by the Other Player in a Prisoner's Dilemma Game," *Journal of Abnormal and Social Psychology* 67 (1963), 139–147; see also M. Pilisuk and P. Skolnick, "Inducing Trust: A Test of the Osgood Proposal," *Journal of Experimental Social Psychology* 11 (1968), 53–63; Gerald Marwell, David Schmitt, and B. Boyesen, "Pacifist Strategy and Cooperation Under Interpersonal Risk," *Journal of Personality and Social Psychology* 28 (1973), 12–20.

25. V. Bixenstein and J. Gaebelein, "Strategies of 'Real' Opponents in Eliciting Cooperative Choice in a Prisoner's Dilemma Game," *Journal of Communication Research* 15 (1971), 157–166; see also S. S. Komorita and

A. R. Brenner, "Bargaining and Concession Making under Bilateral Monopoly," *Journal of Personality and Social Psychology* 9 (1968), 15–20.

26. Bixenstein and Wilson, "Effects of Level of Cooperative Choice by the Other Player in a Prisoner's Dilemma Game."

27. Frank Tutzauer and Michael Roloff, "Communication Processes Leading to Integrative Agreements: Three Paths to Joint Benefits," *Communication Research* 15 (1988), 360–380.

28. Robert N. Bostrom, *Persuasion* (Englewood Cliffs, NJ: Prentice Hall, 1983), p. 223.

29. R. J. Klimoski, "The Effects of Intragroup Forces on Intergroup Conflict Resolution," *Organizational Behavior and Human Performance* 8 (1972), 363–383; see also Michael E. Roloff and Douglas E. Campion, "On Alleviating the Debilitating Effects of Accountability on Bargaining: Authority and Self-Monitoring," *Communication Monographs* 54 (1987), 145–164.

30. Barry R. Schlenker, B. Helm, and James T. Tedeschi, "The Effects of Personality and Situational Variables on Behavioral Trust," *Journal of Personality and Social Psychology* 32 (1973), 664–670.

31. J. W. Bowers, "Guest Editor's Introduction: Beyond Threats and Promises," *Speech Monographs* 41 (1974), ix–xi.

32. Max Bazerman, "Why Negotiations Go Wrong," *Psychology Today,* June 1986, pp. 54–58.

33. William W. Wilmot and Joyce L. Hocker, *Interpersonal Conflict,* 5th Ed. (Boston: McGraw-Hill, 1998), p. 210.

34. Fred E. Jandt, with Paul Gillette, *Win-Win Negotiating: Turning Conflict into Agreement* (New York: John Wiley & Sons, 1985), p. 135.

35. Roger Fisher, "Fractioning Conflict," in Claggett G. Smith (Ed.), *Conflict Resolution: Contributions of the Behavioral Sciences* (Notre Dame, IN: University of Notre Dame Press, 1971).

36. Roger Fisher and William Ury, *Getting to Yes: Negotiating Agreement without Giving In* (Boston: Houghton Mifflin, 1981).

37. Dean G. Pruitt, *Negotiation Behavior* (New York: Academic Press, 1981), p. 148.

38. Ibid., p. 148.

39. Ibid., p. 154.

40. Steven R. Wilson and Linda L. Putnam, "Interaction Goals in Negotiation," in James A. Anderson (Ed.), *Communication Yearbook* 13 (Newbury Park, CA: Sage, 1990), p. 381.

41. Ibid., p. 388.

Part V

Escalating and De-Escalating Conflict

The biggest problem I have in conflict is that, although I try to stay calm, I generally end up yelling at the other person and making a fool out of myself. Then I have to apologize. Lately, especially with my wife, an apology just doesn't seem to be enough. More and more she keeps reminding me that I blow up over things that don't matter. How can I learn to control my temper so that I don't say things I have to make up for in the long run?

This section introduces the reader to four areas of research that have lent insight into why conflict escalates out of hand or is contained by those involved. These four areas are anger, stress, impression management, and forgiveness.

Chapter 14 examines anger and its effect on conflict, and the effects of stress on conflict behavior. Contrary to what some others say, we believe that both anger and stress lead to conflict; they are not simply the result of conflict interaction. Expressing anger appropriately and using our stress in productive ways are important means for controlling the escalation of conflict.

In Chapter 15, the idea of impression management is explored and the impact on conflict by our need to maintain our image of ourselves in the eyes of others is explained. A related line of research concerns the effects of embarrassment on conflict behavior. Not surprisingly, people who feel embarrassed about the situation giving rise to conflict have a harder time resolving it than people who have not been embarrassed. Thus, we discuss some ways to avoid embarrassing the other person and ways to avoid getting embroiled in face issues during the course of a conflict.

Finally, Chapter 16 summarizes some research areas on behaviors that make conflict difficult to resolve: relational transgressions, deception, and violence. In addition, the chapter explores the idea of forgiveness and how learning to forgive may ameliorate the effects of destructive conflict in our lives. We believe that it makes no sense to talk about how to resolve conflicts without pointing to some of the most useful means of eliminating the effects of conflict from our lives.

14

The Escalation of Conflict: Anger and Stress

Objectives

At the end of this chapter, you should be able to

1. diagnose your own general anger level.
2. explain how anger affects your communication behavior in a conflict situation.
3. identify sources of stress in your life.
4. explain how stress affects your communication behavior in a conflict situation.
5. list ways to deal constructively with stress.

Key Terms

anger controllers
anger-ins
anger-outs
defensive coping mechanisms
displacement
distress

eustress
hyperstress
hypostress
projection
rationalization
reaction formation

repression
secondary emotion
stress
stressor
sublimation

Why do some conflicts get out of hand? Why are there times when we feel out of control? Why is it that sometimes we can deal with an issue calmly and at another time the same issue will set off an emotional reaction in us? In this chapter we will deal with these factors that contribute greatly to the escalation of conflict: anger and stress.

The Emotion of Anger

Lee likes to begin his unit on anger by pairing the students in class and asking them to hold hands. He then tells them that one is sitting in a seat that the other has been occupying since the beginning of the semester. So he assigns one of the students the task of getting angry with the other student and to tell her off *while holding hands.* Some can't get angry, others drop the student's hand even though they weren't supposed to, and others start pinching the other's hand. During discussion afterward, students report that when in such a conflict, they don't want to be nice. They want to do injury, so holding hands makes no sense.

Whereas conflict, by definition, does not have to include anger, most of us think conflict and anger are synonymous. What does the feeling of anger do to you? Does it feel threatening? Do you feel that it may make you lose control? Or does it work as an impetus for change?

Their discovery of their rage, its appropriateness and its "beauty," liberated them. Anger felt fully and shared with others moved them beyond their anger. This proudly affirmed and openly shared rage to avenge and punish energized them not to avenge or punish, but to confront . . . and act pragmatically to lessen the abuse and injustice they suffered.[1]

In the preceding, who do you think is feeling the anger? Workers in the labor union movement, African Americans in the civil rights movement, women in their push for equality? The description is actually of the latter. Rage, a form of focused anger, "is essential to the first phase of a social movement. It unifies disparate members of the group against a common enemy . . . public rage calls attention to an issue and the importance the protesters attach to it."[2] Anger in the form of rage may serve a useful social function when it is a call to change. Where anger takes control of one or both partners, it has no place in interpersonal relationships, however. This is not to say that we should not experience anger. "Anger simply is. To ask, 'Is my anger legitimate?' is similar to asking 'Do I have a right to be thirsty?'"[3] Because we experience anger, it is important to understand what anger is and how to manage it.

General Irritability

There are a number of different kinds of anger. One kind arises from a tendency to be irritable in general. Because of a general irritation level that a person carries around, anger arises easily and spontaneously when a frustrating event occurs. For example, an easily irritated person will probably react quite vocally when another car wants to occupy the same part of the road he or she is currently traveling on. For the easily irritated person, this anger is pretty hard to avoid—it arises from the instinctual flight-fight response we have to the threat of danger. Dealing with this kind of anger is generally a matter of creating new responses in ourselves, so that we don't yell an obscenity before we even think about it, or strike back, or do something equally negative, such as this person suggests:

It may make me sound like Pollyanna to say this, but I do find that if I say, "Thanks for missing me," rather than accusing another driver of "not having the brains God gave an amoebae," my blood pressure generally doesn't rise and my anger is momentary rather than lasting. In addition, if I try to assume that a person cutting me off simply didn't see me rather than assuming he or she is an idiot, I also contain the amount of anger I feel while driving. It takes practice, and quite honestly, it's harder on a day when I'm tired or upset about something else or when I am stressed out.

Some people claim to be calm when they are not; others have a fairly good idea of what irritates them. However, general irritability can be diagnosed using an instrument such as the Novato Anger Scale.[4] This questionnaire assesses how you react to various situations in which you may or may not have control over what is happening. For example, how irritated are you if you bring home a new appliance, unpack it, plug it in, and find it doesn't work? How angry do you get if you are waiting for someone to repair an appliance and that person doesn't show up when expected? How angry do you get if someone makes a mistake and blames it on you?

In cases such as these, anger becomes a way to express the general irritation a person feels toward the world. It is a safety valve. Recall in Chapter 7 the explanation of psychodynamic theory—our psyche tends to discharge negative energy along the path of least resistance. It's easier to discharge irritation toward a stranger, or an appliance, or an injustice (or unfortunately toward a spouse or child who appears incapable of defending themselves) than to simply not get angry at all.

APPLICATION 14.1

What things do you get really angry about? For one day, keep a journal of the way you are reacting to things around you. You can do this by keeping track of your data in three columns. In the first, list the situation to which you reacted angrily. In the second column, rate how angry you were, with 1 = mildly irritated, 5 = extremely angry. In the third column, write down why you thought you were angry. How many of these situations could be changed? How might you have reacted differently?

Situation creating anger	How angry were you?	Why were you angry?

What are some alternatives for expressing anger?

1. physical aggression, force
2. verbal aggression
3. passive-aggressive behavior
4. nonassertiveness, avoidance, accommodation
5. compromise
6. talk to someone else about how you feel
7. Stop, think, listen, communicate: Use assertive communication behavior, collaboration, interpersonal confrontation ritual

Anger as a Secondary Emotion

General irritability is one source of anger. The other kind of anger is the kind that builds up over time. This anger is generally a **secondary emotion.** That is, we call it anger, but its origin is in things like disappointment, hurt, frustration, pain, unmet expectations, and so on. We often call it anger because it is another-directed emotion. According to Hocker and Wilmot, it is important to realize that anger is a secondary emotion based on "frustration of unmet needs or thwarted desires."[5] Other communication scholars suggest that the primary emotion is fear that occurs when your security is threatened, self-esteem attacked, or our feelings are hurt. If you are angry at or with someone, you feel more righteous about your emotions, and it is easier for you to lay the responsibility at the other person's feet, than if you say, "I am hurt" or "I am disappointed." Anger protects us; admitting hurt or disappointment may make us feel vulnerable.

The Process of Anger

Anger follows an event that disrupts a calm state. How we express our anger depends on our mental processes, our physical responses, and our verbal responses. The mental process of anger is a place where we can best control the process. When someone is late, when someone has disappointed you, when someone has said something hurtful, how do you frame the event? Your interpretation of the event is probably the best indicator of how angry you will get and how you will express it. Do you assume that the other person has hurt you on purpose? Do you look for other things that might be behind the person's behavior? Do you look for things that might be beyond the other person's control? We are not suggesting that you consistently make excuses for another person. Recall, however, from Chapter 13 that the kinds of attributions you make about another in a conflict situation will affect the way that you respond to the other. When you believe the other has acted in a way that constrains your behavior, that such action was intended to harm you, and that such action is illegitimate, you will respond with anger. Furthermore, we tend to make different attributions about others than we make about ourselves—we make excuses for our failures but attribute the failures of others to personal shortcomings. So, how are you making attributions about the other? Is it possible that the other is innocent of an intent to harm you? A second question to ask is how you are responding physically to the situation. Anger creates a stress on the body: your heart rate increases, you may perspire, your breathing rate may increase, your muscles may tense. Sometimes we are not even aware of these changes, as this narrative suggests:

> I had invited my work group over to my house for a Christmas party. I guess I assumed that not everyone would show up, and I really had hoped a particular person would not. I like entertaining and don't find it stressful, but within a half-hour of his arrival I had a headache that wouldn't stop. I realized that my neck was really tense and my leg muscles hurt. He came into my house and I was ready for a fight, even though he was polite and cheerful.

When you find yourself in a situation in which you are becoming angry, there are four sets of techniques that have proven useful for most people: Take time out, relaxation exercises, self-talk, and find the fear.

Take time out. Exit temporarily if you can. Some people report that counting backward from twenty (or ten or fifty) helps them cool off.

> A student visited her teacher at his office to discuss her grade on the last test. She was unhappy about it and would not accept responsibility for her grade. The teacher tried to explain how the grade was derived and could be improved in the future, but the student became angry. Suddenly she stood up and bolted out of the room. The teacher thought the situation unfortunate, especially for the student who probably would continue to be angry at the

teacher to her own detriment. But after twenty minutes, the student suddenly appeared at the teacher's office door and in a nice manner, said "I shouldn't have acted like that. I was upset and started to lose it. I thought it best to leave and cool off. Now I want to find out what I have to do so that I can do better on the next test."

Using relaxation exercises to control your physical responses also can be helpful. Shut your eyes, tighten your muscles (clench your fist, tense your body), and fantasize your anger—imagine it, feel it all over your body, and then suddenly release the tension and picture something serene and relaxing. Monitor your body as you release the different muscles. Breathe slowly and regularly. Concentrate on relaxing your muscles—tense them up and then release them again. Being aware of how you are physically responding to the situation can help.

Engage in helpful self-talk before, during, and after a conflict. Before a potential conflict (if you expect it), tell yourself that "I'm not going to let so-and-so get to me." During the encounter, tell yourself that the other doesn't know what she or he is saying, she must be really upset at something, he doesn't mean to hurt you psychologically. After successfully surviving a potentially threatening situation, compliment yourself for getting through it. Tell yourself that you have really improved in the way you handle situations like that.

Find the fear. Recall that we said that anger is actually a secondary emotion based on "frustration of unmet needs" that are aroused when our security is threatened, self-esteem attacked, or our feelings are hurt. The trick to controlling emotion is to determine what unmet need or desire is being frustrated. For example, a teacher may fear that all members of her class will fail an exam, which suggests that she is not teaching as well as she could. So if she gets a lot of questions during a review session prior to the exam, the teacher may suddenly turn angry and accuse her students of not studying enough. Her apparent anger is really a response to her fear that the students will fail and make her look bad. Once the teacher realizes that, she is much less likely to act angry toward her students.

Of course, the best verbal response to anger is contained in the skills we discussed in Chapters 10 and 11. Express anger responsibly, and choose the assertive option for communication rather than aggressive or passive-aggressive.

Controlling Anger

Controlling anger, then, is a matter of two things: practicing new habits so that we don't lash out during our flight-fight anger episodes and learning to express the underlying emotion when we experience the slow-building kind. How we learn to control anger depends on the more general habits we have about it.

Generally, people are anger-ins or anger-outs. **Anger-ins** are people who have a hard time even admitting that they are angry. Their response to anger is generally passive. They may sulk around, expecting you to read their minds, and become even more angry because you haven't figured out the problem. They might go so far as to burn dinner or forget to give you a telephone message. Eventually, they might become bitter or resentful toward the object of their anger. Anger-ins generally aren't the people who respond with instant hostility to fight-flight situations. But they probably have the hardest time figuring out what the underlying issue is. Anger-ins need to be given a safe space where they can express their thoughts. They need to figure out why they're really angry.

Anger-outs are people who express their anger, often quite vocally. They can erupt like a volcano. Anger-outs need to learn productive ways to blow off steam. They express their energy outward rather than hold it in. These are the door slammers and screamers. If they continue in their anger, they may humiliate the object of their anger, slander, or ostracize that person. Sometimes they are moved to bully the other or damage that person's reputation. Physical exertion, like running or other exercise, helps to focus the anger-out. Housework, particularly cleaning toilets, can be helpful (and quite symbolic!). Art and music are also ways anger-outs can learn to express anger in healthy ways. Once the energy of the anger has worn off, the anger-out needs to be introspective and work to discover the source of the anger. Overall, dealing with anger requires first that we build habits of positive rather than negative response to anger-provoking situations. It is also necessary that we get to the underlying source of the anger and that we decide what, if anything, we will do to alleviate that source of anger.

APPLICATION 14.2

Are you a person who tends to blow up? Do you express your anger calmly, or do you simply not express it at all? What are the effects of expressing anger in this way?

Understanding Sources of Anger

In her treatise on anger, Tavris argued that we need to understand the sources of our anger and the explanations we provide for feeling angry. If I decide that I am really angry at myself instead of at you, I will take very different steps to deal with that anger than if I had decided you were responsible. Tavris explained as follows:

> If Jane believes that she is not really angry with Arnold for leaving the bathroom in a mess, but "really" angry with her mother for teaching her to be angry with men who leave bathrooms in a mess, her relationship with her mother is likely to be affected; her relationship with Arnold, unchanged. If she attributes her anger to the day's stress, she may be the one who apologizes. If she thinks her anger with Arnold is legitimate, and if she convinces him that it is, she may get him to be more sensitive to her feelings. If she thinks her anger is really directed to sex-role inequities of social and cultural magnitude, she may join the women's movement and leave Arnold to do his own cleaning up.[6]

Our concern then, should not be with the issue of having anger but with the causes, effects, and appropriate and effective response to anger-arousing situations.

Tavris took issue with what she termed the *myths of suppressed anger* and the *myths of expressed anger.* Those who argue against suppressing one's anger claim that suppression can lead to stress, depression, and illness (e.g., ulcers and heart disease). Although Tavris did not deny that suppressed emotions pose some risk for those experiencing them, she noted that the connection between suppressed anger and illness has been overstated. Equally overstated are the benefits of expressing anger. The contemporary view of anger is that it is better to let everything out so that it does not build up inside; the result is that rage is reduced. Such advice "tends to overlook the social context and the consequences of anger. If your expressed rage causes another person to shoot you, it won't matter that you die with very healthy arteries."[7]

Sometimes we are advised to talk out our anger with someone else, such as a friend, parent, colleague, or bartender. This is called the ventilation approach in which we vent our anger but not to the person who we are blaming for it. The biggest problem with the ventilation approach is that simply expressing anger, without directing it toward the person responsible or toward problem solving, actually increases it. Ventilating through aggressive behavior is not an instinctive catharsis for anger. It lowers our inhibitions about acting aggressively and makes us more prone to aggressive behavior. Talking out anger does not get rid of it: Talking rehearses the anger and makes us feel it even more deeply. Tantrums and rages do not forestall neurosis: They increase it. Anger expressed in these ways is "primitive":

> It has failed to develop into mature anger and reach its optimal functioning as a positive fighting force. . . . [I]nstead of being of service to the individual, reliably available for self assertion, achievement and other ego-preserving necessities, it is not under control and spills easily into violence. . . . While this is acceptable in an infant and a normal developmental phenomenon, the manifestation of uncontrollable rage in an adult is an indication of developmental failure. In order to function as it should, anger must become a controlled, reliable weapon in the hands of a responsible but assertive individual.[8]

As we discussed earlier, people have different styles of responding to anger: anger-outs, anger-ins, and **anger controllers** (those who try to be patient and are able to stop themselves from sounding off). Anger controllers get angry less often and behave less aggressively than those with the other two styles.[9] And contrary to popular conceptions of the way men and women act, males score consistently more highly on the tendency to be anger-ins. There are no sex differences on the tendency to be anger-outs. In fact, "men and women are equally likely to keep quiet when they feel angry, or talk it out, or scream it out, or even get violent. . . . It does not depend on gender and it does not depend on personality."[10]

Anger is best expressed and most effective when several conditions are met.[11]

1. Anger must be directed at the target of the anger. Suppose, for example, you are really angry at your boss because your hours were changed without consulting you, and they now conflict with your classes. You probably do not feel you can yell at your boss, so instead you go home and slam things around the house and yell at your roommate. The trouble is that such actions are unlikely to reduce your anger. Instead, you will probably be more angry when you are done because you will find additional things wrong with your boss as you remember all the other inequities you have experienced in your job.

2. Expressing anger has to restore a person's sense of justice and of control over the situation while inflicting appropriate harm on the other person. Going into your boss's office and screaming might feel very good, but it is unlikely to get your hours changed. And if your boss changed your hours simply because of forgetfulness rather than because of a malicious intent, screaming at the boss is too great a reaction for the situation.

3. Expressing anger gives a person a sense of control over the situation if that expression changes the behavior of the other person (your boss says, "I'm sorry, I forgot that you had class on Monday and Wednesday afternoons") or if it provides new insights. (You realize the boss frequently changes employees' hours without consulting them and that because work hours are important to you, you need a new job).

4. It is best to express anger not when angry but after cooling down.

5. For the expression of anger to be effective, there must be no angry retaliation from the target. This last condition is unfortunately the hardest to create. We have yet to meet more than a handful of people who can let someone else express anger at them without responding in kind. To help meet this last condition, anger must be expressed responsibly. Tavris noted that "the result of the ability to control anger is that people feel less angry, not more."[12]

APPLICATION 14.3

Under what conditions have you found yourself expressing your anger appropriately? How was the situation different from a time that you felt your anger got the best of you? What do you think you could do to duplicate the situation in which you expressed your anger constructively?

Responding to Another's Anger

One of the more difficult things we must face in a conflict is the anger and possible rage another person is feeling. Often our fear about the way another will react affects our ability to solve a problem, as this narrative suggests:

> Over the years, my husband has become more calm, but he still can lose his temper over small things pretty easily. When he loses his temper, he scares me. He's a big guy, and seeing all that muscle tense up makes me want to hide. I kept trying to hide a credit card bill from him because I was afraid to tell him what a mess I had made. I was afraid he might even hit me when he found out. He finally got to the mail before I did, and I got ready for the worst. I was really relieved when he controlled himself.

When you are dealing with someone who is extremely angry, it is important to do what you can to stay calm and not feed their anger. Often people are loudly angry because they fear no one will listen to them unless they yell and scream. Listening and reflecting are important skills in responding to another person's anger. Equally important is acknowledging the importance of the source of anger. If you say something to the effect of "I can't believe you are reacting this way" or "I think you are being childish" you will fuel that person's anger rather than subdue it. When a person is on the verge of rage, it is not the time to express *your* anger about the situation. You need to focus on calming that person down before raising any issue of your own. If your attempts to acknowledge the other person's source of anger and the legitimacy of their feelings fail, and the person continues to rage and fume, it is often a good idea to exit the situation. Saying something such as "I can see you're really angry, and I think I'd like to give you some time to cool off before we talk about it" acknowledges that you sympathize with the other and have a commitment to work out whatever problem is there, but postpones the conflict until both people are calm and ready to talk about it.

Containing Escalation

Controlling anger has the biggest impact on controlling the escalation of a conflict. The research discussed in Chapter 9 suggests that it is not the absence of conflict that makes marital couples happy, but their ability to contain its escalation. In addition to getting really angry and erupting like a volcano, we think the following list of behaviors are virtually guaranteed to escalate a conflict into a small-scale war, so they are best avoided.

- Tell everyone but the person involved about the conflict.
- When the other person says what is bothering him or her, come back with a "Well, you" response and tell that person what you don't like in the situation.
- Listen closely so that you can pick apart what the other person is saying.
- Argue over the way something is stated rather than what is being said.
- Call the other person names.
- Remind the other person of every stupid thing he or she has ever done with respect to the issue at hand.
- Disregard the other person's feelings. Especially effective: "You shouldn't feel that way."
- Tell people that you know their situation better than they do. Especially effective: "I know exactly how you feel."
- Make threats. Especially effective: "If I can't have it my way, I won't do anything at all."
- Indicate that nothing can change and you're both doomed to failure anyway.
- Ask the impossible of the other person.

These things will help contain the escalation of conflict. Do these:

- Be aware of your behavior.
- Try to anticipate the effect that your words and actions will have on others. It does minimize the amount of conflict you need to experience.
- Try to keep the other focused on the here and now. Past history should stay out of the conversation as much as possible.
- Be open to what others have to say. Let them say what they are feeling and accept it as a legitimate feeling, if not a legitimate criticism.
- Negotiate acceptable boundaries with others. Not everything a person says needs to be acted on. Consider Aesop's fable of the man, his son, and the donkey. A man and his son are walking from the countryside into town alongside the donkey. In response to one person's criticism that they are not using the donkey efficiently, the man puts his son on the donkey. Another person criticizes, so he rides the donkey while the boy walks. Another person criticizes, so both ride the donkey. Another person criticizes, and they decide to carry the donkey, strung upside down on a stick over their shoulders. On the town bridge over a river, they accidentally drop the donkey into the river, and being bound, the donkey drowns. *Don't drown the donkey!*

Stress and the Escalation of Conflict

There's a bumper sticker that reads "If you're not living on the edge, you're taking up too much space." There are people who like stress. They like to live fast, drive fast, eat fast. They even like conflicts! But these people are generally the exception.

Many people believe that conflicts cause stress in our lives. We believe the opposite: The stress we are feeling intrapersonally in our lives often erupts into conflict with others. Usually, interpersonal conflict textbooks stress the idea that conflict is stressful. Of course, when we are focused on an upsetting problem, dreading a confrontation with someone in authority, and looking at conflict negatively, we are likely to experience stress. To the extent that you accept our philosophy and welcome the techniques and skills offered in this book, you should find that conflict management and resolution will reduce your stress and make your life more enjoyable.

In this section, we take a different view of stress based on the observation that when others explode, jump all over us, or overreact in a conflict situation, we usually find that they have other personal problems that make it difficult for them to behave more predictably. These outside problems have produced stress and one more problem is too much for them. So here we consider the situation in which stress contributes to the escalation of conflict. We'll talk about what stress is, sources of stress, its impact on conflicts you have with others, and how to deal with it.

Walker and Brokaw define **stress** as something that "arises when the perceived demands of a situation exceed the perceived capacities for meeting the demands"; we would add that stress also occurs when we fear that the demands on us might exceed our capacities, even when we have not been given a reason to fear.[13] Both negative and positive events can be stressful. Few people would doubt that an IRS audit is stressful, and almost all people will find enduring a root canal to be a high-stress situation. On the other hand, getting married, we presume, is a happy occasion, and yet it causes a great deal of stress as the bride and groom make arrangements, get to know their new in-laws, and commit themselves to one another. Giving a dinner party is also pleasurable, but the demands of preparation may cause stress.

Selye has identified four kinds of stress.[14] **Eustress** is a good kind; it is short-term stress that allows us to engage in important activities. For example, a hitter stepping up to the plate in a major league baseball game experiences eustress—he is psyched up to perform. A student getting ready to write a paper about a subject he or she has mastered also is experiencing eustress. We experience eustress when we feel control over the situation. We know that we are able to make choices and have the necessary resources to meet the demand.

A second kind of stress is **distress.** This arises when we don't feel control over the situation, or when the source of stress may be unclear. Generally, distress arises over a period of time. For example, if you are harassed by someone at work once, it may be uncomfortable but probably will not cause distress. However, if over a period of time you are unable to predict how this coworker will respond to you, and you are harassed repeatedly despite requests to the coworker to stop, you will experience distress.

Hyperstress is a kind of stress frequently experienced by students. This happens when many things pile up on us and we are unable to adapt to the changes or cope with all that is happening at once. If in the same week that you have three midterms, your parents call you to tell you they are divorcing, and you receive notice of several bounced checks, you will be a candidate for hyperstress.

Finally, people may experience **hypostress,** or underload. This happens when we're bored or unchallenged by our situations. If you are employed in a job that is repetitive and requires little adaptation on your part, you may experience hypostress and find yourself more and more unwilling to go to work.

APPLICATION 14.4

What are the various sources of stress you have in your life? Which are good stress factors? Which are not? How can you reduce the bad stress factors?

Sources of Stress

Stress can arise from a number of sources in our lives. Sometimes we experience stress as an internal conflict over the things that we should do or over a disparity between how we see ourselves and the kinds of activities we are engaged in. **Stressors** or sources of stress can include:

1. anticipated life events, such as graduation
2. unexpected life events, such as the death of a loved one or the loss of a job, or too much happening at once
3. the need to make a decision (e.g., should I go to grad school or get married?)
4. struggle among the various roles we play and how much time and attention we should give to each one (e.g., you're all these things: a student, a child, a friend, a part-time worker, and a romantic partner)

Some people respond to stress negatively through **defensive coping mechanisms,** or methods we have learned through experience that will help us to feel less stress, at least in the short run. Some of these are external—eating too much, drinking, using drugs, driving dangerously, taking unnecessary risks. Some are internal and consist of various messages we create for ourselves in order to make sense of a situation. As you will recall from Chapter 7, psychodynamic theory examines the relationship between intrapersonal states and nonsubstantive types of conflict, discussed in Chapter 4, such as bickering and aggression. We make sense of our engagement in these nonsubstantive conflicts by producing defense mechanisms such as rationalization, repression, projection, reaction formation, sublimation, and displacement.

We **rationalize** when we defend questionable behavior or our reactions to stress with reasons that simply aren't connected to the behavior. "I blew up at you because I am having a really bad day" is a reason. Is it a good one? Many people will accept it occasionally, but not as a regular reason for behavior. We expect others to contain their stress and not take it out on us. We **repress** when we try not to think about our situation. Sometimes we manage to hide the painful thought so well that we "forget" about an important (but stressful) event we were to attend. Scarlett O'Hara vocalized this process in *Gone With the Wind* when she would say, "I won't think about that today. I'll think about that tomorrow." Some people **project** when they are stressed. They attribute what they are feeling to others rather than owning the feeling themselves. If you really would rather not room with your roommate any longer, you may accuse him or her of wanting to move out rather than admitting it yourself. Another means of negative coping is **reaction formation,** when people do the opposite of their true feelings. Homophobia is seen by some as a reaction formation—those who are most afraid that they are homosexual, or who sometimes have homosexual urges, rage about how wrong it is to be one.

People can also negatively cope through **sublimation.** This happens when they put their efforts toward something socially desirable in order to deal with the stress of some event in their life. For example, sometimes people who feel their parents don't approve of them cope by working hard and achieving a great deal in life. But the achievements aren't meaningful to them because they haven't dealt with the source of the stress and substantive conflict issue, which is parental disapproval. A final means of negative coping with stress is **displacement.** Displaced conflict is a type we talked about in Chapter 4—when people do conflict with a "safe" person rather than the person who is actually involved in the conflict. This is the "kick the dog" syndrome, and certainly is negative for the dog!

APPLICATION 14.5

Which of the negative stress coping mechanisms do you tend to use? How can you reduce your reliance on these negative mechanisms?

You'll probably agree that these nonsubstantive conflicts are negative means of coping and should be avoided. But how do you cope with stress in a positive way? Personal characteristics affect the way people respond to stress. Some people, for example, are simply "hardier" than others. They are involved in their jobs and families, they believe they can control their lives, and they see change as a challenge rather than as a threat. Can you become hardy? It is partly a matter of the way you think about stressors, and, as we will show, you can change your thinking.

Probably the most important tool available for managing stressful events is our thought processes. How we think about things affects the way we perceive the events we experience. This in turn has a major impact on how we choose to respond to them, and whether we engage in conflicts with others. McKinnon, Wiesse, Reynolds, Bowles, and Baum claim, "The way in which a stressor is interpreted, more than the stressor's properties, predicts the intensity, nature, and duration of physiological and psychological response."[15] We can't escape decisions. We will nearly always be experiencing the pressure of time and role demands.

We begin with the observation that the same event produces different reactions in people. Practically any event is interpreted by some as good, others as indifferent, and still others as a disaster. We believe that the difference lies in our way to thinking about the event. Perhaps our approach to stress management will be clearer if we refer to it as the ABC approach:

A = the activating event or stressor

B = our relevant beliefs or thoughts

C = consequences or effects and reaction to the stressor

Of course, it would be nice to change A and eliminate the stressor from our lives. There are two ways to do that: change the environment (turn off the computer if it is stressing you today) or change environments (pick up and leave; go somewhere else). Unfortunately, each life event we encounter (courtship, weddings, childbirth, taxes, death, applying for jobs, promotions, etc.) all produce some degree of stress. So we don't always want to eliminate the stressor or can't even if we want to. In such cases, we can change B and interpret, perceive, or label the activating event in a more constructive or positive way. We are saying that when you cannot easily change your circumstances, then change yourself (or at least the way you think).

Let's begin with a common activating event (A)—someone rejects you. Maybe she or he doesn't ask you to go shopping, or vote for you, or call you when you would like. It is at this point that we want to impress upon you that you have a choice as to what to think (B). Here are two alternatives (perhaps more will occur to you):

1. I must be awful; I shouldn't be rejected by anyone, I will never be accepted by others, I am a worthless person, I deserve to be damned for being so unpopular, I wish someone could do some magic and change me into a better person.
2. I don't like this, I wish it hadn't happened, it was unfortunate, undesirable, we would have had a lot of fun together, I am good company, she or he doesn't know what she or he is missing, I'll go do something I know that I want to do.

If you choose to think #1, the consequences (C) are likely to be that you will get very upset, become disorganized, panic, suffer severe anxiety, and maybe even go into depression. The next person to say or do the wrong thing may push you over the edge and you will explode. If you choose to think #2, the consequences (C) are likely to be that you will feel sorrowful initially, perhaps a bit regretful, irritated, or frustrated. However, there is no need to overreact and get down on yourself. You can figure out a way to make the best of the situation. The next person to say or do the wrong thing is not adding fuel to a raging fire, so you can respond in a constructive or positive way if you find yourself in a conflict situation.

The key point here is that if you choose #1, you upset yourself. This is like a self-fulfilling prophecy in that if you expect the worse, you are likely to get it. Here is a list of thoughts that contribute to stress and the escalation of conflict: irrational thinking, ineffectual thinking, self-damaging thinking habits, self-damning, wishful thinking, intolerance, pessimism, expecting the worst, perfectionistic thinking, expecting some magic, being superstitious, being dogmatic, blaming, damning others for everything, Type A or Type B personality. In addition, being too other-directed (or accommodating) can be a problem when you think too much about what others think of you. If your self-acceptance depends on what others think, you lose control of who you are—which is a very stressful event! On the other hand, being too self-directed (or competitive) is also a problem when you think you must win every argument, always come out on top, and have to show up the opposition. If your self-acceptance depends on being number one, the fear of failure will be a constant source of stress.

So how can you control your thoughts to reduce your stress? The first step is to discover the ways in which your self-talk can be contributing to your stress. Table 14.1 shows how different ways of thinking about the same event can increase or reduce stress.

We're not suggesting that you ignore the reality of the situation when you engage in supportive self-talk. What we are suggesting, however, is that if you can avoid "doom and gloom" thinking about situations and focus on the power and choices you do have within them, you can reduce your stress level. Ellis claims that it is not events that cause us to be stressed but how we talk to ourselves about the events that causes our stress.[16] Consider how this person handled a stressful situation:

> There's a person at my work who is really unpredictable. I never know if he's going to snarl at me or say hello. It really began to get me down, and I'd slink around the hallways hoping I wouldn't run into him. But whose life was being ruined? Mine. So I decided I'd be cheerful and greet him and to heck with him if he wants to be nasty. At least I'll know I acted like a nice person.

TABLE 14.1   *The Effect of Self-Talk on Stress*

Situation	*Self-Talk Increasing Stress*	*Self-Talk Decreasing Stress*
Romantic	I'll never find someone like him (her) again.	I enjoyed my time with him (her) and I know there's someone else out there.
Failing a test	I'm so stupid. I won't pass.	I can do other things to bring up my class grade. I can study differently next time.
Getting a speeding ticket	A bunch of people were going faster. Why me?	I was going over the speed limit. I will concentrate more on my driving.

Self-talk, in order to be helpful, needs to be rational. Three unhelpful kinds of statements are *shoulds, awfuls,* and *overgeneralizations.* Shoulds have to do with the expectations we have for ourselves, for others close to us, and for the world in general. Should statements also contain words like *ought, must,* and *have to.* Some of the shoulds are unreasonable and create expectations that are impossible to meet. Consider how this person responds to shoulds:

> Three of us meet regularly to gripe and complain to each other as well as encourage each other. All three of us came from rotten families and we have committed to letting go of the negative messages of our childhood. All three of us have lots of "shoulds" in our lives—I should be a better parent, I should spend more time with my spouse, I should be a better worker, I should this, I should that. When one of us starts to talk this way, we tell that person to stop "shoulding" on himself.

Recognizing when you are "shoulding on yourself" is one way to escape negative self-talk. Another kind of negative self-talk is the awful statements. When people talk about how horrible their circumstances are, or the fact that it is simply unbearable, it is pretty easy to start thinking that nothing can change. Continuing self-talk that makes change seem unlikely will probably result in situations that do not change.

A final means of negative self-talk is overgeneralizations. Overgeneralizations have words such as *always, never, everyone,* and *no one* in them. Overgeneralizations happen when people think one event is indicative of their entire life. You failed a test, so you're a complete failure. Someone didn't listen to you in this one instance, and that person never listens to you. And so on.

Negative self-talk is a poor means of controlling your thoughts in a situation. It leads to stress and the need for more self-talk. When you are in a situation in which you cannot control other people's responses, you still have control over your own. Recognizing that is a way of reducing the stress that you feel about the situation. In the following sections, we give you some questions to ask yourself when you are faced with various types of stressors in your life.

APPLICATION 14.6

List two or three stressors you are facing right now. What kind of negative self-talk are you engaging in that makes the stress worse? How can you turn your self-talk around so that it will reduce your stress level?

Facing the Expected Event

A source of stress with expected events is that we want them to be perfect and memorable, and we are stressed when they don't turn out as we wish. You'll only graduate with your bachelor's degree once, and you want your relatives there not fighting and looking proud. You don't want them to get lost on the way to the ceremony, or for them to be angry because they couldn't find you in the crowd, and so on. This narrative describes one person's response to an expected event stressor:

> Christmas only comes once a year. I love Christmas. I love singing the carols in church. So when my son is misbehaving and I can't really sing, it bothers me a lot. This year was no different. I keep thinking "Isn't he old enough to just settle down?" and I keep hoping it is this year and it's not. I just began to cry. And then he got upset because I was crying. I realized it was because I want this perfect family standing in the pew singing carols together and we are so far from perfect that it is depressing to me.

The source of stress in this situation is unrealistic expectations of the event. The answer, then, is creating some realistic ones. Are there perfect ceremonies? Or perfect families? Of course not. Could this person choose to think differently about how the family should behave at Christmas? Ellis recommends these four steps to deal with irrational thoughts that cause stress:

1. Monitor your emotional reactions. List all the unpleasant feelings you are having.
2. Describe the activating event. Identify what seems to be triggering these unpleasant feelings and your present stressful condition.
3. Record your self-talk. Determine what you say to yourself that is causing you to interpret these activating events in a way that produces so much stress. What are you thinking? Why are you worried? What are you saying to yourself that is making you depressed or angry?
4. Dispute your irrational beliefs. Go back to step 3, and (a) decide whether each statement is a rational or an irrational belief; (b) determine why the belief does or does not make sense; and (c) create some different statements that you can say to yourself in the future to prevent such stress.[17]

Facing Unexpected Events

A significant source of stress is too many unanticipated things at one time. People easily become overwhelmed by the demands on their time. In addition, stress can be created through unanticipated personal setbacks or losses. When stress is created through loss of a loved one or setbacks (e.g., being fired, failing an important test, etc.), it is helpful to find external support systems. Talk to your friends, find people who have experienced the same kind of loss. Don't get locked into an "ain't it awful" game, in which you exchange increasingly awful comments about the situation, but try to get focused on what you can do to respond to the situation.

When stress is created through too many competing demands, it helps to start off with a basic understanding of time: Everything has an opportunity cost associated with it. If you play now, you have to work later. If you date one person, you may not be able to date another. If you do well in one class, you may have to sacrifice another. Dealing with competing demands becomes a matter of asking questions and setting priorities.

1. Ask yourself, "Am I being driven by the tyranny of the urgent?" We are not suggesting that everyone live with appointment books and priority lists. But often we let something control us in the present that does not have to.
2. Try to determine which of the demands made on you will have a greater impact on your life in the long run. For example, if you are choosing between doing well on a paper for a major class, or a paper for a class outside your major, you need to ask which paper you will learn more from in the long run. It may be the one outside your major.
3. Try to stave off competing demands by having at least a loosely defined priority list and schedule. Becoming too schedule-bound is counterproductive—then you are a slave to your organizational scheme. It needs to serve you, not you to serve it.
4. Remember that in the long run, many things will not matter as much to you in retrospect.

Facing Decision-Making Events

According to Deutsch, problems in decision making lead to three types of situations:[18]

1. Approach-approach: A person is torn between two desires. A variation on this is when the achievement of one desire makes the other impossible, and the alternatives are not mutually substitutive.
2. Avoidance-avoidance: A person is caught between two fears.
3. Approach-avoidance: A person fears to approach something that is desired.

The strength of your response tendency, to approach or to avoid, is determined by your closeness to your desired or feared object, as well as your habit strength, the strength of the drive associated with it, and the stimulus intensity or incentive value of the stimulus. As each competing response tendency gains strength, the stress, and therefore the conflict associated with it, becomes harder to avoid.

> Thus, a conflict will be more difficult to resolve if each conflicting behavior tendency has an intense motivation underlying it, has a strong habit strength as a result of the prior history of reward associated with it, and has strongly activating stimuli connected with it. One can also assume that the more equal the competing tendencies are in strength, the greater will be the difficulty in resolving the conflict.[19]

Suppose you are a graduating senior who is considering graduate school. You also are seriously dating someone whom you might marry. If you feel that these situations are not compatible with each other, you are in an approach-approach conflict—torn between two desires. You have a habit strength associated with going to school if you generally have felt successful in doing so. If you have earned good grades and have perceived that you have been rewarded for doing so, the strength of the drive toward continued schooling will be strong. If relationships are something you have not felt as successful in, you will have a lower drive strength associated with the relationship. Given the phenomenon of the "senior clutch," in which everyone seems to be picking life partners, you will have a stronger set of activating stimuli associated with getting married than you will with going to graduate school.

Or suppose you are thinking of starting a relationship with someone, but you have had bad experiences in the past. This would be an approach-avoidance conflict. You want the relationship, but you fear that you will not be successful. Your approach side has intense motivation, but your habit strength is associated with avoidance (due to lack of rewards in prior relationships). On the other hand, if all of your friends are in relationships and you are not, you will have strongly activating stimuli pushing you toward the relationship.

In an avoidance-avoidance situation, one overwhelming desire is to simply leave the situation and refuse to make a decision at all (if this is possible).

Facing a Situation of Competing or Difficult Roles

Often we are asked to be different things to different people. We need to ask what the roles are that are being assigned to us, which are in conflict with one another, and what part of the roles present problems to us. Deutsch argues that:

> Although an individual may be both adequately and appropriately socialized, he [she] may nevertheless find himself [herself] confronted with conflicting expectations that exceed his [her] ability, and, as a consequence, he [she] may experience inner conflict and exhibit deviant behavior.[20]

Viewing deviance as a failure to conform to norms governing goals or means gives us four ways of understanding role conformity and deviance.

1. Innovation—the person accepts the prescribed goals and rejects the prescribed means, and may involve either the covert use of forbidden methods or the attempt to introduce and obtain public acceptance of new methods as a substitute for old ones. For example, Roxane considers herself "innovative" as a mother—she accepts the prescribed goals of raising her children, clothing them, and educating them, but she often rejects conventional schooling methods for them (she will take them out for a good experience elsewhere like travel or performing in a play here at the college), and she doesn't see providing food as the primary means of demonstrating love.

2. Ritualism—the person conforms to culturally approved means but fails to strive for the culturally accepted goals. For example, a woman may do all the household chores expected of her in raising children but never really interacts with them. She goes through the motions.

3. Retreatism—the person rejects both the culturally approved goals and means without any attempt to change them. It is expressed by withdrawal from direct involvement. Continuing the example of mothering, it would be the mother who neither provides for the basic needs of her children nor cares about their needs for love, belonging, and so on.

4. Rebellion—the person rejects both the culturally accepted goals and means and makes an active attempt to substitute new ones. Families living separatist lifestyles within cultlike groups like the Freemen may be examples of this (with respect to mothering).

Dealing with role stress is partly a matter of deciding how you will respond with respect to the role you have been given. What are your options? What are your resources? What choices can you make in the situation?

Ways to Alleviate Stress

We argued earlier in this chapter that stress is often a cause of conflict, rather than the other way around. Walker and Brokaw suggest several ways to avoid and alleviate stress.[21]

First, we can avoid stress by minimizing the number of irrational thoughts we entertain. We can monitor our emotional reactions to things and ask what feelings different events are arousing in us. We can attempt to find the trigger event and determine why it caused stress for us. We can record our self-talk and make sure it is positive rather than negative. When you write down what you are saying to yourself, for example, "I am a failure because I got an F on this algebra test," it is easier to see that it is irrational. By writing down your self-talk, you can also dispute your irrational beliefs by writing down rational statements instead. If your negative self-talk includes a statement such as "I'll never understand this subject," you can dispute that by listing the things you already do understand and listing places where you can seek help on this section.

Managing stress once it occurs can also head off the escalation of conflict that occurs because of it. Walker and Brokaw suggest these steps:

- work off stress through physical exertion
- enjoy yourself by rewarding yourself with some pleasure
- talk it out with a trusted friend who will move you toward doing something about it (not the same as venting anger)
- give in occasionally when in a quarrel
- do something for others
- have some real close friends
- eat sensibly
- get organized
- rehearse stressful situations ahead of time
- do your most difficult task first (or as the saying goes, "Eat a frog first thing in the morning and it's the worst thing you'll have to do all day.")
- learn to say "no"
- learn to accept what you cannot change
- avoid self-medication (alcohol, drugs, etc.)
- live a balanced life
- get enough sleep and rest
- get involved with others
- don't try to be a superhero
- exercise regularly
- take care of yourself
- learn to relax

If you are doing your best to alleviate stress as it occurs, and to avoid bad stress when you can, you are much less likely to engage in destructive conflicts. When we are stressed, it is more difficult to practice good communication skills. It is difficult to be empathic. It is difficult to hear another person out and want to respond to them. Keeping stress at an optimum level is a way of ensuring competence in communication situations.

From Theory to Action

Anger and stress have three things in common. First, they both arise from other events. We feel anger because we are hurt, or disappointed, or frustrated. We feel stress because of things outside our control and because of how we are perceiving our life events. Both anger and stress, therefore, are secondary kinds of emotions. We will deal with them most effectively if we can change how we view the events that are producing anger and stress for us.

Second, both anger and stress serve to escalate conflicts and muddy the waters within them. When we are angry, or stressed, it is difficult to communicate competently. It is difficult to remember that assertive, not aggressive or avoiding, responses will be most effective.

Most importantly, though, we are going to feel both anger and stress. They are unavoidable. What we do with each, though, is within our control. We can learn to express anger constructively. We can learn to rid ourselves of thoughts that contribute to stress, and to manage other sources of stress as they arise. And we can choose not to let our conflicts be driven by anger and stress-related behaviors.

Notes

1. J. Giles Milhaven, *Good Anger* (Kansas City, MO: Sheed and Ward, 1989), p. 106.

2. Carol Tavris, *Anger: The Misunderstood Emotion* (New York: Touchstone, through Simon and Schuster, 1989), p. 272.

3. Harriet Goldhor Lerner, *The Dance of Anger: A Woman's Guide to Changing the Patterns of Intimate Relationships* (New York: Harper and Row, 1985), p. 3.

4. Tim LaHaye and Bob Phillips, *Anger Is a Choice* (Grand Rapids: Zondervan, 1982).

5. Joyce Hocker and William Wilmot, *Interpersonal Conflict,* 4th Ed. (Dubuque, IA: Wm. C. Brown, 1995), p. 175.

6. Tavris, *Anger,* p. 19.

7. Ibid., p. 129.

8. Meira Likerman, "The Function of Anger in Human Conflict," *International Review of Psychoanalysis* 14 (1987), p. 152.

9. Charles Spielberg, Susan S. Krasner, and Eldra P. Solomon, "The Experience, Expression and Control of Anger," in M. P. Janisse (Ed.), *Health Psychology: Individual Differences and Stress* (New York: Springer-Verlag, 1988), pp. 89–108.

10. Tavris, *Anger,* p. 203.

11. Ibid., pp. 152–154.

12. Ibid., p. 1899.

13. V. Walker and L. Brokaw, *Becoming Aware,* 6th Ed. (Dubuque, IA: Kendall Hunt, 1995), p. 315.

14. H. Selye, *Stress without Distress* (New York: J. B. Lippincott, 1974).

15. W. McKinnon, C. S. Wiesse, C. P. Reynolds, C. A. Bowles, and A. Baum "Chronic Stress, Leukocyte Subpopulations, and Humoral Response to Latent Viruses," *Health Psychology* 8 (1989), pp. 389–402.

16. Albert Ellis, "Overview of the Clinical Theory of Rational-Emotive Therapy," in Grieger and J. Boyd (Eds.), *Rational-Emotive Therapy: A Skills-Based Approach* (New York: Van Nostrand Reinhold, 1980).

17. Alfred Ellis, *A New Guide to Rational Living* (N. Hollywood: Wilshire Book, 1975).

18. Morton Deutsch, *The Resolution of Conflict* (New Haven: Yale University Press, 1973).

19. Ibid., p. 35.

20. Ibid., p. 38.

21. Walker and Brokaw, *Becoming Aware.*

15

Impression Management in Conflict Situations

Objectives

At the end of this chapter, you should be able to

1. explain the difference between positive face and negative face.
2. identify at least three preventative strategies you can use to avoid threatening the other person's face in a conflict situation.
3. use the accounting sequence to explain a conflict you have experienced.

Key Terms

account
acknowledgment
apologies
concessions
disclaimers
excuses
face

facework
impression management
justifications
legislation
negative face
positive face
reaffirmation

remediation
remedy
reproach
social confrontation
social predicament

In the preface to this book, we made clear a fundamental assumption that underlies our approach to interpersonal conflict: People are motivated to create and maintain favorable impressions of themselves with others and this motivation may generate or exacerbate conflict situations. In this chapter, we want to address an important skill in developing competent conflict behavior and that is the ability to maintain one's own impression and that of others to avoid escalating the conflict and to restore a relationship if face is lost.

Understanding the Demands of Face

Defining Face

By impression, we mean what sociologist Goffman termed **face** (people's image of themselves).[1] Chapter 5 discussed competitive conflict escalation cycles, a pattern exacerbated by the introduction of face issues, or issues that threaten the way in which participants see themselves. Conflict literature is pretty clear in this point: The introduction of face issues into a conflict can escalate the severity of the conflict, making it very difficult for people to resolve the original issue. This chapter discusses the concept of face and impression management in more detail to show its importance in conflict situations.

The concept of face is fundamental to whom we think we are. According to Goffman, we all have images of ourselves and we project that image (our face) in interactions with others. As we interact, we also look for confirmation of the face we present. The projection of face is cooperative—as long as the image we project seems consistent and believable, you will accept it and respond to it as presented. Likewise, as long as you present a consistent image, we will cooperate with you and accept the image you have presented. The mutual cooperation involved in projecting face is a taken-for-granted principle of interaction. Being able to create and sustain an identity for oneself, as well as helping the other person to create and maintain an identity for himself or herself, is a fundamental component of communication competence, according to Cupach and Metts. It is through the establishment and maintenance of identities that we create rewards for ourselves in social interaction; as a consequence, facework has important consequences for relationships. The authors note, "At its best, effective face support permits us to achieve (however fleeting) relationship nirvana. At its worst, persistent face loss can create bitter enmity and personal agony."[2]

As you read in Chapter 8, competence includes appropriateness and effectiveness. Now we add the idea of consistency. Impression management issues frequently concern problems of continuity in the impression that is being presented. For example, Bill may accuse Steve of acting inconsistently with Steve's previously stated beliefs. An accusation of inconsistency is a threat to Steve's face, and he must work to restore it. The term **facework** includes the many behaviors people use in order to attack, defend, and maintain face with each other: preventative strategies, accounts, apologies, and confrontation.

APPLICATION 15.1

You can support another's face in a general way or specifically. In a general way, people want to be liked, respected, encouraged, consulted, included, appreciated, rewarded, referred to, asked, greeted warmly, helped when needed, and made to feel safe. Ask yourself if you do the following when in a conflict:

- Do I try to make the other feel like an important person?
- Do I try to make the other look good to other people?
- Do I try to make the other feel that he or she is winning?
- Do I try to make the other feel secure?
- Do I try to make the other believe that I am honest and trustworthy?

We can support others in a general way by what we do and what we say. If we don't include, consult, ask, reward, or help others, they may feel put down by our actions. It is also possible to put people down verbally by insulting them or showing disrespect.

We can also support others in a more specific way. To do this, you need to determine what traits or characteristics the other perceives in himself or herself and point out the ones you have in common or are capable of supporting.

- You like to fish? Well, so do I.
- I like people with red hair.
- You're a jogger, so let's jog together next time.
- You have taken three classes from Professor Hamad. I hope to take a class from her soon.
- We both want to lose weight.

If our goal in a conflict is to inflict serious mental harm on another person, we can resort to verbal abuse and put down the other. If our goal is to solve a problem, then we want to avoid abuse in favor of face support.

The concept of face is important to the study of conflict because threats to face are most likely to occur (and to need addressing) within conflict situations. According to Tracy, any interaction is potentially face threatening;[3] but in conflicts, in which people face incompatible goals or activities and share the feeling that the other is somehow interfering with their own pursuit of rewards and goals, face threats are bound to be present.

Positive and Negative Face

In a seminal work, Brown and Levinson concluded that people experience two kinds of face needs.[4] Positive face is the desire people have to be liked and respected by those important to them. A person's **positive face** is supported when others appear to value what the person values, or express admiration for the person, or show acceptance of the person as a competent individual. **Negative face** is the desire people have to be free from constraints and impositions. When others respect a person's autonomy and independence, the person's negative face is supported. The desires for positive and negative face, under the best of circumstances, can create a dilemma. One may communicate support of another's positive face by expressing admiration for that person, spending time with that person, and so on but, by doing so, can encroach on the person's autonomy. So supporting a person's positive and negative face requires a balance under the best of circumstances. Consider how these competing needs are threatened in a conflict situation:

> I would say that the biggest conflict in my life arises when my girlfriend gets emotional. Of the girlfriends I have had, I have never dated one as emotional as my current girlfriend. The conflict usually comes when I have had a hard day and still have things to do in the evening. My girlfriend will come over and yell at me for ignoring her and not really loving her because I have been gone all day. When I try to tell her I have been busy and I still have things to do, the conflict becomes worse. She starts to cry and becomes crazy. At this point, I cannot deal with the situation and want to hide under a rock. The conflict usually has to defuse itself by me leaving and not speaking to her until later that evening or the next day. When she becomes calm, things start to work out and the situation is resolved, but sometimes it can last for a week or so.

Whereas the man's positive face is supported by his partner's desire to be with him, his negative face is threatened by her need for too much of his limited time. Their conflicts arise out of the need to support both positive and negative face. To help solve the dilemma posed by competing desires for positive and negative face, people engage in preventive facework: avoiding or minimizing threats to face. If a threat to face is made, they use corrective facework: alleviating the problem through corrective action.

APPLICATION 15.2

How have you seen issues of negative and positive face create conflicts in your experience? What have you done to resolve issues of negative and positive face? Are the strategies you use for each different?

Preventing Face Threats

How can we avoid getting embroiled in face-saving issues during conflict situations? One way is to try to see the situation from the other's perspective—how the issue affects the other and the other's self-image. Another way is to accept what the other person says at face value (no pun intended). Unless there is a very good reason to the contrary, it is best to accept what the other person says as an accurate reflection of his or her feelings. Probes for more information can be made by asking, "What do you mean by that?" but it should not sound threatening. A third way to avoid face-saving issues is to accept the other person's right to change his or her mind. No one can predict the future with any degree of accuracy. The fact is that goals change, people change, life changes. To treat a change in goals as a sign of the other person's insincerity or instability threatens the other person and sets up future conflicts concerning that very issue.

People can also avoid threats to face by avoiding face-threatening topics (which is almost impossible in a conflict situation) or by employing communication practices that minimize threats to face. Communication practices such as politeness and **disclaimers** (additions to the message that soften the forcefulness of the message) help to minimize threats to face before they happen. This narrative illustrates how to maximize a face threat.

> Just recently, my mother was expressing her dissatisfaction to me about the host in the dining room at the retirement home where she lives. She came a little late to lunch and found that "her" table had dishes all over it. Instead of moving to a different table or asking that the dishes be removed, she turned to the host and said, "When are you going to start doing your job?" As she told me the story, she was amazed that the host had subsequently been rude to her. I tried explaining conflict message skills to her, but someone with as much practice at doing things nastily as my mother is disinclined to change.

In the preceding conflict situation, for example, the person making the complaint could have used either of the following disclaimers to soften the effect of the complaint:

- hedging—which indicates uncertainty and receptivity to suggestions. "Is this my table? It doesn't seem to have gotten cleared yet."
- cognitive disclaimer—you assert that the behavior is reasonable and under control, despite appearances. "I don't want to sound demanding, but I'd really like to sit down now and the dirty table is bothering me."

Other disclaimers available in a conflict situation include:

- credentialing—which indicates you have good reasons and appropriate qualifications for the statement you will make. For example, "I am your friend and I care about you, so I want to say . . ."
- sin license—which indicates that this is an appropriate occasion to violate the rule and the violation should not be taken as a character defect. (For example, "Well, this is a special occasion and . . .")
- appeal for suspended judgment—which asks the other to withhold judgment for a possibly offensive action until it has been explained. ("Hear me out before you get upset . . .")[5]

When a threat to face has been made, corrective action needs to be taken. One means of corrective action is simply to act as though no threat to face has been made, ignoring the action that caused a face threat. Although this works for minor infractions, Goffman warned that it can backfire in the long run:

> When an individual's projected self is threatened during interaction, he may with poise suppress all signs of shame and embarrassment. No flusterings, or efforts to conceal having seen them, obtrude upon the smooth flow of the encounter; participants can proceed as if no incident has occurred.
>
> When situations are saved, however, something important may be lost. By showing embarrassment when he can be neither of two people, the individual leaves open the possibility that in the future, he may be effectively either. His role in the current interaction may be sacrificed, and even the encounter itself, but he demonstrates that, while he cannot present a sustainable and coherent self on this occasion, he is at least disturbed by this fact and may prove worthy at another time. To this extent, embarrassment is not an irrational impulse breaking through socially prescribed behavior but part of this orderly behavior itself.[6]

Other forms of corrective action have been generated by Thomas and Pondy, who viewed **impression management** (ensuring that the image one projects is the one that others perceive) as critical in moving a conflict to its resolution phase. People's beliefs about the other's intent, or their attributions about the other, affect the conflict strategies they choose and how they interpret the other's strategies. Thomas and Pondy found that when people were asked to recall what conflict resolution mode they had used, the majority (74 percent) were most likely to recall using cooperative modes: collaboration, compromise, and accommodation. However, the majority (73 percent) also recalled that the other person in the conflict had been competitive rather than cooperative. Thus, people are not being perceived as cooperative even when they think they are being cooperative.

The authors claimed that because people tend to be unaware of their own manner and how it might be interpreted and because they tend to be overly sensitive to others' competitive behavior, people often view their own behavior in cooperative terms. The authors identified a number of ways in which people can work to manage the impression they make in a conflict to help ensure that the image they project is the one the other person perceives. Table 15.1 lists impression management activities and sample statements.

TABLE 15.1 *Activities for Managing Impressions of Own Intent*

Activities	Sample Statements
Scanning	"Is anything wrong?" "What is your reaction to that?"
Explaining	"What I meant to say . . ." "I think you misunderstood . . ."
Preparing	"I regret having to do this." "Unfortunately, circumstances require . . ."
Excusing	Unintentional "It was an accident." "I had no idea that . . ." Intentional "I was forced to . . ." "I had no choice." "It was unavoidable." Legitimate "You deserved it." "We were only protecting ourselves."
Repairing	Apologies "We were in error." "I am sorry."
Penance	"Please accept this . . ." "Let us make it up to you." "What can I do?"

The first activity is scanning, or checking out the perceptions being created. We can question the other to confirm that we are seeing things the same way. A second activity is explaining, used when we perceive that the other has not taken our message in the way we meant it to be taken. The third activity is preparing the other for what we are about to say, using disclaimers like "I don't want to do this, but . . . ." Excusing can demonstrate that an action was unintentional, beyond control, or required by the situation. The final activity is repairing the impression we have made by apologizing or offering to perform some kind of penance.

In a more recent study, Benoit and Drew examined the ways in which people respond to impression management strategies. They had people rate how appropriate and effective various strategies might be when one's impression had been damaged. The scenario was one in which a one person (A) bumps into another (B), spilling something on B's favorite coat. B accuses A of ruining B's clothes, and A replies with denial ("I didn't do it"), evasion of responsibility for the event ("it was an accident, it wasn't my fault"), reducing the offensiveness of the event ("it's not that bad"), corrective action (offering to have the clothing cleaned), or apology ("I'm so sorry"). The results indicated, not surprisingly, that apologies and offering some corrective action were seen as the most appropriate and effective ways to restore one's image in this kind of circumstance.[7]

Reasons to Avoid Face Issues in Conflict

The skills of face saving are important. They require a consciousness on our part, a sensitivity to our behavior and what that behavior means to others. Competence in enacting conflict episodes comes from self-consciousness and awareness, which make us sensitive to situational and relational requirements.

Studies of business negotiations have found that one of the biggest obstacles to agreement is extreme demands issued early in the negotiation process.[8] Both parties lay out what they want, in no uncertain terms, hoping to compromise somewhere down the line. However, later compromise looks like they are selling out. Extreme demands automatically create a face-saving issue. Competent communicators learn to avoid extreme position statements that leave no room for maneuvering. If I say, "I want my way or I want out of the relationship," I may very well get the latter even if it was only a threat.

The important thing to remember is that the more people feel that the image they are projecting is not being accepted, the harder they will work to restore the image. As discussed in Chapter 5, one source of competitive conflict escalation cycles is the introduction of face issues, which add an extra issue to the initial conflict problems. Because face is so important to people, they feel that the image must be repaired before the initial conflict issue can be settled. Threatening the other person's face is a good way to guarantee that the conflict will not enter the resolution phase.

Embarrassment as a Face-Threatening Situation

When we are embarrassed, we lose face. If you are clumsy, for example, you want people to think that it was a momentary aberration in behavior, not an enduring characteristic. Roxane, for example, observed a student trip over a smooth rug in a hallway outside some classrooms. The student looked up sheepishly, and said, "Did you see that rug rear up and bite my foot? They ought to do something about it." When we're embarrassed, we almost always feel a need to restore impressions people have made about us.

Cupach has coined the term **social predicament** to cover a number of problematic situations in which impression management strategies are necessary to restore one's image of oneself.[9] He argues that a predicament can be created when people fail to perform as they expect. The failure may be at the level of one's "idealized social self," which is the perception of oneself following the rules of the situation and performing with a level of poise within it—essentially, this concerns whether one has acted appropriately. A second level of failure may be at the level of "accomplished role performer," which has to do with skills and abilities—this essentially concerns whether one has acted effectively. The third level of failure is at the level of "idealized self-image," or whether one has acted consistently with one's image of self and consistently with audience expectations of self. An actor's failure at any of these levels can lead to a social predicament. Failures may be forgetting important dates, being physically clumsy, lying, and so on.

People can also be placed into a social predicament by another. If a person receives unexpected praise or blame in public, embarrassment may be the outcome. In addition, a person may be made to look clumsy or foolish by another, which also results in embarrassment. A failure at all these levels is shown in the following narrative:

> I received a flyer from the planning commission in my city that appeared to indicate that my neighbor wanted to erect apartment buildings in the place of his house. At least, that's what I thought it said because it was a request for a zoning variance for more "units." So I showed up to register my disapproval. Before the meeting started, I picked up an agenda, and there was no more information on the agenda than I had been sent. Those wishing to address the commission have to register their names and their positions prior to the meeting starting, so I did so. When they finally came to my neighbor's request (an hour and a half later after struggling over what I thought were asinine issues), I discovered that it *was* a request to have more land covered with structures than zoning allowed, but it was because he wanted to erect a patio cover. I didn't want to say anything, but they called my name several times, and I thought it would be really unfair of me to go on record against something so simple, so I stood up and made an idiot of myself in front of the planning commission and on cable television (as the meetings are televised locally). To make matters worse, I was so embarrassed that I left in the middle of the interchange (probably in contempt of the proceedings!). I don't even want to walk around in my town anymore.

In this narrative, the person fails at the level of an idealized self because he did not act appropriately when he left the planning commission meeting. He failed at the level of accomplished role performer because he apparently did not understand the information on the flyer and showed his lack of understanding in the planning commission meeting. Finally, his idealized self-image is threatened by having an audience to his apparent blunder. Embarrassment at this level can create an enormous conflict for those involved.

Embarrassing situations, like conflicts, may also occur when some communication or relational rule has been violated.[10] For example, this narrative explains how embarrassment results from the breaking of a relational rule:

> I was telling a friend about the time my daughter (as a toddler) misbehaved in a department store. I have told the story many times and can embellish it quite well. In the middle of telling the story, my now teenaged daughter came into the room and yelled, "You promised you wouldn't tell that story anymore." She was terribly embarrassed that anyone would know this story about her.

There are four conditions of embarrassment. One condition is that something triggers a feeling of embarrassment. This happens generally because a behavior or an action violates a rule that is known to both parties, or when the action is incongruent with the social image that person desires. So the trigger event can be external, as when Person A says something or does something to Person B that is rule violating, or when Person A does something to himself or herself that doesn't fit with his or her social image. A second condition is that the person who is embarrassed is aware of the incongruent action and believes that others are making negative attributions about the incongruent action. Third, the trigger event is usually perceived as something unintentional, even though it might have been part of a larger action or behavior that was intentional. Fourth, the person who is embarrassed has reason to believe that others have witnessed the embarrassing action and will talk to someone else about it.[11]

The concept of embarrassment is associated with Goffman's notion of face. In embarrassment, a person's actions, either directly or indirectly, are incongruent with the image that person wants others to accept.[12] Feelings of embarrassment inevitably lead to the need to restore one's self-image, and the embarrassment a person feels has shown a demonstrated effect on the strategies that a person uses to restore face.

Research on embarrassment has examined the kinds of situations people find embarrassing, the strategies they use to reduce their embarrassment, and the strategies people who witness embarrassing events use to reduce the embarrassment of those in it.[13] The need to restore face as a result of embarrassment can complicate conflict situations; some authors argue that the introduction of a face issue will distract people from the original conflict issue and will take precedence until it is dealt with in some way.[14] In addition, embarrassment or shame may make forgiveness or reconciliation after the conflict difficult.[15]

Besides ignoring the threat to face when it arises, someone whose face has been threatened and who is embarrassed can use humor to deflect the face threat. "Making a joke can show that the offending person acknowledges blameworthiness . . . while also allowing the person to demonstrate poise and social competence."[16] A person may also nonverbally display anxiety or discomfort over having caused a threat to face in another; research indicates that blushing and other signs of discomfort help to mitigate negative attributions made by others over an offending action.[17] Physical remediation may be made by correcting the physical damage that might have occurred in the loss of face, for example, offering to clean up a mess. Or a person may show empathy for the other person by pointing out that the embarrassing situation happens to many people and is not unique. Other strategies available to the person offering a face threat to another are apologies, which are discussed later in this chapter.

APPLICATION 15.3

Recall a conflict in which the element of embarrassment was present. What was the conflict issue? Why were you embarrassed? What did you do to cope with your embarrassment?

Of particular interest is research on the effects of embarrassment in bargaining situations, which indicates that people who have been made to look foolish by another in simulated conflict games will seek revenge particularly when they believe no one knows their cost of seeking retaliation.

> The results of the experiment leave little room for doubt; when bargainers have been made to look weak and foolish before a salient audience, they are likely to retaliate against whoever caused their humiliation. Moreover, retaliation will be chosen despite the knowledge that doing so may require the sacrifice of all or large portions of the available outcomes. Such behavior will be most apparent, however, when bargainers believe that their costs are unknown to their opponent. A significant finding is that humiliated subjects soon discovered a means of retaliation that . . . spread the conflict beyond the limits set by the "rules" of the game.[18]

Seeking retaliation when people think another has humiliated them or has caused the embarrassment to occur is also demonstrated in recent studies: Aggressive responses to embarrassing situations are more likely when people feel the other person in the situation has caused the embarrassment.[19] Such situations may be as mild as being criticized in public (e.g., a teacher criticizing a student in class) or being teased. It may be more serious, such as one friend picking a fight with another in public. Embarrassment within a conflict situation can make the conflict worse and can add another issue that must be resolved. In order to move past difficult conflicts, people often must deal with their embarrassment about the conflict issue, where the conflict was enacted, or what they said within the conflict episode.

In developing conflict competence and skills of analysis, then, one needs to be aware of the situations that may cause a threat to face and embarrassment to the other. Threatening the other person's face or causing embarrassment can complicate the nature of the conflict and add new issues to those already existing. Conflict competence requires the ability to allow flexibility in the faces presented by oneself and others. As discussed previously, threatening another person's self-image in a conflict puts the focus on restoring the image rather than on dealing with the issue of the conflict. Threats to face are created largely when people lock themselves and others into untenable positions because they equate flexibility with inconsistency. Concern for the way one appears to others is a driving issue in the following case study.

Case Study 15.1 ■ *The Lucky Cat*

A long-lasting conflict centered on the amount of time and affection my wife was spending on our cat, Lucky. This conflict took place a number of times, usually whenever I was feeling neglected. Whenever Judy entered the house, she lavished our cat with affection. In fact every time she passed the cat in the hallway, she would stop and caress her, talk to her, and go out of her way to make the cat feel loved. From my perspective, I felt that Judy always had time to give the cat the affection she needed (and more) while never having time to provide the affection I felt that I needed. It had become natural for her to seek out our cat and make a fuss over her while I had to ask or make an appointment. Although it wasn't intended, I had inferred from her actions that she was never too busy for the cat but rarely had enough time for me.

From Judy's perspective, the cat was helpless and she lavished attention only because the cat was so "cute and defenseless." Judy shared later that she didn't realize I would really enjoy short, quick doses of affection throughout the day like she was giving the cat. Because of a few instances where Judy interrupted me while I was working intensely on something and I responded

a bit negatively, she also felt that I might put a damper on her affectionate overtures toward me by not being responsive, or by failing to "purr."

I was beginning to get a little more jealous, and so I decided to talk with Judy about my need for affection—I needed to feel more important than our cat. I had a number of options I could have pursued to achieve my goal: I could have gotten rid of the cat or told her of my deprivation and then begin to respond to her in the manner in which I would have liked for her to respond to me. Of course, to these two things she would have replied that getting rid of the cat was not necessary because I was much more important than the cat. She would have apologized for neglecting me and concluded with her perception of me rebuffing all of her affectionate advances. The very least that I felt I needed was for Judy to treat me as being just as important as the cat.

I had brought this subject up several times over the months, but Judy never seemed to grasp what I was asking for. I decided to bring up the conflict one evening while we were watching a video. I snuggled close to her, and when she responded with affection, I complimented her and responded in a way that affirmed her behavior. It was at this point that I brought up the issue of the cat. I told her that every time she enters the room she goes into raptures over the cat. She always finds a moment or two for the cat but not for me. She responded by saying that whenever she felt affirmed, she tended to repeat the same behavior. I realized that maybe the cat was more affirming than I was and that maybe I could learn something from our cat. I haven't begun rubbing against Judy's leg with my head yet, but I have been much more affirming. Judy has begun giving me the affection that I need, and it has helped me to see our cat in a different light.

The need to consider face and threats to it is illustrated in Case Study 15.1. Consider the man's feelings about how his wife treated the cat. He wants affection from his wife; he knows his wife is capable of it (because she gives it to the cat); yet it must be pretty embarrassing to consider telling one's spouse: "I think you love the cat more than you love me." Furthermore, because he recognized that he had sometimes been unreceptive when his wife wanted to be affectionate, he knew that he sometimes threatened her positive face by not valuing her attempts to initiate affection. He worried about how to confront the problem without appearing ridiculous, but his wife seemed to understand his concerns while stating her reasons for being more affectionate with the cat than with him. By overcoming his concerns about looking ridiculous, he was able to resolve the conflict fairly well.

Concern for the way we appear to others can keep us from acting effectively in conflict situations. How many times have you gone ahead and done something you were not committed to because you did not want people to see you as wishy-washy? We get uneasy with people who change their minds frequently. It creates too much unpredictability in interaction. Yet goals can and will change in the course of a conflict. If we accuse the other person of inconsistency, rather than trying to see his or her point of view, we risk creating a conflict over face issues instead of over real issues.

Methods for Correcting One's Impression

People do not simply manage their impressions when they are embarrassed. Problematic situations take on a number of different forms, as we described at the beginning of the chapter. What all of them have in common is this:

- Problematic situations create a need for us to explain our behavior to others or to call other people to account for theirs.
- Frequently, problematic situations are created by the breaking of relational rules.
- When one is caught in a rule violation, one's face is threatened and must be restored. Explanations must be offered for the rule violation.
- When a person catches another in a rule violation, the person who has discovered the rule violation often feels a face threat and must work to restore his or her impression. Having an acceptable explanation offered may reduce the face threat.

Conflicts constitute one part of this class of problematic events. One way that people respond to complaints or conflict initiations is with accounts.

Accounts

The study of accounts derives largely from a classic article by Scott and Lyman, who defined an **account** as:

> . . . a linguistic device employed whenever an action is subjected to valuative inquiry. Such devices are a crucial element in the social order since they prevent conflicts from arising by verbally bridging the gap between action and expectation.[20]

Accounts may prevent conflicts by providing explanations for behavior that is likely to be called into question. They may also be part of the conflict interaction (when a person is challenged on an issue and must respond) or part of the aftermath of conflict (when a person tries to explain things done and said in a conflict situation). Accounts serve an important function in that they explain how people interpret the situation at hand. Through the process of requesting and providing accounts, people in problematic situations come to establish, manage, and change the meanings of the situation.[21] Research on accounts has examined such diverse situations as managing instances of failure in organizations, reasons for the break-up of marital and romantic relationships, and distressed marriages locked into a blaming-accounting cycle.[22]

Accounts may take the form of **excuses** (a person admits that a questioned act took place but denies responsibility for it) or **justifications** (a person admits responsibility for an act but denies that the act was as bad as it appeared). Generally, an excuse serves to minimize the link between the person and the questioned behavior or serves to minimize the negative valence of the behavior.[23] If a person misses an important exam, the person will probably use an excuse: "My alarm clock did not go off; I forgot to set it; I forgot we had an exam; my hamster died"; and so on. The act in question took place, but circumstances prevented the person from being held responsible for his or her actions. If a person cheats on an exam, the person probably will use a justification: "Yes, I cheated, but everyone else did, too; I had to cheat in order to maintain my GPA"; and so on. For the most part, excuses are generally less effective in repairing one's image than justifications because excuses give the impression that a person is not willing to be held responsible for his or her actions.

Other research has gone from identifying accounting strategies to explicating the process of accounting: the nature of offenses that lead to different types of reproaches, the accounts given in response to reproaches, and the means by which accounts are accepted or rejected within an interaction.[24] An accounting sequence has three phases following an offense: a **reproach** (or request for an explanation of an offense), a **remedy** (or an account supplied by an offender), and an **acknowledgment** (or evaluation of the account). The model is similar to the process of conflict: A triggering event is followed by initiation, differentiation, and resolution. The difference is mainly in the relationship of the issue to the episode. Whereas in conflict both people perceive that the other is interfering with their goals or engaging in incompatible activities, in an accounting sequence there is a clear distinction between the offender and the offended party. The offender has created a problem (that is, she or he has not acted in accordance with the face she or he has created for the other person) and must explain his or her actions.

The various factors involved in an accounting sequence are listed in Table 15.2. The reproaches, accounts, and responses are listed in order from "most mitigating" (i.e., most likely to elicit a nondefensive response) to "most aggravating" (i.e., most likely to elicit a

TABLE 15.2 *Factors in the Accounting Sequence*

Most Mitigating						Most Aggravating
Types of reproach	Silence	Nonverbal cues	Projected concession	Projected excuse	Projected justification	Projected refusal
Types of accounts	Ignore reproach		Concession	Excuse	Justification	Refuse to account
Types of response	Drop or switch topic		Honor	Retreat	Reject, take issue with account, reinstate, reproach as if no account given	

defensive response). One of the most striking characteristics of the research in this area was that aggravating forms of reproach lead to aggravating forms of accounting: People tend to match negative remarks with negative responses. Although a mitigating or mild reproach does not necessarily bring a mild response, a mild response to a reproach almost always results in either the acceptance of the account or the offended party retreating from a position of reproach.[25] This corroborates Benoit and Drew's findings discussed previously—people are more likely to see mild responses (like concessions, apologies, and offers to make restitution) more appropriate than counterattacks. Thus, if you are asked to account for some behavior, and your response indicates that you accept your responsibility in the situation and were not intending to hurt anyone, it is likely that the one demanding an account will accept what you have to say. The advice in Chapter 12 concerning calm responses even in the face of not-so-calm remarks from others is supported by this research as well. Conflict is less likely to escalate out of control when mild responses are used.

This makes sense when you consider how a person's face is involved in the accounting sequence. If Terry has offended Kelly, and Kelly uses a mild strategy to suggest Terry was out of line, Terry does not have that much facework to do in order to restore Kelly's impression of her. However, if Kelly uses a highly negative strategy to bring Terry to account, Terry will feel a greater face threat and is likely to respond more negatively to the task of restoring Kelly's impression of her.

An offender may be made aware of the offense even though the offended party is silent. The offended party may also use nonverbal cues (e.g., slamming doors, dirty looks, etc.) to let the offender know a transgression has occurred. The offended party may use projected concession (e.g., "What do you have to say about the broken window?") to let the offender know that an apology or restitution is expected. Projected excuse lets the offender know that the offended party anticipates that the offender will try to avoid responsibility for the action (e.g., "You're not going to tell me you ran out of gas again, are you?"). More aggravating are the projected justification and projected refusal reproaches, in which the offended party presumes that the offender will try to deny the impact of the offense or refuse to account for his or her actions.

Offenders, in turn, respond to reproaches in ascending amounts of aggravation. The offender can simply remain silent—a tactic often used if the offender is embarrassed or feels that accounting would only make things worse. **Concessions** admit the offender's guilt and include apologies and offers of restitution (apologies are covered in more detail later).

Excuses admit that the offense occurred but deny responsibility for it. Excuses can take many forms. The offender can claim impairment (e.g., "I was drunk"), diminished responsibility (e.g., "I didn't know"), or scapegoat (e.g., "they made me do it"). Excuses may also take the form of a "sad tale," in which the offender recounts a series of misfortunes that has resulted in the way the offender is today. Sad tales are often the staple of courtroom drama, in which defense attorneys try to prove their client incapable of responsibility in a crime.

The offender may choose to diminish the meaning of the offense rather than diffuse responsibility within it; a justification changes the offense's meaning. Justifications may acknowledge that an act was committed while claiming that it hurt no one (e.g., "it was just a practical joke"), or they may acknowledge that the act took place but claim that the victim deserved it (e.g., "he hit me first"). The offender may try to reduce the seriousness of the offense by pointing to other people who have committed similar offenses without being punished or may emphasize that he or she had good intentions when choosing to commit the offense. Another form of justification emphasizes the need for the offense because of loyalty to others (e.g., the reasons used by various political subordinates when explaining why they broke various laws).

A final way an offender may respond to a reproach is by refusing to account, the most aggravating response. Refusals include denying that one was even involved in the offending event or that the event took place. A person can also refuse to account by turning the reproach around and questioning the right of the offended person to make a reproach.

After an account has been rendered, the offended party responds in one of several ways. The most mitigating way is to honor the account, accepting its content and signaling, verbally or nonverbally, that the "score is even." The offended party may retreat from the reproach, dropping his or her right to make it (e.g., "I didn't know that you were forced into action"). More aggravating is rejection of the account, either by taking issue with it (e.g., "I can't believe you expect me to believe you") or by simply restating the reproach as though no account was given. The offended party may also simply drop or switch the topic, moving away from the reproach without resolving the issue.

An example of an accounting sequence using silence and nonverbal cues, concessions and excuses, and honoring is found in the following story:

> My husband often has too much to drink, but usually it makes him more cheerful. He always hands over the keys to the car, and I drive home. At this one party, though, he was exceptionally rude to me. He told me to get out of his way and mind my own business. When we left he insisted on driving home, scaring me to death. For three days I didn't say anything more to him than I had to: breakfast is ready; dinner is ready—you know. Finally, he said, "I don't know what I said or did at that party, but you haven't talked to me since then. I was really drunk. What did I do?" I told him he insulted me and scared me to death driving home. He was shocked. First he apologized, then said he never had been so drunk that he couldn't remember anything. He promised to swear off tropical drinks.

Accounts may form a part of the conflict episode, especially if one person feels more of a right to feel conflict exists than the other. The form of account used affects the response of the offended person and the type of resolution to the accounting sequence. When a person claims to be offended, it is obviously less aggravating for the offending party to concede or excuse than to justify or refuse to account. The offender who justifies or refuses accounting essentially denies the content of the offended person's feelings: "Yes, this action happened, but you have interpreted it incorrectly," or worse, "you have no right to question it."[26] The following section provides more detail about apologies, which are especially mitigating to conflict situations.

APPLICATION 15.4

Recall a time when someone required an account from you for your actions. Describe the situation, and then provide a message that would fit each of these account categories: concession, excuse, justification, and refusal to account.

Apologies

Apologies are a means of impression management used to restore or minimize damage done to one's identity and to stave off potential punishment from the person offended. **Apologies** are admissions of blameworthiness and regret on the part of the offender.[27] Apologies allow a person to admit blame for an action, but they also attempt to obtain a pardon for the action by convincing the offended person that the transgression is not representative of what the offender is really like.[28]

> If the apology is viewed as sincere by the audience, the actor appears to have repented, appears not to require further rehabilitative punishment, and should be forgiven. The social interaction can then return to its normal course and the actor has minimized the negative repercussions.[29]

Several levels of apology have been identified; they are used progressively by actors as the offense committed becomes more serious and as the actor's responsibility for the offense increases. An apology can be a simple "pardon me" or may be more complicated, including statements of remorse (e.g., "I'm sorry"), offering to help the injured party, self-castigation, or direct attempts to obtain forgiveness. In one study, respondents were asked to imagine that they had bumped into another person in a public place, either in a crowded shopping mall or in a hallway at school between classes. The degree of felt responsibility was manipulated by explaining that the actor was either knocked from behind, thus bumping into the victim, or had not been paying attention and bumped into the victim without noticing. Consequences for the transgression were that the victim had been bumped on the arm (low), knocked to the ground but was unhurt (medium), or knocked to the ground and was moaning in pain (high). Respondents were asked whether they would use one of the levels of apology, respond in nonapology (e.g., saying or doing nothing, or responding nonverbally), or respond in justification ("I'm glad to see you're not hurt") or excuses ("I didn't see you").

The results indicated that people were very unlikely to walk away from a transgression without saying anything at all. Only when the consequences were minimal would a person choose the option of acknowledging the victim nonverbally and walking away. People were likely to use an excuse in conditions of low responsibility, but there was no difference across the various conditions for the use of justifications. Apologies were used in the predicted manner, becoming more complex as the consequences of the action and responsibility for the action increased. However, apologies may not always have a favored status as a response to events. In this study, the event in question was clearly an accident; the actor would not have been seen as acting intentionally.

The authors concluded that self-serving accounts in this event were probably not used as the action in question was clearly accidental and the actor would be unlikely to be accused of intending harm. However, they predicted that in ambiguous situations in which intention was less clear, a person committing some harm might be more inclined to use a self-serving kind of explanation of his or her actions (in order to try to restore face) in addition to some kind of apology. In this study, it may be that the situation used created a sense of social obligation, leading actors to believe that they must apologize.[30]

As we reflect on this research, it makes sense that someone who has done something that might be imputed to be intentional and harmful would want to restore his or her impression. But we believe that one would think that the person who has made a transgression needs to focus more on the needs of the one who has been hurt and less on his or her own needs to restore his or her impression of self. Arguably, a cynic would say that it is self-serving in the long run to do so. But we think that by submerging self and making remedy for the harm done, one implicitly does restore face to oneself. If you have done a harm to someone, and you focus more on what that person thinks of you than what you can do to undo the harm, we believe the other person will see you as conniving and insincere. If a person's remedy is so focused on what the other thinks of him or her, it is possible that the person who has been offended will not think that the one who has committed the offense really regrets the offense, but only regrets the consequences.

In related research, two studies tested children's reactions to apologies used in circumstances similar to the first study and in circumstances in which good or bad motives could be ascribed to the offender. The more severe the predicament in terms of responsibility and consequences, the more likely children were to think that the offender should be punished. Apologies helped to reduce the negative effects of the offense; more elaborate apologies created more feelings that the offender should be forgiven, more liking and less blame for the offender, and less desire for punishment of the offense. Children were also sensitive to the level of apology used; elaborate apologies were always more effective than perfunctory ones, even when an elaborate apology was not really needed. The age of the child had an effect only with respect to the amount of punishment recommended and the factors taken into account when deciding how sorry the offender was, with younger children more likely to say the offender was sorry regardless of the apology offered and less likely to take the degree of remorse into account when recommending punishment.

In the second set of circumstances the scenarios were varied somewhat to include the ascription of good or bad motives and intentionality or nonintentionality to the offense. Actors with bad motives were blamed more frequently for the offense, had more punishment recommended, and were evaluated less favorably and liked less. The more elaborate the apology, however, the less blame ascribed to the offender, and the offender was evaluated more favorably, liked more, seen as more genuinely sorry, forgiven more, and punished less. Whether or not the offense was seen as intentional also affected the effectiveness of apologies. When the behavior was accidental, a more elaborate apology reduced the amount of punishment recommended; when the offense was seen as deliberate, apologies had little effect on the amount of punishment recommended.[31] Apologies, it would seem, are not "magic bullets"—a person cannot expect to deliberately inflict harm and hope that an apology will alleviate the consequences.

A study of the relationship between the adequacy of apologies and the extent of forgiveness granted by the offended found that the power of the offender affects the relationship.[32] When the offender was in a position of low power and offered what the offended considered to be an adequate apology or explanation for his or her behavior, the result was higher levels of forgiveness, effort to forgive, maintenance of the relationship, empathy for the offender, and belief in the veracity of the explanation or apology. When the offender was in a position of high power and the explanation or apology was considered inadequate, the offended was more likely to rate the offense as serious, be resentful, make negative dispositional attributions, want to retaliate, and want to terminate the relationship. Research demonstrates, then, that we expect longer, more elaborate apologies when an action is considered to be a serious offense.[33]

Advice in rendering apologies offers several steps: (1) acknowledge and explain your role in the situation; (2) explain the problem in immediate terms; (3) offer a solution to the immediate problem; (4) explain controls (why the problem will not recur) and make assurances that the problem will not recur; and (5) explain the impact of the situation and how that impact can be mitigated (if possible).[34]

APPLICATION 15.5

What kinds of apologies work on you? When someone has offended you, what are you most likely to accept? Least likely? Why?

Relationship Outcomes When Accounts and Apologies Are Used

Accounts and apologies are ways that people manage their impressions in problematic situations. In addition to the accounting sequence discussed previously, a different line of research by Newell and Stutman discusses the way in which people discuss rule violations in relationships.[35] Again, it is important to understand the relationship between rule violations and impression management. To break a rule in a relationship creates a threat to the face of the other (you have treated that person in a way that is inconsistent with what he or she expects). In addition, to break a rule in a relationship creates a face threat to yourself as you are confronted by the other person. The other will want to know that you did not act in violation of the rules in order to embarrass or hurt; you will want the other to know that you are the same good person you were before the accusation of a rule violation was made. As you read about the theoretical model, you will be reminded of the practical approach we recommended in the preceding chapter to confront others.

You will recall from Chapter 8 that rules tell us what we must do, what we should do, and what we may not do in relationships. When one person perceives that the other has broken a relational rule, an accounting sequence or alternatively a **social confrontation** may be the result. A social confrontation is considered to be a communication episode—an event with relatively clear expectations for behavior.

Cahn wrote of the conflict episode as an interpersonal confrontation ritual of which many people are aware of, which involves "sitting down to talk." Most people, he claimed, are aware of the significance of the action and strive for a setting that is private and relatively free of interruption. The person initiating the sitting-down-to-talk episode guides the interaction by bringing up the topic or by suggesting some problem exists that can be solved by talking about it.[36] The other person in the situation acknowledges the problem and indicates a willingness to discuss it, and this is followed by a negotiation stage in which the problem is explored and solutions are sought. The episode ends with a reaffirmation step that mitigates the threat of the conflict resolution episode to the relationship. Essentially, this reaffirmation step is the "kiss and make up" part of conflict, reassuring those in it that the conflict did not threaten the relationship even though it might have been an important issue. This core sequence of events in the confrontation episode, then, is one of reproach, account, and evaluation.[37]

Newell and Stutman have been involved in a long-term investigation into the nature of social confrontation. Using interview, survey, and conversational data recorded from role-played confrontation, the authors generated a model of social confrontation and explored some of the reasons people confront one another.[38] They characterized social confrontation episodes as a type of "problematic situation, as opposed to routine situations which are characterized by ease and almost unconscious fulfillment of expectations and goals . . . [D]ifficulty and discomfort characterize problematic situations."[39] Problematic situations include those of embarrassment and disagreement, but Newell and Stutman view social confrontation as a particular type of communication episode, having its own structure and course. They defined a social confrontation (SC) episode as something

> . . . initiated when one person communicates to another that his or her behavior has violated (or is violating) a rule or expectation for appropriate conduct within the relationship or situation. The function of social confrontation may generally be descried as working through disagreement over behaviors. . . . The unifying element of the SC episode appears to be the negotiation of expectations or relational rules.[40]

The SC episode is initiated when the confronter makes a claim about the other person's behavior, and the response of the "accused" will determine the direction of the episode. There are several issues that may be confronted within the episode. The confrontation may include questions of whether the rule thought to be broken is actually a legitimate and binding rule within the relationship—for example, most relationships include a rule that one partner should not lie to the other. If those in the confrontation agree that a legitimate rule has been broken, they may try to determine whether another rule takes precedence over the rule thought to be broken. Sometimes partners agree to a higher rule than the "don't lie" rule, such as when one partner tells less than the truth in order not to hurt the other person's feelings. Finally, confrontations may encompass questions of whether the person actually broke a rule, whether he or she accepts responsibility for his or her behavior, and what kinds of behaviors will be expected in the future when a similar situation arises.

The initiation of a confrontation episode may take the form of hinting, acting angry so that the other has to ask, directly saying something, and so on. The resolution is an attempt to deal with the problem and end the episode by ameliorating the effects of damages through remediation or clarifying future expectations, or both. Remedies (making restitution for the damage) include terminating the offending behavior, expressing remorse for the offending behavior, offering to make up for any damages due to the offending behavior, or accepting punishment for the behavior. Clarification of future behavior occurs through **legislation** (developing a new rule to guide behavior in similar situations), **remediation** (clarifying or modifying an existing rule), or **reaffirmation** (restating the existence and value of the rule, with a pledge to adhere to it in the future). If remedy or clarification fails, the participants may be left with no resolution, which means the problem will be set aside until future interaction can address it.

Here is a way that a conflict might unfold if the people in the situation were following this model: Dante and Diane have been dating for over a year. During this time, Dante has remained friends with his ex-girlfriend, Amy. Diane has tried not to be jealous of this friendship, but it has often seemed as though Dante was inappropriate in the way he acted toward Amy. Diane heard that he had lunch with Amy and seemed to be talking very intimately with her. She also saw them working out together in the gym, and was concerned about how much touching they were doing. Diane has just found out that Dante broke a date with her so that he could drive Amy to the airport, and Diane decides it's time to confront Dante.

When Diane initiates the conflict by pointing out to Dante that it is not appropriate for him to break a date with her in order to drive an ex-girlfriend to the airport, Dante can respond in one of two ways: He can deny that it is a legitimate rule, or agree that it is a legitimate rule.

If he denies the legitimacy of the rule, he might argue that an ex-girlfriend is like anyone else in need. There is no reason to say no to her. Diane could respond by trying to legislate a new rule ("From now on, you won't break a date with me to spend any kind of time with her"). Or Dante could offer a remedy by promising to make it up to her through an extra-special date. A final thing that might happen if the episode went in this direction is that no resolution is reached: Diane would raise the issue, Dante would deny that it is a problem, and Diane would drop the subject.

If Dante agrees that the rule is legitimate, then he has two options. He can try to argue that a superseding rule exists, or he can take issue with the behavior itself. If he argues that a superseding rule exists, for example, "Yes, I shouldn't break a date with you, but she didn't have a ride," Diane must decide whether the rule is legitimate or nonlegitimate. If she decides that the superseding rule is legitimate (i.e., a person in need should not be ignored), she can respond in one of four ways. She can legislate a new rule ("From now on, you'll find someone else to help"). She can remediate the old rule ("Make sure there's no one else who could help before you say yes"). She can reaffirm the old rule ("I don't mind you helping if it's really an emergency"). Or she can demand a remedy from Dante ("Okay, I guess you had to do this, but I expect a great dinner next time"). If Diane denies that the superseding rule is legitimate, she'll need to legislate one or demand a remedy in order to resolve the conflict along this path.

If Dante decides to argue about the behavior itself, he has two options. He can admit or deny his behavior. If he denies his behavior, it will be difficult for Diane to proceed. Either he did it or he didn't. The resolution stage along this unfolding of the episode would be dropping the issue (no resolution), or reaffirmation of the rule ("If it's really an emergency, it's okay.").

According to the research on accounting sequences, the most mitigating thing for Dante to do, particularly if Diane can prove that he performed the behavior in question, is to follow the sequence of admitting the legitimacy of the rule, admitting the behavior, admitting the rule was broken, accepting responsibility, and offering a remedy. Other authors refer to such a sequence of events as going *one-down* to the other person. Such behavior is likely to prevent a conflict from escalating out of control because it will not become embroiled in issues of whether the behavior was performed (it was), or whether the expectation was legitimate (apparently it was), but instead will move to an offer of remedy and reconciliation. Thus, Dante may lose some face in the short run, but he restores Diane's by recognizing the legitimacy of her complaint, and his desire to move the conflict to resolution by coming to some remedy will restore his face in the long run.

Overall, Newell and Stutman's model is useful for examining interpersonal conflicts that concern behaviors and rules for interactions. It is especially noteworthy that when people have conflict over the rules of the relationship, they are likely to renegotiate those rules, and the outcomes offered by Newell and Stutman are reasonable explanations of what might happen as a result of a confrontation. One possible limitation of their work is the assumption that a lack of consensus on rules is due to a lack of understanding or communication.

As Morris pointed out, people often misbehave to see how much they can get away with before someone calls them into line.[41] The issue is not so much "Do we both understand the rule" but "How can I get you to act in accordance with this rule to which we agreed?" Moreover, it is unclear how the model would account for conflict manifested by an issue that masks a deeper one, for example, a conflict over a resource, such as money, when the underlying issue is one of power and relationship. Frequently, people are not aware of the rule that governs their behavior and often need third-party intervention to recognize that they are dealing with more issues than the ones within their awareness.

In addition, Folger pointed out that the definition of social confrontation depends on the participants' shared cultural assumptions about the way an episode should be enacted, much as Cahn described.[42] Folger argued, however, that those in a social confrontation episode may be affected by the definition of the situation surrounding the confrontation episode and may not act according to cultural expectations. For example, if one spouse decides to confront the other in public over a broken rule, the confrontee may respond that the confronter has broken a rule about where confrontation will take place. Although Newell and Stutman claimed that people in a social confrontation episode *either* conform to the intent of the episode (e.g., Dante and Diane negotiate the boundaries of Dante's relationship with Amy) *or* transform it into a different kind (e.g., Dante and Diane negotiate the boundaries of their own relationship and what Diane can actually expect from Dante), Folger pointed out that they may simultaneously do both. Despite these concerns, Newell and Stutman's research has significance for a variety of reasons: It is grounded in the study of interaction, it is concerned with the content of conflict episodes, and it is combined with a concern for the social-psychological aspects of episodes that affect people's behaviors.

APPLICATION 15.6

When you have had a confrontation with another person over the rules of the relationship, where have you been able to see remedy, remediation, reaffirmation, or legislation as an outcome of the conflict?

From Theory to Action

Whether we are involved in a conflict or not, how we see ourselves and how we think others see us are an important part of the communication process. People will undertake a number of different strategies to create, maintain, change, or restore the images other people have of them. Some problems of impression management may be prevented by being attentive to the way in which our messages may be seen as face threatening. The various face management strategies, like hedging and credentialing, may help us to be less offensive on a face level.

When such strategies fail, however, we need to work to repair images. Accounts, apologies, and confrontation are all ways in which relationships can be repaired and impressions can be restored to previous levels. Although research would suggest that preventing face issues from becoming a part of the conflict to begin with would be the most effective course of action, there are times when it is necessary for us to clarify our relationships to one another and to reestablish the rules and boundaries of those relationships.

Despite all of the strategies available to us, there are times when accounting for one's behavior and apologizing do not seem to be enough. If important relationship rules have been broken or trust has been violated, there is a relational transgression. When relational transgressions occur, forgiveness processes are necessary to restore the relationship, or, if that is not possible, to help those involved make sense of the situation so that they do not carry the hurt into other relationships.

Notes

1. Erving Goffman, *The Presentation of Self in Everyday Life* (New York: Overlook Press, 1959); *Interaction Ritual: Essays on Face-to-Face Behavior* (New York: Pantheon Books, 1967).

2. William R. Cupach and Sandra Metts, *Facework* (Thousand Oaks: Sage Publications, 1994), pp. 15–16.

3. Karen Tracy, "The Many Faces of Facework," in H. Giles and W. P. Robinson (Eds.), *Handbook of Language and Social Psychology* (New York: John Wiley & Sons, 1990), pp. 209–226.

4. Penelope Brown and Stephen Levinson, *Politeness: Some Universals in Language Usage* (Cambridge: Cambridge University Press, 1987).

5. J. Hewitt and R. Stokes, "Disclaimers," *American Sociological Review* 40 (1975), 1–11.

6. Erving Goffman, "Embarrassment and Social Organizations," *American Journal of Sociology* 26 (1956), 270–271.

7. William L. Benoit and Shirley Drew, "Appropriateness and Effectiveness of Image Repair Strategies," *Communication Reports* 10 (1997), 153–163.

8. Max Bazerman, "Why Negotiations Go Wrong," *Psychology Today* (June 1985), 54–58.

9. William R. Cupach, "Social Predicaments," in William R. Cupach and Brian H. Spitzberg (Eds.), *The Dark Side of Interpersonal Communication* (Hillsdale, NJ: Lawrence Erlbaum, 1994), pp. 159–180.

10. Sandra Petronio, "The Use of a Communication Boundary Perspective to Contextualize Embarrassment Research," in James A. Anderson (Ed.), *Communication Yearbook* 13 (Newbury Park, CA: Sage, 1990), pp. 365–373.

11. William R. Cupach and Sandra Metts, "Remedial Processes in Embarrassing Predicaments," in James A. Anderson (Ed.), *Communication Yearbook* 13 (Newbury Park, CA: Sage, 1990), p. 324.

12. Erving Goffman, "Embarrassment and Social Organization," pp. 264–271.

13. See, for example, William R. Cupach, Sandra Metts, and Vince Hazelton, "Coping with Embarrassing Predicaments: Remedial Strategies and Their Perceived Utility," *Journal of Language and Social Psychology* 5 (1986), 181–200; and William F. Sharkey and Laura Stafford, "Reponses to Embarrassment," *Human Communication Research* 17 (1990), 315–342.

14. Joseph Folger and Marshall Scott Poole, *Working through Conflict* (Glenview, IL: Scott Foresman, 1984).

15. John Patton, *Is Human Forgiveness Possible?* (Nashville: Abington Press, 1985).

16. Cupach and Metts, *Facework*, p. 10.

17. C. Castelfranchi and I. Poggi, "Blushing as Discourse: Was Darwin Wrong?" in W. R. Crozier (Ed.), *Shyness and Embarrassment: Perspectives from Social Psychology* (Cambridge: Cambridge University Press, 1990), pp. 230–251.

18. Bert R. Brown, "The Effects of Need to Maintain Face on Interpersonal Bargaining," *Journal of Experimental Social Psychology* 4 (1968), 107–112; see also Bert R. Brown, "Face Saving Following Experimentally Induced Embarrassment," *Journal of Experimental Social Psychology* 6 (1970), 255–271.

19. Sandra Metts and William R. Cupach, "Situational Influence on the Use of Remedial Strategies in Embarrassing Predicaments," *Communication Monographs* 56 (1989), 151–162; William R. Cupach and Sandra Metts, "The Effects of Type of Predicament and Embarrassability on Remedial Responses to Embarrassing Situations," *Communication Quarterly* 40 (1992), 149–161.

20. Marvin B. Scott and Stanford M. Lyman, "Accounts," in Gregory B. Stone and Harvey A. Farberman (Eds.), *Social Psychology through Symbolic Interaction* (Waltham, MA: Xerox Publishing, 1970), pp. 489–509.

21. Richard Buttny, "Accounts as a Reconstruction of an Event's Context," *Communication Monographs* 52 (1985), 57–77.

22. Gail T. Fairhust, Stephen G. Green, and B. Kay Snavely, "Face Support in Controlling Poor Performance," *Human Communication Research* 11 (1984), 272–295; William R. Cupach and Sandra Metts, "Accounts of Relational Dissolution: A Comparison of Marital and Non-Marital Relationships," paper presented at the International Communication Association Convention, Honolulu, May 1985; Richard Buttny, "Blame-Account Sequences in Therapy: The Negotiation of Relational Meanings," *Semiotica* 78 (1990), 219–247.

23. C. R. Snyder and Raymond L. Higgins, "Reality Negotiation and Excuse-Making: President Reagan's 4 March 1987 Iran Arms Scandal Speech and Other Literature," in Michael J. Cody and Margaret L. McLaughlin (Eds.), *The Psychology of Tactical Communication* (Clevedon, Avon, England: Multilingual Matters, Ltd., 1990), pp. 207–228.

24. See, for example, Peter Schonbach, "A Category System for Account Phases," *European Journal of Social Psychology* 10 (1980), 195–200; Margaret L. McLaughlin,

Michael J. Cody, and Dan O'Hair, "The Management of Failure Events: Some Contextual Determinants of Accounting Behavior," *Human Communication Research* 9 (1983), 208–224; Margaret L. McLaughlin, Michael J. Cody, and Nancy E. Rosenstein, "Account Sequences in Conversations between Strangers," *Communication Monographs* 50 (1983), 102–124; Michael J. Cody and Margaret L. McLaughlin, "Models for the Sequential Construction of Accounting Episodes: Situational and Interactional Constraints on Message Selection and Evaluation," in Richard L. Street and Joseph N. Capella (Eds.), *Sequence and Pattern in Communicative Behavior* (London: Edward Arnold Publishers, 1985), pp. 50–69.

25. Cody and McLaughlin, "Models for Sequential Construction of Accounting Episodes," p. 66; see also Peter Schonbach and Petra Kleibaumhuter, "Severity of Reproach and Defensiveness of Accounts," in Michael J. Cody and Margaret L. McLaughlin (Eds.), *The Psychology of Tactical Communication* (Clevedon, Avon, England: Multilingual Matters, Ltd., 1990), pp. 229–243; Margaret L. McLaughlin, Michael J. Cody, and Kathryn French, "Account-Giving and the Attribution of Responsibility: Impressions of Traffic Offenders," in Michael J. Cody and Margaret L. McLaughlin (Eds.), *The Psychology of Tactical Communication* (Clevedon, Avon, England: Multilingual Matters, Ltd., 1990), pp. 244–261; Charles Antaki, "Explaining Events or Explaining Oneself?" in Michael J. Cody and Margaret L. McLaughlin (Eds.), *The Psychology of Tactical Communication* (Clevedon, Avon, England: Multilingual Matters, Ltd., 1990), pp. 268–283; Jerald M. Jellison, "Accounting: Societal Implications," in Michael J. Cody and Margaret L. McLaughlin (Eds.), *The Psychology of Tactical Communication* (Clevedon, Avon, England: Multilingual Matters, Ltd., 1990), pp. 283–298.

26. For more on problematic situations, see Nikolas Coupland, Howard Giles, and John W. Wiseman (Eds.), *"Miscommunication" and Problematic Talk* (Newbury Park, CA: Sage, 1991); Margaret L. McLaughlin, Michael J. Cody, and Stephen J. Read, *Explaining Oneself to Others: Reason-Giving in a Social Context* (Hillsdale, NJ: Lawrence Erlbaum Associates, 1992).

27. Barry R. Schlenker and B. W. Darby, "The Use of Apologies in Social Predicaments," *Social Psychology Quarterly* 44 (1981), 271–278.

28. Barry R. Schlenker, *Impression Management* (Monterey, CA: Brooks/Cole, 1980).

29. Schlenker and Darby, "The Use of Apologies in Social Predicaments," p. 272.

30. Ibid., pp. 276–277.

31. B. W. Darby and Barry R. Schlenker, "Children's Reactions to Apologies," *Journal of Personality and Social Psychology* 43 (1982), 742–753.

32. David M. Droll, "Forgiveness: Theory and Research," Doctoral dissertation, University of Nevada, Reno, 1985.

33. B. Fraser, "On Apologizing," in F. Coulmas (Ed.), *Conversational Routines: Explorations in Standardized Communication Situations and Prepatterned Speech* (The Hague: Mouton, 1981).

34. E. Goodman, "Processes of Conflict Resolution," lecture at New York University, Summer 1983; quoted in Deborah Borisoff and David A. Victor, *Conflict Management: A Communication Skills Approach* (Englewood Cliffs, NJ: Prentice-Hall, 1989).

35. See, for example, Sara E. Newell and Randall K. Stutman, "A Qualitative Approach to Social Confrontation: Identifying Constraints and Facilitators," paper presented at the annual meeting of the Speech Communication Association Convention, Louisville, KY, November 1982; Sara E. Newell and Randall K. Stutman, "Negotiating Confrontation: The Problematic Nature of Initiation and Response," *Research on Language and Social Interaction* 23 (1989/1990), 139–162; Sara E. Newell and Randall K. Stutman, "The Episodic Nature of Social Confrontation," in James A. Anderson (Ed.), *Communication Yearbook* 14 (Newbury Park: Sage, 1991), pp. 359–392; Sara E. Newell and Randall K. Stutman, "The Social Confrontation Episode," *Communication Monographs* 55 (1988), 266–285.

36. Dudley Cahn, *Letting Go: A Practical Theory of Relationship Disengagement and Reengagement* (New York: SUNY Press Albany, 1987).

36. Bradford "J" Hall, "An Elaboration of the Structural Possibilities for Engaging in Alignment Episodes," *Communication Monographs* 68 (1991), 79–100.

37. Sara E. Newell and Randall K. Stutman, "The Social Confrontation Episode," *Communication Monographs* 55 (1988). See also, "A Qualitative Approach to Social Confrontation: Identifying Constraints and Facilitators," paper presented to the Speech Communication Association Convention, Louisville, KY, November 1982; "Negotiating Confrontation: The Problematic Nature of Initiation and Response," *Research on Language and Social Interaction* 23 (1989/1990), 139–162; "The Episodic Nature of Social Confrontation," in James A. Anderson (Ed.), *Communication Yearbook* 14 (Newbury Park: Sage, 1991), pp. 359–392; Randall K. Stutman and Sara E. Newell, "Rehearsing for Confrontation," *Argumentation* 4 (1990), 185–198.

38. Newell and Stutman, "The Social Confrontation Episode," p. 267.

39. Ibid., p. 271.

40. G. H. Morris, "Alignment Talk and Social Confrontation," in James A. Anderson (Ed.), *Communication Yearbook* 14 (Newbury Park: Sage, 1991), pp. 393–402.

41. Joseph P. Folger, "Interpretive and Structural Claims about Confrontations," in James A. Anderson (Ed.), *Communication Yearbook* 14 (Newbury Park: Sage, 1991), pp. 393–402.

16

After the Conflict: Forgiveness and Reconciliation

Objectives

At the end of this chapter, you should be able to

1. discuss the various communication research areas that impact our understanding of forgiveness.
2. explain the nature of forgiveness.
3. explain why conflict management requires forgiveness afterward.
4. identify the means you should use to forgive others and be forgiven following conflict interaction.

Key Terms

argumentative skill deficiency	healing	relational transgressions
deception	problematic situation	self-fulfilling prophecy
emotional residues	reconciliation	social lies
forgiveness	regrettable messages	truth bias
forgiveness/reconciliation loop		

The academic literature on conflict contains little mention of what happens after a conflict episode is "over," although the assumption is that each conflict episode within a relationship is affected by previous episodes and will in turn affect future ones. Whether a particular episode is productive or destructive will affect how the next episode unfolds. In distinguishing destructive conflict from productive conflict, Hocker and Wilmot argued that "the best index of destructive conflict is when one or both of the parties has a strong desire to 'get even' or damage the other party."[1]

Various researchers have shown that conflict within a relationship can evolve into competitive escalation or avoidance cycles. The goals, therefore, in teaching people how to manage conflict are generally geared toward teaching them

- how to keep conflicts from escalating out of control.
- how to express their feelings.
- how to negotiate mutually satisfactory solutions.
- how to enhance their relationship by managing and resolving conflicts.

These are laudable goals, which are reflected by the information contained in previous chapters of this book.

These goals, however, do not encompass all of what people need to learn about interpersonal conflict. Sillars and Weisberg say it involves more than simple techniques:

> Serious personal conflicts may represent nothing less than the dissolution of consensus about the core issues and basic ground rules of a relationship. Yet the implication often drawn from conflict research is that a relationship could be set back on its proper course if a few simple changes in communication were instituted.[2]

Changing our attitudes about conflict and acting to manage or resolve conflict are not enough. All the good conflict skills available to us will not help us if we are unable to put the hurt of the past behind us. We need to deal with our deeper feelings such as resentment, hatred, or hurt that we may use to justify our own hostility, revengeful behavior, and aggression. Productive conflict interaction, "rational behavior," is a goal, a valued goal, in teaching people to manage their conflicts more effectively. But what if previous conflict encounters have been destructive? What will allow people to act in productive ways the next time? If people have been hurt by the issue of conflict and the way it was handled, will that hurt not spill into the next conflict between the two people? Some conflicts leave residues that change the nature of the relationship between those involved:

> Many escalating conflicts are characterized by a series of semipermeable boundaries: thresholds that, once passed, do not readily permit retreat. Like a rubber band stretched beyond its normally tolerable limits, the relationship between individuals in an intensifying conflict may pass a psychological or collective threshold—a point of no return—that transforms the relationship into a new, more conflict-intensified state. . . . [This behavior has] introduced a residue that changes things.[3]

A destructive conflict cycle is characterized by the introduction of unresolved issues—issues suppressed, ignored, or put off in the last conflict episode only to become issues again in the next episode. One reason for the recurrence of destructive conflict is the inability or unwillingness of those involved to forgive and let go of the past. One student, who comes from a highly dysfunctional family, wrote in her conflict journal about a visit home:

> The whole situation is very sad. Sometimes I feel like everyone is so busy trying to make everyone else pay for their wrongdoing that no one is willing to just let it all go and move

on. Sometimes I get angry with myself for the same reason. Growing up in my house was no bed of roses, or at least the roses prickled more than your average garden variety. We had some very real, very deep problems. But the unforgiveness runs just as deep, and I think it is the unforgiveness, rather than the wrongdoing, that is doing the most damage in the long run.

Researchers in communication are only now beginning to look at how people repair broken relationships. Although the word *forgiveness* is rarely found in communication literature, it is a common concern in psychotherapeutic literature, and popular writings are beginning to reflect the need to teach people how to make amends both interpersonally and in organizational settings.[4] The desire of people to know how to deal with issues of forgiveness is demonstrated in the success of Louis Smedes's book *Forgive and Forget: Healing the Hurts We Don't Deserve.*[5]

Conflicts and Relational Transgressions

In Chapter 15 we introduced the idea of a **problematic situation.** These situations exist when people have acted in ways that threaten the face of another person, or have acted in ways that are not appropriate to the relationship. Accounts and apologies are ways of rectifying problematic situations. But some problematic situations take on crisis implications and become more intense than a simple face management problem. Problematic situations may evolve into **relational transgressions,** situations in which core rules of a relationship have been violated.

This chapter first examines the research on relational transgressions, describing the conflict behaviors that lead to a need for forgiveness and reconciliation between those involved in the conflict. We then discuss the nature of forgiveness, its effects, the means people use to forgive one another, and the ways in which we may reconcile our differences.

Relational Transgressions

When I arrived back at school after spring break, my roommate said that he needed to talk to me. From his nonverbal behavior I judged that this was going to be an important discussion. We sat down and began our talk; actually I mostly listened. My roommate proceeded to tell me that he had taken "a bold step of faith" and that he believed God had led him to destroy all of my records and compact discs. He said that they were hindering me from being all that God desired me to be. As I listened to my roommate, I became very confused because this action seemed irrational, unbalanced, and incorrect. Yet previously I had valued my roommate's judgment and wisdom. Also, we had a close relationship and this violation of trust damaged that respect and our friendship. When he finished talking, I didn't say a word. My roommate left, and I went to seek the advice of a wise friend. Later I talked with my roommate and told him that, whereas in principle he might be right, his actions were wrong. He agreed to repay me for all of my music, but it will take a long time to restore our friendship, particularly because I'm not sure he is really sorry for what he has done.

Transgressions and Their Effects

Preliminary research has attempted to identify behaviors that would be considered relational transgressions—violations of the implicit or explicit expectations of those involved in the relationship. According to Metts, relational transgressions have three characteristics:

1. they are events that the offended person has discovered or has been told about;
2. they are tied to particular rules; and
3. they are consequential enough to require a good explanation from the other person.[6]

The student whose roommate, whom he considered a good friend, destroyed his music collection experienced a relational transgression on a large scale.

Metts used an open-ended questionnaire to explore the concept of relational transgressions: what constitutes one, who commits it, how it is committed, and what is done about it. About half the respondents said the transgression "just happened," rather than appearing to be a deliberate act. Of those questioned, 46 percent said the person who had been offended initiated confrontation, and 39 percent said the offender initiated the conversation about the transgression. About half said the explanation offered or received was accepted; 15 percent said it was rejected (some in this number terminated the relationship). As might be expected, some (21 percent) said the explanation had been accepted but with emotional residue. Metts noted that "at least in continuing relationships, the preference is to let the transgressor 'off the hook' though on occasion there is latent affect which may resurface at later points."[7]

Metts also asked her respondents to rate relational transgressions in order of their difficulty in resolution, both for the respondent and for the respondent's relational partner. Transgressions most difficult to deal with for the person responding were (in order of importance): sexual infidelity, emotional attachment or intimacy (to someone else), attraction exceeding friendly association, deception, physical abuse, not being supportive, psychological abuse, and other behaviors receiving only a few responses. When respondents listed difficult transgressions as their partner might see it, the order was slightly different, encompassing sexual infidelity, deception, emotional attachment or intimacy (to someone else), not being supportive, psychological abuse, physical abuse, and others. Metts noted that respondents appeared to confuse what she would classify as a threat to the relationship (e.g., a physical attraction to the other) with relational transgressions; however, given her assertion that a transgression is a behavior that violates relational rules, a behavior that threatens the relationship can easily be seen as a transgression.

In explaining behavior to the offended party, the person who committed the relational transgression most often used justification (21 percent), followed by description (19 percent), apology plus justification (14 percent), no explanation offered (11 percent), excuse (10 percent), apology (6 percent), and apology plus excuse (5 percent). In examining the relationship between the type of explanation used and relationship characteristics, she found that (1) the use of justification was associated with higher commitment to the relationship; (2) a greater expression of affection was associated with use of apologies, whereas less expression of affection was associated with excuses; and (3) the type of transgression committed affected feelings that the relationship was special, especially when the transgression was one of sexual infidelity.

Other research in the area of relational transgressions has focused solely on the effects of sexual infidelity in relationships. In a series of studies examining the effects of relationship length, intent to commit infidelity, desire for revenge, and alcohol consumption on guilt and responsibility following infidelity, some interesting findings occurred. Most surprising was the finding that, in reading these various scenarios, respondents claimed they would feel less guilty when they intended to commit sexual infidelity and did so rather than when it happened accidentally. When a person intends to commit a relational transgression, he or she has time to rationalize the behavior ahead of time; committing a transgression spontaneously leaves no time for rationalization and so the transgressor feels more guilt. In addition, definite sex differences occurred in terms of the blame assigned to a transgressor. Women reading scenarios about male and female transgressors assigned equal guilt to both. Men, on the other hand, assigned higher levels of guilt to a female committing sexual infidelity than to a male. Women were also more likely to use alcohol consumption as an excuse for sexual infidelity than were men. This program of research initiated work in the area of relational transgressions, but its exclusive focus on sexual infidelity as a relational transgression has limited its application.[8]

Relational transgressions, depending on their seriousness, produce **emotional residues** in a relationship; that is, people experience lingering emotional responses to the memory of the transgression. One model proposed a trajectory of reconciliation, explaining the process people go through in responding to transgressions. Transgressions result in negative emotional, cognitive, and behavioral responses. For the student losing his entire music collection, emotions of anger, disappointment, and disbelief replaced his originally positive feelings for his roommate. He had to think about the level of responsibility to which he would hold his roommate, and he had to decide what to do about the situation.

APPLICATION 16.1

What constitutes a transgression in your relationships? Compare two relationships you are in, one with a close friend and one with an acquaintance, and list three transgressions in order of their importance to the relationship. How are the lists different?

	Close Friend	Acquaintance
Not very important		
Important		
Would end relationship		

After a relational transgression, the offended person actively copes and comes to change the meaning of the incident and its place within the relationship. An inability to place the relational transgression into the larger context of the relationship results in termination of the relationship. In the case of the student, the relationship is still strained, and that strain is made worse by the fact that full restitution has not yet been made for the destroyed music collection. A person comes to terms with a transgression by focusing on the costs and rewards of the relationship or by focusing on the offense. If the person focuses on the relationship, then cognitions, emotions, and behaviors probably interact with one another and become more positive over time. After a relational transgression, people rarely reconcile instantly, but rather do so over a period of time.[9] Space does not permit us to explore all the various forms of relational transgressions that would necessitate forgiveness processes, but Metts identified two areas of relational transgressions of interest to communication researchers: communicative acts (including regrettable messages, and lies and deception) and physical abuse (which may be viewed as nonverbal communication as presented in Chapter 11).

Regrettable Messages

> Every week I take a total of 800 kids out of their classrooms to release their bottled up energy. I am known for my patience, but it ran dry one day. The thing I did not ever want to do, I did. There was a group of twelve-year-old boys that just would not line up. I said something like, "You guys are just too stupid to know how to line up!" with an accusative tone. I could not believe my ears. But I was ticked off! Nevertheless, that was no excuse.

All of us have experienced foot-in-mouth disease at one time or another. Maybe you blurted out an irrelevant answer in class and everyone stared at you. Saying something regrettable is almost like an out-of-body experience: You know it was your voice, and you know that you said it, but it is hard to believe that you did. What effect do these regrettable messages have on relationships?

Preliminary research into **regrettable messages** asked people to recall instances of their communication blunders. Generally, regrettable messages happen in close relationships and are classified in several different types (see Table 16.1). The most frequent messages were blunders, direct attacks, group references, direct criticism, and revealing or explaining too much. The most frequent reasons for a regrettable message were selfishness (e.g., wanting to get one's own point across without thinking about the other), stupidity (e.g., it just slipped out), being out of control (e.g., being drunk), and good intentions—in other words, not considering the impact of the message before uttering it. Most people realize their mistake immediately and regret the message primarily because it hurt the other person, hurt themselves, hurt the relationship, or was inappropriate. The short-term effects of regrettable messages are generally in the form of negative feelings, but the long-term effects appeared to be minimal in this study.

> Perhaps this can be explained by the fact that most participants recalled cases that occurred with close relationships and these relationships may have had enough credits to withstand problems brought about by these remarks. Narrative accounts indicated that when relationship damage was severe, the regrettable message was perceived as "just one more" statement in a relationship typified by such remarks. But sometimes this one was the fatal blow.[10]

Deception and Lies

Sticking one's foot in one's mouth unintentionally has very different effects than does intentional deception and lies. **Deception** has generally been classified as "the conscious alteration of information a person believes to be true in order to significantly change another's perceptions from what the deceiver thought they would be without the alteration."[11] Deception is a mutually negotiated communication act, according to some writers, because our own needs, values, and expectations help to create situations in which we will be told lies. Recent writers in the field of communication question whether deception should be con-

TABLE 16.1   *Types of Regrettable Messages*

Type	Description	Example
Blunder	Often occurs during small talk	"How's your mother?" to someone whose mother is dead
Direct attack	General critical statements directed at a person, person's family, or person's friend	"Your friend's a nerd."
Group reference	Remarks about a group (often racial or ethnic), or stereotypical references to personal characteristics	"What do you expect from a ____?"
Direct criticism	Criticize something specific about the other person, without qualification	"You never clean the house."
Reveal/explain too much	Remarks that involve too much openness, telling more than the situation calls for	Giving a string of highly personal excuses when asked to contribute to a task
Agreement changed	Statements later regretted because the person changes his or her mind about agreeing	Agreeing to go to a movie, then not wanting to go
Expressiveness/catharsis	Not specifically directed toward other, but expression of feelings and emotions	"I hate my life!"
Lies	Purposeful deceit	Telling another that a task was finished when it was not
Implied criticism	Sometimes teasing, where criticism is below the surface of the remark	"Are you really going to wear that to the party?"
Behavioral edict	Tells someone else what to do in no uncertain terms with no options or alternatives	"Put up with it or go away."
Double entendre	Remark that can be taken different ways	Father speaking to son reluctant to eat the host's meal: "Look at me. I'm eating it."

sidered in a negative light. For some, "deception is seen as a 'normal' part of interpersonal communication rather than as a form of social or moral deviance."[12] Others argue that judgments concerning the acceptability of lies depend on the motives of the liar and the consequences of the lie—for a deceiver who has good intentions and who is motivated to serve the interests of others, deception is an acceptable form of communication.[13]

Few deny that deception is a frequent part of communication. Research examining the frequency of lies has found that they constitute as much as 62 percent of communication,[14] although more conservative research puts the frequency of lies at about five a week.[15] People lie for a number of reasons: to benefit themselves, to benefit the other person in the conversation, to benefit a relationship. They lie to save face, to guide social interaction, to avoid tension or conflict, to affect interpersonal relationships, or to achieve interpersonal power. Lies may be deliberate or simply a reflex (e.g., "It was such a nice party; I had a lovely time"). Generally, a person moves through four stages before resorting to a lie. The person must decide that authentic communication will not accomplish the desired response, that deceptive communication can accomplish the desired response, that deceptive communication will not be detected, and that if it is detected, it will not result in unacceptable negative outcomes.[16] When people kept track of the deceptions they engaged in over a three-week period, most reported that they lied as a response to questions they did not want to answer rather than deliberately generating lies.[17]

Certainly, **social lies** and lies used to get us out of sticky situations (e.g., "I really can't go with you to the beach—I have to study") are part of the social fabric. They become a relational transgression, however, when the lie breaks relational rules. Lying to an acquaintance about why you do not want to go to the beach is different than lying to your best friend. This is particularly true because as we develop relationships with others, we tend to develop a **truth bias** toward them: We assume that they tell us the truth.[18] This truth bias makes us less accurate in detecting deception when it occurs. And although its opposite, suspiciousness, may make us better detectors of deception, this gain is offset by lower intimacy and relational satisfaction,[19] as well as higher cynicism and negativism.[20]

> The effects of uncovering a deception are both cognitive and emotional. When an individual discovers that a message previously processed, interpreted, and stored was in fact deceptive, the individual must go through a cognitive process involving several different steps. First, the information must be retrieved, relabeled as deceptive, and re-stored. Second . . . this newly processed information will be analyzed in relationship to already existing cognitive structures in order for its complete meaning to be determined. . . . [S]uch a comparison with already stored information may lead an individual not only to interpret the processed information thoroughly, but also to reinterpret additional information that had been previously stored but that now becomes suspect.[21]

In addition to the cognitive effects, research indicates that the more involved people are with another person, the more intense their negative emotions when they discover that person has lied to them. In addition, the more important the information lied about, the more intense negative emotions will be on discovering the deception. The more important the issue that is lied about, the more likely it is that a relationship will end.[22]

The effects of lying in a close relationship are seen in Case Study 16.1. The woman in this relationship had no reason to suspect that her dating partner would lie about the concert, particularly since both of them had made such a big deal about it, at least initially. It was devastating to her to find that he went to the concert she so wanted to attend without her and with someone else. The effects of the deception eventually terminated the relationship.

Case Study 16.1 ■ *The Missed Concert*

Trust and honesty are the two most important issues in developing a relationship. Today I had to make the decision of whether my relationship with David was worth working out a very big conflict that caused him to lie to me, and me not to trust him. I care about him a lot; I love him. I don't know where I went wrong in making him feel he couldn't be completely honest with me.

David and I had tickets to see Harry Connick, Jr., in concert. We had the tickets for about three months. We had just started going out when we bought the tickets and planned to attend the concert. It finally came down to one week before the concert, and I was beginning to get really excited about going, whereas David, for some reason, would avoid the excitement and just agreed with me about how fun it would be. It was Monday, and the concert was on Wednesday. David came to my house late that night to tell me he had a ton of studying to do on Wednesday because he had a huge midterm on Thursday that he had to get an "A" on. He made me understand, after hours of continuous explanation, how he really felt it was best to give the tickets to his cousin because he couldn't afford not to study the night before the exam. I understood, but I was really bummed out. I sort of wished David would give me the tickets so I could still go to the concert, but he felt it was unfair that I go to the concert while he stayed home and studied. He said that he would make it up to me with something better, and assured me it would be best if I just understood.

I chose to understand. I did so for exactly 24 hours. Man, he blew it. I went over to his house the next day so we could spend some time together and celebrate his doing well on the test. David and I went over to his friend's house for pizza, but David wasn't acting normal. He was exceptionally quiet. He hardly said two words the entire evening.

Finally, I suggested we go home because I was bored. David wouldn't talk to me, and I sensed something was wrong. We went to his house and up to his room. David went over and shut the door—he never does that because it's against his parents' house rules. Then he walked over to his desk and threw a Harry Connick, Jr., T-shirt at me. I looked at him in confusion because I didn't know how he got it. David said that his cousin bought the T-shirts for us because we

gave him the tickets. Then I asked what was bothering him because he was so quiet. David said in a strong voice, looking out the window, "I lied, okay. I said it. I went to the concert." My face dropped to the ground and all I kept thinking was *why? Why? Why?*

I got up and looked at him and said, "Please tell me why you felt you couldn't tell me that you didn't want to go with me? What did I do? Who went instead of me?" David took a deep breath and said, "It's my fault. I lied. I didn't want to tell you. I didn't think I would feel this bad about it. I wasn't thinking, so I didn't tell you that I took Tina instead of you."

"Tina? Why would you take your ex-girlfriend instead of me? You promised to take me. What about your test? Was that a lie too?" I didn't give him a chance to explain; I just told him I couldn't accept him lying to me, that it wasn't fair because I really loved him and now all the trust in him I had was gone. How can I ever trust someone who doesn't know what the concept of honesty is? I slammed the door with my eyes full of tears and drove home. I didn't even care if what I said made any sense to him. I wanted so badly for him to realize that the best thing that ever happened to him just walked out the door and wasn't ever coming back. I didn't want to listen to him. I was so angry that nothing could change the way I felt.

David finally called me and explained to me the real issue that he avoided telling me. He explained that before we started going out he and Tina had agreed to be just friends and it had turned into a really good friendship. He said that he had originally bought the tickets for them to go to the concert together, but then we started dating, and he wasn't sure how I would feel about Tina. David explained that he didn't know what to do. He avoided telling me, thinking I would never find out.

Not all lies can be considered relational transgressions. When important information is withheld or distorted in an intimate relationship, though, the need to reconcile such behavior in the context of the relationship becomes paramount.

When Conflict Turns to Violence

Although most research on violence between relational partners is generated in the socio-logical and psychological literature, some researchers in communication have turned their attention to situations in which efforts to communicate fail and people turn to physical ag-gression to get their way. As Chapter 11 explained, escalation follows a pattern from ver-bal aggression to physical violence, and cultural expectations are that verbal aggression will turn to violence eventually. DeTurck studied the ways in which people change their persuasive tactics when faced with noncompliance. Using hypothetical scenarios and checklists of persuasive tactics, he found that people in noninterpersonal contexts (with strangers or acquaintances) were more likely to resort to punishment-oriented tactics and to decrease their use of reward-oriented tactics when faced with noncompliance, but peo-ple in interpersonal contexts were more likely to increase their use of both punishment- and reward-oriented tactics.[23]

More frightening than the use of punishment-oriented verbal tactics is the move to-ward physical means of expression in persuasion and conflict situations. Previous research has shown that men are far more likely to employ violence than women both against women and against other men.[24] Using a hypothetical scenario and checklist method again, deTurck examined the effects of gender and intimacy on the likelihood of using physical violence to achieve one's persuasive ends. Men are far more likely than women to use vi-olence when faced with noncompliance, particularly if the noncompliant person is a male with whom they have no strong interpersonal relationship, and men are almost as likely to use violence against a noncompliant female with whom they have no strong interpersonal relationship.[25] A study using naturalistic observation of parent-child dyads found that physical punishment was the second most frequently used compliance-gaining strategy, after commanding the child to obey.[26]

Writers in the field of communication have proposed that the movement from verbal aggressiveness to physical violence stems from **argumentative skill deficiency**—the in-ability to think of responses in the heat of an argument.[27] Violence is most likely when both people involved in the conflict have difficulty framing arguments. Research testing this re-lationship found that those in violent marriages are less argumentative (i.e., making claims and giving reasons for those claims) and more verbally aggressive than people in nonvio-lent marriages. Violent couples are not able to talk through issues. Further research indi-cated that attacks on the other person's character are most frequently associated with the movement from verbal aggressiveness to physical violence, along with swearing, attacks on the other person's competence, and threats. Verbal aggressiveness is present in all re-called instances of violence but does not necessarily lead to violence. Some couples are able to end an aggressive episode, but when one person has a predisposition to physical vi-olence, verbal aggressiveness can trigger it.[28]

How often does physical violence occur in relationships? It is estimated that 2 to 6 million women a year will be physically abused by their husbands; between 2,000 and 4,000 of them will be beaten to death. Of the women murdered each year, 40 percent will be killed by their spouse or lover.[29] Despite its popularity as a topic on talk shows, do-mestic violence toward men is rarely reported. Research examining the dynamic process of domestic violence has found a recognizable pattern to the use of violence in marital re-lationships. Similar to the model of aggression in general, three stages of violent domes-tic episodes have been proposed:

1. a verbal confrontation, which is followed by
2. threats by the person who will employ the violence and evasive action taken by the victim in an effort to stave off the violent attack, which is followed by
3. physical violence.[30]

This cycle of violent behavior was confirmed through intensive interviews with battered wives.[31] Sources of conflict leading to physical violence usually centered on possessiveness and jealousy, money, and demands for domestic labor and service. Men were most likely to become violent at the point at which the woman was seen as questioning their authority, challenging their behavior, or asserting herself in some way. Most assaults took place in the home—in the living room or the hallway—rather than the bedroom (which is frequently speculated to be the scene of the attack). Most attacks took place between 10:00 P.M. and 2:00 A.M. on Friday and Saturday nights.

Contrary to previous findings, research found that witnesses to an attack rarely encouraged or initiated it but rather attempted to appease the aggressors in order to discourage the violence. Once an argument began, the women generally tried various tactics to resolve the argument and avert the use of violence, generally through trying to withdraw from the situation, reasoning, or arguing. Once violence started, most women took a passive stance, claiming that resistance aggravated the assailant and made their injuries worse.

Also contrary to one argument that violent episodes between domestic partners are followed by an apologies-and-forgiveness stage, which makes the violence seem acceptable and the woman an accomplice to her own injury,[32] violent episodes are rarely followed by apologies, asking for forgiveness, or "loving" behavior. After a "typical" assault, 80 percent of the men acted as though nothing had happened, although 35 percent apologized if it was the first time they used violence against their mate. In response to the argument that women help perpetuate the cycle of violence, Dobash and Dobash claimed the following:

> Space does not allow us to consider the fallacies of the idea of equating the forgiveness of an act with its acceptance, and construing this as some form of agreement as to the continuation of the act in the future. . . . [A] detailed analysis of such events in terms of what people actually do and how this changes over time challenges [the] notion that this loving and forgiving stage is characteristic of violent events in general. . . . [T]here is almost no empirical support for the notion that it continues with subsequent acts and, thereby, forms a usual part of the violent event.[33]

Clearly, violence in an interpersonal relationship constitutes a relational transgression, a violation of expected behavior. Violence, when it occurs, is an event progressing from an out-of-control conflict episode, and it creates an issue that the relational partners will have to deal with if they are to remain in relationship with one another.

Conflict, Forgiveness, and Reconciliation

The need to study forgiveness and reconciliation is based on the assumption that conflicts are cyclical and repetitive (see schismogenesis, URP, competitive escalation cycle, and chilling effect in Chapter 5), affected by what has come previously and affecting what will come after. Forgiveness and reconciliation are related, but separate, processes. **Forgiveness** is a cognitive process that consists of letting go of feelings of revenge and desires to retaliate. **Reconciliation** is a behavior process in which we rebuild trust in a relationship and work toward restoration. Together, forgiveness and reconciliation may have a greater effect on long-term relationships than does message behavior.

APPLICATION 16.2

Is there an event in your life that you find difficult to forgive? What is it? What makes it so difficult to forgive the other person? If you are not experiencing a difficult event now, describe a past event that you found difficult to forgive.

Part of the Social Fabric

Teachings on the necessity of forgiveness and reconciliation between estranged individuals are at least as old as recorded civilization. The concept of forgiveness is a core value of the Judeo-Christian culture, as well as a central concept in all major religions.[34] Surviving excerpts of Babylonian Wisdom Literature, predating the biblical exodus out of Egypt and the giving of Jewish law, exhort:

> When confronted with a dispute, go your own way; pay no attention to it. Should it be a dispute of your own, extinguish the flame. . . . Do not return evil to the (person) who disputes with you; requite with kindness your evildoer, maintain justice to your enemy, smile on your adversary. . . . Do not let evil sleep affect your heart; banish misery and suffering from your side.[35]

Virtually every culture has a concept of transgression or sin against the gods, a particular god, or others, and most address the process by which sin is erased or forgiven.[36] Philosopher Hannah Arendt claimed that forgiveness is an essential characteristic of the human condition:

> The discoverer of the role of forgiveness in the realm of human affairs was Jesus of Nazareth. The fact that he made this discovery in a religious context and articulated it in religious language is no reason to take it any less seriously in a secular sense . . . aspects of [his] teaching . . . are not primarily related to the Christian religious message but sprang from experiences in the small and closely knit community of his followers, bent on challenging the local authorities in Israel.[37]

Conflicts arise largely because we feel as though someone has "transgressed" against us; we enact conflicts so as to correct the transgression. Forgiveness and reconciliation are processes that occur after the conflict has been enacted. Still, one author noted the following:

> Forgiveness has often been considered a problematic virtue because it can be difficult to justify in practice, particularly if it is not conditioned by repentance, judgment, or restitution. . . . Saints or saintly people, those at the point of death, and those at a great temporal or physical distance from an offense are more easily portrayed as forgiving or receiving forgiveness.[38]

Why People Don't Forgive or Restore Relationships

"Don't get mad—get even" reads a popular bumper sticker. Why should we forgive? Do people not deserve to be punished when they have hurt us? And why would we want to restore a relationship with a person who has hurt us? Several lines of research explain the need for forgiveness. One study examined the way people describe transgressions, how they have come to forgive or not forgive the other person, and whether or not they attempted reconciliation. When people report that they have not forgiven the person who offended them, the primary reason for not forgiving is that they have not received an apology or an explanation from the other. Because the other has admitted no wrongdoing, they are not willing to forgive. In addition, people report refusal to forgive when the other continues in offensive behavior.[39] One study found that college-aged students, whose primary report of issues requiring forgiveness is hurts from dating relationships, found it more difficult to forgive than any other age group.[40]

There are other reasons why people don't forgive. Sometimes being hurt has created a loss of face for the person who has been offended, and forgiving the transgressor would cause an even greater loss of face. Others do not want to give up their right to hold a grudge; it gives them a sense of power to hold their hurt over the other's head. Fear of being vulnerable and experiencing anxiety over that possibility is a barrier to forgiveness.[41] Some people don't forgive because they enjoy being a victim and not being held responsible for what they do in the here and now. And, perhaps most importantly, some people don't forgive because there is no support in their social system for doing so. It is difficult to forgive when others are saying that one should not.[42]

Those who have not forgiven rarely continue a relationship with the other. Any interaction with the other is a matter of obligation (e.g., at a family gathering, or working in the same organization) rather than a matter of choice. However, forgiving the other does not necessarily lead to reconciliation. Many people forgive, but at a distance. They let go of their need for revenge, but do not choose to put themselves in a position where they can be hurt again. It is a rare account that reports both forgiveness and reconciliation, or restored relationship, with the other.[43]

Whereas some have argued that forgiving a wrongdoing too soon, particularly a criminal one, is a sign of insufficient self-respect,[44] most writers in the area of forgiveness have argued that holding onto grief and hurts is the sign of a psychologically unhealthy person. Holding grudges constitutes an egocentric position wherein we view those who have hurt us only in terms of what we need, what we wish, or what we long for.[45] It puts us in the position of judge, a position that few of us are qualified to hold.

> [Revenge] is based on the belief that . . . it is possible to measure the magnitude of an offense, to receive an equal amount of retribution somehow balances the account. An unforgiving attitude assumes that how one feels about past events is based on an economy similar to that of money and that a person will thus feel poor and deprived if he or she has not sought an equal measure for all the wrongs committed against them. Revenge is a zero-sum game.[46]

By placing blame on other people, we relinquish our control over our emotions and give that control to another.[47] Research examining social adjustment and the ability to forgive found a high correlation between the two: As a person's social adjustment score went up, so did the person's ability to forgive.[48] More recent research on the role of forgiveness in counseling and mental health has demonstrated that teaching people about forgiveness and training them in forgiveness strategies helped increase recovery from divorce (restoring positive feelings about oneself, etc.), decreased feelings of guilt, and decreased feelings of depression and anxiety.[49] A lack of forgiveness accompanied by resentment and bitterness is a stress factor leading to burnout.[50] Linn and Linn argued that "forgiveness is at least as important a discovery for treating emotional illness as penicillin is for treating physical illness."[51]

APPLICATION 16.3

Seven years ago a thief broke into your home, went through your personal belongings, and stole many of your possessions. He was caught, much of your property was returned to you (but some was damaged), and he was sentenced to seven years in a state prison. Are you now in a position to forgive him for what he did to you? Should all convicted felons be forgiven after they serve their time in prison? Do you feel differently if the crime was committed against you? Would you feel differently if you were the one convicted?

Not only is forgiveness related to our psychological health, it is related to our physical health as well. Research on cancer patients has discovered four personality traits characteristic of people prone to get cancer. The first trait is a tendency to hold resentments and an inability to forgive. The second trait is a tendency toward self-pity, and the third is a very poor self-image (related to one's inability to forgive oneself). The fourth trait was a poor ability to develop and maintain a meaningful long-term relationship.[52] Senior citizens who manifested greater abilities to forgive others reported better physical health than those who reported less ability to forgive others.[53]

The relationship between anger, nonforgiveness, and physical illness comes from the stress of experiencing ongoing anger and failing to forgive. Anger is part of the flight-fight response to stressors: Fear underlies how we respond to a situation that turns to anger as our unmet needs are frustrated. We experience physical damage when this flight-fight mechanism, which was designed for short-term emergency responses to situations, becomes a longer-term ongoing response.

> Except in the case of trauma (physical damage from a car accident, house falling, radiation, etc.) anger and guilt play a role in triggering most physical damage to our body. . . . Tensions and frustrations lower the immunization mechanism of the body, thus opening the door for bacteria and viruses to cause physical illness.[54]

The evidence would indicate that forgiveness is an important mental process that should follow traumatic conflict. Reconciliation, on the other hand, is a communication process that we may choose to avoid, particularly if we are likely to be violated by the other again. Unfortunately, most of us are not predisposed to forgive or reconcile with others. Nonforgiveness seems more "reasonable" because through it we can save face and impose a punishment on the person who hurt us. There is not a great deal of social pressure to forgive; in fact, people often think a forgiving person is stupid or naive to be that way.[55]

What Is Forgiveness?

There is virtual agreement in the literature that forgiveness is a process in which a person lets go of feelings of revenge and his or her right to retaliate against the other person. With few exceptions, forgiveness is not equated with forgetting what has happened. Nor is forgiveness equated with the immediate restoration of trust. Forgiveness is generally conceived of as a process through which people get on with their lives after experiencing some hurt.

Research has begun to measure what forgiveness feels like to those who forgive and what it looks like to those observing it. McCullough and Rachal claim that the ability to feel empathy for the offender is the primary way in which people move toward forgiveness.[56] Enright, a leading researcher on the topic of forgiveness, disagrees, arguing that forgiveness includes cognitive, emotional, and behavioral dimensions.[57] Cognitively, forgiveness is characterized by a reduced focus on the other person (in unforgiveness, one might be obsessive about the source of hurt), affirmation of the other as an individual, lack of desire for revenge, and a rejection of a definition of self as a victim. The affective dimensions of forgiveness include the presence of positive feelings and absence of negative feelings toward the other. Forgiveness is defined behaviorally as movement toward reconciliation (not avoiding the other or withdrawing) and giving up a grudge against the other.[58]

One study examined forgiveness as described by people who had experienced instances of forgiveness or nonforgiveness with an important person in their life. The subjects wrote descriptions of their situations, and then the researcher analyzed the content of the account, looking for descriptions of communication and relational rules that were broken and how those situations were remedied. Confirming previous models of forgiveness, the researcher concluded that forgiveness is a process that starts with anger over a transgression and moves toward transforming the meaning of the event.[59]

Several models of forgiveness have been developed. Only one concerns the process of asking for forgiveness from another person. It includes stages of guilt over the transgression, confession to the other person concerning the fault, feelings of remorse (indicating a desire for reconciliation), restitution (reestablishing conditions of the relationship), mutual acceptance, and reconciliation. The remaining models illustrate the process of forgiving another person. They are shown in Table 16.2.

As you can see, there are few similarities between the models. All agree that forgiveness is a process, but the way in which it unfolds varies widely. Linn and Linn's model is based on the Kubler-Ross model of death and dying and is primarily a therapeutic model for healing past hurts. In the first stage, we deny that we ever were hurt. Once we acknowledge a hurt, we feel anger toward the one who hurt us. In the next stage, we set up conditions that must be met before we will forgive the other person. Depression sets in when we blame ourselves for letting others hurt us. In the final stage, we look forward to growing from the hurt we have experienced. Donnelly's model starts with an acknowledgment of the hurt, followed by a decision to forgive with reminders of the consequences of not forgiving. There is no resolution stage in this model.[60]

Smedes has a simple, four-stage model: We hurt, we hate, we heal, and then we reconcile (i.e., we come together again). **Healing** happens as a matter of reframing the event: We are given "magic eyes" to see the person who hurt us in a different light. Augsburger's model starts after the decision to forgive: We value the other person, seeing that person as having worth regardless of the hurt he or she caused us; we love, seeing the other as equally precious again; we cancel demands and recognize that we cannot change the past; we

TABLE 16.2   *Models of the Process of Forgiveness*

Linn and Linn	Donnelly	Smedes	Augsburger
Denial			
	Acknowledge the hurt and affirm the pain	Hurt	
Anger		Hate	
Bargaining			
Depression			
	Decide to forgive		
		Healing	Valuing
			Loving
			Canceling demands
			Trusting now
	Remember that forgiveness is not easy		
	Forgive the self		
	Consider the consequences of nonforgiveness		
Acceptance		Coming together	Opening the future
			Celebrating love

decide to trust again and risk until it is seen by both people as authentic; we open ourselves to the future and allow ourselves to be spontaneous; and, finally, we celebrate love in recognition that the relationship has been restored.[61] Central to all these models of forgiveness is an acknowledgment of the hurt, a decision to let go of the past, an attempt to reframe the event so that it becomes less central in a person's life and/or in the life of a relationship, and an acceptance that the past is past.[62]

A model that acknowledges alternative outcomes in a relationship in which forgiveness does not happen was developed by Johnson and is shown in Figure 16.1. In this model, the process of forgiveness starts with a decision about a presumed violation in the relationship. This violation causes a person to decide how to change the relationship. If the person decides on vulnerability, then the decision is made to reinitiate intimacy, to rebuild trust, and to reconcile. Where a hurt is denied, superficial acceptance results, hurt continues, and the relationship deteriorates.

Enright and Gassin argue that there are different kinds of forgiveness that correspond to different levels of moral development.[63] At the most primitive level, forgiveness is granted only if the person who has been hurt can punish the offender with a similar level of pain—the "eye for an eye" mentality. At the second level, a person grants forgiveness if he or she can be given back what was taken from him or her. The first and second levels are actually preforgiveness levels because something is required before forgiveness will be granted. At the third level, a person grants forgiveness because others expect him or her to

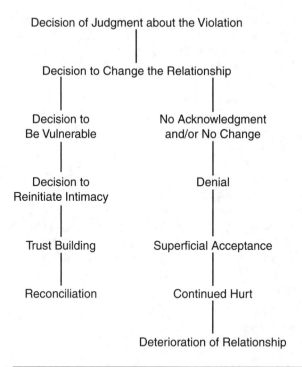

FIGURE 16.1 *Johnson's Model of Forgiveness*

Adapted from Karen Johnson, "A Model of Forgiveness," diss., Biola University, La Mirada, CA, 1986.

do so. At the fourth level, a person forgives because his or her religion demands it. Stages three and four depend on external demands for forgiveness to happen; the person doesn't actually choose to forgive on his or her own. At the fifth level, a person forgives because it will promote social harmony and help to maintain good relationships among people. At the highest level of forgiveness, a person grants forgiveness out of deep love for others that is not altered because of an offense; forgiveness is granted without the need for a response on the part of the other person. As a person experiences forgiveness at higher levels of the model, more complex thinking and perspective taking is required.

Clearly, forgiveness is a process that takes time. Whereas some therapists think that forgiveness can be grasped quickly in some cases, most researchers in the field argue that the process of forgiveness is one that unfolds over time and cannot be rushed.[64] The key in getting to the point of forgiveness is the ability to reframe the event that has occurred, to see it as an event among many in a relationship instead of the central event that defines the quality of the relationship. It is time-consuming and cannot occur if people are not willing to explore and reconcile the different feelings that arise as a result of transgressions.

What Forgiveness Is Not

Forgiveness is a letting go of past hurt and letting go of the desire for revenge. Forgiveness opens us, but does not obligate us, to reconciliation. It is not simply forgetting that something happened. It does not release the other person from the consequences of his or her behavior. It does not deny anger. It does not put us in a position of superiority. It is not a declaration of the end of all conflict, of ever risking again with the other person (or anybody else). It is not one way.[65] According to Hunter,

> There is an obtrusive and onerous quality to the "forgiving" so that one feels the need for protection against such "righteousness" . . . [It] seems to nurture the memory of past injustice, to precipitate fresh "injustice," or to broodingly fantasize injustice yet to come.[66]

We do not forgive in order to be martyrs to the relationship. We forgive because it is better for us, and better for the other person. We forgive because we want to act freely again, not react out of past pain. Smedes said that the best indicator we have forgiven is when we can think of the person who has hurt us, and we feel the power to wish that person well.

Some things, Smedes argued, are not worth forgiving, largely because they are not worth doing conflict over: annoyances, slights, disappointments. "It is wise not to turn all hurts into crises of forgiving. . . . We put everyone we love on guard when we turn personal misdemeanors into major felonies."[67]

Strategizing for Forgiveness

The preceding discussion covered various models of forgiveness and research concerning it. But how do we go about forgiving and opening ourselves to reconciliation? The first step is to decide whether we want to create, alter, or restore the relationship. It is appropriate to forgive at a distance, so to speak, when the other person has not changed, has shown no willingness to change, continues to engage in offensive behavior, or poses a harm to us mentally or physically. Under these conditions, we forgive for our own sake—to let go of the offense, to move on with our lives, and to approach new relationships freely. But under these conditions, contacting the other and becoming vulnerable again by expressing our anger and our hurt may cause more harm than good.

If we believe that the relationship may be restored eventually, then it is important to risk telling the other about our hurt. It is a risk because, as accounts research shows, the other person may tell us that our feelings are not justified or that we have no right to be hurt. Reconciliation, however, is an interpersonal concept based on the intrapersonal process of forgiveness. Moving toward reconciliation without ever bringing an offense to light may simply be a way of "keeping books" on the relationship until the other person has emptied the account. In this case, timing and preparation for the encounter are important. You will need to choose a time and place where you and the other person may talk freely, and you will need to prepare yourself for the possibility that the other may not acknowledge your feelings as valid.

It is easier to forgive when the other person admits guilt. Even so, depending on the offense, we may have a problem in trusting again. A frequent question asked is "Does this mean I have to trust the other person like I did before?" We think the answer is no. Forgiveness means releasing the offense and moving toward creating, altering, or reestablishing a relationship; it is going forward, not going back. A relationship is changed by a relational transgression. Trust needs to be rebuilt. But acting from a state of distrust is dysfunctional. What you can try to do is act from a position of neutrality and work up to previously established levels. You give the other person the same benefit of doubt you would give others in your life; as trustworthiness increases, so does trust. The internal process of forgiving is described in Table 16.3.

The best analogy for explaining the healing that occurs after relational transgressions is the healing process after physical injury. Depending on the level of injury, you may experience mild or intense pain and may need varying lengths of time for the injury to heal. If you broke your leg, for example, you will limp even after the bone has set. You may favor the leg for a while or may avoid putting weight on it. Eventually, though, the fact that you broke your leg does not define your movements anymore. You have adjusted to the injury and learned to live with it. The bone will always reflect the injury: The occurrence of the injury is a fact. But it need not always dictate the way you behave. We believe that forgiveness has occurred when we no longer define our emotions, our desires, or our behaviors in terms of the injury. The injury becomes a part of who we are, not the whole of what we are.

APPLICATION 16.4

Return to the incident you described in Application 16.2. What will it take for you to forgive the other person? What are the consequences of forgiving the other person? Of not forgiving the other person?

The Importance of Creating Reconciliation

If we wish to create, alter, or reestablish our relationship, forgiving the other person is not enough. That forgiveness must also be communicated to the person so that reconciliation can begin. The need for communicating forgiveness is found in research examining self-fulfilling prophecies. A **self-fulfilling prophecy** is one in which people act toward us in the way that we expect. It was first demonstrated quite dramatically in classroom situations in which teachers were told that students were exceptional or average (there was actually

TABLE 16.3   *Forgiving Another Person*

- Understand that forgiveness is a process.
- Start with a recognition of how you have been hurt.
- Allow yourself to be angry about the hurt.
- Don't get stuck in the victim stage.
- Find people to support your forgiveness process.
- Recognize that you may not be able to get the other person to treat you any differently than in the past. Focus then on your responsibility in the situation and your responses to it.
- Try to see the other person as someone like yourself—human, having flaws, and making mistakes. This helps you escape from the villain/victim mentality.
- Try to see yourself as a person like the other—capable of hurting people, capable of doing something wrong (not necessarily that you are capable of the same offense). This helps you escape from a position of superiority with respect to the other.
- Think about what you have learned from the situation, and how you have grown as a result of it.

no difference in the students). As the teacher communicated expectations, though, students responded accordingly: Those in "exceptional" classes performed better than average; those in "average" classes performed adequately but did not do outstanding work.[68]

Later research attempted to map the cognitive changes that take place as a result of expectations being met and behavior being changed. In a study that combined different research methods in which coders "blind" to the experiment's purpose classified behavior, Fazio and others found that expectations not only influence a person's behavior but also can create lasting cognitive changes in that person. Suppose, for example, that Dana has been told that Chris is an outgoing, extroverted person. Dana develops an expectation regarding Chris's behavior and acts toward Chris on the basis of that expectation. Chris, in turn, responds to the expectation, acting in an extroverted way even though Chris's original conception of self did not include extroversion. In turn, Dana sees Chris acting in an extroverted way, confirming the original expectations, whereas Chris looks at the behavior and thinks, "I act in an extroverted way. I guess I am an extrovert." The researchers point out that this last step can actually be enacted in one of three ways. Chris may decide that he is an extrovert only when he is around Dana; so his behavior will only be changed for future interaction with Dana. Chris may decide that he is an extrovert only in the type of situation that he shared initially with Dana, and so his behavior would only be changed for situations of that type. Or Chris may decide he is, in general, an extrovert, changing his behavior for future interactions across types of situations.[69]

So what does this have to do with the process of forgiveness? If someone has said something to offend you, and you say, "It's all right," but act as though it is not, the other person is going to take your actions as the best indicator of your feelings. If you act toward the other as though he or she is not trustworthy, there is a pretty good chance that the other will begin to act in untrustworthy ways. If you act toward the other as though the relationship is strained, he or she will come to believe it is strained and will act in ways that reflect this belief.

> Normal life ceases [when we do not feel forgiven]. . . . [W]e feel forgiven when we get back to the familiar routine. . . . This return to normalcy may be an illusion. Logic tells us that life can never be quite the same after monumental hurt. Even if the wound has healed there will still be scar tissue. But the more the present mirrors the past, the greater the assurance of pardon.
>
> Although some heard the statement, "I forgive you," the words themselves had little impact. Offenders look for confirmation in deed. If the victim's response mirrored reconciliation, the assurance of pardon was unnecessary.[70]

As discussed in the previous section, reconciliation does not mean you simply forget what happened, but you do move forward in your relationship, rebuilding trust and reestablishing intimacy. Acting in ways that signal forgiveness creates expectations of renewed relationship and the possibility of change. Reconciliation means acting in ways that do not lock the relationship into constant reexamination of the offense.

The process of communicating forgiveness and creating reconciliation is illustrated in Figure 16.2, which depicts a **forgiveness/reconciliation loop.**[71] Social construction theory suggests that we make our social worlds by the way we talk about them, and we act within our social worlds based on the way we have made them through our talk. For example, a couple that is beginning to date might say, "We are just friends," and act accordingly, but as the relationship progresses and they move to a definition of "dating partners,"

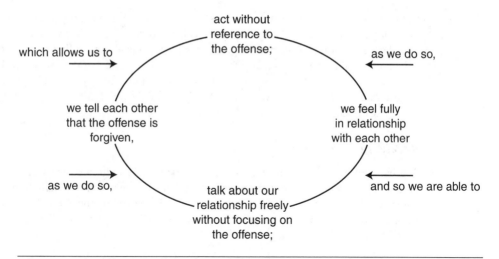

FIGURE 16.2   *The Forgiveness/Reconciliation Loop*

their behaviors will change also. In a sort of circular way, their affectionate behaviors increase because they change the definition of the relationship, and as the affectionate behaviors increase they give labels to their relationship that define it as more serious. Thus, in the communication-reality loop, the way we communicate about our behavior helps to constitute the reality of it. As we describe our behavior, we affect the way we behave; as we behave, we affect the way we describe our behavior.

The process of forgiveness and reconciliation works in the same way: We tell each other that the act is forgiven, which allows us to act without reference to the offense; in turn, we feel more fully in relationship with one another and can talk about our relationship without reference to the offense; so in turn we tell each other that all is forgiven. Some evidence for this kind of reconciliation loop was found in a study of married couples who had enacted forgiveness; three of the means used to communicate that forgiveness had taken place were a return to mundane rituals (signaling that the relationship is "back to normal"), expressions of nonverbal affection, and the use of empathy to understand why the other had committed the offense.[72]

This model is a good example of a communication approach to conflict resolution (see the transactional model of communication in Chapter 8). Within this forgiveness/reconciliation loop, reconciliation is a social construction: Those in a fractured or stressed relationship must create a meaning for the concept they term forgiveness, and must create the actions necessary to make forgiveness seem real to them. Constructing reconciliation is the process of integrating what has become problematic into the realm of the unproblematic in relationships. Small conflicts may only cause people to temporarily pause and ask about the fit of the conflict into the total relationship. Transgressions interrupt their everyday reality, forcing them to reconcile vastly different pieces of the relationship. Accounts and apologies offer new definitions for the offense and its role within the relationship; reconciliation is the process of enacting that new definition so that it becomes permanent.

Thus, expressing forgiveness after conflict becomes a self-fulfilling prophecy when enacted correctly: We say forgiveness is possible; we act toward the other as though we have forgiven; the other, in turn, feels forgiven; and we are able to have a relationship that has moved beyond a relational transgression to where the transgression no longer defines the relationship. Here we have a communication process (involving verbal and nonverbal language, attributions, expectations, confirmation) that is also a conflict resolution process. When any of these steps break down—if we say we forgive but do not act as though we have or if we continue to refer to the offense as though it has not passed—forgiveness is almost impossible. Instead, we become victims of the relational transgression, and the transgression defines us and our relationship with the other.

Receiving Forgiveness

A great deal more has been written on the process of communicating forgiveness to the other than on receiving forgiveness from the other. But clearly, if reconciliation is to be accomplished, forgiveness must be both granted and received by those involved. Enright developed a process model of receiving forgiveness,[73] which was recently tested by Gassin.[74] Enright's model has four stages:

1. an uncovering phase, in which a person admits the hurt that he or she has inflicted on another person;
2. a decision phase, in which a person feels a need for a change in relationship with the other and decides to accept the other's forgiveness;
3. a work phase, in which the person who committed the offense tries to understand the person who was hurt;
4. an outcome phase, in which the person who committed the offense feels genuinely forgiven by the other.

Gassin's research indicated that the primary emotions experienced by those receiving forgiveness are joy and relief, followed by a desire not to hurt the other person again. Few people reported immediate reconciliation or reestablishment of trust. Gassin argues that the forgiveness and reconciliation are sequential. First, a person experiences a sense of relief that he or she has been forgiven. Next, trust is reestablished. Third, reconciliation begins to take place. Finally, a sense of closure is perceived by those in the fractured relationship.

The conclusions of the various studies examining forgiveness appear to be these: Forgiveness takes time, trust needs to be reestablished when relationship rules have been broken, and reconciliation occurs after forgiveness and the reestablishment of trust. It is not easy to forgive, but it is absolutely necessary if a relationship is to grow past the offense.

Moving beyond Victimization

There is a tendency in our society to look for others outside of ourselves to blame. But it is the ability to move beyond the feeling of being a victim that leads to a state of forgiveness:

> [W]hile the victim phase may be a useful part of recovery, it is not sufficient as a total approach to recovery. . . . [W]hat survivors have in common, among other things, is that they do not accept the label or identity of victim. . . . Forgiving has nothing to do with memory loss. There is no need to forget injustices and injuries, or pretend they never happened, and some events must never be forgotten. But that is quite different from letting them dominate one's present state of mind.[75]

We had a family friend who lived with us throughout my childhood years. He molested me numerous times over the course of my childhood. I never told my parents until long after he had died. I thought I had worked through most of my forgiveness issues when I found out that my parents had let him live with us knowing that he had served time in jail for child molesting. What were they thinking of? How could they let him spend time alone with me? How couldn't they know? I had forgiven my molester, and I had stopped thinking of myself as a child-abuse victim, but in some ways it was harder to forgive my parents.

You may never experience a traumatic event like physical or sexual assault, or have someone lie to you about an important issue, and so on.[76] In the course of your everyday conflicts, however, you will at times feel as though you have been victimized (used, manipulated, abused) by another. Perhaps the feeling results from having things you told to the other in trust used as weapons against you in a conflict. It may arise from having your personal possessions taken or destroyed.

Forgiveness is a process. It may take days, weeks, or years. Forgiveness is a process that allows us to act freely again. Without it, we are held by the event that victimized us; with it, we move forward. It is "reframing of how one views the world. . . . [It is] in reality a case of acting in one's own enlightened self-interest."[77] Forgiveness is the final stage of conflict and is the one thing that is most likely to prevent repetitive, destructive cycles of conflict.

I will never forget the time I took a trust and openness class in which the topic was "Someone in my life whom I want to forgive." As a group exercise, we discussed the steps to forgiveness and then we each had to contribute a personal experience of unresolved and unforgiving conflict with someone. You would not believe what happened. Adult men and women alike told shocking stories of wrongs done to them, and they talked about their anger and rage. The facilitator told us that we have been suffering long enough. He asked us to picture our antagonists as children. Picture what was being done to us as being done to them as little children. He said we know that people do to others that which was done to them often as children. He asked us to free them from their wrongs and see them as the wronged, needy people they are. Instead of distancing us from those who had wronged us, he brought us together as mutual victims who are suffering together. I have difficulty believing what then happened. There were changes and healing like I have never seen before. We were all overwhelmed by what was happening. Some cried, some held hands, some hugged the facilitator and then one another. I couldn't help but wonder what would happen if everyone in the world went through a group experience like this.

If you cannot disengage people from their past and see them as the victims they are, too, you will enslave yourself to an ugly emotional affair. Quite often we have unresolved conflicts with others, especially with family members. These unforgiving experiences are now serving as a barrier between you and that person, preventing you from having the positive relationship both of you need. Someday you will realize that these people were only doing the best they knew how. They brought "past baggage" with them. Now you are in a good position to drop the baggage you have been carrying in favor of new tools. You no longer have to act out what was done to you. As we move forward in our new ways, we can also let go of our feelings that "justified" our old ways. We can stop seeking revenge and choose to forgive. A new outlook, it is hoped, will alter or reestablish a much needed relationship. If the other doesn't respond, let it be. Forgiveness will be your benefit alone to enjoy.

From Theory to Action

This chapter has focused on research that helps us understand how to make amends after a conflict has occurred and has been handled poorly. Like the ability to analyze conflicts and the ability to effectively communicate feelings and desires, the use of forgiveness and reconciliation strategies to cope with difficult conflicts is a skill that can be learned. Through the processes of forgiveness and reconciliation, we can forge new relationships or repair former ones and move forward by letting go of the past. Understanding the kind of response necessitated by various transgressions is important, as is developing a repertoire of responses designed to remediate problematic situations. Of all the skills in conflict, the ability to put the conflict into perspective and move forward is probably the most important—without repairs, our relationships become unstable; without forgiveness, our relationships eventually come to an end.

Notes

1. Joyce Hocker and William W. Wilmot, *Interpersonal Conflict,* 3rd Ed. (Dubuque, IA: Wm. C. Brown, 1991), p. 36.

2. Allan L. Sillars and Judith Weisberg, "Conflict as a Social Skill," in Michael E. Roloff and Gerald R. Miller (Eds.), *Interpersonal Processes: New Directions in Theory and Research* (Newbury Park: Sage, 1987), p. 140.

3. Dean G. Pruitt and Jeffrey Z. Rubin, *Social Conflict: Escalation, Stalemate, and Settlement* (New York: Random House, 1986), pp. 111–112.

4. See, for example, Mary Murray, "When You've Done Wrong," *Reader's Digest* (March 1992), 149–154; Diane Cole, "So You Made a Mistake!" *Working Mother* (August 1991), 29–30.

5. Louis B. Smedes, *Forgive and Forget: Healing the Hurts We Don't Deserve* (San Francisco: Harper & Row, 1984).

6. Sandra Metts, "Relational Transgressions," in William R. Cupach and Brian H. Spitzberg, *The Dark Side of Interpersonal Communication* (Hillsdale, NJ: Lawrence Erlbaum, 1994), p. 218.

7. Ibid., p. 4.

8. Paul A. Mongeau, M. A. Clason, and Jerold L. Hale, "Attributions of Responsibility, Guilt, and Blame Following a Relational Transgression," paper presented at the International Communication Association Convention, San Francisco, May 1989; Paul A. Mongeau and Jerold L. Hale, "Attributions of Responsibility for Relational Transgressions," paper presented at the Western Speech Communication Association Convention, Sacramento, CA, February 1990; Paul A. Mongeau, Jerold L. Hale, and P. E. Griffin, "The Impact of Intentionality and Alcohol Consumption on Attributions Following a Sexual Transgression," paper presented at the Central States Communication Association Convention, Detroit, MI,

April 1990; Paul A. Mongeau and Jerold L. Hale, "The Influence of Intent and Revenge on Attributions and Communication Following a Relational Transgression," paper presented at the Communication Association, Chicago, November 1990; see also K. M. McGraw, "Guilt Following Transgression: An Attribution of Responsibility Approach," *Journal of Personality and Social Psychology* 53 (1987), 247–256.

9. David M. Droll, "Forgiveness: Theory and Research," Doctoral dissertation, University of Nevada, Reno, 1985.

10. Mark L. Knapp, Laura Stafford, and John A. Daly, "Regrettable Messages: Things People Wish They Hadn't Said," *Journal of Communication* 36 (1987), 58.

11. Mark L. Knapp and Mark E. Comadena, "Telling It Like It Isn't: A Review of Theory and Research on Deceptive Communications," *Human Communication Research* 5 (1979), 271.

12. Paula V. Lippard, " 'Ask Me No Questions, I'll Tell You No Lies: Situational Exigencies for Interpersonal Deception," *Western Journal of Speech Communication* 52 (1988), 91.

13. Dan O'Hair and Michael J. Cody, "Deception: The Darkside of Interpersonal Communication?" paper presented at the Western Speech Communication Association, Phoenix, February 1991.

14. R. E. Turner, C. Eagly, and G. Olmstead, "Information Control in Conversation: Honesty Is Not Always the Best Policy," *Kansas Journal of Sociology* 11 (1975), 69–89; Dale Hample, "Purposes and Effects of Lying," *Southern Speech Communication Journal* 46 (1980), 33–47.

15. Lippard.

16. S. Booth-Butterfield and M. Booth-Butterfield, "Untangling the Tangled Web: Theory and Empirical

Tests of Interpersonal Deception," paper presented at the International Communication Association Convention Montreal, Canada, May 1987.

17. Lippard, "Ask Me No Questions."

18. Steven A. McComack and Malcolm R. Parks, "Deception Detection and Relationship Development: The Other Side of Trust," in Margaret L. McLaughlin (Ed.), *Communication Yearbook* 9 (Beverly Hills: Sage Publications, 1986), pp. 377–389; James B. Stiff, Hyun J. Kim, and C. N. Ramesh, "Truth-Biases and Aroused Suspicion in Relational Deception," paper presented at the International Communication Association Convention, San Francisco, May 1989.

19. Steven A. McComack and Timothy R. Levine, "When Lovers Become Leery: The Relationship Between Suspicion and Accuracy in Detecting Deception," *Communication Monographs* 57 (1990), 219–230.

20. Timothy R. Levine and Steven A. McComack, "The Dark Side of Trust: Conceptualizing and Measuring Types of Communicative Suspicion," *Communication Quarterly* 39 (1991), 325–340.

21. Steven A. McComack and Timothy R. Levine, "When Lies Are Uncovered: Emotion and Relational Outcomes of Discovered Deception," *Communication Monographs* 5 (1990), 121.

22. Ibid.

23. Mark A. deTurck, "A Transactional Analysis of Compliance-Gaining Behavior," *Human Communication Research* 12 (1985), 54–78.

24. R. J. Gelles, "Violence in the Family: A Review of Research in the Seventies," *Journal of Marriage and the Family* 42 (1980), 143–155.

25. Mark A. deTurck, "When Communication Fails: Physical Aggression as a Compliance Gaining Strategy," *Communication Monographs* 54 (1987), 106–112.

26. Steven T. McDermott, "Naturalistic Observations of Parental Attempts at Gaining Compliance," paper presented at the Speech Communication Association Convention Chicago, November 1986.

27. Dominic A. Infante, Teresa A. Chandler, and Jill E. Rudd, "Test of an Argumentative Skill Deficiency Model of Interspousal Violence," *Communication Monographs* 5 (1989), 163–177.

28. Dominic A. Infante, Teresa Chandler Sabourin, Jill E. Rudd, and Elizabeth A. Shannon, "Verbal Aggression in Violent and Nonviolent Marital Disputes," *Communication Quarterly* 38 (1990), 361–371.

29. Gary P. Liaboe, "The Place of Wife Battering in Considering Divorce," *Journal of Psychology and Theology* 13 (1985), 129–138.

30. R. B. Felson and J. Steadman, "Situational Factors in Disputes Leading to Criminal Violence," *Criminology* 21 (1983), 59–74.

31. R. Emerson Dobash and Russell P. Dobash, "The Nature and Antecedents of Violent Events," *British Journal of Criminology* 24 (1984), 269–288.

32. Lenore Walker, "Treatment Alternatives for Battered Women," in Jane Roberts Chapman and Margaret Gates (Eds.), *The Victimization of Women* (Beverly Hills, CA: Sage, 1987).

33. Dobash and Dobash, "The Nature and Antecedents of Violent Events," p. 281.

34. Donald Hope, "The Healing Paradox of Forgiveness," *Psychotherapy* 24 (1987), 240–244.

35. W. G. Lambert, *Babylonian Wisdom Literature* (London: Oxford University Press, 1960), pp. 101, 109.

36. James Hastings (Ed.), *Encyclopedia of Religion and Ethics* (Edinburgh: T. & T. Clark, 1974), pp. 528–571.

37. Hannah Arendt, *The Human Condition* (Chicago: University of Chicago Press, 1956), pp. 238–239.

38. Thomas Trzyna, "Forgiveness and Time," *Christian Scholar's Review* 22 (1992), pp. 7, 8.

39. Roxane S. Lulofs, "Swimming Upstream: Creating Reasons for Unforgiveness in a Culture That Expects Otherwise," paper presented to the Speech Communication Association Convention, San Antonio, TX, November 1995.

40. Michael J. Subkoviak, Robert D. Enright, Ching-Ru Wu, Elizabeth A. Gassin, Suzanne Freedman, Leanne M. Olson, and Issidoros Sarinopolous, "Measuring Interpersonal Forgiveness," paper presented at the American Educational Research Association Convention, San Francisco, April 1992.

41. R. P. Fitzgibbons, "The Cognitive and Emotional Uses of Forgiveness in the Treatment of Anger," *Psychotherapy* 23 (1986), 629–633.

42. For an excellent illustration of the variability of people's support or lack of support for forgiveness, see Simon Wiesenthal's *The Sunflower: On the Possibilities and Limits of Forgiveness* (New York: Schocken Books, 1997).

43. Lulofs, "Swimming Upstream."

44. Joshua Dressler, "Hating Criminals: How Can Something That Feels So Good Be Wrong?" *Michigan Law Review* 88 (1990), 1454.

45. Heinz Kohut, "Narcissism and Narcissistic Rage," *The Psychoanalytic Study of the Child* 27 (1972), 379–392; Jared P. Pingleton, "The Role and Function of Forgiveness in the Psychotherapeutic Process," *Journal of Psychology and Theology* 17 (1989), 27–35.

46. Hope, "The Healing Paradox of Forgiveness," p. 240.

47. Gershen Kauhnan, *Shame: The Power of Caring* (Cambridge, MA: Shenkinan Publishing, 1980), p. 95.

48. James G. Emerson, *The Dynamics of Forgiveness* (Philadelphia: The Westminster Press, 1964) used the Rogers and Dymond q-sort test of emotional adjustment, adding items concerning feelings about one's ability to forgive, Carl R. Rogers and Rosalind F. Dymond, *Psychotherapy and Personality Change* (Chicago: University of Chicago Press, 1954).

49. Mary F. Trainer, "Forgiveness: Intrinsic, Role-Expected, Expedient, in the Context of Divorce," Doctoral dissertation, Boston University, 1984; Mellis I. Schmidt, "Forgiveness as the Focus Theme in Group Counseling," Doctoral dissertation, North Texas State University, 1986; John H. Hebl, "Forgiveness as a Counseling Goal with Elderly Females," Doctoral dissertation, University of Wisconsin, 1990.

50. F. Minirth, D. Hawkins, P. Meier, and R. Flournoy, *How to Beat Burnout* (Chicago: Moody, 1986).

51. Matthew Linn and Dennis Linn, *Healing Life's Hurts: Healing Memories Through Five Stages of Forgiveness* (New York: Paulist Press, 1978), p. 39.

52. S. Achterberg, S. Matthews, and O. C. Simonton, "Psychology of the Exceptional Cancer Patient: A Description of Patients Who Outlived Predicted Expectancies," *Psychotherapy: Theory and Research and Practice* 6 (1976), 13–14.

53. Judith A. Strasser, "The Relation of General Forgiveness and Forgiveness Type to Reported Health in the Elderly," Doctoral dissertation, Catholic University of America, 1984.

54. Linn and Linn, *Healing Life's Hurts,* pp. 36–37.

55. Doris Donnelly, *Learning to Forgive* (Nashville, TN: Abingdon Press, 1979).

56. Michael E. McCullough and Kenneth C. Rachal, "Interpersonal Forgiving in Close Relationships," *Journal of Personality and Social Psychology* 73 (1997), 321–336.

57. Robert D. Enright, "Counseling within the Forgiveness Triad: On Forgiving, Receiving Forgiveness, and Self-Forgiveness," *Counseling and Values* 40 (1996), 107–127.

58. Susan Helen Wade, "The Development of a Scale to Measure Forgiveness," Doctoral dissertation, Fuller Theological Seminary, 1989.

59. Neil Robert Fow, "An Empirical-Phenomenological Investigation of the Experience of Forgiving Another," Doctoral dissertation, University of Pittsburgh, 1988.

60. Doris Donnelly, *Putting Forgiveness into Practice* (Allen, TX: Argus Communications, 1982).

61. David Augsburger, *Caring Enough to Forgive* (Ventura, CA: Regal Books, 1981).

62. See also David G. Benner, *Healing Emotional Wounds* (Grand Rapids: Baker Book House, 1990) and Michael E. McCullough, Steven J. Sandage and Everett L. Worthington, Jr., *To Forgive Is Human* (Downer's Grove, IL: InterVarsity Press, 1997).

63. Robert D. Enright and Elizabeth A. Gassin, "Forgiveness: A Developmental View," *Journal of Moral Education* 21 (1992), 99–114. This model is Lawrence Kohlberg's stages of moral development, "Moral Stages and Moralization: The Cognitive Development Approach," in T. Licrona (Ed.), *Moral Development and Behavior: Theory, Research and Social Issues* (New York: Holt Rinehart, 1976).

64. Scott Heller, "Emerging Field of Forgiveness Studies Explores How We Let Go of Grudges," *Chronicle of Higher Education,* July 17, 1998, p. A-19.

65. Robert D. Enright and Robert L. Zell, "Problems Encountered When We Forgive One Another," *Journal of Psychology and Christianity* 8 (1989), 52–54; David Augsburger, *Caring Enough to Not Forgive* (Ventura, CA: Regal Books, 1981).

66. R. C. A. Hunter, "Forgiveness, Retaliation, and Paranoid Reactions," *Canadian Psychiatric Association Journal* 23 (1978), 171.

67. Smedes, *Forgive and Forget,* p. 15.

68. See, for example, R. Rosenthal and L. Jacobson, *Pygmalion in the Classroom* (New York: Holt, Rinehart & Winston, 1968).

69. Russell K. Fazio, Edwin A. Efrrein, and Victoria J. Falender, "Self-Perceptions Following Social Interaction," *Journal of Personality and Social Psychology* 41 (1981), 232–242.

70. Em Griffin, "Accountability and Forgiveness: Saying the Tough Words in Love," paper presented at the Speech Communication Association Convention, Denver, November 1985, pp. 18, 26.

71. Roxane Salyer Lulofs, "The Social Construction of Forgiveness," *Human Systems* 2 (1992), 183–198. The model is based on John Shotter's communication/reality loop from *Social Accountability and Selfhood* (Oxford, England: Basil Blackwell, 1984).

72. David L. Palmer, "The Communication of Forgiveness," paper presented at the annual meeting of the Speech Communication Association, New Orleans, November 1994.

73. Enright, "Counseling within the Forgiveness Triad."

74. Elizabeth Gassin, "Receiving Forgiveness as Moral Education: A Theoretical Analysis and Initial Empirical Investigation," *Journal of Moral Education* 27 (1998), 71–88.

75. Carol Tavris, *Anger: The Misunderstood Emotion* (New York: Touchstone through Simon & Schuster, 1989), pp. 314–315.

76. For those who have experienced childhood trauma, two excellent resources are James E. Kepner, *Healing Tasks: Psychotherapy with Adult Survivors of Childhood Abuse* (San Francisco: Jossey Bass, 1995), and Gina O'Connell Higgins, *Resilient Adults: Overcoming a Cruel Past* (San Francisco: Jossey Bass, 1994).

77. Hope, "The Healing Paradox of Forgiveness," p. 242; see also A. Ellis and R. A. Harper, *A New Guide to Rational Living* (North Hollywood, CA: Wilshire Book Co., 1975), who claim that forgiving leaves us sane and realistic.

Appendix A

Mediation as Third-Party Intervention

Up to now, we have concentrated on those concepts, principles, and skills that are most useful when you personally are involved in a conflict with someone you know. You should be able to apply what you have learned so far to better manage or resolve the conflict you yourself are having with someone else.

This appendix is different in that it focuses on what you need to know to help others who are having a conflict. Perhaps they invite you as a neutral party to intervene on their behalf. Moreover, the nature of the conflict is different because it is one that the conflicting parties cannot handle by themselves. They need the help of a knowledgeable, unbiased third party—a role you could perform after you study the subject of mediation and are trained in the various skills associated with mediation.

When Lee first read about mediation services at a local dispute resolution center, he realized that it offered a practical application of many skills taught in undergraduate interpersonal communication and conflict courses. The local mediator training program lived up to his expectations, and he found mediation to be an ideal application of interpersonal communication concepts, principles, and skills. In this appendix, basic information about mediation is provided so that you can help your friends, family, and coworkers resolve their interpersonal conflicts. However, if you want to practice mediation on a more formal basis, you will need to be certified, which means mediation training by an approved agency.

Settling Disputes through the Intervention of a Third Party

We'd like to begin the study of third-party intervention by introducing you to the concept of a dispute. A **dispute** may be defined as "a conflict that has reached a point where the parties are unable to resolve the issue by themselves due to a breakdown in communication, and normal relations are unlikely until the dispute is resolved."[1] Not all conflicts are alike. Conflicts become disputes when participants realize that they confront a communication barrier that must be removed for normal relations to resume. They seek help from a third party because they cannot resolve the issues by themselves.

When a dispute occurs, the conflicting parties sometimes resort to violent means. Our prisons are full of people who took "justice" into their own hands by taking violent action against someone with whom they disagreed. For those who use their heads instead of their fists and guns, the following alternative dispute resolutions options (**ADRs**) exist:

- **conciliation,** in which a neutral third party practices "shuttle diplomacy" by traveling back and forth between conflicting parties who are unable to meet together for any one of a variety of reasons;
- **ombudsperson,** who cuts "through the red tape" on behalf of individuals who feel abused by the larger system (often governmental agencies) in which they work, study, or seek support;
- **arbitration,** in which a neutral third party considers both sides of a dispute and makes a decision, which may be more binding than that of a judge in the legal system, if both parties have agreed in advance to abide by the decision;
- **adjudication,** in which a neutral judge and jury in the legal system hear and decide a case which may be appealed;
- **mediation,** which differs from the foregoing alternatives in that a neutral third party facilitates communication between the conflicting parties so that they may work out their own agreement.

The use of third-party intervention, short of legal involvement, has become quite popular, as Putnam and Folger attested:

> The 1980s have brought renewed interest in studying conflict as alternatives emerge for resolving labor, community, and marital disputes. Alternative dispute resolution (ADR) typically refers to the use of negotiation, mediation, and conciliation as alternatives to the traditional practice of adjudication. The founding of dispute resolution and neighborhood justice centers, the enactment of divorce mediation legislation, and the involvement of third parties in community, environmental, and organizational disputes have made conflict management a growth industry in this country.[2]

Mediators are unbiased third parties, who intervene but have no authority or power in the decision-making process; they do exert considerable influence over the communication process.

> This notion, that mediators regulate procedure without affecting content, is a common theme in writing about mediation programs. The working assumption in mediation is that the procedure should empower disputants to resolve their own dispute, not that the procedure should substitute informal authority for formal authority. Mediators create the conditions in which the two disputants can work together to reach a consensus solution to a problem. While minimally influencing the alternatives considered or the agreement reached.[3]

Basically, mediators facilitate agreement by building a cooperative context in which disputants collaboratively create their own agreement. In this way, mediators help to restore communication and normalize relations. Many disputes consist of elements that identify conflicting needs or interests that are capable of resolution through the mediation process. Community and campus dispute resolution centers offer mediation for a wide range of conflicts including noisy neighbors, sexual and racial harassment, minor assault, breach of contract, landlord-tenant, buyer-seller, small claims, bad checks, trespassing, and a variety of interpersonal issues such as gossip and rumors, misunderstandings, friendship issues, ex-boyfriend–ex-girlfriend disputes.[4]

Mediation Compared to Adjudication

Lawsuits have become increasingly popular in recent years. Therefore, we would like to add a few details to adjudication as an ADR to make more apparent many of the advantages of mediation. In contrast to mediation, the conflicting parties play a small role in adjudication. In the U.S. legal system, the judge and jury decide the outcome of a case and dictate what they think is fair. Because lawyers have been hired to represent their clients, the lawyers typically take over the communication process and often discourage direct communication between the disputants. Essentially, adjudication is designed to take the decision-making process out of the hands of those who must live with the final decision.

You are undoubtedly familiar with many aspects of adjudication. The process begins when one party files charges, a petition, or a suit, requiring the other party to respond. Both usually hire their own lawyers who communicate with one another to see if some settlement can be reached out of court (based on their estimates of what the judge and jury would accept) and who defend their clients in court when ordered to appear before the judge and jury. We should point out that in fact many cases are settled out of court, but disputants may be dissatisfied with the agreement because they feel forced into it. Because parties are supposed to receive "equal protection under the law" and have their own attorneys to defend them, adjudication serves as a power-balancing mechanism. Perhaps for this reason, a complementary conflict in which one of the parties is considerably more dominant, threatening, or abusive is often best resolved through a court decision because the court empowers the weaker party. This is particularly true in cases involving wife and child abuse.

There are other times when adjudication may be preferable to mediation. Weitzman argued that women suffer economically when they do not use lawyers in a divorce.[5] Because divorce leaves most women economically disadvantaged, they are already in a low-power position when they enter the mediation process. Having less power leads them to agree to unfair outcomes. There is little research to support or dispute Weitzman's claim, but the claim is worth some consideration, particularly in light of the finding of Pearson, Thonnes, and Vanderkooi that men are more willing to try mediation when they do not believe their chances of winning in the legal system are very good.[6]

Other limitations to mediation are found in problems of interaction: Sometimes people simply do not want to sit down with "the enemy" to work things out. The conflict has become so entrenched and the relationship so full of enmity that the thought of trying to negotiate in a give-and-take situation is too much for those involved.

Adjudication also has its limitations. To begin with, it is an adversarial system in which the objective is a win-lose result and conflicts often escalate. According to Hocker and Wilmot, "In order to file an action, one has to blow up the magnitude of the conflict to a 'you owe us' or 'we'll get you' frame of mind; one tries to win at the other's expense . . . filing sets an escalatory process in motion."[7] Another author points out, "The client's interest is always perceived as being in opposition to the interests of the other party. The lawyer cannot and does not regard the parties as having a common problem which he or she will help resolve."[8] Initially, the parties retain the services of attorneys who are trained in the adversary role. According to Keltner:

> The ethics of the Bar have traditionally been strongly based on the adversarial relationship between people. The lawyer has been expected to press the advantage of the client being represented and to protect that client's right to due process. Although this is a very important and necessary function in our system of justice, it is not the function of mediation.[9]

Because of the adversarial nature of the system, many disputants see adjudication as a means for "getting even." Then they find themselves caught up in an escalating process with apparently no way out. Another disadvantage with adjudication is that many courts are overburdened with a backlog of cases leading to considerable frustration, expense, and delay, such that even a two-year waiting period between filing and the first court appearance occurs. Trials are often expensive, exhausting one's finances. What if a person does not want to wait months for a trial, hire lawyers, spend many more months in court, and run the risk of feeling dissatisfied with the final decision? One could choose mediation instead.

In contrast to adjudication, mediation allows for full participation by the conflicting parties. Because it is voluntary, they must agree to mediation and approve of the meeting time and place. After the mediator explains the rules or guidelines, the parties are asked if they are willing to abide by them. It is explained to them that either one may terminate the mediation at any time. Perhaps the hardest idea to convey is that the mediator is not a judge. She or he only facilitates the discussion so that the parties can come to their own agreement: To facilitate means to make the process easier, to use "diplomatic language," to discover new ideas, and to exercise good communication and problem-solving skills.[10] Both parties must find the agreement satisfactory before it becomes final, and they have the right to not sign it. It has been estimated that "once the disputants have agreed to mediate, at least 80% of the time they will be able to work out an agreement that is acceptable to both of them."[11] In informal settings, the parties may agree orally rather than in writing, but the voluntary nature of the mediation should still be made clear and preserved throughout.

Because mediation is unique, it is free of the limitations that are associated with adjudication. First, mediation is not set up in an adversarial manner. Instead it is based on a win-win, cooperative model. Parties are encouraged to talk and collaborate with each other toward reaching a mutually satisfactory agreement. It has been said that the mediator's "client" is the relationship. The mediator is intervening into this dispute because the parties need help in overcoming their communication problems and normalizing (restoring, preserving, or restructuring) their interpersonal relationship. To this end, the mediator is working for the relationship, attempting to help the parties create an agreement, save face, prevent verbal aggression, eliminate competition, and encourage cooperation as they move toward agreement.

Second, mediation is normally more satisfying, cheaper, and faster than adjudication. After one party calls the mediation center, a mediation may occur within the next few days or couple of weeks. At schools, mediation may be held when and where conflicts often occur such as on playgrounds or at noon in lunch halls. In any case, community and school mediations are often free or offered on a "sliding scale" that is cheaper than lawyers' fees. Satisfactory agreements may be worked out at a single mediation session lasting one to three hours, although complex cases may require weekly sessions until all the details are worked out. Evidence indicates that parties are more satisfied with mediated agreements than they are with the decisions of judges and juries and are more likely to comply with mediated agreements than they are to court orders.[12] The disputants are more likely to comply because they felt empowered to play an active role in resolving their dispute; they had a mutual stake in the agreement; the contract was theirs, not imposed; and no one was a loser who feels the need for revenge.

> I recall one dispute in which one of the parties brought a lawyer to the mediation. The room was filled with tension as the parties were obviously "not speaking." When the lawyer asked me if he could attend the session, I informed him that normally lawyers were not involved or present during mediation. However, I told him that I had no problem with him being present if he promised to say nothing until after the parties reached an agreement. I said that his client could show him the agreement before she signed it and that signing the agreement was voluntary. I also explained how words spoken in mediation were confidential and may not be permitted later in court. After I explained how I wanted the parties to interact and helped them communicate more effectively with each other, they worked through the issues and reached an agreement that the one party showed her lawyer. He advised her to sign it, which she did. As the parties were leaving the room in a much more jovial mood, talking and even joking a little, the lawyer came over to me with an amazed look on his face. "I don't believe it," he said. "I would not have believed this session if I had not seen it for myself. I thought these two were too angry with each other to peacefully sit down and talk over their differences. I am impressed," he said. After he thanked me for letting him sit in, he turned and walked out.

If mediation is so great, why don't more people choose to mediate their disputes? The reasons are numerous. To begin with, there is usually a lack of publicity. Because there is little money available for advertising the service, mediation is often publicized by word of mouth, by an occasional newspaper article, and by fliers posted on bulletin boards in courthouses, schools, or college campuses. There is also a general misunderstanding as to what it is and how it works. People sometimes think it is similar to a trial without a jury or more costly and more threatening than it is. It is unfortunate that the word *mediation* looks so much like the word *meditation,* which helps to explain why some people see the public announcements but think it is a form of contemplation and reflection rather than a type of dispute resolution. Even when people have an opportunity to benefit from mediation, they may not be encouraged to seek it by their friends, relatives, family therapists, and lawyers. Friends and relatives may be angry and want revenge as much as the offended party, whereas therapists and lawyers may prefer to receive substantial payment for their services rather than advise their client to seek a less expensive alternative. Finally, the intervention by third parties is not as much a cultural value here in the United States as it is elsewhere in the world. Many Americans resent the intrusion of a third party in what they consider to be their personal and private affairs. In spite of these discouraging reasons, many people do seek mediation every year and benefit from it.

Who Are the Mediators?

In the case of community and campus conflict resolution programs, mediators are trained volunteers. First and foremost, mediators must be neutral and unbiased. This means that there is no reason for mediators to take one party's side against the other. In informal cases, it would not be a good idea to mediate for family or friends if one knows one party better than the other. Mediators must also make every effort to demonstrate their neutrality by equalizing the speaking time, giving the same amount of time and attention to both parties, and not spending time alone with one of the parties without spending the same amount of time with the other. Certainly, mediators are not to take sides in the dispute.

As noted earlier, mediators have no decision-making power. Initially, the parties often have expectations about the role of the mediator such as expecting her or him to solve their problems for them. From their perspective, an interventionist is needed because they believe they cannot resolve the issues by themselves. Mediators need to inform the parties that they have no authoritative decision-making power. However, mediators show the conflicting parties how to be more competent in communication. Mediators have discovered that many disputants who enter mediation have found it difficult to communicate, relate, or work with each other in the past.

In formal cases, mediators are trained and certified. In New York State, for example, community mediators are required to complete a state-certified training program.

> Adult training time totals 28 hours, and usually involves one full weekend and supplementary evening sessions. Mediators role play at least three complete mediations in training, in order to build confidence and competence. All role plays are followed by discussion and brainstorming focused on how they might have been improved and affirmation for hard work well done.[13]

Mediators are trained to facilitate communication and to perform additional tasks such as preparation of mediation consent forms and proper recording of the agreement. Mediators must maintain confidentiality. They are not to make public the names of the conflicting parties, disclose the words spoken during the mediation, or retain notes taken during the mediation. Because mediation offers the disputants an opportunity to talk openly to each other about their feelings, needs, goals, and reasons for behaving as they do, mediators must recognize their value as facilitators of communication and not take advantage of the parties by telling anyone else under any circumstances. In formal cases, trained mediators learn rules that cover a few legal exceptions, which they include in their opening remarks and make explicit on the mediation consent form that must be signed by both parties before mediation begins. In informal settings, a mediator can simply state in her or his opening remarks that the mediation will be considered confidential and ask the parties if they will agree to keep what is said "among us." It is this guarantee of confidentially that makes self-disclosure possible in mediation.

In informal situations, people can help others without their being formally trained and state-certified mediators. Thus, everyone can benefit from receiving training that is available to the general public and is similar to that required for certification.

Research has examined perceptual biases that arise as a result of the gender of the mediator. Burrell, Donahue, and Allen examined simulated mediation situations to discover whether disputants judge the effectiveness of male and female mediators differently. Two mixed-sex groups were compared: one in which members were trained to mediate roommate conflicts using an interventionist (i.e., highly control-oriented) strategy and another in which the group received no training. In the trained group, males were seen as more controlling, even though men and women used equally controlling strategies. In the untrained group, women were seen as less controlling, although they used more controlling strategies than the trained group. The authors concluded:

> Men may still maintain an assertive, self-confident image, whereas women are viewed as vague and lacking in confidence. Individuals look beyond objective

reality and assess behavior more globally, relying on their images of how individuals act in those contexts. . . . Perhaps the most perplexing implication about this observation for professional women mediators is that, even though they pursue an interventionist role with as much fervor as their male counterparts, they are perceived to be less in charge of the interactions.[14]

When Should a Third Party Intervene?

When does one decide to bring in a third party to help resolve a conflict? There are several guidelines. When a conflict presents an urgent need for resolution and both parties to the conflict have taken one side or another, an impartial third party will help in resolving the conflict. For example, the parents of a child whom a teacher has continually accused of disrupting class should first talk to the teacher involved about the situation. However, if they conclude that the teacher is simply overreacting or is unable to deal with the demands of the child, it is a good idea to ask the principal to mediate the conflict because the child cannot go on disrupting class and all parties want to resolve the situation. If the complexity of the conflict exceeds the resources available to deal with it, then a third party may be needed. In college roommate situations, coalitions often form among roommates, who may be unable to understand the actions of an individual roommate or may compel that roommate to act in accordance with majority wishes. The intervention of a resident advisor could mediate such a conflict. In addition, if there is little or no trust between the people involved, a mediator may become necessary. Folger and Poole suggested the following guidelines, taken from their review of a large body of research, for determining the involvement of the third party:

1. If there is little time to resolve the conflict and if a quick solution is required for the survival of the group or organization, a highly authoritative style will be more effective than a less authoritative style.
2. If there is a long-standing conflict in which opposing positions have been clearly and definitely drawn, and the two sides express little hope in their ability to work out a solution, a highly authoritative style is more likely to be effective than a less authoritative one.
3. If the conflict is sharp and bitter, with highly charged emotions, a highly authoritative style will be more effective in getting parties to cease hostilities than will a less authoritative style. (Once parties have "cooled down," less authoritative styles may be effective.)
4. The greater the third party's credibility, legitimacy, and respect in the eyes of the members, the more successful the third party will be in his or her attempts to adopt a highly authoritative style.
5. If the group members have the bargaining and communication skills necessary to work out a solution, a less authoritative style will be more effective than a more authoritative style.
6. The group's expectations are the most important determinant of the appropriate style. A style that matches the group's expectations of how a third party should act is most likely to be effective, at least in the early stages of the third-party intervention. Once the third party has shown the group he or she can meet its expectations, deviations from these expectations are more likely to be effective.[15]

Mediator Skills

Mediation skills training enhances the ability of an impartial third party to intervene in an interpersonal conflict and help the parties communicate and resolve conflicts. The relevant skills include basic communication, structuring, reframing, and expanding.

Basic Communication Skills

One of the most important roles of the mediator is to facilitate constructive communication by encouraging cooperation and discouraging competition between the parties. Essentially, a mediator's objective is to create a cooperative environment for the parties to discuss emotional and substantive issues and reach agreement.[16] The process of mediation is successful to the extent that it moves from a competitive to a cooperative orientation. Competition may be viewed as a defensive communication climate and cooperation as supportive. Competitive communication is self-promoting because it serves as a vehicle through which individuals attempt to distort the other's perceptions of the situation in order to obtain an advantage. A cooperative orientation consists of actions characteristic of organized action (e.g., working together) and a thought process known as consensus (e.g., shared understanding, actual agreement). It also facilitates attempts to discover areas of common interest regarding issues.

Mediation sessions usually begin with a broad and confused discussion of issues seen from competitive orientations, but when successful, proceed to more detailed and specific statements out of which cooperation and consensus (shared meanings) emerge. Thus, the mediator must help the parties build confidence in the mediation process, find common ground, and communicate effectively by structuring the interaction, serving as a resource person, and helping the disputants reach their own agreement. To select the appropriate intervention techniques for creating a cooperative environment for reaching agreement, the mediator must also be competent in communication. Competence is generally thought of as a quality or ability. According to Cooley and Roach, communication competence refers to "the knowledge of appropriate communication patterns in a given situation and the ability to use the knowledge."[17] In practice, the mediator follows these communication guidelines:

- Be descriptive rather than judgmental.
- Be specific.
- Deal with things that can be changed instead of "givens."
- Give feedback when it is requested.
- Give feedback as close as possible to the behavior being discussed.
- Speak only for yourself.
- Check your explanations with the other party.[18]

In addition to competence in basic communication skills, mediators are trained to structure the process of mediation, reframe the disputants' statements and positions, and expand the information source.

Structuring the Process of Mediation

This objective is met when the mediator gains control of the mediation. Donohue, Allen, and Burrell detail five tactics that mediators may use to achieve this goal:

- Identifying or enforcing the communication rules.
- Initiating or terminating discussion.
- Identifying or enforcing the agenda or topic.
- Explaining the role and the process of mediation.
- Providing orientation information about mediation and its alternatives.[19]

Reframing the Disputants' Statements and Positions

This goal is achieved when the parties take the information given and reword it in a more usable form, perhaps resulting in the creation of an integrative agreement. Again, Donohue and his colleagues list several tactics that mediators may use to achieve this objective:

- Creating alternative proposals.
- Reframing proposals or reframing the utterances as a proposal.
- Identifying and reinforcing points of agreement and support for the utterance.
- Providing a listening response to signal attentiveness.[20]

Expanding the Information Resource

This objective is realized when more information is provided by the parties to one another and the mediator. Requesting tactics are also available such as:

- Requesting an opinion or evaluation of the other's proposal or opinion.
- Requesting proposals.
- Requesting clarification of a proposal or topic.
- Requesting relational or feeling information.
- Requesting clarification of a prior utterance.[21]

Thus, techniques exist for improving mediator competence to achieve more successful mediation outcomes.

Mediators as Communication Rules Enforcers

To appreciate the idea that mediators primarily control the communication process to give them greater influence over the outcome of the interaction, one must understand how mediators create and enforce communication rules. As we said in Chapter 8, some rules are regulative because they influence our actions whereas others are definitional because they influence how we define and perceive things. Rules tell us what we must say, what we should say, and what we better not say in different situations. We know that a rule exists largely when we have broken it and face some sort of sanction. For example, at a friend's wedding, it is customary to congratulate the groom and convey best wishes to the bride. Saying "congratulations" to the bride is considered to be in poor taste, and if you do so, you may get a disapproving look from someone. The rule is there, but it is not a very strong one—it is a preferred rule. On the other hand, laughing at a funeral is almost unheard of. It is prohibited, and anyone who breaks the rule would probably be escorted out of the room.

Thus, a pattern of behavior is said to be rule governed when there exists mutual expectations regarding what is appropriate in a given situation. Although rules are social conventions that can be violated or changed by individuals or groups, it is argued that, when people know the rules, they tend to conform to them. Mediation may be viewed as a structured social activity guided and defined by rules designed to convert competitive orientations and actions into cooperative ones. According to Allen and Donohue,

> Successful mediators lay down rules at the beginning of the session . . . The rules enforced by the mediator go beyond explaining the legal status of the mediator and mediation. The mediator also establishes rules for behavior during the session. The mediator limits the agenda for the session and the tone of the discussion. If disputants decide to call each other names and dwell on the issues . . . the mediator can and does exercise the option to ask the disputants to stop discussing those issues or change their use of language . . . Unsuccessful or less skilled mediators seem hesitant or unwilling to enforce rules of behavior during the sessions.[22]

It may be no accident that even early practice in divorce mediation was based on a rules approach.[23] Some common rules that are useful for directing the communication process toward positive outcomes are as follows:

- taking turns to talk without interruptions
- talking without expressing hostility to one another
- creating a positive climate with no put-downs
- focusing on the future (what can be done) rather than the past (what was done)
- striving for a win-win solution with no one feeling dissatisfied or agreeing to something he or she finds unacceptable
- striving to solve the problem rather than attacking or blaming the other person
- being honest and sharing your thoughts and feelings without fear of criticism or publicity
- adhering to time constraints set by mediator
- agreeing to abide by additional rules as announced by the mediator during the session

The Mediation Process: Step by Step

Prior to the actual mediation, mediators may examine the environment, rearrange tables and chairs, decide who should be present at the mediation, and divide up their responsibilities if two will be working together as comediators. When the conflicting parties arrive, the mediators greet them, make introductions, and indicate where they are to sit. Sometimes additional people show up at the appointed time (e.g., lawyers, witnesses, family members, or friends) and, if they are to be included in some way, their role needs to be clarified before the mediation begins. In less formal situations such as a disagreement between relatives, friends, or coworkers, an unbiased third party may simply ask the parties to move to a "quiet area" to talk. In any case, the mediation process itself consists of the following six steps.

The Mediator's Opening Statement: Setting the Rules

In formal mediations, it may help to have an opening statement that is written out ahead of time. In informal cases, the following ideas can be worked into one's introductory comments. It should be explained to the parties:

- that the mediation is voluntary and that the participants are to try to resolve the dispute with the mediator's help.
- that the mediators have no prior knowledge of the situation, that they are not acquainted with one party more than the other, and that they must remain impartial throughout the mediation.
- that the mediator's role is not to make judgments or decisions, but facilitate the discussion between the participants, so that they may develop their own agreement.
- that the mediation is confidential; if notes are taken, they are to be destroyed before the parties leave the room. In formal mediations, the parties are given a mediation consent form.
- that specific ground rules must be adhered to, such as taking turns talking, no interruptions, no name-calling, and so on.
- that the goal is to develop an agreement that both will find acceptable. In formal situations, the agreement must be in writing and signed by both parties with the mediator as witness. Even in informal cases, it is often a good idea to at least put the agreement in writing.
- that the participants understand the preceding ideas and are willing to give mediation a try.

An experienced mediator writes:

> This opening statement, ceremonial in tone, sets the scene for all that follows. Often, both parties are anxious and uncertain. Their perception of the mediator's respect for them and control of the situation can encourage them to try for new solutions to old problems—to take risks. The experience can then become educational, and disputants become more competent in coping with life's difficulties. Conversely, if the disputants doubt the reliability or reputation of the third party, his or her actual skills or credentials matter very little. Neutrality and the ability to listen may be honed in training, but if these qualities are not part of an individual's value system, all the training in the world cannot make that person an effective mediator. The mediator must be able to inspire in the disputants the trust and confidence crucial to beginning the process. Without this trust, disputants are not likely to feel that it is worthwhile even to begin.[24]

The Disputants' Opening Statements: Identifying the Issues

Following their opening remarks, mediators ask the party who initially made the complaint to explain the situation (why are we here?) without interruptions. This is done by asking each person what happened and how she or he feels about it. This period often tests the alertness and influence of the mediators because the other party is inclined to try to interrupt or respond. Mediators must be quick to intervene, remind the offending person not to interrupt, and explain that she or he will have an opportunity to speak in a few minutes. Sometimes a disputant's opening statement is short and to the point (e.g., "The landlord wants me to pay the water bill, but that was not what I agreed to do when I signed the rental agreement"), whereas at other times, one might talk for several minutes. It is appropriate for the mediator to intervene to clarify or restate biased language in neutral terms. As soon as the party with the complaint has finished explaining the situation, the other party is asked to respond, without interruptions. Again, the mediator may need to clarify or restate some of these remarks. While listening, the mediator identifies the issues and lists them on paper to refer to throughout the mediation. It helps to do this by drawing a line down the middle of the paper to separate the issues mentioned by one party from those expressed by the other. This not only produces a list of all the issues, but it also identifies differing views on those issues mentioned by both parties.

Exchange: Clarifying the Issues

Following the opening statement by each party, the mediator serves a fact-finding function and encourages each to reply to the other's remarks, asking such questions as "How do you feel about what she said? Would you like to respond to his statement?" During this period, the less said by the mediator the better; however, the mediator should identify and prioritize the issues as they emerge (e.g., "It seems then that who is to pay for the gas is an important issue"). In addition, the mediator should use (a) power balancing, (b) fractionation, and (c) framing and reframing to facilitate discussion. Power balancing occurs when the mediator prevents one of the parties from speaking too loudly, dominating the discussion, interrupting the other, or becoming verbally aggressive.

Participation can be balanced by calling on the more reticent party in a nonthreatening way while restraining the more vocal party. Saying something such as "Thanks for your contributions, Jon; now we need to hear from Jan who is equally involved so we can get a complete picture of what has transpired in this conflict" will often serve to set the stage of balanced participation. Sometimes, of course, the intervener has to be "heavy-handed" and say things such as "Joan, I know this is an important issue for you. But if you keep interrupting him and not letting him talk, you won't get the information you need to figure out a workable solution for both of you."[25]

Fractionation occurs when the mediator helps to break down more complicated issues into smaller, more manageable ones. The intervener can be heard to say things such as "Well, there are a lot of issues here. Let's take them one at a time. The first issue is the concern about how much socialization should be expected of all employees." The third party assures the participants that all issues will be heard but insists on taking them one at a time.[26]

Framing occurs when mediators communicate in a way that helps the disputants clarify the issues. Mediators do this by asking neutral or "friendly" questions (that avoid fixing blame or passing judgment), and by listening effectively, and by emphasizing and summarizing issues. **Reframing** is a different skill, which occurs when the mediator re-states negatively loaded, biased, or accusatory statements in more neutral terminology or restates positions in a way that makes the disputants look at the issues differently.

> Reframing . . . can be done indirectly or directly, giving the person an alterna-tive interpretation of the other party's behavior . . . Reframing is important be-cause the participants are usually engaged in communication practices that make agreement difficult—derogatory statements, not listening to the other side, and other forms of uncooperative communication.[27]

In some cases, where there are strong feelings, the participants may need to get "a load off their chests." They may express anger as long as it is not couched in hostile ver-bal aggression (i.e., name-calling, verbal threats, swearing, etc.). The primary responsibil-ity of the mediator is to make sure the parties adhere to the rules—not interrupt, hear each other out, express their own perceptions and feelings but without blaming, accusing, or threatening one another. In cases where hostility becomes too high, the mediator may need to temporarily enact a conciliatory role by separating the disputants and "shuttle back and forth" between them, a mediation technique known as **caucus.** "Mediators meet individu-ally with each disputant for an equal amount of time. Information disclosed in a caucus can remain confidential or can be disclosed when the parties reunite, depending on the wishes of the parties as stated in the caucus."[28] Usually this caucus technique is reserved for only extreme situations because many disputants will adhere to the rules as laid out ini-tially and not become openly hostile toward one another. As one mediator says:

> The presence of a third party, a silent representative of the larger community, is the ingredient that makes this dialogue different. The dispute is no longer private, but taken seriously by the "public," as represented by the mediator. As a result disputants speak and listen differently than they might when encoun-tering each other alone. Some mediations, when the dispute has been a matter of misunderstanding, are resolved at this stage, without very much mediator assistance . . . The mediator simply provides the proper atmosphere, rather like a strategically placed potted plant.[29]

In situations in which the parties are not listening well to each other or failing to try to understand the other person's point of view, the mediator may ask the parties to engage in role reversal and active listening techniques in which they summarize the issues from the other party's point of view. Although it is necessary that disputants go through this ex-change period, it is important to move to the next stage as soon as possible.

Building an Agreement: Identifying Goals

At the earliest opportunity, the mediator should ask each party, starting with the one who made the initial complaint, what she or he would like to see as the outcome of the media-tion. Another approach is to ask the one charged with the complaint what she or he could do here and now. In either case, the mediator asks the other party to explain how she or he feels or to respond with a counteroffer. Once the outcomes are made clear, the mediator attempts to move the parties to a mutually acceptable solution. The mediator does this by

1. beginning with the easiest issues leaving the most difficult issues until later,
2. highlighting common ground where possible,
3. overcoming impasses by identifying underlying needs and interests and emphasizing those they share in common, and
4. brainstorming alternative ways to satisfy these needs and interests.

According to trained mediators,

> The third party may help participants to work for superordinate goals that transcend the individual interests they brought to the conflict. If a married couple, for instance, is involved in a series of conflicts, some possible superordinate goals might be appealing to "the marriage," "the children," or "your need of one another during these difficult times." Just as nations have a superordinate goal of not destroying the human race, interpersonal conflict participants may be convinced not to destroy the good elements of their relationship.[30]

Working toward agreement is usually the most complex part of the session. It means moving away from what has existed and opening new, clear lines of communication so that a plan for a better future can emerge. The basic rules and the structured process promote this outcome. However, the mediator's skill must be applied in a way that allows the disputants to let go of negative behavior, brainstorming the issues to create a better future for themselves.[31]

These suggestions are helpful in promoting agreement. Whenever consensus occurs, the mediator must draw attention to it and write it down, so that it can later become part of the written agreement. It is a good idea to draw attention to the parties' agreement on a point and to provide consequences by explaining how that instance of cooperation moves the mediation toward a mutually satisfactory resolution. Every effort should be made to instill a sense of optimism that the differences can and will be resolved.

The Written Agreement

Although one may have the impression that the agreement is put in writing at the end of the mediation, this is not really the case. A written agreement begins as soon as the parties find any point on which to agree. In fact, the agreement should include all points of consensus including consensus on principles as well as specific behaviors agreed to by both parties. The mediator must be alert for these instances of cooperation, point them out, and write them down in the initial draft of the written agreement. The mediator should help the parties agree on a resolution that they both feel is fair. To give the appearance of balance, the mediator should solicit offers from both parties, so that each feels that he or she gained something. A line may be drawn down the center of the agreement, separating the gains made by each party, which are outlined in the form of a list or numbered items. The mediator should request additional items for the list to achieve a balance (e.g., "Mike has agreed to do several things. Jennifer, what could you do in return?"). The specific wording on the written agreement is extremely important because future problems can be prevented by a carefully worded agreement. Both parties' names are used throughout, beginning with the items to which both have agreed, for example, "Mike and Terry have agreed to do . . . ." This is followed by the individual items such as "Mike agrees to do . . ." and "Terry agrees to do . . . ." Statements should be kept simple, in their declarative form, and not accusatory. Care should be taken to be specific especially with regard to the date and time of commitments, amount of money, method of payment (check, cash, credit), and so on. Questions with regard to workability should be raised. This does not mean that the mediator declares items as unworkable but rather asks the participants how they intend to make something work.

Toward the end of the mediation, the mediator reads off the points of agreement as a check to ensure that she or he has correctly identified those issues that have been resolved. In formal meetings, an agreement is written down and signed by both parties, with the mediators signing as witnesses. When witnessed by state-certified mediators, these official agreements can have the legally binding force of a contract. In some situations in which only partial agreement was achieved, an agreement on only some of the points in contention is put into writing and signed. In less formal meetings, it may still be a good idea to put the agreement in writing following the principles described earlier to serve as a reminder to live up to each other's commitments. Of course, if there is no agreement, the mediator should discuss options with the disputants. Sometimes disputants contact one another after an unsuccessful mediation and agree to an unwritten arrangement of their own without the assistance of a mediator.

The Closing

Whether or not an agreement is reached, the mediator should thank the participants for giving mediation a try and compliment them.

> It took courage to try, and the relationship will have been altered in some way by the simple fact of the two parties' sitting down and listening to one another. . . . The closing is ceremonial but important. Disputants often have mixed feelings: grateful for the process, yet embarrassed by their need of it. As one disputant said to a mediator, "Thank you very much! I hope I never have to see you again." They need the mediator to be neutral, anonymous, and respectful.[32]

Code of Ethics

Whether one is mediating formally or informally, the practice carries with it ethical responsibilities and duties relating to the conduct of the individual as a mediator. First, mediators have a responsibility toward the parties. Mediators are interveners in the communication process and not the decision-making process, which rests upon the parties themselves. Mediators must recognize that the agreements that are reached are voluntary and that the parties have the right to terminate mediation at any time. It is the mediator's responsibility to assist the parties in reaching a mutually acceptable agreement by providing procedural and substantive suggestions and alternatives but not to criticize the potential solution or insist on one's own idea of a good resolution. In addition, mediators must keep confidential all statements made during the mediation.

Second, when more than one mediator is participating as comediators, they have a responsibility toward one another. They must keep each other informed and extend to one another all possible courtesies. Moreover, prior to the session, mediators should discuss their roles and decide how to share the responsibility of mediating the conflict.

Third, mediators have a responsibility to the organization they represent. Care should be taken to complete all necessary paperwork including mediation consent forms, filing of written agreements, and data forms used for reporting purposes. Moreover, mediation must be terminated in legally required instances that are identified in the mediator's introduction or on the consent form. Finally, for cases in which mediation is provided by a nonprofit community or campus organization, it is inappropriate for mediators to accept money or gifts for the performance of their duties.

Mediation in Educational Settings

Having looked at mediators in general, it is time to consider how they manage conflicts in elementary schools, secondary schools, and colleges. Because disputes have plagued educational systems at all levels, many educators have taken an interest in peer mediation. Peer mediation simply means that the impartial third party is a fellow student specially trained to facilitate communication and problem solving when a conflict occurs between other students. Today there are a number of successful school and college peer mediation programs around the country. The primary goal of all of these programs is to reverse the high rates of student-to-student aggression. Peer mediation training may begin as early as the third grade. Although conflicts at the elementary, middle school, high school, and college differ in type, intensity, and complexity, the goal of every mediation program is to help students resolve their interpersonal conflicts productively.

School-Based Mediation Models

Mediation in the school setting began in New York City when teachers became active in nonviolence training during civil rights actions of the sixties. The Quakers began an educational project (Children's Project for Friends) to link nonviolence training with conflict resolution techniques for children. In 1984, at a small conference involving community mediators, peace educators, and ESR members, the group recognized the need for a national network and formed the National Association for Mediation in Education (NAME).

In public elementary and secondary schools, there are several types of mediation models that vary according to how formally or informally the dispute is dealt with and how immediately the conflict resolution process is enacted. For example, the playground model uses conflict managers to intervene at the time a dispute occurs. Using this informal mediation model, students help their peers resolve their problems during recess, at lunch, or before and after school. Conversely, many schools use a more formal intervention process. In a more formal intervention: (a) The conflict is referred to mediation by an administrator, teacher, or student; (b) those students named in the referral are approached about the possibility of using mediation to resolve their dispute; and (c) if students mutually agree to follow the procedures for mediation described by the student mediator, the session takes place.[33] Because schools' needs vary, program trainers and advisors individually tailor the intervention process, selection and training of school mediators, and program operation. The types of cases handled by student mediators is less diverse than those handled by community mediators, so their training is not quite as extensive. The training of student mediators in New York State for fourth through twelfth graders consists of sixteen hours total, in four-hour sessions.

Peer mediation is a highly visible way to introduce the concepts of problem solving and nonviolent conflict resolution to both faculty and students. A small group of specially trained students, who are able to produce agreement between disputing peers referred by the discipline system, has a positive impact on school climate and especially on the behavior of those directly involved. Skeptical adults notice that properly trained students can become excellent problem solvers.[34]

Mediation training gives students more knowledge to make choices, generate options, make decisions, communicate, and solve problems. They find that there is no one "right" answer or solution but, rather, multiple ways to resolve problems. In short, training programs focus on the need to creatively explore solutions to interpersonal conflict so that all parties may be satisfied with the outcome.

College-Based Mediation Models

Young people operate at different levels of competence with regard to interpersonal conflict. As they age and develop mentally and emotionally, they come to understand and respond to conflict differently.[35] Thus, any program intending to incorporate student peers as mediators must adapt its operation and mediator training to young people at that age level.

As in the community at large, college mediation is especially recommended in cases that involve an established interpersonal relationship. When people must live near one another as in a neighborhood, residence hall, apartment complex, or trailer park, work together at a place of employment, or attend classes at a school or college setting, a breakdown in communication accompanied by harmful, negative emotions may make it difficult for disputing parties to continue living, studying, or working together in close proximity without escalating the conflict. In the college's classroom and residence hall environment, peer rejection and violence may be prevented or relationships reorganized through mediation.

Normally, peer mediation in institutions of higher education is usually tied into the formal grievance, dispute resolution, and college/university judicial system. Folger and Shubert, who conducted in-depth interviews at twenty institutions of higher education, found that disputes between students are likely to come to the attention of college staff in the office of vice president for student affairs, the dean of students, or the director of housing.[36] The initial step in dispute resolution at all twenty institutions calls for informal resolution at the lowest level, that is, direct confrontation between disputing students. For students who are unable to settle their disputes without the intervention of a third party, three different models for incorporating mediation exist.

In the required mediation model, the disputing students must mediate regardless of circumstances. Usually, if mediation fails to resolve the dispute, the matter is then turned over to the campus judicial system for a decision by someone who acts as judge or arbitrator.

In the required adjudication model, the disputing students must first formalize their dispute by submitting their differences to the campus judicial system. After they have entered the formal judicial system, the students may be encouraged to mediate as a step in the overall judicial process. Campus disputes share with the court system the fact that cases are frequently settled prior to judgment through mediation.

The referral model promotes the idea of options, choice, and voluntary participation. It requires that disputing students first go through an intake process. This role is typically assigned to college staff in the office of vice president for student affairs. There the staff member uses the intake process to explore the feasibility of mediation. The disputing students are then referred to either mediation or adjudication with the understanding that they may pursue the other option later. Folger and Shubert also found that institutions typically manage student disputes through a centralized or decentralized operation usually depending on the size of the institution. Smaller colleges and universities may lean toward more centralized programs in which student disputes are coordinated through a single office, usually that of the vice president for student affairs, the dean of students, or director of housing. There are, however, numerous procedures to take into account the diversity of issues (e.g., academic and nonacademic). To simplify the process for students, many smaller institutions have assigned these multiple procedures to staff in a single office.

Larger institutions may lean in the opposite direction toward more decentralized programs where no single office serves a gatekeeping function for all disputes. The administrative responsibility depends on the nature of the allegation (academic or nonacademic), where it originated (in the classroom, in a residence hall, or at a student activity), and where the student is enrolled (undergraduate, graduate, or professional school). In large institutions in which the sheer number of students would be burdensome, the handling of disputes may be better distributed over a larger domain.

In Summary

By studying the subject of mediation, you can learn how to help others resolve their disputes. In third-party intervention, a person unrelated to the conflict helps the involved parties resolve the conflict. Third parties can facilitate the communication process and enhance understanding by helping those involved express their concerns and frustrations about a situation. They can also reduce tension in the situation by focusing the issue and finding areas of agreement. They can establish procedures for decision making and hold participants to those procedures. They help the parties determine the possible solutions and, depending on the extent of their intervention, may help implement that solution.[37] Essential to effective intervention is a balance between focusing on the issues involved and flexibility in seeking out and evaluating possible solutions to the problem.[38] Pruitt and Rabin made the following claim:

> The mere presence of a third party is likely to profoundly change the relationship between the disputants. . . . such a change is likely to be beneficial. . . . However, there are times when inclusion of the third party may have detrimental effects, such as when it occurs in the midst of efforts by the disputants to work directly toward settlement. . . . [A] third party's involvement in a conflictual relationship that is characterized by genuine and effective movement toward settlement of differences may have the costly effect of breaking a newly established—and possibly quite fragile—momentum toward agreement. . . . [T]hird-party intervention is not a panacea in conflict resolutions.[39]

Notes

1. N. A. Burrell and D. D. Cahn, "Mediating Peer Conflicts in Educational Contexts: The Maintenance of School Relationships," in D. D. Cahn (Ed.), *Conflict in Personal Relationships* (Hillsdale, NJ: Erlbaum, 1994), p. 79.

2. Linda L. Putnam and Joseph Folger, "Communication, Conflict, and Dispute Resolution: The Study of Interaction and the Development of Conflict Theory," *Communication Research* 15 (1988), 349.

3. S. Jacobs, S. Jackson, J. Hallmark, B. Hall, and S. A. Stearns, "Ideal Argument in the Real World: Making Do in Mediation," in J. W. Wenzel (Ed.), *Argument and Critical Practices* (Annandale, VA: SCA, 1987), p. 291.

4. C. Danielsson, "A Holistic Approach to Dispute Resolution at a Community Mediation Center," in D. D. Cahn (Ed.), *Conflict in Personal Relationships* (Hillsdale, NJ: Erlbaum, 1994).

5. L. J. Weitzman, *The Divorce Revolution* (New York: The Free Press, 1985).

6. Judy Pearson, N. Thonnes, and L. Vanderkooi, "The Decision to Mediate Profiles—Individuals Who Accept and Reject the Opportunity to Mediate Contested Child Custody and Visitation Issues," *Journal of Divorce* (Winter 1982), 17–35.

7. William W. Wilmot and Joyce L. Hocker, *Interpersonal Conflict,* 5th Ed. (New York: McGraw Hill, 1998), pp. 240–241.

8. O. J. Coogler, *Structured Mediation in Divorce Settlement* (Lexington, MA: Lexington Books, 1978), p. 7.

9. John W. Keltner, *The Management of Struggle: Elements of Dispute Resolution through Negotiation, Mediation and Arbitration* (Annandale, VA: Speech Communication Association, 1994), p. 102.

10. Danielsson, "A Holistic Approach to Dispute Resolution at a Community Mediation Center."

11. B. C. McKinney, W. D. Kimsey, R. M. Fuller, *Dispute Resolution Through Communication,* 2nd Ed. (Dubuque, IA: Kendall Hunt, 1990), p. 146.

12. D. D. Cahn, *Conflict in Intimate Relationships* (New York: Guilford, 1992).

13. Danielsson, "A Holistic Approach to Dispute Resolution at a Community Mediation Center," p. 212.

14. Nancy A. Burrell, William A. Donohue, and Mike Allen, "Gender-Based Perceptual Biases in Mediation," *Communication Research* 15 (1988), 453–464.

15. Joseph Folger and Marshall Scott Poole, *Working through Conflict* (Glenview, IL: Scott Foresman, 1984), p. 191.

16. Cahn, *Conflict in Intimate Relationships.*

17. R. E. Cooley and D. A. Roach, "A Conceptual Framework," in R. N. Bostrom (Ed.), *Competence in Communication* (Beverly Hills, CA: Sage, 1984), p. 25.

18. Joyce L. Hocker and William W. Wilmot, *Interpersonal Conflict,* 4th Ed. (Dubuque, IA: Wm. C. Brown, 1995), p. 238.

19. William A. Donohue, M. Allen, and N. Burrell, "Communication Strategies in Mediation," *Mediation Quarterly* 10 (1985), 75–89.

20. Ibid.

21. Ibid.

22. M. Allen and W. Donohue, "The Mediator as an Arguer," in J. W. Wenzel (Ed.), *Argument and Critical Practices* (Annandale, VA: SCA, 1987), p. 280.

23. Coogler, *Structured Mediation in Divorce Settlement.*

24. Danielsson, "A Holistic Approach to Dispute Resolution at a Community Mediation Center," p. 213.

25. Hocker and Wilmot, *Interpersonal Conflict,* 4th Ed., p. 237.

26. Ibid.

27. Ibid.

28. K. Domenici, *Mediation: Empowerment in Conflict Management* (Prospect Heights, IL: Waveland, 1996), p. 73.

29. Danielsson, "A Holistic Approach to Dispute Resolution at a Community Mediation Center," p. 214.

30. Hocker and Wilmot, *Interpersonal Conflict,* 4th Ed., p. 239.

31. Danielsson, "A Holistic Approach to Dispute Resolution at a Community Mediation Center," p. 214.

32. Ibid.

33. N. Burrell and S. Vogl, "Turf-Side Conflict Mediation for Students," *Mediation Quarterly* 7 (1990), 237–250.

34. Danielsson, "A Holistic Approach to Dispute Resolution at a Community Mediation Center," p. 216.

35. T. Jones and H. Brinkman, "Teach Your Children Well: Suggestions for Peer Mediation Programs in the Schools," in J. Folger and T. Jones (Eds.), *Third Parties and Conflict: Communication Research and Perspectives* (Beverly Hills, CA: Sage, forthcoming).

36. Joseph P. Folger and J. J. Shubert, *Resolving Student-Initiated Grievances in Higher Education: Dispute Resolution Procedures in a Non-Adversarial Setting* (Report No. 3). (Washington, DC: National Institute for Dispute Resolution, 1986).

37. Morton Deutsch, "Conflict and Its Resolution," in Clagett G. Smith (Ed.), *Conflict Resolution: Contributions of the Behavioral Sciences* (Notre Dame, IN: University of Notre Dame Press, 1971), pp. 36–57; see also Roger Fisher, "Third Party Consultation: A Method for the Study and Resolution of Conflict," *Journal of Conflict Resolution* 16 (1972), 67–94.

38. A. M. Levi and A. Benjamin, "Focus and Flexibility in a Model of Conflict Resolution," *Journal of Conflict Resolution* 21 (1977), 405–425.

39. Dean G. Pruitt and Jeffrey A. Rubin, *Social Conflict: Escalation, Stalemate, and Settlement* (New York: Random House, 1986), pp. 165–166, italics omitted.

Appendix B

Example of a Conflict Assessment

I. Write out the narrative of the conflict as if you were telling it to another person. After telling the story, analyze the conflict using the questions in II–V.

Because I am just "waking up" this year and have finally still only progressed to Conflict Management 101, I am going to relate a narrative that will illustrate the point of two of the most powerful sentences I read in the book: "Thus, a *fundamental assumption* of this book is that effective behavior in conflict situations requires an ability to analyze the situation and choose behavior appropriate to it, without sacrificing one's own values and beliefs" and "We are affected by our desire to appear competent to others" (read "boss" in my case).

Anyway, here goes. For a long while, whenever my boss would go out of town to attend meetings and seminars for a couple of weeks, he would ask me if I would mind just checking on his house a couple of times during his absence. He told me where the extra key was hidden, and wanted me to just take a few minutes and check to make sure the house was okay. I thought at the time, "Wow, what an honor, the boss really trusts me," and I said, "Sure, no problem." He would always bring me back a nice present as a gesture of thanks. After a couple of times of this, he asked if I also would take in the newspaper and the mail. I said, "Sure, no problem."

As time went on, the next trip came up, and there was an added-on request of watering the house plants every couple of days. I gritted my teeth, but, feeling like I was in quicksand said, "Okay." The "thank you" gifts from him to me upon his return stopped.

Then, one time during his absence, there was a huge windstorm and some of his windows were shattered. So I went up to the house and arranged for a company to come out and board up his windows until his return when he could have the glass replaced. I asked another employee in our department to go up to the boss's house with me because there was a lot of dangerous shattered glass and it would have been too dangerous for him to walk into if he had come home late at night. This time, he never even thanked me for my trouble and was more narcissistically preoccupied with the annoying hassle of arranging to get his windows replaced. Not even a thank you.

Then his girlfriend moved in with him, and she was mean and jealous, but she had tons of plants. So the next time he went out of town, he asked me if I would check on his house, take in his mail and paper, water not only his plants but also his awful girlfriend's plants because she was going with him on the trip. And they left explicit instructions, just like it was

360

a protocol for an experiment or something, as to how each plant was to be watered and how often. And there was never a thank you gift anymore, let alone a verbal thank you.

Then they broke up, thank God, but his request of me when going out of town became more extensive: continue to do all the other assignments and also water the lawn front and back because it was August and he was worried about fires. He has a gardener, so this made no sense to me, but I just kept getting in deeper and deeper with this abuse of my personal time. And yet he was my boss, and I was addicted to appearing willing and competent and not at all disagreeable.

Finally, one day at work my boss was in the conference room, talking to someone and saying that he was seriously considering getting a dog. The person pointed out that because he traveled so much it would be difficult to care for the dog in his absence. My boss replied, "Oh, I'll just have someone from the office drive up and walk him and give him food and water." This person was a friend of mine, so she came by the office to let me know of my boss's intentions. Something snapped, and I whipped off an e-mail to him (because it is the only way I can get his attention): "Dear B: I just heard through the grapevine that you actually intend to get a dog. Please don't ask me to take care of it in your absence. Thanks, Z." He replied, "Z—I've heard of preemptive strikes before, but . . . B."

I didn't even give it the dignity of an answer because I was deadly serious. Since then, he has never asked me to check on his house, water his plants and lawn, and so on ever again. My feelings are not hurt.

A short time ago he sent me an e-mail stating that, realizing how much I hate to water plants, would I mind watering the ones in his office just once during his absence because his secretary would also be out of the office. I said yes, but since then, nothing more has been asked of me. And my feelings are not hurt. Appearing competent is not an issue for me now. I'm cured.

II. Background of the conflict

A. What set off the conflict?

What set it off was that he had finally gone too far. He is what the book calls a Noble Self (i.e., high concern for self, low concern for other, low adaptiveness). But I didn't know that at the start. I just started out doing what seemed like a simple favor that didn't take much time. I was just trying to be a nice person. Plus, I used to be addicted to appearing competent to him. It wasn't harassment, but it was abusive somehow, and once it escalated I didn't know how to say "no." Bosses can be intimidating just by the fact that they are your boss and they sign your paycheck.

B. Explain the conflict from your perspective.

I believe in retrospect that long before things got out of hand I had made a decision about who I was that later on put me in a position to be abused by my boss.

C. Explain the conflict from the other person's perspective.

Until he received the dog e-mail, he was so self-centeredly oblivious to my inconveniences that, in his view, there was no conflict.

D. What kinds of feelings does the conflict arouse in you?

Anger, frustration, humiliation, shame, fear.

Why do you think you feel the way you do about the conflict?

Because it kind of snuck up on me. All of a sudden I was devoting my free time to taking care of his house, like a servant. I don't look down on servants, but he offered no thanks and no remuneration. *Besides, I already had a job, working for him in the office.* I tried to rationalize the situation to myself by saying that it was nice to be of service, and so on, but there's a difference between being of service and being abused and taken advantage of.

E. **To whom does this conflict seem apparent?**

Me. And then him. And a few people in the office who knew about his intention to get a dog.

F. **Who will be the first to notice if this conflict is resolved in some way?**

Me. And him. He backed away very quickly. Good.

Who else will notice?

Other members of the office. He has put them into similar positions or worse.

III. **Analyzing the situation**

A. **What kind of relationship do you have with the other person?**

Actually, that's a tricky question because our relationship is a professional one. But it overstepped the boundary into a "social" one—or should I not romanticize it and simply say a "slave labor" one?

B. **Who are interested parties to the conflict? Who else has a stake in the way this conflict will be resolved?**

Me. My boss. And some homeless dog out there. Perhaps other people in the office who have been talked into doing favors for him.

C. **How has the situation that gave rise to the conflict been altered as a result of the conflict occurring? That is, has your relationship with the other person changed? Has trust decreased? Have power relations shifted?**

As I mentioned, all requests to even slightly check on the welfare of his home have ceased. This was the first time I set a boundary with him. Since then, it has gotten easier. For example, I now can tell him that work he is giving me should be given to his secretary, not to me.

IV. **Analyzing your choices**

A. **What is your goal in the conflict?**

My goal is to be a professional, competent manager who no longer obsessively seeks a "thank you" from my boss (such a self set-up for abuse), and to keep adding value to my work through lifelong learning and my relationships with colleagues and friends. And to do as the text instructs—"to analyze the situation and choose behavior appropriate to it."

B. **What can you do to achieve your goals?**

Don't be asleep at the switch. And watch my motives.

C. **How do you think the other person will respond to your goal-seeking behavior?**

As time goes on, our relationship could become tricky because I have seen the light. The dance steps are changing. I must learn to be an artful dodger when it comes to his selfishness and to be able to see it coming.

D. **What is the very least you need from the other person in order to say that the conflict is over?**

At this point, that conflict is over. I need no reassurances that we're still "friends." I am changing in my addiction to appear competent. I almost feel a strange sort of freedom.

E. **What kind of person will you be if you achieve your goals?**

A more authentic person; actually, a truly competent person. An effective manager of my time and the office's. A more productive person, with boundaries. My boss has certainly always exercised his with me.

F. **What kind of relationship will you have with the other person if you achieve your goal?**

I truly hope a more mature, productive, adult, nonabusive, professional, and yet friendly relationship.

G. **Do you want to be the kind of person or have the kind of relationship that is likely to result from achieving your goal in the conflict situation?**

Yes, because the inability to set boundaries, and delegate, and say "no" can literally kill you. It is not right for me to be abused and/or to allow abuse from others. It's no good for either party.

V. **Planning the conflict**

A. **How could you bring the conflict up to the other person (assuming you haven't done so already)?**

What can you say to the other person? I brought it up via e-mail—his communication medium of choice. Quick and easy. Just like that—the conflict was over for me. I wasn't even scared after I hit the "send" button. However, I might have added: "When you asked me to do a small favor, that was okay. And when you brought back a thank you present, that was nice. But then when you added on more requests, and stopped with the thank you soap, and not even a verbal thank you, and piled on more requests, and topped it all off by intending to buy a dog without even consulting me as to my willingness to take responsibility for it before your purchase, not only did you put me in a compromising position based on the fact that you are my boss and these escalating tasks are not job related, but you made me feel exploited beyond belief."

B. **What do you think the other person would say about the conflict if he was initiating it?**

It's hard for me to imagine that he ever perceived a conflict until I told him not to get the dog.

References

Achterberg, S., S. Matthews, and O. C. Simonton, "Psychology of the Exceptional Cancer Patient: A Description of Patients Who Outlived Predicted Expectancies," *Psychotherapy: Theory and Research and Practice* 6 (1976), 13–14.

Adler, Peter S., "Beyond Cultural Identity: Reflections of Cultural and Multicultural Man," in Gary R. Weaver (Ed.), *Culture, Communication and Conflict: Readings in Intercultural Relations,* 2nd Ed. (Needham Heights, MA: Simon and Schuster, 1998), pp. 251–252.

Adler, Ronald B., *Confidence in Communication: A Guide to Assertive and Social Skills* (New York: Holt, Rinehart & Winston, 1977).

Albert, E., "Values Systems," in *International Encyclopedia of the Social Sciences* (New York: Macmillan, 1968), p. 287.

Alberti, R. E., and M. L. Emmons, *Your Perfect Right: A Guide to Assertive Behavior* (San Luis Obispo, CA: Impact, 1970).

Alberts, Jess K., "An Analysis of Couples' Conversational Complaints," *Communication Monographs* 55 (1988), 184–197.

Alberts, Jess K., "A Descriptive Taxonomy of Couples' Complaint Interactions," *Southern Speech Communication Journal* 54 (1989), 125–143.

Alberts, Jess K., "Perceived Effectiveness of Couples' Conversational Complaints," *Communication Studies* 40 (1989), 280–291.

Alberts, Jess K., and Gillian Driscoll, "Containment vs. Escalation: The Trajectory of Couples' Conversational Complaints," *Western Journal of Communication* 56 (1992), 394–412.

Allen, M., and W. Donohue, "The Mediator as an Arguer," in J. W. Wenzel (Ed.), *Argument and Critical Practices* (Annandale, VA: Speech Communication Association, 1987).

Alloway, David L., and Janis F. Andersen, "Individual Differences of the Perceptions of Verbal Aggression," paper presented at the annual meeting of the Western Speech Communication Association Convention, San Diego, February 1988.

Altman, Irving, and D. Taylor, *Social Penetration: The Development of Interpersonal Relationships* (Chicago: Holt, Rinehart and Winston, 1973).

Anderson, Stephen A., Candace J. Russell, and Walter R. Schuman, "Perceived Marital Quality and Family Life Cycle: A Further Analysis," *Journal of Marriage and the Family* 45 (1983), 127–139.

Antaki, Charles, "Explaining Events or Explaining Oneself?" in Michael J. Cody and Margaret L. McLaughlin (Eds.), *The Psychology of Tactical Communication* (Clevedon, Avon, England: Multilingual Matters, Ltd., 1990), pp. 268–283.

Arendt, Hannah, *The Human Condition* (Chicago: University of Chicago Press, 1956).

Augsburger, David, *Caring Enough to Forgive* (Ventura, CA: Regal Books, 1981).

Augsburger, David, *Caring Enough to Not Forgive* (Ventura, CA: Regal Books, 1981).

Augsburger, David, *Caring Enough to Hear and Be Heard* (Ventura, CA: Regal Books, 1982).

Azakahi, Walter R., and James C. McCroskey, "Willingness to Communicate: A Potentially Confounding Variable in Communication Research," *Communication Reports* 2 (1989), 96–104.

Bach, G. R., and R. M. Deutsch, *Pairing* (New York: Peter H. Wyden, 1970).

Bach, G. R., and H. Goldberg, *Creative Aggression: The Art of Assertive Living* (New York: Avon Books, 1974).

Bach, G. R., and P. Wyden, *The Intimate Enemy: How to Fight Fair in Love and Marriage* (New York: Avon, 1969).

Baker, William H., "Defensiveness in Communication: Its Causes, Effects and Cures," *Journal of Business Communication* 17 (1980), 33–43.

Bardwick, J. M., *Psychology of Women: A Study of Biocultural Conflicts* (New York: Harper & Row, 1971).

Barnlund, Dean C., *Communicative Styles of Japanese and Americans: Images and Realities* (Belmont, CA: Wadsworth, 1989).

Bateson, Gregory, *Naven,* 2nd Ed. (Stanford, CA: Stanford University Press, 1958).

Bateson, Gregory, *Steps to an Ecology of Mind* (New York: Ballantine Books, 1972).

Baxter, Leslie A., "Accomplishing Relationship Disengagement," in Steven Duck and D. Perlman (Eds.), *Understanding Personal Relationships: An Inter-*

disciplinary Approach (London: Sage, 1985), pp. 243–265.

Baxter, Leslie A., and Tara L. Shepherd, "Sex-Role Identity, Sex of Other and Affective Relationship as Determinants of Interpersonal Conflict Management Styles," *Sex Roles* 6 (1978), 813–825.

Bazerman, Max, "Why Negotiations Go Wrong," *Psychology Today,* June 1986, 54–58.

Bell, E. C., and R. N. Blakeney, "Personality Correlates of Conflict Resolution Modes," *Human Relations* 30 (1977), 849–857.

Bell, Mae Arnold, "A Research Note: The Relationship of Conflict and Linguistic Diversity in Small Groups," *Central States Speech Journal* 34 (1983), 128–133.

Belsky, J., M. E. Lang, and M. Rovine, "Stability and Change in Marriage Across the Transition to Parenthood: A Second Study," *Journal of Marriage and the Family* 47 (1985), 855–865.

Benner, David G., *Healing Emotional Wounds* (Grand Rapids: Baker Book House, 1990).

Benoit, Pamela J., "Relationship Arguments: An Interactionist Elaboration of Speech Acts," *Argumentation* 3 (1989), 423–437.

Benoit, Pamela J., and William L. Benoit, "To Argue or Not to Argue: How Real People Get into and Out of Interpersonal Arguments," in R. Trapp and J. Schuetz (Eds.), *Perspectives on Argument: Essays in Honor of Wayne Brockriede* (Prospect Heights: Waveland, 1990), pp. 55–72.

Benoit, William L., and Pamela J. Benoit, "Everyday Argument Practices of Naive Social Actors," in J. W. Wenzel (Ed.), *Argumentation and Critical Practices* (Annandale, VA: Speech Communication Association, 1987), pp. 465–473.

Benoit, William L., and Pamela J. Benoit, "Accounts of Failures and Claims of Successes in Arguments," in B. E. Gronbeck (Ed.), *Spheres of Argument* (Annandale, VA: Speech Communication Association, 1989), pp. 551–556.

Benoit, William L., and Dudley D. Cahn, "A Communication Approach to Everyday Argument," in D. D. Cahn (Ed.), *Conflict in Personal Relationships* (Hillsdale, NJ: Erlbaum, 1994), pp. 163–181.

Benoit, William L., and Shirley Drew, "Appropriateness and Effectiveness of Image Repair Strategies," *Communication Reports* 10 (1997), 153–163.

Berne, Eric, *Games People Play* (New York: Ballantine Books, 1964).

Bettinghaus, Erwin P., and Michael J. Cody, *Persuasive Communication,* 4th Ed. (New York: Holt, Rinehart & Winston, 1987).

Biggers, Thompson, and John T. Masterson, "Communication Apprehension as a Personality Trait: An Emotional Defense of a Concept," *Communication Monographs* 51 (1984), 381–390.

Billings, Andrew, "Conflict Resolution in Distressed and Nondistressed Married Couples," *Journal of Consulting and Clinical Psychology* 47 (1979), 368–376.

Birchler, G. R., R. L. Weiss, and J. P. Vincent, "Multimethod Analysis of Social Reinforcement Exchange Between Maritally Distressed and Nondistressed Spouse and Stranger Dyads," *Journal of Personality and Social Psychology* 31 (1975), 349–360.

Bixenstein, V., and J. Gaebelein, "Strategies of 'Real' Opponents in Eliciting Cooperative Choice in a Prisoner's Dilemma Game," *Journal of Communication Research* 15 (1971), 157–166.

Bixenstein, V., and K. Wilson, "Effects of Level of Cooperative Choice by the Other Player in a Prisoner's Dilemma Game," *Journal of Abnormal and Social Psychology* 67 (1963), 139–147.

Blake, Robert R., and Jane Srygley Mouton, "The Fifth Achievement," in Fred E. Jandt (Ed.), *Conflict Resolution through Communication* (New York: Harper & Row, 1973).

Blood, R. O., and D. M. Wolfe, *Husbands and Wives: The Dynamics of Married Living* (New York: Free Press, 1960).

Bograd, M., "Why We Need Gender to Understand Human Violence," *Journal of Interpersonal Violence* 5 (1990), 132–135.

Booth-Butterfield, S., and M. Booth-Butterfield, "Untangling the Tangled Web: Theory and Empirical Tests of Interpersonal Deception," paper presented at the annual meeting of the International Communication Association Convention, Montreal, Canada, May 1987.

Borisoff, Deborah, and David A. Victor, *Conflict Management: A Communication Skills Approach* (Englewood Cliffs, NJ: Prentice-Hall, 1989).

Bostrom, Robert N., *Persuasion* (Englewood Cliffs, NJ: Prentice Hall, 1983).

Bowers, J. W., "Guest Editor's Introduction: Beyond Threats and Promises," *Speech Monographs* 41 (1974), ix–xi.

Braiker, H., and H. Kelley, "Conflict in the Development of Close Relationships," in R. Burgess and T. Huston (Eds.), *Social Exchange in Developing Relationships* (New York: Academic Press, 1979), pp. 135–168.

Brilhart, B. L., "Relationships of Speaker-Message Perception to Perceptual Field Dependence," *Journal of Communication* 20 (1970), 153–166.

Brown, Bert R., "The Effects of Need to Maintain Face on Interpersonal Bargaining," *Journal of Experimental Social Psychology* 4 (1968), 107–112.

Brown, Bert R., "Face Saving Following Experimentally Induced Embarrassment," *Journal of Experimental Social Psychology* 6 (1970), 255–271.

Brown, Charles T., Paul Yelsma, and Paul W. Keller, "Communication-Conflict Predispositions:

Development of a Theory and Instrument," *Human Relations* 34 (1981), 1103–1117.

Brown, Penelope, and C. Grazer, "Speech as a Marker of Situation," in K. Scherer and H. Giles (Eds.), *Social Markers in Speech* (Cambridge: Cambridge University, 1979).

Brown, Penelope, and Stephen Levinson, *Politeness: Some Universals in Language Usage* (Cambridge: Cambridge University Press, 1987).

Brunner, Claire C., and Judy C. Pearson, "Sex Differences in Perceptions of Interpersonal Communication Competence," paper presented at the annual meeting of the Speech Communication Association Convention, Chicago, November 1984.

Burggraf, Cynthia S., and Alan L. Sillars, "A Critical Examination of Sex Differences in Marital Communication," *Communication Monographs* 54 (1987), 276–294.

Burke, Kenneth, *Permanence and Change* (Indianapolis: Bobbs Merrill, 1954).

Burke, R. J., "Methods of Resolving Superior-Subordinate Conflict: The Constructive Use of the Subordinate Differences and Disagreements," *Organizational Behavior and Performance* 5 (1970), 393–411.

Burrell, Nancy A., and Dudley D. Cahn, "Mediating Peer Conflicts in Educational Contexts: The Maintenance of School Relationships," in D. D. Cahn (Ed.), *Conflict in Personal Relationships* (Hillsdale, NJ: Erlbaum, 1994), pp. 79–94.

Burrell, Nancy A., William A. Donohue, and Mike Allen, "Gender-Based Perceptual Biases in Mediation," *Communication Research* 15 (1988), 453–464.

Burrell, Nancy A., and S. Vogl, "Turf-Side Conflict Mediation for Students," *Mediation Quarterly* 7 (1990), 237–250.

Buttny, Richard, "Accounts as a Reconstruction of an Event's Context," *Communication Monographs* 52 (1985), 57–77.

Buttny, Richard, "Blame-Account Sequences in Therapy: The Negotiation of Relational Meanings," *Semiotica* 78 (1990), 219–247.

Cahn, Dudley D., "Communication Competence in the Resolution of Intercultural Conflict," *World Communication* 14 (1985), 85–94.

Cahn, Dudley D., *Letting Go: A Practical Theory of Relationship Disengagement and Reengagement* (New York: SUNY Press Albany, 1987).

Cahn, Dudley D., "Communication and Self-Management in Yugoslavia," *World Communication* 18 (1989), 1–22.

Cahn, Dudley D., *Intimates in Conflict* (Hillsdale, NJ: Erlbaum, 1990).

Cahn, Dudley D., *Conflict in Intimate Relationships,* (New York: Guilford, 1992).

Cahn, Dudley D., and Sally Lloyd (Eds.), *Family Violence from a Communication Perspective* (Thousand Oaks, CA: Sage, 1996).

Canary, Daniel J., B. G. Brossmann, Alan L. Sillars, and S. Lovette, "Married Couples Argument Structures and Sequences: A Comparison of Satisfied and Dissatisfied Dyads," in J. W. Wenzel (Ed.), *Argument and Critical Practices* (Annandale, VA: Speech Communication Association, 1987).

Canary, Daniel J., Ellen M. Cunningham, and Michael J. Cody, "Goal Types, Gender and Locus of Control in Managing Interpersonal Conflict," *Communication Research* 15 (1988), 426–446.

Canary, Daniel J., and William R. Cupach, "Relational and Episodic Characteristics Associated with Conflict Tactics," paper presented at the annual meeting of the Western Speech Communication Association Convention, Fresno, February 1985.

Canary, Daniel J., and William R. Cupach, "Relationship and Episodic Characteristics Associated with Conflict Tactics," *Journal of Social and Personal Relationships* 5 (1988), 305–325.

Canary, Daniel J., and Kimberly Hause, "Is There Any Reason to Research Sex Differences in Communication?" *Communication Quarterly* 41 (1993), 129–144.

Canary, Daniel J., and Alan L. Sillars, "Argument in Satisfied and Dissatisfied Married Couples," in W. L. Benoit, D. Hample, and P. J. Benoit (Eds.), *Readings in Argumentation* (Dordrecht: Foris, 1992).

Canary, Daniel J., and Brian H. Spitzberg, "Appropriateness and Effectiveness in the Perception of Conflict Strategies," *Human Communication Research* 14 (1987), 93–118.

Canary, Daniel J., and Brian H. Spitzberg, "A Model of the Perceived Competence of Conflict Strategies," *Human Communication Research* 15 (1989), 630–649.

Canary, Daniel J., and Brian H. Spitzberg, "Attribution Biases and Associations Between Conflict Strategies and Competence Outcomes," *Communication Monographs* 57 (1990), 139–151.

Canary, Daniel J., and H. Weger, "The Relationship of Interpersonal Argument to Control Mutuality: An Observational Analysis of Romantic Couple's Conversations," in B. E. Gronbeck (Ed.), *Spheres of Argument* (Annandale, VA: Speech Communication Association, 1989).

Canary, Daniel J., H. Weger, and Laura Stafford, "Couples' Argument Sequences and Their Associations with Relational Characteristics," *Western Journal of Speech Communication* 55 (1991), 159–179.

Carey, Colleen M., and Paul A. Mongeau, "Communication and Violence in Courtship Relationships," in Dudley D. Cahn and Sally A. Lloyd, *Family Violence* from a Communication Perspective (Thousand Oaks, CA: Sage Publications, 1996), pp. 127–150.

Carnevale, P. J. D., Dean G. Pruitt, and S. Seilheimer, "Looking and Competing: Accountability and Visual Access in Integrative Bargaining," *Journal of Personality and Social Psychology* 28 (1973), 12–20.

Castelfranchi, C., and I. Poggi, "Blushing as Discourse: Was Darwin Wrong?" in W. R. Crozier (Ed.), *Shyness and Embarrassment: Perspectives from Social Psychology* (Cambridge: Cambridge University Press, 1990), pp. 230–251.

Cegala, Donald J., "Interaction Involvement: A Cognitive Dimension of Communicative Competence," *Communication Education* 30 (1981), 109–121.

Cegala, Donald J., "Affective and Cognitive Manifestations of Interaction Involvement During Unstructured and Competitive Interactions," *Communication Monographs* 51 (1984), 320–338.

Chang, Hui-Ching, and G. Richard Holt, "A Chinese Perspective on Face as Inter-Relational Concern," in Stella Ting-Toomey (Ed.), *The Challenge of Facework: Cross-Cultural and Interpersonal Issues* (Albany, NY: SUNY, 1994).

Chmielewski, Terence L., "Communicator Orientations: Attitudes Underlying the Rhetorical Sensitivity Archetypes," paper presented at the annual meeting of the International Communication Association Convention, San Francisco, May 1984.

Clark, Ruth Anne, and Jesse G. Delia, "Topoi and Rhetorical Competence," *Quarterly Journal of Speech* 65 (1979), 187–206.

Cloven, Denise H., "Relational Effects of Interpersonal Conflict: The Role of Cognition, Satisfaction, and Anticipated Communication," Master's thesis, Northwestern University, Evanston, IL, 1990.

Cloven, Denise H., and Michael E. Roloff, "Sense-Making Activities and Interpersonal Conflict: Communication Cures for the Mulling Blues," *Western Journal of Speech Communication* 55 (1991), 134–158.

Cloven, Denise H., and Michael E. Roloff, "Sense-Making Activities and Interpersonal Conflict, II: The Effects of Communicative Intentions on Internal Dialogue," *Western Journal of Communication* 57 (1993), 309–329.

Cloven, Denise H., and Michael E. Roloff, "The Chilling Effect of Aggressive Potential on the Expression of Complaints in Intimate Relationships," *Communication Monographs* 60 (1993), 199–219.

Cloven, Denise Haunani, and Michael E. Roloff, "Cognitive Turning Effects of Anticipating Communication on Thought about an Interpersonal Conflict," *Communication Reports* 8 (1995), 1–9.

Cody, Michael J., and Margaret L. McLaughlin, "Models for the Sequential Construction of Accounting Episodes: Situational and Interactional Constraints on Message Selection and Evaluation," in Richard L. Street and Joseph N. Capella (Eds.), *Sequence and Pattern in Communicative Behavior* (London: Edward Arnold Publishers, 1985), pp. 50–69.

Cole, C., and R. Ackerman, "A Change Model for Resolution of Stress," *Alternative Lifestyles* 4 (1981), 134–141.

Cole, Diane, "So You Made a Mistake!" *Working Mother* (August 1991), 29–30.

Collier, Mary Jane, "Culture and Gender: Effects on Assertive Behavior and Communication Competence," in Margaret L. McLaughlin (Ed.), *Communication Yearbook* 9 (Beverly Hills, CA: Sage, 1986).

Condon, John, ". . . So Near the United States: Notes on Communication between Mexicans and North Americans," in Larry A. Samovar and Richard E. Porter (Eds.), *Intercultural Communication: A Reader,* 6th Ed. (Belmont, CA: Wadsworth, 1991), pp. 106–112.

Conrad, Charles, "Gender, Interactional Sensitivity, and Communication in Conflict: Assumptions and Interpretations," paper presented at the annual meeting of the Speech Communication Association Convention, Denver, November 1985.

Conrad, Charles, *Strategic Organizational Communication,* 2nd Ed. (Fort Worth, TX: Holt, Rinehart & Winston, 1990).

Conrad, Charles, "Communication in Conflict: Style-Strategy Relationships," *Communication Monographs* 58 (1991), 135–155.

Coogler, O. J., *Structured Mediation in Divorce Settlement* (Lexington, MA: Lexington Books, 1978).

Cooley, R. E., and D. A. Roach, "A Conceptual Framework," in R. N. Bostrom (Ed.), *Competence in Communication* (Beverly Hills, CA: Sage, 1984).

Coomb, Clyde H., and George S. Avrunin, *The Structure of Conflict* (Hillsdale, NJ: Lawrence Erlbaum Associates, 1988).

Coser, Lewis, *The Functions of Social Conflict* (New York: Free Press, 1956).

Coupland, Nikolas, Howard Giles, and John W. Wiseman (Eds.), *"Miscommunication" and Problematic Talk* (Newbury Park, CA: Sage, 1991).

Cronen, Vernon E., W. Barnett Pearce, and Lonna M. Snavely, "A Theory of Rule-Structure and Types of Episodes and a Study of Perceived Enmeshment in Undesired Repetitive Pattern ('URPs')," in Dan Nimmo (Ed.), *Communication Yearbook* 3 (New Brunswick, NJ: Transaction Books, 1979), pp. 225–240.

Cross, Gary P., Jean H. Names, and Darrell Beck, *Conflict and Human Interaction* (Dubuque, IA: Kendall Hunt Publishing, 1979).

Cummings, H. Wayland, Larry W. Long, and Michael Lewis, *Managing Communication in Organizations,*

2nd Ed. (Scottsdale, AZ: Gorsuch Scarisbrick Publishers, 1987).

Cupach, William R., "Perceived Communication Competence and Choice of Interpersonal Conflict Message Strategies," paper presented at the annual meeting of the Western Speech Communication Association Convention, Denver, February 1982.

Cupach, William R., "Social Predicaments," in William R. Cupach and Brian H. Spitzberg (Eds.), *The Dark Side of Interpersonal Communication* (Hillsdale, NJ: Lawrence Erlbaum, 1994), pp. 159–180.

Cupach, William R., and Sandra Metts, "Accounts of Relational Dissolution: A Comparison of Marital and Non-Marital Relationships," paper presented at the annual meeting of the International Communication Association Convention, Honolulu, May 1985.

Cupach, William R., and Sandra Metts, "Remedial Processes in Embarrassing Predicaments," in James A. Anderson (Ed.), *Communication Yearbook* 13 (Newbury Park, CA: Sage, 1990), pp. 323–352.

Cupach, William R., and Sandra Metts, "The Effects of Type of Predicament and Embarrassability on Remedial Responses to Embarrassing Situations," *Communication Quarterly* 40 (1992), 149–161.

Cupach, William R., and Sandra Metts, *Facework* (Thousand Oaks: Sage Publications, 1994).

Cupach, William R., Sandra Metts, and Vince Hazelton, "Coping with Embarrassing Predicaments: Remedial Strategies and Their Perceived Utility," *Journal of Language and Social Psychology* 5 (1986), 181–200.

Cupach, William R., and Brian H. Spitzberg (Eds.), *The Dark Side of Interpersonal Communication* (Hillsdale, NJ: Lawrence Erlbaum, 1994).

Cushman, Donald, and Dudley D. Cahn, *Communication in Interpersonal Relationships* (Albany, NY: SUNY 1985).

Daly, John A., Anita L. Vangelisti, and Suzanne M. Daughton, "The Nature and Correlates of Conversational Sensitivity," *Human Communication Research* 14 (1987), 167–202.

Danielsson, C., "A Holistic Approach to Dispute Resolution at a Community Mediation Center," in Dudley D. Cahn (Ed.), *Conflict in Personal Relationships* (Hillsdale, NJ: Erlbaum, 1994), pp. 203–221.

Darby, B. W., and Barry R. Schlenker, "Children's Reactions to Apologies," *Journal of Personality and Social Psychology* 43 (1982), 742–753.

Darnell, Donald K., and Wayne Brockriede, *Persons Communicating* (Englewood Cliffs, NJ: Prentice-Hall, 1976).

Davis, L., "An Experimental Investigation of Tolerance of Ambiguity and Information in Interpersonal Bargaining," *Dissertation Abstracts International* 2 (1975), 970-B.

Derr, C., "Managing Organizational Conflict," *California Management Review* 21 (1978): 76–83.

deTurck, Mark A., "A Transactional Analysis of Compliance-Gaining Behavior," *Human Communication Research* 12 (1985), 54–78.

deTurck, Mark A., "When Communication Fails: Physical Aggression as a Compliance Gaining Strategy," *Communication Monographs* 54 (1987), 106–112.

Deutsch, Morton, "Trust and Suspicion," *Journal of Conflict Resolution* 2 (1958), 265–279.

Deutsch, Morton, "Conflicts: Productive or Destructive?" *Journal of Social Issues* 25 (1969), 7–41.

Deutsch, Morton, "Conflict and Its Resolution," in Clagett G. Smith (Ed.), *Conflict Resolution: Contributions of the Behavioral Sciences* (Notre Dame, IN: University of Notre Dame Press, 1971).

Deutsch, Morton, "Toward an Understanding of Conflict," *International Journal of Group Tensions* 1 (1971), 42–54.

Deutsch, Morton, *The Resolution of Conflict* (New Haven, CT: Yale University Press, 1973).

DeVito, Joseph, *The Interpersonal Communication Book,* 6th Ed. (New York: HarperCollins, 1992).

Dillard, James Price, C. Segrin, and J. M. Harden, "Primary and Secondary Goals in the Production of Interpersonal Influence Messages," *Communication Monographs* 56 (1989), 19–38.

Dobash, R. Emerson, and Russell P. Dobash, "The Nature and Antecedents of Violent Events," *British Journal of Criminology* 24 (1984), 269–288.

Dobash, R., and R. Dobash, "Research as Social Action: The Struggle for Battered Women," in K. Yllo and M. Bograd (Eds.), *Feminist Perspectives on Wife Abuse* (Newbury Park, CA: Sage, 1988).

Domenici, K., *Mediation: Empowerment in Conflict Management* (Prospect Heights, IL: Waveland, 1996).

Donnelly, Doris, *Learning to Forgive* (Nashville, TN: Abingdon Press, 1979).

Donnelly, Doris, *Putting Forgiveness into Practice* (Allen, TX: Argus Communications, 1982).

Donohue, William A., "Analyzing Negotiation Tactics and Development of a Negotiation Interact System," *Human Communication Research* 7 (1981), 273–287.

Donohue, William A., M. Allen, and N. Burrell, "Communication Strategies in Mediation," *Mediation Quarterly* 10 (1985), 75–89.

Donohue, William A., Mary E. Diez, and Mark Hamilton, "Coding Naturalistic Interaction," *Human Communication Research* 10 (1984), 403–425.

Dressler, Joshua, "Hating Criminals: How Can Something That Feels So Good Be Wrong?" *Michigan Law Review* 88 (1990), 1454.

Droll, David M., "Forgiveness: Theory and Research," Doctoral dissertation, University of Nevada, Reno, 1985.

Druckman, Daniel, "The Importance of the Situation in Interparty Conflict," *Journal of Conflict Resolution* 15 (1971), 523–554.

Duvall, Evelyn M., *Family Development,* 2nd Ed. (New York: Lippincott, 1962).

Eadie, William F., "Influence of Attitudes Toward Communication and Relational Factors on Rhetorical Force," paper presented at the annual meeting of the Western Speech Communication Association Convention, Albuquerque, February 1983.

Edwards, Renee, James M. Honeycutt, and Kenneth S. Zagacki, "Imagined Interaction as an Element of Social Cognition," *Western Journal of Speech Communication* 52 (1988), 23–45.

Eisenberg, Eric, "Ambiguity as a Strategy in Organizational Communication," *Communication Monographs* 51 (1984), 227–242.

Ellis, A., "Overview of the Clinical Theory of Rational-Emotive Therapy," in Russell Grieger and John D. Boyd (Eds.), *Rational-Emotive Therapy: A Skills-Based Approach* (New York: Van Nostrand Reinhold, 1980).

Ellis, A., and R. A. Harper, *A New Guide to Rational Living* (N. Hollywood: Wilshire Book, 1975).

Ellis, Donald, and B. Aubrey Fisher, "Phases of Conflict in Small Group Development," *Human Communication Research* 1 (1975), 195–212.

Emerson, James G., *The Dynamics of Forgiveness* (Philadelphia: The Westminster Press, 1964).

Enright, Robert D., "Counseling within the Forgiveness Triad: On Forgiving, Receiving Forgiveness, and Self-Forgiveness," *Counseling and Values* 40 (1996), 107–127.

Enright, Robert D., and Elizabeth A. Gassin, "Forgiveness: A Developmental View," *Journal of Moral Education* 21 (1992), 99–114.

Enright, Robert D., and Robert L. Zell, "Problems Encountered When We Forgive One Another," *Journal of Psychology and Christianity* 8 (1989), 52–54.

Etzioni, Amatai, *A Comparative Analysis of Complex Organizations* (New York: Free Press, 1961).

Fairhust, Gail T., Stephen G. Green, and B. Kay Snavely, "Face Support in Controlling Poor Performance," *Human Communication Research* 11 (1984), 272–295.

Faludi, Susan, *Backlash: The Undeclared War Against American Women* (New York: Crown Publishers, 1991).

Fazio, Russell K., Edwin A. Efrein, and Victoria J. Falender, "Self-Perceptions Following Social Interaction," *Journal of Personality and Social Psychology* 41 (1981), 232–242.

Felson, R. B., and J. Steadman, "Situational Factors in Disputes Leading to Criminal Violence," *Criminology* 21 (1983), 59–74.

Filley, Alan C., *Interpersonal Conflict Resolution* (New York: HarperCollins Publishers, 1975).

Fink, Clinton F., "Some Conceptual Difficulties in the Theory of Social Conflict," *Journal of Conflict Resolution* 12 (1968), 412–460.

Fisher, B. Aubrey, *Interpersonal Communication: Pragmatics of Human Relationships* (New York: Random House, 1987).

Fisher, Roger, "Third Party Consultation: A Method for the Study and Resolution of Conflict," *Journal of Conflict Resolution* 16 (1972), 67–94.

Fisher, Roger, and William Ury, *Getting to Yes: Negotiating Agreement Without Giving In* (Boston: Houghton Mifflin, 1981).

Fitzgibbons, R. P., "The Cognitive and Emotional Uses of Forgiveness in the Treatment of Anger," *Psychotherapy* 23 (1986), 629–633.

Fitzpatrick, Mary Anne, "A Typological Approach to Communication in Relationships," in Dan Nimmo (Ed.), *Communication Yearbook* 1 (New Brunswick, NJ: Transaction Books, 1977).

Floyd, Sally, and Beth Emery, "Physically Aggressive Conflict in Romantic Relationships," in Dudley D. Cahn (Ed.), *Conflict in Personal Relationships* (Hillsdale, NJ: Lawrence Erlbaum Associates, 1994), pp. 27–46.

Foa, U. G., and E. G. Foa, *Societal Structures of the Mind* (Springfield, IL: Thomas, 1974).

Folger, Joseph P., "Interpretive and Structural Claims about Confrontations," in James A. Anderson (Ed.), *Communication Yearbook* 14 (Newbury Park: Sage, 1991), pp. 393–402.

Folger, Joseph P., Marshall Scott Poole, and Randall K. Stutman, *Working Through Conflict,* 2nd Ed. (New York: HarperCollins, 1993).

Folger, Joseph P., and J. J. Shubert, *Resolving Student-Initiated Grievances in Higher Education: Dispute Resolution Procedures in a Non-Adversarial Setting* (Report No. 3). (Washington, D.C.: National Institute for Dispute Resolution, 1986).

Fow, Neil Robert, "An Empirical-Phenomenological Investigation of the Experience of Forgiving Another," Doctoral dissertation, University of Pittsburgh, 1988.

Fraser, B., "On Apologizing," in F. Coulmas (Ed.), *Conversational Routines: Explorations in Standardized Communication Situations and Prepatterned Speech* (The Hague: Mouton, 1981).

Freeman, Sally A., Stephen W. Littlejohn, and Barnett W. Pearce, "Communication and Moral Conflict," *Western Journal of Communication* 56 (1992), 311–329.

French, John R. P., and Bertram Raven, "The Basis of Social Power," in Dorwin Cartwright and A. Sander (Eds.), *Group Dynamics,* 2nd Ed. (New York: Harper and Row, 1960).

Frey, Lawrence R., Carl H. Botan, Paul G. Friedman, and Gary L. Kreps, *Investigating Communication: An Introduction to Research Methods* (Englewood Cliffs, NJ: Prentice Hall, 1991).

Fritz, Janie M. Harden, "Responses to Unpleasant Work Relationships," *Communication Research Reports* 14 (1997), 302–311.

Galvin, Kathleen M., "Communication and Well-Functioning Families," paper presented at the annual meeting of the Western Speech Communication Association Convention, Fresno, February 1985.

Galvin, Kathleen M., and Bernard J. Brommel, *Family Communication: Cohesion and Change,* 2nd Ed. (Glenview, IL: Scott Foresman, 1986).

Gamson, William A., "A Theory of Coalition Formation," in Claggett C. Smith (Ed.), *Conflict Resolution: Contributions of the Behavioral Sciences* (Notre Dame, IN: University of Notre Dame Press, 1971).

Gassin, Elizabeth, "Receiving Forgiveness as Moral Education: A Theoretical Analysis and Initial Empirical Investigation," *Journal of Moral Education* 27 (1998), 71–88.

Gayle, Barbara Mae, "Sex Equity in Workplace Conflict Management," *Journal of Applied Communication Research* 19 (1991), 152–169.

Gelles, R. J., "Violence in the Family: A Review of Research in the Seventies," *Journal of Marriage and the Family* 42 (1980), 143–155.

Georing, Elizabeth M., "Context, Definition, and Sex of Actor as Variables in Conflict Management Style," paper presented at the annual meeting of the Speech Communication Association Convention, Chicago, November 1986.

Gibb, Jack, "Defensive Communication," *Journal of Communication* (September 1961), 141–168.

Girdner, L. K., "Adjudication and Mediation: A Comparison of Custody Decision-Making Processes Involving Third Parties," *Journal of Divorce* 8 (1985), 33–47.

Goffman, Erving, "Embarrassment and Social Organizations," *American Journal of Sociology* 26 (1956), 270–271.

Goffman, Erving, *The Presentation of Self in Everyday Life* (Garden City, NY: Doubleday, 1959).

Goffman, Erving, *Interaction Ritual: Essays on Face-to-Face Behavior* (New York: Pantheon Books, 1967).

Gottman, John M., *Marital Interaction: Experimental Investigations* (New York: Academic, 1979).

Gottman, John M., "Emotional Responsiveness in Marital Conversations," *Journal of Communication* 32 (1982), 108–133.

Gottman, John M., "Temporal Form: Toward a New Language for Describing Relationships," *Journal of Marriage and the Family* 44 (1982), 943–962.

Gottman, John M., and R. Krokoff, *Marital Interaction: A Longitudinal View* (Unpublished manuscript University of Washington, Seattle, WA, 1989).

Gottman, John M., H. Markman, and C. Notarius, "The Topography of Marital Conflict: A Sequential Analysis of Verbal and Nonverbal Behavior," *Journal of Marriage and the Family* 39 (1977), 461–477.

Griffin, Em, "Accountability and Forgiveness: Saying the Tough Words in Love," paper presented at the annual meeting of the Speech Communication Association Convention, Denver, November 1985.

Gudykunst, William B., and Young Yun Kim, *Communicating with Strangers: An Approach to Intercultural Communication* (New York: McGraw Hill, 1997).

Guerrero, Laura K., and Walid A. Afifi, "Some Things Are Better Left Unsaid: Topic Avoidance in Family Relationships," *Communication Quarterly* 43 (1995), 276–296.

Guetzkow, H., and J. Gyr, "An Analysis of Conflict in Decision-Making Groups," *Human Relations* 7 (1954), 367–381.

Haight, Larry, and Charles Pavitt, "Implicit Theories of Communication Competence 1: Traits, Behaviors, and Situation Differences," paper presented at the annual meeting of the Speech Communication Association Convention, Louisville, November 1982.

Hall, Bradford "J.," "An Elaboration of the Structural Possibilities for Engaging in Alignment Episodes," *Communication Monographs* 68 (1991), 79–100.

Hall, C. S., *A Primer of Freudian Psychology,* 2nd Ed. (New York: World, 1979).

Hample, Dale, "Predicting Immediate Belief Change and Adherence to Argument Claims," *Communication Monographs* 45 (1978), 219–228.

Hample, Dale, "Purposes and Effects of Lying," *Southern Speech Communication Journal* 46 (1980), 33–47.

Hample, Dale, and Judith M. Dallinger, "A Lewinian Perspective on Taking Conflict Personally: Revision, Refinement, and Validation of the Instrument," *Communication Quarterly* 43 (1995), 297–319.

Harper, N. L., and Randy Y. Hirokawa, "A Comparison of Persuasive Strategies Used by Female and Male Managers," *Communication Quarterly* 36 (1988), 157–168.

Harris, Thomas A., *I'm Okay, You're Okay* (New York: Avon Books, 1967).

Hart, Roderick P., and Don M. Burks, "Rhetorical Sensitivity and Social Interaction," *Speech Monographs* 39 (1972), 75–91.

Hart, Roderick P., Robert E. Carlson, and William F. Eadie, "Attitudes Toward Communication and the Assessment of Rhetorical Sensitivity," *Communication Monographs* 47 (1980), 1–22.

Harvey, J. H., A. L. Weber, K. L. Yarkin, and B. E. Stewart, "An Attributional Approach to Relationship

Breakdown and Resolution," in Steven Duck (Ed.), *Personal Relationships 4: Dissolving Personal Relationships* (New York: Academic Press, 1982).

Harvey, Thomas R., and Bonita Drolet, *Building Teams, Building People: Expanding the Fifth Resource* (La Verne, CA: Department of Educational Management, University of La Verne, 1992).

Hastings, James, (Ed.), *Encyclopoedia of Religion and Ethics* (Edinburgh: T. & T. Clark, 1974).

Hayakawa, S. I., *Language in Thought and Action,* 4th Ed. (New York: Harcourt, Brace, Jovanovich, 1978).

Healey, J. G., and R. A. Bell, "Assessing Alternate Responses to Conflicts in Friendship," in Dudley D. Cahn (Ed.), *Intimates in Conflict: A Communication Perspective* (Hillsdale, NJ: Erlbaum, 1990), pp. 25–48.

Hebl, John H., "Forgiveness as a Counseling Goal with Elderly Females," Doctoral dissertation, University of Wisconsin, 1990.

Heller, Scott, "Emerging Field of Forgiveness Studies Explores How We Let Go of Grudges," *Chronicle of Higher Education,* July 17, 1998, p. A-19.

Hess, Herbert J., and Charles O. Tucker, *Talking About Relationships,* 2nd Ed. (Prospect Heights, IL: Waveland Press, 1980).

Hewitt, J., and R. Stokes, "Disclaimers," *American Sociological Review* 40 (1975), 1–11.

Higgins, Gina O'Connell, *Resilient Adults: Overcoming a Cruel Past* (San Francisco: Jossey Bass, 1994).

Hilyard, Delmar M., "Research Models and Designs for the Study of Conflict," in Fred E. Jandt (Ed.), *Conflict Resolution Through Communication* (New York: Harper & Row, 1972).

Hocker, Joyce, and William Wilmot, *Interpersonal Conflict,* 4th Ed. (Dubuque, IA: Wm. C. Brown, 1995).

Holmes, John, "The Exchange Process in Close Relationships: Microbehavior and Macromotives," in M. J. Lerner and S. C. Lerner (Eds.), *The Justice Motive in Social Behavior* (New York: Plenum, 1981).

Holmes, John G., and John K. Rempel, "Trust in Close Relationships," in Clyde Hendrick (Ed.), *Close Relationships* (Newbury Park, CA: Sage, 1989), pp. 187–220.

Homans, G. C., *Social Behavior: Its Elementary Forms* (New York: Harcourt Brace Jovanovich, 1961).

Honeycutt, James M., B. L. Woods, and K. Fontenot, "The Endorsement of Communication Conflict Rules as a Function of Engagement, Marriage and Marital Ideology," *Journal of Social and Personal Relationships* 10 (1993), 285–304.

Honeycutt, James M., Kenneth S. Zagacki, and Renee Edwards, "Imagined Interaction and Interpersonal Communication," *Communication Reports* 3 (1990), 1–8.

Hope, Donald, "The Healing Paradox of Forgiveness," *Psychotherapy* 24 (1987), 240–244.

Howell, William S., *The Empathic Communicator* (Belmont, CA: Wadsworth Publishing, 1982).

Hughey, Jim D., "Interpersonal Sensitivity, Communication Encounters, Communication Responsiveness, and Gender," paper presented at the annual meeting of the Speech Communication Association Convention, Washington, DC, November 1983.

Hunter, R. C. A., "Forgiveness, Retaliation, and Paranoid Reactions," *Canadian Psychiatric Association Journal* 23 (1978), 171.

Infante, Dominic A., Teresa A. Chandler, and Jill E. Rudd, "Test of an Argumentative Skill Deficiency Model of Interspousal Violence," *Communication Monographs* 5 (1989), 163–177.

Infante, Dominic A., Bruce L. Riddle, Carl L. Horvath, and S. A. Tumlin, "Verbal Aggressiveness: Messages and Reasons," *Communication Quarterly* 40 (1992), 116–126.

Infante, Dominic A., Teresa Chandler Sabourin, Jill E. Rudd, and Elizabeth A. Shannon, "Verbal Aggression in Violent and Nonviolent Marital Disputes," *Communication Quarterly* 38 (1990), 361–371.

Infante, Dominic A., J. D. Trebing, P. E. Shepherd, and D. E. Seeds, "The Relationship of Argumentativeness to Verbal Aggression," *Southern Speech Communication Journal* 50 (1984), 67–77.

Infante, Dominic A., and C. J. Wigley, "Verbal Aggressiveness: An Interpersonal Model and Measure," *Communication Monographs* 53 (1986), 61–69.

Isard, Walter, and Christine Smith, *Conflict Analysis and Practical Conflict Management* (Cambridge, MA: Ballinger Publishing, 1982).

Ivy, Diana K., and Phil Backlund, *Exploring Gender-Speak: Personal Effectiveness in Gender Communication* (New York: McGraw Hill, 1994).

Jacobs, Scott, Sally Jackson, J. Hallmark, B. Hall, and S. A. Stearns. "Ideal Argument in the Real World: Making Do in Mediation," in J. W. Wenzel (Ed.), *Argument and Critical Practices* (Annandale, VA: SCA, 1987).

Jain, Nemi C., "World View and Cultural Patterns of India," in Larry A. Samovar and Richard E. Porter (Eds.), *Intercultural Communication: A Reader,* 6th Ed. (Belmont, CA: Wadsworth, 1991).

Jakubowski, P., and A. Lange, *The Assertive Option: Your Rights and Responsibilities* (Champaign, IL: Research Press, 1978).

Jandt, Fred E., with Paul Gillette, *Win-Win Negotiating: Turning Conflict into Agreement* (New York: John Wiley & Sons, 1985).

Jellison, Jerald M., "Accounting: Societal Implications," in Michael J. Cody and Margaret L. McLaughlin (Eds.), *The Psychology of Tactical Communication* (Clevedon, Avon, England: Multilingual Matters, Ltd., 1990), pp. 283–298.

Jones, R., and B. Melcher, "Personality and the Preference for Modes of Conflict Resolution," *Human Relations* 35 (1982), 649–658.

Jones, T., and H. Brinkman, "Teach Your Children Well: Suggestions for Peer Mediation Programs in the Schools," in J. Folger and T. Jones (Eds.), *Third Parties and Conflict: Communication Research and Perspectives* (Beverly Hills, CA: Sage, forthcoming).

Kabanoff, B. "Predictive Validity of the MODE Conflict Instrument," *Journal of Applied Psychology* 72 (1987), 160–163.

Kahn, Lynn Sandra, *Peacemaking: A Systems Approach to Conflict Management* (Lanham, MD: University Press of America, 1988).

Kaslow, F. W., "Divorce Mediation and Its Emotional Impact on the Couple and Their Children," *American Journal of Family Therapy* 12 (1984), 58–66.

Kauhnan, Gershen, *Shame: The Power of Caring* (Cambridge, MA: Shenkinan Publishing, 1980).

Kelly, C., T. L. Huston, and R. M. Cate, "Premarital Relationship Correlates of the Erosion of Satisfaction in Marriage," *Journal of Personal and Social Relationships* 2 (1985), 167–178.

Kelley, Harold H., and John W. Thibault, *Interpersonal Relations: A Theory of Interdependence* (New York: John Wiley & Sons, 1978).

Kelman, Herbert C., "Compliance, Identification and Internalization: Three Processes of Attitude Change," *Journal of Conflict Resolution* 2 (1958), 51–60.

Kepner, James E., *Healing Tasks: Psychotherapy with Adult Survivors of Childhood Abuse* (San Francisco: Jossey Bass, 1995).

Kilmann, Ralph H., and Kenneth W. Thomas, "Developing a Forced-Choice Measure of Conflict-Handling Behavior: The Mode Instrument." *Educational and Psychological Measurement* 37 (1977), 309–325.

Kimmel, M. J., Dean G. Pruitt, J. M. Magenau, E. Konar Goldband, and P. J. D. Carnevale, "Effects of Trust, Aspiration and Gender on Negotiation Tactics," *Journal of Personality and Social Psychology* 38 (1980), 9–22.

King, Andrew, *Power and Communication* (Prospect Heights, IL: Waveland Press, 1987).

Klimoski, R. J., "The Effects of Intragroup Forces on Intergroup Conflict Resolution," *Organizational Behavior and Human Performance* 8 (1972), 363–383.

Klopf, Donald W., and Myung-Seok Park, *Korean Communicative Behavior* (Seoul, Korea: The Communication Association of Korea, 1994).

Knapp, Mark L., *Interpersonal Communication and Human Relationships* (Boston: Allyn and Bacon, 1984).

Knapp, Mark L., and Mark E. Comadena, "Telling It Like It Isn't: A Review of Theory and Research on Deceptive Communications," *Human Communication Research 5* (1979), 270–285.

Knapp, Mark L., Laura Stafford, and John A. Daly, "Regrettable Messages: Things People Wish They Hadn't Said," *Journal of Communication* 36 (1987), 40–59.

Kohlberg, Lawrence, "Moral Stages and Moralization: The Cognitive Development Approach," in T. Licrona (Ed.), *Moral Development and Behavior: Theory, Research and Social Issues* (New York: Holt Rinehart, 1976), pp. 31–53.

Kohut, Heinz, "Narcissism and Narcissistic Rage," *The Psychoanalytic Study of the Child* 27 (1972), 379–392.

Komorita, S. S., and A. R. Brenner, "Bargaining and Concession Making under Bilateral Monopoly," *Journal of Personality and Social Psychology* 9 (1968), 15–20.

Koren, P., K. Carlton, and D. Shaw, "Marital Conflict: Relations Among Behaviors, Outcomes, and Distress," *Journal of Consulting and Clinical Psychology* 48 (1980), 460–468.

Kriegsberg, Louis, *The Sociology of Social Conflicts* (Englewood Cliffs, NJ: Prentice Hall, 1973).

LaHaye, Tim, and Bob Phillips, *Anger Is a Choice* (Grand Rapids: Zondervan, 1982).

Lambert, W. G., *Babylonian Wisdom Literature* (London: Oxford University Press, 1960).

Lane, Shelley D., "Empathy and Assertive Communication," paper presented at the annual meeting of the Western Speech Communication Association Convention, San Jose, February 1981.

Lansky, B., *Mother Murphy's Second Law: Love, Sex, Marriage and Other Disasters* (New York: Simon and Schuster, 1986).

Larzalere, R., and T. L. Huston, "The Dyadic Trust Scale: Toward Understanding Interpersonal Trust in Close Relationships," *Journal of Marriage and the Family* 42 (1980), 595–604.

Lasswell, Marcia, and Thomas Lasswell (Eds.), *Love, Marriage, Family: A Developmental Approach* (Glenview, IL: Scott Foresman, 1973).

Lax, David A., and James K. Sebenius, *The Manager as Negotiator* (New York: Free Press, 1986).

Lerner, Harriet Goldhor, *The Dance of Anger: A Woman's Guide to Changing the Patterns of Intimate Relationships* (New York: Harper and Row, 1985).

Leung, Kowk, "Some Determinants of Conflict Avoidance," *Journal of Cross Cultural Psychology* 19 (1988), 125–136.

Levi, A. M., and A. Benjamin, "Focus and Flexibility in a Model of Conflict Resolution," *Journal of Conflict Resolution* 21 (1977), 405–425.

Levine, Timothy R., and Steven A. McComack, "The Dark Side of Trust: Conceptualizing and Measuring

Communicative Suspicion," *Communication Quarterly* 39 (1991), 325–340.

Lewicki, R. J., "Lying and Deception: A Behavioral Model," in Max Bazerman and R. J. Lewicki (Eds.), *Negotiation in Organizations* (Newbury Park, CA: Sage, 1983).

Liaboe, Gary P., "The Place of Wife Battering in Considering Divorce," *Journal of Psychology and Theology* 13 (1985), 129–138.

Likerman, Meira, "The Function of Anger in Human Conflict," *International Review of Psychoanalysis* 14 (1987), 152.

Linn, Matthew, and Dennis Linn, *Healing Life's Hurts: Healing Memories Through Five Stages of Forgiveness* (New York: Paulist Press, 1978).

Lippard, Paula V., "'Ask Me No Questions, I'll Tell You No Lies: Situational Exigencies for Interpersonal Deception," *Western Journal of Speech Communication* 52 (1988), 91–103.

Louis, Meryl Reis, "How Individuals Conceptualize Conflict: Identification of Steps in the Process and the Role of Personal/Development Factors," *Human Relations* 30 (1977), 451–467.

Lulofs, Roxane Salyer, "The Social Construction of Forgiveness," *Human Systems* 2 (1992), 183–198.

Lulofs, Roxane S., "Teaching Forgiveness: A Social Construction Approach," paper presented at the annual meeting of the Central States Speech Communication Association, Oklahoma City, April 1994.

Lulofs, Roxane S., "Swimming Upstream: Creating Reasons for Unforgiveness in a Culture That Expects Otherwise," paper presented at the annual meeting of the Speech Communication Association Convention, San Antonio, November 1995.

Mack, Raymond W., and Richard C. Snyder, "The Analysis of Social Conflict: Toward an Overview and Synthesis," in Fred E. Jandt (Ed.), *Conflict Resolution through Communication* (New York: Harper and Row, 1973), pp. 25–87.

Mack, Raymond W., and Richard C. Snyder, "Cooperators and Competitors in Conflict: A Test of the 'Triangle' Model," *Journal of Conflict Resolution* 22 (1978), 393–410.

Margolin, L. "Beyond Maternal Blame: Physical Child Abuse as a Phenomenon of Gender," *Journal of Family Issues* 13 (1992), 410–423.

Marshall, Linda L., "Physical and Psychological Abuse," in William R. Cupach and Brian H. Spitzberg (Eds.), *The Dark Side of Interpersonal Communication* (Hillsdale, NJ: Erlbaum, 1994), pp. 281–311.

Marwell, Gerald, David Schmitt, and B. Boyesen, "Pacifist Strategy and Cooperation Under Interpersonal Risk," *Journal of Personality and Social Psychology* 28 (1973), 12–20.

McComack, Steven A., and Timothy R. Levine, "When Lies Are Uncovered: Emotion and Relational Outcomes of Discovered Deception," *Communication Monographs* 5 (1990), 219–230.

McComack, Steven A., and Timothy R. Levine, "When Lovers Become Leery: The Relationship Between Suspicion and Accuracy in Detecting Deception" *Communication Monographs* 57 (1990), 219–230.

McComack, Steven A., and Malcolm R. Parks, "Deception Detection and Relationship Development: The Other Side of Trust," in Margaret L. McLaughlin (Ed.), *Communication Yearbook* 9 (Beverly Hills: Sage Publications, 1986), pp. 377–389.

McCorkle, Suzanne, and Janet L. Mills, "Rowboat in a Hurricane: Metaphors of Interpersonal Conflict Management," *Communication Reports* 5 (1992), 57–66.

McCroskey, James C., "Oral Communication Apprehension: A Summary of Recent Theory and Research," *Human Communication Research* 4 (1977), 78–96.

McCullough, Michael E., and Kenneth C. Rachal, "Interpersonal Forgiving in Close Relationships," *Journal of Personality and Social Psychology* 73 (1997), 321–336.

McCullough, Michael E., Steven J. Sandage, and Everett L. Worthington, Jr., *To Forgive Is Human* (Downer's Grove, IL: InterVarsity Press, 1997).

McDermott, Steven T., "Naturalistic Observations of Parental Attempts at Gaining Compliance," paper presented at the annual meeting of the Speech Communication Association Convention, Chicago, November 1986.

McGoldrick, M., and E. A. Carter, "The Family Life Cycle," in F. Walsh (Ed.), *Normal Family Processes* (New York: Guildford Press, 1982), pp. 167–195.

McGraw, K. M., "Guilt Following Transgression: An Attribution of Responsibility Approach," *Journal of Personality and Social Psychology* 53 (1987), 247–256.

McKinney, B. C., W. D. Kimsey, and R. M. Fuller, *Dispute Resolution Through Communication,* 2nd Ed. (Dubuque, IA: Kendall Hunt, 1990).

McKinnon, W., C. S. Wiesse, C. P. Reynolds, C. A. Bowles, and A. Baum, "Chronic Stress, Leukocyte Subpopulations, and Humoral Response to Latent Viruses," *Health Psychology* 8 (1989), 389–402.

McLaughlin, Margaret L., Michael J. Cody, and Kathryn French, "Account-Giving and the Attribution of Responsibility: Impressions of Traffic Offenders," in Michael J. Cody and Margaret L. McLaughlin (Eds.), *The Psychology of Tactical Communication* (Clevedon, Avon, England: Multilingual Matters, Ltd., 1990), pp. 244–261.

McLaughlin, Margaret L., Michael J. Cody, and Dan O'Hair, "The Management of Failure Events: Some

Contextual Determinants of Accounting Behavior," *Human Communication Research* 9 (1983), 208–224.

McLaughlin, Margaret L., Michael J. Cody, and Stephen J. Read, *Explaining Oneself to Others: Reason-Giving in a Social Context* (Hillsdale, NJ: Lawrence Erlbaum Associates, 1992).

McLaughlin, Margaret L., Michael J. Cody, and Nancy E. Rosenstein, "Account Sequences in Conversations between Strangers," *Communication Monographs* 50 (1983), 102–124.

Mead, D. E., G. M. Vatcher, B. A. Wyne, and S. L. Roberts, "The Comprehensive Areas of Change Questionnaire: Assessing Marital Couples' Presenting Complaints," *American Journal of Family Therapy* 18 (1990), 65–79.

Metts, Sandra, "Relational Transgressions," in William R. Cupach and Brian H. Spitzberg, *The Dark Side of Interpersonal Communication* (Hillsdale, NJ: Lawrence Erlbaum, 1994).

Metts, Sandra, and William R. Cupach, "Situational Influence on the Use of Remedial Strategies in Embarrassing Predicaments," *Communication Monographs* 56 (1989), 151–162.

Metts, Sandra, and William R. Cupach, "The Influence of Relationship Beliefs and Problem-Solving Responses on Satisfaction in Romantic Relationships," *Human Communication Research* 17 (1990), 170–185.

Milhaven, Giles, *Good Anger* (Kansas City: Sheed and Ward, 1989).

Minirth, F., D. Hawkins, P. Meier, and R. Flournoy, *How to Beat Burnout* (Chicago: Moody, 1986).

Mongeau, Paul A., M. A. Clason, and Jerold L. Hale, "Attributions of Responsibility, Guilt, and Blame Following a Relational Transgression," paper presented at the annual meeting of the International Communication Association Convention, San Francisco, May 1989.

Mongeau, Paul A., and Jerold L. Hale, "Attributions of Responsibility for Relational Transgressions," paper presented at the annual meeting of the Western Speech Communication Association Convention, Sacramento, February 1990.

Mongeau, Paul A., and Jerold L. Hale, "The Influence of Intent and Revenge on Attributions and Communication Following a Relational Transgression," paper presented at the annual meeting of the Communication Association, Chicago, November 1990.

Mongeau, Paul A., Jerold L. Hale, and P. E. Griffin, "The Impact of Intentionality and Alcohol Consumption on Attributions Following a Sexual Transgression," paper presented at the annual meeting of the Central States Communication Association Convention, Detroit, April 1990.

Morrill, Calvin, and Cheryl King Thomas, "Organizational Conflict Management as a Disputing Process: The Problem of Social Escalation," *Human Communication Research* 18 (1992), 400–429.

Morris, G. H., "Alignment Talk and Social Confrontation," in James A. Anderson (Ed.), *Communication Yearbook* 14 (Newbury Park: Sage, 1991), pp. 403–413.

Murray, Marry, "When You've Done Wrong," *Reader's Digest* (March 1992), 149–154.

Nadeua, Robert L., *S/he Brain* (Westport, CT: Praeger, 1996).

Nemeth, Charlan, "A Critical Analysis of Research Utilizing the Prisoner's Dilemma Paradigm for the Study of Bargaining," in Leonard Berkowitz (Ed.), *Advances in Experimental Social Psychology,* Vol. 6 (New York: Academic Press, 1982).

Newell, Sara E., and Randall K. Stutman, "A Qualitative Approach to Social Confrontation: Identifying Constraints and Facilitators," paper presented at the annual meeting of the Speech Communication Association Convention, Louisville, November 1982.

Newell, Sara E., and Randall K. Stutman, "The Social Confrontation Episode," *Communication Monographs* 55 (1988), 266–285.

Newell, Sara E., and Randall K. Stutman, "Negotiating Confrontation: The Problematic Nature of Initiation and Response," *Research on Language and Social Interaction* 23 (1989/1990), 139–162.

Newell, Sara E., and Randall K. Stutman, "The Episodic Nature of Social Confrontation," in James A. Anderson (Ed.), *Communication Yearbook* 14 (Newbury Park: Sage, 1991), pp. 359–392.

Newton, Deborah A., and Judee K. Burgoon, "Nonverbal Conflict Behaviors: Functions, Strategies, and Tactics," in Dudley D. Cahn (Ed.), *Intimates in Conflict: A Communication Perspective* (Hillsdale, NJ: Erlbaum, 1990).

Nicotera, A., (Ed.), *Conflict and Organizations: Communicative Processes* (Albany, NY: SUNY 1995).

Nierenberg, Gerald I., *The Complete Negotiator* (New York: Nierenberg & Zeif Publishers, 1986).

North, R. C., R. A. Brody, and O. R. Holsti, "Some Empirical Data on the Conflict Spiral," *Peace Research Society (International) Papers 1* (1964), 1–14.

Norton, Robert W., "Foundations of a Communicator Style Construct," *Human Communication Research* 4 (1978), 99–112.

Norton, Robert W., and Barbara Warnick, "Assertiveness as a Communication Construct," *Human Communication Research* 3 (1976), 62–66.

Nowak, Mary Helen, "Conflict Resolution and Power Seeking Behavior of Androgynous and Traditional Married Couples (Sex Roles)," Doctoral dissertation, Michigan State University, 1984.

Nye, R. D., *Conflict among Humans* (New York: Spring Publishing, 1973).

O'Hair, Dan, and Michael J. Cody, "Deception: The Darkside of Interpersonal Communication?" paper presented at the annual meeting of the Western Speech Communication Association, Phoenix, February 1991.

O'Keefe, Barbara J., and G. J. Shepherd, "The Communication of Identity During Face-to-Face Persuasive Interactions: Effects of Perceiver's Construct Differentiation and Target's Message Strategies," *Communication Research* 16 (1989), 375–404.

Olson, David H., and Hamilton McCubbin, *Families: What Makes Them Work?* (Beverly Hills: Sage, 1983).

Osgood, Charles E., *An Alternative to War or Surrender* (Urbana: University of Illinois Press, 1962).

Osgood, Charles E., *Perspective in Foreign Policy,* 2nd Ed. (Palo Alto, CA: Pacific Books, 1966).

Palmer, David L., "The Communication of Forgiveness," paper presented at the annual meeting of the Speech Communication Association, New Orleans, November 1994.

Papa, Michael J., and Elizabeth J. Natelle, "Gender, Strategy Selection and Discussion: Satisfaction in Interpersonal Conflict," *Western Journal of Speech Communication* 53 (1989), 260–272.

Parsons, Talcott, "On the Concept of Influence," *Public Opinion Quarterly* 27 (1963), 37–62.

Patton, John, *Is Human Forgiveness Possible?* (Nashville: Abington Press, 1985).

Pearce, W. Barnett, "Keynote Address: Communication Theory," Institute for Faculty Development: Communication Theory and Research, Hope College, Holland, MI, July 1992.

Pearce, W. Barnett, *Interpersonal Communication: Making Social Worlds* (New York: HarperCollins College Publishers, 1994).

Pearce, W. Barnett, Vernon Cronen, and F. Conklin, "A Hierarchical Model of Interpersonal Communication," paper presented at the annual meeting of the International Communication Association, Berlin, 1977.

Pearson, Judy C., *Interpersonal Communication: Clarity, Confidence, Concern* (Glenview, IL: Scott Foresman, 1983).

Pearson, Judy C., *Communication in the Family: Seeking Satisfaction in Changing Times* (New York: Harper & Row, 1989).

Pearson, Judy C., and Tom D. Daniels, "Oh, What Tangled Webs We Weave: Concerns About Current Conceptualizations of Communication Competence," *Communication Reports* 1 (1988), 95–100.

Pearson, Judy C., N. Thonnes, and L. Vanderkooi, "The Decision to Mediate Profiles—Individuals Who Accept and Reject the Opportunity to Mediate Contested Child Custody and Visitation Issues," *Journal of Divorce* (Winter 1982), 17–35.

Peterson, Candida C., and James L. Peterson, "Fight or Flight—Factors Influencing Children's and Adult's Decisions to Avoid or Confront Conflict," *Journal of Genetic Psychology* 151 (1990), 451–471.

Petronio, Sandra, "The Use of a Communication Boundary Perspective to Contextualize Embarrassment Research," in James A. Anderson (Ed.), *Communication Yearbook* 13 (Newbury Park, CA: Sage, 1990), pp. 365–373.

Pike, G. R., and Alan L. Sillars, "Reciprocity of Marital Communication," *Journal of Social and Personal Relationships* 2 (1985), 303–324.

Pilisuk, M., and P. Skolnick, "Inducing Trust: A Test of the Osgood Proposal," *Journal of Experimental Social Psychology* 11 (1968), 53–63.

Pingleton, Jared P., "The Role and Function of Forgiveness in the Psychotherapeutic Process," *Journal of Psychology and Theology* 17 (1989), 27–35.

Planalp, Sally, and James M. Honeycutt, "Events That Increase Uncertainty in Personal Relationships," *Human Communication Research* 11 (1985), 593–604.

Planalp, Sally, Diane K. Rutherford, and James M. Honeycutt, "Events That Increase Uncertainty in Personal Relationships II," *Human Communication Research* 14 (1988), 516–547.

Porter, Richard E., and Larry A. Samovar, "Basic Principles of Intercultural Communication," in Larry A. Samovar and Richard E. Porter (Eds.), *Intercultural Communication: A Reader,* 6th Ed. (Belmont, CA: Wadsworth, 1991).

Poundstone, William, *Prisoner's Dilemma* (New York: Doubleday, 1992).

Pruitt, Dean G., *Negotiation Behavior* (New York: Academic Press, 1981).

Pruitt, Dean G., and Melvin J. Kimmel, "Twenty Years of Experimental Gaming: Critique, Synthesis and Suggestions for the Future," *Annual Review of Psychology* 28 (1977), 363–392.

Pruitt, Dean G., and S. A. Lewis, "Development of Integrative Solutions in Bilateral Negotiation," *Journal of Personality and Social Psychology* 31 (1975), 621–633.

Pruitt, Dean G., and Jeffrey Z. Rubin, *Social Conflict: Escalation, Stalemate, and Settlement* (New York: Random House, 1986).

Putnam, Linda L., "Bargaining as Organizational Communication," in Robert D. McPhee and Phillip K. Tompkins (Eds.), *Organizational Communication: Traditional Themes and New Directions* (Newbury Park: Sage, 1985).

Putnam, Linda L., and Joseph P. Folger, "Communication, Conflict, and Dispute Resolution: The Study of

Interaction and the Development of Conflict Theory," *Communication Research* 15 (1988), 349–359.

Putnam, Linda L., and Trisha S. Jones, "The Role of Communication in Bargaining," *Human Communication Research* 8 (1992), 262–280.

Putnam, Linda L., and M. Scott Poole, "Conflict and Negotiation," in Fred M. Jablin, Linda L. Putnam, Karlene H. Roberts, and Lyman W. Porter (Eds.), *Handbook of Organizational Communication: An Interdisciplinary Approach* (Newbury Park, CA: Sage, 1987), pp. 549–599.

Rahim, M. A., "A Measure of Styles of Handling Interpersonal Conflict," *Academy of Management Journal* 26 (1983), 368–376.

Rausch, H., W. Barry, R. Hertel, and M. Swain, *Communication, Conflict, and Marriage* (San Francisco: Jossey-Bass, 1974).

Reardon, Kathleen Kelly, *Interpersonal Communication: Where Minds Meet* (Belmont, CA: Wadsworth, 1987).

Reinard, John C., *Foundations of Argument: Effective Communication for Critical Thinking* (Dubuque: William C. Brown, 1991).

Remer, Rory, and Paul de Mesquita, "Teaching and Learning the Skills of Interpersonal Confrontation," in D. Cahn (Ed.), *Intimates in Conflict: A Communication Perspective* (Hillsdale, NJ: Lawrence Erlbaum Associates, 1990), pp. 225–252.

Rempel, John K., "Trust and Attributions in Close Relationships," unpublished doctoral dissertation, University of Waterloo, Ontario, 1987.

Rempel, John K., John G. Holmes, and M. P. Zanna, "Trust in Close Relationships," *Journal of Personality and Social Psychology* 49 (1985), 95–112.

Rettig, K. D., and M. M. Bubolz, "Interpersonal Resource Exchanges as Indicators of Quality of Marriage," *Journal of Marriage and the Family* 45 (1983), 497–509.

Rieke, Richard D., and Malcolm O. Sillars, *Argumentation and Critical Decision-Making,* 3rd Ed. (New York: HarperCollins, 1993).

Roberts, Marc, *Managing Conflict from the Inside Out* (San Diego: Learning Concepts, 1982).

Rogers, Carl R., *On Becoming a Person* (Cambridge, MA: The Riverside Press, 1961).

Rogers, Carl R., and Rosalind F. Dymond, *Psychotherapy and Personality Change* (Chicago: The University of Chicago Press, 1954).

Rokeach, Milton, *Beliefs, Attitudes, and Values* (San Francisco: Jossey-Bass, 1969).

Rollins, Boyd C., and Harold Feldman, "Marital Satisfaction over the Family Life Cycle: A Re-Evaluation," *Journal of Marriage and the Family* 32 (1970), 20–27.

Roloff, Michael E., "The Impact of Socialization on Sex Differences in Conflict Resolution," paper presented at the annual meeting of the International Communication Association Convention, Acapulco, Mexico, May 1980.

Roloff, Michael E., "The Catalyst Hypothesis: Conditions Under Which Coercive Communication Leads to Physical Aggression," in Dudley D. Cahn and Sally A. Lloyd, *Family Violence from a Communication Perspective* (Thousand Oaks, CA: Sage Publications, 1996), pp. 20–36.

Roloff, Michael E., and Douglas E. Campion, "On Alleviating the Debilitating Effects of Accountability on Bargaining: Authority and Self-Monitoring," *Communication Monographs* 54 (1987), 145–164.

Roloff, Michael E., and Denise H. Cloven, "The Chilling Effect in Interpersonal Relationships: The Reluctance to Speak One's Mind," in Dudley D. Cahn (Ed.), *Intimates in Conflict: A Communication Perspective* (Hillside, NJ: Lawrence Erlbaum Associates, 1990), 49–76.

Rosenberg, Shawn W., and Gary Wolsfeld, "International Conflict and the Problem of Attribution," *Journal of Conflict Resolution* 21 (1977), 75–103.

Rosenthal, R., and L. Jacobson, *Pygmalion in the Classroom* (New York: Holt, Rinehart & Winston, 1968).

Ruben, Brent, "Communication and Conflict: A Systems Perspective," *Quarterly Journal of Speech* 64 (1978), 202–210.

Rubin, Rebecca R., "Communication Competence," in Gerald M. Phillips and Julia T. Wood (Eds.), *Speech Communication: Essays to Commemorate the 75th Anniversary of the Speech Communication Association* (Carbondale, IL: SIU Press, 1990), pp. 94–129.

Rummel, R. J., *Understanding Conflict and War: The Conflict Helix,* Vol. 2 (Beverly Hills, CA: Sage Publications, 1976).

Rummel, R. J., "A Catastrophe Theory Model of the Conflict Helix, with Tests," *Behavioral Science* 32 (1987), 241–266.

Rusbult, C. E., D. J. Johnson, and G. D. Morrow, "Determinants and Consequences of Exit, Voice, Loyalty, and Neglect: Responses to Dissatisfaction in Adult Romantic Involvements," *Human Relations* 39 (1986), 45–63.

Rusbult, C. E., and I. M. Zembrodt, "Responses to Dissatisfaction in Romantic Involvements: A Multidimensional Scaling Analysis," *Journal of Experimental Social Psychology* 19 (1983), 274–293.

Sabourin, Teresa Chandler, "The Role of Communication in Verbal Abuse between Spouses," in Dudley D. Cahn and Sally A. Lloyd, *Family Violence from a Communication Perspective* (Thousand Oaks, CA: Sage Publications, 1996), pp. 199–217.

Saine, T. A., "Perceiving Communication Conflict," *Speech Monographs* 41 (1974), 49–56.

Salyer, Roxane, "Communication: A Resource, Not a Panacea," *Southern California Business,* August 13, 1980, p. 23.

Sarason, I., "Life Stress, Self-Preoccupation, and Social Supports," in I. G. Sarason and C. D. Speilberger (Eds.), *Stress and Anxiety,* Vol. 7 (Washington, DC: Hemisphere, 1980).

Satir, Virginia, *Peoplemaking* (Palo Alto, CA: Science and Behavior Books, 1972).

Schellenberg, James A., *The Science of Conflict* (New York: Oxford University Press, 1982).

Schelling, Thomas C., *The Strategy of Conflict* (Cambridge, MA: Harvard University Press, 1980).

Schlenker, Barry R., *Impression Management* (Monterey, CA: Brooks/Cole, 1980).

Schlenker, Barry R., and B. W. Darby, "The Use of Apologies in Social Predicaments," *Social Psychology Quarterly* 44 (1981), 271–278.

Schlenker, Barry R., B. Helm, and James T. Tedeschi, "The Effects of Personality and Situational Variables on Behavioral Trust," *Journal of Personality and Social Psychology* 32 (1973), 664–670.

Schmidt, Mellis I., "Forgiveness as the Focus Theme in Group Counseling," Doctoral dissertation, North Texas State University, 1986.

Schonbach, Peter, "A Category System for Account Phases," *European Journal of Social Psychology* 10 (1980), 195–200.

Schonbach, Peter, and Petra Kleibaumhuter, "Severity of Reproach and Defensiveness of Accounts," in Michael J. Cody and Margaret L. McLaughlin (Eds.), *The Psychology of Tactical Communication* (Clevedon, Avon, England: Multilingual Matters, Ltd., 1990), pp. 229–243.

Schwarz, Benjamin, "The Diversity Myth: American's Leading Export," in Gary R. Weaver (Ed.), *Culture, Communication and Conflict: Readings in Intercultural Relations,* 2nd Ed. (Needham Heights, MA: Simon and Schuster, 1998), pp. 473–481.

Scott, Lorel, and Robert Martin, "Value Similarity, Relationship Length, and Conflict Interaction in Dating Relationships: An Initial Investigation," paper presented at the annual meeting of the Speech Communication Association Convention, Chicago, November 1986.

Scott, Marvin B., and Stanford M. Lyman, "Accounts," in Gregory B. Stone and Harvey A. Farberman (Eds.), *Social Psychology through Symbolic Interaction* (Waltham, MA: Xerox Publishing, 1970), pp. 489–509.

Sears, J., E. Maccoby, and H. Levin, *Patterns of Childrearing* (Evanston, IL: Row Peterson, 1957).

Selye, H., *Stress without Distress* (New York: J. B. Lippincott, 1974).

Sereno, Kenneth K., and C. David Mortenson, "The Effects of Ego-Involved Attitudes on Conflict Negotiation in Dyads," in Fred E. Jandt (Ed.), *Conflict Resolution through Communication* (New York: Harper and Row, 1973), pp. 145–152.

Sharkey, William F., and Laura Stafford, "Responses to Embarrassment," *Human Communication Research* 17 (1990), 315–342.

Shepherd, Tara L., "Content and Relationship Dimensions of a Conflict Encounter: An Investigation of Their Impact on Perceived Rules," paper presented at the annual meeting of the Speech Communication Association Convention, Anaheim, November 1982.

Sherif, Mustafer, *In Common Predicament* (Boston: Houghton Mifflin, 1966).

Shichman, Shula, "Constructive and Destructive Resolution of Conflict in Marriage," Doctoral dissertation, Columbia University, 1982.

Shiminoff, Susan, *Communication Rules: Theory and Context* (Beverly Hills, CA: Sage Publications, 1980).

Shockley-Zalabak, Pamela S., and Donald D. Morley, "An Exploratory Study of Relationships Between Preferences for Conflict Styles and Communication Apprehension," *Journal of Language and Social Psychology* 3 (1984), 213–218.

Shotter, John, *Social Accountability and Selfhood* (Oxford, England: Basil Blackwell, 1984).

Sillars, Allan L., "Attributions and Communication in Roommate Conflicts," *Communication Monographs* 47 (1980), 180–200.

Sillars, Allan L., "The Sequential and Distributional Structure of Conflict Interactions as a Function of Attributions Concerning the Locus of Responsibility and Stability of Conflicts," in Dan Nimmo (Ed.), *Communication Yearbook* 4 (New Brunswick, NJ: Transaction Books, 1980), pp. 217–235.

Sillars, Allan L., Stephen F. Coletti, D. Parry, and Mark A. Rogers, "Coding Verbal Conflict Tactics: Nonverbal and Perceptual Correlates of the 'Avoidance-Distributive-Integrative' Distinction," *Human Communication Research* 9 (1982), 83–95.

Sillars, Allan L., Gary R. Pike, Tricia S. Jones, and Kathleen Redmon, "Communication and Conflict in Marriage," in Robert N. Bostrum (Ed.), *Communication Yearbook* 7 (Newbury Park, CA: Sage, 1983).

Sillars, Allan L., and Judith Weisberg, "Conflict as a Social Skill," in Michael E. Roloff and Gerald R. Miller (Eds.), *Interpersonal Processes: New Directions in Theory and Research* (Newbury Park, CA: Sage, 1987).

Simons, Herbert W., "Persuasion in Social Conflicts: A Critique of Prevailing Conceptions and a Framework for Future Research," *Speech Monographs* 39 (1972), 227–247.

Simons, Herbert W., "The Carrot and the Stick as Handmaidens of Persuasion in Conflict Situations," in

Gerald R. Miller and Herbert W. Simons (Eds.), *Perspectives on Communication in Social Conflict* (Englewood Cliffs, NJ: Prentice Hall, 1974), pp. 172–205.

Skow, Lisa, and Larry Samovar, "Cultural Patterns of the Maasai," in Larry A. Samovar and Richard E. Porter (Eds.), *Intercultural Communication: A Reader,* 6th Ed. (Belmont, CA: Wadsworth, 1991).

Smedes, Louis B., *Forgive and Forget: Healing the Hurts We Don't Deserve* (San Francisco: Harper & Row, 1984).

Snyder, C. R., and Raymond L. Higgins, "Reality Negotiation and Excuse-Making: President Reagan's 4 March 1987 Iran Arms Scandal Speech and Other Literature," in Michael J. Cody and Margaret L. McLaughlin (Eds.), *The Psychology of Tactical Communication* (Clevedon, Avon, England: Multilingual Matters, Ltd., 1990), pp. 207–228.

Snyder, Mark, "Self-Monitoring of Expressive Behavior," *Journal of Personality and Social Psychology* 30 (1974), 526–537.

Snyder, Mark, "Self-Monitoring Processes," in Leonard Berkowitz (Ed.), *Advances in Experimental Social Psychology,* Vol. 12 (New York: Academic Press, 1979), pp. 85–128.

Solomon, Muriel, *Working with Difficult People* (Englewood Cliffs, NJ: Prentice Hall, 1990).

Spector, Bertram, "Negotiation as a Psychological Process," *Journal of Conflict Resolution* 21 (1977), 607–618.

Speilberg, Charles, Susan S. Krasner, and Eldra P. Solomon, "The Experience, Expression, and Control of Anger," in M. P. Janisse (Ed.), *Health Psychology: Individual Differences and Stress* (New York: Springer-Verlag, 1988).

Spitzberg, Brian H., "Cans of Worms in the Study of Communicative Competence," paper presented at the annual meeting of the International Communication Association Convention, Honolulu, May 1985.

Spitzberg, Brian H., "The Dialectics of (In)Competence," paper presented at the annual meeting of the Western Speech Communication Association Convention, Phoenix, February 1991.

Spitzberg, Brian H., and Claire C. Brunner, "Toward a Theoretical Integration of Context and Competence Inference Research," *Western Journal of Speech Communication* 55 (1991), 28–46.

Spitzberg, Brian H., Daniel Canary, and William R. Cupach, "A Competence-Based Approach to the Study of Interpersonal Conflict," in Dudley D. Cahn (Ed.), *Conflict in Personal Relationships* (Hillsdale, NJ: Lawrence Erlbaum Associates, 1994), pp. 183–202.

Spitzberg, Brian H., and William R. Cupach, *Interpersonal Communication Competence* (Beverly Hills, CA: Sage, 1984).

Spitzberg, Brian H., and Michael L. Hecht, "A Component Model of Relational Competence," *Human Communication Research* 10 (1984), 575–599.

Stamp, Glen H., Anita L. Vengelisti, and John A. Daly, "The Creation of Defensiveness in Social Interaction," *Communication Quarterly* 40 (1992), 177–190.

Sternberg, R. J., and D. M. Dobson, "Resolving Interpersonal Conflicts: An Analysis of Stylistic Consistency," *Journal of Personality and Social Psychology* 52 (1987), 794–812.

Sternberg, R. J., and L. J. Soriano, "Styles of Conflict Resolution," *Journal of Personal and Social Psychology* 47 (1984), 115–126.

Stewart, John, *Bridges Not Walls: A Book About Interpersonal Communication* (New York: Random House, 1986).

Stiff, James B., James Price Dillard, Lilnabeth Somera, Hyun Kim, and Carra Sleight, "Empathy, Communication, and Prosocial Behavior," *Communication Monographs* 55 (1988), 199–213.

Stiff, James B., Hyun J. Kim, and C. N. Ramesh, "Truth-Biases and Aroused Suspicion in Relational Deception," paper presented at the annual meeting of the International Communication Association Convention, San Francisco, May 1989.

Strasser, Judith A., "The Relation of General Forgiveness and Forgiveness Type to Reported Health in the Elderly," Doctoral dissertation, Catholic University of America, 1984.

Strauss, M. A., "A General Systems Theory Approach to a Theory of Violence Between Family Members," *Social Science Information* 12 (1973), 103–123.

Strodtbeck, L., and R. Mann, "Sex-Role Differentiation in Jury Deliberation," *Sociometry* 19 (1956), 3–11.

Stutman, Randall K., and Sara E. Newell, "Rehearsing for Confrontation," *Argumentation* 4 (1990), 185–198.

Subkoviak, Michael J., Robert D. Enright, Ching-Ru Wu, Elizabeth A. Gassin, Suzanne Freedman, Leanne M. Olson, and Issidoros Sarinopolous, "Measuring Interpersonal Forgiveness," paper presented at the annual meeting of the American Educational Research Association Convention, San Francisco, April 1992.

Suzuki, Shinobu, and Andrew S. Rancer, "Argumentativeness and Verbal Aggressiveness: Testing for Conceptual and Measurement Equivalence Across Cultures," *Communication Monographs* 61 (1994), 256–279.

Swanson, D., and Jesse Delia, *The Nature of Human Communication* (Palo Alto, CA: SRA, 1976).

Swensen, C. H., R. W. Eskew, and K. A. Kohlhepp, "Five Factors in Long-Term Marriages," *Lifestyles* 7 (1984), 94–106.

Syna, Helena, "Couples in Conflict: Conflict Resolution Strategies, Perceptions About Sources of Conflict, and Relationship Adjustment," Doctoral dissertation, State University of New York at Buffalo, 1984.

Tavris, Carol, *Anger: The Misunderstood Emotion* (New York: Touchstone through Simon and Schuster, 1989).

Tavris, Carol, *The Mismeasure of Woman* (New York: Simon and Schuster, 1990).

Tedeschi, James T., *The Social Influence Processes* (Chicago: Aldine Publishing, 1972).

Tedeschi, James T., and Paul Rosenfeld, "Communication in Bargaining and Negotiation," in Michael R. Roloff and Gerald R. Miller (Eds.), *Persuasion: New Directions in Theory and Research* (Beverly Hills, CA: Sage, 1980).

Tedeschi, James T., Barry R. Schlenker, and T. V. Bonoma, *Conflict, Power & Games: The Experimental Study of Interpersonal Relations* (Chicago: Aldine Publishing, 1973).

Thibault, John W., and Harold H. Kelley, *The Social Psychology of Groups* (New York: John Wiley, 1959).

Thomas, Kenneth W., "Conflict and Conflict Management," in M. D. Dunnett (Ed.), *The Handbook of Industrial and Organizational Psychology* (Chicago: Rand McNally, 1976).

Thomas, Kenneth W., and Ralph H. Kilmann, *Conflict Mode Instrument* (Tuxedo, NY: XICOM, Inc., 1974).

Ting-Toomey, Stella, "An Analysis of Verbal Communication Patterns in High and Low Marital Adjustment Groups," *Human Communication Research* 9 (1983), 306–319.

Ting-Toomey, Stella, "Coding Conversation Between Intimates: A Validation Study of the Intimate Negotiation Coding System (INCS)," *Communication Quarterly* 31 (1983), 68–77.

Ting-Toomey, Stella, "Intercultural Conflict Competence," in William R. Cupach and Daniel J. Canary (Eds.), *Competence in Interpersonal Conflict* (New York: McGraw-Hill, 1997), pp. 122–139.

Tracy, Karen, "The Many Faces of Facework," in H. Giles and W. P. Robinson (Eds.), *Handbook of Language and Social Psychology* (New York: John Wiley & Sons, 1990), pp. 209–226.

Trainer, Mary F., "Forgiveness: Intrinsic, Role-Expected, Expedient, in the Context of Divorce," Doctoral dissertation, Boston University, 1984.

Trzyna, Thomas, "Forgiveness and Time," *Christian Scholar's Review* 22 (1992), 7, 8.

Turner, Lynn H., "Women, Men and Conflict Management: When Do the Differences Make a Difference?" paper presented at the annual meeting of the Speech Communication Association Convention, Louisville, November 1982.

Turner, Lynn H., and S. A. Henzl, "Influence Attempts in Organizational Conflicts: The Effects of Biological

Sex, Psychological Gender, and Power Position," paper presented at the annual meeting of the Speech Communication Association Convention, Boston, November 1987.

Turner, Lynn H., and Helen M. Sterk, "Introduction: Examining 'Difference,' " in Lynn H. Turner and Helen M. Sterk (Eds.), *Differences That Make a Difference: Examining the Assumptions in Gender Research* (Westport, CT: Bergin & Garvey, 1994).

Turner, R. E., C. Eagly, and G. Olmstead, "Information Control in Conversation: Honesty Is Not Always the Best Policy," *Kansas Journal of Sociology* 11 (1975), 69–89.

Tutzauer, Frank, and Michael Roloff, "Communication Processes Leading to Integrative Agreements: Three Paths to Joint Benefits," *Communication Research* 15 (1988), 360–380.

Ury, William, *Getting Past No: Negotiating with Difficult People* (New York: Bantam Books, 1991).

Vincent, John P., Robert L. Weiss, and Gary R. Birchler, "A Behavioral Analysis of Problem Solving in Distressed and Nondistressed Married and Stranger Dyads," *Behavior Therapy* 6 (1975), 475–487.

Viscott, D., *Risking* (New York: Pocket Books, 1977).

Vissing, Yvonne, and Walter Baily, "Parent-to-Child Verbal Aggression," in Dudley D. Cahn and Sally A. Lloyd, *Family Violence from a Communication Perspective* (Thousand Oaks, CA: Sage Publications, 1996), pp. 85–107.

Wade, Susan Helen, "The Development of a Scale to Measure Forgiveness," Doctoral dissertation, Fuller Theological Seminary, 1989.

Wall, J. A., *Negotiation: Theory and Practice* (Glenview, IL: Scott Foresman, 1985).

Waller, W., and R. Hill, *The Family: A Dynamic Interpretation* (New York: Dyden, 1951).

Walker, Lenore, "Treatment Alternatives for Battered Women," in Jane Roberts Chapman and Margaret Gates (Eds.), *The Victimization of Women* (Beverly Hills, CA: Sage, 1987).

Walker, Lenore, "Psychology and Violence Against Women," *American Psychologist* 44 (1989), 695–702.

Walker, V., and L. Brokaw, *Becoming Aware,* 6th Ed. (Dubuque, IA: Kendall Hunt, 1995).

Walster, E., G. W. Walster, and E. Berscheid, *Equity Theory and Research* (Boston: Allyn and Bacon, 1978).

Walton, Richard E., *Managing Conflict: Interpersonal Dialogue and Third-Party Roles,* 2nd Ed. (Reading, MA: Addison Wesley, 1987).

Watzlawick, Paul, Janet Beavin, and Don D. Jackson, *Pragmatics of Human Communication* (New York: Norton, 1967).

Watzlawick, Paul, J. H. Weakland, and R. Fisch, *Change* (New York: W. W. Norton, 1974).

Weaver, Gary R., "Contrasting and Comparing Cultures," in Gary R. Weaver, (Ed.), *Culture, Communication and Conflict: Readings in Intercultural Relations,* 2nd Ed. (Needham Heights, MA: Simon and Schuster, 1998), pp. 72–77.

Weeks, Dudley, *The Eight Essential Steps to Conflict Resolution* (New York: G. P. Putnam's Sons, 1992).

Weick, Karl, *The Social Psychology of Organizing,* 2nd Ed. (New York: Addison-Wesley Publishing, 1979).

Weinstein, Eugene A., "The Development of Interpersonal Competence," in D. A. Goslin (Ed.), *Handbook of Socialization and Theory and Research* (Chicago: Rand McNally, 1969), pp. 753–775.

Weitzman, L. J., *The Divorce Revolution* (New York: The Free Press, 1985).

Werner, B. L., " 'I Want the Kids!' Parents' Conversational Strategies During Child Custody Mediation," paper presented at the annual meeting of the Speech Communication Association, Chicago, November 1990.

Wheeless, Lawrence R., Robert Barraclough, and Robert Stewart, "Compliance-Gaining and Power in Persuasion," in Robert Bostrum (Ed.), *Communication Yearbook* 7 (Beverly Hills, CA: Sage, 1983), pp. 105–145.

White, L. K., and A. Booth, "The Transition to Parenthood and Marital Quality," *Journal of Family Issues* 6 (1985), 435–449.

Whitehead, Alfred, and Bertrand Russell, *Principia Mathematica,* III, 2nd Ed. (Cambridge: Cambridge University, 1910–13).

Wiesenthal, Simon, *The Sunflower: On the Possibilities and Limits of Forgiveness* (New York: Schocken Books, 1997).

Wilmot, William W., *Dyadic Communication: A Transactional Perspective* (Reading, MA: Addison-Wesley, 1979).

Wilmot, William W., and Joyce L. Hocker, *Interpersonal Conflict,* 5th Ed. (Boston: McGraw-Hill, 1998).

Wilson, Charmaine E., "The Influence of Message Direction on Perceived Conflict Behaviors," paper presented at the annual meeting of the Western Speech Communication Association Convention, Denver, February 1982.

Wilson, Steven R., and Linda L. Putnam, "Interaction Goals in Negotiation," in James A. Anderson (Ed.), *Communication Yearbook* 13 (Newbury Park, CA: Sage, 1990), pp. 374–406.

Winter, D. G., *The Power Motive* (New York: Free Press, 1973).

Wiseman, Richard, "Towards a Rules Perspective of Intercultural Communication," *Communication* 9 (1980), 30–38.

Witteman, Hal, "Interpersonal Problem Solving: Problem Conceptualization and Communication Use" *Communication Monographs* 55 (1988), 336–359.

Witteman, Hal, "Analyzing Interpersonal Conflict: Nature of Awareness, Type of Initiating Event, Situational Perceptions, and Management Styles," *Western Journal of Communication* 56 (1992), 248–280.

Witteman, Hal, and Mary Anne Fitzpatrick, "Compliance-Gaining in Marital Interaction: Power Bases, Processes and Outcomes," *Communication Monographs* 53 (1986), 140.

Yum, June Ock, "The Impact of Confucianism on Interpersonal Relationships and Communication Patterns in East Asia," in Larry A. Samovar and Richard E. Porter (Eds.), *Intercultural Communication: A Reader,* 6th Ed. (Belmont, CA: Wadsworth, 1991).

Zietlow, P., and A. Sillars, "Life-Stage Differences in Communication During Marital Conflicts," *Journal of Social and Personal Relationships* 5 (1988), 223–245.

Zimmerman, D. H., and C. West, "Sex-Roles, Interruptions, and Silences in Conversation," in B. Thorne and N. Henley (Eds.), *Language and Sex: Differences and Dominances* (Rowely, MA: Newbury House, 1975), pp. 105–129.

Index

Accommodation, as conflict style, 101,
  207–208
Accounts
  and accounting sequence, 304–307
  defined, 304
Acknowledgment, 304
Adaptation, vs. control, 155
Adjudication, 342
Aggressive communication, 208–210
Aggressor-defender model, 81
Alternative dispute resolution, 342
Ambiguity (*see also* Uncertainty)
  defined, 139
  purposeful, 31
Analyzing conflicts, 192–202
  goal of, 193
  importance of, 192
  methods for, 201–203
  specific questions for, 202
Anger
  and anger controllers, 280
  and anger-ins, 278
  and anger-outs, 278
  control of, 278–279
  vs. general irritability, 275–276
  myths about, 279
  process of, 277–278
  responding to, 281
  as secondary emotion, 276–277
Apologies, 307–309
Appropriateness, 153
Arbitration, 342
Argument, 62
Argumentative skill deficiency,
  212–213, 324
Aspiration level, 251
Assertive communication, 216–220
Attitudes
  assessing, 36
  defined, 22
  fostering conflict resolution,
    35–36
Attribution theory, 126–127
Avoidance
  as conflict strategy, 105

  as conflict style, 101
  productive, 30

Bargaining
  defined, 250
  effects of embarrassment on,
    301–302
  in formal situations, 250–252
  range, 251
  research on, 252–254
BATNA, 259–260
Behavioral conflicts, 66–67
Behaviors, 100
Beliefs
  defined, 22
  functional, 28–35
Bickering, 62
Bridging, 268

Case Studies
  alcohol abuse, 174–176
  children of divorced parents,
    134
  conflict about conflict, 164
  conflict dimensions, 194–195
  conflict resolution in former
    Yugoslavia, 117–118
  conflict resolution in Japan,
    114–116
  conflict resolution in United
    States, 116–117
  lying, 322–323
  management troubles, 18–20
  morality and reality, 71–72
  ongoing conflict, 83
  reconciliation, 261–264
  threats to face, 302–303
Caucus, 353
Chaining approach, 201–202
Chilling effect, 79–80
Climate (*see also* Context)
  cooperative vs. competitive,
    198–199
  defensive vs. supportive, 228
Coalitions, 94

Collaboration (*see also* Integrative
    strategy)
  as conflict strategy, 104, 106
  as conflict style, 102
  phases of, 112–114
  as preferred style, 109–112
  requirements for, 35
Communality, vs. instrumentality, 155
Communication
  aggressive, 208–210
  apprehension of, 27–28
  assertive, 216–220
  choosing best option for, 220–222
  and conflict competence (*see*
    Competence)
  nonassertive, 207–208
  and nonverbal aggression, 210
  options for, 206
  as panacea, 30–31
  passive-aggressive, 214–215
  rights, 216–217
  rules for (*see* Rules)
  skills, 226
  and verbal aggression, 211–213
Communicator style, 23
Comparison level, 129
Compensation, 267
Competence
  as appropriateness, 153
  defined, 153
  dialectics of, 154–156
  differences in, between men and
    women, 50
  as effectiveness, 153
  vs. incompetence, 155–156
Competition
  as conflict dimension, 198–199
  as conflict strategy, 104
  as conflict style, 101
  converting to cooperation, 268–270
  as part of conflict, 3
  as type of conflict, 63
Competitive conflict escalation cycle,
  81–87
Complementary relationships, 7

381

Compromise, as conflict style, 102
Concessions, 305
Conciliation, 342
Conflict
  analysis of, 193
  deciding to engage in, 193–194
  defined, 3–6
  destructive, 14–15
  dimensions of, 194–196
  as fact of life, 9–11
  functions of, 12–13
  fundamental assumptions about,
    xi–xii
  metaphors, 6–7
  moral, 69–72
  phase, 74
  pollutants, 196–198
  preparing for, 227–228
  productive, 16–17
  spiral, 81
  structural change model of, 82
  structure of, 156
  styles of (*see* Styles of conflict)
  theory (*see* Theories of conflict)
  traps, 197
  types of (*see* Types of conflict)
  viewed negatively, 6–9
Conflict avoidance cycle, 79–80
Conflict issues
  behavioral, 66–67
  defined, 66, 157
  intangible, 248
  marital, 170
  normative, 67–68
  about personality, 68–69
  tangible, 248
Conflict messages
  consequences statements, 236
  feeling/needs statements, 230, 236,
    237
  goal-statements, 236
  I-statements, 233–239
  personalized communication, 234
  problematic behavior statements, 236
  responsibility, 234–235
  wants, 231
Conflict process
  differentiation, 93–96
  initiation, 92–93
  prelude, 88–91
  resolution, 96
  triggering event, 87, 91–92
Confrontation
  vs. avoidance, 29–30
  decision to engage in, 193–195
  defined, 225
  steps in, 226–233

Consequences statement, 236
Content goals, 33
Context
  as cultural variable, 43
  effect on interaction, 32, 90–91
Conversational sensitivity, 27
Corrective facework, 303–312
Cost-cutting, 267
Counterattack/countercomplaints,
  85–86, 95
Couple type, 178
Cross-complaining, 180–181
Cultural variability, 44–47
Culture
  defined, 40
  and differences in assertiveness, 219
  and perspective, 41
Cycles of conflict
  avoidance cycle, 77–79
  chilling effect, 79–80
  competitive conflict escalation cycle,
    81–87
  defined, 75
  schismogenesis, 77
  undesired repetitive pattern (URP),
    77

Deception, 320–323
De-escalating conflict, 281–282
Defensive coping mechanisms, 284
Defensiveness, vs. supportiveness, 228
Defensive spiral, 82
Definitional rules, 152
Depersonalized communication,
  234–235
Destructive conflict, 14–15
Developmental changes (in family),
  172
Dialectical tensions, in conflict
  competence, 154
Differentiation phase, 93–96
Difficult people, 240–243
Disagreements, vs. interpersonal
  conflicts, 65
Disclaimers, 296
Displaced conflict, 60
Displacement, 125, 285
Dispute, 341
Distress, 283
Distressed couples, 180
Distributive strategy, 104, 106
Diversity, 47–48

Effectiveness, 153
Ego, 125
Embarrassment, 299–302
Emotional residues, 319

Empathy, 219–220, 232
Escalation, containing, 281–282
Ethnocentrism, 40
Eustress, 283
Evaluative ability, 200
Evidence, 159
Excuses, 304
Exit, 107–108
External resources, 177

Face
  defined, 45, 294–295
  effect on conflict, xi-xii
  and facework, 294
  negative, 295
  positive, 295
  preventing threats to, 296–299
False conflict, 59
Feeling/needs statements, 230, 236,
  237
Fidelity, 149
Forgiveness
  concepts misconstrued as, 331–332
  defined, 326
  and forgiveness/reconciliation loop,
    335
  importance of communicating, 333
  models of, 329–331
  and moving beyond victimization,
    336–337
  receiving, 336
  and reconciliation, 326, 333–336
  strategizing for, 332–333
  and unforgiveness, 327–328
Fractionating conflict, 352
Framing, 352
Functional beliefs, 28–35

Game-playing, vs. game-mastery, 122
Games, 239–240
Game theory of conflict
  application to bargaining situations,
    252–254
  defined, 132–133
Gender and sex
  and communication, 49–50
  and conflict, 48–52
  defined, 48
  essentialist view of, 48
  and perceptions of assertiveness,
    220
  and perceptions of competence,
    50
  and sexism, 211–212
  stereotypes about, 50
General irritability, 275–276
Goal-centeredness, 199

Goals
  defined, 33
  identity, 161–163
  instrumental, 158–159
  relational, 159–161
  types of, 33
Goal-statement, 236
Gunny-sacking, 219

Healing, 329
Healthy trust, 137
Hierarchical model of culture, 42–44
High-context culture, 45
Hyperstress, 283
Hypostress, 283

Id, 125
Identity goals, 33, 161–163
Imagined interactions, 227–228
Impression management
  correcting impressions for,
    303–312
  defined, 297–299
  disclaimers for, 296
  results of apologies and accounts in,
    309–312
Independents, 178
Individual differences, 180
Inevitability, of conflict, 9–11
Initiation phase, 92–93
Instrumental goals, 158–159
Intangible issues, 248
Interaction involvement, 26
Intercultural communication, 40
Intercultural conflict, 41
Interdependence, 4–5
Interests, 265
Internal resources, 177
Interpersonal conflicts, 5
  vs. mere disagreements, 65
Interpersonal violence, 11, 210,
    324–325
Issues (*see* Conflict issues)
I-statements, 233–239

Justifications, 304

Language of cooperation, 269
Last tags complex, 197
Latent conflict (*see* Prelude to conflict)
Legislation, 310
Libido, 125
Lies, 320–323
Linear model of communication,
    149–150
Listening, 203–204
Log-rolling, 267

Low-context culture, 45
Loyalty, 107–108

Marital conflict
  couple type and conflict style in,
    178–180
  individual differences and style in,
    180
  issues in, 170
  patterns of interaction in, 180–181
  types of complaints and responses
    in, 182
Mediation, 342
  compared to adjudication, 343–345
  in educational settings, 356–358
  ethics of, 355–356
  guidelines for use of third parties, 347
  process of, 350–355
  rules for structural approach to,
    349–51
Mediators, 342, 345–347
  skills of, 348–349
Metaphors, for conflict, 6
Misassumptions, about conflict
  leading to avoidance, 77–78
  leading to competitive escalation,
    86–87
Misplaced conflict, 61
Mixed motives, 32, 132–133
Monochronic time, 46
Moral conflict, 69–72
Mushroom syndrome, 197

Negative face, 295
Neglect, 107–108
Negotiation
  defined, 250
  informal, 254
  research on tactics and strategies
    for, 254–256
Noble Self, 23
Nonassertive communication, 207–208
Nonsubstantive conflict, 62
Nonverbal aggression, 210
Normative conflict, 67–68

Objective standards, 200, 268
Ombudsperson, 342
One-down moves, 311
Overblown expectations, 197

Paraphrasing, 232
Passive-aggressive communication,
    214–215
Pathological trust, 137
Patterns and cycles in conflict (*see*
    Cycles of conflict)

Perception
  defined, 24
  effect on conflict, 25, 31–32
Personality, 68–69
Personalized communication, 234
Personal stress, 109
Phases of conflict (*see* Conflict process)
Phase theory, 75–76
Physical aggression, 62, 210, 324–325
Politeness, vs. assertiveness, 154–155
Pollutants, 196–198
Polychronic time, 46
Positions, 265
Positive face, 295
Power
  assessment of, 141
  bases of, 142
  communication and, 143
  defined, 140
  traditional views of, 141
Preferences over principles, 197
Prelude to conflict
  defined, 88
  elements of, 88–91
Prisoner's Dilemma, 132–133
Problematic behaviors, 172
Problematic behavior statement, 236
Problematic situations, 317 (*see also*
    Social predicament)
Process goals, 33
Productive conflict, 16–17
Projection, 284
Psychodynamic theory, 124–125
Punctuation, 32

Racism, 211
Rationalization, 284
Reaction formation, 284
Reaffirmation, 310
Real conflicts, 58
Real and substantive conflicts, 65
Reciprocated diatribe, 69–70
Reconciliation, 326
  principles of, 261
Redefinition, 199
Reframing, 329, 353
Regrettable messages, 320
Regulative rules, 152
Relational conflict, 67
Relational goals, 33, 159–161
Relational stress, 109
Relational transgressions
  deception and lies, 320–323
  defined, 317
  effects of, 318–320
  regrettable messages, 320
  violence, 324–325

Remediation, 310 (*see also* Accounts)
Remedy, 304, 310
Repression, 284
Reproach, 304
Resistance point, 251
Resolution phase, 96
Responsibility, for behavior, 28–29, 234–235
Rhetorical Reflector, 23
Rhetorical sensitivity
    vs. conflict styles, 103
    defined, 23
Rights, 216–217
Rules
    defined, 152
    definitional, 152
    regulative, 152
    theory approach to conflict, 151–153

Schismogenesis, 77
Scripted behavior, 76
Secondary emotion, 276–277
Self-fulfilling prophecy, 333
Self-monitoring, 25–26
Self-talk
    defined, 227
    effect on stress, 286–287
Separates, 178
Sex differences (*see* Gender and sex)
Sexism, 211
Social competence, vs. relational
    competence, 155
Social confrontation, 309–312
Social environment (*see* Context)
Social exchange theory, 129–131
    comparison level, 129
    comparison level of alternatives, 129
    options for changing outcomes, 130–131
Socialization, 22
Social lies, 322
Social predicament, 299–300
Status quo point, 251
Stereotypes, 211
S-TLC, 190–191
Strategies and tactics
    avoidance, 105
    collaborative/integrative, 104, 107
    competitive/distributive, 104, 106
    defined, 94, 100

exit, 107–108
    loyalty, 107–108
    neglect, 107–108
    voice, 107–108
Stress
    defined, 283
    effects of conflict style on, 110–112
    impact on conflict, 291–292
    personal, 109
    relational, 109
    self-talk and, 286–287
    and stressors, 284–288
    types of, 283
Structural change model, 82
Structural theory, 136–144
    power and, 140–144
    trust and, 137–139
    uncertainty and, 139–140
Styles of conflict
    accommodation, 101
    attribution of, to others, 297
    avoidance, 101
    collaboration, 102
    competition, 101
    compromise, 102
Styles theory, 99–100
Sublimation, 284
Substantive conflict, 62
Superego, 125
Supportiveness, vs. defensiveness, 228
Symmetrical relationships, 8
Systems theory, 133–136

Tactics (*see* Strategies and tactics)
Taking conflict personally (TCP), 85
Tangible issues, 248
Theories of conflict
    attribution, 126–127
    game, 132–133
    phase, 75–76
    psychodynamic, 124–125
    rule, 151–153
    social exchange, 129–131
    structural, 136–144
    styles, 99–100
Theory
    defined, 123
    importance of, 121
Third-party effect, 90
Third-party intervention (*see* Mediation)

Threats and promises, 255
Thromise, 255
Traditionals, 178
Trained incapacities, 199–200
Transactional model of communi-
    cation, 150–151
Traps, 197
Triggering events, 87, 91–92
Trust, 137–139
Truth bias, 322
Types of conflict
    argument, 62
    bickering, 62
    competition, 63
    false conflict, 59
    mere disagreements, 65
    misplaced conflict, 61
    moral, 69–72
    nonsubstantive conflict, 62
    physical aggression, 62
    real conflict, 58
    real and substantive conflict, 64
    substantive conflict, 62
    unreal conflict, 58
    verbal abuse, 62
    verbal aggression, 62

Uncertainty, 139–140 (*see also*
    Ambiguity)
Undesired repetitive pattern (*see*
    Cycles of conflict)
Unreal conflicts, 58
Unresponsiveness pattern, 95

Values
    defined, 22
    instrumental, 22
    intercultural, 44–48
    terminal, 22
Verbal abuse and aggression, 61, 62,
    211–213
Violence, 324–325
Voice, 107–108

Wants, 231
Willingness to communicate, 27

You-language, 234

Zero-sum, 252